Germany and the Americas

Other Titles in ABC-CLIO's

Transatlantic Relations Series

←══════════════════→

Germany and the Americas

the Americas

Culture, Politics, and History

A Multidisciplinary Encyclopedia

VOLUME I

EDITED BY

Thomas Adam

Transatlantic Relations Series

Will Kaufman, Series Editor

A B C ❧ C L I O

Santa Barbara, California   Denver, Colorado   Oxford, England

Library of Congress Cataloging-in-Publication Data
Germany and the Americas : culture, politics, and history / edited by
Thomas Adam.
   v. cm.— (Transatlantic relations series)
   Also available on the World Wide Web as an eBook from ABC-CLIO
   Includes bibliographical references and index.
   Contents: Vol. 1: A-F — v. 2: G-N — v. 3: O-Z.
   ISBN 1-85109-628-0 (hardback : alk. paper) — ISBN 1-85109-633-7
(ebook) 1. America—Relations—Germany—Encyclopedias. 2.
Germany—Relations—America—Encyclopedias. 3.
America—History—Encyclopedias. 4. Germany—History—Encyclopedias. 5.
North America—History—Encyclopedias. 6. Latin
America—History—Encyclopedias. 7. South
America—History—Encyclopedias. 8. America—Politics and
government—Encyclopedias. 9. Germany—Politics and
government—Encyclopedias. I. Adam, Thomas. II. Series.

E18.75.G48 2005
303.48'27043—dc22

                          2005021064

08 07 06 05 10 9 8 7 6 5 4 3 2 1

This book is also available on the World Wide Web as an e-Book. Visit abc-clio.com
for details.

ABC-CLIO, Inc.
130 Cremona Drive, P.O. Box 1911
Santa Barbara, California 93116-1911

This book is printed on acid-free paper ∞.
Manufactured in the United States of America

*The Acquisitions Editor for this title was Simon Mason, the Project Editor was Carla
Roberts, the Media Editor was Sharon Daugherty, the Media Manager was Caroline
Price, the Assistant Production Editor was Cisca Schreefel, the Production Manager was
Don Schmidt, and the Manufacturing Coordinator was George Smyser.*

To my parents

CONTENTS

ADVISORY BOARD

SERIES EDITOR'S PREFACE

The transatlantic relationship has been one of the most dynamic of modern times. Since the great age of exploration in the fifteenth and sixteenth centuries, the encounters between the Old World and the New have determined the course of history, culture, and politics for billions of people. The destinies of Europe, Africa, North and South America, and all the islands in between have been intertwined to the extent that none of these areas can be said to exist in isolation. Out of these interconnections comes the concept of the "Atlantic world," which Alan Karras describes in his introductory essay to *Britain and the Americas* in this series: "By looking at the Atlantic world as a single unit, rather than relying upon more traditional national (such as Britain) or regional (such as North or South America) units of analyses, scholars have more nearly been able to re-create the experiences of those who lived in the past." This perspective attempts to redefine and respond to expanding (one might say *globalizing*) pressures and new ways of perceiving interconnections—not only those rooted in history ("the past") but also those that are ongoing. Just one result of this conceptual redefinition has been the emergence of transatlantic studies as an area of inquiry in its own right, growing from the soil of separate area studies, whether European, North American, African, Caribbean, or Latin American. Students and scholars working in transatlantic studies have embarked on a new course of scholarship that places the transatlantic dynamic at its heart.

In this spirit, the Transatlantic Relations Series is devoted to transcending, or at least challenging, the boundaries of nation/region as well as discipline: we are concerned in this series not only with history but also with culture and politics, race and economics, gender and migration; not only with the distant past but also with this morning. The aim, in a phrase, is to explore the myriad connections and interconnections of the Atlantic world. However, although the Atlantic world concept challenges the isolation of smaller, national perspectives, nations do continue to exist, with boundaries both physical and conceptual. Thus this series acknowledges the intractability of the national and the regional while consistently focusing on the transcending movements—the connections and interconnections—that go beyond the national and the regional. Our mode of operation has been to build an approach to the Atlantic world through attention to the separate vectors between the nations and regions on both sides of the Atlantic. We do this by offering the six titles within the series so far commissioned, devoted respectively to Africa, Britain, France, Germany, Iberia, and Ireland in their engagements with the Americas. In each case, the transatlantic exchanges are those of all kinds: cultural, political, and historical, from the moment of the first contact to the present day. With this organizing principle in mind, the object is to offer an accessible, precisely focused means of entry into the various portals of the Atlantic world.

Finally, a word about this series' origins: in 1995, Professor Terry Rodenberg of Central Missouri State University invited scholars and teachers from eighteen universities on both sides of the Atlantic to establish an educational and scholarly institution devoted to encouraging a transatlantic perspective. The result was the founding of the Maastricht Center for Transatlantic Studies (MCTS), located in the Dutch city whose name, through its eponymous treaty, resonates with transnational associations. Since its foundation, MCTS has continued to bring together students and scholars from a host of worldwide locations to explore the intricate web of Atlantic connections across all disciplines. It has been a dynamic encounter between cultures and people striving to transcend the limitations of separate area and disciplinary studies. I am pleased to acknowledge the extent to which the Transatlantic Relations Series grows out of the discussions and approaches articulated at MCTS. Therefore, although the separate titles in the series carry their own dedications, the series as a whole is dedicated with great respect to Terry Rodenberg and the students and scholars at Maastricht.

Will Kaufman
University of Central Lancashire
Maastricht Center for Transatlantic Studies

EDITOR'S PREFACE

The German-speaking world has had an impact on the history of the Americas for more than five hundred years. In 1507, Martin Waldseemüller of Freiburg provided the first world map showing the shape of the American continent explored by Christopher Columbus and Amerigo Vespucci—it was in fact Waldseemüller who suggested naming this new land "America" after Vespucci. Since then, Germans have been among the major ethnic groups and nationalities to settle the American continents, especially in the United States, Canada, Brazil, and Argentina. In contrast to other European settler groups of the nineteenth century (Spanish, Portuguese, French, and English), Germans migrated to all parts of the American continents. This appears to be even more intriguing if one considers that Germany was the only major European power without American colonies. For the millions of people who left Germany for political, religious, and economic reasons between the seventeenth and twenty-first centuries, Ontario, Pennsylvania, Wisconsin, Texas, Rio Grande do Sul, and Santa Catarina—among many other regions—became home.

Yet, the majority of these migrants did not leave Germany but one of the many Germanies: the Holy Roman Empire, the German Confederation, the German Empire, the Weimar Republic, Nazi Germany, and the two German states founded on the ruins of World War II. After their arrival in the New World, Palatines, Saxons, Bavarians, and Prussians became Germans only in the eyes of the British, Spanish, and Portuguese. Language was the major indicator of ethnic belonging. That these Germans spoke very different dialects and represented distinct social and cultural backgrounds was lost in translation. However, New World Germans did not only arrive from "Germany proper." Siebenbürgen Saxons, Sudeten Germans, and Volga Germans left their homes for North and South America. In addition, German speakers from the Austro-Hungarian Empire, Austria (after 1918), and Switzerland joined in this transatlantic migration.

Germans left Europe for several reasons: The first settlers who immigrated to Pennsylvania were attracted by its religious tolerance. For them the New World offered opportunities and freedom of thought and belief. After the failed revolution of 1848/49 many liberal and progressive German revolutionaries left for North America in order to avoid political persecution and in search for personal freedom and civil liberties. However, the majority of the ca. 5.5 million German-speaking immigrants, who arrived in the United States alone between 1815 and 1914, left for economic reasons. To them the United States represented the land of unlimited opportunities and social advancement. Disillusionment with the Treaty of Versailles and the Weimar Republic caused Germans to seek their fortunes elsewhere. Strict limitations on immigration imposed by the American government resulted in an increased migration to South America. Adolf Hitler's appointment as Reich chancellor on January 30, 1933, forced left-leaning intellectuals and Jews to flee their home country. In contrast to the Forty-Eighters a century earlier, Jews and left-leaning intellectuals could not count on unlimited access to the United States or Canada. While the United States, Canada, and even Brazil refused to accept larger numbers of Jewish refugees from Nazi Germany, it was Argentina that welcomed thousands of refugees who were in need of a new home. Argentina, as Holger M. Meding points out in his article, accepted per capita more Jewish refugees than any other country in the world besides Palestine. The forceful removal of Germans from all of Eastern Europe after World War II as well as the attempts to escape denazification trials and judicial persecution for war crimes spurred Germans again to leave Germany in large numbers.

According to Frederick C. Luebke, 90 percent of all German migrants went to North America. By the time of the American Revolution about 8 or 9 percent of the population of the United States were of German extraction. More than two hundred years later, in 1980, about 52 million U.S. citizens (out of 226 million) claimed German heritage in a nationwide census. This made the Germans the largest ethnic group in the country "exceeding both the Irish and the English" (Luebke 1990, 174).

German American relations include the wide variety of social, cultural, economic, political, military, literary, and intellectual encounters of German speakers with this New World. It is common knowledge that during the twentieth century, the United States (together with other North and South American countries) faced Germany in two world wars and, after the second, contributed to the transformation of authoritarian Germany into a democracy. Many know, too, of Germany's pivotal position between the contending forces in the cold war. Nevertheless, German American relations cannot merely be reduced to military or political engagements: the first German settlers contributed to the emerging national cultures in the Americas, and their descendants have continued to exert their influence. They established their own subcultures, printed their own newspapers, imported their cuisine, music, literature, art, and cinema, and greatly enriched the cultural life of the American societies. German actors, producers, and composers gave Hollywood its image. German universities educated the elite of the United States before 1900. Bauhaus and German landscape art shaped American cities. Emanuel Leutze produced one of the foremost American paintings depicting Washington crossing the Delaware. In turn, the Americas have acted upon Germany through a host of historical, political, and cultural developments. German cuisine without potatoes is now unthinkable. Tropical fruits (bananas) are taken for granted by German consumers. Coca-Cola, chewing gum, and McDonald's are common elements of modern German life. Thanks to Karl May, Liselotte Welskopf-Henrich, and many more authors and film producers, Indians populated German novels, movies, and the fantasies of German children and adults.

This encyclopedia contains hundreds of articles on all aspects of the German American encounter written by scholars from several countries including Austria, Brazil, Canada, France, Germany, Great Britain, Israel, South Korea, the Netherlands, and the United States. Following five introductory essays on the migration of German-speaking people to North and South America, the bulk of articles follows the A to Z format. I would like to thank James M. Bergquist, Alexander Emmerich, Yves Laberge, Gabriele Lingelbach, Christof Mauch, Holger M. Meding, Michael Rudloff, and Ralf Roth for agreeing to write articles on very short notice. Many students and scholars in Arlington, Texas, helped in the translation of articles, which were submitted in German. Further, I would like to thank Linda Wiencken Williams, Sarah E. Wobick, Michael L. Dailey, Deana Covel, and Scott G. Williams for their continued and tireless support in the translation of the German articles. In addition, I would like to thank Scott G. Williams and his students Martin Boyd, Michael Daily, Steffany Fischer, Phillipp Foroughi-Esfahani, Steven Hagle, Marina Kljucevic, Hildegard Lombardo, Eva McKendrick, Angela Moritz, Kiet Nguyen, Scott Strough, Jennifer Kraig Takacs who translated biographical articles as part of fulfilling the requirements in their spring 2004 course on *German Translation Theory and Practice*. All translations have been authorized by the contributors to this encyclopedia. For the sake of comprehension, I have insisted on translating all book, journal, and newspaper titles to give the English-speaking reader at least a general idea about the many German titles listed in this work.

Thomas Adam
The University of Texas at Arlington

References

Colin G. Calloway, Gerd Gemünden, and Susanne Zantop, eds. *Germans and Indians: Fantasies, Encounters, Projections.* Lincoln and London: University of Nebraska Press, 2002.

Frederick C. Luebke. *Germans in the New World: Essays in the History of Immigration.* Urbana and Chicago: University of Illinois Press, 1990.

Frank Trommler and Joseph McVeigh, eds. *America and the Germans: An Assessment of a Three-Hundred-Year History.* 2 vols. Philadelphia: University of Pennsylvania Press, 1985.

TOPIC FINDER

CHRONOLOGY OF GERMANY AND THE AMERICAS

1507 Martin Waldseemüller publishes a collection entitled *Cosmographiae Introductio* (Introduction to Cosmography) with a world map, in which he suggests naming the newly discovered continent *America*.

1519 Ulrich von Hutten publishes his book *De Guaiaci Medicina et morbo gallicus liber unus* (Of the Wood Called Guaiacum). It confirms his status as the most prominent early European victim of syphilis, which was introduced to Europe by Spanish sailors returning from the New World after 1492.

1525 The printer Jacob Cromberger and his son-in-law Lazarus Nürnberger are the first Germans to receive permission to enter the American trade, which has until now been exclusively reserved for Spaniards.

1527 Representatives of the Welser firm of Augsburg contract with the Spanish crown to transport fifty miners from Saxony to the American continent, where they are to extract precious metals on the island of Santo Domingo and in other provinces.

1528 Heinrich Ehinger and Hieronymus Sailer, acting for the Augsburg firm of Bartholomäus Welser, conclude a treaty with Emperor Charles V of Spain that gives them jurisdiction over the territory that will become known as Venezuela.

1557 Hans Staden publishes his *Wahrhaftige Historia und Beschreibung eines Landes der wilden, nackten und grimmigen Menschenfresser, in der Neuen Welt Amerika gelegen* (True History and Description of a Country of Wild, Naked, Terrible Man-eaters Who Dwell in the New World Called America) in Marburg. Staden's *Wahrhaftige Historia* represents one of the earliest American Indian captivity narratives—if not *the* earliest captivity narrative of all.

1567 Ulrich (Utz) Schmidel from Straubing publishes a description of his trip and twenty-year sojourn in the La Plata region of Argentina under the title *Wahrhafftige Historien einer Wunderbaren Schiffart* (True Stories from a Marvelous Journey). With this book Schmidel becomes the first historian of Argentina.

c. 1598 The first German Jesuit to serve as a missionary overseas appears to be Peter de Gouveia from Edister, who is made coadjutor of the village of San Bernabé in Brazil.

1683   Thirteen Dutch Quaker families from Crefeld arrive in Philadelphia and settle in what is to become the first self-conscious attempt to create a German settlement in North America. Francis Daniel Pastorius, the agent of the German settlers, envisions this community as a "Germanopolis" or "little German city."

1691   German Jesuit Samuel Fritz produces the first accurate map of the Amazon River.

       Eusebius Franciscus Kino makes the first of many expeditions to what will become modern Arizona, and by locating the source of the Colorado River he definitively proves that (Baja) California is not an island.

1710   Samuel Güldin is the first ordained German Reformed minister to arrive in Pennsylvania.

       The first-known significant German immigrant group from the Palatinate arrives in New York City.

1720   John Law, a Scottish emigrant to France and the founder of the Compagnie des Indoes (Company of the Indies), brings the first German settlers to Louisiana.

c. 1728   Conrad Beissel founds a monastic community of Sabbatarians in northern Lancaster County, Pennsylvania, which he names Ephrata.

1731   German-speaking Silesian Schwenkfelders immigrate to Pennsylvania in six waves of migration between 1731 and 1737.

1732   Benjamin Franklin is the first to print a German-language newspaper, the *Philadelphische Zeitung* (Philadelphia News), in Britain's North American colonies. The paper, however, soon fails.

1734   German Lutherans living in the Tyrol region are forced into exile by the archbishop of Salzburg. These "Salzburg Germans" cross the Atlantic and arrive in Charleston, South Carolina, before continuing on to Savannah, Georgia. Their arrival marks the beginning of German settlement in Georgia. They call their new town "Ebenezer."

1735   German American printer John Peter Zenger is charged with libel for criticism of New York governor William Cosby published in the *New York Weekly Journal,* which was printed in Zenger's establishment. A jury, however, acquits him of any guilt. This verdict is considered the first landmark decision in the history of American press freedom.

1737   The Pennsylvania German Indian agent Conrad Weiser develops a pacifist colonial policy for dealing with the Iroquois Confederacy. His successful negotiations on behalf of the Pennsylvania provincial government with the Iroquois authority in Pennsylvania avoid military confrontation between settlers and Indians.

1738   The German printer Christoph Sauer of Germantown, Pennsylvania, begins publishing the *Hoch-Deutsch Pennsylvanische Geschichts-Schreiber* (High German Pennsylvania Chronicle), later known as the *Pennsylvanische Berichte* (Pennsylvania Reports).

1741   Nikolaus Ludwig von Zinzendorf founds the Pennsylvania Synod, a preecumenical gathering of pietists.

1748   Pennsylvania German Lutheran clergyman Henry Melchior Muhlenberg organizes the Lutheran churches into the first Lutheran Church synod in the American colonies, officially known as the Ministerium of Pennsylvania.

1750   The first significant German-speaking settler groups arrive in Halifax, Nova Scotia. They come from the German Palatinate, Switzerland, the Netherlands, and other German-speaking areas.

1753   The British establish the predominantly German settlement of Lunenburg in Nova Scotia.

1764 The German Society of Pennsylvania is founded with the purpose of protecting new immigrants.

1776 Pennsylvania German minister John Peter Gabriel Muhlenberg delivers his famous farewell sermon to his parish. According to legend, he concludes with the phrase: "There is a time to pray and a time to fight, and that time has now come!" With that statement, he throws off his gown at the pulpit, revealing the uniform of a Continental Army colonel.

Prince Friedrich II of Hesse-Cassel enters into a treaty with his brother-in-law, George III of England, according to which Hesse-Cassel promises to supply about 12,000 troops annually for military duty in Britain's North American colonies. This is the basis for German large-scale support for British troops during the American War of Independence.

1777 Benjamin Franklin, the American ambassador to Paris, offers Friedrich Steuben a place in the Continental Army as a drillmaster. Franklin liberally exaggerates his qualifications to George Washington, promoting Steuben to major general and emphasizing the "von" title, which the Steuben family had never used. After Steuben arrives in Britain's North American colonies, he trains a "model company" in European-style military drill in order for them to train the remaining rebel forces.

1778 The brothers Johann Anton and Peter Paul (von) Obwexer of Augsburg establish a trading house on the Caribbean island of Curaçao, where their representative Pierre Brion markets central European textiles imported via Amsterdam and purchases tropical goods.

1779 August Ludwig von Schlözer publishes his *Vertrauliche Briefe aus Kanada und Neu-England vom Jahre 1777 und 1778* (Confidential Letters from Canada and New England, 1777 and 1778).

1781 The decisive battle at Yorktown, Virginia, becomes the most "German" of all battles during the American War of Independence as both sides, Americans as well as the British, rely on German support.

1784 The German Society of the City of New York is formed after the model of the German Society of Philadelphia. Its goal is to aid German immigrants to New York City.

1785 The United States and Prussia conclude their first commercial treaty.

1786 The first Mennonite settlements are established in Ontario, Canada.

1788 German immigrant Anton Heinrich publishes Canada's first German newspaper, the *Neu-Schottlaendischer Kalender* (Nova-Scotian Calendar) in Halifax.

1789 Pennsylvania German politician Frederick Augustus Conrad Muhlenberg is elected the first Speaker of the U. S. House of Representatives.

1793 The Reformed Coetus formally severs its European connection and constitutes itself as the Synod of the German Reformed Church in the United States of America.

1799 Alexander von Humboldt, together with the French botanist Aimé Bonpland, embarks on his South American expedition.

1804 George Rapp brings a group of German religious dissenters from Württemberg to Pennsylvania, where they found one of the most successful communal societies in nineteenth-century America—the Harmony Society.

1806 Pennsylvania German immigrant Abraham Erb founds Waterloo, Ontario. Located in the center of a large Pennsylvania German colony, Waterloo over the years develops into Waterloo County's agricultural center.

1806
(cont.)

German linguists Johann Christoph Adelung and Johann Severin Vater begin publication of the *Mithridates.* This eminent work of comparative linguistics includes the first comprehensive analysis and reference work of the known American Indian languages.

1807

The Mennonite bishop Benjamin Eby leads members from his community in Pennsylvania to settle in Ontario, Upper Canada. The hamlet is established under the name Ebytown and later renamed Berlin.

1815

Prince Maximilian von Wied-Neuwied embarks on his expedition to Brazil. After a stay in Rio de Janeiro he sets out for the coastal region north of Rio, together with the ornithologist Georg Wilhelm Freyreiss and the botanist Friedrich Sellow. Although only a few miles from the coast, this jungle area had scarcely been explored. The Indian peoples of the Coropó, Coroado, Purí, Pataxó, and Camacan live here largely untouched by European civilization. Prince Maximilian spends several months among the Botokude before reaching Bahia (Salvador) in April 1817. The detailed ethnological observations that he publishes in his travel account (*Reise nach Brasilien in den Jahren 1815 bis 1817* [Journey to Brazil in the years 1815 to 1817], 2 vols., 1820–1821) provide the first comprehensive description of this area. The expedition to Brazil makes Maximilian famous, and his home at Neuwied becomes a meeting place for numerous learned visitors.

1817

The marriage of Princess Leopoldine, the daughter of Emperor Francis I, with Portuguese crown prince Dom Pedro sparks a large-scale Austrian expedition into Brazil. Fourteen explorers, physicians, and painters are invited to join this expedition. However, after their arrival in Brazil, conflicts break out among them over the goals and objec-

tives of this enterprise. In the end, the expedition splits up. Johann Christian Mikan and his team return to Europe in 1818 with about 700 drawings and paintings, as well as extensive zoological, botanical, and mineralogical collections. Johann Emanuel Pohl remains in Brazil until 1821 and returns with two Botokude natives to Austria. The last to return from this expedition is Johann Natterer (1836) who collects over 12,000 birds and nearly 33,000 insects.

The Hessian nobleman Wilhelm Ludwig von Eschwege becomes general director of Brazil's gold mines.

1818

The first German settlements are established in southern Bahia and Nova Friburgo in the state of Rio de Janeiro, Brazil.

1821

German globetrotter and Russian consul general to Brazil Georg Heinrich von Langsdorff publishes his book *Bemerkungen über Brasilien. Mit gewissenhafter Belehrung für auswandernde Deutsche* (Remarks on Brazil: With Careful Advice for Germans Who Are Considering Emigration) to promote German emigration to Brazil.

1823

Harvard professor George Ticknor presents his reform of Harvard University, which is inspired by his experiences at the University of Göttingen. Ticknor proposes two major reorganizations. First, the students are to be grouped by ability. Second, traditional classes will be abolished and the college organized by departments. As at Göttingen, students may advance at their own pace through examination, rather than as a group by recitation.

1824

A group of Rhenish and Westphalian merchants and manufacturers in Elberfeld creates the Deutsch-Mexikanischer Bergwerks-Verein (German-Mexican Mining Society), later renamed Deutsch-Amerikanischer Bergwerksverein (German-American Mining Society).

1825   The first theological seminary of the German Reformed Church in the United States is opened in Carlisle.

1826   Prussia and Mexico conclude their first trade treaty based on the principle of mutual preferential treatment.

1827   Johann Wolfgang von Goethe writes his famous poem "Den Vereinigten Staaten" (To the United States).

1828   German American scholar Charles Follen publishes his German grammar. It is the first to be used widely in American schools and eventually appears in over twenty editions in the next three decades. In addition, he publishes his *Deutsches Lesebuch für Anfänger* (A German Reading Book for Beginners) in the United States, which includes selections from the writings of numerous authors, including Gotthold Ephraim Lessing, Christoph Martin Wieland, Novalis, and Friedrich Schiller. This textbook is used for several decades in American colleges.

1829   Gottfried Duden publishes his famous *Bericht über eine Reise nach den westlichen Staaten Nordamerikas und einen mehrjährigen Aufenthalt am Missouri in den Jahren 1824, 25, 26 und 27. In Bezug auf Auswanderung und Übervölkerung* (Report on a Journey to the Western States of America and a Stay of Several Years Along the Missouri during the Years 1824, 1825, 1826, and 1827).

Bremerhaven is opened and facilitates much of German immigration to North America.

Francis Lieber begins the publication of the famous thirteen-volume *Encyclopaedia Americana, Popular Dictionary of Arts, Sciences, Literature, History, Politics and Biography, Brought Down to the Present Time; Including a Copious Collection of Original Articles in American Biography; On the Basis of the Seventh Edition of the German Conversations-*

Lexicon in Philadelphia. This encyclopedia represents the successful transfer and adaptation of the German type of encyclopedia, namely Brockhaus's twelve-volume *Allgemeine deutsche Real-Encyclopaedie für die gebildeten Stände* or *Conversations-Lexikon* (Universal German Encyclopedia for the Educated Classes, 1827–1829).

The Vienna-based Leopoldine Foundation, which will support the development of the Catholic Church in North America during the nineteenth century, is founded. The goal of the society is to support Catholics in North America through the donation of funds and spiritual articles.

German writer Charles Sealsfield, after Karl May the most popular German novelist using American settings, publishes his first novel *Tokeah and the White Rose,* which is apparently written first in English.

1830   German American philologist Johann Gottfried Flügel publishes his *Complete Dictionary of the English and German Languages,* which also contains a great number of americanisms. Enlarged, updated, and newly edited by his son Felix, it becomes a standard work, appearing in its fifteenth edition in 1891.

Karl C. Satorius brings German settlers to Veracruz, Mexico, and assembles a small colony of Germans in the tropics.

1833   The Frankfurt banker August Belmont moves to New York City, where he represents the banking house of the Rothschilds.

1834   Detlef Dunt publishes one of the earliest German guidebooks to Texas entitled *Reise nach Texas, nebst Nachrichten von diesem Lande; für Deutsche, welche nach Amerika zu gehen beabsichtigen* (Journey to Texas: With Information about This Land for Germans Planning to Go to America).

1834
(cont.)

German Jacksonian Democrats establish the *New Yorker Staats-Zeitung* (New York Public News), which becomes the most important German-language publication in the city and by far the most successful German newspaper in the United States after the American Civil War. Its circulation rises above 50,000 in the 1880s, making it the sixth-largest newspaper in the United States. It will become the longest-lasting German newspaper in America and, by the end of the nineteenth century, the largest and most powerful. It is the oldest German-language newspaper still operating in the United States.

1835

The *Anzeiger des Westens* (Western Informer) in St. Louis, Missouri, is the first German-language newspaper to be published west of the Mississippi River.

The first German immigrants arrive in Jamaica and settle around Seaford Town.

The *Canada Museum und Allgemeine Zeitung* (Canada Museum and General Newspaper) is launched as Ontario's first German-language paper.

1836

John Jacob Astor opens the Astor House in New York City as the finest hotel in the United States.

1837

Hermann, Missouri, is founded by a group of Philadelphia Germans. It attracts freethinkers, left-liberals, and eventually Forty-Eighters.

1838

The Ludwig-Missionsverein is formed with the permission of King Ludwig I of Bavaria and directed by the archbishop of Munich-Freising. It is charged with promotion of the Roman Catholic Church in the United States.

1839

Prince Maximilian von Wied-Neuwied publishes his *Reise in das innere Nord-Amerika* (Travels in the Interior of North America), which is illustrated by Karl Bodmer.

John Lothrop Motley publishes his first novel, *Morton's Hope*. Its main character

is the dueling, drunken, and rebellious Otto von Rabenmarck, who represents Otto von Bismarck with whom Motley is befriended from their student days at Göttingen and Berlin.

c. 1840

From the 1840s on, the Little Germany on Manhattan Island becomes the largest residential area and most important settlement of German immigrants in New York City.

1840

The Sons of Hermann is founded in New York City as a German American fraternal order. It works for solidarity among German immigrants in the United States through the promotion of their common heritage and traditions.

1842

Twenty-one German noblemen interested in founding a German colony in Texas create the Verein zum Schutze deutscher Einwanderer in Texas (Society for the Protection of German Immigrants in Texas) at Biebrich on the Rhine.

The first Jewish Reform congregation in the United States, the Har Sinai Verein (Har Sinai Association), is established in Baltimore by a group of German Jewish laymen and modeled after the Hamburg Temple.

1843

Twelve German Jews establish the Jewish fraternal order B'nai B'rith (Sons of the Covenant) in New York City.

1844

The German American brewer Jacob Best establishes the Pabst Brewing Company in Milwaukee, Wisconsin.

1845

Prince Carl of Solms-Braunfels establishes the hamlet of New Braunfels in Texas. A few weeks later, Baron Otfried Hans Freiherr von Meusebach founds Fredericksburg in Texas.

1846

The Bavarian monk Boniface Wimmer founds St. Vincent Archabbey, near Latrobe, Pennsylvania, as the first Benedictine monastery in the United States and one of the first Roman Catholic institutions in the United States to see to the needs of German Catholic immigrants. The monastery, located in the Diocese of Greensburg (formerly part of the Diocese of Pittsburgh), forms a college and sends out missions to establish many of the early Benedictine monastic communities in the country.

American travel writer Bayard Taylor publishes his widely popular travel account of Germany *Views A-Foot, or, Europe Seen with Knapsack and Staff.*

A group of young German Jewish women of the newly founded Temple Emanu-El in New York City, guided by Henriette Bruckman, the wife of a German Jewish medical doctor in New York's Little Germany, establish the Unabhängiger Orden Treuer Schwestern (UOTS). This American Jewish sororal order is supposedly the first such organization exclusively for women in the United States.

1847   The Darmstaedters or "The Forty," a group of thirty-four young men from the duchy of Baden, immigrate to Texas to form a utopian communistic settlement.

A group of Hamburg ship owners comes together to form a shipping line, christening it the Hamburg-Amerikanische-Paketfahrt-Aktien-Gesellschaft (Hapag).

Die Deutsche Evangelisch-Lutherische Synode von Missouri, Ohio und anderen Staaten (The German Evangelical-Lutheran Synod of Missouri, Ohio, and Other States) is founded.

The Deutsche Gesellschaft (German Society) of New Orleans is established with the goal of providing support for the numerous German immigrants in the New Orleans area by arranging for housing, helping them to find employment, and assisting them in reaching their ultimate destinations.

1848   In his last will German American merchant John Jacob Astor gives orders to build the Astor Library, which will become at the end of the nineteenth century, together with two other libraries, the New York Public Library.

Frankfurt citizens found the Frankfurter Verein zum Schutz der Auswanderer (Frankfurt Association for the Protection of Emigrants). Its purpose is to organize individual, as well as group, emigration in a safe and modest way.

The *Illinois Staatszeitung* (Illinois Public News) is founded. It will become one of the leading German American daily newspapers during the nineteenth century.

1848–1849 The failure of the national liberal revolutions in central Europe forces many liberal intellectuals to flee the German-speaking countries. These Forty-Eighters settle mostly in the United States and Brazil.

German refugees of the failed German revolutions found the first Turner societies in the United States.

1849   German American painter Emanuel Gottlieb Leutze begins working on his famous painting *Washington Crossing the Delaware* in Düsseldorf.

Moravian brothers (Herrnhuter Brüdergemeine) establish their first mission in Bluefields (Mosquito Coast).

The Wendish migration to Texas begins.

1850   Blumenau, Santa Catarina (Brazil), is founded by seventeen German immigrants. The city will be dominated by German architecture and culture into the twenty-first century.

1851   The Brummer, German mercenaries who had fought in the war of independence for the two duchies of Schleswig and Holstein from Denmark in 1848 and 1849, emigrate to Brazil where they will serve in the army in exchange for land to be given to them upon completion of their four years of military service.

1851
(cont.)

German immigrants begin to settle around Lake Llanquique in Chile. By 1861, several communities will have developed around the lake.

The Socialistischer Turnerbund von Nordamerika (Socialist Turner Union of North America) is founded.

German socialist Wilhelm Weitling creates his Socialist colony Communia in County Clayton, Iowa.

1852

The German translation of Harriet Beecher Stowe's *Uncle Tom's Cabin* sets the paradigm for a German discussion of slavery. A point of reference for expository texts and an influential model for many novels on slavery, it will have a vital impact on German attitudes toward slavery during the nineteenth century.

Cincinnati businessman Robert B. Bowler, an avid horticulturalist, hires German landscape architect Adolph Strauch to design the landscape of his new seventy-three-acre estate, Mount Storm (a public park in 2005) in the picturesque hilltop village of Clifton, newly incorporated just north of the old city of Cincinnati. Strauch also "improves" the landscapes of Robert Buchanan's forty-three-acre Greenhills, George Neff's twenty-five-acre The Windings, Henry Probasco's thirty-acre Oakwood, William Resor's Greendale, and George Schoenberger's forty-seven-acre Scarlet Oaks—all without walls or fences so that the whole neighborhood looks like a large, unified park reached by sinuous drives through undulating terrain for a processional revealing "a sequence of carefully designed, gradually unfolding views." Clifton, one of the first picturesque designed suburbs, is acclaimed the "Eden of Cincinnati Aristocracy" by Emperor Dom Pedro of Brazil and the prince of Wales.

1853

The German American politician Gustave Koerner is elected lieutenant governor of Illinois.

1854

A group of prominent Germans in Philadelphia founds Egg Harbor as a pure German hamlet outside the city. Envisioned as "a new German home in America. A refuge for all German countrymen who want to combine and enjoy American freedom with German *Gemütlichkeit*" it has the distinction of being the most "German" town in America. As late as 1900 virtually everyone in Egg Harbor will still be speaking German.

Wendish immigrants found the settlement of Serbin in Texas.

1855

The Amana Society establishes the Amana Colonies in Amana, East Amana, Middle Amana, High Amana, West Amana, South Amana, and Homestead located in the Iowa River valley in Iowa County in east-central Iowa.

Chicago witnesses the so-called Beer Riot, a violent protest of German and Irish immigrants against a ban on the public sale and consumption of alcohol by the city.

The German Catholic Central-Verein is founded in Baltimore. Originally organized as a confederation of parish-based mutual aid societies, it is at first oriented to the social, economic, and religious needs of first-generation immigrants.

Roman Catholic missionary priest Francis Xavier Pierz publishes his book *Die Indianer in Nord-Amerika* (The Indians of North America). This book is intended to encourage Catholic immigrants to come to Minnesota (Minnesota Holy Land).

1856

One of the very first German Brazilian almanacs, *Der neue hinkende Teufel. Deutscher Volkskalender für das Jahr 1856 für die Provinz S. Pedro do Sul* (The New Limping Devil. German Popular Calendar for the Year 1856 for the Province of S. Pedro do Sul, 1856–1858) is published.

Margarethe A. Schurz opens the first kindergarten in the United States in Milwaukee.

1857   Two Bremen shippers, Carl Eduard Crüsemann and Hermann Henrich Meier, form the Norddeutscher Lloyd (North German Lloyd). It will become one of the world's largest shipping firms before World War I. Its main route covers the Atlantic and it serves as a major tie between the United States and Europe as it takes out emigrants and brings back staple goods. Luxury liners ferry elite passengers between Germany and America.

1858   New York City's Central Park opens. This first landscaped public park in the United States could not have been envisioned, let alone built, without a profound knowledge of German garden theory and German garden design.

Heinrich Balduin Möllhausen (the "German James Fenimore Cooper") publishes his first book *Tagebuch einer Reise vom Mississippi nach den Küsten der Südsee* (Diary of a Journey from the Mississippi to the Coasts of the Pacific).

1859   Friedrich Rittinger and John Motz found the weekly German-language newspaper *Berliner Journal* that will be published every Thursday, without interruption, from now until 1918 in Berlin (Kitchener), Ontario.

Robert Avé-Lallemant, a physician from Lübeck returning from Brazil, reports about the horrible conditions of German colonists at the Mucury River in Minas Gerais, who have been deprived of their rights and are being exploited by lack of sufficient nourishment and medical care as well as rising indebtedness. Avé-Lallemant speaks of "human butchery" and labels any further immigration to Brazil as "unsafe and dangerous." Prussian authorities react immediately. An edict is issued that revokes all concessions permitting recruitment granted previously and forbids all further recruitment for emigration to Brazil. The edict soon becomes known as the *von-der-Heydt'sches Rescript* (Heydt Edict) after Baron August von der Heydt, the Prussian minister for trade and industry whose department handles emigration.

1861   Frankfurt banking houses financially support the Union in the American Civil War, holding nearly 40 percent of the North's debts, which will rise from $90 million to $2.74 billion between 1860 and 1865.

Emmanuel Gottlieb Leutze receives a government commission for a painting to be called *Westward the Course of Empire Takes Its Way* (popularly *Westward Ho!*). After an excursion into the Rocky Mountains, Leutze paints the mural directly upon the wall of the great stairway in the U.S. House of Representatives in Washington, D.C.

1862   The 82nd Illinois Volunteer Infantry Regiment, which includes numerous German volunteers, is mustered into service for fighting in the American Civil War.

In the Battle of the Nueces, German militiamen from Texas who want to join the Union army are massacred by Texas Confederate troops at the Nueces River, near where the town of Comfort will be established.

1863   With U.S. aid, the first German Protestant church in Chile is built in Osorno.

1864   Austrian-born Emperor Maximilian ends discriminatory legislation in Mexico that had discouraged immigration. Enticed by the prospect of living under the rule of Maximilian, thousands of German-speaking immigrants flock to Mexico. The vast majority of these immigrants are young, male, and single, and many of them will return home after Maximilian's execution in 1867.

1864   For his role in the capture of Atlanta, Georgia, German American Peter J. Osterhaus is promoted to major general of the Union army. He is one of five German Americans (the others being August Willich, Franz Sigel, Carl Schurz, and Edward S. Salomon) to reach the rank of major general in the American Civil War.

1865   German American Mathilde Franziska Anneke, together with Cecilia Kapp, opens her Töchter Institut (Daughters Institute) in Milwaukee.

Henry Wirz, a German-speaking Swiss immigrant to America who fought for the Confederacy during the Civil War and commanded the Andersonville prisoner-of-war camp from April 1864 to the end of the war in April 1865, is put on trial for war crimes. Arrested by Union military forces, he is questioned, released, rearrested, and sent to Washington for a war crimes trial relating to his treatment of prisoners at the Andersonville camp. He is convicted and executed for "murder in violation of the laws and customs of war."

1867   German American engineers John Augustus and Washington Augustus Roebling begin planning the construction of the suspension bridge that will link Manhattan with Brooklyn across the East River.

1870   U.S. president Ulysses S. Grant appoints Edward S. Salomon, the highest-ranking German Jewish officer in the Union army during the American Civil War, to the position of territorial governor of the Washington Territory.

1871   Simon Peter Paul Cahensly founds the St. Raphaels-Verein zum Schutz der katholischen deutschen Auswanderer (St. Raphael's Association for the Protection of German Catholic Emigrants) in Mainz.

c. 1871   Brazil's government propagates the *perigo alemão* (German scare) that will continue until World War I. German

Brazilians living in the southern provinces of Brazil are feared to be a fifth column of the German Empire that might eventually help Wilhelm I to establish colonies in Brazil.

1872   German Brazilians in Porto Alegre organize the first *Kaiserfeier* to celebrate the birthday of Wilhelm I.

German priest John Joseph Jessing establishes the *Ohio Waisenfreund* (Ohio Orphan's Friend), which quickly gains a significant voice in the German American Catholic press of Ohio.

Several Waterloo County, Ontario, publishers found the Deutsch-Kanadischer Pressverein (German-Canadian Press Association) to lobby for German-language education in Ontario's public schools.

St. Louis's daily Catholic newspaper, *Die Amerika,* begins publication. It will become the largest and most successful German Catholic daily in the United States.

The Canadian government adopts a proactive immigration policy, resulting in a system of immigration agencies in Europe. Jakob Emil Klotz of Preston becomes Canadian emigration agent in Hamburg, while Wilhelm Hespeler of Waterloo is appointed Canadian immigration agent in charge of all German-speaking territories in Europe and takes up his post in Straßburg, Alsace. Berlin industrialist Jacob Yost Shantz becomes a leading organizer and activist for the settlement of several thousand German-speaking Russian Mennonites in Manitoba, and later establishes his own colony in Didsbury, Alberta, which attracts many descendants of German pioneers from Waterloo County.

1873   Reform Jewish congregations of the West and South launch the formation of a national lay union of Jewish congregations in the United States, the Union of American Hebrew Congregations (UAHC), in Cincinnati, Ohio.

1874   James Morgan Hart publishes his book *German Universities: A Narrative of Personal Experiences. Together with Recent Statistical Information, Practical Suggestions, and a Comparison of the German, English and American Systems of Higher Education.*

1875   Philip Becker and Henry Overstolz are the first German immigrants to serve as mayors of major American cities—Buffalo (New York) and St. Louis (Missouri).

The Hebrew Union College (HUC) is founded in Cincinnati and begins training American rabbinical students.

1876   Johns Hopkins University is founded. It will come to be considered the most "German" of all American universities.

German American educator Karl Gottfried Maeser is appointed principal of the Brigham Young Academy in Provo, Utah.

Karl May begins publishing his famous *Winnetou* in three volumes.

An average of 30,000 Volga Germans from Russia per year begin arriving in the United States and settling in Kansas, the Dakotas, and Oregon along the lines of the Northern Pacific Railroad. Aided by the U.S. Homestead Act and subsidized loans from the railroads, Volga German communities spread across the upper Midwest. The influx will continue at these levels until 1914.

1877   U.S. president Rutherford B. Hayes appoints Carl Schurz secretary of the interior. Schurz effectively reorganizes the Indian affairs administration and introduces many civil service reforms.

The Socialist Labor Party of the United States is founded. The party has a predominantly German working-class membership.

1878   The German parliament passes the Anti-Socialist Laws, which force many Social Democrats to leave Germany and emigrate to North America.

1881   The two first German assemblymen are elected to the provincial assembly in Rio Grande do Sul, Brazil.

Henry Higginson founds the Boston Symphony and puts the German George Henshel in charge of the new orchestra, which is staffed heavily by German and Austrian players.

Jacobo Schaerer builds the first permanent German colony in Paraguay at San Bernardino.

Several German-speaking colonies are established in Paraguay in the late 1800s, of which Nueva Germania, San Bernardino, and Hohenau are the largest.

1882   Johann Most moves *Freiheit* (Freedom), one of the longest-running anarchist periodicals, from London to New York City.

1884   Karl von den Steinen embarks on his first South American expedition. His expedition will find the source of the Rio Xingú, and a member of his team, the physicist Otto Clauss, will produce the first map of the Rio Xingú river system.

1885   At the Pittsburgh Conference, Reform rabbis agree upon the "Pittsburgh Platform" that becomes the basis for "Classical Reform." This movement stresses the Reform principle (i.e., that Judaism's basis is spirit, not law, so that continuous religious progress can be achieved) over communal unity. In Pittsburgh, Reform Jews define themselves as a community of belief. They give up the idea of Jewish nationhood and instead stress their identity as *American* Jews. The conference decides to use David Einhorn's prayer book *Olat Tamid* as a model for the *Union Prayer Book* of the American Reform movement.

1886   An alliance of Chicago factory owners, media concerns, and members of the political establishment seize the opportunity of the Haymarket bombing to destroy Chicago's popular (and mostly German American) radical left, especially the anarcho-syndicalist groups.

The German antisemite Bernard Förster establishes his settlement Nueva Germania in Paraguay. Together with his wife, Elizabeth Nietzsche (sister of the philosopher Friedrich Nietzsche), Förster attempts to establish a "pure" racial living space of Aryans.

Wilhelm Rotermund creates the Synod of Rio Grande do Sul, which will serve as a model for the creation of three other synods: the Evangelical Lutheran Synod of Santa Catarina, Paraná and Other States (1905); the Evangelical Synod of Santa Catarina and Paraná (1911); and the Synod of Central Brazil (1912).

The first English translation of August Bebel's influential book *Woman and Socialism* appears in the United States. The original German book, first published in 1879, will go through over fifty reprintings and new editions in German by 1913 and achieve translation into more than twenty languages. It will rank among the world's first best-sellers. Certainly, it will inspire many women throughout the world to rethink their social situation and some to join the Socialist or women's movements. Its main point is that "[t]he freedom of humanity is not possible without the establishment of the social independence and equality of the genders."

1888   The International Council of Women (ICW) is founded in Washington, D.C. Its intention is not merely to bring together women from across the globe, but also to provide coordination for national women's movements. As such, the ICW is intended as a federation of national organizations.

1889   Richard Sapper, a wealthy German coffee planter, becomes president of the German Society of Guatemala.

1890   German Canadian publisher and journalist John Adam Rittinger begins writing his "Briefe vun Joe Klotzkopp, Esq." (Letters of Joe Klotzkopp, Esq.). These letters, 120 of which he will write until his death in 1915, will all be published in the *Ontario Glocke* and the *Berliner Journal.* The letters are composed in the Pennsylvania German dialect.

1890–1891   Buffalo Bill's Wild West Show goes to Germany. By the end of its travels it will have performed in the German cities of Munich, Dresden, Leipzig, Magdeburg, Brunswick, Hanover, Berlin, Hamburg, Bremen, Cologne, Düsseldorf, Frankfurt, Stuttgart, Karlsruhe, Strassburg, Dortmund, Duisburg, Baden-Baden, Mannheim, Darmstadt, Koblenz, and Aachen. It also visits the Austrian cities of Innsbruck and Vienna.

1891   German American conductor Thedore Thomas founds the Chicago Symphony.

German geologist and explorer in South America Moritz Alphons Stübel offers the city council of Leipzig to present his collections to the city in return for a suitable museum space. The city council agrees to this, and when a new building for the Museum of Ethnology is opened in 1896 the Stübel Collections find a home as the Department of Comparative Regional Geography in a separate room. Stübel's donation includes 82 oil paintings, 100 drawings (including more than 30 large-format Andean panoramas), about 2,000 photographs, and 3,000 geological samples, as well as ethnological artifacts. He develops this unique geographical museum with his own funds, including a library with a map collection—also deriving from his private collection. His expedition notes will form the basis of an *Archiv für Forschungsreisende* (*Archives of Exploration*) that will open in 1902.

1892   German American politician John Peter Altgeld is elected governor of Illinois.

German priest John Joseph Jessing creates the Pontifical College Josephinum in Columbus, Ohio, which will become a leading educational center for German American Catholic priests during the late nineteenth and early twentieth centuries. Instruction is provided in both English and German.

1894   The Deutsche Schule von Mexico/ Colegio Alemán de México opens its doors in Mexico City.

On March 29, the Bund Deutscher Frauenvereine (BDF, or Federation of German Women's Clubs) is founded in Berlin. It is the first umbrella organization with the specific aim of connecting and centralizing the broad spectrum of women's interests and concerns.

1895   German parliament revokes the *von-der-Heydt'sches Rescript* (Heydt Edict) for the three southern states (Rio Grande do Sul, Santa Catarina, and Paraná), but not for the rest of Brazil.

1897   The Hermann monument in New Ulm, Minnesota, financed by contributions from the Sons of Hermann lodges, is opened to the public.

1898   Herrmann Meyer creates his colony Neu-Württemberg in Rio Grande do Sul, Brazil.

Victor L. Berger cofounds the Social Democratic Party of the United States, Branch 1, and is soon recognized as the unchallenged leader of the Socialist movement in the most German city in the United States, Milwaukee, Wisconsin, at the turn of the twentieth century.

1899   Charles Hexamer founds the German-American Central Alliance of Pennsylvania and becomes its first president. The stated goal of the organization is to preserve German culture in America and to establish a national organization for German Americans.

1901   Booker T. Washington agrees to help the German government to improve the cotton output of the German colony of Togo in West Africa from 1901 to 1909. For this purpose he sends an expedition consisting of three Tuskegee graduates, Allen L. Burks, Shepherd L. Harris, and John W. Robinson, led by a German-speaking Tuskegee faculty member, James N. Calloway, to Togoland. The four establish a model plantation at Tove that will operate throughout the German colonial period.

The Deutsch-Amerikanische National Bund (National German-American Alliance, NGAA) is founded, and Charles Hexamer is elected president. The NGAA focuses on promoting the teaching of the German language in public schools, preserving German culture, praising the achievements of German Americans, and fostering closer ties between the United States and Germany.

1902–1903   The clash of German and American interests in Venezuela leads to the Venezuela Crisis.

1904   Richard Wagner's *Parsifal* premieres at the Metropolitan Opera House in New York City, violating the Wagner family's wishes that it not be performed outside of Germany.

1905   U.S. president Theodore Roosevelt mediates between Germany and France in resolving the First Moroccan Crisis peacefully.

1908   Georg von Bosse publishes his history of Germans in the United States, *Das deutsche Element in den Vereinigten Staaten* (The German Element in the United States, 1908), which becomes a standard work.

1910   German American leading academic Hugo Münsterberg organizes the Amerika Institut in Berlin for the purpose of maintaining and furthering academic relations and cooperation between Germany and the United States.

1910
(cont.)

Victor Berger, a German American politician from Milwaukee, is the first member of the Socialist Party elected to the U.S. Congress.

Due in large part to efforts by the National German-American Alliance, a statue of Baron Friedrich Wilhelm von Steuben is unveiled in Washington, D.C.

1911

The Waterloo Lutheran Seminary is founded as Canada's first institution to train pastors for Lutheran congregations within the country. Prior to this, Canada's Lutheran clergy has been exclusively trained in Germany and the United States. Placed in the midst of a predominantly Lutheran and German community, the seminary contributes greatly to Waterloo's German Canadian identity. It later becomes integrated into Wilfrid Laurier University.

1912

German conductor Ernst Kunwald is hired by the Cincinnati Symphony Orchestra.

German conductor Karl Muck, one of history's greatest Wagnerians, is engaged as the conductor of the Boston Symphony Orchestra.

1913

B'nai B'rith founds the Anti-Defamation League (ADL) to fight antisemitism.

The Nebraska legislature passes the Mockett Law. This law calls for instruction in modern European languages for students in the fifth grade and higher if requested by the parents of fifty or more pupils. Given the large percentage of German Americans in Nebraska, the legislation results in German becoming an "official" second language.

1914

Following Great Britain, Canada declares war on Germany.

The War Measures Act gives the Canadian government powers of "arrest, detention, exclusion and deportation" of individuals, and specifically denies the rights of bail and habeas corpus to anyone arrested "upon suspicion that he is an alien enemy."

The Canadian government begins to intern Germans. During the war about 8,000 enemy aliens, mostly Ukrainians but also Germans and Austro-Hungarians are held at 24 locations (e.g., at Amherst and in the national parks at Banff, Jasper, Yoho, and Mount Revelstoke).

Kuno Meyer, professor of Celtic Philology at Berlin University, embarks on a propaganda tour throughout the United States to facilitate the collaboration between German American and Irish American organizations with the goal of ensuring American neutrality in World War I.

Felix Moritz Warburg and Jacob H. Schiff are instrumental in creating the American Jewish Joint Distribution Committee (JDC). The JDC is originally conceived as a short-term project. It originates as a war-relief committee aiming to assist its overseas brethren during the Great War. In the interwar period, following the Russian Revolution, Warburg and the JDC will assist Soviet Jewry by creating the American Jewish Joint Agricultural Corporation (the "Agro-Joint"). Following the Nazi rise to power, Jews from Germany and later from Nazi-occupied Europe will receive the JDC's assistance in emigration and absorption elsewhere. The JDC will help persecuted Jews during World War II and assist displaced persons and Holocaust survivors in its aftermath.

1915

The German-born Carl Laemmle opens one of the first film studios, Universal City, thus contributing to the rapid growth of the film industry in Hollywood.

Mexican revolutionary Victoniano Huerta meets with German representatives in New York City. The Germans promise to provide Huerta and Pascual Orozco with $895,000, along with rifles and ammunition. In return, Germany hopes that Orozco and Huerta will overthrow the Mexican government and set up a pro-German government, thus giving them an ally geographically close to the United States.

The German Admiralty issues a declaration announcing all waters around the United Kingdom to be a war zone and threatening any merchant vessels found within the zone with destruction. Importantly, the declaration indicates that no guarantee can be given as to the safety of the crew and passengers. Neutral shipping will be treated the same as that from combatant nations. This includes American merchant vessels. For the first time, German submarines are directly threatening American ships and American lives.

The German policy of unrestricted warfare soon makes itself clear when the *William P. Frye,* an American vessel carrying a shipment of wheat to England, is sunk in the South Atlantic. This is the first loss of an American ship, and U. S. president Woodrow Wilson's reaction is to warn Germany that it will be held responsible for the safety of American lives.

The sinking of the liner *Lusitania* by torpedo off the coast of Ireland with the loss of 128 American lives and of the British passenger liner *Arabic* inflames public opinion in the United States, with Wilson threatening to break diplomatic relations with Germany.

1916 In a show of patriotism, Berlin, Ontario, is renamed Kitchener after the late British minister of war, Lord Horatio Herbert Kitchener.

Torontonians form an Anti-German League, aiming at the dismissal of all Canadians of German heritage from public office and the administration, as well as taking measures considered necessary against German Canadians.

Bilingual schools (English and German) are abolished in Manitoba, Canada.

German American Catholic women form the Catholic Women's Union (CWU) in St. Louis, Missouri, which is modeled after the Katholischer deutscher Frauenbund (Catholic German Women's Organization, KDF).

Since the Chilean Allied Statutory or Black Lists interrupted German Chilean and German businesses, the German Chamber of Commerce (now Camara Chileno Alemana de Comercio e Industria) is established.

The Liga Chilena Alemana (DCB, German-Chilean Association) is created as an umbrella organization in response to Allied propaganda and black lists to protect German Chilean institutions (especially the schools), to lobby for Chilean neutrality, and to protect the interests of German citizens.

The Lafayette Escadrille (initially known as the *Escadrille Americaine*) is formed under the command of a French officer, Captain Georges Thenault. This unit is made up of American volunteer pilots. Although the U.S. government granted the volunteers' petition to undertake military service abroad, the United States still maintains its neutrality.

1917 After Germany returns to unrestricted submarine warfare, U.S. president Woodrow Wilson breaks off diplomatic relations and begins to arm American merchant vessels. This "armed neutrality" is the final step before American entry into the war.

The German navy torpedoes the Brazilian ship *Paraná*.

Brazil declares war on Germany.

The Brazilian government prohibits the circulation of German newspapers and orders the closing of German schools. A state of siege is declared in the states of Rio de Janeiro, Rio Grande do Sul, Santa Catarina, Paraná, São Paulo, and the Federal District.

1917
(cont.)

The Canadian War-Times Election Act disfranchises all Germans (and other "enemy aliens") who were naturalized but had arrived after 1898, which includes the vast majority of Germans in western Canada. All Mennonites lose the vote without exception. Both groups are also exempted from the draft.

In the Zimmermann Telegram, Germany offers Mexico an alliance. Germany asks that Mexico attack the United States should it attack Germany. In return, Germany, after winning the war, will make sure that Mexico receives back lands that the United States had taken from it in the nineteenth century.

The Zimmermann Telegram and the unrestricted submarine warfare practiced by Germany force the United States to enter World War I.

The American Expeditionary Force (AEF) arrives at Saint-Nazaire, France.

U.S. president Woodrow Wilson creates the Committee on Public Information (CPI) to disseminate American propaganda about World War I.

U.S. president Woodrow Wilson signs the Espionage Act. This act is intended to catch and punish German spies and to stop the subversive activities of enemies.

The U.S. Trading with the Enemy Act requires that foreign-language papers file translations with proper officials of any article dealing with the Red Cross, the Liberty Loan program, the draft, or the war in general. It also gives A. Mitchell Palmer, the alien property custodian, the authority to confiscate tangible or intangible property in the form of land, patents, money, and securities that belong to the enemy. The term *enemy* applies to any citizen of Germany or person residing in Germany even if American-born who owns property in the United States.

The selective internment of Germans in the United States begins. In the begin-ning nonnaturalized male Germans are interned in local jails and at Ellis Island. During the war between 8,500 and 10,000 nonnaturalized German civilians will be interned in camps at Fort Oglethorpe, Georgia; Fort Douglas, Utah; Fort McPherson, Georgia; and Hot Springs, North Carolina.

1918

Bilingual schools (English and German) are abolished in Alberta and Saskatchewan, Canada.

Woodrow Wilson presents his famous Fourteen Points to Congress and to the world. Promising "open covenants of peace, openly arrived at" and national self-determination, his speech is to give the first democratically elected German government some hope for a just peace.

In an extreme instance of violence directed against German Americans during World War I, a lynch mob murders a German American worker, Robert Prager, in Collinsville, Illinois.

1919

The Treaty of Versailles is concluded between Germany and the four Allies (the United States, France, Great Britain, and Italy). It ends World War I and imposes harsh conditions on Germany (limitation of armed forces, territorial and population losses, loss of industrial facilities, colonial losses, acknowledgement of war guilt, and reparation payments). The U.S. Senate refuses to ratify the treaty.

The enactment of Prohibition forces German brewers to fold or retool to produce flavored soda, "near beer," cheese, and candy and to close down the traditional beer gardens.

German and Colombian businessmen found the Sociedad Colombo-Alemana de Transportes Aéreos (SCADTA, Colombian German Air Transport Company) in Barranquilla, Colombia. It is one of the earliest and, for more than a decade, will be one of the most successful ventures in civil aviation in Latin America.

A small group of German Americans in New York City that suffered from considerable anti-German sentiment following World War I creates the Steuben Society of America, which is named after the hero of the American War of Independence, Frederick von Steuben. The organization's goal is to combat anti-German sentiment by celebrating the numerous social, cultural, political, and scientific contributions of German Americans to American society.

1921 The Treaty of Berlin formally ends the war between Germany and the United States.

Henry Ford's blatantly antisemitic *Der Internationale Jude* (*The International Jew*), is published in Germany. Ford's book, which will still be praised and published by antisemites worldwide on the Internet in 2005, also catches the attention of men like Adolf Hitler, who comes to deeply respect and admire Ford as an industrialist and fellow antisemite.

The Germanic Collection at Harvard University, housed in the Adolphus Busch Hall is opened. It combines Renaissance, Gothic, and Romanesque styles to highlight the history of German architectural achievements.

1922 The position of Germans living in South and Central America taken in the *Flaggenstreit* (debate over the German flag) displays their predominantly conservative attitude. The official flag of the Weimar Republic is black, red, and gold—since the Napoleonic Wars the flag of German democrats. The vast majority of Germans in Latin America refuse to recognize these colors, preferring the black, white, and red flag of the Empire. A poll taken by the Verband Deutscher Reichsangehöriger (Confederation of Citizens of the German Reich) in Mexico favors the imperial over the republican flag by a vote of 1,800 to 2.

German American brewer Frank X. Schwab is elected mayor of Buffalo, New York. Schwab acquires national publicity in the 1920s for his open hostility to both Prohibition and the Ku Klux Klan.

Peter Jonas Weissmueller, descendent of a *Donauschwaben* (Danube Swabian) family, swims to his first world record: the 200-meter in 2:15.5 minutes, and thus beats the three-time Olympic gold medalist Norman Ross.

1923 The Heidelberger Austauschstelle (Heidelberg Exchange Center) is founded as an institution to further academic contacts between the United States and Germany and especially to further German American student exchange.

1924 The U.S. government introduces a quota system to limit immigration (25,957 German immigrants per year).

An Allied Reparations Commission headed by the American financier Charles G. Dawes calls for lower reparations payments as part of a comprehensive reform of the German economy (Dawes Plan).

Hugo Eckener pilots the zeppelin (LZ *126*) from Friedrichshafen across the Atlantic to Lakehurst, New Jersey. Eckener receives a ticker tape parade through Manhattan and is praised as the "modern Columbus" by U.S. president Calvin Coolidge.

The crossing of the Atlantic by LZ *126* leads to the founding of Goodyear-Zeppelin in Akron, Ohio. This new enterprise employs thirteen German engineers and begins construction of American airships in 1928. Ten of these ships were to be employed in the crossing of the Pacific.

German Brazilians celebrate *Der 25. Juli. Unser Tag* (The 25th of July. Our Day) for the first time. It commemorates the arrival of the first German immigrants in São Leopoldo in 1824.

1925   Wrigley's establishes its first German production facility in Frankfurt am Main, where it produces the P. K. gumball.

The Akademischer Austauschdienst (Academic Exchange Service, AAD) is founded to increase academic contacts between Germany and the United States.

1926   The German American Gertrud Ederle is the first woman to swim the English Channel.

Concordia University at Austin is founded by thirteen Lutheran congregations in central Texas, the majority membership of which is of Wendish descent. The university regards itself as the only university in the world founded largely by people of Wendish ancestry and will continue to have strong percentages of Wends among its student body, faculty, and staff.

1927   Fritz Lang releases his film *Metropolis.* Lang had the idea for this film back in 1924, while arriving on a ship in New York City. The vision of the skyscrapers seen in the sunrise inspired him to write a story about an inhuman, gigantic city of the future.

1929   The first Coca-Cola vending machines are installed in Germany.

The Young Plan, a new American-led effort to reduce Germany's reparations burden after World War I, is published.

The German Protestant Church in Rio Grande do Sul enters into an affiliation with the German Federation of Protestant Churches, which becomes part of the German Protestant Church in 1933.

The Great Depression spreads from the United States to Germany because of close connections in the financial market.

Leonhard Sigmund Schultze-Jena embarks on his research trip to Central America during which he records the everyday speech of the Indian peoples. He first stays in the Mexican provinces of Guerrero and Oaxaca among the Tlapaneca, Mixteca, and Aztec language groups. Subsequently he travels to the western highlands of Guatemala to study the Mayan language of the Quiché; his last project is to record the language of the Pipil in Salvador.

1930   The German branch of the Coca-Cola Company is founded in Essen.

Marlene Dietrich moves to Hollywood to become one of its most glamorous and provocative stars.

1931   The Austrian Creditanstalt is the first major European bank to fail as the Great Depression spreads to Europe. It causes a chain reaction, and a run at all major German banks ensues.

The Hoover Moratorium effectively cancels all German reparation payments.

The National Socialist German Worker's Party (NSDAP) opens its first Latin American branch in Paraguay.

American journalist Dorothy Thompson publishes her interview with Adolf Hitler (*I Saw Hitler!*). In a somewhat sensational lapse, Thompson emerges convinced of the insignificance and ridiculousness of the führer, but she also introduces him as the "apotheosis of the little man," thus shifting attention to the sociopolitical problem of the masses that will continue to cheer and support him.

1932   Albert Einstein accepts an appointment at the Institute for Advanced Study in Princeton, New Jersey.

Adolf Hitler appoints his friend Ernst Hanfstaengl, the heir of a prominent German art publishing firm and closely connected with American upper society, to be foreign press chief of the NSDAP.

The novelist Plínio Salgado founds the Ação Integralista Brasileira, which represents the Brazilian version of fascism.

The former swimmer Peter Jonas Weissmueller begins his movie career as Tarzan in Hollywood. Within sixteen years he will play in twelve *Tarzan* movies and act in another sixteen films as the star of the *Jungle Jim* series. With his well-trained body and innocent looks, he is considered to be the ideal person to play the role of Tarzan.

1933   After the Nazi seizure of power, the German Parliament passes the Law for the Prevention of Progeny with Hereditary Diseases. It states that anyone with a hereditary illness may be sterilized against his or her will if a medical expert determines that he or she is likely to produce children with a serious hereditary defect. This law is based on several state laws in the United States.

The Friends of the New Germany (FONG) is founded as a Nazi organization in the United States.

1934   The journal *Aufbau* (Construction) is founded in New York City by the German Jewish Club. This German Jewish periodical will achieve considerable influence and standing in the years around World War II.

The Frankfurt School moves to New York where it becomes affiliated with Columbia University. It continues as the Institute for Social Research.

The pro-Nazi Deutscher Bund Kanada (German Association Canada), thinly disguised as a cultural and social club, is founded.

The U.S. Congress creates the Special House Committee to Investigate the Extent, Character, and Objects of Nazi Propaganda in the United States. This is the predecessor for the Committee to Investigate Un-American Activities that will become infamous in the 1940s and 1950s for excesses in its hunt for alleged Communists in the United States.

The Austrian composer Erich Wolfgang Korngold goes to Hollywood, where his film music—written in the tradition of Wagner, Puccini, and Strauss—contributes to the power of the pictures and becomes the prototype of American film music. His musical style becomes the style of Hollywood.

1935   Inspired by current events in Germany, Sinclair Lewis publishes his warning novel, *It Can't Happen Here,* in which he depicts his own country in the iron grip of a 100 percent American dictator.

1936   The African American Jesse Owens wins the 100 meters, the 200 meters, the long jump, and the 4 x100-meter relay at the Olympic Games in Berlin. His success spoils Nazi ambitions to showcase its notion of Aryan racial superiority on the athletic field. After congratulating the Finnish medal winners in the 10,000 meters, German leader Adolf Hitler refuses to congratulate black American Cornelius Johnson, who had won the high jump. Hitler refrains from congratulating medal winners after the IOC informs him that he must congratulate all or none.

Fritz Kuhn founds the German American Bund (GAB) in Buffalo, New York, as the successor to the Friends of the New Germany. In contrast to its predecessor, which had many German nationals among its members, the GAB insists that members must be American citizens of German origin.

Max Schmeling travels to New York City for a boxing match with African American Jesse Jones.

1937   After the Nazi seizure of power, the Bauhaus is closed and its members leave Germany for the United States. Industrialists succeed in bringing Laszlo Moholy-Nagy to Chicago to head the New Bauhaus, soon to be reorganized as the School of Design.

1937
(cont.)
Harvard's Graduate School of Design offers Walter Gropius a professorship of architecture and then the departmental chair from 1938 to 1952, positions through which he makes modernism the dominant international style for a generation of students and emulators, breaking the American architectural establishment away from the Beaux-Arts style.

Brazil introduces a system of immigration quotas. According to this system, immigration is reduced to an annual maximal number of 2 percent of the total number of immigrants of a certain nationality that had immigrated in the previous fifty years.

The Brazilian constitution prohibits all political activities and in the beginning of 1938 all foreign political parties, including the NSDAP.

The zeppelin LZ *129,* christened *Hindenburg,* explodes over Lakehurst, New Jersey. It is the largest and last zeppelin used to transport passengers from Germany to North and South America.

1938
James Mooney, Henry Ford, Charles Lindbergh, and Benito Mussolini receive the *Verdienstkreuz Deutscher Adler* (Grand Cross of the German Eagle), the highest award available to foreigners to reward invaluable service to the Third Reich.

The Ford Motor Company's German subsidiary Ford-Werke AG begins producing troop transport trucks for the German military.

The McCormack Act, which requires the registration of "Agents of Foreign Principals" and outlaws alien political activists in the United States, is passed by the U.S. Congress.

1939
The S.S. *St. Louis,* a German passenger ship with Jewish refugees, is denied entry to Havana and thus forced to return to Europe.

One week after Great Britain, Canada declares war on Germany.

Canada introduces the Defence of Canada Regulations (DCR) under the War Measures Act. Under the DCR, the justice minister may detain without charge anyone who might act "in any manner prejudicial to the public safety or the safety of the state."

1940
With the passage of the Alien Registration Act in the United States, the Alien and Sedition Laws of 1798 are reactivated and aliens have to register with government authorities.

Charlie Chaplin produces the only full-length anti-Nazi movie, *The Great Dictator,* before the U.S. declares war on Germany.

1941
Stefan Zweig publishes his book *Brasilien. Ein Land der Zukunft* (Brazil: A Land of the Future), which praises and romanticizes Brazil. The book is seen as an homage to Brazilian dictator Getúlio Vargas and is even considered to have been commissioned by him.

The U.S. government issues the Trading with the Enemy Act that sets legal prohibitions on trade with Axis nations.

A group of German-speaking exiles in Mexico that includes Egon Erwin Kisch and Anna Seghers founds the political and cultural monthly *Freies Deutschland* (Free Germany).

Germany declares war on the United States.

The U.S. government, fearing Nazi subversion in Latin America, organizes the expulsion of over 4,000 German residents from 15 Latin American countries and their internment in U.S. camps in Texas, Louisiana, and other states.

1942
Stefan Zweig and his wife commit suicide in Brazil and receive a pompous state funeral.

In "Operation Pastorius" German Nazis use recently remigrated German Americans and Nazi sympathizers as agents for acts of sabotage in the United States and land them in two groups by submarine on the shores of Long Island and Florida.

Franz L. Neumann publishes his book *Behemoth: The Spirit and Structure of National Socialism,* which makes him widely known both within and outside academic circles as an expert on contemporary Germany.

Canadian forces engage in a disastrous raid on Dieppe in France. In a matter of hours, the 5,000 Canadian soldiers who composed the bulk of the 6,000-man attacking force were decimated—with more than 900 killed and another 2,000 taken prisoner, most of them wounded, more prisoners than the Canadian army would suffer in the entire 10-month-long Northwest Europe campaign.

American forces land in French Morocco and Algeria as the initial part of the North African campaign.

1943   At the end of the British American conference in Casablanca, Franklin D. Roosevelt, with Winston Churchill at his side, explains that the elimination of Axis war power means their unconditional surrender.

The enforced ban on all political parties and the prohibition of political activities of foreigners in Brazil leads to the end of exile groups such as the Movimento dos Alemães Antinazis (Movement of German Anti-Fascists), the committee Das Andere Deutschland (The Other Germany), and the Movimento dos Alemães Livres (Movement for a Free Germany), which was related to the Communist Bewegung Freies Deutschland (Movement for a Free Germany) in Mexico.

Mildred Fish Harnack is executed for her involvement in the German resistance group known as the Red Orchestra. She is the only U.S. civilian the Nazi government will execute during World War II.

At the Tehran Conference, Winston Churchill, Franklin D. Roosevelt, and Joseph Stalin decide key points of their grand strategy in the European theater and the treatment of defeated Nazi Germany (occupation, division).

Canadian soldiers participate in the invasion of Sicily and subsequent liberation of Italy. During the Christmas Battle of Ortona—"Little Stalingrad" as the exhausted Canadian infantry ruefully names it—vicious house-to-house fighting against fanatic German paratroopers wins the enemy more respect than hatred.

The Royal Air Force (RAF) and the U.S. Army Air Force (USAAF) bomb Hamburg. Incendiary bombs, filled with phosphorus or petroleum jelly (napalm), create a firestorm that kills over 44,000 people. In addition to the heavy civilian casualties, the bombing reduces half the city to rubble and the remainder must be evacuated.

1944   Nineteen left-liberal political and cultural representatives (among them Bertolt Brecht, Hermann Budzislawski, and Paul Hagen) under the chairmanship of the Protestant theologian Paul Tillich establish the Council for a Democratic Germany (CDG) in New York City to add an organized voice of the "other Germany" to the American public wartime debate and in the hope of influencing the official U.S. planning for postwar Germany.

Henry Morgenthau publishes his pamphlet *Program to Prevent Germany from Starting a World War III* (commonly known as the Morgenthau Plan). It is

1944
(cont.)

the most comprehensive scheme for the reconstruction of German society. Morgenthau argues that a powerful, industrialized Germany would inevitably attempt to wage war on its neighbors and the world again. He postulates that Adolf Hitler's rise to power was the logical consequence of the German national character that had earlier produced Prussian authoritarianism and militarism. Only the country's territorial dismemberment and its political and economic impotence would assure future peace.

At the conference of Yalta the United States, the Soviet Union, and Great Britain agree to establish an Allied Control Council (ACC), comprised of the Allied commanders in chief.

The American government drafts JCS 1067, a postsurrender interim occupation directive. It prohibits any steps toward Germany's economic rehabilitation and clarifies that the country had not been liberated but defeated. Yet, the same text gives the U.S. military commander substantial leeway to determine actual occupation policies, further enhanced through provisions granting him the explicit authority to ensure the production of goods and services essential for the prevention of disease and civil unrest.

American and Canadian troops participate in the Normandy (D-Day) landing on the coast of France. Altogether 57,500 American troops and 75,215 British and Canadian troops are landed on D-Day and the assaulting forces suffer 6,000 American casualties and 4,300 British and Canadian ones on the first day of the operation.

1945

The Royal Air Force (RAF) and the U.S. Army Air Force (USAAF) bomb Dresden. Some 650,000 bombs fall on the city from February 13 to 15, 1945, and Dresden is almost totally destroyed as a result of the ensuing firestorm. Estimates vary as to the number of civilian casualties caused by the bombing from 40,000 to 50,000.

American, British, and Russian troops cross the rivers Rhine in the west and Oder in the east, thus advancing deeply into the German heartland. At the end of April, Russian troops encircle Berlin and American and Russian troops meet at the river Elbe.

On May 7 and 8 the remaining German military leadership unconditionally surrenders to the American and Russian forces.

American military forces establish the American Occupation Zone in the territories of the German states of Bavaria and parts of Württemberg, Baden, the former Prussian province of Hesse, the U.S. enclave in the city of Bremen with Bremen's port at Bremerhaven, and a sector of western Berlin.

American occupation forces enforce a strict denazification policy by requesting that every adult German complete a lengthy questionnaire (*Fragebogen*), detailing the subject's personal, professional, and political past.

The Conference of Potsdam, with Harry S. Truman as the new U.S. president, leads to the creation of an additional zone of occupation for the French and accommodates the Soviets on the reparations issue. Germany is to be treated as an economic and administrative unity under the supervision of the Allied Control Council. It is to be subjected to a policy of democratization, decartelization, demobilization, and denazification.

American military forces move into the six districts that will become part of the American sector of occupation in the city of Berlin (Kreuzberg, Neukölln, Schöneberg, Steglitz, Tempelhof, and Zehlendorf) in the middle of the Soviet Zone of Occupation, later to become the German Democratic Republic.

The Nuremberg Trials start. They are a series of thirteen trials that begin on November 20, 1945, and last until April 1949. Indictments are brought against 207 Nazis, who are charged with conspiracy to wage war, crimes against humanity, crimes against peace, and war crimes. The trials are held at the Palace of Justice in Nuremberg, because this was one of the few courthouses that had not been damaged during the air raids and because the city of Nuremberg had been the site for all the NSDAP rallies. The International Military Tribunal (IMT), directed by France, Great Britain, the Soviet Union, and the United States against major Nazi war criminals, leads the first trial. The IMT not only sentences individuals but also bans organizations such as the Gestapo (Geheime Staatspolizei, Secret Political Police), the SS (Schutzstaffel, Protective Squadron), and the SS Totenkopfverbände (SS Death Head Special Units).

The German colony Neu-Württemberg in Rio Grande do Sul, Brazil, is renamed Panambi.

Chicago entrepreneur Walter Paul Paepcke develops Aspen, Colorado, into a modern ski resort with the longest ski lift in the world to create a successful economic basis for his wider schemes: to establish a modern Weimar (the city the famous Johann Wolfgang von Goethe lived in from 1775 until his death in 1832) in America together with his friend Walter Gropius.

1946   Margaret Boveri publishes her anti-American *America Primer for Grown-up Germans. An Attempt to Explain What Has Not Been Understood.*

The Council of Relief Agencies Licensed for Operation in Germany (CRALOG) is founded. It collects donations in the United States for the purpose of humanitarian aid to Germany.

The first German American club in West Germany, the Bad Kissingen Cos-

mopolitan Club, is founded by Captain Merle Potter, a local military governor who sees the need for friendly interaction between Germans and Americans.

Aloisius Münch, bishop of the diocese of Fargo and apostolic visitor to Germany, publishes his controversial pastoral letter *One World in Charity,* in which he rejects the notions of "collective" guilt and responsibility for Germany's population during the Nazi dictatorship.

The Radio Inside the American Sector (RIAS) is created in West Berlin.

1947   Siegfried Kracauer publishes his famous book *From Caligari to Hitler: A Psychological History of the German Film* with Princeton University Press. This study purports to find the ideological roots of National Socialism in some silent films from the Weimar Republic. For Kracauer, the German films produced between 1915 and 1933 already included many of the ideological values that unconsciously prepared German society for Nazism, such as a "collective complex of inferiority," the cult of authority, and the awaiting of a strong chief.

The U.S. secretary of state, George C. Marshall, announces the European Recovery Program (ERP, or Marshall Plan) at Harvard University.

1948   Conflict over currency reform in West Berlin leads the Soviets to block all access into West Berlin sectors by land or on water. In response, the U.S. Air Force and the British Royal Air Force organize the Berlin Airlift that will support the population and military garrisons in West Berlin during the eleven months that the blockade will last before it is suspended after successful U.S.-Soviet negotiations in May 1949. These eleven months will achieve legendary status for German American relations and will strengthen the U.S. commitment to West Berlin.

1949 German nuclear physicist Klaus Fuchs is sentenced to prison for espionage. He participated in the British and American projects to produce an atomic bomb and is convicted of relating some of the information to the Soviet Union.

The Petersberg Agreement restricts the dismantling of German industrial plants and gives West Germany the right to establish consular relations with foreign nations and to join international organizations. At the same time, West Germany concludes a bilateral economic agreement with the United States on Marshall Plan aid and joins the Council of Europe as an associate member.

1950 Radio Free Europe (RFE) is created with headquarters in Munich as part of the National Committee for a Free Europe. It is secretly funded and controlled by the CIA.

West Berlin's government receives a replica of Philadelphia's Liberty Bell, which is installed in the City Hall of Schöneberg following an extensive fundraising drive across the United States. This move symbolizes the mutual identification of America and West Berlin with the cause of freedom and strengthens emotional ties.

George Nauman Shuster is named land commissioner of Bavaria, presiding over the continuing denazification program and preparing for home rule at the close of the American occupation.

West Germany and the United States sign the Marshall Plan agreement.

1951 East German author Liselotte Welskopf-Henrich begins to publish her three-volume epic novel that begins with *Die Söhne der grossen Bärin* (The Sons of Great Mother Bear), which deals with Dakota Indians.

A comprehensive revision of the Occupation Statute not only brings virtually complete internal self-government but

also permits the establishment of a foreign ministry for West Germany.

1952 The German American Fulbright Program is established to facilitate the bilateral exchange of German and American students, instructors, professors, researchers, and professionals.

Soviet leader Joseph Stalin offers in his famous Stalin Note the reunification of Germany to the former Western Allies. The Stalin Note proposes an end to the "abnormal situation" in Germany by (1) a peace treaty between the Four Powers and Germany, (2) administrative unification of the four occupied zones of Germany, and (3) holding of all-German elections (in that order). The proposal also asserts the right of a sovereign Germany to arm itself, with the conspicuous proviso that it is to remain neutral. The Stalin Note is finally rejected by the Western powers and the West German government.

The Volkswagen Company opens its Volkswagen Canada, Ltd., division with headquarters in Toronto.

1953 The Volkswagen Company opens its Volkswagen do Brasil S.A. in São Bernardo do Campo near São Paulo. In the same year the Verkaufsgesellschaft Volkswagen of America, Inc. (Volkswagen Marketing Company of America) is established with its seat in Inglewood, New Jersey.

1954 Alfredo Stroessner, the son of German Paraguayan parents, becomes president of Paraguay and creates a dictatorship that will last until 1989.

1955 The High Commissioner for Germany is dissolved and West Germany receives full sovereignty from the Allies.

The Convention on Relations between the Three Powers (United States, Great Britain, and France) and the Federal Republic of Germany lays out the rationale and circumstances of the deployment of Allied troops in West Germany.

The document declares that the Allied powers have the right to station troops in West Germany, and, although the Americans often state that they will return a property if the Germans insist, such events rarely occur.

The Leo Baeck Institute is founded to document, research, and publish the distinct history of German Jewry and its impact on German society from the Enlightenment to the Holocaust. It is established in the three main centers of German Jewish immigration and German Jewish life after the Holocaust: London, New York, and Jerusalem.

West Germany is admitted to NATO and introduces general male conscription.

1956   German political scientist and Harvard professor Carl Joachim Friedrich publishes, together with Zbigniew K. Brzezinski, *Totalitarian Dictatorship and Autocracy.* This book is best known for its exposition of the conservative theory of totalitarianism that postulates that the similarities between Nazi Germany and Stalinist Russia far outweigh the differences.

1958   Soviet leader Nikita Khrushchev declares the 1944 London Protocol invalid. The Western powers of France, Great Britain, and the United States had forfeited their rights to stay in West Berlin, he says, and the latter should become an "independent political unit, a free city."

The rock legend Elvis Presley lands by boat in Bremerhaven to serve with the U. S. Army in Germany. When he arrives, he is greeted by hundreds of German fans eager to catch a glimpse of the young rock 'n' roll star.

1959   The Paraguayan government issues a Paraguayan identification certificate to war criminal Josef Mengele, who is also known as the "Angel of Death." He is awarded full citizenship under the thinly disguised pseudonym "José Mengele."

1960   Ex-Nazi Wernher von Braun becomes director at the George C. Marshall Space Flight Center, a part of the National Aeronautics and Space Administration (NASA).

Israeli secret service agents find the Nazi war criminal and organizer of the Holocaust, Adolf Eichmann, living on Garibaldi Street in Buenos Aires. The spectacular kidnapping of Eichmann and his secret abduction to Israel result in his trial in Jerusalem.

Following the equipping of the West German army with tactical nuclear weapons (1958), the West German peace movement initiates the Easter Marches.

1963   American president John F. Kennedy visits West Berlin and gives his famous speech in which he declares "Ich bin ein Berliner."

1964   The Volkswagen Company establishes a production facility in Puebla, Mexico, where it produces the VW Beetle.

The Neue Heimat, an organization that is concerned with good relations of East Germans with citizens of German descent in non-Socialist countries, is founded in East Berlin. This society takes full control of East German activities in the United States and provides assistance for Americans in the German Democratic Republic.

1965   The Group 47, a loose organization of West German poets and writers, distances itself publicly from Chancellor Ludwig Erhard's assurance to President Lyndon B. Johnson that West Germany fully supports U.S. policy in Vietnam. The Group 47 denounces the American Vietnam War as a "scorched-earth" tactic and tantamount to genocide.

1966   Canadian folk singer Perry Friedman founds the Hootenanny-Klub Berlin in East Germany, which is later renamed the Oktoberklub.

1966
(cont.)
The East German Deutsche Film Aktiengesellschaft (DEFA) starts to produce a cycle of fourteen highly popular films featuring American Indians as the main characters.

1968
The West German extraparliamentary opposition organizes an international conference on the Vietnam War.

1971
The first German McDonald's restaurant is opened in Munich.

Encouraged and organized by the East German government, thousands of East Germans write protest letters to the U.S. government demanding the release of civil rights activist and Marxist Angela Davis from prison.

1972
American singer-songwriter, actor, film director, and peace activist Dean Reed, the "Red Elvis," decides to move to East Germany.

1973
German-born Henry Kissinger is appointed secretary of state by President Richard M. Nixon.

1974
German Brazilian Ernesto Geisel becomes president of Brazil.

The United States government establishes diplomatic relations with the German Democratic Republic and opens an embassy in East Berlin.

1975
The International Research and Exchanges Board (IREX), which was founded in 1968 by the American Council of Learned Societies to negotiate exchanges with Socialist and other countries, begins to support study trips of American scholars to the German Democratic Republic.

1979
The NATO "dual-track" decision, which calls for modernization of the nuclear arsenal in Western Europe and simultaneous offers of negotiations, causes peace demonstrations in both East and West Germany that will continue for years to come.

Petra Kelly, influenced by the American antiwar and civil rights movements, plays a vital role in the founding of the West German Green Party.

1982
The Easter Marches in West Germany are resumed to protest the dual-track strategy of NATO.

1983
Peru extradites Nazi war criminal Klaus Barbie to France.

The German Democratic Studies Association of the USA is founded.

An agreement between the German Democratic Republic (GDR) and the International Research and Exchange Board (IREX) in Washington, D.C., facilitates the exchange of academics between both countries, but is clouded by the GDR's intention to send primarily natural and engineering scientists to obtain technological knowledge banned from trade with Western countries.

1985
American president Ronald Reagan visits Bitburg War Cemetery to honor German soldiers who died in World War II. Intended as a symbolic act of German American reconciliation, the ceremony provokes strong protests from U.S. veterans of World War II and the American Jewish community after approximately forty-eight graves of Waffen-SS soldiers are discovered and Reagan equates victims of the concentration camps with fallen German soldiers.

Günther Walraff publishes his book Ganz unten (Totally Down Under). After having worked under the disguise of a Turkish national at a McDonald's restaurant, Walraff details McDonald's mistreatment of employees. His book becomes a big success and results in high losses for the West German McDonald's.

1986
German American writer and scholar Richard Plant publishes his study of the fate of homosexuals under the Nazis, The Pink Triangle.

1987   The German Historical Institute in Washington, D.C., is founded to further German American academic and intellectual exchange.

1989   Visa requirements to enter West and East Berlin are waived on December 22. Farcically, passport checks remained in place until June 30, 1990.

1990   The Two-Plus-Four Accord, involving the four World War II Allies (the United States, Great Britain, France, and the Soviet Union) and the two Germanies, pave the way for the Second German Unification.

1997   German legal expert Christian Tomuschat is appointed head of the Guatemalan Commission for Historical Clarification (Comisión para el Esclarecimiento Histórico, CEH). Its mandate is to undertake the clarification of human rights violations and acts of violence that occurred during over thirty years of armed confrontation between government forces and guerilla insurgents. Based on its findings, the CEH is supposed to formulate recommendations with the objective of promoting peace and national harmony in Guatemala.

1999   McDonald's opens its 1,000th restaurant in Berlin-Treptow (former East Berlin).

2002   German chancellor Gerhard Schröder distances himself from the war-mongering policy of U.S. president George W. Bush. Struggling for his reelection, Schröder refuses to support any military action against Iraq. After his reelection, Schröder steers Germany closer to France and Russia who also oppose an American invasion in Iraq.

2003   The last VW Beetle (No. 21,529,464) rolls off the assembly line in Puebla, Mexico, after an unexpected and unprecedented lifespan of fifty-eight years. Sold in the United States until 1978, the VW Beetle and VW Bus became the symbols of an alternative counterculture during and after the 1968 student revolutions. No longer just a car, the Beetle has become the center of a cult since the 1960s and its association with the hippie movement. It still has a very strong fellowship of believers worldwide. It even became the star, "Herbie," of a Walt Disney movie *The Love Bug* (1968), followed by three sequential movies: *Herbie Rides Again* (1974); *Herbie Goes to Monte Carlo* (1977); and *Herbie Goes Bananas* (1980).

Austrian American world-champion bodybuilder and actor Arnold Schwarzenegger is elected governor of California.

INTRODUCTORY ESSAYS

← →

GERMAN-LANGUAGE MIGRATION TO THE AMERICAS

NORTH AMERICA

Dirk Hoerder

German-speaking men and women departed Europe for many parts of the world but in particularly large numbers for North America. Agricultural settlers, miners, and skilled workers came from the contiguous German-language territories in Central Europe and, toward the end of the nineteenth century, in secondary migrations from earlier migration destinations and settlement enclaves in SouthEastern and Eastern Europe. Until the early nineteenth century German speakers who reached North America were mainly indentured servants. In the next decades, large numbers came in search of agricultural land; from the mid-nineteenth century on, migrants were predominantly laboring men and women. Refugees reached the Americas first after the unsuccessful revolutions of 1848 and 1849 in Europe; then under Otto von Bismarck's anti-Socialist laws after 1878; finally, and most importantly, after the Nazi rise to power in 1933. From the 1880s to 1918, at the height of its nationalism and imperialist designs, the German Reich attempted to use the migrants, designated *Auslandsdeutsche,* for expansionist designs and thus warped the processes by which these immigrants became part of their host societies.

Origins and Diasporas: The Many German-Language Societies

"German" migrants originated in many cultures, came from different states, and were differentiated by class and gender, as well as by their stages of economic and political development at the time of departure. In contrast, nationalist historiography has for a long time constructed a German continuity and unity from the medieval Hohenstaufen Empire via the small ("dwarf") principalities to the Habsburg and Hohenzollern empires and, with the "interruption" of the refugee-generating Third Reich, to the Federal Republic of Germany and to unified Germany after 1989. People, however, do not migrate from historians' constructs but from regional societies into which they have been socialized. Thus, the territories and societies from which speakers of the many German dialects departed need to be described first.

The early modern German-language settlement areas constituted only a part of what had been the medieval transeuropean Holy Roman Empire, later called the Holy Roman

Empire of German Nation. Around 1500, when the dynasties of the Iberian peninsula reached out for the Americas, the German-language territories were differentiated by cultures and dialects, consisted of culturally mixed borderlands, and were in contact with neighboring non-German societies. The contiguous region of German dialects included Holstein and Lower Saxony in the northwest; formerly Slavic Mecklenburg and Pomerania in the northeast; Saxony, Franconia, Bavaria, Austria, Styria, and Carinthia in the central and southeast; Tyrol and several Swiss cantons in the south; Alsace, Swabia, and Lorraine in the southwest; and the Rhenisch, Palatine, and Hessian regions in the west. This core region was ringed by mixed borderlands: Schleswig and the Baltic region; Bohemia, Silesia, Moravia; regions in which Italian dialects were spoken; and mixed German French and German Dutch territories. By the time of the nineteenth-century mass migrations, the Habsburg dynasty had incorporated historic Hungary, the Hohenzollern dynasty, and the western third of Poland into their realms. From all of these regions men and women moved outward, first mainly eastbound, but subsequently mainly westbound to the Americas.

From the medieval and early modern period to the beginning of the twentieth century, migrations were artisanal, rural-urban, interurban, but also circular—men and women returned to their places of origin after periods of work elsewhere and with experience of different lifestyles. Even when migrants to other cultures intended to establish a cultural enclave, as was the rule in dynastic states, they interacted with the surrounding society, whether as "Germans" in the Slavic lands or as Huguenots in one of the German states. A bird's-eye view reveals a complex pattern of mobility and settlement: In the late Middle Ages, along the shores of the eastern Baltic, a *rural* Balto-Slavic-German-Flemish mixed population emerged and, halfway between Belgrade and the Black Sea, the Transylvania Saxons established themselves. In subsequent centuries, migrants established an East Central European and Eastern European *urban* German-language culture based on special *ius civitatum urbanum* (the law of particular cities, especially of Magdeburg, and their burghers), not on "German" *ius teutonicum* (a generic law of a German polity). *German* was not a designation found useful at the time because people identified themselves by region and religion. The Ashkenazim communities in Poland, Lithuania, and Russia and their *shtetl* cultures of German Jewish origin used the Yiddish dialect of the German-language family. Migrating artisans reached eastward to St. Petersburg, southeastward via Budapest to the cities of the eastern Mediterranean, and westward to Paris and London. An artisanal German dialect became the lingua franca of Europe's craftspeople and, in the nineteenth century, in competition with English, of technological innovation. In a new eighteenth- and nineteenth-century eastward movement, the Danube Swabians, the Black Sea and Volga Germans, the Mennonites in East Prussia and South Russia, and ethnic German workers in Polish towns and cities established their many distinct cultures. While the craftsmen voluntarily adopted German as the lingua franca, the Habsburg and Hohenzollern bureaucracies imposed it on other peoples. In the early nineteenth century, emigrants changed direction westward to North America, where settlements as differentiated as in Eastern Europe, although in a nineteenth-century industrializing context, emerged. Others moved southwestward to Latin America, South Africa, and Australia, where islands of settlement developed.

Throughout these centuries, the contiguous German-language region also received immigrants from many other cultures. Traders from as far as Africa visited the early modern South Germany commercial towns. After the Reformation and the resulting schism of western Christendom in 1517, German principalities generated masses of religious refugees and admitted coreligionists sent fleeing from elsewhere. These included the French-language Huguenots as well as the Moravians. Religion served as the marker of identity and belonging rather than language or ethno-culture. Whether in Lübeck, Cologne, or Vienna, urban populations were culturally mixed: The language of Hamburg's stock exchange was Flemish. Vienna had a Greek colony, and Cologne its important Jewish quarter. Along the rivers and the littorals of the northern seas sailors of many origins arrived; courts called administrators and military officers from afar and hired soldiers wherever they could be had for comparatively low wages. With commercial and industrial development, Italians, Poles, Swiss, Swedes, Dutch, and many others came as laborers and technicians from their internally diverse societies. By the end of the nineteenth century, Germany, Britain, France, Switzerland, the Netherlands, and the United States ranked as the largest importers of labor migrants. In all of these countries, industrial and societal development depended on migrants.

The origin of Germans in America has never been one Germany but many Germanies, as well as culturally mixed regions and colonies of settlement further afield. While transatlantic migration began in the sixteenth century for Iberian colonization in Latin America as well as the establishment of the Caribbean plantation societies, the vast majority of migrants chose North America as a destination. From the end of the Napoleonic Wars to the aftermath of World War II, some 7 million people left that segment of the culturally diverse, politically divided but geographically contiguous Central European German-language region that was to become the German Empire in 1871. To these, German-speaking migrants from other states and distant destinations of earlier migrations have to be added. German emigration was second only to that from the United Kingdom until Italian emigration surpassed it in 1900. Per thousand of population it ranked tenth among European sending countries. Remittances of emigrants' savings to relatives in their home countries contributed to an image of an America of considerable opportunities. *German* thus is a mix of many influences that developed dynamically over the centuries, and the Germany after 1871 was a society influenced to some degree by emigrants, in particular those in the United States.

North America: From Many-Cultured German Immigrants to German Americans

Although event-oriented historical memory usually dates the commencement of German migration to the founding of Germantown in Pennsylvania in 1683 by Mennonite and Quaker families from the Krefeld region, the New Amsterdam/New York colony (founded in the 1620s) had accommodated English and Scottish dissenters, Mennonites and Quakers, as well as German Lutherans even earlier. In the seventeenth and eighteenth centuries, when some 75,000 (or according to other estimates: 110,000) men, women, and children migrated across the Atlantic, areas of origin coincided for east- and westbound transcontinental and transatlantic departures: the southwestern principalities, the German Swiss territories, Alsace, and the Palatinate (Fertig 1994). Settlement opportunities in Pennsylvania mobilized Mennonites and pietists who formed compact colonies like their coreligionists in the east. When, in the 1750s, the British government attracted Protestant settlers to Catholic and French-speaking Acadia, renamed Nova Scotia in 1713, some 1,500 came from British-ruled Hanover and Brunswick, but also from Switzerland and elsewhere (Bell 1990). The German-language so-called foreign Protestants of Nova Scotia formed their own municipality, and in the Pennsylvania legislature procedures were bilingual up to the era of the American Revolution.

In the early phase, migration involved mass recruitment of "redemptioners" or indentured servants of German as well as English and French origin. Under this system, ship captains and entrepreneurs transported migrants and sold them "for time" to recover the cost of the transatlantic voyage. People without means thus had a chance to move upon their own decision, outside of the often collective migrations based on religious ties. Poverty in the regions of origin, an efficient labor market in the region of arrival, and post-contract independent lives explain why between one-half and two-thirds of all white immigrants before 1776 came to North America under this system. At first, these migrants were mainly destined for the mid-Atlantic colonies' staple-crop production, especially tobacco. They subsequently also settled as skilled artisans in seaboard cities. Demand directed men and women from the Germanies to Philadelphia as a port of arrival and from there to Pennsylvania's hinterlands—that is, to the German-language segment of the North American labor markets. After serving their time, usually seven years, they could move freely. For them, Pennsylvania became the "best poor man's country" and information sent back home induced sequential migrations. Such relational continuity is characteristic of migration networks.

A further group of migrants, the so-called Hessians, came against their will when central German princes sold male subjects as soldiers to the British Hanoverian ruler during the American War of Independence after 1775. As in warfare in Europe—for example, the Habsburg campaigns in the Balkans—such involuntary soldier-migrants became scouts: They took note of opportunities, sent information back to their communities of origin, and thus induced others to follow. Land could easily be acquired and, while in Germany one grain of wheat sowed produced three grains at harvest, the crop yield in Pennsylvania amounted to ten grains.

At the founding of the United States in 1789, the population consisted of English (49 percent), African slaves and free blacks (20 percent), Germans and Scots (7 percent each), as well as of Irish, Dutch, French, Swedish, and Spanish. Because of the revolutionary and Napoleonic Wars in Europe, few migrants came in the next quarter century. When, in 1815, the Congress of Vienna reversed the changes of the Age of Revolution and reestablished the reactionary regimes and when, in the 1820s, the Habsburg and Romanov governments restricted in-migration of ethnic German peasant families, the importance of transatlantic destinations increased. Furthermore, the particularly cold winter of 1816 and 1817 resulted in famine-induced departures from the traditional regions. These then expanded from the German southwest to the Hessen principalities in the

1840s, to Mecklenburg in the 1850s, and to the agrarian northeast and to cities across the Germanies in the 1870s. Departures in the century from 1815 to 1914 peaked from the mid-1840s to the mid-1850s, from the mid-1860s to the mid-1870s, and from 1880 to the early 1890s.

The nineteenth-century economic migrants, rather than also seeking religious self-determination like those of the seventeenth and eighteenth centuries, wanted to rid themselves of their respective principalities' overbearing bureaucracy and reactionary regimes. Peasant families were aware of the far lower taxes and the absence of tithes in North American societies. Notwithstanding some aristocrats' attempts to establish a German-cultured state in Texas, they migrated in networks to areas where earlier migrants from the same (micro)region of origin had established themselves and where soil and climate suited their intentions, where land prices were low and market access easy. In their letters, many reported home that they could elect their local officials themselves. From the mid-1840s on, an ever-larger percentage came as labor migrants from both rural and urban origins. At this time, internal mobility in the German Federation increased while Europe-wide migrations of German-language artisans and skilled workers declined. In contrast, German American neighborhoods in New York, New Orleans, Galveston, and especially in the cities of the Midwest experienced vigorous growth as part of the rapidly expanding U.S. economy. Skilled artisans left the Germanies when incipient factory production threatened the survival of their crafts and their social position. In North America, with no institutionalized craft apprenticeship, they could become foremen in the new factories.

The refugees from the revolutions of 1848 and 1849, the Forty-Eighters, carried genuinely German reformist political convictions across the Atlantic. As a political and intellectual elite, they were outspoken and some—Carl Schurz, for example—became prominent in U.S. politics. Because of their high visibility, their influence has been as overemphasized in public memory as that of the Puritan migrants in English American memory. They numbered but a few hundred out of the 1 million arriving in the decade after 1848. The anti-Socialist laws of the Bismarckian government (1878–1890) resulted in another political refugee movement to the United States. But, again, activists were few in relation to the mass migration of proletarians.

Rapid industrialization, rigid class structure, as well as antilabor legislation, induced 2.4 million working men and women to leave Germany between 1871 and 1893 (Marschalck 1973), despite appeals by the Social Democratic Labor Party to stay in Germany and struggle for better conditions at home. Some emigrated because of the harsh, obligatory military service and because, after the German wars against Denmark and France, they feared further warfare. The migrants, predominantly from cities and the regions east of the Elbe River, were of agrarian and proletarianized backgrounds and selected cities as destinations. Thus, Chicago became one of the largest centers of the German American working class. A Social Democratic diaspora developed and, by sending back money, contributed to the survival of social democracy under Bismarckian repression.

Acculturation in both Canadian and U.S. societies involved cultural interaction with mainstream society and other immigrant groups, ethno-cultural diversity as well as homogenization, and internal social stratification. In rural areas, German Catholics and

German Lutherans often settled separately, but among Americans, Canadians, and immigrants from many countries of Europe. Insertion into communities was quick because these communities were built by the newcomers. Even in so-called ethnic-bloc settlements, cultural interaction was ever present. Socialized in multiethnic interaction, Germans from Russia or the Balkans often spoke several languages. Children mingled in school. Men in need of cash for their families frequently worked far from their homesteads and mingled with Galicians, Irish, Scots, English, Italians, Russians, Norwegians, Swedes, and others.

Self-organization usually occurred along regional lines, in *Landsmannschaften* (associations of people from the same region), and, often, separately in Catholic and Protestant communities. The position of German citizens of Jewish faith was ambivalent. Some joined the German American communities; others became part of Jewish American organizations. At the same time, a postmigration Germanization process began, comparable to developments in other immigrant groups. From the outside, the newcomers were quickly reduced to generic "Germans" by their Anglo-American and immigrant neighbors who could not distinguish between the many regional cultures of origin. Within their communities, the multiregional *Landsleute* (countrymen and countrywomen) established common institutions to pool resources for political action. Their cultural Germanness developed in the frame of U.S. or Canadian society in interaction with non-German cultures. Because an ethnic group's status depended in part on its host society's image of its state of origin, the imagined community of Germans identified with the new German Empire when it became a factor in international affairs, but many dissociated themselves from it when Wilhelm II's increasing arrogance and the declaration of war in 1914 resulted in hostility in the U.S. and Canadian host societies.

The continuing connections immigrants had to kin in their respective regions of origin, return migration, and migrants shuttling between labor markets on the two continents by the 1870s had resulted in the emergence of diasporic-stratified ethnic communities with an urban bourgeoisie, a working class, and rural clusters from New York to Wisconsin—as well as in Texas and Missouri. Ethno-culturally German men and women americanized, crossed the group's boundaries, and mingled with other ethno-cultural groups. Some, in particular those who disagreed with German policies, did so quickly, the majority in the course of two or three generations. In Canada, the emergence of a German Canadian group was even more complex because of the country's regional diversity and lower level of urbanization in the early 1900s, as well as because of the German-speaking immigrants' diversity.

In the 1890s a caesura occurred in the patterns of German migration. After 1893 the German Empire's economy was able to absorb surplus agrarian labor. In the two decades before 1914, only between 20,000 and 40,000 German migrants arrived annually in U.S. ports (Marschalck 1973). Between 15 and 20 percent of these migrants returned to Germany (Kamphoefner 1988). Beginning in the mid-1880s, German *Junkers* and industrialists hired Poles for low-paying seasonal labor on the eastern estates or for mining jobs in the industrialized Ruhr district. Italians and western Ukrainians (Ruthenians) came; Russian Jews migrated to major cities. After 1900 Germany—an exporter of human labor a

German emigrants for New York embarking on a Hamburg steamer, 1874. (Corbis)

mere decade earlier—had become the second-largest labor importer after the United States in absolute figures (Herbert 1986).

This caesura is less evident as regards migration to Canada. As in the case of Germantown, Pennsylvania (founded 1683), a few men and women arrived early but, in general, Canada became a destination only in the nineteenth century. Migrants aimed for the cities and, when settlement of the prairies began in the 1870s, for the West. When the United States began to reduce immigrant admission after 1917, Canada's populationist policy kept its borders open, and German and other European immigrants increasingly selected this society. However, during the worldwide depression of 1929, entry into Canada became more difficult, too.

In both North American states, the multiple German-speaking groups diversified even more when Russian Germans and Russian Mennonites, as well as Hutterites, decided to move to North America in semivoluntary or compelled secondary migrations. From the 1880s, the age of nationalizing dynastic societies, the czarist government abolished the settler colonies' privileges: self-administration with separate schools and exemption from military service. Thereafter, all children were required to attend Russian schools. The Mennonites' pacifist convictions were violated. At first in the U.S. Dakotas, then increasingly on the Canadian prairies, these migrants once again attempted to achieve an enclave-type cultural retention through patterns of bloc settlement. A comparison from 1881 to 1941 of the ethnic-origin with the mother-tongue immigration statistics of the

Canadian census shows that many of the non-Mennonite immigrants, self-designated "Germans from Russia," no longer spoke the German language (Szabo 1996, 11–31). At the same time, the Danube and Transylvanian Saxons left their economically marginal regions for wage labor in North America. These migrations lasted into the 1920s.

From the North American German-(Empire)-origin community, the Mennonite and Amish "Pennsylvania Dutch" and the Hutterite and other ethno-religious groups remained distinct. They continued their traditional ways of life, and when land in Pennsylvania became increasingly scarce for new generations, some migrated to Ontario to the area around Berlin (now Kitchener) and nearby St. Jacobs, where this Mennonite community continues to exist into the twenty-first century. Similarly, German-speaking migrants from Austria and Switzerland and from the mixed areas in east-central Europe—Hungary, for example—preferred to organize among themselves. Their cultural ways and dialects were different and they resented a hierarchy in which Germans from the German Empire placed themselves at the top of "Germanness" in the two North American societies. Nevertheless, interaction among these groups occurred when it was mutually beneficial.

Boundaries were constructed and reconstructed; they were never clearly delineated and always permeable. The migrants were neither dislocated, nor uprooted, nor even hyphenated. They lived, according to recent concepts, transculturally. Migrating in a period that has been labeled the apogee of nationalism, they had, in fact, left empires that were yet to be transformed into state-nations or self-described nation-states. While the German Empire emphasized "Germanness" (although citizenship was still that of the constituent states), the Habsburg monarchy—despite rampant German Austrian nationalism—still referred to itself as a state of many peoples. The Romanov Empire, which had never disputed its many-cultured composition, from the 1880s began to abrogate the special status accorded to immigrants of earlier centuries.

Though divided by region of origin, dialect, class, religion, and time of arrival (making newcomers "greens" or greenhorns), as well as by urban or rural lifestyle, gender, generation, or nationalist or working-class political views, a sizable part of those labeled or self-defined as Germans in the United States combined into a full-fledged community with institutions, a press, and group politics. The continuing transatlantic migration, up to the 1890s in the United States and into the 1920s in Canada, reinvigorated communities with each new cohort of immigrants and prevented memories from becoming "frozen in time" and relationships to the communities of origin from withering. Even though farming communities in the American Midwest or the Canadian prairies could retain culture over generations and though they struggled for German-language schools, interaction with neighbors and in the market prevented the emergence of a separatist mentality. In multiethnic urban neighborhoods, acculturation lurked at every street corner, as some immigrants put it. The period from the 1870s to the early 1900s was the apogee of German American visibility and organizational activity.

With the end of mass emigration from Germany in 1893, however, German Americans began to lose their connectedness to their society of origin. At the same time, at the height of its nationalism and imperialist designs, the German Empire's government attempted to utilize the emigrants as *Auslandsdeutsche* and, for those who accepted this rein-

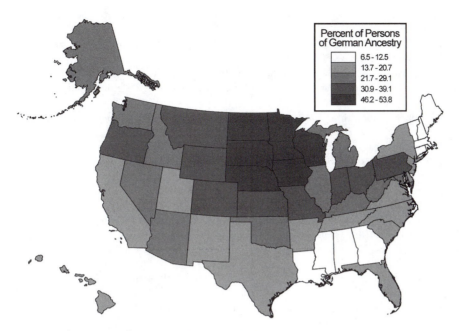

Percent of Persons of German Ancestry: 1990

Source: U.S. Census Bureau, 1990 Census of Population and Housing.

corporation, this warped the processes of acculturation into their host societies. When in 1914 war began in Europe, German American institutions had stagnated for two decades, and *Auslandsdeutsche* supporters of the German aggression were viewed as subversives. When public opinion labeled the German Americans "enemy aliens" after U.S. entry into the war in 1917, many of their institutions folded. The interpretation that such anti-German feelings destroyed a lively and viable community is contradicted by the decline of immigration since the 1890s, the declining interest in the community's press, and the attrition of membership in its associations. After the war, the censuses of 1920 (United States) and 1921 (Canada) indicated a sharp decline in number of those who designated themselves as "German," while the numbers of "Dutch" increased almost correspondingly. The war accelerated a process of becoming part of mainstream society that had been underway already for a long time.

> **See also** Amish; Assimilation of Germans in the United States; Berlin/Kitchener, Ontario; Bismarck's Anti-Socialist Laws; Canada, Germans in (during World Wars I and II); Chicago; Forty-Eighters; Germantown, Pennsylvania; Hessians; New Orleans; New York City; Newspaper Press, German Language in the United States; Nova Scotia; Ontario; Pietism; Politics and German Americans; Schurz, Carl; Texas; World War I and German Americans

References and Further Reading

Bade, Klaus J., ed. *Deutsche im Ausland—Fremde in Deutschland. Migration in Geschichte und Gegenwart.* München: Beck, 1992.

Bell, Winthrop P. *The 'Foreign Protestants' and the Settlement of Nova Scotia.* First ed., 1961, repr. Sackville, NB: Mount Allison UP, 1990.

Chmelar, Hans. *Höhepunkte der österreichischen Auswanderung.* Vienna: Österreichische Akademie der Wissenschaften, 1974.

Conzen, Kathleen Neils. *Making Their Own America. Assimilation Theory and the German Peasant Pioneer.* Oxford, UK: Berg, 1990.

Engelmann, Frederick C., Manfred Prokop, and Franz A. J. Szabo, eds. *A History of the Austrian Migration to Canada.* Ottawa: Carleton University, 1996.

Fertig, Georg. "Migration from the German-Speaking Parts of Central Europe." *Europeans on the Move. Studies on European Migration 1500–1800.* Ed. Nicholas Canny. Oxford: Oxford UP, 1994, 210–218.

Harzig, Christiane. *Familie, Arbeit und weibliche Öffentlichkeit in einer Einwanderungsstadt. Deutschamerikanerinnen in Chicago 1880–1910.* Ostfildern: Scripta Mercaturae, 1991.

Harzig, Christiane, ed. *Peasant Maids—City Women.* Ithaca, NY: Cornell University, 1997.

Herbert, Ulrich. *Geschichte der Ausländerbeschäftigung in Deutschland 1880 bis 1980. Saisonarbeiter, Zwangsarbeiter, Gastarbeiter* (Berlin-West, 1986); English translation under the title *A History of Foreign Labor in Germany 1880–1980. Seasonal Workers, Forced Laborers, Guest Workers,* transl. by William Templer (Ann Arbor: University of Michigan Press, 1991).

Hoerder, Dirk. "The German-Language Diasporas. A Survey, Critique, and Interpretation." *Diaspora: A Journal of Transnational Studies* 11, no. 1 (Spring 2002): 7–44.

Hoerder, Dirk, and Jörg Nagler, eds. *People in Transit. German Migrants in Comparative Perspective, 1820–1930.* Cambridge, UK: Cambridge University, 1995.

Kamphoefner, Walter D. *The Westfalians. From Germany to Missouri.* Princeton, NJ: Princeton University, 1987.

———. "Umfang und Zusammensetzung der deutsch-amerikanischen Rückwanderung." *Amerikastudien* 33 (1988), 291–307.

Keil, Hartmut, and John B. Jentz, eds. *German Workers in Industrial Chicago, 1850–1910: A Comparative Perspective.* DeKalb: Northern Illinois University, 1983.

Lehmann, Heinz. *The German Canadians 1750–1937. Immigration, Settlement and Culture.* Trans. and ed. Gerhard P. Bassler. St. John's, NF: Jesperson, 1986.

Marschalck, Peter. *Deutsche Überseewanderung im 19. Jahrhundert. Ein Beitrag zur soziologischen Theorie der Bevölkerung.* Stuttgart: Klett, 1973.

Moltmann, Günter, ed. *Deutsche Amerikaauswanderung im 19. Jahrhundert: Sozialgeschichtliche Beiträge.* Stuttgart: Metzler, 1976.

Rippley, LaVern J. *The German-Americans.* New York: American University, 1976.

Sauer, Angelika E., and Matthias Zimmer, eds. *A Chorus of Different Voices. German-Canadian Identities.* New York: Lang, 1998.

Scherer, Karl, ed. *Pfälzer-Palatines.* Kaiserslautern: Arbeitskreis für Familienforschung, 1981.

Szabo, Franz A. J., ed. *Austrian Immigration to Canada. Selected Essays.* Ottawa: Carleton University, 1996.

———. "German-Speaking Immigrants of Many Backgrounds and the 1990s Canadian Identity." *Austrian Immigration to Canada. Selected Essays.* Ottawa: Carleton University Press, 1996, 11–31.

Wokeck, Marianne. *Trade in Strangers. The Beginnings of Mass Migration to North America.* Philadelphia: Pennsylvania State University, 1999.

Yedlin, Tova, ed. *Germans from Russia in Alberta: Reminiscences.* Edmonton, AB: Central and East European Studies Society, 1984.

GERMAN JEWISH MIGRATION TO THE UNITED STATES

Adi Gordon and Gil Ribak

The immigration of German-speaking Jews to North America began long before both the United States and Germany were born as independent countries. The circumstances that brought about Jewish migration out of Central Europe in the eighteenth and nineteenth centuries were socioeconomic and political. The situation was much different after 1933, however, when Nazi Germany engaged in a systematic persecution of Jews. Between 1933 and 1940, when German Jews were still able to leave the Third Reich (though it became harder and harder), the United States remained their favored destination. British-ruled Palestine came second.

While the first Jews with Ashkenazic (denoting Jews who originated in Medieval Germany) names arrived in North America as early as 1654, Jewish migration from German- and Austrian-ruled regions to America remained minuscule until the 1820s. Between the 1820s and 1870s, some 150,000 to 180,000 Jews emigrated from Central Europe to the United States (Diner 1992, 35; Cohen 1984, 12). This migration virtually constituted American Jewry before 1880. The period stretching between the 1880s and 1933 saw German Jewish immigration to the United States coming almost to a halt. In those years (before the United States curtailed immigration in 1924), Germany primarily served as a transit point for the masses of Jewish immigrants from Eastern Europe en route to the United States. The Austro-Hungarian Empire witnessed the migration of masses of mostly Yiddish-speaking Jews from Austrian-ruled Galicia to the United States.

Early Emigration from Central Europe to North America (1654–1820)

Several Jews with Ashkenazic names were among the first group of Jews who sailed to North America and landed (1654) on Manhattan Island, New Amsterdam (renamed New

York when England captured it in 1664). During the second half of the seventeenth century, many German states expelled their Jewish populations in the wake of the Thirty Years' War (1618–1648). Many of those Jews emigrated to Holland and later to England, and the push westward was increased by a general economic decline in the German states during the eighteenth century. Yet only a handful of German and Polish Jews continued and crossed the Atlantic to North America before 1820: by the time of the American Revolution (1776) the number of Jews in the thirteen colonies was estimated at between 1,500 and 2,000 (mostly of Ashkenazic origin), usually residing in cities along the eastern seaboard and involved in commerce and artisanship (Faber 1992, 107; Sarna 1986, 359). Most American Jews at the time were already completely acculturated and often indifferent to Jewish religious practices.

Not every Central European Jew emigrated to North America due to poverty: some belonged to families of merchants in Europe seeking to widen their trading sphere by sending a family member to the New World. Ashkenazic Jewish immigrants had been considered somewhat uneducated and uncouth by Sephardim (Jews who originated in the Medieval Iberian peninsula), who made up a minority among the colonies' Jewry. Still, most Jewish congregations in eighteenth-century North America adhered to the Sephardic rite of worship.

Emigration between the 1820s and World War I

Up to 1820 Jewish migration to the United States remained a trickle. The census of 1820 estimated that only about 2,700 Jews lived in the young republic. But within sixty years the number would mushroom to almost 280,000 (Faber 1992, 107–108; Cohen 1984, 12; Barkai 1994, 9). In the decades between the 1880s and World War I, the immigration of Central European Jews to the United States significantly waned, while more than 2 million Eastern European Jews left their homes for America. Yet despite their shrinking numbers, German-speaking Jews continued to play an important role in the life of American Jewry.

The reasons for that wave of migration were manifold. In the aftermath of the Napoleonic Wars (which ended in 1815) Central Europe witnessed the first signs of profound changes, mainly urbanization and industrialization. These changes brought about a gradual dissolution of the agrarian and feudal society, which prompted a wave of immigration to America from across Western and Central Europe, in which Jews were only a small fraction. There were other upheavals as well. At the same time, Europe's monarchs were determined to restore the political order that prevailed before the French Revolution (1789) and to clamp down on any expression of liberalism or nationalism. Jews found themselves in an especially precarious situation: after centuries of imposed separation and degradation among Christians, some Jews (like Moses Mendelssohn) were imbued with the ideas of the Enlightenment, such as universal human rights. But Jewish hopes for legal and social emancipation were frustrated by the prevailing political regression. In addition, many in the German national movement were openly hostile toward Jews, as the latter were considered non-Germans or "backward." Some German nationalists also saw the Jews as the alleged financers of the erstwhile French occupation forces, hence unworthy of emancipation. Those factors and others retarded Jewish emancipation in Germany (achieved fully only after Germany's unification in 1871). Even more troubling were the economic dislocations. The gradual dissolution of traditional peasant society, in which the Jews had played an important role as middlemen, small merchants, and peddlers, left some of them with little hope for earning a living.

Those changes happened, moreover, when many German Jews were moving from small towns to larger cities and becoming more integrated into German culture (language, clothing). Among the most profound responses to the pressures of partial emancipation and modernization involved the emergence of Reform Judaism. Supported initially by the urban economic elite of German Jewry in the 1810s and 1820s, reformers sought to modernize the beliefs and practices of Judaism. Reform rabbis like Abraham Geiger and David Einhorn emphasized the universal and nonnational essence of Judaism, while asserting the right of Jews to amend ancient laws to fit a modern setting. By harmonizing Judaism with modern conditions, reformers believed they would both prevent Jews from abandoning their religion while demonstrating to their Gentile neighbors that Jews were ready for full emancipation.

The United States was well advertised by the second quarter of the nineteenth century in Europe as the "common man's utopia." Shippers and American consuls circulated guidebooks on the young country, and letters from relatives and friends in America fed an "immigration fever." Among Central European Jews, the poorer one was, the more likely one was to go to America. Nevertheless, it was not only the promise of prosperity that lured them but also the vision of a country where neither guilds, nor a state church, nor Jewish origin would limit one's success. In America emancipation was guaranteed.

Many of the Jewish immigrants hailed from areas where German was not the only (or not even the more common) language—such as Galicia, Hungary, Moravia, and Bohemia in the Austrian Empire, and western Poland in Prussia. Jews from German states, particularly Bavaria, still made up the single-largest group in the Jewish migration to the United States between the 1820s and the 1870s. Immigration reached its peak in the early 1850s, when increased government repression following the abortive revolutions of 1848 and 1849 combined with economic depression.

Jewish settlement spread across the country. Central European Jews could be found not only on the eastern seaboard (New York, Philadelphia, Baltimore), but also along the Mississippi River (New Orleans, St. Louis, Louisville, Minneapolis), or the Ohio River (Cincinnati), throughout the Great Lakes area (Buffalo, Chicago, Detroit, Milwaukee), the Deep South (Jackson, Mobile, Birmingham), and the Pacific West (San Francisco, Portland), to name but a few. Most Jewish immigrants concentrated on what they knew best: small commerce (peddlers, shopkeepers). As a group, American Jews achieved a high degree of economic mobility, though only a small group of bankers and businessmen struck gold (Joseph Seligman, Jacob Schiff, Meyer Guggenheim, Lazarus Strauss, and Julius Rosenwald). Jewish upward mobility in America can be explained by the fact that Jews pursued occupations closely resembling those they knew in Europe; strove for self-employment and were willing to defer marriage and family until they could afford them; and relied heavily on family and community networks of support, especially for credit, and drew on the labor of relatives. In short, the very economic pattern that made Jews pariahs in Bavaria or Bohemia made them respectable citizens in the United States, where self-made businessmen were admired.

The development of most small congregations usually followed a similar path: first came a burial society, then a synagogue, and only later a school. To overcome the sense of isolation, Jews opted to live, work, socialize, and fulfill religious obligations with one another. Philanthropy became the backbone of institutions formed by American Jews. Despite the success of many, Jewish communities did not lack poor people, particularly in large cities. Dozens of charitable societies soon proliferated to aid the sick, widows, orphans, and poor brides. Combining Jewish tradition of communal charity and American philanthropy, these organizations were established to counter the influence of Christian societies who might target Jews in need in order to convert them. Furthermore, Jewish leaders were concerned over how American society perceived them and resolved to prove that Jews were never a burden on the community at large, as seen in the creation of the fraternal society B'nai B'rith (Sons of the Covenant) and others. Formed by German Jews, organizations such as the Hebrew Emigrant Aid Society, the United Hebrew Charities, and the Educational Alliance aided the masses of their Eastern European brethren who came to the United States between 1881 and 1924. A different national organization was the Young Men's Hebrew Association (YMHA), whose first association was founded in Baltimore (1845). Influenced by the emergence of the YMCA, the YMHA offered intellectual leisure activities for middle-class, urban Jewish youth, including lecture courses, classes in different languages, and musical programs. Though the YMHA watered down traditional Judaism, it emphasized themes such as pride in one's Jewish identity and the importance of Jewish fellowship.

The immigration of Central European Jews brought about a tremendous growth of Reform Judaism in the United States. Reformers and laity alike sought shorter services, prayers in German or English, and improved decorum (like the introduction of choirs and organs, mixed seating for men and women, and uncovered heads in synagogue). One of the prominent reformers, Rabbi Isaac Mayer Wise, founded the Union of American Hebrew Congregations in Cincinnati (1873), which was Reform Judaism's laity organization, and two years later a rabbinical seminary (the oldest seminary in the United States), Hebrew Union College. The movement's rabbinical organization, the Central Conference of American Rabbis, was established in 1889. The essence of nineteenth-century Reform Judaism was expressed in the "Pittsburgh Platform" (1885) adopted by nineteen American Reform rabbis. The platform rejected laws relating to diet or priestly purity, abolished most passages in prayers relating to a return to Zion, and stressed that Jews share only religious beliefs and do not constitute a nation. By the 1930s, however, Reform Judaism reversed its course and abandoned its antinational stance due to mounting antisemitism in the United States and abroad; the growing influence of Eastern European Jews and their children, who became the vast majority among American Jews; and the emergence of a strong Zionist movement in America.

Jewish Reform ideology and American middle-class decorum enabled Jewish women to play a greater role in communal life. Jewish women's organizations in America usually began as local charities, study societies, and synagogue sisterhoods. By the 1870s mixed choirs were already quite common in synagogues, and gradually women's galleries were replaced by mixed seating. In the latter half of the nineteenth century, acculturated middle-class Jewish women became involved in communal activities beyond the Jewish fold. Hannah Solomon of Chicago worked with Jane Addams to improve the conditions of the city's poor. Solomon was also among the chief organizers of the Jewish Women's Congress that was held in Chicago (1893) and included ninety-three delegates, mainly of German origin, aimed at organizing a body that would represent all Jewish women in America.

German Jewish women also had been active in propagating Jewish education. Rebecca Gratz, who led many philanthropic programs in Philadelphia, established there in 1838 the first Jewish Sunday school. Gratz and her students recited prayers, read chapters from the Bible, and sang hymns. The Philadelphia school grew rapidly and soon branched out to other cities, becoming the most popular form of Jewish education in America. Still, many in the newly organized German congregations opposed the Sunday school, seeing it as a distasteful imitation of the Gentiles.

Hearing about some of the innovations in American Reform Judaism, many observant Jews in Germany came to believe that, religiously speaking, *in Amerika geht alles!* (in America anything goes). Unlike Germany, where the government lent some support to the orthodox, the separation of state and church in the United States precluded traditionalists from appealing to the government. Yet even though Reform Judaism made considerable progress in nineteenth-century America, it met traditional opposition. Influential German Jewish leaders like Isaac Leeser of Philadelphia and Samuel Isaacs of New York rebuked the innovations by reformers and argued that the changes in Jewish law should be limited to what is absolutely necessary (such as Sunday schools that would defend Jewish children from Christian missionaries).

The Jewish press was a main forum for the dispute about religious reforms, as well as for communal news, discussions of Jewish history, Jewish Gentile relations, American politics, and Jewish life around the world. Anglo-Jewish periodicals outnumbered those in German and survived longer. In 1855 reformer Isaac Mayer Wise founded in Cincinnati the first German-language periodical of any longevity, the monthly *Die Deborah,* as a women's supplement to his weekly English-language *Israelite* (later *The American Israelite*). The following year another Reform rabbi, David Einhorn of Baltimore, began publishing *Sinai.* Yet, already before 1914, the last Jewish periodical in German ceased publication.

Among the first generation of German Jewish immigrants there were many who proudly accepted the label "Germans" and were active in German American cultural life. Many spoke German at home and kept records and prayed in German. Jews were prominent in German musical and theatrical societies and regularly contributed as writers and subscribers to German newspapers. During the Civil War, some northern Jews joined units of German volunteers to fight on the side of the Union. Still, not all immigrants shared the special bond to the German language and culture. Some immigrants, especially those hailing from the Slavic regions of Prussia or Austro-Hungary, did not speak German very well or were deterred by anti-Jewish sentiments harbored in some German organizations. The more traditional Jewish immigrants preferred to stay within the confines of their own community. Others, who sought rapid Americanization, urged immigrants to conduct their lives only in English.

After 1870 the German Jewish link dissolved quite quickly. Americanization weakened foreign customs and loyalties. Moreover, the eruption of antisemitism in the newly unified Germany disenchanted many German Jews with their former country. The rise of racial theories highlighting the differences between "lowly" Jews and Aryans pulled German American and Jewish American communities farther apart.

German Jews entered politics mostly at the local level as established businessmen and in the nineteenth century did not climb higher than mayor, or less often, U.S. congressman. Though Simon Wolf of Washington, D.C., became an unofficial Jewish lobbyist, especially among the Republicans, most Jewish leaders warned their public to refrain from voting as a bloc; and, indeed, no party received an overwhelming majority among nineteenth-century American Jews. Jewish communities usually preferred to keep a low profile and disapproved of partisanship. During the Civil War, American Jews were split and tended to side with their home state. There were exceptions, however, such as antislavery reformer David Einhorn, who had to flee proslavery Baltimore in 1861, or Rabbi Morris Raphall of New York who supported slavery. As a rule, most communities tried to muzzle their rabbis on the issue of slavery.

American Jews usually came together against antisemitism at home or abroad. When in 1862 General Grant ordered "Jews as a class" to be expelled from the military zone under his command (later rescinded by President Abraham Lincoln), Republican and Democratic Jews fought together. In a similar manner Jews struggled to abolish restrictions on office holding by Jews or Christian missionary influence in public schools. German Jews in the United States were also active in attempts to help their persecuted brethren around the world, whether during the blood libel in Damascus (1840) or Russian pogroms (1880s, 1900s). Prominent German Jews established early defense agencies like the American Jewish Committee (1906) and the Anti-Defamation League (1913). German Jewish financiers like Jacob Schiff and Felix Warburg played a major role in founding the Joint Distribution Committee (1914) to help East European Jewry, which suffered immensely after the outbreak of World War I. Yet many times it was the Jewish press that was crucial for alerting the Jewish public to antisemitic occurrences.

Emigration from the Weimar Republic (1918–1932)

The German defeat in World War I and the subsequent years of political crisis and economic hardships prompted a considerable emigration from the short-lived German democracy (1918–1932). This immigration of more than 420,000 Germans to the United States included an estimated number of more than 7,000 Jews (Niederland 1998, 172). Jewish immigrants did not differ in essence from the broader German immigration to the United States in both motivations and figures (increasing steadily before 1924 and decreasing until 1933). Though this immigration included some ideologically driven exiles (e.g., a notable group of left-wing intellectuals disillusioned by the crushed Socialist revolutions in Germany), most left for America out of different motivations. These were, for the most part, young single men of the World War I generation. Most of them were academics, professionals, or merchants, though initially many had to practice manual labor to make ends meet. A German Jewish periodical (*Israelitisches Familienblatt* 20.4.1932, 2) claimed in those years that German Jewish emigrants formed their own organizations in response to rising antisemitism in the German immigrants' organizations in the United States and their own alienation toward the Eastern European Jews now dominant in the Jewish American street.

Like other potential emigrants to the United States, Central European Jews were influenced by the growing restrictions in American immigration policy prior to the Great Depression. These restrictions were fateful to the history of Central European Jewish emigration: The Immigration Act of 1917 initiated the principle of blocking applications of "persons who were likely to become public charges" (LPC Clause). The 1921 Emergency Immigration Restriction Act (Johnson Act) originated the quota system (i.e., the principle of a fixed yearly quota of immigrants from any given country respectively; 25,000 from Germany, which was still much higher than Eastern European quotas). The Immigration Act of 1924 (National Origins Act) required that emigrants apply for a visa in their native countries, which would then be accepted or rejected according to the above-mentioned categories. And finally, during the Great Depression, came a stricter interpretation of the LPC Clause and the Hoover Directive of September 13, 1930, which demanded exacting proofs from applicants on these qualifications, thus drastically limiting the numbers of immigrants even without a cut in the quota itself. This rigorous immigration policy proved tragic for European Jews seeking to flee Nazi persecution.

Emigration from the Third Reich (1933–1945)

The last and most important chapter in the history of the German Jewish immigration to the United States started with the Nazi rise to power in Germany in 1933. The state policy of Nazi Germany was to ruthlessly encourage and accelerate Jewish emigration. Though an overtly proclaimed policy, it did take both German Jews and the Western world—the United States included—some time to fully acknowledge and react accordingly. Prior to World War II, some two-thirds of the Jews left Germany (Rosenstock 1956, 373). Approximately 85,000 of them left for the United States, rendering it the major destination of Jewish emigrants (supplanting Palestine as early as 1937) (http://www.ushmm .org/wlc/article.php?lang=en&ModuleId=10005139).

The Third Reich inflicted an escalating series of unprecedented blows on its Jews during the first years, from the exclusion of "non-Aryans" (Jews) from an ever-growing circle of professions, positions, and associations starting in 1933, to the endorsement of the racial Nuremberg Laws of 1935, which deprived German Jews of their citizenship and outlawed marriage and sexual relations between Jews and "Aryans." This unbearable situation in the first seven years of Nazi rule generated a relatively steady stream of emigrants. During these years a significant change occurred in the consciousness and self-confidence of the Jews and their vision of the future: Whereas in its early months, Nazi rule was perceived by most Jews as provisional, in the following years most would accept that, in the long run, Jews had no future in Germany. Accordingly, Jewish organizations and leadership, both in Germany and in the free world, embraced a policy aimed at preparing the prospective emigrants and rendering this almost-inevitable emigration as orderly as possible. This was conducted without any panic: one envisaged a process of many decades, and thus in the mid-1930s a tenth of the Jewish emigrants had even returned to Germany.

Historian Herbert Strauss described German Jewish immigrants as "basically urban, an aging and overaged group, concentrated in commerce and selected professions" (Strauss 1980, 325). This professional profile was molded to a large extent by Nazi persecution policy in the 1930s that initially focused on select professions (e.g., Jewish civil servants, academics, lawyers) earlier than on others (e.g., big business) out of pragmatic considerations. The need for an affidavit from American friends and relatives sustained the dominance of southern and western Germans among the Central European Jewish emigrants to the United States. Compared to other destinations for Jewish emigration from the Reich, emigration to the United States seems to have included a larger percentage of entire families.

In 1938 a new Nazi policy turned this stream of emigrants to a wave of refugees. Following the unparalleled actions of the SS in brutally forcing Jews from newly annexed Austria, Nazi Germany redefined its anti-Jewish policy, using unrestricted terror measures to force Jewish emigration from all over the country. This brutal policy reached new peaks at the end of 1938 with the October expulsion of 17,000 Polish-born Jews from Germany (October 28), and the *Kristallnacht* ("Night of Broken Glass") pogrom of November 9 and 10, during which synagogues all over Germany were demolished and set ablaze, as well as houses and enterprises of Jews. Hundreds of Jews were beaten, more than 90 murdered, and some 30,000 were arrested and sent to concentration camps (Breitman and Kraut 1987, 53). At this stage, most German Jews wished to immigrate to nearly any place that would accept them.

American immigration policy remained strict all through these years, permitting but a small percentage of the fixed immigration quota and creating a years-long waiting list for American visas. According to the Hoover Directive, prospective immigrant affidavits from friends and family in the United States were needed under the LPC Clause. But due to the virtual halt of Central European Jewish immigration to the United States since the 1870s, Jews from Nazi Germany found it very hard to meet this demand. Thus, for example, during the first year of Nazi rule, only some 1,450 German Jews were permitted to immigrate to the United States (see Table 1.1). But by the late 1930s the humanitarian challenge was too big to ignore. In 1938, following the public assault on Jews in the cities of newly annexed Austria, President Franklin D. Roosevelt convened an international conference to address together the deteriorating refugee problem. This conference took place in Evian (France) with the participation of thirty-two states and the attendance of twenty-four voluntary organizations. But beyond the symbolic gesture, the conference was adjourned with no breakthrough and no new hope for Central European Jews. The United States did not take any drastic measures, such as increasing its quota. Even though Roosevelt somewhat eased the LPC Clause in 1936, only in 1939 did the United States admit, for the first time, the full yearly fixed quota of 27,370.

During World War II, Nazi Germany moved from a policy of persecution to a policy of systematic murder. By late 1941—as Jewish emigration from the Reich was closed off

Number of German Immigrants, 1933–1944

Year	Percentage of German Quota Filled	Number of Immigrants
1933	5.3	1,450
1934	13.7	3,740
1935	20.2	5,530
1936	24.3	6,650
1937	42.1	11,520
1938	65.3	17,870
1939	100.0	27,370
1940	95.3	26,080
1941	47.7	13,500
1942	17.4	4,760
1943	4.7	1,290
1944	4.8	1,351

Source: Straus, Herbert A. "The Immigration and Acculturation of the German Jew in the United States of America," *Leo Baeck Institute Yearbook* 16 (1971): 68.

and the first deportations of Jews from the Reich were leaving to the camps and killing sites—most (around 60 percent) German Jews had already managed to emigrate (Rosenstock 1956, 373). Being the first victims of Nazi persecution in the 1930s, many German Jews understood earlier the danger and emigrated; some, however, did not flee far enough and were caught by the Germans in Belgium, Holland, and France. Still, this emigration proved to be the rescue of many, and it explains the relatively high percent of survival among Central European Jews compared with their Eastern European counterparts.

In the summer of 1945, soon after the end of the war, there were some 100,000 Jewish survivors in Germany and Austria (Dinnerstein 1982, 24). By the end of 1946, their number rose to approximately 250,000 Jewish displaced persons (DPs), most of them of Eastern European descent (Dinnerstein 1982, 111, 278). After the Holocaust they wished to rebuild their lives outside Europe—primarily in Palestine—but stayed in the central European DP camps until the gates of emigration opened. A directive by President Harry S. Truman provided very partial aid by enabling 28,000 of them (mostly German citizens) to enter the United States between May 1946 and June 1948. The solution to the refugees' problem came with the establishment of the state of Israel (1948) and the implementation of new U.S. immigration laws shortly thereafter. Some two-thirds immigrated to Israel, but a good third immigrated to the United States (Lavsky 1990, 377).

Physicist Albert Einstein, intellectual Hannah Arendt, novelist Franz Werfel, composer Arnold Schönberg, and future secretary of state Henry Kissinger are but a few examples of the significant contribution of individual Jewish immigrants from the Third Reich to American life. At the same time, it is important to note the magnitude of Central European Jewry's contribution in terms of the overall development of the American Jewish community. It was Central European Jews, wrote historian Naomi W. Cohen, "who laid the foundations of the modern American Jewish community. They set the institutional framework and the codes of behavior that, with relatively few important qualifications, obtain today" (Cohen 1984, xi) on remained intact even decades after the German component became numerically minor among American Jews. They left a legacy of integration and progress built in the plethora of organizations they established as well as in the cultural manifestations of their time; for example, Reform Judaism, the Jewish press, and philanthropic activities. Through these endeavors they strove to maintain their Jewish identity, yet for them this identity assumed a religious rather than a national form.

See also Antisemitism; B'nai B'rith; Einhorn, David; Einstein, Albert; Judaism, Reform (North America); Kissinger, Henry; Leeser, Isaac; Schiff, Jacob Henry; Schönberg, Arnold; Warburg, Felix Moritz; Wise, Isaac Mayer

References and Further Reading

Barkai, Avraham. *Branching Out: German-Jewish Immigration to the United States 1820–1914*. New York: Holmes & Meier, 1994.

Breitman, Richard D., and Alan M. Kraut. *American Refugee Policy and European Jewry 1933–1945*. Bloomington: Indiana University, 1987.

Cohen, Naomi W. *Encounter with Emancipation: The German Jew in the United States 1830–1914*. Philadelphia: Jewish Publication Society, 1984.

Diner, Hasia R. *A Time for Gathering: The Second Migration 1820–1880*. Baltimore, MD: Johns Hopkins University, 1992.

Dinnerstein, Leonard. *America and the Survivors of the Holocaust*. New York: Columbia University, 1982.

Faber, Eli. *A Time for Planting: The First Migration, 1654–1820*. Baltimore: Johns Hopkins University Press, 1992.

Genizi, Haim. "New York Is Big—America Is Bigger: The Resettlement of Refugees from Nazism 1936–1945." *Jewish Social Studies* 46 (Winter 1984): 61–72.

Gurock, Jeffrey S., ed. *Central European Jews in America 1840–1880: Migration and Survival*. New York: Routledge, 1998.

Lavsky, Hagit. "Displaced Persons, Jewish." In Israel Gutman (ed.), *Encyclopedia of the Holocaust*. New York: Macmillan Publishing Company, vol. 1, 1990: 377–394.

Niederland, Doron. "Leaving Germany: Emigration Patterns of Jews and Non-Jews during the Weimar Period," *Tel Aviver Jahrbuch für deutsche Geschichte* 27 (1998): 169–194.

Rosenstock, Werner. "Exodus 1933–1939: A Survey of Jewish Emigration from Germany." *Leo Baeck Institute Year Book* 1 (1956): 373–390.

Sarna, Jonathan D., ed. *The American Jewish Experience: A Reader*. New York: Holmes & Meier, 1986.

Straus, Herbert A. "The Immigration and Acculturation of the German Jew in the United States of America." *Leo Baeck Institute Yearbook* 16 (1971): 63–94.

———. "Jewish Emigration from Germany: Nazi Policies and Jewish Responses (I)." *Leo Baeck Institute Yearbook* 25 (1980): 313–361.

———. "Jewish Emigration from Germany: Nazi Policies and Jewish Responses (II)." *Leo Baeck Institute Yearbook* 26 (1981): 343–409.

Wyman, David S. *The Abandonment of the Jews: America and the Holocaust 1941–1945*. New York: Pantheon, 1984.

SOUTH AMERICA

Dirk Hoerder

Sixteenth- and seventeenth-century Latin America was a destination for miners and soldiers. The craft of warfare (*Kriegshandwerk*) was an itinerant one, and in mining German-speaking experts had a long history of mobility. The Spanish crown, in general reluctant to admit foreigners to New Spain, during a liberal phase after 1526 leased Venezuela to the South German Welser Company. In later centuries, German and Iberian miners brought ore-refining technology to Spanish Mexico. Other commercial connections to Latin America, originally to Dutch Suriname and Dutch Brazil, originated with a Portuguese Sephardic Jewish community from Amsterdam that had reestablished itself in seventeenth-century Danish Altona, adjacent to the port of Hamburg.

Of the approximately 55 million European migrants to the Americas from the 1830s to the 1950s, about one-fifth went to Latin America. Arrivals increased from 1850 to 1885, then rose rapidly to 1914. Commerce, stock ranching, and plantation agriculture attracted settlers, merchants, entrepreneurs, and laborers in large numbers. They mingled with Flemings, Germans, Neapolitans, Genoese, Greeks, and others. Their children often migrated internally to regions of sustained economic growth or, in search of riches, to new mining districts. Some, however, chose to seclude themselves in small agricultural settlements, which sometimes have been romanticized as, for example, the German Blumenau colony in southern Brazil (f. 1850). Such rural colonies professed a "Germanness" that was frozen in time because of distance, separation, and isolation.

Most of the European migrants to the Afro-Native-Latin societies originated in the Mediterranean cultures. From the 1850s to 1924, 38 percent came from Italy, 28 percent from Spain, 11 percent from Portugal, and the rest from Russia (Jews), Germany, and France. Argentina and Brazil received almost four-fifths of the newcomers. In Brazil, the first postindependence phase of European immigration from the 1820s to the 1860s brought German, Italian, and Polish settlers to the coffee plantations of Rio Grande do Sul. Because the politically powerful planters imposed miserable working conditions, many of the immigrants fled their regime. This oligarchic rule made Brazil different from any other country in the Americas.

Some 400,000 German-speaking migrants, at the most, reached *Ibero-America,* the German term for the countries from Mexico to Chile. Five phases of migration may be discerned: The first took place after the disastrous winter in Europe of 1816 and 1817 spurred flight from famine for a decade and a half, mainly to Brazil. The second phase was a consequence of the agrarian crisis of 1846 and 1847, which was delayed by the Revolution of 1848 and 1849, and involved a decade-long emigration to the independent states. Parallel to the initial phase of southern European mass migration from 1850 to 1885, a third phase of German migration began to grow after 1865. However, while the former rose rapidly from 1885 to 1914, German migration "boomed" only between 1885 and 1894. As in North America, a fourth—brief—migration peak after the end of World War I (86,000 from 1920 to 1924) was caused by disgust about the war, disagreement with the conditions of the Versailles Peace Treaty, or discontent with economic prospects in general. The fifth discernable phase of German migration to South America occurred from 1933 to the late 1940s. It was a new, trifurcated sizeable migration: first of German Jews, then of political and intellectual refugees, and finally of Nazi fugitives from justice after the collapse of fascism.

Diversity of destination and of patterns of insertion characterized the German-speaking immigrant communities. Most selected Portuguese-speaking Brazil and Spanish-speaking Argentina as destinations; smaller numbers chose Uruguay and Chile; and a few ended up in Mexico, Central America, the Caribbean, Venezuela, and Colombia. The time lags between the five phases indicate that each cohort of newcomers came from different socio-economic conditions in Germany and, even if destined for the same regions as earlier migrants, met partly or fully acculturated immigrant populations. In the two major receiving countries, the different cohorts also often settled in different regions. The southernmost Brazilian states were the destination of phase-one migrants; those of phase two settled in São Paulo, often as plantation labor, or as first settlers in southern Chile. Groups of them formed agricultural colonies similar to those in eighteenth-century Eastern Europe, but numerically smaller, without special privileges, and with fewer connections to the society of origin. Geographic isolation permitted autonomy but retarded economic integration of the rural colonies. Low wages retarded integration of plantation laborers. The pre-1933 Brazilian, Argentine, and Chilean communities—often perceived in Latin America as a single German group—formed clusters of rural islands in different regions, separated from the surrounding culture; clusters of urban elites with ties to the Latin indigenous elites and a certain communality of interests; and, third, clusters of rural and urban laborers.

Although in Eastern Europe and in North America the elites emerged out of the German-speaking immigrant communities, elite formation in Latin America involved a distinct movement of merchants, entrepreneurs, and financiers, as well as teachers, scholars, engineers, and military officers. The close connection of the elites to Germany was based on economic interest and the "esteem value" to be derived from German culture, merchandise, and authoritarian political rule.

These diverse communities formed neither a diaspora nor full-fledged ethnic groups. They remained an appendix. Politically and economically, the German state from 1871 to

1945, with its high level of diplomatic exchange and trade, considered the emigrants bridgeheads to fuller exploitation of the New World.

See also Argentina; Brazil; Brazil, German Exile in; Chile; Conquista; German Migration to Latin America (1918–1933)

References and Further Reading

Bade, Klaus J. *Europa in Bewegung: Migration vom späten 18. Jahrhundert bis zur Gegenwart.* München: Beck, 2000.

———. *Migration in European History,* transl. Allison Brown. Oxford: Blackwell, 2003.

Bade, Klaus J., ed. *Deutsche im Ausland—Fremde in Deutschland. Migration in Geschichte und Gegenwart.* München: Beck, 1992.

Fröschle, Hartmut, ed. *Die Deutschen in Lateinamerika. Schicksal und Leistung.* Tübingen: Erdmann, 1979.

Hoerder, Dirk. "The German-Language Diasporas. A Survey, Critique, and Interpretation." *Diaspora: A Journal of Transnational Studies* 11, no. 1 (Spring 2002): 7–44.

Luebke, Frederick C. *Germans in Brazil: A Comparative History of Cultural Conflict during World War I.* Baton Rouge: Louisiana State University, 1987.

Marschalck, Peter. *Deutsche Überseewanderung im 19. Jahrhundert. Ein Beitrag zur soziologischen Theorie der Bevölkerung.* Stuttgart: Klett, 1973.

Mühlen, Patrick von zur. *Fluchtziel Lateinamerika. Die deutsche Emigration 1933–1945. Politische Aktivitäten und soziokulturelle Integration.* Bonn: Verlag Neue Gesellschaft, 1988.

German Migration to Latin America (1918–1933)

Stefan Rinke

After World War I, a wave of Germans emigrated to Latin America. Between 1919 and 1933 more than 140,000 people left for that continent. This number was almost as high as the total of German emigration to Latin America between 1846 and 1918. Most of these migrants left Germany in the six years following the end of the war. In several years Latin America attracted more Germans than even the United States, usually the preferred choice of immigrants. In 1924 the number of Germans leaving for South American shores reached an all-time high of more than 32,000 people. After 1924 the number sank almost continuously until 1932, when it did not reach more than some 2,600 (Statistik 1930, 229; Bickelmann 1980, 143, 149).

The reasons for this development were manifold. Most important were World War I and the social and economic crisis in Europe after the war. The dissatisfaction with the Peace Treaty of Versailles, the November Revolution, and the new system of republican government in Germany were additional factors. Hyperinflation, unemployment, lack of housing, and fear of the future dominated postwar German society. The importance of this latter factor can easily be measured by looking at the drastic decline in the numbers of emigrants after the situation in Germany stabilized somewhat in 1925.

An important factor in stimulating emigration to Latin America was the migratory policy of the United States. Until 1921, German immigrants were prohibited from coming to that country and after that date a quota continued to restrict their number. No such quota existed in Latin America. Nevertheless, immigration to Latin America was not simply a diversion of people who would otherwise have gone to the United States.

Additional pull factors included Latin American and German emigration agencies that advertised the possibilities for the purchase of land and social mobility in that region in an aggressive and often misleading manner. The economic potential of countries such as Argentina or Brazil was overestimated immediately after the war. News of the failure of settlement projects, economic problems, and the large number of returning emigrants contributed to the strong decline in German emigration to Latin America after 1925.

The constitution of the Weimar Republic allowed emigration in principle, yet the German state considered it a loss of potential. Legislative measures tried to regulate emigration to prevent the abuse of the migrants abroad that had frequently happened before the war. Hence, starting in 1924 private settlement enterprises and emigration agencies were placed under governmental control. In general, German policy was not to support emigration but to steer those who still wanted to leave into suitable countries where they would remain "useful" for the mother country by buying German products and preserving their German culture and language. Although the state thus remained largely passive, German shipping lines took an active interest in promoting immigration to Latin America for the sake of profit. In addition, a mushrooming number of private enterprises openly advertised the advantages of emigration.

Within Germany, emigration experts preferred Latin America to the United States as a destination for German emigrants. As World War I had proven beyond doubt, Germans in the United States assimilated rapidly and—according to the biologistic discourse of the time—became "cultural fertilizer" (*Kulturdünger*) contributing to the positive development of that country. On the contrary, in Latin America German migrants usually settled in tight communities and remained loyal to their cultural heritage for many generations. In addition, contemporary German experts emphasized the fact that in the weak countries of Latin America, the German government had more freedom to support and to guide its emigrants than in the United States. Some even claimed that the German emigrants could become compensation for the German colonies lost as a result of the Treaty of Versailles. Thoughts like these inspired the foundation of the Gesellschaft für wirtschaftliche Studien in Übersee (Society for Economic Studies Overseas) in 1927, a central institution for the coordination of emigration to Latin America. Yet, the activities of that organization remained negligible due to the declining number of emigrants.

The main destination of German emigrants to Latin America in this period remained Brazil, despite the fact that the country had joined the Allies in 1917. According to the Brazilian statistics, the German share of immigrants was above average, reaching a climax of 22.6 percent in 1924 (Statistik 1930, 266–267). According to an estimation of 1932, about 685,000 Germans and people of German descent lived in Brazil, which accounted for 1.9 percent of the Brazilian population (Grothe 1932, 45). The main reason for Brazil's attractiveness was its land policy that offered convenient credit for the purchase of government land. In addition, immigrants received a number of benefits upon their arrival, such as free transportation to their destination and free meals and medical care for an initial period. From 1919 on, Brazilian agencies started an advertising campaign that achieved good results. Most Germans who came to Brazil settled in the southernmost federal states of Rio Grande do Sul, Santa Catarina, and Paraná, where they mingled with a relatively large population of German settlers from the prewar period. A new destination for Germans who came to Brazil after 1919 was the federal state of São Paulo with its booming capital. The state government subsidized trips from Germany to Brazil, and its fledgling industry offered jobs to numerous Germans. Yet there were many complaints by Germans who reported maltreatment, especially on the coffee plantations. These reports seemed to suggest that the German immigrants experienced a modern form of indentured servitude. In addition, the numerous revolutionary upheavals and economic crises affected the German immigrants in this period negatively. The number of people who wanted to return to Germany increased steadily in the later 1920s, but only a small percentage could afford the passage or benefited from the offers of the various German auxiliary associations in the big cities.

Argentina was almost as important as Brazil for German emigration after 1918. More than 48,000 people migrated to the Rio de la Plata in this period (Statistik 1930, 229; Bickelmann 1980, 143, 149). After 1926, Argentina was the preferred destination within Latin America. The decline of German emigration to Argentina in the late 1920s was below the Latin American average. Argentina had remained neutral during the war and positive economic development had a strong attractive effect. In addition, exaggerated news about the Argentinean Homestead Act of 1917 opening up government lands in the northern territories of Entre Ríos and Santa Fé heightened expectations. Argentinean immigration policy, though explicitly excluding anarchists and sick people from entering the country, granted benefits to immigrants, including temporary lodging and free transportation to the projected settlement. The capital city of Buenos Aires remained the most important destination for German migrants to Argentina. Yet it was in this metropolis that social problems among Germans reached new proportions, especially when the Argentinean boom drew to a close by the end of the 1920s. In addition, there were several settlement projects in the subtropical northern territories of Chaco and Misiones. Although some of these colonies worked in close cooperation with agencies in Germany, such as the Gesellschaft für wirtschaftliche Studien in Übersee, not all were successful. Problems increased in the wake of the Great Depression. The Argentinean government reacted by restricting immigration, and thus in 1933 fewer than 1,000 Germans entered the country (Bickelmann 1980, 42–43).

The third traditional country of destination for German emigrants to Latin America was Chile. In comparison to Argentina and Brazil, however, it did not reach the same proportions as in the prewar period. For lack of statistical material, we do not know the exact number of Germans who emigrated to Chile during the whole period. Yet, with 133 immigrants in 1924, it is clear that this migration was negligible (Statistik 1930, 229; Bickelmann 1980, 143,149). Those who came to Chile went into the already existing settlements in the south or stayed in the cities of Valparaíso and Santiago. In 1929 the settlement at Peñaflor was the only coordinated German settlement effort sponsored by the Chilean government. Reasons for the relative failure to attract German immigrants included high passage prices, the passive Chilean immigration policy, and the news about Chilean economic problems.

To a certain degree, Paraguay took the place of Chile in becoming the thirdmost important destination for German emigration to the region. Although neither German nor Paraguayan statistics list exact numbers, an estimate for 1927 gives a number of 7,000

German Immigration to Brazil and Argentina (1919–1932)

Year	Total number of immigrants to Brazil	Number of Germans among the immigrants to Brazil	Total number of immigrants to Argentina	Number of Germans among the immigrants to Argentina
1919	37,898	466	41,299	1,992
1920	71,027	4,120	87,032	4,798
1921	60,784	7,920	98,086	4,113
1922	66,967	5,038	129,263	6,514
1923	86,679	8,254	195,063	10,138
1924	98,125	22,168	159,939	10,238
1925	84,886	7,185	125,366	4,933
1926	117,695	7,674	135,011	5,112
1927	96,880	4,878	161,548	5,165
1928	76,586	4,228	129,047	4,165
1929	94,931	4,351	140,086	4,581
1930	61,099	4,180	135,403	5,171
1931	26,183	2,621	64,922	3,045
1932	34,683	2,273	37,626	2,089
total	1,014,423	85,356	1,639,691	72,054

Germans in the country as compared to some 4,500 in 1918 (Grothe 1932, 81). In particular, contemporary observers evaluated the region of the Alto Paraná as a promising settlement area for Germans. Much like Argentina, the Paraguayan government tried to support immigrants by various measures, such as free transportation from Buenos Aires to the destination in Paraguay, free lodging and meals for an initial period, and—last but not least—cheap government lands. Despite problems due to revolutionary upheaval and economic crises in the 1920s, the German settlements in Paraguay continued to grow on a modest scale, and in 1932 more than 20 German colonies were counted in the country (Grothe 1932, 86).

In the rest of Latin America, only Mexico and Uruguay received some German settlers. In addition, given the low number of Germans in the prewar period, the number of Germans increased considerably in countries such as Guatemala and Nicaragua after the war. In Germany, some agencies even investigated the opportunities for major settlement projects in Venezuela, Peru, Bolivia, and Ecuador. Yet, these projects were never realized. Apart from the countries discussed, there was no German mass emigration to Latin America in this period. Yet capitals and major cities such as Mexico City, Lima, Caracas, and Bogotá continued to attract German professionals, such as businessmen and teachers. Although quantitatively negligible, these German immigrants often made important contributions to the economy and culture of their host countries.

See also Argentina; Brazil; Chile; Mexico; World War I

References and Further Reading

Bernecker, Walther L., and Thomas Fischer. "Deutsche in Lateinamerika." *Deutsche im Ausland— Fremde in Deutschland: Migration in Geschichte und Gegenwart.* Ed. Klaus J. Bade. München: Beck, 1992, 197–214.

Bickelmann, Hartmut. *Deutsche Überseeauswanderung in der Weimarer Zeit.* Wiesbaden: Steiner, 1980.

Blancpain, Jean Pierre. *Les Allemands au Chili, 1816–1945.* Köln-Wien: Böhlau, 1974.

Grothe, Hugo. *Die Deutschen in Übersee: Eine Skizze ihres Werdens, ihrer Verbreitung und kulturellen Arbeit.* Berlin: Zentralverlag, 1932.

Illi, Manfred. *Die deutsche Auswanderung nach Lateinamerika: Eine Literaturübersicht.* München: Fink, 1977.

Kellenbenz, Hermann, and Jürgen Schneider. "La emigración alemana a América Latina desde 1821 hasta 1930." *Jahrbuch für Geschichte von Staat, Wirtschaft und Gesellschaft Lateinamerikas* 13 (1976): 386–403.

Newton, Ronald C. *German Buenos Aires, 1900–1933: Social Change and Cultural Crisis.* Austin: University of Texas, 1977.

Rinke, Stefan. "Der letzte freie Kontinent": Deutsche Lateinamerikapolitik im Zeichen transnationaler Beziehungen, 1918–1933. Stuttgart: Heinz, 1996.

Statistik des Deutschen Reiches, vol. 360, *Die Bewegung der Bevölkerung in den Jahren 1925 bis 1927.* Berlin. 1930.

CHANGES IN MIGRATION PATTERNS IN THE TWENTIETH CENTURY

Dirk Hoerder

The decline of emigration in the 1890s reduced cultural transfer from Germany to the societies in the Americas. The role of Auslandsdeutsche imposed by Germany's nationalism imperiled insertion into the host societies. This unsolicited conceptual unification from outside was detrimental to the communities after 1914. In protest or simply in order to escape discrimination, many Germans changed ethnic affiliation to Dutch when in 1920 and 1921 the U.S. and Canadian censuses were taken. The further development of the ethnic communities in Canada, the United States, and Latin America, as well as migration to the three regions, followed different patterns. Immigration caesurae varied from country to country. The United States first legislated restrictions on immigration during World War I, while Canada and Latin American imposed restrictions only during the Great Depression.

In the United States, two brief twentieth-century peaks of immigration came after each of the world wars. Men and women who saw no chance in devastated Germany left for the better options and less militaristic attitudes in the United States. In Canada, immigration continued in the decades before World War I, and after the Treaty of Versailles, so-called *Volksdeutsche* from territories outside of the post-1918 German borders came in considerable numbers. Economically far less secure than earlier immigrants from Germany proper, they were also marginalized by the latter's attitude of superiority. From 1919 to 1929, half a million Germans departed (Marschalck 1986). Immigration slowed with the beginning of the worldwide depression after 1929, and the Canadian state tightened immigration regulations. However, throughout the 1920s, Russian Mennonites and Russian Germans from the Soviet Union were accepted as settlers for prairie communities. As in Canada, doors remained open in Latin America, and Germans continued to arrive in the 1920s.

The rise of fascism to power in 1933 resulted in the flight of Germans of Jewish faith and of those politically persecuted. However, racism was not confined to Europe's Fascist regimes. Many states in the Americas, like the West European democracies, were slow in accepting Jewish refugees—the Canadian immigration authorities being particularly adamant in this respect. At the July 1938 refugee conference in Evian, France, U.S. diplomats insisted on establishing an Inter-Governmental Committee on Refugees to negotiate an end to the chaos of expulsions and procedures of property transfer. The latter would free receiving societies from the cost of support. This was a subterfuge to keep refugee admission low. In the decade before 1939, a mere 120,000 immigrants from Germany were admitted into the United States (Marschalck 1986).

In Latin America, the refugees from fascism had little in common with either the rural or the urban communities of earlier migrants. They came ill prepared and impoverished, selecting Latin American countries because visas were available, rather than because of cultural or economic preference. On the other hand, after 1945 the fugitives from prosecution for war crimes found a certain receptiveness in the prewar ethnic communities. The capture of, or rumors about, hiding Nazi officials have made headlines from time to time.

At the end of World War II, the Allies prohibited German emigration but, after a short period of hesitation, accepted displaced persons (DPs) from the forced labor, prisoner-of-war, and concentration camps. A total of 450,000 had received visas by the end of 1951. The figures included Germans of Jewish faith who had survived the Holocaust. A mere 118,000 people designated as Germans immigrated to the United States in the 1940s (Marschalck 1986). In Canada, migration resumed in the late 1940s with further *Volksdeutsche* being admitted under humanitarian demands by the churches. Because of the economic dependency of the Latin American economies on the United States, these societies no longer attracted migrants from West Germany after the 1950s. In the Federal Republic of Germany, authorities attempted to slow down emigration of able-bodied men; under a still-racial concept of the unity of the *Volk,* they were needed to rebuild the ruins. The government, however, supported emigration of unwanted members of the *Volk*—single women and refugee landowners from eastern, formerly German, territories. Even with these restrictions, approximately 577,000 still migrated to the United States. With the economic upswing in the mid-1950s, the post–World War II peak of emigration came to an end. Less than a quarter of a million left for the United States in the 1960s (Marschalck 1986). Since then small numbers have continued to depart, in particular to the United States and, increasingly, to Canada.

See also Argentina; Barbie, Klaus; Eichmann, Karl Adolf; Great Depression; Latin America, Nazis in

References and Further Reading

Bade, Klaus J., ed. *Deutsche im Ausland—Fremde in Deutschland. Migration in Geschichte und Gegenwart.* München: Beck, 1992.

Fröschle, Hartmut, ed. *Die Deutschen in Lateinamerika. Schicksal und Leistung.* Tübingen: Erdmann, 1979.

Goñi, Uki. *The Real Odessa: Smuggling the Nazis to Perón's Argentina.* London: Granta, 2002.

Hoerder, Dirk. "The German-Language Diasporas. A Survey, Critique, and Interpretation." *Diaspora: A Journal of Transnational Studies* 11, no. 1 (Spring 2002): 7–44.

Hoerder, Dirk, and Jörg Nagler, eds. *People in Transit. German Migrants in Comparative Perspective, 1820–1930.* Cambridge, UK: Cambridge University, 1995.

Marschalck, Peter, comp. *Inventar der Quellen zur Geschichte der Wanderung, besonders der Auswanderung in Bremer Archiven.* Veröffentlichung aus dem Staatsarchiv der Freien Hansestadt Bremen, Bd. 53. Bremen: Staatsarchiv, 1986, 47–51.

Meding, Holger. *Flucht vor Nürnberg?* Köln: Böhlau, 1992.

Sauer, Angelika E., and Matthias Zimmer, eds. *A Chorus of Different Voices. German-Canadian Identities.* New York: Lang, 1998.

A

ADAMS, JOHN QUINCY
b. July 11, 1767; Braintree, Massachusetts
d. February 23, 1848; Washington, D.C.

John Quincy Adams served as the first U.S. minister to Prussia from 1797 to 1801. Adams, his wife, and his brother (serving as secretary of legation) arrived at Hamburg on October 26, 1797, and at Berlin on November 7 of the same year. Two days later Count Finckenstein, one of the three Prussian foreign ministers, received him. The illness and subsequent death of King Friedrich Wilhelm II on November 16 prevented a formal reception until June 5, 1798, when Adams met Friedrich Wilhelm III. In the interim, Adams made the rounds of the diplomatic receptions in Berlin, encountering many diplomats who had known his father, John Adams (1735–1826).

Adams's mission was to secure a renewal of the Prussian-American Treaty of 1785. The new treaty had to be compatible with the Jay Treaty, signed between the United States and Great Britain in 1794. The first casualty was article 12, which stated that free ships made free goods, meaning that goods belonging to a belligerent carried in a neutral vessel were considered neutral. The principle was at the heart of American diplomacy during the American Revolution but was repudiated by the Jay Treaty. Secretary of State Timothy Pickering also ordered an expansion of the contraband list (the list of goods that neutrals could not trade with a belligerent and still be considered neutral), the removal of the mutual exemption from general embargoes, and a reversal of the ban on privateering (outfitting private vessels as warships) in the event of war between the United States and Prussia. Neither Adams nor the Prussian government was prepared to give up the principle of neutral rights—the idea that neutral nations should be able to trade in a wide variety of goods, ship the goods of other nations in their own ships, and carry belligerent goods without being subject to capture—embodied in the 1785 treaty. Formal negotiations began in June 1798. Because there were no real controversies between the two countries, only slow communications prevented a rapid conclusion. The final treaty, signed on July 11, 1799, marked a significant revision of the 1785 treaty. Article 12 was rewritten to exclude the principle that free ships make free goods, citing a general lack of respect for the idea from the belligerent powers. Yet Prussia and the United States formally expressed the hope that with the return of peace there might be a general agreement among maritime powers protecting neutral rights. The Senate ratified the treaty on

February 18, 1800, and the two nations exchanged ratifications on June 22, 1800.

During his time in Berlin, Adams studied the German language by translating Christoph Martin Wieland's *Oberon*. He also sought to introduce German literature and culture to Americans. To this end, he translated Friedrich von Gentz's *Der Ursprung und die Grundsätze der Amerikanischen Revolution, verglichen mit dem Ursprunge und den Grundsätzen der Französischen* into English (*Origin and Principles of the American Revolution Compared with the Origin and Principles of the French Revolution,* 1800). In July 1800 Adams toured Silesia and wrote a series of letters to his brother describing the society and productions of that province (*Letters on Silesia,* 1801). Like many commentators before and after, Adams noted that Silesian linens were a perfect article for Prussian American trade.

Robert W. Smith

See also Treaty of 1785
References and Further Reading
Adams, Henry M. *Prussian-American Relations, 1775–1871.* Cleveland: Case Western Reserve University Press, 1960.
Adams, John Quincy. *Memoirs of John Quincy Adams.* Vol. 1. Ed. Charles Francis Adams. Philadelphia: J. B. Lippencott, 1874.
Scott, James Brown, ed. *The Treaties of 1785, 1799, and 1828 between the United States and Prussia.* New York: Oxford University Press, 1918.

ADDAMS, (LAURA) JANE

b. September 6, 1860; Cedarville, Illinois
d. May 21, 1935; Chicago, Illinois

One of the founders of Chicago's Hull-House settlement and an internationally known peace activist, Jane Addams was one of the best-known reformers of the Progressive Era and one of the most widely admired women of her day. Adams graduated from Rockford [Illinois] Female Seminary in 1881. As part of the first generation of college-educated women in the United States, Addams struggled for a way to put her talents to use. Uninterested in careers traditionally open to women, such as teaching, Addams sought a way to better the world. In 1889, she joined with Ellen Gates Starr to found Hull-House in a run-down mansion built decades earlier by Charles Hull. Located in the largely immigrant Nineteenth Ward, it served as the initial settlement house in Chicago and the model for many others. Designed initially to allow wealthy women to uplift the poor by sharing their knowledge of literature and art, Hull-House quickly shifted into a provider of social services and an employer of women eager to find some socially worthwhile use for their brains. Just as importantly, it served as a means of preserving the culture of the Old World. Hull-House offered visiting nurses, legal services, a nursery and kindergarten for the children of working mothers, a theater, a music school, multiple reading groups, a museum of immigrant crafts, a butcher shop, a coffee shop, and a bakery. German immigrants, often better educated than other newcomers to the United States, came to Hull-House to pursue courses in German history and literature. They used the settlement to introduce German arts, especially music, to their American-born offspring. At a time when the sons and daughters of immigrants dismissed all of the Old World and wholeheartedly embraced Americanization, Hull-House promoted respect for German heritage. Hull-House would remain as Addams's home until her death, and its accomplishments made her into a national figure.

During the 1890s and 1900s, she lobbied city, state, and national authorities for an eight-hour day, employment regulations for women and children, unemployment insurance, improved sanitation, factory legislation, municipal playgrounds, public kindergartens, a juvenile court system, and the enforcement of antiprostitution and antidrug laws. Addams served on the Chicago School Board and as a vice president of the National American Woman Suffrage Association and helped found the National Association for the Advancement of Colored People.

One of the first public intellectuals, Addams wrote and spoke prolifically. Peace activism and suffrage were among her favorite topics, all of which centered on the obligation of citizens to redefine government to be more responsive to the needs of the people. Although she occasionally published in scholarly journals, most of her work went into mass-circulation magazines such as *Ladies Home Journal* and *McClure's*. Addams wrote six books during her lifetime, including the best-selling autobiographicy *Twenty Years at Hull-House* (1910).

A self-possessed woman, Addams did not fear to take the side of unpopular causes. Advocacy of a role for women in public life had cost her the goodwill of many conservatives, and in 1901, she spoke out for the civil rights of anarchists arrested by the police in the wake of President William McKinley's assassination. But she did not expect to be vilified for her pacifist beliefs during World War I. When Addams broke with most Progressives by opposing U.S. entry into the war, she experienced ostracism for the first time. She

Jane Addams of Hull-House, Chicago, Illinois, ca. 1913. (Library of Congress)

had once believed that immigration, commerce, the telephone, and the telegraph would establish a truly international culture that would make violence between western European states and the United States virtually unthinkable, but the war crushed these hopes.

Addams viewed World War I as a twofold threat because it halted progress toward civilized methods of conflict resolution while diverting resources away from community projects and toward military spending. As a founder of the Woman's Peace Party, the chair of the Emergency Federation of Peace Forces, and the symbol of feminine conscience in the United States, Addams sought to stop the fighting. Politicians and the public attacked her activities as treasonous and foolish. Undeterred, Addams helped create the Women's International League for Peace and Freedom immediately after the war in 1919.

Addams did her best to fight the cruelty and self-righteousness shown by the United States in dealing with Germans during and after World War I. The American Protective League, a vigilante organization with quasi-official status from the U.S. government, singled out the city of Chicago as a hotbed of pro-German sympathizers and placed Hull-House under a cloud of suspicion of disloyalty for its work with German Americans. Addams did not attack her attackers. Instead, she responded to verbal assaults by bemoaning the general acceptance of standardization and advocating an America that permitted voluntary assimilation at the immigrant's pace. As a member of the International Congress of Women, Addams issued a call in 1915 for the lifting of the wartime blockade of Germany so that food could get to noncombatants. During a 1919 fact-finding mission to Germany, she documented widespread starvation among children as a result of the blockade.

By the late 1920s, Addams had regained most of her reputation and her place as one of the greatest Americans. The culmination of this restoration came when she won the Nobel Peace Prize in 1931.

Caryn E. Neumann

See also Anarchists; Chicago; International Council of Women

References and Further Reading

Davis, Allen F. *American Heroine: The Life and Legend of Jane Addams.* Chicago: Ivan R. Dee, 2000.

Elshtain, Jean Bethke. *Jane Addams and the Dream of American Democracy.* New York: Basic Books, 2002.

———. *The Jane Addams Reader.* New York: Basic Books, 2002.

ADELSVEREIN (SOCIETY FOR THE PROTECTION OF GERMAN IMMIGRANTS IN TEXAS)

The Adelsverein was initially organized on April 20, 1842, at Biebrich on the Rhine by twenty-one German noblemen interested in founding a German colony in Texas. The organization was officially dubbed Verein zum Schutze deutscher Einwanderer in Texas (Society for the Protection of German Immigrants in Texas). It is varyingly referred to as the Texas-Verein, the Mainzer Verein, and the German Emigration Company.

The noblemen who founded the Adelsverein were heavily influenced by positive news about life in Texas spread in Europe by authors such as Carl Postl, who wrote historical novels under the penname Charles Sealsfield. During a prolonged illness, Prince Carl of Leiningen, a leading light in the Adelsverein, read several works expounding the virtues of Texas, serving to shape his favorable opinion of the newly minted republic. Further, early immigrants such as Friedrich Ernst sent glowing reports of Texas back to their friends and families, which received wide circulation. As a result, a limited amount of German immigration was already underway in Texas. In the minds of the noblemen who founded the Adelsverein, Texas presented itself as the perfect laboratory for their colonial experiment.

In May 1842 Counts Joseph of Boos-Waldeck and Victor August of Leiningen-Westerburg-Alt-Leiningen were given the assignment of traveling to Texas, surveying the land firsthand, and purchasing property on which to build a colony. Republic of Texas president Sam Houston had been authorized under a law of February 5,

1842, to provide generous grants of land to those willing to bring settlers to Texas. The counts entered into negotiations with Houston for a colonization grant but ultimately declined the president's offer when he refused to provide an exemption from taxation to the colonists.

Boos-Waldeck and Alt-Leiningen spent some time exploring Texas. Impressed by the lands in the vicinity of Ernst's settlement at Industry, in January 1843 Boos-Waldeck purchased a league of land nearby, which he dubbed Nassau Farm in honor of the Adelsverein's protector, Duke Adolf of Nassau. Alt-Leiningen returned to Europe in May 1843, while Boos-Waldeck remained in Texas to develop his farm. The two men split their decision on whether to recommend a colonization effort in Texas. Alt-Leiningen heartily backed the adventure, whereas Boos-Waldeck, fearing the expense, recommended against it. Although unable to receive official backing from the Prussian government, the Adelsverein was reorganized as a joint-stock company on June 18, 1843, and was capitalized at 200,000 gulden ($80,000) for the purpose of purchasing land in the Republic of Texas.

The Adelsverein was approached in September 1843 by Alexander Bourgeois d'Orvanne, a speculator, who along with his partner, Armand Ducos, had received a colonization grant in Texas. The Adelsverein was interested in purchasing the right to settle Bourgeois's cession, which was situated to the west of San Antonio. The Adelsverein formally organized itself under its official title on March 25, 1844, naming Prince Carl Emich III of Leiningen president and Count Carl of Castell-Castell vice president and secretary, a position that was the equivalent of business manager.

Prince Carl of Solms-Braunfels was selected as commissioner-general and put in charge of the colonization project, and Bourgeois was named colonial director. These two men arrived in Texas to begin the colonization project on July 1, 1844.

Shortly after his arrival in Texas, Prince Carl realized that Bourgeois's colonial grant was worthless. It had expired, and it quickly became clear that the Republic of Texas would not renew it. However, the Adelsverein had already negotiated a replacement. The Adelsverein had been approached in May by Henry Francis Fisher, who along with his partner Burchard Miller held the right to colonize lands between the Colorado and Llano rivers in what is today known as the Hill Country of Texas. Fisher was himself a German native and had been appointed by Sam Houston to serve as Texas consul at Bremen. On June 26, 1844, the Adelsverein purchased the right to the Fisher-Miller Colony, and Castell-Castell acted quickly to inform Prince Carl of these changes. On August 28, 1844, Bourgeois resigned as colonial director, with Fisher taking his place.

The first colonists began arriving at the port of Carlshafen (later Indianola) in December 1844. Prince Carl had established the port on the Texas coast as a central point of entry for the immigrants. The Fisher-Miller Colony was some 300 miles inland and thus too far for an easy trek by the would-be settlers. As a stopgap measure in order to handle the influx of immigrants, in March 1845 Prince Carl established the hamlet of New Braunfels along the Comal River north of San Antonio to act as a way station. He named this new settlement for his home, Braunfels, on the Lahn River.

Baron Otfried Hans Freiherr von Meusebach succeeded Prince Carl as commissioner-general in May 1845. It quickly became apparent to the new commissioner-general, who took the egalitarian name of John O. Meusebach, that the Adelsverein had deep financial troubles. He was allotted only $5 per person to transport colonists from the coast to the Fisher-Miller Colony. Nevertheless, Meusebach went to work immediately. In August 1845 he established another village, dubbed Fredericksburg, for Prince Friedrich of Prussia, this time closer to the Adelsverein's colonial cession.

It was under the very capable leadership of Meusebach that the Adelsverein enjoyed its greatest success. During his tenure as commissioner-general (May 1845–July 1847), over 5,000 German immigrants made their way to Texas. Five small settlements (Bettina, Castell, Leiningen, Meerholz, and Schoenburg) were established within the Fisher-Miller cession, and the towns of New Braunfels and Fredericksburg were on their way to great success by the time Meusebach stepped aside. His successor, Hermann Spiess, functioned as little more that a caretaker. By the close of 1847 it was apparent that the Adelsverein was facing financial ruin. Although a special business manager was appointed to deal with the crisis, very little could be done to save the company. Henry Francis Fisher attempted to keep the enterprise going as the German Emigration Company, but in September 1853 it was finally forced to turn all of its assets over to its creditors.

As a financial venture, the Adelsverein was a disaster. However, it accomplished its chief goal of inspiring German immigration to Texas. Germans became the largest European immigrant group to settle in Texas, a process of continual colonization that lasted into the twentieth century. The Adelsverein was built on a foundation of ideals. The noblemen who created it sought to build a satellite state of Germany in Texas that would better the lives of those who chose to settle in the colony and strengthen Germany proper with expanded access to goods and trade. Ultimately, it was the noblemen themselves who undermined the enterprise through simple lack of experience in the complex business matters of building a foreign colony. For the most part, the settlers prospered, building lasting communities in their new homeland.

Jerry C. Drake

See also Darmstaedters; Ernst, Friedrich; Fredericksburg, Texas; Meusebach, John O.; New Braunfels, Texas; Sealsfield, Charles; Solms-Braunfels, Prince Carl of

References and Further Reading

Benjamin, Gilbert Giddings. *The Germans in Texas: A Study in Immigration.* Austin: Jenkins Publishing, 1974.

Biesele, Rudolph Leopold. *The History of the German Settlements in Texas, 1831–1861.* Austin: Von Boeckman Jones, 1930.

Jordan, Terry G. *German Seed in Texas Soil: Immigrant Farmers in Nineteenth-Century Texas.* Austin: University of Texas Press, 1975.

King, Irene Marschall. *John O. Meusebach: German Colonizer in Texas.* Austin: University of Texas Press, 1967.

Lich, Glen E. *The German Texans.* San Antonio: Institute of Texan Cultures, 1981.

Lich, Glen E., and Dona B. Reeves, eds. *German Culture in Texas: A Free Earth; Essays from the 1978 Southwest Symposium.* Boston: Twayne Publishers, 1980.

ADELUNG, JOHANN CHRISTOPH

b. August 8, 1732; Spantekow, Prussia
d. September 9, 1806; Dresden,
Saxony

Eminent German linguist with significant works about the German language and comparative linguistics, including the first comprehensive analysis and reference work of the known American Indian languages (*Mithridates*, 1806–1817). Work on the *Mithridates* was continued by Johann Severin Vater (1771–1826).

Adelung, chief librarian at the court in Dresden, became widely known for his *Versuch eines vollständigen grammatisch-kritischen Wörterbuches der hochdeutschen Mundart, mit beständiger Vergleichung der übrigen Mundarten, besonders aber der Oberdeutschen* (German Dictionary, 1774–1786), which was the most substantial and methodologically most advanced dictionary of the time; he also gained recognition for his other works in German grammar, lexicography, stylistics, and language history. His last project, the *Mithridates*, is a comparison and classification of all the known languages of the world at the time, mainly by using translations of the Lord's Prayer. The *Mithridates* consists of four volumes. Adelung completed volume 1 and parts of volume 2. Vater continued the work by adding the first comprehensive comparison and analysis of American Indian and African languages in volume 3. The fourth volume contains corrections and an article about the Basque language by Wilhelm von Humboldt. Before the *Mithridates*, Adelung had already published four American Indian poems with translations in 1799, and Vater had pub-

lished the first results of his studies about American Indian languages in 1810. In the *Mithridates*, language samples and their German translations, typological and grammatical information, and ethnographic information about the speakers are given. Adelung's goal was to find relationships between peoples by finding the relationships between their native languages. The *Mithridates* was the only widely recognized work by Adelung for several decades but is nevertheless missing in many linguistic bibliographies in Europe during the nineteenth century. Its volume covering the American Indian languages gained recognition from contemporary U.S. linguists, however.

Adelung's ethnographic-historical concept saw language as being closely connected to society, history, and culture. Thus every chapter of the *Mithridates* starts with ethnographic information about the language users, including the settlement areas of the tribes and possible relationships to each other. Chosen by Adelung to complete the *Mithridates*, Vater applied Adelung's language concept to his analysis of American Indian languages and emphasized the influence of historical migration of the tribes on the ethnic and linguistic structure of the Americas. Vater favored the theory of migration movements of Asian tribes from Asia to the Americas, pushing autochthonous American tribes toward South America. Consequently, Vater started his analysis of American Indian languages in South America, where he assumed he would find the oldest American peoples. Influenced by the evolving discipline of comparative anatomy, Vater also integrated anatomical data in his analysis, mainly to clarify the possible genealogical relationship between the North, Central, and South American Indians and between American Indian and Asian peoples. Vater concluded that some anatomical and linguistic similarities pointed to connections between the Americas and Asia, and he emphasized the linguistic diversity of the Americas, caused by communicative isolation in those sparsely populated continents.

The core of the *Mithridates* is the comparison of language samples, mainly versions of the Lord's Prayer in different languages, but it also includes shorter texts, poems, and word lists. Adelung considered a broad database as crucial and therefore collected as many text samples as possible from earlier language studies and synoptic collections of the Lord's Prayer, which were already used as sources by other linguists before him. Adelung chose the Lord's Prayer as the main language sample to have a text long enough to contain grammatical structures that was also available in numerous different languages around the world. Adelung and Vater also compiled all available grammars for American Indian and African languages, which were mostly written by missionaries or explorers, or derived grammars themselves from language samples.

One problem for Adelung and Vater was that they did not know most of the languages they analyzed and had never heard those languages spoken. Nevertheless, they tried to give an impression of the phonology of the language with their transcription of the language samples. To provide as much accessible data as possible, Adelung and Vater also included unpublished information from other researchers. (For his study about American Indian languages, for example, Vater used Alexander von Humboldt's unpublished data about American Indians.) Nevertheless, few reliable sources were available for most of the languages. Adelung saw this as a basic problem of his study. Vater pointed out that the inconsistent availability of sources made a totally balanced comparison of all languages impossible because the selection of languages depended on the availability of material. Nevertheless, he expressed surprise about the large amount of data he could find about African and American Indian languages.

Language classifications in the *Mithridates* are determined by the restricted database and Adelung's language concept. Adelung theorized that languages historically evolve from basic words with one syllable to more and more complex structures with multiple syllables and elaborate grammar. Adelung considered such a morphologic and grammar-based language classification as impossible without detailed linguistic information and therefore only classified the Asian languages according to this scheme as monosyllabic or polysyllabic; however, they are subdivided according to geographical distribution, as is typical in other language collections of the eighteenth century. For the European languages, he choose roughly the classification (e.g., Slavic, Romantic, or Germanic language groups, etc.) still used today, even though he did not describe all relationships correctly. Vater did utilize Adelung's syllabic categorization for African and American Indians languages but classified them according primarily to geographical and historical-genealogical factors. Linguistic similarities were secondary factors. He characterized the American Indian languages as mainly nonelaborate (*kunstlos*), but he considered some of them to be more developed and linguistically more complex.

For the American Indian languages, Vater identified several language groups: eleven for South America, four for Central America, and five for North America, including Greenland. However linguistically determined, the language groups are named and organized according to their geographical distribution.

Adelung and Vater did not use completely new methodological or theoretical approaches to linguistics but differed from their immediate successors by using social and ethnographical data for their language analysis. The *Mithridates* is widely recognized for its vast collection of data, typological descriptions, and classifications of languages, especially of the African and American Indian languages.

Jörg Meindl

See also Humboldt, Alexander von; Humboldt, Wilhelm von; Vater, Johann Severin

References and Further Reading
Adelung, Johann Christoph. "Proben der Dichtung ungebildeter Völker: Erstes Dutzend." *Erholungen* (1799): 194–208.
———. *Mithridates oder allgemeine Sprachenkunde mit dem Vater Unser als Sprachprobe in bey nahe fünfhundert Sprachen und Mundarten.* 4 vols. Berlin: Vossische Buchhandlung, 1806–1817.
Bahner, Werner, ed. *Sprache und Kulturentwicklung im Blickfeld der deutschen Spätaufklärung: Der Beitrag Johann Christoph Adelungs.* Berlin: Akademie-Verlag, 1984.

Admiral Graf Spee

This armor-plated ship, operating as a privateer at the beginning of World War II, was named after Count Maximilian Graf von Spee, the commandant of the German East Asia squadron. After an overwhelming victory over British units in front of Coronel (Chile), Spee's squadron was sunk near the Falkland Islands by an enemy unit of modern battleships in December 1914.

The *Admiral Graf Spee,* commissioned in 1936, was a so-called pocket battleship with a crew of 1,100 sailors. It was of light construction and equipped with modern location devices. From the beginning of the war, it operated very successfully against enemy merchant ships in the South Atlantic and Indian Ocean. Severely damaged during a sea battle with three British cruisers off the Rio de la Plata estuary, the *Graf Spee* succeeded in freeing itself, but it had to dock in the harbor of Montevideo, Chile. Diplomatic pressure from London forced the *Admiral Graf Spee* to leave the harbor shortly afterward. In view of the ship's unfitness for battle and his assessment of the situation as hopeless, Commandant Captain Hans Langsdorff decided to scuttle the ship. On December 17, 1939, he permitted the crew to climb into lifeboats and gave the order to blow up the ship.

While the *Admiral Graf Spee* sank, over 1,000 German seamen crossed the Rio de la Plata and landed in Argentina. Langsdorff had arranged this coup jointly with the German naval attaché in Buenos Aires and a friendly shipping company, thus confronting neutral Argentina with a fait accompli. After leading the crew into safe internment, Langsdorff shot himself. The commandant's suicide greatly affected public opinion at the Rio de la Plata. It simultaneously irritated and impressed the Argentines, caused a wave of admiration even in circles not sympathetic to Germany, and led to the largest funeral since that of deposed President Hipólito Yrigoyen: 100,000 Argentines joined Langsdorff's funeral at the German section of Chacarita Cemetery.

Launching of the new German armored ship, Admiral Graf Spee, *Wilhelmshaven, Germany, 1939.*
(Underwood & Underwood/Corbis)

The crew of the *Admiral Graf Spee* enjoyed extensive liberty, although they were officially interned. Argentina firmly rejected British demands for extradition and even permitted the internees' wearing of uniforms during liberty. Two hundred and eighty-five *Speegrafen* (Spee counts) married at the Rio de la Plata. Quite a number of crewmen managed to escape. Some of them reached Germany through the Soviet Union and rejoined the war as marines.

In response to Allied pressure, the internees living at the Rio de la Plata were forcefully repatriated to Germany on February 16, 1946. However, as many as 500 returned to Argentina during the Peron era. United in the Kameradenkreis Admiral Graf Spee (Admiral Graf Spee circle of comrades) the former seamen still celebrate the day of their captain's and savior's death annually.

The sea battle at the Rio de la Plata and the scuttling of the ship was Argentina's only direct contact with World War II. This incident caused Argentines to view neutrality more positively than at the beginning of the war. In Germany, the honorable and courteous treatment of the German soldiers raised Argentina's reputation, so that after World War II, the La Plata Republic became a destination for many refugees.

The wreck of the *Admiral Graf Spee* remained where it had been scuttled. With the goal of establishing an *Admiral Graf Spee* Museum in Montevideo, the first attempts to raise it were made at the beginning of 2004.

Holger M. Meding

See also Argentina; Chile; World War I;
World War II

References and Further Reading

Lascano, Diego M. *Historia en imágenes del acorazado* alemán Admiral Graf Spee. *Buenos Aires: (Author's edition) 1998.*

Laurence, Ricardo E. *Operativo Graf Spee: Uruguay, Diciembre 17 de 1939, Argentina, Febrero 16 de 1946.* Rosario: (Author's edition) 1996.

Rasenack, Friedrich Wilhelm. *Panzerschiff Admiral Graf Spee.* Hamburg: Koehler, 1999.

ADORNO, THEODOR WIESENGRUND

b. September 11, 1903; Frankfurt am Main, Prussia

d. August 6, 1969; Visp, Wallis

An eminent member of the Frankfurt School who lived from 1938 to 1953 in the United States, Adorno deeply influenced the intellectual discourse in both Germany and the United States. He coined the phrase that after Auschwitz there can be no poetry.

Adorno grew up in Frankfurt, where he studied music and philosophy at university. He studied neo-Kantianism under Hans Cornelius, and while attending his seminars, he met Max Horkheimer. Both men were interested in Edmund Husserl's phenomenology. Adorno received his doctorate in philosophy in 1924. In 1930 he traveled to Berlin, where he met Ernst Bloch, Siegfried Kracauer, Walter Benjamin, and Bertolt Brecht, all of whom were trying to create an aesthetic based on Karl Marx's critique of capitalist society and the bourgeoise. Adorno became enamored with George Lukács's *History and Class Consciousness* (1923). At the beginning of his studies, Adorno gained an interest in expressionism and wrote Ernst Bloch, whom he considered the philosopher of expressionism. He found in this philosophy the very real possibility of cultural disintegration. Around this same time, he met Alban Berg, a student of Arnold Schönberg, the creator of atonal music. He soon agreed to go with Berg to Vienna as his student. Adorno's two years in Vienna had considerable influence on his aesthetic and philosophical pursuits.

When he returned from Vienna, Paul Tillich had become chair of philosophy at the University of Frankfurt. Tillich was a good friend of Horkheimer and Friedrich Pollock, the early founders of the Institute for Social Research, which Adorno would later join. Before that, he had already published some of his first essays on music in the *Zeitschrift für Sozialforschung* (Journal of Social Research), the institute's journal. Tillich helped Adorno become a lecturer (*Privatdozent*) while he finished his Habilitationsschrift, a postdoctoral study of Søren Kierkegaard's aesthetics.

When in 1933 Jews were excluded from academic professions, Adorno hoped to find refuge in Vienna but was unable to receive a position at the university. In 1934, he moved to England, where he remained for three and a half years. While there, he continued to publish articles on the aesthetics of music in the *Zeitschrift für Sozialforschung,* and he also began a thorough study of Husserl. Through his studies over the years, he did not dwell solely on music but turned again to Marx in order to understand the influence of capitalist society on the rational subject. In 1938 he moved to the United States and became an "official" member of the Institute of Social Research in New York. Alienated from American life, he began to investigate the culture industry and mass culture in a capitalist society. While in New York, he encountered the true nature of the technological and managerial control created by a growing monopolistic capitalism. As he watched the order of capitalist society move more and more toward rationalization and mechanization, Adorno paradoxically claimed it to be even more irrational than bourgeois society. The commodification and homogenization of capitalist society destroyed in his eyes the foundations of bourgeois society and led to the disintegration of the individual. He believed this loss of subjectivity was a major threat to the future of society. During this time he published some of his best known works, *Dialectic of Enlightenment* (1947), a collaboration with Horkheimer; *The Authoritarian Personality* (1950), a collaborative project; and *Minima Moralia* (1951).

While in New York, his doubts about capitalism increased, and his ideas made him even more of a cultural elitist. He began his first research project in the United States with Paul Lazarsfeld at the Princeton University Radio Research project. He at once disliked the empirical and quantitative nature of the study and felt the study of audience response to radio programming displayed a form of commercialism in which consumers would eventually dictate radio programming. As a result, real art itself would become a commodity. He saw music within mass culture as a commodity judged more by exchange value than use value. Returning to his belief in the destruction of the individual, he felt the music of mass culture destroyed subjectivity. The mass media was creating a reified culture that destroyed mediation and reconciliation and created instead a passivity that completely eliminated the possibility of a negation. He believed the culture industry merely imitated existing social

patterns, whereas true art went beyond such social arrangements. For Adorno, the power of mass culture was greater than any economic theory in strengthening the success of capitalism. He claimed it did not allow people to question social conditions and instead created for them false needs.

After living in California, Adorno returned to Frankfurt in 1953 and became director of the Institute for Social Research in 1959. During this time he wrote as prolifically as before. He engaged in debates with the social positivists and with Martin Heidegger, and he completed his *Negative Dialectics* (1966). His *Aesthetic Theory* was published posthumously in 1970. His books and essays greatly influenced postmodernism and poststructuralism.

Jim Varn

See also Brecht, Bertolt; Frankfurt School; Horkheimer, Max; Intellectual Exile; Kracauer, Siegfried; Schönberg, Arnold

References and Further Reading

Dallymar, Fred. *Between Freiburg and Frankfurt: Toward a Critical Ontology.* Amherst: University of Massachusetts Press, 1991.

Jay, Martin. *The Dialectical Imagination: A History of the Frankfurt School and the Institute of Social Research, 1923–1950.* Berkeley: University of California Press, 1973.

Lunn, Eugene. *Marxism and Modernism: An Historical Study of Lukacs, Brecht, Benjamin, and Adorno.* Berkeley: University of California Press, 1982.

AFRICAN AMERICANS

African Americans occupied a noteworthy place in German American relations throughout the twentieth century. For African Americans, Germany could serve as an analogue or counterpoint to white American society as they fought pervasive racial discrimination in the United States. Germans could also use developments in African American history to comment on German concerns, but they more frequently articulated critiques (racist or antiracist) of the United States based on the position of African Americans in American society.

Consideration of African Americans in Germany can appropriately begin with William Edward Burghardt Du Bois, who pursued graduate study of social science at the Friedrich-Wilhelm University in Berlin from 1892 to 1894. Du Bois's thought shows influences from his studies in Germany and reading of German writers. More fundamentally, Du Bois's time in Germany and Europe provided him with a broader perspective on American society and the question of race. His *Autobiography* describes his feelings of liberation from American racism and parochialism, although Du Bois at times confronted racial prejudice in Germany.

African Americans have sometimes significantly shaped German views of the United States and American culture, especially American music. From the 1920s through at least the 1950s Germans typically regarded jazz as both fundamentally black and quintessentially American music, a discomfiting assessment for white and black American opponents of jazz. During the short life of the Weimar Republic, numerous African American entertainers, including most famously Josephine Baker, performed in Germany. A minority of German listeners enthusiastically greeted African American music as a tonic for European culture, which they regarded as increasingly sterile. Ernst Krenek's successful 1927 opera, *Jonny spielt auf* (Jonny Strikes Up), whose title character was an African American, exemplified that kind of reading

of black music, which would find echoes in the eagerness of postwar German youth for jazz and rock 'n' roll. Conservative Germans, however, derided jazz. Racist critiques of jazz typically argued that the musical export revealed the essence of uncultured America. Nazi rhetoric decried the threatened "negrification" of German culture, and the printed guide for the Nazis' 1938 "Degenerate Music" exhibit carried an apelike caricature of a saxophonist.

Nazi antipathy toward jazz represented but one aspect of the movement's thoroughgoing antiblack racism. African Americans appeared as the object of National Socialist racial scorn. Nazi Party organs commented approvingly on white supremacist practices like lynching and segregation in the American South. Jesse Owens's victories at the 1936 Berlin Olympics and the boxing matches between Joe Louis and Max Schmeling acquired their special charge in both the German and American public imaginations because they publicly refuted Nazism's insistence on the biological inferiority of African Americans.

The establishment of the expressly racist Nazi regime under Hitler had far-reaching consequences for the struggles of African Americans for civil rights in the United States. White and black Americans recognized that racism, both antisemitic and antiblack, was a central tenet of Nazism. As the Third Reich carried the logic of racist dogma to its genocidal conclusion, racism generally came under increasing attack. American civil rights rhetoric thus analogized segregationist policies in the United States to Nazi measures against the Jews. During World War II, African American leaders linked American racism to Nazism in calling for a "double victory" against fascism abroad and racism

Spurred by the crowd's cries of "go, go, go" the Lionel Hampton band, and especially its "King" Lionel, played themselves into a sweat for the entertainment of the jazz-hungry audience, Frankfurt, Germany, 1946. (Bettmann/Corbis)

at home. In the 1940s and into the 1950s, the example of Nazi racism served to buttress the critique of racial segregation in the American South.

African Americans had been present in Germany since 1945 as members of the U.S. armed forces stationed there. First arriving as part of a segregated army charged with democratizing the Germans, black GIs comprised just below 10 percent of the U.S. forces through the years of the military occupation. The interactions between African American soldiers and the local population produced some conflict, as well as friendships, romantic attachments, and a number of marriages between Germans and African Americans. Relationships be-

tween German women and African American soldiers aroused considerable concern among Germans and white Americans in the 1940s and 1950s. During the 1950s, West Germans publicly debated how to integrate children of African American and German parents into West German society as Germans began to consider in a new way ideas about race and Germanness.

In Germany, a tradition of criticizing American racial discrimination against African Americans and of forging a sympathetic affiliation with African Americans continued from the nineteenth into the twentieth centuries. In the interwar years, German Communists protested as unjust the rape convictions of the celebrated

African American "Scottsboro Boys." In a more attenuated fashion, antiracist allegiances continued during the Third Reich as "swing youth" imitated African American music and styles as a means of signaling their nonconformity. The African American communist Angela Davis has described her feeling of solidarity with members of the German radical student Left during her postgraduate studies in 1960s Frankfurt. After Davis was arrested in the United States on charges of kidnapping and murder, Germans in the Federal Republic and especially in the German Democratic Republic participated actively in the international campaign to free her. Following her acquittal in 1972, she toured a number of Socialist countries, where her case had become a cause célèbre in efforts to expose racism and anticommunism in the United States. She reported receiving an especially enthusiastic reception in East Germany.

Timothy Schroer

See also American Students at German
    Universities; Davis, Angela Yvonne; GIs in
    West Germany; *Hindenburg* Disaster;
    Olympic Games; U.S. Bases in West
    Germany

References and Further Reading

Fehrenbach, Heide. "Of German Mothers and
    'Negermischlingskinder': Race, Sex, and the
    Postwar Nation." In *The Miracle Years: A
    Cultural History of West Germany,
    1949–1968.* Ed. Hanna Schissler. Princeton:
    Princeton University Press, 2001, 164–186.
Lewis, David Levering. *W. E. B. Du Bois:
    Biography of a Race.* New York: Henry
    Holt, 1993.
McBride, David, Leroy Hopkins, and C. Aisha
    Blackshire-Belay, eds. *Crosscurrents: African
    Americans, Africa, and Germany in the
    Modern World.* Columbia, SC: Camden
    House, 1998.
Miller, James A., Susan D. Pennybacker, and
    Eve Rosenhaft. "Mother Ada Wright and
    the International Campaign to Free the
    Scottsboro Boys, 1931–1934." *American
    Historical Review* 106 (2001): 387–430.

ALTGELD, JOHN PETER

b. December 30, 1847; Nieder Selter
(Taunus mountain range)
d. March 8, 1902; Chicago, Illinois

Governor of Illinois from 1892 to 1896, John Peter Altgeld may well be the German American politician who gained the largest amount of national notoriety and fame in the smallest amount of time, addressing the most controversial of issues.

Altgeld's father was a wagon maker by trade, and when his parents decided to emigrate only three months after his birth, they followed Mrs. Altgeld's brother and took up farming in north-central Ohio, in a township largely settled by Germans and similar in landscape and farming methods to what they had known in their previous home. For the next twenty years John Peter Altgeld was trapped in endless, hard farm labor and a narrow-minded, unsupportive family environment. His desire to receive an education had to be realized against his father's wishes and without any financial support except John's ability to sell his labor. In 1864 he briefly escaped home by enlisting in the army, though his experiences on the battlefield remained limited due to illness and the disbanding of his regiment in the same year. In 1868, on the day of his twenty-first birthday, he left his family, embarked on a journey through the Midwest, and finally arrived in Andrew County, Missouri. Here, with the charitable support of influential people, he was able to work and to study law and was admitted to the Andrew County Bar in 1871. He practiced law until 1874, became involved in activities of the farmers' movement, the Grange, and moved on to Chicago in 1875.

Altgeld established a law practice, worked hard and lived frugally, and in

1877 married Emma Ford, a woman he had known since childhood. He began to successfully invest in real estate, gained a reputation by publishing in law journals, networked with supportive people in his profession and in politics, and was nominated for the state legislature on the Democratic ticket in 1884. In 1886 he became a judge for the Cook County Supreme Court, from which he retired in 1890, having found the complacency and routine of the court not challenging enough. His professional life in Chicago was marked by a moderately successful practice as a lawyer and by great esteem for his performance as a judge. He had also been able to accumulate great wealth in real estate deals, which he later lost on an ill-conceived financial scheme related to the "United Building," a project in which he had great financial and emotional interest. When he embarked on his political career in 1892, he was reputed to be an earnest, hardworking, intelligent, socially responsible man, this being noteworthy in a political climate marked by financial depression, industrial disputes, and growing public annoyance over corruption. That he was also able to address issues of concern to the German American citizens of Chicago and Illinois (i.e., the right to be taught in German in school) certainly helped. In 1880 one-third of Chicago's population was of German descent. When Altgeld won the gubernatorial race, Illinois, for the first time in forty years, had a Democratic governor.

Altgeld's term as governor, though brief and turbulent, was nonetheless effective. Besides the highly controversial pardoning of the Haymarket riot martyrs and the equally publicized conflict over the Pullman strike, he was able to pursue a number of reform projects related to the penal system, charitable institutions, industrial relations, and education. His most notable accomplishments were the factory reform legislation that brought Florence Kelley, whom he appointed as the first factory inspector, into the national limelight, and the support he was able to muster for the University of Illinois. This support not only helped to turn the university into a first-rate educational institution but also changed the way the legislature and politicians dealt with higher education in Illinois.

Upon taking up office, Altgeld was immediately approached by representatives from the amnesty movement asking clemency for Samuel Fielden, Michael Schwab, and Oscar Neebe, who were still serving life sentences in prison, allegedly for being involved in the Haymarket square riot of 1886. Today, it is widely understood that had Altgeld issued the pardons on grounds of executive clemency, the move would have found widespread public support. However, after close investigation of the documents, Altgeld came to the conclusion that the prisoners had received gross injustice and that the preceding trail, by all legal standards, had been a scam. So the decision to pardon was not an act of mercy; since the three men had been unjustly convicted, nothing but a full pardon was in order. This critical assessment of the legal procedures of that trial was Altgeld's downfall. The press accused him of being a foreign agitator, if not an anarchist himself. It is said that he was aware of the political consequences when he delivered the Pardoning Message in June 1893.

The controversy over the use of federal troops during the 1894 railroad strike again found Altgeld on the other side of the political-capitalist power structure. President Grover Cleveland had readily aligned himself with the railroad magnates when he, upon their request, sent federal troops to Chicago and allowed for local gunmen to be invested with federal authority. This transaction not only disturbed the local peace but effectively broke the strike, rendered the American Railway Union powerless, and completely alienated the working people. Altgeld had refrained from sending in the Illinois National Guard because the strikers, for the most part, had maintained civil order. He had not wanted to forgo the union's chances to achieve an agreement with the railroad. But President Cleveland had other ideas. He set a precedent by using the Sherman Anti-Trust Act as an effective tool against workers' organizations, which would become a legal device of great consequence in the years to come, putting workers at a great disadvantage in any disputes between capital and labor. When Altgeld protested Cleveland's actions and demanded a withdrawal of troops, the press once again denounced him as a foreign agitator not in tune with the principles of the U.S. Constitution.

It was obvious that Altgeld would have no chance of reelection after these two controversial political affairs. He thus retired from public view in 1896, only to become active in Democratic circles, promoting the "silver issue"; that is demanding the free coinage of silver, and shaping the "Chicago Platform" that became the Democratic credo in the 1896 election. He was arguably the brain behind William Jennings Bryan's presidential campaign, and had he not been disqualified due to his German birth, he may well have been the presidential candidate himself.. The "Silver Plan" did not materialize, and Altgeld continued

to defend workers' rights as a lawyer in Chicago.

Altgeld's personality defies easy categorization. His political credo, nevertheless, was in accordance with the great reformers of his time: Jane Addams, Henry D. Lloyd, and Clarence Darrow all respected him. He was among the earliest of a generation of reformers whose political influence would shape American urbanism a decade later.

Christiane Harzig

See also Addams, (Laura) Jane; Anarchists; Chicago; Haymarket; Illinois; Politics and German Americans

References and Further Reading

Barnard, Harry. *Eagle Forgotten: The Life of John P. Altgeld*. New York: Bobbs Merill, 1938.

Browne, Waldo R. *Altgeld of Illinois: A Record of His Life and Work*. New York: B. W. Huebsch, 1924.

Ginger, Ray. *Altgeld's America: The Lincoln Ideal versus Changing Realities*. New York: Funk and Wagnalls, 1958.

AMANA COLONIES

The Amana Colonies are a settlement comprised of seven small villages (Amana, East Amana, Middle Amana, High Amana, West Amana, South Amana, and Homestead) located in the Iowa River valley in Iowa County, in east-central Iowa. They were founded by the Amana Society in Iowa in 1855. The society's origins date back to an early eighteenth-century religious sect with congregations predominantly in southern and central Germany. The Amana people successfully practiced communal living in Iowa for almost eighty years. Today Amana residents (about 1,650 people), especially the younger generation, embrace a more secular, individualistic lifestyle strongly influenced by

American mainstream culture. Traces of the German culture can still be found in architecture, customs, crafts, and food preparation. Other German traditions, such as the Oktoberfest and *Fachwerk* (half-timbering construction) architecture, have only recently been introduced. Current membership in the Amana Church is around 400. One of the Sunday church services is still held in German. Over the years, residents' use of Amana German (*Kolonie-Deutsch*) has steadily declined. In 1965 the seven villages of Amana were designated a National Historic Landmark. The Amana Heritage Society, founded in 1968, aims at collecting, preserving, and interpreting the heritage of the Amana community.

The history of the Amana people is rooted in the Community of True Inspiration (*Wahre Inspirations-Gemeinde*), a religious movement strongly influenced by German pietism and mysticism. The former Lutheran clergyman Eberhard Ludwig Gruber (1655–1728) and saddle maker Johann Friedrich Rock (1678–1749), both originally from Württemberg, are regarded as the primary founders of this religious society. Like the pietists, the two men and their followers were dissatisfied with the dogmatic practices of the orthodox Lutheran Church. As a result, in 1714 they established their own religious movement in Himbach (Hessen), which had a more liberal government. Although most of the members of the Community of True Inspiration settled in central and southern Germany, a number of smaller communities could also be found in other European countries, such as Holland and Switzerland.

Central to the inspirationist's belief system is the idea that God would reveal his wishes and guide his people through the divine inspiration of the Bible and through messages transmitted by specially endowed individuals, called *Werkzeuge* (instruments). During the state of divine inspiration, these instruments or prophets would violently shake while delivering *Bezeugungen* (testimonies). The *Schreiber* (scribe) recorded their inspired testimonies to provide guidance for the community on their journey through life in the true spirit of God. Many *Bezeugungen* have been preserved in collections, such as the *Diarium*, the *Tagebücher* of the Congregations of Inspiration, the *Sammlungen*, and the yearbooks entitled *Jahrbücher der Wahren Inspirations-Gemeinden oder Bezeugungen des Geistes des Herrn (Yearbooks of the Community of True Inspiration or Testimonies of the Spirit of God)*. Rock and Christian Metz (1794–1867) were among the first documented *Werkzeuge,* and Barbara Heinemann (married name: Landmann), who died in 1883, was the last. Several documents can be considered the foundation for the community's religious practices: *Der Glauben* (The Faith), *The Twenty-four Rules of True Godliness, The Twenty-one Rules for the Examination of Our Daily Lives, The Ten Commandments,* and the *Lord's Prayer.* These materials promote a simple, pietist faith, inward devotion, and avoidance of secular celebrations and amusements.

After the death of Gruber in 1728 and Rock in 1749, the membership of the inspirationist communities started to decline drastically, and the movement was on the wane. In 1817, a tailor journeyman from Straßburg, Michael Krausert, a devoted follower of Gruber and Rock's preachings, declared himself a *Werkzeuge* and revived the movement. As a result, inspirationist communities were established in the German region of Palatinate (Zweibrücken, Edenkoben, Bergzabern, Hambach), in Alsatia (Straßburg, Bischweiler), in Hessen (Lieblos), and in Switzerland (Zurich). Taking advantage of the more liberal political climate in Hessen, Krausert settled with his followers in the Ronneburg Castle (northeast of Hanau, Hessen), which soon became the center of the inspirationist movement.

Due to the inspirationists' continued refusal to perform military duty, take the legal oath, and send their children to public schools grounded in orthodox Lutheranism, they came into conflict with the Lutheran Church and political authorities. Metz, a carpenter from Neuwied, took over leadership of the sect and leased four estates near Ronneburg in Marienborn, Herrnhaag, Arnsburg (called Armenburg by the inspirationists), and Engelthal, where the inspirationists could—at least temporarily—seek refuge from growing government hostility and persecution. When economic conditions became increasingly severe, and following Metz's inspired testimonies, the community emigrated to the United States to lead their lives in peace and liberty.

On October 26, 1842, Christian Metz and three other members of the community reached New York. From the Ogden Land Company they purchased the Seneca Indian Reservation, a tract of 5,000 acres near Buffalo, Erie County, in New York State. By 1845 more than 800 inspirationists, mostly craftsmen and peasants, had come from Germany. The first village they built on Erie County land was named "Ebenezer," ("Hitherto hath the Lord helped us"), a biblical term that can be found in 1 Samuel 7:12. Within seven years from the founding of Ebenezer (later called Middle Ebenezer), three additional, self-sustaining villages (Upper Ebenezer, Lower Ebenezer, and New Ebenezer) were laid out, each with its own school, store, and church. Later two small outposts, Canada Ebenezer and Kenneberg, were constructed across the Canadian border. The community prospered due to its successful farming practices and its operation of a large woolen mill, saw mills, flour mills, and tanneries, as well as other branches of industry.

In 1843 the group legally organized as the Ebenezer Society. The society adopted a constitution that united its members by religion and its communal economic system of property sharing (except for clothing and some household items). The thirteen members of a board of trustees, the *Bruderrath* (Council of Brethren), took leadership of the society, making all church and secular decisions. The New York State Assembly incorporated the community under the name "Community of True Inspiration" in 1846. Yet in order to find more affordable territory for expansion and to gain greater distance from the secular world, the community decided to leave New York for the Midwest.

In 1855 the Ebenezer Society, under Metz's guidance, purchased a tract of 18,000 acres (later expanded to 26,000 acres) in the Iowa River valley, Iowa County, in the new state of Iowa. At the same time, the group started to sell their land in New York. Over a period of ten years, the entire community (approximately 1,200 people) moved from Ebenezer to Iowa to realize their religious ideals and goals in greater seclusion and on expanded territory. They built six villages and purchased the already existing town of Homestead to gain access to its railroad station (Mississippi and Missouri Railroad). The settlers named their first village *Bleibtreu* (remain faithful) but soon changed it to the biblical name "Amana." Amana (a mountain range in Lebanon), referred to in the Song of Solomon 4:8, signifies "*glaub treu*" (believe faithfully). In 1859 the group became a legal corporation under the name Amana Society and adopted a new constitution and bylaws.

People in the Amana Colonies enjoyed a simple lifestyle filled with communal work, religious activities, and time spent with family. The villages featured churches, schools, general stores, craft shops, bakeries, meat markets, locksmiths, basket makers, cabinet shops, and so on. To this day, outsiders consider Amana craftsmanship (e.g., fine needlework, furniture making) to be quality work. Profits from agricultural and industrial enterprises (such as woolen, calico, and flour mills) were shared to sustain the community. Food was prepared and eaten in communal kitchens. Amana residents also embraced modern technologies, such as electric lights, a society-owned telephone system, and society-owned cars and trucks.

Members of the Amana Society attended eleven church services each week. Apart from praying and singing a cappella hymns from the hymn collection *Psalter-Spiel,* worship included readings from the Bible and from the testimonies of the *Werkzeuge.* One of the most solemn religious ceremonies, which lasted for several days, was the biannual *Liebesmahl* (Love Feast), or celebration of the Lord's Supper.

In 1932, strong external influences and internal changes forced the Amana people to reorganize their economic system. The main reasons for the implementation of this "Great Change" are regarded to be the loss of charismatic religious leadership, reduced isolation and increased secularism, a youth revolt against "outdated" Amana traditions, and severe financial problems aggravated by the Great Depression. The Amana Society separated its business interests from religious affairs by establishing two separate bodies, the Amana Society and the Amana Church Society. The Amana Society was transformed into a joint-stock company and introduced profit-seeking business ventures with an increased emphasis on external markets. Residents started to manufacture on a large scale electric appliances such as freezers and air-conditioning systems for homes. After changing hands several times, today Amana Appliances, with headquarters in Middle Amana, is a division of the Maytag Corporation. Next to the successful marketing of agricultural and industrial products, tourism has become a profitable major business enterprise for the people in the Amana Colonies.

Siegrun Wildner

See also Buffalo; Iowa, German Dialects in; Pietism

References and Further Reading

Barthel, Diane L. *Amana: From Pietist Sect to American Community.* Lincoln: University of Nebraska Press, 1984.

Hoehnle, Peter. *The Amana People: The History of a Religious Community.* N.p.: Penfield Books, 2003.

Shambaugh, Bertha M. *Amana That Was and Amana That Is.* Iowa City: Torch Press, for the State Historical Society of Iowa, 1932.

Webber, Philip E. *Kolonie-Deutsch: Life and Language in Amana.* Ames: Iowa State University Press, 1993.

AMERICAN CHURCHES IN GERMANY

Most churches original to Germany have correlate bodies in North America, and many churches original to North America are derived from movements with roots in Europe that have also touched Germany. There are, however, some peculiarly "American" churches in Germany, including the Seventh-Day Adventists (SDA); the Mormon Church, or the Church of Jesus Christ of Latter-Day Saints (LDS); and the Church of Christ, Scientist (CCS). Each of these groups is based on unique teachings of a particular leader that are given authority tantamount to Holy Scripture. It may thus be argued that they are not technically Christian churches. However, the SDA strove to become a part of the clear mainstream of Christian activity and faith. Stretching the definitions yet further, there is the Church of Scientology, which, aside from its name, makes no pretense of being Christian but is visibly present as an American institution in German cities. Jehovah's Witnesses (JW) are also clearly visible, selling the internationally known publications of the Watchtower Society on German street corners.

The LDS was founded by Joseph Smith in New York in 1830 and took its current name in 1838. It counts 36,000 members in 183 congregations in Germany. "Christian Science," based on Mary Baker Eddy's book *Science and Health with Key to the Scriptures* (1875), is taught in various "churches" in Germany. Like all other congregations of this church, they are directly subordinate to the First Church of Christ, Scientist, in Boston, which Eddy founded in 1895. The church has no ordained ministers, since Eddy in her author-ity "named the Bible and *Science and Health* as the Pastor for worldwide Churches of Christ, Scientist" ("About the Church of Christ, Scientist" 2004). In a certain parallel to CCS, the Church of Scientology is also centrally administered much like a business enterprise. It, too, is based on the one work of one individual, *Dianetics* by L. Ron Hubbard (1950).

Charles Taze Russell started the Zion's Watch Tower Tract Society, which controls the Jehovah's Witnesses, in 1881 in Allegheny (Pittsburgh, Pennsylvania). There are 165,935 "witnesses" in 2,175 congregations in Germany.

Aside from the groups above, the success of free church groups in Germany has been based on the vitality and accessibility of the American and British religious experience, which has created an interest among Germans in such American groups. Both those churches rooted in the American tradition that seek to work among people native to Germany and those groups that seek to minister to expatriates can generally be contrasted to traditional German Protestant religious groups on the basis of (1) a lively and family-like fellowship among the faithful, as opposed to an individualistic and often highly intellectual or abstract experience of faith and worship; and (2) the expectation of personal decision and personal involvement on the part of the faithful, which includes voluntary commitment of heart, mind, lifestyle, and financial resources, rather than quiet assent to largely impersonal, often bureaucratic structures of governance, pastoral care, worship, and finances.

Church groups that have found their way to Germany from the United States have often come simultaneously or at an earlier time from Great Britain, where the American and British manifestations had common or similar origins. Methodists, for example, arrived in Germany in at least four different thrusts. The Wesleyan Methodist Missionary Society in London acquiesced to pleas from people in Winnenden, Württemberg, for a missionary to revitalize moribund extrachurch pietistic societies there by sending a "native son," Christoph Gottlob Müller (1785–1858), as missionary in 1832. After Müller's death, these British efforts moved primarily eastward to Augsburg, Munich, Vienna, Budapest, and beyond. By 1897 long-standing efforts to combine British and American Methodist missionary endeavors in Germany resulted in a unified mission under American leadership, ending a specifically British presence.

The wish of immigrants to America to be at work in Germany, explicitly stated by German American publicist Wilhelm Nast after a tour in 1844, was especially encouraged in 1848, after the national-liberal revolution had begun to succeed in overthrowing the princes of the German petty states and replacing their regimes with democratic structures but before the ultimate failure of this effort. Ludwig Sigismund Jacoby, a German of Jewish origin who had converted to Methodism in the United States, returned to Germany as missionary superintendent in 1849, with a base in Bremen, where a book publishing mission began under the banner of the Methodist Episcopal Church (MEC, Bischöfliche Methodistenkirche). Both the MEC, the Evangelical Association (EG, Evangelische Gemeinschaft) and the United Brethren in Christ Church (UB) charged German-born and German-speaking Americans to fulfill their strong

calling to bring their respective varieties of Methodism to friends and relatives in Germany.

The UB lacked the typically strict structure of other early Methodist bodies. It later united with the Methodists in Germany (MEC) and with the EG in the United States (EUB). The EG found its origins among Methodists in Pennsylvania, when founder Jacob Albright (Jakob Albrecht) lost his membership in the local Methodist society for lack of attendance at meetings. He was spending his time preaching to Germans, while the early Methodists found enough to do working only with English speakers. The first MEC leader, Francis Asbury, turned down Albright's offer to create a German-speaking branch of that church. Rebuffed but not discouraged, Albright organized the Newly Formed Methodist Connection (Albrechts-Leute) and translated Methodist foundational documents word-for-word for this German American Methodist church.

Methodist efforts met with moderate success, creating strongholds in Saxony and Württemberg and enjoying widespread acceptance in Bremen and Hamburg but facing an uphill struggle in most other parts of the countryside. Their task was made more difficult by the presence of hundreds of different jurisdictions without unity of law or policy—duchies, grand duchies, counties, principalities, electoral principalities, as well as imperial free cities, and free and Hanseatic cities. In 1850 leaders of the EG felt that they were in part answering the call of German church leaders like Johann Hinrich Wichern for spiritual renewal when they established a mission board to send two missionaries, one of them Conrad Link, to Stuttgart. The UB did not establish a German missionary effort until

1869, when Bavarian-born American Reverend Christian Bischoff went back to his native Naila. The work was turned over to the MEC in 1905. In 1940 a church union in the U.S. changed the name of the German MEC to "The Methodist Church" (MC). A second union in 1968 of the MC and EUB united EG and MC units in Germany in the United Methodist Church (UMC=Evangelisch-methodistische Kirche). In the year 2000, the United Methodist Church in Germany counted about 65,000 members in just over 600 congregations.

Baptists had a similar introduction into Germany, but their beginnings were much more of a one-man project. Johann Gerhard Oncken had emigrated to Great Britain in 1814 as teenage apprentice to a Scots tradesman. In a Methodist congregation in London he experienced a personal conversion and became an agent for the Continental Society for the Diffusion of Religious Knowledge over the Continent of Europe. In April 1834, two years after the London Methodists sent Müller to Winnenden, Oncken was ordained elder in the Baptist congregation in Hamburg that he had founded. Oncken then founded a Federation of Baptist Congregations, conceived of as a "great congregation" uniting all German Baptists. By the time of his death, however, the individual congregations had taken upon themselves a much greater autonomy than he had envisioned, as was typical in many other branches of World Baptism. The Baptist call, "we consider every member as a missionary," became a rallying cry for German Baptists. In response to this call, Gottfried Wilhelm Lehman engaged in missionary activities that led to the honorific title "Father of Baptists in Prussia." And Julius

Köbner, a Dane of Jewish origin, led the Baptist mission in the Rhineland and in Copenhagen. At the time of the 1848 revolutions he published the *Manifesto from Free Primal Christianity to the German People,* appealing for religious freedom in the new German social order, expected soon to be introduced. English and American Baptists are largely identified in the minds of many as sources of this movement, and although it was not strictly an "American" incursion onto German soil, contacts with Baptists in North America, Great Britain, and Scandinavia were clearly evident. The first director of the Oncken Publishing House in Hamburg was a German American. The European Baptist Federation (EBF) is a body separate from North American Baptist federations and conventions, but it is not aloof from issues known there in recent times. In more recent years, the EBF has included ministry in many languages, including English, throughout Europe. Additionally, the U.S. Southern Baptist Convention has been involved in providing expatriate Americans with congregational ministry in Europe, especially "off-base" from U.S. military units, where only "General Protestant" chaplaincy is available, with all the vicissitudes and compromises such a name implies. As of the year 2000, the German Baptists counted 87,000 members in 900 congregations.

After the forging of the German nation-state in 1871, the country's leaders focused on deciding what was "German" and what was not. Slowly, the sentiment grew that Socialist thinking, Roman Catholicism, and the so-called free churches were "foreign growths" (Dwyer 1978, 27) in the body politic of the German imperial state and were not to be encouraged. This view did not substantially change even with the Weimar Constitution of 1919, but at least the seeds were sown at that time for a general acknowledgment of the positive contributions of many free churches when National Socialist rule was ended in 1945. Both during and after the Third Reich, some free churches were learning a new degree of cooperation in the Federation of Evangelical Free Churches (Vereinigung Evangelischer Freikirchen, VEF), which continues today alongside the Evangelical Alliance (Evangelische Allianz) as an instrument of free church and evangelical cooperation. These same churches have played a role in the greater ecumenical picture in modern Germany, especially in the local and national councils of churches, normally called "working associations" to avoid conflict with Catholic concepts of conciliarism. The national Association of Christian Churches (Arbeitsgemeinschaft christlicher Kirchen, ACK) provides a broad base for consultation and cooperation.

Among churches related to one or another of these cooperative efforts, the following can also be named among the "American" churches: The Church of the Nazarene (Kirche der Nazarener), a union of various Wesleyan and holiness groups created in Texas in 1908, formed its first congregation in Germany in 1959. Since 1966 it has maintained a seminary in Büsingen near the Swiss German border. Today it counts 2,300 members in twenty congregations. The Muehlheim Federation of Free Church Protestant Congregations (Mühlheimer Verband Freikirchlicher Evangelischer Gemeinden) grew out of the international Pentecostal awakening at the beginning of the twentieth century. It understands its foundation to have been specifically precipitated by the rejection of Pentecostal phenomena by the innerchurch societies and other free churches brought to expression in the Berlin Declaration of 1909. The first congregation formed in 1905, and the association came into being between 1911 and 1913. Today it counts 2,900 members in fifty congregations. The Federation of Free Church Pentecost Congregations (Bund Freikirchlicher Pfingstgemeinden), first organized in 1954 but using that name only since 1982, is another of the associations of Pentecostal congregations that grew out of the worldwide Pentecostal awakening that started in Asuza Street in Los Angeles. It currently has 32,000 members in 500 congregations. The Freikirchlicher Bund der Gemeinde Gottes (Church of God, Anderson, Indiana) has been present in Germany since 1901. Founded by D. S. Warner in 1881, the church published its "Gospel Trumpet" in a German edition as early as 1885. It proposes to provide "light and salt" to German society and to contribute to the building of the kingdom of God. It counts 2,500 worshipers in thirty congregations. The Seventh-Day Adventists (Gemeinschaft der Siebenten-Tags-Adventisten) has been present in Germany since 1876. It has 36,000 members in 569 congregations. For the sake of completeness, the Salvation Army (Heilsarmee) should be mentioned. Founded in London in 1878 by Methodists, it is widely known in North America as well and was already present in Germany in 1886. Perhaps because of its military structure, the Salvation Army was banned by the NS regime in 1933 and was not readmitted to the territory of the former German Democratic Republic until 1990. It counts 2,000 "soldiers" (members) in 140 "corps" (congregations).

James A. Dwyer

See also Lutheran Church–Missouri Synod;
U.S. Bases in West Germany
References and Further Reading
"About the Church of Christ, Scientist."
Church of Christ, Scientist.
http://www.tfccs.com/aboutthechurch/
(cited September 9, 2004).
"Bund Evangelisch-Freikirchlicher
Gemeinden in Deutschland: Ein
Überblick des Kirchengeschichtlers
Günter Balders" (Erscheinungsdatum:
2003-06-01).
http://www.baptisten.org/faq/news_show.
php?sel=100&select=FAQ&show=9&cat
=Eine percent20Freikirche percent20stellt
percent20sich percent20vor (cited
September 9, 2004).
Dwyer, James A. "The Methodist Episcopal
Church in Germany, 1933–1945."PhD
diss., Northwestern University, 1978.
EKD: Evangelische Kirche in Deutschland—
EKD and Kirchen. "Gliedkirchen der
EKD."
http://www.ekd.de/ekd_kirchen/3221_gli
edkirchen_adressen.html (cited
September 9, 2004).
Freikirchenhandbuch—Informationen—
Anschriften—Berichte. Wuppertal:
Borkhaus-Verlag, June 2000.
Voigt, Karl Heinz. "Die Methodistenkirche
in Deutschland." *Geschichte der
Evangelisch-methodistischen Kirche: Weg,
Wesen und Auftrag des Methodismus unter
besonderer Berücksichtigung der
deutschsprachigen Länder Europas.* Eds.
Karl Steckel and C. Ernst Sommer.
Stuttgart: Christliches Verlagshaus, 1982,
85–112.
Watchtower: Official Web Site of Jehovah's
Witnesses. "Statistics: 2003 Report of
Jehovah's Witnesses Worldwide."
http://www.watchtower.org/statistics/worl
dwide_report.htm (cited September 9,
2004).
Wüthrich, Paul. "Die Evangelische
Gemeinschaft im deutschsprachigen
Europa." *Geschichte der Evangelisch-
methodistischen Kirche: Weg, Wesen und
Auftrag des Methodismus unter besonderer
Berücksichtigung der deutschsprachigen
Länder Europas.* Eds. Karl Steckel and C.
Ernst Sommer. Stuttgart: Christliches
Verlagshaus, 1982, 149–211.

AMERICAN CIVIL WAR, FINANCIAL SUPPORT OF FRANKFURT BANKERS FOR

Frankfurt bankers lent money to the U.S. government in the form of six large war bonds during the American Civil War. Frankfurt was the most powerful banking city in Germany, and in the trading of state bonds it was certainly as important as London, Paris, or Vienna. Its relationship to the American capital market had flourished after the middle of the nineteenth century. For over half a century, the financial relations between Germany and the United States could, with very few exceptions, be identified as those existing between the Frankfurt and the New York money powers. Frankfurt nevertheless managed to bolster its position as the principal German capital market by acquiring a new measure of importance in the 1860s, not only as an underwriting and trading center for German bank and railroad issues but above all as the gateway for Germany's capital exports, especially to the United States. After its debut on the Frankfurt market in the early 1850s, American debt and equity paper inundated Frankfurt in second and third waves in the early and late 1860s, respectively. The city became, after London, the second-largest outlet for U.S. government and railroad bonds in Europe. Since London sympathized with the South for both practical (cotton supplies) and political (free trade) reasons, it took over the majority of the Confederate issuance of bonds. Frankfurt seems to have placed the overwhelming portion of the Union issues during the American Civil War. By 1864, the bonds of the United States—whose public debt between 1860 and 1865 rose from $90 million to $2.74 billion—had fallen to a low of 38 percent on the Frankfurt market.

Frankfurt achieved a key position in the financing of the American Civil War for two reasons: the efforts of the U.S. consul general, William Walton Murphy, and the influence of a group of Frankfurt's top bankers, which, over the years, had established a strong economic relationship with the United States. Murphy became the U.S. consul general in the free city of Frankfurt in 1861. After he arrived on November 7 in Frankfurt, he immediately began to search for support for the Union. His initial attempts were, however, unsuccessful. He never received a reaction to his offer of 50,000 rifles for 12 Taler each, and his suggestion to hire German soldiers was repudiated by the U.S. government, which asked instead for German immigrants to farm the lands. Murphy's time came when he put his experience as a newspaper publisher and banker into action. He made sure that the press remained supportive and "friendly" toward the affairs of the Union in Frankfurt. This was of great importance at a time when the Confederacy was engaging well-known writers to influence public opinion against the Union. It even publicized a £30-million loan from the Parisian branch of the Frankfurt bank of Raphael Erlanger in Europe in 1863. Murphy personally wrote articles and essays against these activities and discredited the loan to the Confederacy in the *Neue Frankfurter Zeitung* (New Frankfurt Journal) or the *Ober-Post-Amts-Zeitung* (Major-Post-Office-Journal). Indeed, the honor of Erlanger's bank was successfully damaged. In return for this activity, Murphy managed to convince many of the Frankfurt banking houses, including Seligman and Stettheimer, Lazard Speyer-Ellissen, Philipp Nicolaus Schmidt, Karl Pollitz, M. A. Gruenebaum and Ballin, to support six

large war bonds for the Union. At the end of the Civil War their bonds were quoted at an almost dreamlike height and upon redemption brought hundreds of millions in profits to their shareholders. It was especially J. and W. Seligman that harvested most of the wealth. They founded branches in London, Paris, and the business metropolises of the United States.

Ralf Roth

See also Frankfurt am Main Citizens in the United States
References and Further Reading
Heyn, Udo. *Private Banking and Industrialization: The Case of Frankfurt am Main, 1825–1875.* New York: Arno Press, 1981.
Roth, Ralf. *Stadt und Bürgertum in Frankfurt am Main: Ein besonderer Weg von der ständischen zur modernen Bürgergesellschaft 1760 bis 1914.* Munich: Oldenbourg, 1996.
Sterne, Margaret. "Ein Amateur wird Diplomat: Die politische Karriere von William Walton Murphy, amerikanischer Generalkonsul in Frankfurt am Main 1861–1869." *Archiv für Frankfurts Geschichte und Kunst* 48 (1962): 119–132.

AMERICAN CIVIL WAR, GERMAN PARTICIPANTS IN

When Wilhelm Kaufmann claimed, in his 1911 volume *Die Deutschen im Amerikanischen Bürgerkriege* (*The Germans in the American Civil War*), that the Union side could not have won the war without the Germans, he was clearly exaggerating. However, at more than 180,000 German-born soldiers, the ethnic German element provided a slightly overproportional percentage of the Union force. Most of those soldiers were volunteers who joined up during the first six months of the war.

The Northern German Federation strongly supported the Union war effort politically, and the liberal press then described the refugees of the revolutions of 1848–1849 as German heroes. Officially, Union efforts at recruiting German nationals were discouraged, though some 20,000 emigrants went to the war from German states. A few more joined the crews of U.S. warships in European ports. In 1863, the wife of Illinois vice governor Gustav Körner initiated a nationwide series of advertisements in newspapers, addressing particularly relatives of German Union soldiers and offering to transport medical and other supplies to Union hospitals. The public opinion in most of the German states was strongly pro-Union; only some of the Junkers in the Prussian officer corps sympathized with the secessionists.

Arguably the most important contribution Germans made to the Union war effort came early on in the war in Missouri, where pro-secessionist governor Claiborne Jackson attempted a coup d'etat. In return, Unionists organized forces in excess of the regiments President Abraham Lincoln's proclamation had called for and on May 10 marched against the encampment of the state militia. More than 80 percent of the volunteer force that saved the city of St. Louis and the state for the Union were Germans, and throughout the war, they supplied about one-third of the Missouri soldiers fighting for the Union. Most of the officers and men in the Missouri volunteer infantry regiments 2, 3, 4, 5, 12, 15, 17, and 31 were Germans or of German descent, as were most of the members of several batteries. Other states contributed similar numbers and even entire units: the 9th Ohio; the 32nd Indiana; the 7th, 9th, 20th, 29th, 41st, 43rd, 45th, and 52nd New York; the 27th and 74th Pennsylvania; and the 9th Wisconsin were other famous all-German units, at least during the early stages of the war. After the summer of 1862, few regiments maintained their original ethnic formats, and only two new units—the "2nd Hecker" (named for the commanding officer, 1848 revolutionist Friedrich Hecker) 82nd Illinois and the 26th Wisconsin—were formed as German regiments.

The artillery was the one arm of the army where the presence of trained and skilled veterans of the various German armies, including the revolutionary forces of 1848–1849, was most strongly felt. German cannoneers turned the tide at Pea Ridge and helped to save the day on July 2 at Gettysburg. Clemens Landgräber's Missouri battery was known as the "Flying Dutchmen." Captain Hubert "Leather Breeches" Dilger won the Congressional Medal of Honor for his retreat-by-recoil support of the remnants of Adolph Buschbeck's brigade at Chancellorsville (May 1863); among the German soldiers his name was legendary.

Particularly this battle and the rout of the 11th Corps by Thomas Jonathan "Stonewall" Jackson's veterans were used by newspapers and politicians in the East to denigrate the effort and importance of the "foreign" element, despite the fact that the commander of the ill-fated corps, General Oliver Otis Howard, had been notified repeatedly of ominous movements in front of his badly deployed troops. He tried to exculpate himself by blaming the responsibility for the defeat on the Germans among his soldiers.

They were easy targets: exaggerated expectations and incompetence had, by 1863, resulted in a rather checkered record for the ethnic German units with the Army of the Potomac, which was eagerly exploited by the nativist press. At First Bull Run, General Ludwig Blenker's division had covered the retreat to Washington, but the same units had fared badly during John Frémont's Shenandoah Valley campaign in 1862. Out west, ethnic German units performed well at Pea Ridge, Shiloh, Perryville, Stones River, and Vicksburg and in the Tullahoma campaign, but the public focus was on the eastern theater. The Chancellorsville disaster was followed by similar accusations and blame when the 11th Corps was forced to withdraw again during the first day at Gettysburg.

Reorganized as the 20th Corps, many of the German veterans of the Army of the Potomac were sent west after Chickamauga. The German units from East and West more than redeemed themselves when they stormed Missionary Ridge (November 1863). The next year, the same units participated in the advance on Atlanta, where many of the regiments formed early in the war were mustered out after the fall of the city in September 1864.

Ethnic Germans account for 5 major generals (August Willich, Franz Sigel, Carl Schurz, Edward S. Salomon, and Peter Osterhaus, all of them Forty-Eighters), about 25 brigadiers, and more than 100 colonels. Since ethnic officers were not as easily promoted as native-borns, let alone graduates of West Point, some of these colonels might have deserved a brigadier's star—like Adolph Buschbeck of the 27th Pennsylvania, whose brigade covered the retreat at Chancellorsville, or like Bernhard Laiboldt of the 2nd Missouri, who commanded brigades at Perryville and Stones River and successfully defended posts at Wauhatchie, Tennessee, and Dalton, Georgia, in 1863

and 1864. The most successful German Union general, Peter Osterhaus (1824–1917), fought in thirty-four engagements and lost none of the seventeen, where he was in command of the Union forces he himself led.

Of course, not all German officers were paragons of virtue and loved by their men: General Henry Bohlen was shot by his own soldiers, Generals Blenker, Stahel, Schurz, and of course Franz Sigel were all at some point accused of incompetence. Not all German Union soldiers were volunteers; nor did all Germans support the Union effort. There were pockets of archconservative Catholics in Wisconsin who were reluctant to fight and served poorly when they did. Some prewar supporters of the Democrats never switched their allegiance. Poorer immigrants from the most recent waves of immigration often let themselves be hired as substitutes. Cases of "crimping" Germans occurred: in one case some 1,000 immigrants had been promised work contracts by agents operating for the state of Massachusetts but upon arrival found themselves sold to serve in state regiments.

Most German immigrants and second- and third-generation Germans in the loyal states, however, supported the idea of the Union, and many were also in favor of abolition. Pronounced the "nigger-loving Dutch," surrendering German soldiers were sometimes mistreated or murdered because of their supposed or real association with African Americans. Ethnic Germans provided a considerable percentage of the officers in the U.S. Colored Troops. Several German officers, such as General Wilhelm Peter Heine, and Colonels Joseph Weydemeyer and Adolph Dengler, supported the formation of U.S. colored regiments; General Osterhaus's old German Brigade sponsored the 1st Mississippi (African Descent [A.D.]) in 1863.

In the secession states, the situation of the German element was more various and ambiguous. Emigration societies and associations organizing immigration to the states before the war had often screened potential immigrants and directed only those with a positive attitude toward slavery to southern ports. Strong pro-slavery and pro-secession pockets existed in South Carolina, Virginia, and Louisiana, where one of the richest slaveholders was the former Prussian consul in New Orleans. In Texas, the situation was mixed: many Germans tried to evade the draft, hiding or fleeing the country. In 1862, Texas militia overtook a column of refugees trying to escape to Mexico on the Rio Nueces and killed many of the men.

An estimated 5,000 to 10,000 native-born Germans fought in the Confederate forces, about half of this number volunteers in the early days of the war, often members of all-German militia companies like Company K, 1st Virginia Infantry. There were no ethnic German units larger than company size on the Confederate side. Later in the war, Germans in Confederate units were often draftees, and many soldiers defected to the Union side.

Wolfgang Hochbruck

See also 82nd Illinois Volunteer Infantry Regiment; Forty-Eighters; Hecker, Friedrich; Koerner, Gustave Philipp; Nueces, Battle of the; Osterhaus, Peter J.; Salomon, Edward S.; Schurz, Carl; Sigel, Franz; Willich, August (von)

References and Further Reading

Kaufmann, Wilhelm. *Die Deutschen im amerikanischen Bürgerkriege.* München/Berlin: R. Oldenbourg, 1911.
Loeffler, Michael. *Preußens und Sachsens Beziehungen zu den USA während des Sezessionskrieges, 1860–1865,* Münster: LIT, 1999.
Lonn, Ella. *Foreigners in the Union Army and Navy.* New York: Greenwood, 1969.
Mehrländer, Andrea. "'Ist daß nicht reiner Sclavenhandel?' Die illegale Rekrutierung deutscher Auswanderer für die Unionsarmee im amerikanischen Bürgerkrieg." *Amerikastudien/American Studies* 44, no. 1 (1999) 65–93.

AMERICAN OCCUPATION ZONE

The American Occupation Zone was the region of postwar Germany occupied and administered by the United States from 1945 to 1955, the most extensive occupation ever undertaken by U.S. military and civilian authorities. It was administered from 1945 to 1949 by the Office of Military Government, United States (OMGUS), and from 1949 to 1955 by a civilian high commissioner for Germany (HICOG).

The American zone encompassed the German states of Bavaria and parts of Württemberg, Baden, the former Prussian province of Hessen, the U.S. enclave in the city of Bremen with Bremen's port at Bremerhaven, and a sector of western Berlin. It was the second largest (after the Russian) in terms of territory, encompassing 45,047 square miles, and the third largest in terms of population, with approximately 16.7 million inhabitants in 1949 (24 percent of the overall German population). With the influx of millions of ethnic German refugees from Eastern Europe, the American zone's population grew within the first years of the occupation by about 17 percent to a total of 18.2 million inhabitants.

Planning for U.S. worldwide postwar occupation duties was principally the responsibility of the War Department and its Civil Affairs Division (also known as "G-5"), which was created in 1943. In the case of Germany, Civil Affairs Division staff comprised civilian specialists and émigrés from Germany and other European countries. Personnel received training at various military camps and in special civilian programs in the United States and England. Other branches of the government—the State and Treasury departments—competed for influence in shaping occupation policies. In general, the War Department wanted a short occupation that limited the military's responsibility for civilian affairs. State Department officials believed that occupation policies should be aimed primarily at Germany's reconstruction based on the transfer of an American model of democratic political practices and liberal capitalist economics. Outside the government, a variety of private associations and informal circles of academics and intellectuals (many of them German refugees) promoted their own occupation policy agenda, one that emphasized extensive political, economic, and social change. Their collective influence on occupation planning and execution was limited, however, even though many refugees served in important positions in the occupation.

In the fall of 1944, Secretary of the Treasury Henry Morgenthau briefly convinced President Franklin D. Roosevelt that Germany would have to be completely stripped of its industrial infrastructure and effectively "pastoralized." Though Roosevelt soon backed away from the "Morgenthau Plan," he avoided reconciling the various conflicting agendas for postwar Germany, thus allowing policy planning to drift. The result of this drift was a belated and vague occupation direc-

tive drafted by the Joint Chiefs of Staff that offered little by way of constructive policies for occupation officials to follow. The course of the occupation, then, would be shaped largely by a combination of improvisation on the ground in Germany and by wider diplomatic developments among the wartime allies.

At the Yalta conference, the United States, the Soviet Union, and Great Britain agreed to establish an Allied Control Council (ACC) comprising the Allied commanders in chief. The ACC would govern the country; make decisions on policies dealing with Germany as a whole; and administer a program of political and economic decentralization, denazification, demilitarization, and democratization (the "Four D Program"). The council had to operate under the proviso of unanimity, a regulation France used to veto decisions successfully to prevent any policies that would have restored a functioning central authority for its old enemy. The Declaration of Potsdam on August 2, 1945, confirmed the decisions taken at Moscow and Yalta, and subsequently Germany was divided into four zones, which were administered by the U.S., British, French, and Soviet military governments.

The U.S. Army's forces in Germany were ordered to implement the "Four D Program" upon cessation of hostilities. In May 1945 at war's end, combat troops became occupation troops charged with maintaining law and order in the American zone. At the same time, trained military government detachments numbering 13,000 officers and soldiers at the occupation's peak in September 1945 took over control of particular German cities, counties, districts, and states. To guide its efforts, the army used Joint Chiefs of Staff

Directive 1067 (JCS 1067), drafted in September 1944, and the Handbook for Military Government in Germany, published in December 1944.

The occupation itself was initially administered by the Supreme Headquarters Allied Expeditionary Forces Europe (SHAEF; after July 1945, the U.S. Forces European Theater, which included G-5) and the U.S. Group of the Allied Control Council. In the fall of 1945, OMGUS assumed overall responsibility for the occupation. As Supreme Allied Commander, U.S. Army general Dwight D. Eisenhower was the first military governor of occupied Germany. In April 1945, the Office of Deputy Military Governor was created to represent Eisenhower at the ACC in Berlin. The first deputy military governor was U.S. Army general Lucius D. Clay, who became military governor in March 1947. Clay, a civil engineer by training, took a pragmatic approach toward administering the American zone, emphasizing the rapid restoration of transportation networks and other basic services and the fostering of local democratic self-government. In both endeavors, he was remarkably successful.

As U.S. troops entered Germany, they were faced with an enormous array of problems resulting from vast physical destruction, population displacement, and the collapse of political authority. Very often improvising with what material and personnel were available on the spot, troops restored order and oversaw the restoration of many basic services. They contended with thousands of prisoners of war and displaced persons (including concentration camp survivors). They also arrested suspected war criminals and began the process of denazification, which initially required the automatic dismissal of any member of the Nazi

Party or individual who had supported the regime in more than a "nominal" manner. Relations between U.S. soldiers and Germans were generally peaceful and cooperative. Attacks on U.S. personnel were rare. An American ban on fraternization was ignored from the outset and quickly abandoned. U.S. soldiers generally treated Germans humanely, and marriages or the formation of long-lasting friendships were common. The pillaging of private property was limited, though several U.S. government agencies netted millions of dollars worth of patents, blueprints, and industrial equipment for U.S. military and commercial purposes. The United States also recruited a number of former Nazi intelligence officers and scientists to secure their expertise in the emerging confrontation with the Soviet Union.

Following Germany's surrender, the Americans banned political activity of any kind. In August 1945, however, OMGUS allowed political parties to reorganize under its supervision. The reestablishment of local and state governments became a priority, and military governors began reviving political life according to democratic principles in preparation for local elections in municipalities as early as September 1945. The effort included the licensing of political parties, registering voters, drafting election laws, formulating balloting procedures, identifying candidates, and other related matters. Elections in villages with fewer than 20,000 inhabitants (*Gemeinden*) occurred in January 1946, whereas larger villages and counties (*Landkreise*) elected their new administrations in April. City (*Stadt*) dwellers chose their representatives in May.

As preparations for a return to elected government proceeded, the U.S. military government ordered the four appointed minister-presidents of Bavaria, Hesse, Württemberg-Baden, and Bremen to draft constitutions for their states. The minister-presidents were supposed to submit the constitutions to popular referendum in order to provide the states with democratic constitutions and democratically elected governments. The minister-presidents finished their work in October 1946, when they submitted their constitutions for final approval to the military government. All were later ratified in popular referenda that also elected state parliaments. All four jurisdictions thus entered 1947 with elected governments subject only to an Allied directive published in September defining the powers of the military government, which included a right to exercise supreme authority on matters involving Allied objectives.

The U.S. military government established a Council of States in Stuttgart in October 1945, comprising the lands within the American zone. It dealt with matters of common interest to all states. During its existence, the council took on difficult issues, such as treatment and integration of expellees into society, administration of denazification starting in March 1946, food rationing, providing redress for Nazi wrongs, land resettlement and reform, and revision of civil as well as criminal codes and court procedures. When the United States and Great Britain decided to merge their zones economically, a Bizonal Council continued its work. With relations between the western Allies and the Soviet Union deteriorating, the U.S. Congress passed legislation in 1947 designed to resurrect the shattered German economy through the European Recovery Program (Marshall Plan).

Further, the United States also tried to "reeducate" the German population by overseeing the reopening of schools and universities and attempted reforms of the entire educational system that were generally resisted by the Germans. More successful was a major initiative aimed at facilitating communications between occupation authorities and the German public and restoring a free German media establishment. The Information Control Division (ICD) was created in 1945 to license new newspapers, book publishers, radio stations, film productions, and musical performances with an eye toward eventually returning full control of these media to the Germans.

On the diplomatic front, four-power administration collapsed rapidly. The ACC was never effective and broke down completely in January 1948, when the Soviet delegation walked out in protest over American, British, and French moves toward establishing a West German state. Concurrently, the foreign ministers of each Allied nation met in 1946 and 1947 to negotiate a final peace treaty and were unsuccessful. The main problem was that American, British, and French visions of Germany's future could not be reconciled with those of the Soviet Union. On the U.S. side, the State Department's position of rehabilitating Germany—if necessary at the expense of division—came to dominate Washington's actions. In September 1946, U.S. secretary of state James F. Byrnes delivered a speech in Stuttgart in which he gave priority to Germany's economic reconstruction above all other endeavors. Three months later, the Americans and British agreed to the joint economic administration of their two zones (the French zone was added in 1948). On the Soviet side, Joseph Stalin initially hoped that Germany would remain unified and "neutral" but vulnerable to the Moscow-controlled German Communists. When this outcome appeared increasingly unlikely, he began to plan a separate East German state. American, British, and French moves toward division in late 1947 and early 1948 led Stalin to blockade the land access routes to western Berlin in June 1948 in order to force the Allies back to the negotiating table or out of Berlin or both. The Americans and British responded with an unexpectedly successful airlift, handing the Soviets a humiliating diplomatic defeat and forcing them to lift the blockade in May 1949. Formal division was now a certainty, and in September 1949, the Federal Republic of Germany was created out of the three western occupation zones and western Berlin. A month later, the German Democratic Republic, or East Germany, was created out of the Soviet zone.

In May 1949, the U.S. secretary of state ordered the State Department to assume nonmilitary responsibilities for the occupation under a civilian "high commissioner." John J. McCloy, a lawyer and former assistant secretary of war and World Bank president, would serve in this position until HICOG was dissolved in 1955 and West Germany gained full sovereignty.

Steven Remy and Bianka J. Adams

See also Barbie, Klaus; Bremerhaven; Denazification; Halvorsen, Gail S.; Morgenthau Plan; Nuremberg Trials; U.S. Plans for Postwar Germany; West Berlin; World War II

References and Further Reading

Clay, Lucius D. *Decision in Germany.* Garden City: Doubleday, 1950.

Ermarth, Michael, ed. *America and the Shaping of German Society, 1945–1955.* Providence: Berg, 1993.

Höhn, Maria. *GIs and Fräuleins: The German-American Encounter in 1950s West Germany.* Chapel Hill: University of North Carolina Press, 2002.

Schwartz, Thomas A. *America's Germany: John J. McCloy and the Federal Republic of Germany.* Cambridge, MA: Harvard University Press, 1991.

Standifer, Leon C. *Binding up the Wounds: An American Soldier in Occupied Germany, 1945–1946.* Baton Rouge: Louisiana State University Press, 1997.

Wolfe, Robert, ed. *Americans as Proconsuls: United States Military Government in Germany and Japan, 1944–1952.* Carbondale: Southern Illinois University Press, 1984.

Ziemke, Earl F. *The U.S. Army in the Occupation of Germany, 1944–1946.* Washington: Center of Military History, United States Army, 1975.

AMERICAN STUDENTS AT GERMAN UNIVERSITIES

Throughout the nineteenth century, a large number of American students who aspired to an academic career enrolled at German universities for part of their university training. Before World War I, about 9,000 to 10,000 Americans had traveled to Germany to pursue academic training. The influx of American students began slowly: In 1835–1836, only a handful of American students was enrolled at German institutions of higher learning. Their numbers grew to more than 170 in 1880 and to about 400 each year during the 1890s. After the turn of the century, the number of American students decreased again, and in 1910 only 200 American students were found on the enrollment lists of German universities. World War I virtually ended the American student migration to Germany.

American students were the largest contingent of foreign students in Germany before 1914. Between 5 and 10 percent of all foreign students in Germany came from the United States. Germany attracted more students from the United States than from neighboring France. Among these students were George Bancroft, George Ticknor, and Nicholas M. Butler, who later became renowned scholars and eminent public figures in their home country. A significant number of nineteenth-century American university professors had received parts of their academic training at a German university.

Two world wars, the state intrusion into academia during the Nazi period, and the success of American universities throughout the twentieth century contributed to the diminishing attraction of German universities for American students. In 2002, only 3,100 American students chose to enroll in a German university, a tiny fraction of the overall number of students in both countries.

During the first half of the nineteenth century, small-town universities like those of Göttingen and Halle an der Saale attracted most of the American students; the universities of Leipzig and Berlin became the favored institutions in the second half of the century. However, not only the choice of alma mater but also the motivation for American students to study in Germany underwent changes. The most important reason why Americans choose to cross the Atlantic was undoubtedly the excellent reputation of German universities. In addition, eminent scholars such as Gustav Schmoller, Theodor Mommsen, and Wilhelm Wundt attracted students who wanted to work with them. Furthermore, the highly esteemed training at a German university was a guarantee of a university career in the United States.

However, there were also a couple of much simpler reasons: American universities did not offer the PhD until the 1870s. Therefore, many students went to Germany because they knew that they could acquire this prestigious title in a brief period of time and with a rather small amount of work. Further, living expenses for Americans in German cities were lower than in the United States. In addition, for many American students, studying at a German university was simply part of the traditional Grand Tour, which included travel all over Europe. Sitting in German lecture courses was thus part of the experience of European culture and was not taken as seriously as one would have expected. In other cases, a period of study in Germany was for the purpose of learning German, which was important for future scholars since Germans were leaders in many academic disciplines.

Depending on their motivation, American students returned home with different experiences of German academia. Some spent just one or two semesters in Germany and acquired only a fairly superficial impression of German scholarship, whereas others stayed for years and took their studies very seriously. However, especially those who came to Germany during the 1880s and 1890s rarely had contact with their German professors and fellow students because the overall number of students was increasing tremendously, turning them into a more or less anonymous mass. In cities such as Göttingen and Leipzig, American students formed enclaves, thereby avoiding contact with their fellow German students. They lived together in the same student residences, frequented their own gathering places, and spent their free time with each other. This helped to establish tight networks among the future academic elite of the United States, but it hindered the development of relationships with German academics.

Gabriele Lingelbach

See also Bancroft, George; German Students at American Universities; Göttingen, University of; Ticknor, George; U.S.-German Intellectual Exchange

References and Further Reading

Diehl, Karl. *Americans and German Scholarship, 1770–1870.* New Haven: Yale University Press, 1978.

Drewek, Peter. "'Die ungastliche deutsche Universität': Ausländische Studenten an deutschen Hochschulen 1890–1930." *Jahrbuch für Historische Bildungsforschung* 5 (1999): 197–224.

Jarausch, Konrad H. "American Students in Germany, 1815–1914. The Structure of German and U.S. Matriculants at Göttingen University." *German Influences on Education in the United States to 1917.* Ed. Henry Geitz. Cambridge and New York: Cambridge University Press, 1995, 195–211.

AMERICANISMS IN THE GERMAN LANGUAGE

An americanism is a word or a linguistic characteristic of American English that has become part of another language. Whereas *anglicism* refers generally to an exported English word or linguistic characteristic, *americanism* specifically refers to those anglicisms originating from the United States. Some americanisms have adapted to German spelling, grammatical, and/or pronunciation conventions (e.g., nouns are capitalized); others occur in their original form. Americanisms are found in spoken as well as written German, especially in mass media and specialty fields. The converse phenomena, Germanisms, are readily found in the English language.

History

German, like all languages, has been and continues to be influenced by other languages. Although French and Latin were the primary influences from the fifteenth to nineteenth centuries, anglicisms have been noted as early as the thirteenth century, mainly in the fields of trade and maritime. Anglicisms comprised less than 1 percent of all foreign words in the seventeenth century but increased to more than 6 percent by the middle of the eighteenth century, in part due to the influence of English literature.

There was a notable influx of English words into the German language in the nineteenth century (from 8 percent of all foreign words at the beginning of the century to nearly 36 percent by the end) as England influenced areas such as commerce, travel, journalism, and politics. The portion of anglicisms in the German language was estimated to have been slightly more than 1 percent of the total vocabulary by the end of the nineteenth century. There was a steady increase throughout the twentieth century, so that by 1980, approximately 88 percent of foreign words in German were anglicisms (slightly less than 3.5 percent of the total vocabulary).

Although some anglicisms (e.g., *Bestseller, Babysitter,* and *Stress*) can be traced to American English, others are of British origin, still others came to German via a third country, and yet others are of ambiguous origin. As the economic and political influence of the United States increased beginning in the early decades of the twentieth century, the portion of anglicisms of American origin became much more significant. And since the mid-twentieth century, the frequency of americanisms has continued to increase consistently. Researchers have identified anywhere from four to nineteen americanisms per newspaper page in the mid-twentieth century, climbing to as many as twenty-four per page in 1974.

Americanisms have altered both written and spoken German and both formal and colloquial language. Indeed, some americanisms have become such a standard part of German vocabulary that they may no longer be perceived as foreign words (e.g., *Okay, Star, Jeans, Training*). Virtually all areas of German life—music, dance, theater, film, newspapers, magazines, radio, television, literature, travel, science, technology, industry, economy, politics, and the military—have witnessed an influx of americanisms. In addition, fashion, food, and tourism have been affected, as have the modern branches of the sciences such as information technology, atomic energy, air travel, and certain sports (e.g., "bowling," "roller-skating," "surfing," and "aerobics"). The use of americanisms is especially noticeable among German youth due to the strong influence of the American music industry and television. There are an estimated 6,000 to 7,000 americanisms in the German language today.

Sources of Americanisms

The means of transfer of americanisms into German are manifold. As the political and social contacts between speakers of German and English have grown over the last centuries, most notably since World War II, the influence of American English on the German language has increased as well. Specific sources of americanisms include the translation of many specialized texts into German; the prominence of English in international press agencies as well as in international politics; increasing numbers of exchange students and professors travel-

ing between German-speaking and English-speaking countries; the presence of American military service members and their families in the post–World War II years; the popularity of American films, television shows, and hit songs; and the increasing number of native German speakers who study the English language and American culture at German schools and universities. Another important source of increased contact between the cultures is the return to Germany of many German emigrants who lived in the United States. The German press, including newspapers and magazines, has played a key role in facilitating the process of adoption and circulation of americanisms.

Although residents of the former German Democratic Republic (GDR) did not have this same degree of contact with American English, some americanisms also existed there largely because of the media influence of their western neighbors. The social and political changes of 1989, when the Berlin Wall came down, the subsequent unification with West Germany, and access to a wider variety of media, led to a wave of American influence—and consequently many more americanisms—in that part of the country in the 1990s.

Types of Americanisms

Americanisms include English words in their original form that have been incorporated into German, such as *Ticket, Party,* and *Makeup,* as well as words that have adapted to German conventions such as *Komputer, Musikbox,* and *Additiv.* Other americanisms combine American and German words, as in *Twistschritt* (twist step), *Fußballfan* (football fan), and *Jetflug* (jet flight). Still others are newly constructed words based upon English yet not found in the English language (e.g., *Twen,* "someone in his or her twenties"; *Dressman,* "male model"; *Beamer,* "data projector"; *Handy,* "mobile phone"; *Happy end,* "happy ending"; and *Shakehand,* "handshake"). Another type of americanism is the translation of an English word into German, such as *Beiprodukt* from "byproduct," *Herzattacke* from "heart attack," and *Fiskaljahr* from "fiscal year."

Americanisms also demonstrate the impact of American English on German morphology, semantics, pronunciation, syntax, and writing conventions. For example, some americanisms undergo additions or changes. Imported verbs frequently take on German patterns of conjugation, as with the americanisms *campen, joggen,* and *coachen,* although spelling changes are not always consistent (e.g., *recyclen* and *recyceln*). Another form of adaptation is the addition of a German prefix to an English root word: *aufstylen,* "to make more stylish"; and *vertrusten,* "to form into a trust."

In most cases, the meaning of an americanism is the same or nearly the same as in English. However, the definition of an americanism may differ from the closest corresponding German word, adding to the vocabulary choice of the speaker (e.g., *Job,* meaning "temporary employment to earn money," as distinct from the German words *Beruf,* "career"; and *Arbeit,* "work"). Or, the connotation may be slightly different from the German equivalent (e.g., *Baby* as a more affectionate term for the German word *Säugling,* "infant"). In other cases, the americanism may take on an entirely different meaning (e.g., *clever,* to mean "cunning" or "crafty," as compared to the more common English definition of "smart" or "witty,"; and *Keks,* which came from "cakes," to mean "biscuit").

Generally, americanisms are pronounced as they are in English; infrequently they are spoken using German conventions or a combination of the two, depending in part upon the speaker's knowledge of English. Evidence of americanisms in German syntax includes, for example, the phrase *in 1980,* which imitates English rather than the German *im Jahre 1980.*

English nouns typically are written with a capital letter as soon as they are established in German (e.g., *Teenager, Trend,* and *Test*). Other changes in writing conventions are not implemented universally. Some examples are the use of "k" instead of the original "c" in *Klown* and *Kockpit,* "sch" instead of "sh" in *Schock,* and the replacement of a single consonant with a double one in *Stopp* and *Tripp.*

Motives for Using Americanisms

German speakers may use americanisms to refer to items for which there is no German equivalent, as in the case of the jazz styles *Hard Bop* and *West Coast* or the advent of *Supermarket* and *Park and Ride,* which came into the German language with the inventions themselves. Americanisms may refer to items that were founded or popularized in the United States (e.g., the verbs *snowboarden, skateboarden, mountainbiken*), or that specifically designate American cultural features (e.g., *Cowboy, Western, High School, Hippie,* and *Yuppie*). Some americanisms, such as *Checkpoint* and *Displaced Persons,* come in and out of usage if they are connected with trends or time-sensitive events. In still other cases, americanisms offer synonyms and stylistic variations, may provide an American flavor or color to the topic being discussed, and may be used to create a desired tone or affect.

Americanisms can allow German speakers to be more precise or brief since the German equivalent may be longer than the americanism; many americanisms are one syllable (e.g., *Snob, Box, Quiz,* and the adjective *fair*). Americanisms may be required for communication in specialty areas where the terminology dictates it. Germans may also use americanisms out of a desire to imitate the publicity styles used in the United States; some believe that the use of americanisms, especially in advertising, can add an air of modernity and prestige to the speaker or writer. Youth subculture and the entertainment industry have contributed to the popularity of americanisms, as have political organizations, making their use not solely connected to pro-Americanism. Indeed, the use of americanisms can also be found among members of alternative political movements and those espousing anti-Americanism.

Reception of Americanisms

The existence of americanisms and their increasing number have brought both positive and negative reactions from German speakers. Enthusiasm for and openness to americanisms are common, given their prevalence and popularity and the recognition that they are continuing to increase over time. Moreover, the advent of thousands of americanisms in the German language can be viewed not so much as an Americanization of German as an internationalization of the language, not unlike what has occurred in other countries.

However, already in the late nineteenth century, there was a movement against the rising tide of anglicisms and other foreign words in the German language that mirrored the nationalist sentiment of that time.

The language purists campaigned to encourage German speakers to use their mother tongue as opposed to foreign words whenever possible. During the National Socialist era, americanisms and other foreign expressions were discouraged as a more pure German language was linked to intense nationalist sentiments. Official campaigns against English words in the GDR focused selectively on americanisms as a representation of U.S. imperialism.

Nowadays, some native German speakers feel that the use of americanisms, and anglicisms in general, devalues the language, especially where there are equivalent German terms, as with the popular words *cool, Kids,* and *happy.* Debates on this topic and organizations that encourage the use of German words in place of English imports are not uncommon. Some who fear degradation of German have dubbed the mixture of the two languages *Denglisch* or *Engleutsch.* It is true, on occasion, that many americanisms are not fully understood by the German listener or reader and that their use can create communication problems. Nonetheless, researchers have found very little structural change in the German language due to the influx of americanisms, and americanisms are widely viewed as an enrichment of the German language.

Germanisms in the English Language

The German language has also influenced the English language. As early as 1520, there is evidence that the Reformation left its mark on English vocabulary from newly created German words (e.g., *Protestant,* and *papist*) as well as from new Bible translations (e.g., *weakling* and *mercy seat*). In the seventeenth century, German scientific and technical terms, including some in the field of mining, were added to the English vocabulary (e.g., *satellite, inertia, focus,* and *cobalt*). The number of germanisms increased in the second half of the eighteenth century with an influx of mineralogical, chemical, and geological terms such as *quartz* and *graphite.* Even more germanisms entered the English language in the second half of the nineteenth century and the first half of the twentieth century from fields including biology and psychology. An estimated 3,000 germanisms in English fall into the following main categories: geology, chemistry, physics, medicine, and other sciences. Some better known germanisms are *kindergarten, glockenspiel, leitmotiv, ersatz, lieder, U-boat, Nazi, kitsch, wunderkind, blitzkrieg, achtung, gesundheit,* and *angst.* Few germanisms have replaced English words; most have expanded the English vocabulary and continue to be extremely useful in a variety of fields.

Diane Guido

See also American Occupation Zone; U.S. Bases in West Germany

References and Further Reading

Carstensen, Broder, and Hans Galinsky. *Amerikanismen der Deutschen Gegenwartssprache.* Heidelberg: Carl Winter Universitätsverlag, 1975.

Carstensen, Broder, Ulrich Busse, and Regina Schmude. Anglizismen-Wörterbuch: *Der Einfluss des Englischen auf den Deutschen Wortschatz nach 1945.* 3 vols. Berlin: Walter de Gruyter, 2001.

Fink, Hermann, Liane Fijas, and Danielle Schons. *Anglizismen in der Sprache der Neuen Bundesländer: Eine Analyse zur Verwendung und Rezeption.* Frankfurt am Main: Peter Lang, 1997.

Galinsky, Hans. *Amerikanisch-deutsche Sprach- und Literaturbeziehungen: Systematische Übersicht und Forschungsbericht, 1945–1970.* Frankfurt am Main: Athenäum Verlag, 1972.

Pfeffer, J. Alan, and Garland Cannon. *German Loanwords in English: An Historical Dictionary.* Cambridge: Cambridge University Press, 1994.

Polenz, Peter von. *Deutsche Sprachgeschichte vom Spätmittelalter bis zur Gegenwart.* 3 vols. Berlin: Walter de Gruyter, 1991–1999.

AMERICANIZATION

Americanization refers to a process by which ideas, practices, and patterns of behavior that were developed and widely spread in the United States first aroused the interest of some Germans. They studied them and introduced them into public discussion in their country, raising the question of transferability and applicability. Those who were convinced that what they saw and scrutinized was transferable began to import these ideas and practices. Not the United States as a whole, but selected aspects of American society, became to them a model to be emulated. They were helped in this transaction by Americans who not only believed that their model was superior to existing alternatives (e.g., the British one) but who also had a vested interest in exporting the American model. These two groups are Americanizers. Americanization, seen as a process in which elements and practices first developed in the United States were introduced into Germany, invariably met with resistance from those who rejected these elements as alien and unsuitable to German society and its economic, political, and cultural traditions.

What emerged from the Americanization process was not a simple replica of conditions in the United States but a blending of both those imports that came to be accepted and indigenous traditions. They formed a peculiar mixture, the specific American content of which varied from issue to issue, from social group to social group, and from region to region. This is illustrated by the large, impersonal, profit-driven multinational corporation, McDonald's, which imposes its alien, uniform, and low standards on a helpless world. Though McDonald's has a standardized menu, featuring hamburgers, Big Macs, shakes, and fries, the chain does not impose a worldwide model. If you have ever had a cup of coffee in a French McDonald's, you know you are not in the United States. In India, McDonald's serves lamb burgers; in southern France, they substitute aubergine for pickles; in Germany, there is beer. Instead of insisting on doing things its own way, it adapts to local tastes.

The process that Americanizers, both foreign and indigenous, set in motion resulted in a stance that became known as Americanism, which had a flip side: it extolled the need to uphold German traditions that the American imports were thought to undermine. Over the past fifty years, anti-Americanism has evolved in fits and starts and experienced both ups and downs. In the 1950s and 1970s, for example, anti-Americanism was at a low point; more recently, it has been on the rise.

The progression of Americanization depends not just on the relative balances of power between Americanizers and their indigenous critics but is also related to the hegemonic pressure that the United States is willing and able to exert upon a foreign society. This pressure can take a variety of forms: political, economic, and cultural. It could be quite direct or it could be indirect, subtle, and covert.

U.S. hegemonic pressure may be said to have been very weak before 1914. It became stronger during and immediately after World War I, before it weakened again as a consequence of U.S. isolationism. It partially revived in the mid-1920s, when American industry became a model for Germany and American investments propelled a rise in commercial mass culture. German entrepreneurs and trade unionists went to the industrial centers of Michigan, Ohio, and Pennsylvania to study the transferability, to their country, of what they saw.

During the 1920s, Germany imported jazz, Hollywood, and the Tilly sisters. There was both acceptance and integration of these imports and resistance to them.

With the onset of the Great Depression in 1929, the United States retreated into isolationism. However, American cultural offerings continued to intrigue the Germans. Joseph Goebbels was mesmerized by American film and thought of a "counter-Hollywood"; Albert Speer built scale models of assembly halls, railroad stations, and bridges for Adolf Hitler's proposed urban reconstruction program, and time and again American architecture provided the models; and Ferdinand Porsche inspected Henry Ford's factories before he began to construct what came to be called the Volkswagen Works at Wolfsburg. Of course, Hitler's societal utopia, driven as it was by racism, military conquest, and mass murder, was fundamentally different from the "American dream." Yet even for Hitler, who began to establish an exclusive Germanic folk community, the United States never completely disappeared from his ideological radar screen. However fierce the regime's anti-Americanism may have been, even then the penetration of ideas, practices, and patterns of behavior from the United States did not stop completely.

In 1945, U.S. hegemonic pressure on Germany was greater than ever before because of the occupying forces in the American zone. The mistakes of the interwar period had made the U.S. political, economic, military, and cultural elites absolutely determined, from 1941–1942 onward, to shape the structures and mentalities of the Europeans and of the Germans in particular in their own image.

The process of Americanization affected West Germany's political, economic, and cultural system after 1945 in several ways. Although the reshaping of the political system began in 1949, first at the local and regional levels and later at the interzonal level, West Germany did not import the U.S. Constitution en bloc. What the Basic Law therefore reflects is a mix of American and indigenous traditions and principles. General Lucius D. Clay exerted direct pressure, but he left it to the Germans to design a constitution that broadly fitted the principles of parliamentary-representative government, a division of powers, democratic elections, and basic rights. In a very broad sense it might be said that the German political system was westernized in that it was wrenched away from its authoritarian traditions and practices that had spelled the end of Weimar democracy. But the specific forms that this transformation took were British or French at best in a marginal sense. The blending occurred between what the American hegemon and the West German constitutional experts envisioned.

The Americanization of West Germany is perhaps even more striking when Germany's economic system is considered. The economy that had emerged in Germany by the late 1930s was fundamentally different from the liberal, multilateral, competitive, open-door world system that the Americans wanted to reestablish after the war. The Nazi economy was still capitalist, at least for the time being, in the sense that in general it upheld the principle of private ownership. It was also industrial and, within limits, wedded to constant technological innovation. But beyond this there was little left to compare. It was totally cartelized. The market and competition had been virtually abolished. Collective bargaining, workers' rights, and trade unions had been proscribed. It had been largely decoupled from the world economy and aimed at the creation of an autocratic system within which the economies of Germany's neighbors would be blatantly exploited and geared exclusively to the needs of the German economy and financial system. It was a system of trade based on barter and bilateralism. The Nazis spoke of the creation of a consumer society, but it was one based on the idea of ethnic exclusion and the murder of "undesirables."

American planners were determined to decartelize the Nazi economy and to establish, at the earliest opportunity, competitive market conditions. They also wanted to deconcentrate some of the virtual monopolies, such as IG Farben and Vereinigte Stahlwerke, but did not envisage a total breakup. Rather they envisaged the creation of units of production that were large enough to act as engines of growth in the European reconstruction effort and to be able to compete in the open-door world trading system. In using their hegemonic clout, the Americans could rely on a number of German businesspeople and politicians as their Americanizing allies.

There was considerable opposition to the introduction of American-style antitrust law and decartelization, mainly from heavy industry in the Ruhr. This legislation, which was finally ratified in 1957, was not a mirror of the American antitrust laws preventing businesses from engaging in practices, such as forming anticompetitive agreements, that would allow them to dominate the market. Instead, German antitrust legislation blended German and American tradition. It pushed German business away from their ancient cartels and syndicates in the direction of a competitive oligopolistic capitalism very similar to the American version.

U.S. hegemonic pressures also brought social and cultural changes in West Germany during the postwar period. German Americanizers, it seems, were very much young people who responded positively, indeed enthusiastically, to what arrived from the United States. The resistance to these imports came from an older generation who rejected rock and jazz, James Dean and Coca-Cola as products of an *Unkultur*. For a while they thought that West Germany's youth was immune to American youth culture, and they were shocked when riots broke out at the end of rock concerts. The arguments that could be heard were the familiar ones dating back to the 1920s. But the attractiveness of this culture to the young was something that intellectuals, academics, parents, clergy, and politicians could not contain. There was something inexorable about the way American mass culture began to blend into West German society.

This wave of acculturation was inseparably connected with something that West German business had embraced as part of the recasting of the country's industrial system: Fordism. In the 1920s, German industry had begun to experiment with rationalized production. It sought to gain the economic benefits of modern technology and factory organization without any of the leveling effects of Americanism. They wanted higher productivity without mass production, greater exports without mass consumption, and higher profits without higher wages. In other words, German business refused to accept the other side of Ford's equation; that is, that the transition to mass production would be incomplete if it did not result in a lowering of prices, thus making products that were hitherto reserved for the few within the budget of the many. It was with this principle that Ford had initiated the motorization of the United States in the 1920s. The German car industry refused to adopt Fordism in this sense, with the exception of Opel Cars, acquired in 1927 by General Motors, which began to produce the Laubfrosch, the first popular German motorized vehicle manufactured on an assembly line.

After World War II, confronted with the need to adapt to an American-dominated, competitively organized, multilateral economy, the German economy made the transition to mass production and embraced the idea of mass consumption. The marketing of mass-produced consumer goods may not immediately have led to levels of consumption comparable to the United States in the 1950s. Many Germans could not yet afford a car, a refrigerator, or a washing machine and invested their rising wages in the replacement of essential household items. However, all this does not mean that the introduction of Fordism—defined here not just as mass production but also as the initiation of mass consumption—did not arouse consumerist desires and dreams of a better life.

Michael McGregor

See also American Occupation Zone; Coca-Cola; Ford, Henry; Fordism; Hollywood; McDonald's Restaurant; Volkswagen Company and Its VW Beetle

References and Further Reading

Berghahn, Volker. *The Americanization of West German Industry.* Leamington Spa: Berg, 1986.

Diner, Dan. *America in the Eyes of the Germans: An Essay on Anti-Americanism.* Princeton: Markus Wiener, 1996.

Kroes, Rob. *If You've Seen One, You've Seen the Mall: Europeans and American Mass Culture.* Urbana: University of Illinois Press, 1996.

Nolan, Mary. *Visions of Modernity.* New York: Oxford University Press, 1994.

Willett, Ralph. *The Americanization of Germany, 1945–1949.* New York: Routledge, 1989.

AMERIKADEUTSCHER VOLKSBUND

see German American Bund

AMERIKA INSTITUT

The Amerika Institut was founded in 1910 in Berlin and took responsibility for maintaining and furthering academic relations and cooperation in the intellectual sphere between Germany and the United States. Its creation is to be seen in the context of the societal discourse in the United States on what constitutes an American identity. Figuring prominently in the discourse was the perceived antagonism between German and Anglo-Saxon culture. The debate thus reflected not only the numerical predominance of British and German immigrants, or rather their descendants, among the population of the United States but also political and ideological developments in Europe.

The Amerika Institut concerned itself with matters that were considered traditionally and generally to be German success stories: scientific thoroughness and higher education. The institute thus aimed at those sections of American society that could be expected to be German-friendly; that is, academics and the educated elites. Almost 10,000 U.S. citizens had received an education at German universities in the nineteenth century, and the German system of higher education was recognized by many among the U.S. academic elite to be exemplary.

There was, however, an increasing chorus of voices pointing to the authoritarian, grandiose, elitist, and inflexible character of German scholarship and its incompatibility with the American ideal of a democratic educational system. The Amerika Institut therefore may have served to counter those tendencies that threatened to undermine German exemplariness in the one field where it had hitherto gone virtually unchallenged. The importance of the founding of the institute among German Americans was shown by the fact that financial contributions were sent to Berlin even before the institute was set up. The Prussian Education Department received a check for 100,000 Reichsmark from the New York banker Jakob Henry Schiff, co-owner of the banking house Loeb and Co. The New York German American James von Speyer sent $200,000 to Germany as a contribution toward the institute's library.

The institute's founder-president was Hugo Münsterberg; he was succeeded by Karl O. Bertling, who headed the institute until his death in 1945. During World War I, the Amerika Institut and its connections in the United States became part of the propaganda efforts of the German government; the institute continued to serve as a covert propaganda tool during the Weimar Republic and the Third Reich, establishing a working relationship with the German intelligence community. The Allies closed the Amerika Institut after World War II.

Joachim Lerchenmüller

See also American Students at German Universities; Johns Hopkins University; Münsterberg, Hugo; U.S.-German Intellectual Exchange

References and Further Reading

Lerchenmüller, Joachim. *Keltischer Sprengstoff: Eine wissenschaftsgeschichtliche Studie über die deutsche Keltologie von 1900 bis 1945.* Tübingen: M. Niemeyer, 1997.

AMISH

The Amish are a Christian nonstate church community whose members live today in twenty-two states of the United States (Ohio, Illinois, Indiana, Pennsylvania, New York, and others) and in Ontario, Canada. All Amish groups together probably number about 100,000 members. The center of Amish life is Ohio, where about 45,000 Amish live. Amish culture is rooted in Swiss German religious beliefs dating back to the sixteenth century. Any discussion of the Amish has first of all to take into account their religious practice of "Anabaptism," or adult baptism, as practiced also by today's Mennonites. The Anabaptists' movement originated in Switzer-

land and Germany at a time when Ulrich Zwingli and Martin Luther proclaimed their new understanding of the Christian faith. The Anabaptists, however, were even more radical in their reformatory thinking and soon became visible in the whole of central western Europe. As a result of their beliefs, which stress voluntary entry into the church, the separation of church and state, the idea of individual priesthood, and the dominance of faith over good deeds, they were persecuted by both Catholic and Protestant state churches. The climax of the Anabaptist movement came in 1535, with the creation of a kingdom in Münster, North-Rhine Westphalia. After the military defeat of the Anabaptists in that city at the end of June 1535, the leaders of the Baptists were captured, tortured, and put into cages hanging from the top of the Lambertus Church. The survivors of the massacre fled to the Netherlands, where they found refuge with the former Catholic priest Menno Simons (1496–1561). He reorganized the movement whose members were known thereafter as Mennonites. Attracted by the prospect of religious freedom, many fled to the United States during the first half of the eighteenth century. The Amish are a splinter group named after their founder, the Swiss-born Jakob Ammann, who disagreed with more liberal Mennonites in 1693 over the issue of whether or not to shun baptized members who had subsequently left the church.

Amish links with Germany are still clearly evident today on all cultural levels, particularly on the linguistic one. Pennsylvania Dutch is their first language, despite the fact that English is taught at schools, which are usually Amish operated. Early modern High German, the language of the

Luther translation of the Bible and other scriptures like the *Ausbund,* a hymnal of lyrics and verse, is used during worship. Members that sin severely against the *Ordnung* (order, or church discipline) might be temporarily banned from the community (*Meidung*), and after a life spent in *Gelassenheit* (spiritual comfort resulting from trust in God's will), Amish couples usually retire to so-called *Grossdadi* (grandpa) houses.

The most traditional group, the "Old Order Amish," interpret the pursuit of happiness in a way different not only from other Christian churches but even more so from capitalist America. The Amish believe with Luther that being a Christian is a gift of God and therefore requires a special frame of mind and form of conduct. However, there is no missionary activity on their part, although the church is open to anyone willing to accept the lifestyle that comes with being Amish. Due to the practice of adult baptism, the young are allowed to test the water before joining the church, but commitment is then usually for life. Surrounded by a nation that propagates a belief in the latest technological equipment and progress in general, the Amish deliberately prefer tilling their soil with archaic equipment. On their highly productive farms, there is yet no electricity, and there are no cars, only horse-driven buggies. At a time when lifelong learning has become so commonplace that knowledge has been reduced to a marketable commodity, the Amish object to higher education in the sense of refusing the acquisition of what they perceive as "worldly" knowledge. However, they have sound expertise in farming: like their forefathers, most Amish still work in agriculture or related professions.

If individuality and freedom can be seen as the main characteristics of modernity, the Amish live a communitarian life, curbing what they interpret as the excessive and disruptive freedom of the individual. Against the sense of depression and isolation that often strike modern individuals, the Amish maintain the value of a protective community based on and revolving around intact three-generational families. Although careers for women have become a regular feature of modern life, the Amish share jobs according to gender. They preach and practice a frugal life in the way that Luther and Ammann had advertised. Throughout life (and beyond), discipline, submission to the will of God, and modesty are of essential importance to the Amish and become manifest, for example, in their austere outfit made according to the traditional German fashion, as well as in the graveyard monuments that do not single out any individual. In times of war the Amish remain pacifist to the level of suffering hostility and punishment up to imprisonment.

Markus Oliver Spitz

See also Iowa, German Dialects in; Pennsylvania German (Dutch) Language

References and Further Reading

Hostetler, John A. *Amish Life*. Scottdale: Herald Press, 1983.
———. *Amish Society*. Baltimore: Johns Hopkins University Press, 1993.
Nolt, Steven. *A History of the Amish*. Intercourse, PA: Good Books, 1992.

ANARCHISTS

For the Anarchist, freedom is not an abstract philosophical concept, but the

*vital concrete possibility for every human
being to bring to full development all
capacities and talents with which nature
has endowed him, and turn them to
social account.*
—Rudolf Rocker, *Anarcho-Syndicalism*

In the United States, with its at least theoretically uninhibited possibility to exercise one's rights and freedoms, anarchist idealism—the idea that, as Immanuel Kant has it, "freedom and order" are possible "without the use of force"—found enough ground to flourish on in the mid- to late nineteenth century. In reality— other than in nationalist fiction and myth—the United States never were a "melting pot" but rather a heterogeneous conglomerate of groups and class fragments, immigrant associations, and upwardly mobile individuals. This left spaces for local (mostly rural) utopian projects, as well as for urban associations and cooperative projects. Consequently, almost all known variants of anarchist beliefs found a following in North America, ranging from religiously inspired sectarians to free-market extremists. Due to the background of anarchism in the ideals of the Enlightenment, many of the early anarchists were German and French immigrants. Among their representatives were such diverse activists as Wilhelm (Christian) Weitling (1808–1871), August Becker (1813– 1871), and Karl Heinzen (1809–1880). Important figures later in the century were August Willich (1810–1878), the apostate priest Robert Reitzel (editor of *Der Arme Teufel* [The Poor Devil], 1849–1898), August Spies (1855–1887), and Johann Most (1846– 1906), ranging in their ideologies from syndicalism to radical action and utopian terrorism.

To draw a clear line between the various forms of anarchist idealism is almost impossible. To simplify, three main brands of anarchist thinking can be distinguished: one syndicalist, trade union, and cooperative-based form of leftist socialism that tries to overcome hierarchical order and oppression by establishing a grassroots form of counterhegemony and one radical and often militant form that believes in the necessity of destroying existing order before anything new can be erected, are usually (over-)identified with two theorists of anarchism, Petr Krapotkin (1842–1921) and Mihail Bakunin (1814–1876). The third direction is indebted to Max Stirner's (1806–1856) radical individualism. His belief in the absolute independence and therefore irresponsibility of the individual toward any form of society, however, has been less influential in anarchist circles than among free-market capitalists and the followers of Ayn Rand.

Among the unifying principles of all subforms of anarchism are the following: (1) anarchism is different from communism in that it rejects party control; (2) the ultimate goal is liberty from any form of institutionalized power; (3) and anarchism is based on the individual's free choice of association, thus also transcending the (artificial) borderlines of nation, race, class, creed, and even gender. The sexual libertinage in some anarchist theories (viz. the campaign in *Der Arme Teufel*) met with fierce opposition from Puritan quarters in the United States; many of the demands have since been adopted by feminism. Anarchist freedom naturally came into confrontation with the interests of invested capital and the political power system in the United States. Notably, those anarchist groups whose ideals included social responsibility and opposed the established form of government-supported and profit-oriented market economy soon became the objects of misrepresentation in the media and worse. From the beginning in the late eighteenth century (*The Anarchiad*, 1787) to the stage melodrama of the late nineteenth century, anarchism had usually been identified with chaos and terror. On this pretext, persecution by state and federal agencies as well as by private security companies like the Pinkerton Agency was made to appear necessary. Measures against anarchists ranged from intimidation and physical violence to assassinations and, as in the case of the Haymarket anarchists in 1886, the International Workers of the World (IWW) spokesman Joe Hill in 1915, and the famous case of Nicola Sacco (1891–1927) and Bartolomeo Vanzetti (1888–1927) in the 1920s, to judicial murder.

Individual militant anarchists and anarchist groups contributed their share to this confrontation. The Arbeiter Lehr- und Wehrvereine (Workingmens' Education and Defense Associations) stood in the tradition of the prewar socialist Turner Societies and rejected violence. The 1886 Haymarket incident changed the situation. Not only was it the first challenge to representatives of state order (in this case police trying to disperse a crowd of striking workers), but it also signaled a new quality in the fight. Though anarchist operations in the United States never reached the level or the impact they had in czarist Russia, for example, the assassination of President William McKinley in 1901 is usually attributed to a self-styled anarchist, Leon Czolgosz (1873–1901). His actual connections with anarchism are, however, doubtful.

After 1886, the anarchist movement in the United States lacked theoreticians and intellectual figureheads, with August Spies and Albert Parsons (1848–1887) dead, and Johann Most, the Russian immigrant Emma Goldman (1869–1940), and others like Reitzel constantly under surveillance and repeatedly imprisoned. The practical side and value of anarchism, however, remained visible in and behind many strikes for better working and living conditions and in countless acts of solidarity among miners, sailors, and transportation and steelworkers, notably in the eastern states and in the Great Lakes region. Out of this practical anarchism rose the anarcho-syndicalist IWW in the early 1900s, which again met with stiff resistance and relentless persecution, including a court decision to have the IWW archives destroyed. As a consequence, and also because of IWW opposition to the Communist Party, anarchist groups dwindled in size and effectivity. After the demise of figures like the syndicalist theorist Rudolf Rocker (1873–1958), who escaped Nazi Germany to the United States, or Sam Dolgoff (1902–1990), the various anarchisms are now mainly clandestine theoretical ideologies, advanced by intellectuals like Murray Bookchin (1921–) and Noam Chomsky (1928–). The notable exception is the Stirnerian form of anarcho-capitalism, first introduced in the Reagan era and advanced by the George W. Bush administration. The heyday of the German anarchists, however, had ended already before World War I.

Wolfgang Hochbruck

See also Bismarck's Anti-Socialist Law; Haymarket; Most, Johann; Schwab, Justus H.; Turner Societies; Weitling, Wilhelm

References and Further Reading

Diefenbacher, Hans, ed. *Anarchismus: Zu Geschichte und Idee der herrschaftsfreien Gesellschaft.* Darmstadt: Primus, 1996.

Foner, Philip Sheldon. *History of the Labor Movement in the United States.* Vol. 2. New York: International Publisher, 1977.

Most, Johann. *Revolutionäre Kriegswissenschaft.* Millwood: Kraus Reprint, 1983.

ANNEKE, MATHILDE FRANZISKA

b. April 3, 1817; Leveringhausen, Westphalia
d. November 25, 1884; Milwaukee, Wisconsin

The most important German American social activist, feminist, educator, and writer of the second half of the nineteenth century.

Moderately successful as a journalist and dramatist before her political career, Anneke was one of the prominent women among the Forty-Eighters. She married the former artillery lieutenant Fritz Anneke in 1847 and through him came in contact with the Cologne Socialist circle. With him and all by herself while he was in prison, she wrote, edited, and printed the *Neue Kölnische Zeitung* (New Cologne Newspaper), a working-class daily. When the censors closed down the paper, she reopened it as the *Frauen-Zeitung* (Women's Journal), only to see it closed down again. The Annekes escaped from Germany in 1849 and eventually arrived in Milwaukee, where in 1852 Mathilde Anneke started editing the *Deutsche Frauen-Zeitung* (German Women's Newsletter), the first feminist U.S. periodical. She also published the diary she had kept during the 1849 campaign as *Memoiren einer Frau aus dem badisch-pfälzischen Feldzüge* (A Woman's Memoir of the Campaign in Baden and the Palatinate), wrote short stories and essays for newspapers, and saw her pre-1848 stage success, *Oithono oder die Tempelweihe* (O., or the Dedication) produced in Milwaukee. Of major importance were her contact and cooperation with Elizabeth Cady Stanton and Susan B. Anthony, which led to her appearance as speaker at the 1853 Seneca Falls Conference of women's rights activists.

The outbreak of the American Civil War found Anneke and her family in Switzerland en route to Italy, where her notoriously improvident husband had hoped to join Giuseppe Garibaldi. He returned to the United States immediately for a tumultuous career during the war. Mathilde Anneke remained in Switzerland and supported her family by writing correspondence and reports for German newspapers like the liberal *Augsburger Allgemeine* (Augsburger Gazette), based on letters she received from the United States. She also wrote and published magazine stories. These stories often contained interesting heroines, some of them slave women. Doubly enslaved as African Americans and as women, they actively fought for their own freedom, transgressing the borderlines set by, for example, Harriet Beecher Stowe's female characters in *Uncle Tom's Cabin.*

After the close of the war, Anneke returned to Milwaukee with her three surviving children, where she started her last major project, a women's academy. She had realized that women could only hope for equality in their lives and workplaces if their level of education and their training compared favorably to that of men. She directed this academy and spoke and wrote on behalf of women's rights and emancipation until her death.

Wolfgang Hochbruck

See also Forty-Eighters; Milwaukee; Slavery in German American and German Texts

References and Further Reading

Gebhardt, Manfred. *Mathilde Franziska Anneke.* Berlin: Neues Leben, 1988.

Steucher, Dorothea Diver. "Double Jeopardy: Nineteenth Century German-American Woman Writers." PhD diss., University of Minnesota, 1981.

Wagner, Maria. "Mathilde Anneke's Stories of Slavery in the German-American Press." *MELUS* 6, no. 4 (1979): 9–21.

ANTISEMITISM

Antisemitism, discrimination against Jews as a religious or ethnic group, has been an important factor in German American relations, particularly since 1933. In the nineteenth century, antisemitism, along with economic factors, spurred emigration of German Jews to the United States. With the rise of National Socialism, the American Jewish community worked to call attention to German antisemitism and to make it a central issue in German American political relations. This effort, impacted by the legacy of the Holocaust, continued after 1945, and in recent years Jewish-related issues, including antisemitism and Holocaust memorialization, have had a prominent place on the agenda of German American political and cultural relations.

Despite the large wave of German Jewish immigration to the United States in the nineteenth century, antisemitism was seldom the primary motivating factor for leaving Germany. A sclerotic economy induced millions of Germans of all faiths to emigrate to the United States during the course of the 1800s, and likewise, German Jews most frequently emigrated for economic reasons, particularly beginning in the 1840s. After the defeat of Napoleon by the German states in the Wars of Liberation (1813), Jewish emancipation was partially or totally repealed by restoration governments throughout Germany. German Jews lost most of the political and economic rights granted to them by liberalizing governments in the early nineteenth century, and societal antisemitism manifested itself in more hostile forms, most notably the Hep-Hep riots of 1819. However, most German Jews sought to acclimate to the altered situation through acculturation or assimilation during the course of the nineteenth century.

In the nineteenth century, German Jewry dominated American Jewish life, and German Jews soon formed a majority of the Jewish community in many midwestern and southern cities. Milwaukee, St. Louis, and Cincinnati were centers for German Jewish life well into the twentieth century. In the antebellum United States, Jews were not subject to nativist discrimination specifically as Jews, and Catholic Irish and German immigrants were more frequent targets of xenophobic prejudice. German Jewish immigrants also participated in German American organizations on an equal or near-equal basis in the early to mid-1800s. In Chicago, four of the five founders of the Republican Party's German-language wing were Jews, and the abolitionist movement numbered German Jews among its members. However, Jews faced rising societal antisemitism at the time of the Civil War, and they responded with increased patriotism. Although German Jews fought for both the Union and the Confederacy, antisemitism and economic hardship in the post–Civil War South persuaded many to migrate to the Northeast.

German Jews in the United States established B'nai B'rith, a Jewish fraternal society, in 1843, and this organization founded the Anti-Defamation League (ADL) in 1913 to fight antisemitism. However, German Jews in the United States did not always respond to antisemitism in such a proactive and insistent manner. Many German Jews perceived the rise in American antisemitism in the late nineteenth century to be a direct response to the increased numbers of eastern European Jewish immigrants entering the country and not a reaction to their own conspicuous success. They established schools to Americanize the recent arrivals, teaching them English and vocational skills. Others attempted to shunt new immigrants into the less densely populated and less Jewish American West. Some German Jews in the United States denied the existence of pervasive antisemitism in their new homeland.

Antisemitism was clearly on the rise in Germany in the late nineteenth century. Liberal German American circles deplored this trend as reported by German-language newspapers in the United States. German American political leader Carl Schurz frequently attacked German antisemitism in the *New York Evening Post*. He also criticized German chancellor Otto von Bismarck for refusing to accept official condolences from the U.S. Congress on the death of Jewish German politician Eduard Lasker. Lasker, a rival of Bismarck and a leader of the National Liberal Party, died while visiting New York in 1884.

In the early years of World War I, many American Jews sympathized with the Central Powers rather than the Allies. For some it was a matter of residual sympathy for their erstwhile homelands, Germany and Austria-Hungary. Others fervently supported the Central Powers' struggle against antisemitic, czarist Russia. Regardless, this support evaporated with U.S. entry into the war in 1917. After the war, American Jewish groups, fearing for the position of Jews in the new Polish republic, exercised great pressure on the Allied governments to induce the Polish government to sign a treaty protecting the rights of non-Polish minorities. The provisions of the treaty applied both to Jews and to Germans, and until 1933 there was a joint German Jewish interest in protecting the rights of minorities in Poland.

The rise of National Socialism in Germany placed antisemitism at the forefront of German American relations. American discontent did not immediately lead to a policy of overt confrontation, but rather a slow atrophy of German American relations. Soon after the Nazi seizure of power, the U.S. embassy in Berlin reported to Washington on regular acts of violence directed against Jews, and President Franklin D. Roosevelt received frequent briefings on the situation. The president expressed his distress to Reichsbank president Hjalmar Schacht, visiting the United States in May 1933, but Roosevelt repeatedly declined to make any public statement about the Jews' plight in Germany. According to William E. Dodd, U.S. ambassador to Germany from 1933 to 1937, Roosevelt was fully aware of the persecution of the German Jews and regretted it, but noted that it was "not a governmental affair. We can do nothing except for American citizens." Roosevelt felt that only personal influence and unofficial channels should be used. Secretary of State Cordell Hull was equally reluctant to condemn German antisemitism. During his tenure in office, Ambassador Dodd struggled to formulate an adequate response to German aggression, including German policy toward the Jews. Dodd was personally critical of Nazi policy and helped many Germans of Jewish descent to emigrate; however, his public statements on the issue were seldom forceful. Moreover, Dodd, a history professor, not a career diplomat, failed to receive support from the State Department for more vigorous action. Ineffective against the implementation of antisemitic policy in Germany and isolated within the State Department, Dodd was recalled from his position in 1937. His successor, career Foreign Service officer Hugh R. Wilson, felt that a less confrontational course of action would be more effective. He disapproved of attacks on Germany in the American press. After the pogrom of November 9–10, 1938, known as *Reichskristallnacht,* Roosevelt, acting upon the recommendation of Assistant Secretary of State and former Consul General in Berlin George Messersmith, recalled Wilson to Washington for consultations, and Wilson did not return to Germany.

Seeing the reluctance of their government, American Jewish groups and their non-Jewish allies pursued their own course of action in response to increasingly virulent German antisemitism. They staged rallies, most notably a giant protest assembly at Madison Square Garden in New York on March 27, 1933. Speakers included New York mayor John O'Brien, German-born U.S. senator Robert F. Wagner, and Episcopal bishop William T. Manning. Jewish groups also organized a boycott of German products. Although it had some success in New York City, it ultimately proved ineffectual. The U.S. government maintained a neutral position on the boycott. German officials, meanwhile,

complained about the boycott to Secretary Hull, who refused to place pressure on Jewish groups to end the action. The government also refused to squash a mock trial of Adolf Hitler held by the American Federation of Labor and the American Jewish Congress in 1934, despite official German protests.

Antisemitism also shaped official German perceptions of the United States. Although Adolf Hitler spoke of the United States' supposed Nordic racial core and Anglo-Saxon settlers who had colonized an entire continent, he also viewed the United States as a land where Jewry had flourished. For propagandistic purposes the Nazis continually overstated and exaggerated the influence of American Jews over their government's policies. Hitler, who neither spoke English nor had been to an English-speaking country, considered Anglo-American democracy a Jewish invention, and he blamed the Jews for U.S. participation in World War I. He considered Roosevelt to be the pawn of an international Jewish cabal. Moreover, cultural antimodernism accompanied antisemitism in Nazi perceptions of the United States as an increasingly degenerate land of racial mixing. Some Americans of German descent supported the policies of the Nazi regime, including antisemitism. The most infamous of these groups was the Friends of the New Germany, later renamed the German American Bund, which gathered 20,000 for a rally at Madison Square Garden in February 1939. It activities fell under the scrutiny of an investigation launched by Jewish congressman Samuel Dickstein into Nazi propaganda activities in the United States. His inquiry gave rise to the House Un-American Activities Committee. Meanwhile, as Bund leader Fritz Kuhn was prosecuted for embezzlement, the group lost any prestige it had and eventually dissolved.

Many Americans perceived the 1936 summer Olympic Games, hosted by Germany, to be a propaganda show for Hitler's Germany, and negative press reports colored their impressions. However, German officials, aware of the potential for negative publicity, removed anti-Jewish signs from public view for the duration of the games. Prior to the Olympics, U.S. Olympic officials were divided over whether to boycott the games. Ernest Lee Jahnke, a German American and member of the International Olympic Committee (IOC), encouraged a boycott, for which he was expelled from the IOC. He was replaced by Avery Brundage, who opposed any boycott. At the Berlin games, some Jewish American athletes were not allowed by their coaches to compete in their events. It remains a topic of controversy whether this was in deference to German wishes or for competitive reasons.

As virulent antisemitism persuaded German Jews to emigrate, it was very difficult for them to seek refuge in the United States. Fears of economic competition and xenophobia had led in 1924 to the establishment of a quota system to limit immigration. Under popular pressure, these quotas were not relaxed in the 1930s to admit Jewish refugees facing Nazi persecution. In 1938, Roosevelt responded to the mounting refugee crisis by calling for an international conference, which was held in Evian, France, that summer. Thirty-two countries, including the United States, sent delegates; however, the United States was represented not by any State Department official but by Myron Taylor, an American industrialist and friend of the president. Despite universal regret ex-

pressed for the refugees' plight, only the Dominican Republic agreed to accept more immigrants. Nazi officials considered it astounding that the United States, Britain, and others criticized Germany for its treatment of the Jews but refused to admit them as immigrants.

The late 1930s marked a high point in American antisemitism, and many U.S. State Department officials, themselves antisemitic, refused to make full use of the quota allotments available to Germans. Notable among these antisemitic officials was Assistant Secretary of State Breckenridge Long, who ordered U.S. consulates to hinder Jewish immigration as far as possible and who personally acted illegally to do so. Nonetheless, between January 1933 and September 1939, approximately 95,000 German Jews did emigrate to the United States, where they made important contributions to American public and academic life, notably at the New School in New York, the Institute for Advanced Studies in Princeton, and historically black colleges in the American South. Most notable among them were Albert Einstein, Max Horkheimer, Theodor Adorno, and Herbert Marcuse.

The U.S. Army was also not immune to antisemitism, and many important officers held the Jews collectively accountable for the Bolshevik revolution in Russia. Xenophobia was rife in the officer corps. Although completely committed to the military defeat of Nazi Germany, many officers hoped for a postwar alliance of the United States and Germany against the Soviet Union. During the war, army officials did not press for the bombing of rail lines to concentration camps or the camps themselves, and some officers and War Department officials openly opposed such bombings, claiming them to be a diversion from tactical objectives. In the American Occupation Zone of Germany, some senior officers, most notably George S. Patton, did not hide their anti-Jewish prejudice. The physical appearance and general attitude of Jewish Holocaust survivors, compared to the healthy appearance, cleanliness, and deferential attitude of German civilians, repelled many U.S. soldiers and disposed them against the Jews. Others continued to support a U.S.-German alliance against the Soviets, whom they regarded in overtly racist terms.

Since 1945, fears of renewed antisemitism have affected German American relations. In the immediate postwar years, U.S. occupation officials considered antisemitism and Germany's position on the Jews to be a barometer of German democratization. Despite their policy, U.S. officials were loathe to interfere in the affairs of West Germany regarding the Jews or manifestations of antisemitism, including a wave of cemetery desecrations in the 1950s and a riot in Munich in 1952 in response to an antisemitic letter published in the *Süddeutsche Zeitung* (*South German News*). The U.S. government approved of West German reparations to Israel and to Jewish Holocaust survivors, initiated in the early 1950s, but it placed no pressure on Konrad Adenauer's government to conclude an agreement for restitution. Jewish groups in the United States, including the American Jewish Committee (AJC) and B'nai B'rith, maintained a skeptical attitude regarding West German efforts to combat reappearances of antisemitism. The participation of former Nazis and fellow travelers in public life exacerbated their fears, and they lobbied for a more critical and reserved embrace of West Germany as a U.S. ally.

These sentiments found little support within the U.S. government as increasing cold war tensions induced U.S. officials to overlook sensitive issues that had the potential to alienate support within the West German government or public.

In the 1950s, German antisemitism frequently accompanied nationalism, but after 1968, anti-Jewish sentiments became more frequent on the political Left. Anticapitalism, anti-Americanism, and support for so-called Third World liberation movements often merged with antisemitism. Israel's strongest public detractors in Germany were members of the political New Left. Frequently their anticapitalist and anti-Zionist rhetoric merged and strayed into the realm of antisemitism. Israel's strongest supporters in West Germany were political conservatives who embraced U.S. foreign policy marked by global anticommunism and support for Israel.

In the 1980s, the seeming irrelevance of antisemitism to German American diplomatic relations forced Jewish groups to reconsider their earlier agendas. In 1985, U.S. president Ronald Reagan visited Bitburg cemetery accompanied by West German chancellor Helmut Kohl, to the dismay and outrage of Jewish groups. In response to Jewish censure, Reagan also visited Bergen-Belsen concentration camp, but criticism did not abate. The following year, the so-called *Historikerstreit* (historians' debate) over the uniqueness and relative significance of the Holocaust raged within German and German American intellectual circles. Surprised at the general reaction to both events, American Jewish groups established permanent ties to German nongovernmental organizations, and the German embassy in Washington engaged more actively with Jewish issues.

East Germany, which had been seen by many Jews as having the potential to be a genuinely anti-Fascist Germany, embarked on an official campaign of antisemitism in 1952. Moreover, the new state rejected calls for reparations to Holocaust survivors and denied any responsibility for the actions of the Nazis. East German Jews fleeing renewed persecution received aid from Jewish charitable organizations, including the American Joint Distribution Committee. After Joseph Stalin's death in 1953, antisemitism abated, but throughout its existence, East Germany maintained an anti-Zionist position that negatively affected its relations with Jews in the United States. Nonetheless, Jewish groups hoped that East Germany would change its position, and the Conference on Material Claims against Germany, which had negotiated a reparations agreement with West Germany in 1952, continued to maintain loose ties to East German front organizations. Only in the 1980s, as the East German regime faced financial catastrophe, did relations improve. Erich Honecker's government, seeking most-favored-nation trade status and guarantees for foreign loans, approached American Jewish groups and initiated discussions regarding Holocaust reparations. The East German government believed that if it curried favor with American and world Jewry, Jews might use their supposed influence with the U.S. government on behalf of East Germany. This seemingly pro-Jewish attitude was based on older, antisemitic stereotypes of Jews exercising great power over policy formation, including in the United States. East Germany's only democratically elected government continued these efforts in 1990, but no conclusive agreement was reached, and the German Democratic Re-

public soon ceased to exist as a separate state. Meanwhile, many American Jews initially opposed German reunification or were ambivalent to it, primarily out of fear of a resurgent Germany.

By the 1990s, Jewish groups had evolved from a reactive stance regarding antisemitism and German American relations to an active one in which they pursued specific agendas. As a result, Jewish issues, including the memory of the Holocaust, have become major factors in German American relations. In the late 1990s, Undersecretary of State Stuart Eizenstat negotiated Holocaust reparations agreements with representatives of German government and industry. The ADL regularly reports on German neo-Nazism, and in 1998 the American Jewish Congress opened an office in Berlin. Its representatives frequently meet with German cabinet officials to discuss their concerns. In 1999 the German Bundestag voted to erect a giant Holocaust memorial designed by American Jewish architect Peter Eisenman. In 2001, after decades of discussions and planning, the city of Berlin opened a Jewish museum designed by Polish-born, American Jewish architect Daniel Libeskind. Despite these German efforts to memorialize the German Jewish experience and the Holocaust, the actualization of these efforts has been largely a reactive process. Beginning in the late 1970s, the United States made plans for a Holocaust memorial in Washington, D.C., and that proposal led to the United States Holocaust Memorial Museum, which opened in 1993. Since that time, the Washington museum has become an international focal point for Holocaust research and has contributed significantly to an "Americanization" of Holocaust memorialization. Similarly, the Simon Wiesenthal Center in Los Angeles has served as one of the world's leading institutions devoted to researching and combating antisemitism. Despite its strong presence in Europe, the center does not maintain an office in Germany or Austria, where Wiesenthal operates his own research and documentation center on crimes against the Jews.

In the years since 1945, antisemitism has also had influence on a more nefarious variant of German American relations. Because *Mein Kampf* (*My Battle*) and other antisemitic propaganda are banned in the Federal Republic of Germany, many American neo-Nazis and white supremacists have reimported Nazi antisemitism to Germany. German right-wing extremists and Holocaust deniers or minimizers have come to rely on foreign groups to supply them with propaganda materials, including reprints of *Mein Kampf.* The United States, whose Constitution guarantees free speech and whose courts have overturned public censorship of neo-Nazi groups, has been home to many individuals assisting German groups. From the 1970s to the 1990s, the most infamous of these was Gary Lauck, who led the so-called National Socialist German Worker's Party/Overseas Organization (NSDAP/AO). Lauck, the most important importer of neo-Nazi propaganda to Germany during that time, was arrested in Denmark and extradited to Germany in 1995. Since the late 1990s, right-wing American Internet sites have superseded earlier patrons of the movement. The United States has also been the source of much white power or skinhead rock music imported to Germany.

Jay Howard Geller

See also Adorno, Theodor Wiesengrund; Bitburg; B'nai B'rith; Chicago; Cincinnati; Einstein, Albert; Frankfurt School; Friends of the New Germany; German American Bund; Horkheimer, Max; Kuhn, Fritz Julius; German-Jewish Migration to the U.S.; Marcuse, Herbert; Milwaukee; Morgenthau Plan; Schurz, Carl

References and Further Reading

Barkai, Avraham. *Branching Out: German Jewish Immigration to the United States, 1820–1914.* New York: Holmes and Meier, 1994.

Bendersky, Joseph W. *The "Jewish Threat": Anti-Semitic Politics of the U.S. Army.* New York: Basic Books, 2000.

Gassert, Philipp. *Amerika im Dritten Reich: Ideologie, Propaganda und Volksmeinung, 1933–1945.* Stuttgart: Franz Steiner, 1997.

Geller, Jay Howard. "Das Bild Konrad Adenauers vom Judentum und seine Beziehungen zu Vertretern jüdischer Organisationen nach 1945." *Adenauer, Israel, und das Judentum.* Ed. Hanns Jürgen Küsters. Bonn: Bouvier, 2004, 137–155.

Junker, Detlef. "The Continuity of Ambivalence: German Views of America, 1933–1945." *Transatlantic Images and Perceptions: Germany and America since 1776.* Eds. David E. Barclay and Elisabeth Glaser-Schmidt. Cambridge and Washington: Cambridge University Press and German Historical Institute, 1997.

Mauch, Christof, and Joseph Salmons. *German-Jewish Identities in America.* Madison: Max Kade Institute for German American Studies, 2003.

Offner, Arnold A. *American Appeasement: United States Foreign Policy and Germany, 1933–1938.* Cambridge: Harvard University Press, 1969.

Shafir, Shlomo. *Ambiguous Relations: The American Jewish Community and Germany since 1945.* Detroit: Wayne State University Press, 1999.

Wyman, David S. *Paper Walls: America and the Refugee Crisis, 1938–1941.* Amherst: University of Massachusetts Press, 1968.

ANZEIGER DES WESTENS (WESTERN INFORMER)

The *Anzeiger des Westens,* established in St. Louis, Missouri, in 1835, was the first German-language newspaper to be published west of the Mississippi River. During its lifetime it served many German immigrants as an introduction to American politics, and was especially active in the decade before the Civil War, when the newly arrived refugees of the 1848 revolutions sought a new role for the Germans in a period of political flux. The *Anzeiger* was a strong force in rallying the Germans of Missouri to support the Union cause in the opening stages of the Civil War. Until its merger with another paper in 1898, it remained a widely read political and social force in the Midwest.

The first issue of the *Anzeiger* came off the press October 21, 1835; it remained a weekly until 1842, then became a tri-weekly, and was published daily from 1846 until the end of its life. The founder and first editor of the paper was Heinrich Bimpage, but the dominant editor from 1836 to 1850 was William Weber, a former law student from Jena who had taken part in the revolutions of 1830. Weber enlisted the help of prominent German leaders such as Friedrich Münch of rural Missouri and Gustave Philipp Koerner of nearby Illinois. The paper was known for its liberal anti-slavery position, a bold stance for a publication in a slave state.

In 1851 Heinrich Börnstein took over as editor and later publisher of the *Anzeiger.* In 1854 Börnstein, a fiery, radical Forty-Eighter, employed as an editor Carl Dänzer, another Forty-Eighter. Börnstein also hired as editor in chief Karl L. Bernays, who had previously been associated with him in the publication of the radical *Vor-*

wärts (Forwards) in Paris. Börnstein spread his liberal opinions across the pages of the *Anzeiger;* his outspokenness aroused controversy, especially because of his strident anticlericalism, which raised antagonisms among religious elements and became a source of division in St. Louis's German community. Börnstein also was a strong promoter of German culture, publishing a literary supplement to the newspaper and promoting the German theater, which he managed for a time.

After the passage of the Kansas-Nebraska Act of 1854, the paper threw its support to the free-soil section of the Missouri Democratic Party, led by Francis Preston Blair Jr., and ultimately, after 1856, supported the new Republican Party. When the southern states began to secede in 1860–1861, the St. Louis Germans were a strong element in keeping Missouri in the Union and remained as defenders of the Union after the outbreak of the Civil War.

In 1857 Dänzer, after some differences with Börnstein, left the *Anzeiger* and founded the *Westliche Post* (Western Post), which became the strongest rival to the *Anzeiger* for the rest of the century. After the outbreak of the war, Börnstein served as a Union army officer, then accepted an appointment as U.S. consul at Bremen. He never returned to the United States. The *Anzeiger* languished during Börnstein's absence and suspended publication in early 1863. Several months later, Dänzer left the *Westliche Post* and revived the *Anzeiger.* He remained as editor until 1898.

In the post–Civil War era, the *Anzeiger des Westens* and the *Westliche Post* competed to be the principal German newspaper in St. Louis. Both circulated through the expanding West, especially into Illinois and westward into Missouri, Iowa, and Kansas.

Both published weekly and Sunday editions and generally followed liberal Republican politics. The *Anzeiger* had the steady editorship of Dänzer, while the *Westliche Post* had at various times associations with Emil Preetorius, Carl Schurz, and Joseph Pulitzer. The circulation figures of the two newspapers were about the same, each approaching 30,000 in the late 1890s. In 1898 the *Anzeiger des Westens* merged with the *Westliche Post;* the *Anzeiger* then was issued as the evening edition of the merged papers, under the title *Abend-Anzeiger* (Evening Informer). It ceased publication on April 30, 1912. The *Westliche Post* continued publication until 1938.

James M. Bergquist

See also Forty-Eighters; Koerner, Gustave
  Philipp; Newspaper Press, German
  Language in the United States; Schurz, Carl
References and Further Reading
Arndt, Karl J. R., and May E. Olson. *German-
  American Newspapers and Periodicals,
  1732–1955: History and Bibliography.*
  Heidelberg: Quelle and Meyer, 1961.
Bergquist, James M. "The German-American
  Press." *The Ethnic Press in the United
  States: A Historical Analysis and Handbook.*
  Ed. Sally M. Miller. New York:
  Greenwood, 1987.
Geitz, Henry, ed. *The German-American Press.*
  Madison, WI: Max Kade Institute, 1992.
Rowan, Steven, ed. and trans. *Germans for a
  Free Missouri: Translations from the St. Louis
  Radical Press, 1857–1862.* Columbia:
  University of Missouri Press, 1983.
Wittke, Carl. *The German Language Press in
  America.* Lexington: University of
  Kentucky Press, 1957.

ARGENTINA

Although several Germans participated in Ferdinand Magellan's expedition, spending the winter of 1520 in Patagonia, the earliest documented German interest in the La Plata region was connected with trade. Once Emperor Charles V granted overseas travel and trade privileges to his subjects in Spain and the Holy Roman Empire, two large German companies, Fugger and Welser, established trade routes to the new Spanish colonies in South America. One of the fourteen ships commanded by Pedro de Mendoza in 1534 had been outfitted by the Augsburg trading company of Welser and other German businessmen. Among the 150 German and Dutch crewmen was Ulrich (Utz) Schmidel from Straubing. In 1567, he published a description of this trip and his twenty-year sojourn in *Wahrhafftige Historien einer Wunderbaren Schiffart* (True Stories from a Marvelous Journey). This book included an account of the founding of the fortress Puerto de Nuestra Señora Santa María del Buen Aire. Thus Schmidel became the first historian of Argentina.

In the colonial era, following the abdication of Charles V and the partition of his empire, few Germans except for Jesuit missionaries arrived in the region. From 1616, 117 German Jesuit padres arrived, leaving a lasting impact on the Indian missions of the Upper Paraná and the Rio Paraguay. The first important missionary was Tyrolean Anton Klemens Sepp von Seppenburg (1655–1733), who brought a variety of musical instruments to South America and for forty-three years gained high renown teaching music in several Indian mission communities. His *Reissbeschreibung* (Description of his Journey, 1696) and mission reports are valuable sources for historians. The missionaries Florian Baucke (Paucke) and Martin Dobrizhoffer served among the Mokobian and Abipone tribes in the Chaco for many years. Baucke, a Silesian, became a teacher and modernizer. He introduced the nomadic people to the advantages of: a settled lifestyle, stone houses, planted fields, and cultivated yerba maté (the special herb tea of that region). A careful observer, he wrote an illustrated report—first published in 1829 as *Reise in die Missionen* (Journey to the Missions)—a humorous description full of anecdotal material and ethnographic details. Dobrizhoffer's *Historia de Abiponibus* (History of the Abipones, 1784) is another valuable ethnological description. The Styrian Matthias Strobel (1696–1769) became the highest-ranking German Jesuit and superior of the entire Guaraní missions. Denounced as the "viceroy of the missions" by the opposition to the Jesuits, he, Baucke, and Dobrizhoffer were expelled along with their order after 1767.

With Ibero-American independence after 1810, more Germans arrived, especially businesspeople, but the antirevolutionist policy of the major European countries united in the the Holy Alliance prevented diplomatic recognition of Argentina by the German states. This delayed the development of profitable relations, while an Argentine government commission actively recruited immigrants in central Europe. In 1826, the first major contingent of 200 Germans arrived after great difficulties. They were assigned to settle Chacarita de los Colegiales, where they founded the first colony at the Rio de la Plata. Caudillo Juan Manuel de Rosas (1829–1832, 1835–1852) discouraged immigration until he was removed from power by a coalition force of Argentine unitarians and federalist dissidents with the help of Brazil, Uruguay, and Paraguay. The Brazilian contingent of the coalition included 250 German veterans of the War of Schleswig-Holstein (referred to as "Brum-

mers"). At times, their military efforts were decisive.

Afterward, Argentina opened its doors to European immigration. Considering Germans model immigrants, Argentina's future president, Domingo Faustino Sarmiento, personally promoted emigration in Germany. After some hesitation, German and Austrian immigration resumed, leaving a lasting impact on Argentine society. However, Argentina attracted immigrants along with natural scientists who explored the flora, fauna, and geography of the country. Naturalist Hermann Burmeister, a disciple of Alexander von Humboldt, traveled through Brazil and Argentina in the 1850s and produced a large number of zoological, paleontological, and botanical studies. During the 1860s, he reorganized the Museo Público in Buenos Aires and established the School of Natural Sciences at the University of Córdoba, for which he recruited many German scholars (e.g., the mineralogist Adolf Stelzner from the famous Freiberg mining academy and the chemist Max Siewert from the University of Halle).

Starting in the 1870s, several waves of immigrants from German-speaking countries arrived in Argentina. They escaped crises in Europe, including the Anti-Socialist Laws, the German Empire's authoritarianism, the results of the Treaty of Versailles that ended World War I, and the Great Depression. They included Germans, Austrians, ethnic Germans from the Balkans and eastern Europe, and citizens from the former German colonies in Africa and the Pacific Islands. Among the immigrants were significant numbers of Teuto-Brazilians who, since the mid-nineteenth century, had been moving westward in search of land. The numerically largest group consisted of Volga Germans, who arrived by way of Brazil. In 1940, about 130,000 Volga Germans lived in the country. Currently, the estimate is 300,000 to 350,000, with 40 percent still speaking German.

During the 1860s and 1870s, the first German newspapers were founded in Buenos Aires. German associations and clubs dominated the social, economic, and religious life in the small German colony of Argentina's capital. Germans founded mutual aid societies, sickness-insurance funds, a hospital, and an orphanage. German schools, singing societies (*Gesangvereine*), gymnastic groups (*Turnvereine*), and cooperatives were established. In 1869, Leopold Böhm founded Argentina's first kindergarten according to the ideas of Friedrich Fröebel. The Socialist association *Vorwärts* (Progress) was created in 1882.

German businesses became interested in economic contacts with Argentina in the last third of the nineteenth century. Siemens and Allgemeine Elektricitäts-Gesellschaft (AEG, General Electricity Company) invested into the electronic industry and quickly occupied a leading position in this sector. The Argentine army restructured itself to model the Prussian German army. German military instructors taught at the War Academy of Argentina. German armaments (Krupp cannons, Mauser rifles, etc.) were imported by the Buenos Aires government. Germany and Argentina entered into a close cooperation in the development of an air force, which continues even today.

Under the presidency of Hipólito Yrigoyen (1916–1922, 1928–1930), who was largely influenced by the Saxon philosopher Karl Christian Friedrich Krause (1781–1832), Argentina remained neutral during World War I. Nevertheless, the British naval blockade prevented trade between Argentina and Germany. After Germany's defeat and because of restrictions imposed on immigration to the United States, Argentina became a preferred country for Germans who wanted to escape the economic and political chaos at home. About 30,000 Germans left for Argentina during the 1920s. They settled mostly in Buenos Aires and the region of Misiones. In 1937 about 10,000 Germans lived in Misiones; by 1941 about 39,000 German-speaking settlers were living in the territory (about 20 percent of the population).

After Germany lost World War I, the German Argentine community was as polarized as the population of the Weimar Republic. The two German newspapers, the liberal *Argentinisches Tageblatt* (Argentine Daily News) and the conservative *Deutsche La Plata Zeitung* (German La Plata Newspaper), were forums for heated debates between left- and right-wing Germans. The Socialist association *Vorwärts* turned even more Marxist, favoring world revolution. Long before 1933, National Socialism divided and polarized the German population of Argentina. While a large number of Germans joined the National Socialist *Volksgemeinschaft* (people's community), a smaller segment was rigorously excluded from this new German community. The immigration of about 30,000 to 40,000 German Jews to Argentina from 1933 to 1939 increased tensions between both camps. In relation to its overall population (13 million in 1931), Argentina accepted per capita more Jewish refugees than any other country in the world besides Palestine. Among the Jewish refugees were many intellectuals, scientists, entrepreneurs, and artists who quickly found places in Argentina's economy and culture. Jewish émigrés aligned themselves with Socialist and liberal Germans to attack the conservative and National Socialist German majority in Argentina. They supported the *Argentinisches Tageblatt* and created new weekly and monthly publications such as *Das andere Deutschland* (The Other Germany) and *Die Jüdische Wochenschau* (The Jewish Weekly). However, the Argentine branch of the National Socialist German Worker's Party (NSDAP) foreign organization possessed, with its 2,000 members, an enormous influence among the German population in the country. It dominated nearly all of the German social, cultural, and religious associations and clubs.

The outbreak of World War II reduced contacts between Argentina and Germany to an absolute minimum. Buenos Aires became the hub of German espionage activities in South America. Several Germans volunteered to be spies for their former home country. Throughout the war, Argentina remained neutral. Argentina was the last country in the world that declared war against Germany on March 27, 1945, after the United States threatened Argentina's exclusion from the United Nations. Afterward, all property of Germans and German organizations in 1945–1946 was confiscated. While the Argentine Germans reorganized their lives after the end of the war, Argentina experienced an enormous influx of German refugees from central Europe. Despite the ban on German emigration imposed by the Allies, about 30,000 to 40,000 German refugees came to Argentina during the presidency of Juan D. Perón (1946–1955). Some of the German scientists, technicians, and armament experts were brought into the country in secret. They quickly found employment in Argentina's armaments industry, where they developed rockets and a jet fighter. At the University of Tucumán alone about thirty German professors were hired during the 1950s. Others found employment in Mendoza, La Plata, and Buenos Aires. The German migration largely contributed to the modernization of Argentina's economy, as well as its sciences.

Post–World War II German migration changed the structure of Argentina's German society tremendously. Among the refugees were about 50 to 100 internationally warranted war criminals such as Adolf Eichmann, Josef Mengele, and Josef Schwammberger. They were in hiding from jurists, journalists, and secret services. Further, Argentina attracted many Germans who wanted to escape the reeducation system in occupied Germany and continued to believe in National Socialism. They founded extreme right-wing journals such as *Der Weg* (The Path) and *La Plata Ruf* (La Plata Call). In 1952 Argentina reestablished diplomatic relations with West Germany, and Perón supported the process by returning confiscated German property. Relations between both countries remained strong despite fallouts over violations of basic human rights during the military dictatorship between 1976 and 1983 and especially during the Falklands War with Great Britain in 1982. On the level of cultural relations, the Institución Cultural Argentino-Germana (German-Argentine Cultural Institution) (founded in 1922) and the Goethe Institut Buenos Aires (founded in 1966) support and further cultural exchange and mutual understanding. Today, there are about eighteen German schools in Argentina. The oldest German school is the Goethe school, which has been in existence for more than 100 years.

After immigration came to an end in the 1950s, assimilation increased. Today, there are still about 250,000 German-speaking people in Argentina.

Holger M. Meding

See also Brummer; Burmeister, Carl Hermann Conrad; Dobrizhoffer, Martin; Eichmann, Karl Adolf; Humboldt, Alexander von; Latin America, German Military Advisers in; Latin America, Nazis in; Schmidel, Ulrich

References and Further Reading
Hoffmann, Werner. "Die Deutschen in Argentinien." *Die Deutschen in Lateinamerika: Schicksal und Leistung*. Ed. Hartmut Fröschle. Tübingen/Basel: Erdmann, 1979, 40–145.
Lütge, Wilhelm, Werner Hoffmann, Karl Wilhelm Körner, and Karl Klingenfuß. *Deutsche in Argentinien, 1520–1980*. Buenos Aires: Alemann SRL, 1981.
Meding, Holger M. *Flucht vor Nürnberg? Deutsche und österreichische Einwanderung in Argentinien, 1945–1955*. Cologne: Böhlau, 1992.
Newton, Ronald C. *The "Nazi Menace" in Argentina, 1931–1945*. Stanford: Stanford University Press, 1992.
Saint Sauveur-Henn, Anne. *Un siècle d'émigration allemande vers l'Argentine, 1853–1945*. Cologne: Böhlau, 1995.
Zago, Manrique, ed. *Presencia alemana en la Argentina—Deutsche Präsenz in Argentinien*. Buenos Aires: Zago, 1992.

ASSIMILATION OF GERMANS IN THE UNITED STATES

During their 300-year history in the United States, Germans were often regarded by other Americans as especially resistant to assimilation, mostly because they maintained separate social enclaves with a visibly different culture. The large complex of institutions of "German America" made them appear clannish and averse to "Americanization." These appearances, however, were deceiving. German Americans were assimilating consistently throughout their history, probably at a rate faster than that of most other immigrant groups. Factors facilitating their assimilation included their frequent upward social mobility, the compatibility of their predominantly middle-class culture with mainstream American life, and their high literacy rate and educational level.

The U.S. Census for the year 2000 revealed that nearly 43 million people, about 15 percent of the total population, acknowledged some German ancestry. Only about 700,000 of them were born in Germany. About 1.4 million people said they spoke the German language. Most of the rest of those claiming German ancestry had little except perhaps a German surname to distinguish them from the rest of American society. The numerous ethnic neighborhoods, clubs, taverns, newspapers, and other institutions that once supported a separate ethnicity had almost entirely disappeared. Save for the most recent immigrants, German Americans as a group had almost completely assimilated.

"Assimilation" may be defined as a process involving interaction between two cultures, wherein the adherents of a minority culture take on the cultural attributes of a mainstream or "host" society and are eventually absorbed into the dominant culture. In the process, distinguishing elements between the two cultures gradually disappear. The process is not a sudden transformation but a gradual passage through a series of stages, with individuals undergoing these changes at differing rates. Seen from the perspective of an immigrant group, the process usually occurs across several generations, with the first generation holding more closely to the culture of the mother country, while their children and subsequent generations move more rapidly toward the dominant culture. The interaction of the two cultures operate both ways; the process of assimilation leaves its mark on the dominant society and culture, which acquire some characteristics of the immigrant culture. Both cultures are transformed, even as one is slowly submerged into the other.

Not long after the eighteenth-century migrations of Germans and soon after the American Revolution, some signs of the processes of assimilation could be discerned. Life in the Pennsylvania German region, with its dense concentrations of Germans and the reinforcing influence of conservative pietistic religions, seemed secure against the forces of cultural change. Nevertheless, another kind of cultural change was taking place: the formation of a distinct Pennsylvania German culture, which continued to evolve and increasingly seemed strange to newcomers from Germany. However, out on the frontiers of the Pennsylvania German region, there were signs as early as 1800 of assimilation into the English-speaking American community. In places like the Shenandoah Valley of Virginia, Germans formed their own close-knit communities in close contact with neighboring English and Scots-Irish settlements. The rise of a commercial agricultural economy in such regions drew all groups into an interdependent economic network, tied to markets as far away as Philadelphia. The diminishing use of the German language in favor of English is one clear sign of the acculturation process. The German-language newspapers in the region were mostly defunct by 1815. About the same time, tensions began to appear over the language used in the German churches. Historians of the Virginia Germans see the period 1820–1840 as one of transition of Germans to the primary use of English. In the Virginia example, there were few newcomers after 1815 arriving in the community to revive German customs and language. As the second and third generations came to dominate, integration into the larger American society speeded up.

In Philadelphia, the city that had the largest urban concentration of Germans at the beginning of the nineteenth century, conflicts arose in the first two decades of the 1800s over the use of the English language in the German churches. The proponents favoring English-language services were typically American-born Germans who had attained some status in the larger community and were comfortable with their acculturation. The opponents tended to be older, first-generation Germans who feared not just the loss of the familiar language but the further acculturation that they believed would follow. By the 1820s the arguments were largely settled, and the growing influence of the younger generations easily prevailed, with the use of German considerably reduced.

The decline of German churches and other social and cultural institutions was partly restrained by the revival of new immigration from the German states beginning in the 1820s. By the 1830s new German societies and churches began to appear in cities along the East Coast and the newly established cities in the Ohio Valley, the Great Lakes, and along the Mississippi. In other places along the eastern seaboard that did not receive as many of the new immigrants, German organizations stagnated or declined as the younger generations became more assimilated. The assimilation process was facilitated in the growing urban industrial areas where interaction among diverse social groups was necessary. Germans were brought more frequently into closer contact with other social groups in their workplaces, their marketplaces, and the political arena. Their affinity to the Democratic Party brought them into an uneasy relationship with the Irish, the other major immigrant group of the day. Political activity at any level outside the immediate ethnic neighborhood became an influence toward acculturation. When second-generation immigrants moved partway through the process of assimilation, their offspring were almost certain to move further.

The 1850s were a period of expansion and change in German America (a term first used during this decade). The massive upsurge in new German immigrants (1848–1853) brought fresh additions of the unassimilated first generation into the major cities and spread them across the plains of the Midwest, now being opened up by the railroads. The decade saw an impressive growth of German institutions of all sorts. The visibility of the Germans and their social organizations, churches, and newspapers inspired fear in some native-born Americans and helped to build a nativist movement to one of its highest levels. Nativists tended to argue that the immigrants, both Irish and German, were too numerous and too resistant to American social and political values to ever become a part of American society.

Such perceptions have led some later historians to argue that the anti-immigrant attack did forge a tighter, more resistant German American social structure as a defensive reaction to nativism. A conclusion drawn from this was that Germans in the United States resisted assimilation and huddled within the fortresses of their churches, clubs, mutual aid societies, and rural communities. This German resistance to acculturation and involvement in the larger society, some historians said, would persist for over half a century, until another anti-German attack at the time of World War I would leave the whole edifice of German America in ruins.

Such interpretations, as many more recent historians have argued, are oversimplifications of the complex workings of the German American community and those within it. The decade that saw the nativist attack also saw the Germans drawn increasingly into the political process, partly of course to combat the nativist-organized American or "Know-Nothing" Party. As in earlier times, the move into active participation in the heterogeneous American political parties was a major step toward assimilation. With the coming of the Civil War, many German young men were drawn into the combat, mostly within the Union army. Although a minority of these served in ethnic militia units, as the war went on Germans found themselves increasingly mixed into units with Americans of other backgrounds. The Civil War on both the military and the home front had a considerable influence upon the assimilation of all immigrants.

The great array of German organizations that flourished during the second half of the nineteenth century also fostered a misconception that they constituted a structure designed to prevent assimilation. It is true that many such organizations presented themselves as havens of German ethnicity, where immigrants could find a comfortable replica of traditions from the old country. Their stated objectives were often those of ethnic preservation and the celebration of German culture. Yet, inevitably, as they welcomed new German immigrants, the German societies also had to assist them in their introduction into American society as a whole. Their efforts to aid the immigrants included helping them to find employment, advising them about issues of naturalization, introducing them to American politics, and, in many cases, giving them instruction in the English language. Thus, while fostering ethnicity, the German organizations also had the necessary alternative purpose of facilitating assimilation.

The structures of German America in its heyday can thus be seen as temporary way stations for the thousands of immigrants who entered the country and passed through in the process of assimilation. German America, its neighborhoods, its rural communities, its churches, and its social organizations appeared to external observers to be unchanging and persistent. They might then conclude that all the people within those structures were steadfastly resisting change. In reality, people moved out of the structures in the assimilation process even as new Germans arrived. The first generation might stay close to their ethnic roots; the second generation might then begin to find the larger society more attractive and move into it; the subsequent generations might have little connection to the visible organizational structures of German America.

The constant erosion of the German population became more noticeable as the formal structures reached their peak and then began to decline. This phenomenon clearly was happening in the 1890s. The numbers of German-born counted in the decennial census rose from 1850 to 1890 and then declined in 1900 and thereafter. In the 1890s, those numbers contained

both the wave of the immigrants from the 1850s and the wave of the 1880s. As new immigration from Germany fell off sharply, there were no longer replacements for the first-generation Germans who were passing away. At the same time, the growing numbers of the younger generations continued assimilating and leaving the comfortable confines of the German ethnic world. During the 1890s German ethnic leaders began to voice concern about the endurance of the German structures. Controversy arose over efforts in some states to limit German-language schools. German newspaper editors, who saw language maintenance as absolutely necessary to preserve their own readership, implored the younger generation to learn German. Some German organizations like the Turner gymnastic societies and mutual savings associations began to open their memberships to non-Germans and to use English as their common language. Both the number of German societies and their individual membership rolls began to decline. The 1890s are a crucial period in the story of German assimilation, not because the process was being accelerated, but because the decline in new immigrants revealed that Germans had been steadily assimilating for most of the century.

Around the turn of the twentieth century, many Germans were already finding their work within the larger community rather than in the German ethnic network. This was in part the result of the large corporations and industries that increasingly dominated the American economy. An even more powerful influence was the rise of mass-market consumerism and a mass popular culture. Advertisers displayed the attractions of the general popular culture, even in the German newspapers. The younger generations particularly felt no guilt about deserting the German theater and riding a streetcar to the popular music halls and vaudeville houses downtown. Increasingly, they spent their Sundays at the amusement park at the end of the trolley line, rather than with their elders in the German beer gardens. Department stores, professional baseball, motion pictures, and eventually the radio were attractive forces of acculturation that the most fervent appeals of German leaders could not overcome. German organizations themselves began to appeal to the mass consumer culture and became "acculturated" themselves. German restaurants and taverns, some becoming tourist attractions, opened their conviviality to all. German neighborhood societies downplayed their Germanness and opened their doors to newer immigrant groups who lived there.

In rural areas, factors at work might delay the assimilation process somewhat, largely due to the relative isolation of Germans there from other cultural groups. Pastors of German churches and other ethnic spokesmen argued for German ethnicity against the inroads of American material culture and the American educational system. Small towns and rural communities might retain their ethnic characters longer; but as the land filled up and opportunities for farms or employment for the younger generation decreased, assimilation was often a by-product of the migration of younger members out of the community. Some might go to a nearby county seat; others found their way to the larger cities. The growing movement of population from the countryside to the cities, a phenomenon of American life generally during the years around the turn of the twentieth century, brought Germans into increasing contact with other ethnic groups and with the new mass culture.

In the first two decades of the twentieth century, there were strong efforts to rally Germans around their institutions and their culture. The best-known representative of this effort was the National German American Alliance, which attempted to gather all German societies under one umbrella organization. The traditional divisions among German Americans prevented the alliance from achieving its goal of full unification of German America. For most of its brief history, it stressed the one element upon which nearly all Germans might agree: opposition to Prohibition, which, it was argued, threatened the very basis of German American social life.

The processes of assimilation and the consequent dwindling of traditional German America were well under way in the period before World War I. While the identification of some with the German Empire may have caused a revival of German ethnicity, the attacks upon German American culture after the United States entered the war dealt an additional blow to the surviving institutions, as well as to all public expressions of German ethnicity. The passage of Prohibition laws dealt another blow to the German social organizations, for which beer was a vital element. Suspicions of the use of the German language led to restrictions on the German-language newspapers and prohibitions on the teaching of German in some places. Overwhelming pressures on all things German doubtless caused many to abandon their already tenuous ties to German ethnicity and hastened their assimilation. An unusual drop in the number of German-born recorded in the census of 1920 suggests that many may have been concealing their German birth from the census taker.

But regardless of the events of the wartime crisis, the demographic factors hastening Germans' assimilation continued relentlessly. Immigration from Germany never again attained the level of the boom of the 1880s. The first-generation immigrants from that era now were being replaced by more numerous second and third generations, who were less eager to assert their German heritage. In the new nativist environment of the 1920s, many Germans hastened to identify themselves as members of the "Nordic" race of northwestern Europeans, praised by the immigration restrictionists as superior to other Europeans. But that position, of course, meant that they had to stress their similarities with the Scandinavians, English, and Irish rather than their own distinctive culture. Given the various attractions of mass popular culture and entertainment that appeared in the Roaring Twenties, Germans saw little reason to spend their leisure time within the old German enclave. Fewer remained in the churches and institutions of the old German neighborhoods as upward social mobility led to geographic mobility, and the younger generations were dispersed more often into neighborhoods of mixed social groups.

World War II did not bring any strong pressures on the German Americans as a group, perhaps a sign that the general society did not perceive any strong ethnic loyalties among them. Some German American leaders hoped that new immigration might revive after the war, but the facts did not fulfill their hopes. The new first-generation immigrants of the postwar era included many women who had married U.S. soldiers in Germany, who were subject to many influences to quickly assimilate, and who raised a second generation with little sense of German ethnicity. Increasingly, many "immigrants" coming to America from Germany were transients representing German businesses or governments. By the end of the twentieth century, the once-impressive German network of ethnic institutions had dwindled to a few vestiges of their former selves, with few others remaining to care about them.

But the two-way process of assimilation also left American culture changed. German Americans influenced American life in many ways, even as they were changed by the United States. The most obvious examples are their foodways and the German words (*kindergarten, sauerkraut*) that became part of the English vocabulary. Many American churches bear the marks of their German foundations. The Germans, followed by other immigrants, helped Americans to change from the somber "Puritan" Sunday observance to the more festive European model. Americans adopted the Christmas holiday (complete with Christmas tree) as it was celebrated among the Germans. Public festivities and observances followed the German model, with family celebrations involving both sexes. German music, both classical and popular, transformed American artistic expression. German gymnastics became the model for American physical culture. Professions such as engineering, pharmacy, and chemistry were influenced by German models. The American educational system was formed in many ways by German influences. And not least, lager beer, so much a part of German life, became a part of American life as well. Much of German culture was now preserved in the context of general American life.

James M. Bergquist

References and Further Reading

Bergquist, James M. "German Americans." *Multiculturalism in the United States: A Comparative Guide to Acculturation and Ethnicity.* Eds. John D. Buenker and Lorman A. Ratner. Westport, CT: Greenwood Press, 1992.

Conzen, Kathleen Neils. "Patterns of German-American History." *Germans in America, Retrospect and Prospect: Tricentennial Lectures Delivered at the German Society of Pennsylvania in 1983.* Ed. Randall M. Miller. Philadelphia: German Society of Pennsylvania, 1984.

———. "German-Americans and the Invention of Ethnicity." *America and the Germans: An Assessment of a Three-Hundred-Year History.* Eds. Frank Trommler and Joseph McVeigh. 2 vols. Philadelphia: University of Pennsylvania Press, 1985, vol. 1: 131–147.

Dobbert, Guido A. *The Disintegration of an Immigrant Community: The Cincinnati Germans, 1870–1920.* New York: Arno Press, 1980.

Gjerde, Jon. *The Minds of the West: Ethnocultural Evolution in the Rural Middle West, 1830–1917.* Chapel Hill: University of North Carolina Press, 1997.

Gordon, Milton M. *Assimilation in American Life: The Role of Race, Religion, and National Origin.* New York: Oxford University Press, 1964.

Kazal, Russell M. "Revisiting Assimilation: The Rise, Fall, and Reappraisal of a Concept in American Ethnic History." *American Historical Review* 100, no. 2 (April 1995): 437–471.

———. *Becoming Old Stock: The Paradox of German-American Identity.* Princeton: Princeton University Press, 2004.

ASSING, OTTILIE
b. February 11, 1811; Hamburg
d. August 12, 1884; Paris, France

German journalist who reported about the United States. Ottilie Assing was a mistress and helpmate to Frederick Douglass and a fiercely independent woman. Her mother Rosa Maria Assing (née Varnhagen) was an educated woman of respectable middle-class background, a teacher, and a poet; her father came from a well-to-do Jewish family. When he took up practice as a physician, he preferred to be baptized as a Lutheran. The two sisters Ottilie and Ludmilla (born 1821) received an excellent education from their mother. Ottilie, an exceptionally intelligent child, grew up in a domestic environment marked by unconventionality, liberal ideas, extensive traveling, and the Jewish culture of her grandparents. When the mother died in 1839 and the father in 1842, the two sisters had to fend for themselves. They moved to Berlin to live with their famous uncle, Karl August Varnhagen von Ense. Ottilie, though enjoying the cultural excitement of the big city, soon clashed with her uncle and her sister, and after an attempted suicide in 1843 moved back to Hamburg. Despite having a small independent income, she was determined to work, earn a livelihood, and experience life to the fullest. She learned to paint and began to publish reviews of literature and the arts. She moved in intellectually interesting circles, expressed her radical ideas freely, and scandalized almost everybody by moving in with a prominent, married Hamburg actor, Jean Baptiste Baison, first as a governess to his children and then as his lover. After he died of typhoid fever in 1848, Assing continued to have an amiable and trusting relationship with his wife. In

1851 she published her first article (on emigration) in the distinguished journal *Morgenblatt für gebildete Leser* (Morning News for Educated Readers). In August 1852 she left Hamburg for the United States. She carried with her the verbal agreement to become the *Morgenblatt's* American correspondent. Over the course of 14 years, until 1865, she wrote 125 articles, explaining and interpreting the United States to her German readers, presenting her own view on politics, the arts, and most importantly, on the "Negro question" and race relations.

During her stay in the United States, Assing wanted to investigate the life of African Americans, having but a vague understanding of race through literature, particularly through Carla Mundt's novel *Aphra Behn*. Assing gave an informative account of her crossing in a column entitled "Transatlantische Briefe" (Transatlantic Letters), published in *Jahreszeiten* (*Seasons,* November 1852). Upon her arrival in New York, she was guided by the information networks catering to immigrants, stayed in a boarding house suggested to her by a friend, and settled into life in New York City. Since she wanted to report truthfully about the United States, she traveled extensively through New England and upstate New York, avoiding "the West," which she found lacking in culture and refinement, and all the while reporting to the *Morgenblatt* about what she experienced.

In the United States of the mid-1850s, she could not help but get immersed in the debate over slavery and abolition. Having decided to learn more about the individual experiences of African American slaves, in the summer of 1856 she met Frederick Douglass. He agreed to let her translate his second autobiography, *My Bondage and My Freedom,* which was then published in 1860 in Germany as *Sklaverei und Freiheit: Autobiographie von Frederick Douglass* (*Slavery and Freedom: The Autobiography of Frederick Douglass*). Working together on this translation project established a relationship that lasted almost thirty years. Assing moved to Hoboken, New Jersey, in the winter of 1856–1857 and rented rooms that could accommodate Douglass's frequent visits, where she lived in a circle of like-minded Freethinkers, Forty-Eighters, and Socialists. Her relationship with Douglass developed amid activities related to the abolitionist and women's rights movement and the household routine of the Douglass family. The children made emotional space for the white woman, but Assing condescendingly ignored Mrs. Douglass, Anna Murray. Ottilie continued to work as translator and teacher and became the authoritative voice on all things "Negroe" for the *Morgenblatt* and her German readers. During the Harper's Ferry raid in October 1859, Assing and her German American friends proved their loyalty by helping Douglass to escape, first to Canada and then to England, from which he returned in March 1860.

During the Civil War, Assing continued to report on the plight of African Americans, and, together with Douglass, analyzed the war from an African American perspective as a struggle of black self-liberation. The political issues that dominated the Reconstruction years affected their relationship but never disrupted it. Assing supported the passage of the Fifteenth Amendment with a vengeance, infuriated by the reluctance of the women's movement, but she was rather dismissive about the Republican maneuverings regarding the end of Reconstruction and the lack of equality and support for the African American population. Meanwhile, Douglass had relocated his household to Washington, D.C., enjoying moderate political recognition for his service to the Republican Party. Assing continued to visit over extensive periods of time and supported him publishing a journal, *The New National Era,* for which she wrote many articles.

In July 1876 Assing returned to Europe: she visited her literary and financially successful sister in Florence, traveled extensively in Italy, and went to see friends in Germany. In September 1877 she returned to a rather unstable personal and emotional situation. Helen Pitts had entered the Douglass household. When Assing's sister died in March 1880, leaving her personal estate in disarray, another trip to Europe was inevitable. Assing departed again in the summer of 1881, unknowingly for the last time. Throughout the following years she lived in Italy. In 1882 Anna Murray died, and in 1884 Douglass married Helen Pitts. Six month later, on August 12, 1884, Assing was found dead in Paris; she had poisoned herself. It was said that she had been diagnosed with incurable cancer. Douglass, who was bequeathed a monthly income during his lifetime, did not seem to reflect on whether her suicide had anything to do with him.

Christiane Harzig

See also Forty-Eighters; Slavery in German American and German Texts
References and Further Reading
Diedrich, Maria. *Love across Color Lines: Ottilie Assing and Frederick Douglass.* New York: Hill and Wang, 1999.
Lohmann, Christoph. *Radical Passion: Ottilie Assing's Reports from America and Letters to Frederick Douglass.* New York: Peter Lang, 1999.

ASTOR, JOHN JACOB
b. July 17, 1763; Walldorf, Palatinate
d. March 29, 1848; New York, New York

German American fur trader, merchant, and real estate owner in New York City who, in the early nineteenth century, accumulated fabulous wealth and became the first U.S. multimillionaire.

John Jacob Astor was the fifth child of a poor butcher who was also named John Jacob Astor and his first wife Maria Magdalena vom Berg in the small village of Walldorf, near Heidelberg. At an early age, he saw no other chance but emigrating to the United States in order to climb up the social ladder. He followed in the footsteps of his two older brothers, George and Henry. First, he made his way to London, where he and his brother George founded a store for selling and constructing musical instruments. Right after the Treaty of Paris (1783) between the United States and Great Britain that ended the American Revolution, he moved on to New York City.

As the legend goes, Astor received the idea to trade furs onboard the *North Carolina* during the time the ship lay frozen in Chesapeake Bay, near Baltimore, from a mysterious fur trader of German descent. On March 24 or 25, 1784, Astor arrived in Baltimore. Finally he made his way to New York City in the spring of 1784. There, he met his brother Henry, who had come to North America as a Hessian soldier during the American Revolution. His brother helped him to find a job in the New World.

At first, Astor served as a delivery boy for a German baker. After a while he had earned enough money to found his own store. He traded in German toys, wooden flutes, and other instruments imported

John Astor's first trip for furs. The begining of a great fortune—John Jacob Astor buying furs in western New York. Undated illustration. (Bettmann/Corbis)

from his brother in London. However, his biggest business was the fur trade. As a young immigrant, he walked through the rough wilderness of New York, New Jersey, and Pennsylvania and along the Hudson River valley to Canada to trade furs, following old Native American trails. He bought the furs from Indians, trappers, and Canadian fur traders and on the biggest fur market on the American continent of that time, Montreal. Since he was not allowed to import his furs directly to the United States due to British law, he had to send them to London and from there to New York. The Jay Treaty of 1794 facilitated Astor's import business. As a result of this treaty, it became possible for Astor to import furs directly from Montreal to New York. This improved his business as well as his profits.

Although Astor became a famous fur trader around the turn of the nineteenth century, the major fur trade remained in the hands of two mighty Canadian fur companies: the North West Company and the Hudson's Bay Company. With the encouragement of President Thomas Jefferson and Albert Gallatin, the secretary of the treasury, Astor founded the American Fur Company in 1808 to harness control of the fur trade within the U.S. territory. He established trading outposts from St. Louis to the Rocky Mountains. In 1810 Astor engaged in some new endeavors. He dispatched two expeditions to the Pacific Ocean, one of which was to go overland, winning the confidence of the Indians and exploring locations for new trading posts, while the other was to go by sea around Cape Horn with a full cargo of all supplies needed for the establishment of the settlement on the Columbia River, later known as Astoria. But Astor's plans failed, and he lost his outpost in the War of 1812 to England. Nevertheless, he continued his businesses in fur trade and real estate, as well as in other fields. He bought low-priced farmland outside of New York City, which increased greatly in value and became part of the city of New York during Astor's lifetime, making it expensive real estate. This business became the source of most of his wealth. After three long voyages to Europe, Astor retired from the fur trade in 1834.

After his last trip to Europe and the death of his wife Sarah, he tore down his former residence on Broadway to build a hotel. This building, named the Astor House, opened in 1836 as the finest hotel in the United States. Many statesmen and famous people stayed in the Astor House during their sojourn in New York. At the end of the nineteenth century, two of Astor's descendents used the popularity of the early Astor hotels to build the famous Waldorf-Astoria Hotel in New York.

Astor became an important economic factor for the young republic because he engaged in many fields of business. As the director of the Hudson & Mohawk Railroad Company, he was involved in establishing the New York State railroad; he owned the Park Theater on Broadway—one of the leading theaters of New York; he lent money to important politicians as well as to other citizens of New York; and he was one of the driving powers behind the upcoming China trade following the example of the American trading vessel, *The Empress of China,* in 1784. Furthermore, Astor was one of the financial investors of the War of 1812. Together with other businessmen he persuaded the government to establish the Second Bank of the United States. Astor's funds not only provided the financial foundation of the bank, but Astor himself was appointed by the James Madison administration to be one of the bank's directors. In his last years Astor lived the life of a patron of culture. He encouraged Washington Ir-

ving to write his novel *Astoria* based on the events that happened to the outpost on the Columbia River during the years 1808–1814. He hired the well-known poet Fitz-Greene Halleck, who lived with the multimillionaire on Astor's domicile Hell Gate, as his personal secretary. Furthermore, he supported the famous ornithologist John James Audubon, the well-known writer Edgar Allan Poe, and the political career of Henry Clay. During the years 1837–1840 he was the president of the German Society of New York City and donated a large sum to it every year to facilitate the adjustment of German immigrants to life in New York City.

When he died, Astor left a fortune of $20 million. In his last will he gave orders to build the Astor Library, which at the end of the nineteenth century was combined with two other libraries to form the New York Public Library. Furthermore, he reserved $50,000 to build a poorhouse in his home village, Walldorf. Astor was the first to live the American dream and to advance from a dishwasher to a millionaire.

Alexander Emmerich

See also German Society of the City of New York; Hessians; New York City

References and Further Reading

Emmerich, Alexander W. *The American Dream Made in Germany: The Life of John Jacob Astor.* Forthcoming, 2005.

Haeger, John D. *John Jacob Astor: Business and Finance in the Early Republic.* Detroit: Wayne State University Press, 1991.

Horn, Wilhelm O. von. *Johann Jakob Astor: Ein Lebensbild aus dem Volke für das Volk und seine Jugend.* Wiesbaden: Verlag von Kreisel und Riedner, 1854.

Parton, James. *Famous Americans of Recent Times.* Boston: Ticknor and Fields, 1867.

Porter, Kenneth W. *John Jacob Astor: Business Man.* 2 vols. New York: Harvard University Press, 1931.

AUFBAU (CONSTRUCTION)

A German Jewish periodical published in New York City that gained considerable influence and standing in the years before and after World War II. The *Aufbau* was founded in New York in 1934 by the German Jewish Club, an association that was soon renamed New World Club. In the first years of its existence the *Aufbau* was merely the club's monthly newsletter; its primary purpose was to provide valuable information and tips to the growing community of Jewish refugees (some 85,000 German Jews immigrated to the United States from 1933 onward). Manfred George's nomination as the new editor in early 1939 revolutionized the *Aufbau* and turned it into one of the leading anti-Nazi publications of the German press in exile (*Exilpresse*). George—a well-known left-wing journalist in the Weimar Republic—turned the monthly into a weekly and managed, within the first five years, to increase its circulation from 8,000 to 40,000. This new *Aufbau* was not exclusively Jewish: quite a few of its contributors were not Jewish, and so was also approximately a fourth of the readership. It became a mouthpiece of the central European émigrés, "the diary of us all," as exiled author Hans Habe put it. During World War II the *Aufbau* enjoyed the regular contributions of the brightest exiled intellectuals, including Hanna Arendt, Siegfried Aufhäuser, Julius Bab, Kurt Kersten, Kurt Pinthus, Heinz Pol, and Alfred Polgar. Occasional contributors in those years included novelists Thomas Mann, Lion Feuchtwanger, Fritz von Unruh, Oskar Maria Graf, Franz Werfel, and Carl Zuckmayer. Some of them also served on the *Aufbau*'s advisory board, which was founded in 1941.

Exiled intellectuals from the Third Reich conducted ongoing debates about the German past, present, and future and about the nature of Adolf Hitler's Germany. In these debates between German exiles scattered all over the world—from Moscow to London and from Palestine to Argentina—the New York *Aufbau* was a key participant. And yet the *Aufbau* differed from most publications in two regards: first, it never conceived of itself as the periodical of transient exiles but rather of new Americans and thus was categorical in endorsing thorough Americanization. Second, it remained an essentially Jewish publication and dealt extensively with Jewish matters. Confronting the Nazi persecution of Jews in their old homeland, the *Aufbau* contributors reevaluated not only German history but also the traditional integrationist (or rather assimilatory) path of central European Jewry. The *Aufbau* (whose contributors were originally non-Zionist for the most part) developed an undeviating pro-Israeli standpoint following the establishment of the state of Israel in 1948. The *Aufbau,* however, expressed not only an unequivocal Jewish identity and a deep responsibility for the Jewish cause but also a distinct German cultural identity. One of the most remarkable aspects of its story is the fact that it did not perish with the generation of its founders but continues to this very day (2003). Nowadays it is written for and by the post–World War II generation. It focuses on five major topics—politics, Jewish life, Jewish history, culture, and the German Jewish heritage—and its content appears half in English, half in German.

Adi Gordon

See also Americanization; Ben W. Huebsch et al. and the Viking Press Imprint; Council for a Democratic Germany; Intellectual Exile; Mann, Thomas; Zuckmayer, Carl

References and Further Reading

Bauer-Hack, Susanne. *Die jüdische Wochenzeitung Aufbau und die Wiedergutmachung.* Düsseldorf: Droste, 1994.

Schaber, Will, and Gert Niers. *Aufbau 50 Years, 1934–1984: Eine Ausstellung des Aufbau unter Mitwirkung des Instituts für Zeitungsforschung der Stadt Dortmund.* New York: Verlag des Aufbau, 1984.

Steinitz, Hans. *Der Aufbau: Eine Berliner Zeitung für Deutsche in den USA.* Berlin: Presse- und Informationsdienst des Landes Berlin, 1989.

AVÉ-LALLEMANT, ROBERT CHRISTIAN BERTHOLD

b. July 25, 1812; Lübeck, Holstein
d. October 10, 1884; Lübeck

German physician who spent extensive time in Brazil as a doctor and an explorer. Having graduated from medical school at the University of Kiel in 1837, Robert Avé-Lallemant immigrated to Brazil, where he worked as a doctor for nearly seventeen years. During this time, he quickly advanced to becoming the head of the Yellow Fever Hospital and later was appointed a member of the Highest Health Council of the country. In 1855, Avé-Lallemant returned to Kiel, where he applied for the position of ship's doctor aboard the Austrian vessel *Novara,* which was scheduled to embark on the circumnavigation of the globe. Since Alexander von Humboldt supported his application, Avé-Lallemant was chosen as a member of the crew, which left Kiel on April 30,

1857. This expedition was under the command of Bernhard Freiherr von Wüllerstorf-Urbair and included such eminent explorers as the natural scientist Karl Ritter von Scherzer and the geologist Ferdinand von Hochstetter. The scientific goal of this expedition was the exploration of the islands in the Pacific and in the Indian Ocean. However, the Austrian team's circumnavigation of the world was also to serve their home country's ambitions to be regarded as a world power. Initially enthusiastic about this endeavor, Avé-Lallemant soon had doubts about his decision to join the *Novara.* When the ship arrived at Madeira, he filed his request to be relieved. After successfully crossing the Atlantic, Avé-Lallemant left the expedition and returned to Brazil. Early in 1858 he embarked on a research voyage to the southern provinces of Brazil Rio Grande do Sul, Santa Catharina, Paraná, and São Paulo, where he visited the German settlements and observed the social and economic hardships suffered by its colonists. It was on this trip that he found Aimé Bonpland, the French botanist and long-lost traveling companion of Alexander von Humboldt, in a primitive shack in Corrientes at the Rio Uruguay. Bonpland died shortly after on May 4, 1858.

After Avé-Lallemant returned to Rio de Janeiro, he turned his attention toward the northeastern portion of the country. He went on to explore the coastal provinces of Bahia, Pernambuco, Alagoas, and Sergipe as well as the Amazon to Tabatinga. In October 1859 he returned to Lübeck, where, in addition to working as a doctor, he began writing. In his two-volume *Reise durch Süd-Brasilien im Jahre 1858* (Travels through South Brazil in

1858, published in 1859) and his two-volume *Reise durch Nord-Brasilien im Jahre 1859* (Travels through North Brazil in 1859, published in 1860), Avé-Lallemant descried his exhausting and sometimes life-threatening explorations in detail.

Heinz Peter Brogiato

See also Humboldt, Alexander von; Von-der-Heydt'sches Reskript

References and Further Reading

Ahlers, Olof. "Avé-Lallemant, Robert Christian Berthold." *Neue Deutsche Biographie.* Berlin: Duncker and Humblot, 1953, 1: 465–466.

Hantzsch, Viktor. "Avé-Lallemant, Robert Christian Berthold." *Allgemeine Deutsche Biographie.* Leipzig: Duncker and Humblot, 1902, 46: 144–146.

Henze, Dietmar. *Enzyklopädie der Entdecker und Erforscher der Erde.* Graz: Akademische Druck- und Verlagsanstalt, 1978, 1: 116.

B

BAEGERT, CHRISTOPH JOHANNES JAKOB

b. December 22, 1717; Schlettstadt, Alsace
d. September 29, 1772; Neustadt an der Weinstraße, Palatinate

German Jesuit who traveled to lower California and studied the lives of the native tribes.

Jakob Baegert became a member of the Societas Jesu (Jesuits) in 1736, studied theology, and entered the priesthood. In 1751, he traveled to lower California in order to work as a missionary in San Luis Gonzaga. During the years of his missionary work, Baegert engaged in cultural, ethnographic, and linguistic studies of the native societies in North and Central America. When the Jesuits were forced to leave Mexico in 1767, Baegert returned to his home via Spain. Summarizing his American experiences, Baegert published anonymously in 1772 his *Nachrichten von der amerikanischen Halbinsel Californien mit einem zweyfachen Anhang falscher Nachrichten* (the English translation was published under the title *Observations in Lower California* in 1863–1864). In this book, Baegert analyzed and criticized the writings of other authors, especially the work of his fellow Jesuit Miguel Venegas, who had published his account on California in 1757 in Spanish. The *Nachrichten* was divided into three parts: in part 1, Baegert described the natural conditions of the peninsula; part 2 was dedicated to the living conditions and customs of the native people; and part 3 dealt with the history of the Jesuit mission in this area. In the appendix, Baegert refuted the wrong assumptions of other authors. He presented California as a land lacking sufficient precipitation or vegetation and considered the landscape to be entirely worthless in economic terms. In the second part, Baegert described with open sympathy and envy the simple and uncivilized lifestyle of the natives: their nomadic lifestyle, small and dispersed tribes, customs and traditions, family structures, and language (Guaicura), which he was the first to put into writing. In his concluding part, Baegert detailed the hard life, full of deprivation and sacrifices, of the Jesuits. This part was clearly intended to diminish any prejudgments and stereotypes about the Jesuits. With his *Nachrichten,* Baegert provided the first scholarly introduction to lower California's culture and people.

Heinz Peter Brogiato

See also Mexico, German Jesuits in
References and Further Reading
Dunne, Peter Masten. "Baegert Pictures a
    Lower California Mission." *Mid-America:
    An Historical Review* 30 (1948): 44–65.
Oehme, Ruthardt. "Baegert (Begert),
    Christoph Johannes Jakob." *Neue Deutsche
    Biographie.* Berlin: Duncker and Humblot,
    1953, 1: 517.
Schaefer, Ursula. "Father Baegert and His
    Nachrichten." *Mid-America: An Historical
    Review* 20 (1938): 151–163.

BANANAS AND PINEAPPLES

Nowadays fruits from the Americas are part of the daily diet in Germany. Explorers such as Christopher Columbus brought home descriptions and drawings of an until then unknown variety of edible and colorful fruits. Although the most popular of them, pineapples and bananas, do not have their botanical origin in the New World, it was American enterprises that made them affordable and available in Germany by commercializing and industrializing production in their homelands. Today more bananas are eaten in Germany than in any other European country. Nearly a fourth of all European banana imports go from Central and South America via U.S. enterprises to Germany. Though bananas have been known in Europe since the late fifteenth century, it was not until the beginning of the twentieth century that fresh bananas from the Americas were regularly imported. The precondition for this change was the development of new cooling technologies, which made it possible to transport the delicate fruit over long distances. Beginning in the 1950s, bananas became one of the most important fruits in the Federal Republic of Germany (FRG), but,

their import to the German Democratic Republic (GDR) was limited. There the banana became a symbol for material well-being. The same was true for pineapples, which had been an element of conspicuous consumption since the late eighteenth century. In contrast to bananas, nobles and the wealthy grew pineapples in hothouses or bought the expensive fruit from gardeners. Fresh pineapples had been imported since the beginning of the twentieth century, but they gained popularity only after World War II, when large quantities of canned fruit appeared on the market for modest prices.

Bananas are one of the oldest cultivated plants on earth. Since they are very fertile and grow fast in tropical climates, they spread rapidly throughout the New World—so rapidly that European explorers and chroniclers thought that they were an American fruit. Originally bananas came from Southeast Asia and were brought to the Canary Islands in 1402. The Portuguese missionary and later bishop Tomás de Berlanga planned to make them the people's food, so he took some plants with him on his travels to the Caribbean Islands in 1512. From there bananas were transplanted to Central America. Alexander von Humboldt saw banana trees on his journeys to the New World and calculated that it would be possible to nourish twenty times as many people with bananas grown on a given piece of land than with wheat. Thus, he prophesied that bananas would gain great importance. He marveled at the enormous fertility of the plant and its sweet fruit; though he was not the first to do so, as the Koran speaks of the "paradise tree." The famous botanist Carl von Linné thus classified the plant as *Musa paradisi-*

aca, and during the nineteenth century Germans spoke of "Paradiesfeigen" (paradise figs) instead of bananas. German botanists were familiar with banana plants, their numerous varieties, and different purposes as early as 1850. They had grown numerous varieties in botanical gardens. But due to the cold climate of Germany, the plants never produced fruit, and so bananas were almost unknown before being imported.

Throughout the nineteenth century, English merchants imported smaller quantities of bananas from the Canary Islands to Germany through the large harbors in Bremen and Hamburg. However, around 1900 bananas were still so uncommon that they rotted on the docks because nobody was interested in buying them. Nevertheless, regular imports began around that time, and in 1907 official statistics on the import of bananas began. They show that the import of the fruit to Hamburg was already at 7 million kilograms (15,400,000 lbs) in 1907 and multiplied to 45 million kilograms in 1913. Most of these bananas came, however, from the Canary Islands. Over the years the market share of the United Fruit Company increased, and Germans bought more and more bananas from Central and South America. The invention of cooling techniques and the discovery of methods to control the ripening process were preconditions for long-distance mass transport. The first modern cooling ship, named "Venus," was launched in 1903. From 1910 to 1913 the imports of bananas to Germany nearly doubled, while bananas and banana products were heavily promoted as health foods, especially for children. Pediatricians were eager to advertise their high nutrition content, digestibility,

Bananas ripen in a radio tower, West Berlin, 1956. Today more bananas are eaten in Germany than in any other European country. Nearly a fourth of all European banana imports go from Central and South America via U.S. enterprises to Germany. (Deutsches Historisches Museum, Berlin)

and sweet taste. Since vitamins had become the new food paradigm in the 1920s, the banana's content of Vitamins C and D helped to make it even more popular. During the 1920s German imports of bananas from Spain and the Canary Islands fell from 24 percent to 9 percent (1927), whereas the share of imports from Cuba, Jamaica, Honduras, Colombia, Costa Rica, Guatemala, and Panama increased to over 75 percent.

With the Nazi seizure of power, imports of bananas decreased tremendously. Advertisement for bananas was forbidden, and doctors were asked not to promote them anymore. This policy was backed by the nutritional advice that bananas were not as healthy as previously thought. Nevertheless, 146,800 tons were still imported in 1937. World War II brought further restrictions, and bananas disappeared from the German market. But after the end of the war, Germans longed for bananas and welcomed the first import of 900 tons of bananas in 1949 with great enthusiasm. In 1949 around 50,000 tons were imported, and it is worth noting that the relatively modest price of bananas (1.20 to 0.80 DM per kilogram) was part of their success. Bananas became a symbol of West Germany's new economic power and the first postwar chancellor, Konrad Adenauer, took care that they remained affordable. In 1957 he pushed through a law negating the European Economic Community (EWG) policy that required Germany, like the other European countries, to pay a 20 percent import tax on bananas.

During the 1970s the consumption of bananas was at 10 kilograms per person, the highest consumption rate worldwide. Most of these bananas arrived from South and Central America. The year 1993 marked a milestone in German banana consumption, when the tax exception established under Adenauer was abolished. Since then the European Community has limited the imports of bananas and has subsidized imports from countries bound to the European Community, mostly former colonies of France and Great Britain.

Another landmark in the recent German history of banana consumption is the year 1989. Bananas had been rare in the GDR because the imports, coming mainly from Ecuador, were limited due to lack of convertible currency. Before Christmas and Easter extra contingents were sold, and kindergartens and hospitals were given preference. But per capita consumption amounted to only 3.9 kilograms in 1989, whereas West Germans consumed 13.5 kilograms. Indeed, bananas were a rarity in the former GDR and were sought after as a symbol of economic well-being. In fact, bananas were sold out for months after the fall of the Berlin Wall. East Germans came to West Germany and bought whole boxes because they did not believe that they would be on sale the next day. Consumption rose to 27 kilograms per person in the East immediately after November 1989, whereas West Germans ate only 16 kilograms per person that year. Today the consumption of bananas in East Germany is 20 percent higher than in West Germany.

The pineapple is another fruit that has a special place in the history of the agricultural exchange between the Americas and Germany. According to the diary of Christopher Columbus, pineapples were grown in Guadelupe, on the coast of Panama, and in the delta of the Amazonas River. They were used to provision ships. The Spaniards spread their cultivation across the Pacific to the Philippines and from there to China and the Portuguese from Brazil to Africa and India. Pineapples became rather well known in Europe and were esteemed as the queen of fruit. Unlike bananas, pineapples were often depicted in paintings, and there was a tradition of sculpting goblets in the shape of pineapples from the seventeenth century onward. In 1711 gardeners supposedly managed to grow the first pineapple in the hothouse of the botanical garden in Leipzig, and in 1715 a doctor from Breslau reportedly harvested a fully mature fruit, which he then sent to the emperor's court as a present.

Like bananas, pineapples are available in numerous botanic variations, but the consumer receives only those that are suited for transport and storage and have certain qualities of taste. Since about

1850, pineapples grown for sale have come from Hawaii, Cuba, Puerto Rico, Haiti, Malaysia, Honduras, Costa Rica, and the British Indies. There have been attempts to grow them in nontropical areas, such as Florida. Transportation was hazardous because unlike bananas, pineapples do not ripen after harvesting. Before World War II, fresh pineapples were imported only from Portugal. Thus, the widespread consumption of pineapples in modern-day Germany is linked to the improvement of transportation and to the invention of industrial canning, which started around the 1890s. Two U.S. enterprises, Dole and Del Monte (California Packing Corporation), built a pineapple empire with their own plantations and their own canning factories.

Before World War II, the canning of pineapples was restricted to the colonies. Hawaii served the needs of the United States; Formosa the needs of Japan; and Malaysia the needs of England. But still, pineapples were a luxury, although a fashionable one. In 1911–1913, Germany imported 280,000 kilograms of (fresh) pineapples (in contrast to 37 million kilograms of bananas). By 1928, that number had increased to 9.8 million kilograms, but by 1930, it went down to 6.5 million kilograms. The Nazis abandoned pineapples for the same reasons they reduced the import of bananas. Directly after World War II the quantity increased again, mainly due to an intensification of commercial relations with the United States and to the improvement of canning. German writers have often described the arrival of the tinned pineapple as a sign of the German *Wirtschaftswunder* (economic miracle), marking the shift toward exotic food,

dishes, and preparations, like Toast Hawaii and pineapple Bowle.

Ulrike Thoms

See also Americanization; Humboldt, Alexander von; McDonald's Restaurant
References and Further Reading
Brunner, Ursula, and Rudi Pfeifer. *Zum Beispiel Bananen*. Göttingen: Lamuv, 1993.
Cadot, Olivier Emmanuel, and Douglas Webber. *Banana Splits and Slipping over Banana Skins: The European and Transatlantic Politics of Bananas*. San Domenico, FI: European University Institut, 2001.
Reichart, Thomas. *Die Ananas: Ein neues Wirtschaftsgut?* Nürnberg: Wirtschafts- u. Sozialgeographisches Institut der Friedrich-Alexander-Universität, 1982.
Ritter, Kurt, and Martin Guttfeld. *Weltproduktion und Welthandel an frischen Südfrüchten*. Berlin: Parey, 1933.
Toppel, Johannes. *Die Banane: Eine wirtschaftsgeographische Monographie, ihre Geschichte, Anbaubedingungen und Verwertung sowie der Produktionsländer, des Imports, Handels und Verbrauches*. Berlin-Steglitz: Bodenbender, 1934.
Tschoeke, Jutta. "Die Banane—ein neues Volksnahrungsmittel im 20. Jahrhundert." *Industriekultur: Expeditionen ins Alltägliche: Begleitheft zur Ausstellung*. Nürnberg, 1982, 98–102.

BANCROFT, GEORGE
b. October 3, 1800; Worcester, Massachusetts
d. January 17, 1891; Washington, D.C.

Father of American history who received his university education at the University of Göttingen and who was appointed minister to the Kingdom of Prussia/German Empire from 1867 to 1874.

His father, Aaron Bancroft, a Unitarian minister, had fought in the Revolutionary War and later wrote a popular and often reprinted *Life of Washington* (1807). His mother, Lucretia Chandler, was born on Gardiner's Island, across from New London, Connecticut. This family could trace their ancestry back to Puritans who had come to New England in 1652. Bancroft initially embraced this heritage by "prepping" at Phillips Exeter Academy, and entering Harvard at age thirteen. After graduating from Harvard in 1817, he went on to study for a divinity degree, and money was raised to send him to the University of Göttingen, where he studied theology, languages (Arabic, Hebrew, and Aramaic Greek), the antiquities of Greece and Rome, and a survey of Greek philosophy from 1818 to 1820. He took an MA and earned a PhD. This was the start of his lifelong dedication to academic work. He selected history as a special area for study under August Heeren, his philosophy professor, and learned the idea of scientific history, based upon primary sources and unified in focus. Although his university training was not different from that of the handful of earlier American students, Bancroft distinguished his education in that he created a context by visiting leading European intellectuals. From 1821 to 1822 he toured Europe and met Friedrich Daniel Ernst Schleiermacher and Georg Friedrich Wilhelm Hegel in Berlin; Johann Wolfgang von Goethe in Weimar; Alexander von Humboldt, Marquis de Lafayette, Albert Gallatin, and Washington Irving in Paris; and Lord Byron in Italy.

Upon his return to Worcester, Bancroft experimented in applying this training to a career. He spent a year tutoring students at Harvard, presenting guest sermons and exploring the life of a minister. In the end, he decided against becoming a minister and shifted over to a teaching career. Bancroft took over a private school but eventually gave up teaching. His translation of Heeren's *The Politics of Ancient Greece* (1824) into English indicated his high level of proficiency in German. In 1827, he married Sarah Dwight in Boston (she died in 1837; Elizabeth Bliss was his second wife, from 1838 to 1886) and became involved in politics. In 1830, he was elected to the Massachusetts General Court (the legislature), but he refused to serve. About this time he began researching the colonial period and frequently published historically oriented but politically focused articles in the *North American Review.*

He received popular success and critical acclaim with the 1834 publication of the first volume of his *History of the United States from the Discovery of the American Continent.* Using abundant footnotes and foreign sources, he perfected a polished style of narrative synthesis, which soon won him the title of Father of American History. He succeeded in applying the German idea of scientific history and combined it with the "hidden" influence of Teutonic folkways on the English settlement of the eastern coast of North America. He created elaborate vignettes of individuals that showed their own viewpoint but also incorporated moral judgments from the enlightened view of the 1830s. Bancroft placed a highly normative value upon the "progress" of colonization while dealing with slavery as part of Western civilization. His working assumption was that the importance of an individual's character, for both villains and heroes, rested upon free will, responsibility, and culpability. Bancroft utilized the New England clerical tradition by always looking for the role of Providence in causing historical change.

From his German university training, Bancroft believed that history was an empirical science because it was based upon exact observation of facts. These "facts" created an explanation of causation, and since general laws were assumed to exist, history was based upon truth that was harmonious, just, and permanent. Bancroft fused this historical understanding with the Transcendental belief in God's Providence overruling individual mistakes. Moreover, events were organically connected to earlier decisions so the proto-democratic institutions of colonial America resembled the earlier Teutonic folkways and included personal freedom, a free press, and popular sovereignty. American independence from the British Empire followed the ultimate criteria: acceptance of the "common mind," moderation, activity, and lack of ambition. It is not surprising that Leopold von Ranke praised Bancroft's work as the best history ever written from the democratic point of view.

Bancroft financed his multivolume series of books (10 volumes, 1834–1874) through his career as a politician. He was named to the lucrative patronage post of collector of the Port of Boston for the years 1838 to 1840. The writing of his major work therefore paralleled his political career—there was a twelve-year hiatus, from 1840 to 1852, before other volumes appeared. During this time he was defeated as the Democratic candidate for the governor of Massachusetts in 1844 but was named secretary of the navy (1845–1846) and helped to establish the Naval Academy. When he was named U. S. minister to Great Britain (1846–1849), Bancroft spent this time assiduously collecting primary documents not only in London but also in Paris and Madrid. This research appeared in volumes 4, 5, and 6 in the decade of the 1850s, but volume 7 (1858) contained no citations at all! Volume 8 came out just before the beginning of the Civil War.

Bancroft became a War Democrat who abhorred slavery but still remained true to the party of Andrew Jackson. After the assassination of Abraham Lincoln, Bancroft wrote the speech that Vice President Andrew Johnson delivered, and Bancroft was eventually appointed U.S. minister to the Kingdom of Prussia in 1867. The next seven years that he spent in Berlin were the happiest of his entire career. His early friendship with German scholars provided a sense of homecoming to his appointment, and he was received like an honorary German American. He became intimate friends with German politicians such as Otto von Bismark and Helmut von Moltke; at the same time he was on equal footing with the historians Theodor Mommsen and Leopold von Ranke. He celebrated his fiftieth anniversary of receiving his doctorate from the University of Göttingen at an impressive *Jubilaeum* at the university and received an honorary LLD. Bancroft also was accepted into the *Mittwochs-Gesellschaft für Wissenschaftliche Unterhaltung*, which was limited to sixteen living intellectuals. In 1868 he received diplomatic status by the North German Confederation, and became involved in the issue of naturalization. He negotiated treaties with the kingdoms, duchies, and free cities of the confederation. This led to the first international recognition of the principle of the right of expatriation for emigrants (Bancroft Treaty).

Upon returning to the United States in 1874, he retired from public life to devote himself to historical research. He had scoured the Prussian archives and used his ambassador post as a basis for securing primary documents from throughout Europe. He busied himself with using primary documents to complete volume 10, the final one in the set, and then revising the ten into six volumes for a Centennial Edition in 1876, "The Author's Last Revision." In this edition he corrected mistakes, added new information, and made stylistic elisions. Bancroft accepted the presidency of the fledgling American Historical Association in 1886 and remained active up to the few months preceding his death. With his death, most academics felt that the last truly national figure had died.

William Roba

See also American Students at German Universities; *Encyclopaedia Americana;* Everett, Edward; German Unification (1871); Göttingen, University of; Humboldt, Alexander von; Transcendentalism

References and Further Reading

Howe, M. A. de Wolfe. *The Life and Letters of George Bancroft.* 2 vols. Port Washington, NY: Kennikat Press, 1908.

Nye, Russell B. *George Bancroft: Brahmin Rebel.* New York: A. A. Knopf, 1944.

BARBIE, KLAUS

b. October 25, 1913; Bad Godesberg (Rhineland), Prussia
d. September 25, 1991; Lyon, France

Klaus Barbie was instrumental in the torture and deaths of thousands of French Resistance members and the deportation of thousands of Jews during World War II.

After the end of the war, he was protected by the British and American occupiers. He escaped later to South America.

After he had attended the Friedrich Wilhelm Institute, Barbie joined the Schutzstaffel (SS) in 1933 and became a member of the National Socialist German Worker's Party (NSDAP) in 1937. His sadistic personality reveled in his power as a Gestapo agent. Barbie served as an intelligence officer for Jewish affairs.

In May 1941 Barbie was posted to Amsterdam, where he took charge of putting down the February strike in 1941 by sealing off the Jewish quarter. He is responsible for the deportation of hundreds of Jewish children who were sent to the Buchenwald concentration camp and later transferred to Mauthausen, where they were worked to death in its stone quarry. Barbie was transferred to Lyon in May 1942 and became head of the local Gestapo, where his role was to extinguish the Resistance. He personally tortured men, women, and children—whoever was deemed an enemy of the Reich. Barbie was responsible for the death of Jean Moulin, a leading member of the French Resistance, whom he personally tortured. For his brutality Barbie became quickly known as the Butcher of Lyon. He was involved directly and indirectly in the deportation of over 7,000 people, more than 400 murders, and the arrests of over 14,000 Resistance fighters in Lyon.

After World War II ended, Barbie returned to Germany. The English employed him as an expert in police matters until 1947. He then enjoyed protection and employment from the U.S. Army's Counter Intelligence Corps. He was useful because he could easily penetrate the

Communist Party cells springing up throughout Germany. The U.S. government protected Barbie until 1955, despite the fact that the Military Tribunal of Lyon sentenced Barbie to death in absentia in 1952 and 1954 for war crimes. The Americans refused to extradite him to France and instead created a false identity for him using the name of Klaus Altmann. They sent Barbie and his family to Bolivia, where he became a citizen in 1957. Barbie became a businessman who moonlighted in police investigations for Bolivia's dictators.

In 1971 the Nazi hunters Serge and Beate Klarsfeld found Barbie in La Paz using the name of Klaus Altmann. However, the Bolivian government would not allow Barbie's deportation. He moved to Peru to hide from the Klarsfelds, but in doing so he lost his protection and was extradited to France on January 18, 1983. It took four years of preparation to amass the witnesses, affidavits, and other materials. Barbie stood trial in the Rhône Court of Assizes on May 11, 1987, for crimes against humanity. He did not recognize the court or the proceedings and scarcely attended sessions. Overwhelming evidence led to the jury finding him guilty with no extenuating circumstances. Barbie was sentenced to life imprisonment.

Annette Richardson

See also Argentina; Braun, Wernher von; Latin America, Nazis in
References and Further Reading
Finkielkraut, Alain. *Remembering in Vain: The Klaus Barbie Trial and Crimes against Humanity.* New York: Columbia University Press, 1992.
Murphy, Brendan. *The Butcher of Lyon: The Story of Infamous Nazi Klaus Barbie.* New York: Empire Books, 1983.
Paris, Erna. *Unhealed Wounds: France and the Klaus Barbie Affair.* New York: First Grove Press, 1985.

BARTZ, FRITZ
b. April 8, 1908; Themar, Thuringia
d. June 21, 1970; Spreitenbach, Switzerland

German geographer and professor who became famous for his work on the North American fishing industry.

Fritz Bartz studied geography, biology, and *Volkswirtschaftslehre* (political economy) at the universities of Berlin, Vienna, Kiel, and Bonn. Fascinated by the travels of Sven Hedin, Bartz decided to write his dissertation on the fauna of Tibet and the Himalayan region. He received his doctoral degree for his thesis *Das Tierleben Tibets und des Himalaya-Gebirges* (The Animal Life of Tibet and the Himalaya Mountains) in 1935. Afterward, Bartz went to the United States, first as a scholarship recipient and then as an instructor of geography. He taught from 1935 to 1939 at Stanford University in Palo Alto, at Reed College in Portland, and at the University of California at Berkeley. When World War II broke out in 1939, Bartz was on a trip through East Asia (Japan, Korea, Manchuria, and northern China). He returned to Germany via Siberia.

On extensive travels along the western coast of North America between Mexico and the Bering Strait, including long stays in Alaska and British Columbia, Bartz gathered the material for his *Habilitationsschrift* (postdoctoral degree). This thesis was published in 1942 under the title *Fischgründe und Fischereiwirtschaft an der West-*

küste Nordamerikas (Fishing Grounds and the Fishing Industry of the West Coast of North America). In the following years, Bartz published several books and articles on the fishing trade in the Pacific and on the geography and culture of North America. In 1949 he received an honorary professorship of economic geography at the University of Bonn, though he took a guest professorship in 1950–1951 at Berkeley and also taught at the University of Minnesota. In 1959 he was appointed chair of geography at the University of Freiburg, where he taught until he died.

Bartz traveled repeatedly to the Americas: in 1953 he embarked on a journey from Florida to eastern Canada; in 1966 he traveled to South America; in 1967 he visited the United States again; and in 1969 he toured Central America, Mexico, and Canada. In addition, research led him to the Orient, East Asia, South Africa, and Oceania. He reflected upon his worldwide travels in the three-volume handbook *Die großen Fischereiräume der Welt* (The Great Fishing Areas of the World, 1964–1965). Volume 3 is dedicated to the Americas.

Besides his main field of research, the fishing industry, Bartz also dedicated himself to other topics, such as agrarian and economic geography and the research of cultural landscapes, in which the North American subcontinent stood again and again at the center of his interests. He published a geographical introduction on Alaska in 1950 and an urban-geographical study of the settlement density in the San Francisco Bay region in 1954.

Heinz Peter Brogiato

References and Further Reading

Bartz, Fritz. *San Francisco–Oakland Metropolitan Area.* Dubuque, IA: W. C. Brown, 1968.
Schott, Carl. "Fritz Bartz." *Geographische Zeitschrift* 58 (1970): 241–250.

BAUDISSIN, ADELBERT HEINRICH, COUNT

b. January 25, 1820; Hovegaard, Denmark
d. March 26, 1871; Wiesbaden, Prussia

German American author who wrote *An den Ansiedler im Missouri-Staat: Den deutschen Auswanderen gewidmet* (*The Settler in Missouri: Dedicated to the German Immigrants*) to give potential German migrants a better description of the Missouri River valley. Baudissin, a Forty-Eighter, a journalist, an author, and a member of prominent noble family in Schleswig-Holstein, was the son of Christian Carl Count Baudissin, who had been forced into Danish exile from his northern German estate after an affair with a married woman, Henriette Kungler, Adelbert's mother. Growing up in Denmark and Schleswig, Adelbert experienced the political turbulence surrounding the duchy of Schleswig-Holstein and its principal antagonists, Denmark, Prussia, and Austria. After studying mining in Saxony, he became a civil servant in 1843 for the Habsburg monarchy. Despite their religious differences, he married the Catholic Pauline von Gersdorff in 1844 but divorced her within a year. When Schleswig-Holstein revolted against Danish rule and oppression, he volunteered for the Schleswig-Holstein militia and later rose to the rank of lieutenant in the duchy's army. After the revolt was suppressed, he emigrated to the United States in 1852.

With his brother Julius, Adelbert arrived in New York City in June 1852 on route to settle in Missouri, where two older brothers had settled years earlier; Waldemar in 1840 and Felix in 1847. While in New York City he married Luisa del Strother and arrived with her in the autumn of 1852 in Portland, Missouri, a small town located in central Missouri along the Missouri River, approximately 100 miles from St. Louis. Though he lived in the United States only for another ten years, his time in Missouri is characterized by intensive work on behalf of German immigration, his republican ideals of freedom and liberty, and a commitment to public life.

After two years in Portland, in 1854 Adelbert published *An den Ansiedler im Missouri-Staat,* one of the best examples of immigration literature. In the wake of Gottfried Duden's seminal work *Bericht über eine Reise nach den westlichen Staaten Nordamerikas* (Report on a Journey to the Western States of America, 1829), German immigration to the United States exploded in the late 1840s and continued through the early 1850s, but many of the publications on the United States were general or academic in nature. Baudissin desired to correct misconceptions about life in the United States and offered a detailed account of what awaited German immigrants in one localized area, namely the Missouri River valley. The work reads like a cultural document, outlining social and natural conditions in the state. More than anything, it is a "survival manual" that offers pragmatic suggestions to the potential immigrant; warns him of dangers and pitfalls; and then gives specific advice on how to start a new life, such as purchasing property, clearing land, building a farmhouse, farming, and all other aspects related to life on the farm. Baudissin stresses that a successful German immigrant should have financial means; be knowledgeable about the area where he wishes to settle; and realize that everything, from farming, business, money, and personal relationships to politics is different in the United States and that former experiences in Germany will be useless in the new homeland. Baudissin reveals himself as a master observer and writes candidly about the horrors of the seven-week voyage to the United States and the dangerous trek across the country and then insightfully portrays the culture of the United States, including the concept of democracy, representative government and its institutions, American attitudes toward Germans, nativism, and the problem of slavery. *Der Ansiedler* serves as one of the first and arguably most thorough cultural and natural histories of Missouri whose format sets the standard for subsequent state histories.

Seeking a more prominent role in public life in the rapidly developing West, Adelbert moved with his family to Washington, Missouri, located approximately 40 miles from St. Louis, in 1854. Washington was a bustling town known for its German immigrant community. Civic minded and dedicated to the advancement of the arts, Adelbert founded the German-language newspaper, *Der Courier* (*The Courier*), and became active in local politics. He became a successful businessman, owning a drugstore, and farmer. Like the overwhelming majority of Forty-Eighters, Adelbert opposed slavery and welcomed the outbreak of the Civil War in 1861. Missouri was a slave state, though the population was evenly divided between Unionists and Confederates. This division soon engulfed the state, especially the Missouri River valley, where most German immigrants lived, in a fierce struggle. Disillusioned with initial southern victories, Adelbert returned to Germany with his family in 1862, settled in Hamburg, and resumed his life as a civil servant and author. Ironically, he returned to Germany just when Otto von Bismarck began to unify Germany through a series of wars, culminating with the Franco-Prussian War of 1870–1871, during which Adelbert served as a war correspondent. He became sick in 1870 and died in the next year.

After his return to Germany, Adelbert published considerably on the Schleswig-Holstein wars of 1848–1851 and other political matters but could not forget the United States. In 1866 he published *Peter Tütt: Zustände in Amerika* (Peter Tütt: Conditions in America), in which he attempted to reveal everyday life in the United States to the Germans. His belief in representational government and personal freedoms is still apparent in sections on politics, voting, and July Fourth, but an undercurrent of disappointment in the United States caused by slavery, deception, and greed gives the publication a bitter tone. Unlike in *Der Ansiedler*, he no longer enthusiastically championed German immigration to the United States.

Gregory H. Wolf

See also Forty-Eighters
References and Further Reading
Baudissin, Adelbert Heinrich. *An den Ansiedler im Missouri-Staat: Den deutschen Auswanderen gewidmet.* Iserlohn, Germany: Bädecker, 1854.
Greely, Ralph. "Count Baudissin on Missouri Towns." *The Bulletin* [of the] *Missouri Historical Society* (January 1971): 111–124.
Wilkey, Stanley. *Washington, Missouri: Yesterday through Tomorrow.* Washington, MO: Bicentennial Commission of Washington, MO, 1975.

BAUHAUS

For many Americans the International Style in modern architecture is synonymous with the Bauhaus (building house), the influential German school of art, architecture, and design. This is true in large part because faculty and alumni of the institute, not least its charismatic founding director Walter Gropius, brought many of the forms and methodologies of modernism with them to the United States as refugees from the Third Reich. Although other German-speaking architects and designers contributed to American modernism, nearly all crucial episodes of German American relations in modern design can be traced to the Bauhaus, in the fields of commercial graphics, furniture design, and design education, as well as architecture. Walter Gropius's refusal to limit his school's mission to the teaching of architecture, his insistence that every field of practical design could be an outlet for creativity as well as social betterment, is the key to the Bauhaus's worldwide influence.

The Bauhaus's roots can be traced to currents in design during the German Empire (1871–1918) and the young architect Walter Gropius's concern for design's fate in an industrial mass society. A member of the German Werkbund, an organization of designers, industrialists, and educators founded in 1908, Gropius shared its concern with the inadequacy for modern needs of traditional fine arts training of artists and architects, as well as the apprenticeship and trade school systems in the applied arts. Inspired by fellow Werkbund member Henry van de Velde, who in turn based his ideas on the arts and crafts philosophy of William Morris, Gropius began to plan a school curriculum that erased distinctions between "fine" and "applied" art. It was based on a philosophy of design education that would identify basic laws of form and fitness for use. The resulting products,

Gropius believed, would meet modern needs both practically and spiritually, as they healed the schism between the artist and the ordinary citizen.

By the time he founded the Staatliches Bauhaus (supported by the state of Thuringia) in Weimar in 1919, Gropius, shocked by his experience in World War I, had retreated from his prewar embrace of industrial civilization. He established the school on a handicraft- rather than an industrial-training basis, and its dominant mood was that of a utopian colony divorced from the world. The institute's *Vorkurs* (Basic Course) was taught at first by painters identified with the antimodern Expressionist movement, with the Swiss Johannes Itten as the leading figure and Wassily Kandinsky, a founder of abstract painting, among the staff. (The German American painter Lyonel Feininger, although always essentially detached from the school's practical education, was part of this initial cadre.) Gropius hoped that the investigations into pure form pursued by radical painters would lead to a new basis for design thinking in architecture and applied design, replacing the imitation of classical or Gothic prototypes. The idea of a new beginning in society as well as art was paramount.

It has been suggested that Itten's philosophy of creating form out of the tasks and inspirations of the moment borrowed from American pragmatist John Dewey's philosophy of education as learning through experience instead of memorizing a "correct" curriculum. Itten encouraged students to find laws of basic design, formal and practical, through free experiment with scrap material and exercises with colors and patterns. Itten's Expressionist antimodernism and mysticism pushed the school's meager output toward a rough, heavy, vaguely cubist-influenced style.

The Bauhaus took its mature direction in 1922–1923. Many students, and then Gropius himself, were swayed by the pro-machine arguments, backed up by striking designs, of the Dutch De Stijl movement and the Russian constructivists. Deciding that only by embracing the machine and the forms most in tune with its processes could the school help society, Gropius proclaimed, "Art and Technology—A New Unity." The Hungarian-born constructivist painter Laszlo Moholy-Nagy, an unabashed enthusiast for the machine, replaced Itten in 1923 as director of the *Vorkurs*. He and his pupil, painter Josef Albers, became the bulwarks of Gropius's curriculum. Keeping Itten's *Vorkurs* intact, Moholy-Nagy and Albers encouraged play with smooth surfaces, simple geometric shapes, serene yet dynamic formal compositions, and industrial materials. Under Moholy's direction of the metals workshop, the school created the first mass-production modernist lighting fixtures and pioneered chromed-steel furniture. Gropius's stirring rhetoric and personal charisma quickly made Bauhaus a shorthand term for avant-garde functionalist design throughout Germany. In the process he awakened the enmity of the political and cultural Right, which would dog the school for the rest of its existence.

During the Bauhaus's peak period of 1925–1928, when the school relocated to Gropius's striking white-cubic building complex in Dessau—with its soon-to-be-famous glass-walled workshop wing—the school's credo was a creative process without preconceptions. However, the Bauhaus quickly became identified (not entirely unfairly, since Gropius had pushed the school to find a universal grammar of design) with a style of smooth horizontals, white or glass cubistic forms accented with primary colors, clean sans-serif or lowercase graphics, and the air of machine functionality. In addition, for many students and some faculty, Americanization was a powerfully attractive ideal that steered them away from art and toward bold practicality. As an architect, Gropius thought of himself as a creative experimenter with standardized industrial modules, like Henry Ford with the Model T, and is alleged to have solicited Ford (unsuccessfully) for support. More generally, if nebulously, America's supposed spirit of engagement with the present, its bold embrace of the machine age and spurning of the past, inspired many at the school. American-style jazz was popular among students, and one student declared in the school magazine that Ford and Edison were honorary Bauhausler (along with Pablo Picasso and Albert Einstein). Gropius himself toured the United States in 1928 and became preoccupied both with issues of mass production and the technologies of skyscraper construction.

By this time, however, Gropius had stepped down as the Bauhaus's director. Under his successor, Hannes Meyer, the politically engaged functionalist who had headed the school's architecture department, the school's americanism intensified. However, the school's pursuit of free creativity waned, a consequence of Meyer's insistence on practical design that would serve the industrial masses. Student spirit for engaging with society ran high, but dissatisfaction among those who still valued the fine arts and a fear that the school's po-

litical engagement endangered it led to Meyer's replacement by the apolitical, magisterial Ludwig Mies van der Rohe in 1930. Mies ran the school as an architectural atelier, with only Kandinsky and Albers remaining from the Gropius era, until Nazi elements in the Dessau city government forced the school's closure in early 1932. Mies reopened it in Berlin as a private school, but the Nazis sealed its building under suspicion of Communist activities soon after Adolf Hitler's seizure of power. Rather than accept Nazi demands to alter the curriculum, Mies chose to disband the institution in the summer of 1933.

The Bauhaus had attracted a few American students, beginning with artist Florence Henri in the late 1920s, but for the most part the American presence was limited to male architecture students in the final years under Mies. American avant-garde "little magazines" occasionally spotlighted Bauhaus architectural designs along with other European modernist manifestations, and architectural journals described the "extreme functionalism" of Gropius's architecture, ignoring the rest of the curriculum. Significant American attention to the school began in 1927, when the young Harvard-trained art historian Alfred Barr toured the school and met Gropius. Barr's preoccupation with finding a unified style for all the arts in the machine age seemed to him to have been triumphantly met in Gropius's school. As director of the new Museum of Modern Art (MOMA), Barr exhibited architecture, painting, photography, and typography from the school. Although it featured Gropius only as one of many architects in a worldwide "International Style," MoMA's 1932 "Modern Architecture: International Exhibition" brought the Bauhaus's founder to the attention of American design schools desperate for reform.

After Hitler's seizure of power, Barr's efforts and those of MOMA's architecture curator Philip Cortelyou Johnson (a devotee of Mies) secured teaching positions for Bauhaus alumni in the United States. Albers found a position teaching art at the experimental Black Mountain College (1933). Chicago industrialists brought over Moholy-Nagy as head of a New Bauhaus in Chicago (1937), soon reorganized as the School of Design. Barr and architectural educator Joseph Hudnut secured Gropius's appointment as director of the architecture curriculum at Harvard University (1936–1937). Alumni designers Marcel Breuer, Herbert Bayer, Alexander (Xanti) Schawinsky, Herbert Matter, and Mies soon followed. Even though MOMA's 1938 show on the Gropius years of the Bauhaus was a critical and popular failure, it helped cement a growing idea that functionalist architecture, modernist commercial design, and geometric abstract art were all synonymous with the Bauhaus.

Renewed contact between the former Bauhausler in optimistic circumstances led to new creativity for many, notably in Breuer's imaginative output of small country houses (in practice with Gropius) and Bayer's exhibition designs for MOMA and advertisements for the Container Corporation of America (CCA). The Swiss art historian Sigfried Giedion's book *Space, Time, and Architecture* (1941), based on lectures he had given at Harvard at Gropius's invitation, was influential in cementing the Bauhaus approach as the cornerstone of modern architecture. (Mies and his most loyal Bauhaus faculty, especially Walter Pe-

Chicago Bauhaus School—in the former home of Marshall Field. Dr. Walter Gropius (lt) and Laszlo Moholy-Nagy on the famous circular staircase with students, 1938. (Bettmann/Corbis)

terhans and planner-architect Ludwig Hilberseimer, tended not to associate with the Gropius group.)

The post–World War II years saw both triumph for and growing criticism of the Bauhaus influence in the United States. Gropius uprooted the Beaux-Arts curriculum from Harvard but was unable to introduce the complete Bauhaus *Vorkurs* curriculum. His approach, which influenced all departments of the Graduate School of Design, stressed an unprejudiced approach to problems of architecture as a social environment. In practice, this meant planning exercises that stressed urban decentralization and an approach to building design that turned functional elements into bold formal patterns. Marcel Breuer emerged as the dominant teacher of architecture in the school. Although graduates like I. M. Pei and the Australian Harry Seidler adopted much from his form language, Paul Rudolph and Philip Cortelyou Johnson (who had chosen architectural practice over historical scholarship) increasingly took their own paths. So did Mies, directing the architecture program at the Illinois Institute of Technology and becoming increasingly preoccupied with the steel industrial frame. Moholy-Nagy proved more successful as an inspiring spirit than director of a school, although his impact on younger designers like Charles Eames and Paul Rand was considerable. The élan of the Bauhaus years survived most undiluted at Black Mountain College, where Gropius, Moholy, and other alumni were frequent visitors to Albers's courses and to the school's famous Summer Institute. The school had no architecture or design curriculum, however, and by the late 1940s was increasingly under the influence of writers and teachers of literature.

Albers became head of Yale's fine art curriculum in 1950 and successfully directed its path toward abstract art until 1970. His wife Anni, an important member of the Bauhaus community, gained respect as a leading textile artist. Throughout this period an American Bauhaus style of lightweight planes in bright, simple, primary-colored forms, playful yet machined, could be felt in the best American commercial design until the 1970s, epitomized by Herbert Bayer's work for CCA and Atlantic Richfield.

Unfortunately, Americans who picked up Bauhaus forms and methods often ignored the idealism (social and philosophical) behind them and began to equate Bauhaus style with either blank utility or a formalism of abstract geometry. It might be said that Gropius's decision in the early Weimar days to drop the study of past design, as a drag on individual creativity and an irrelevance to modern conditions, encouraged a reaction toward a more historically rooted (or at least more familiar-looking) forms. The use of apparently Bauhaus-influenced forms in the much-reviled megaprojects of late modernism, such as Wallace Harrison's New York State governmental complex in Albany, discredited (however unfairly and uncomprehendingly) Gropius's philosophy of "total design." By the time Gropius and Mies died in 1969, a looser, more ironic, and historicist pluralism, often casting the Bauhaus as its enemy, had begun to push aside the Bauhaus ideals of learning through doing and exploring the fundamentals of design.

Miles David Samson

See also Americanization; Einstein, Albert; Ford, Henry; Gropius, Walter Adolph; Mies van der Rohe, Ludwig

References and Further Reading

Allen, James Sloan. *The Romance of Commerce and Culture: Capitalism, Modernism, and the Chicago-Aspen Crusade for Cultural Reform*. Chicago: University of Chicago Press, 1983.

Alofsin, Anthony. *The Struggle for Modernism: Architecture, Landscape Architecture, and City Planning at Harvard*. New York: W. W. Norton, 2002.

Harris, Mary Emma. *The Arts at Black Mountain College*. Cambridge: MIT Press, 1987.

Kentgens-Craig, Margret. *The Bauhaus and America: First Contacts, 1919–1936*. Cambridge: MIT Press, 1999.

Naylor, Gillian. *The Bauhaus Reassessed: Sources and Design Theory*. New York: E. P. Dutton, 1985.

Wingler, Hans M. *Bauhaus in Amerika: Resonanz und Weiterentwicklung*. Berlin: Bauhaus-Archiv, 1972.

Wingler, Hans M., ed. *The Bauhaus: Weimar, Dessau, Berlin, Chicago*. Cambridge: MIT Press, 1986.

BECKER, JOÃO
b. February 24, 1870; Sankt Wendel, Rhineland
d. June 15, 1946; Porto Alegre, Rio Grande do Sul, Brazil

Son of Catholic southern German emigrants who was ordained archbishop of Porto Alegre in 1912 and became famous for his public anti-German sentiments.

João Becker's parents left for Brazil in 1878. Raised a Catholic, Becker was ordained in 1897 and served as a priest in Porto Alegre, the capital of Rio Grande do Sul, until he was appointed bishop of Florianópolis, the capital of Santa Catarina, in 1908 and archbishop of Porto Alegre in 1912. Becker was one of the leading representatives of political Catholicism in Brazil. Closely connected to the central government, Becker had far-reaching political ambitions. He tried vehemently to get loyal priests elected to parliament and hoped for a political career for himself. In 1923, Becker acted as a negotiator between the two parties of the so-called Revolution of 1923, between the government of Borges de Medeiros, from the Republic Party of Rio Grande do Sul, and the followers of Francisco de Assis Brasil, from the Federalist Party. He attempted to present himself as a suitable candidate for the Senate.

In spite of his German origin, Becker belonged to the so-called ethnic renegades. During World War I, Becker closed the German-speaking Saint Josephs Community in Porto Alegre and agreed to be appointed as the leader of the nationalistic Liga de Defesa Nacional (Association for National Defense). According to contemporaries, Becker is said to have stated that the German immigration to Brazil was no good for the country and that the Germans had polluted Brazil with their Kantian thoughts, Protestantism, and beer breweries. He even came into conflict with German Jesuits in Rio Grande do Sul.

To avoid any conflict with the governing authorities, Becker supported Luso-Brazilian politicians who were backed by Getúlio Vargas but branded by the Catholic Church as enemies of the Catholic faith. During the 1930s, Becker fully supported the nationalist policy of the central government and approved of the closing of all schools that offered education in non-Portuguese languages (in 1938). In line with Vargas's initial support and admiration for the Fascist and National Socialist regimes in Europe, Becker held a very positive view of Adolf Hitler's and Benito Mussolini's dictatorships. However, when Vargas joined the Allies in 1942, Becker abandoned his earlier opinions and supported the fight against Nazi Germany.

René Gertz

See also Brazil
References and Further Reading
Isaia, Artur Cesar. *Catolicismo e autoritarismo no Rio Grande do Sul.* Porto Alegre: EDIPUCRS, 1998.

BECKER, PHILIP
b. April 25, 1830; Oberotterbach on the Rhine
d. July 4, 1898; Buffalo, New York

Philip Becker and Henry Overstolz of St. Louis, both elected in 1875, were the first German immigrants to serve as mayors of major American cities. Becker was a merchant and Republican mayor (1876–1877, 1886–1889) of Buffalo, New York. He was a committed member and virtual leader of Buffalo's German American community, socially, financially, and politically. His status as the "Uncle Philip" of the German community lasted from his effort to ensure the presence of German instruction in the schools in 1873 to his leadership of local German American opposition to William Jennings Bryan in 1896.

Becker came directly to the emergent "Queen City of the Great Lakes" in 1847. Securing supervisory positions in Buffalo stores, he worked seven years before opening up his own Main Street grocery business. Over the next forty years, Becker became known as the "Merchant Prince." His store was the leading wholesale grocery business of western New York during the last third of the century. One of his two other major concerns, the Buffalo German Insurance Company, also enjoyed remarkable success, erecting a massive building with soaring tent roofs that occupied the prestigious downtown corner of Lafayette Square.

Becker's local fame rose quickly after the Civil War, during a period when he was thought to have become the city's third millionaire. In the early 1870s he was the dominant force in a committee that built Buffalo's City Hall, which remains one of the landmarks of nineteenth-century Buffalo, as the Erie County Hall. Becker became an activist in German circles. As an organizer of those who favored German-language courses on the Anglo-dominated west side of the city in 1873, he played a key role in the successful struggle to maintain German instruction in public schools. This success, his mayoral victory in 1875, and his role as president of the German Insurance Company from 1869 to 1893

made him a central philanthropist and political representative of German American societies. As the very nature of the cultural associations known as *Vereine* moved away from purely cultural pursuits to a stronger business orientation, Becker became a leading voice in the key *Verein* of Buffalo. In 1883 he was elected president of the *Sängerfest* (Singer's Festival) in Buffalo, which drew choirs from around the country. Becker contributed much to making the event memorable, including raising funds for the city's first Music Hall and a triumphal arch over Main Street. He also intervened musically, helping to decide which singing societies would be most prominently displayed and eventually helping to oust a director of only local fame from his position. When a gas chandelier set the first Music Hall ablaze in 1885, Becker led the effort that resulted in the construction of a second one.

Becker showed that a thick German accent and a willingness to promote German causes were not necessarily liabilities in the 1870s and 1880s. Had Buffalo attained the dominant influence in its state, as did St. Louis and Milwaukee, it is conceivable that Becker could have attained higher offices. In an age noted for the scale of civic corruption, Becker, with a youthful countenance and distinctive chin beard, haggled to reduce costs. His approach set a precedent for Grover Cleveland, a rival and later president, whose one-year stint as Buffalo's mayor came after Becker's first administration. Like Cleveland, Becker also convinced opponents of his integrity and gained local support for a gubernatorial bid. In 1891, a large delegation left Buffalo to ramrod Becker through as the Republican choice for New York's governor. Boss

Thomas Platt, however, opposed the scheme, and despite the near unanimity of Buffalo's Republicans and a two-day effort to out-shout downstate opponents, Becker's allies were unable to secure his nomination.

Andrew Yox

See also Buffalo

References and Further Reading

Holli, Melvin G., and Peter Jones, eds. *Biographical Dictionary of American Mayors, 1820–1980.* Westport, CT: Greenwood, 1981, 21.

Yox, Andrew P. "Decline of the German-American Community in Buffalo, 1855–1925." PhD diss., University of Chicago, 1983, 144–240.

BECKMANN, MAX
b. February 12, 1884; Leipzig, Saxony
d. December 27, 1950; New York, New York

One of the most important painters of the twentieth century, who fled Nazi Germany and after World War II emigrated to the United States.

His paintings were included in the infamous Nazi art exhibition "Degenerate Art." Beckmann studied from 1900 to 1903 at the art academy in Weimar and made study trips to Paris, where he was impressed in particular by the art of Paul Cezanne and Vincent Van Gogh. In Germany, the works of Edvard Munch but also paintings by the masters Pieter Brueghel the Elder and Matthias Grünewald (the Isenheim Altarpiece) had an influence on Beckmann. He moved to Berlin in 1905 and joined the avant-garde Secession movement, which counted leading German impressionist painters such as Max

Liebermann and Lovis Corinth among its members. In 1906 Beckmann won the Villa-Romana-Price, which paid for a study trip to Florence. In the same year he married Minna Tube, like him a promising painter who had also trained in Weimar and became later known as an opera singer. In 1913 the famous art dealer Paul Cassirer organized the first major exhibition of Beckmann's works in Berlin.

Beckmann volunteered for World War I in August 1914. He spent several months as a medical orderly in Belgium, producing a number of drawings and etchings that reflect his war experience on the western front. In 1915 he was released from the army after suffering a nervous breakdown. World War I constituted a decisive turning point in Beckmann's life and exerted a major impact on his art. His style became rougher and more expressive. By the mid-1920s, he emerged as one of the leading avant-garde artists in Germany. Beckmann's broadly realistic paintings display circus subjects, cripples, brutal violence, and suffering but also colorful social scenes and still lifes. His art betrays a complex symbolism that in part remains enigmatic to this day. Beckmann did not identify with a movement or group. Art historians debate whether his paintings relate to the Neue Sachlichkeit (new objectivity) and expressionism. Although influences are clearly visible, Beckmann transcends such categorizations. His art is characterized by an intense reflection of his own personality, which is illustrated most strikingly by the numerous self-portraits Beckmann painted. He also produced a number of bronze sculptures.

In 1925 Beckmann divorced Minna Tube and married the much younger Mathilde ("Quappi") von Kaulbach, who would appear in many of his paintings. From 1925 to 1933 Beckmann taught as a professor at the renowned Städel Institute in Frankfurt am Main. In 1932 he began work on the first of his nine monumental Triptychons. In the same year the National Gallery in Berlin devoted a whole room to his paintings. The Nazis, however, despised his paintings and expelled him from the Städel Institute in 1933. They regarded him as one of the leading representatives of "Degenerate Art" and included twenty-four of his paintings in the 1937 exhibition by that name. Shortly after the opening of the exhibition, Beckmann and his wife left Germany, moving to Paris and later to Amsterdam. When German troops marched into the Netherlands in 1940, Beckmann burned his diaries. During the occupation he was not harmed physically but suffered from the oppressive atmosphere, as his deeply pessimistic dark paintings from this period illustrate. In 1947 Beckmann emigrated to the United States. He taught and lectured as a guest professor at several universities in the Midwest, notably at Washington University in St. Louis, and also at the Brooklyn Museum Art School in New York. As a consequence of the Nazi purge of German art museums, many of his most famous paintings are today owned by leading art museums in the United States. His famous *Self Portrait in Tuxedo* (1927), exhibited in the Berlin National Gallery Beckmann Room in the Kronprinzenpalais before 1933, can be viewed today at Harvard University's Busch-Reisinger Museum in Cambridge, Massachusetts. The St. Louis Art Museum also owns a large collection of his works.

Tobias Brinkmann

References and Further Reading
Rainbird, Sean. *Max Beckmann.* New York: Distributed Art Publishers, 2003.

BEER

Beer became the drink of choice for Americans as the result of German influence. An inexpensive, grain-based drink with low-alcohol content, beer has historically come in many varieties, including ale and porter, but it has only been a popular American beverage since the mid-nineteenth century. The German immigrants who flooded into the United States at that time demanded beer and brought the skills to produce a high-quality, light-bodied beer that appealed to a wider market. German Americans with such names as Eberhard Anheuser, Adolphus E. Busch, Frederick Miller, Joseph Schlitz, and Frederick Pabst have dominated the beer industry ever since.

Beer probably originated in southern Europe, both as a way to use grain before it spoiled and as a healthier drink than other available choices. For much of recorded history, water has been a source of such killer illnesses as dysentery. Milk, with pasteurization unknown until the mid-nineteenth century, did not have a noticeably better safety record. Therefore most people, including infants and nursing mothers, drank ale in the morning, noon, and night. The boiling necessary to make beer neutralized most of tainted water's ill effects, although no one realized this for centuries, and the grains added some protein to the diet.

The Romans brought beer to northern Europe around 55 BCE, and the popularity of the beverage gradually spread. The English word *beer* comes from the German word *bier*, a term that originated in the breweries of German monasteries in the eighth century. Beer of this early period would not be recognizable to modern connoisseurs of the drink. Hops were not used, and as a result, the beer appeared very dark with a strong flavor. It also spoiled easily because the active ingredient in hops, lupulin, inhibits the growth of certain types of fungi and bacteria. Sometime around the early sixteenth century, breweries in Germany began adding malt to beer production. Hops were added to the mix about the seventeenth century to produce a light, clear, somewhat bitter, and long-lasting product.

The German process of making beer would become the world standard by the nineteenth century, and despite changes in technology, it remains the essential process employed today by American brewers. Barley kernels are allowed to germinate by immersing them in water until as much as 45 percent of the water is absorbed. After this steeping is completed, the barley is spread out on a stone floor to a depth of 2 feet and constantly turned with a shovel. This five- to seven-day process of germination causes the natural enzyme systems within the barley to begin breaking down the membranes of starch cells so that the starch can be more easily converted into sugars during the brewing process. When the barley is properly germinated to a sprout length of three-fourths of the size of the kernel, the grains are transferred to a kiln and heated to 140° Fahrenheit (60° Celsius). The temperature is raised depending upon the type of malt desired. A lower temperature in the malting process results in a paler malt and a lighter-colored beer. Ground malted barley is mashed with hot water. The liquor, known as wort, is then extracted. A portion of hops is added, and the whole mass is boiled until the aroma of hops is obtained. It is then allowed to cool before being fermented with yeast, which produces a small amount of alcohol. Different brews require different types of yeast.

American brewers in the colonial era used barley to make beer, but the quality of the product may have been poor. Most American brewers had little training, and it was fairly easy to misjudge steeping to produce unevenly germinated barley. Additionally, they did not employ hops and often blended herbs such as rosemary and yarrow together to produce gruit beer. These early brewers produced only enough ale, porter, or stout to meet the needs of their families. Wealthy Americans would purchase beer imported from England. Cider, an alcoholic drink that anyone with an apple tree and a press could easily make, proved a much more popular beverage. Still, home-brewed beer could commonly be found in colonial homes as a drink used from infancy.

During the first half of the nineteenth century, immigrants from northern Europe poured into the United States. Many of the immigrants came from the German states of Bavaria and Württemberg, the biggest beer-producing areas per capita in the world, bringing both a love of beer and excellent beer-making skills. Although many of these immigrants stayed in New York City, over 1,000 Germans per week in the 1840s came through Milwaukee, Wisconsin. This city would soon emerge as the brewing center of the United States because of these immigrants. Milwaukee's substantial German population provided not only a huge base of customers but also a source of experienced brewers.

The influx of German immigrants changed every aspect of American beer from ingredients to manufacturing to marketing. The first German-influenced development came with the introduction of lager beer. This type of beer, a beverage with a 3.5 percent alcohol content that is difficult and time consuming to make, constituted the most popular German variety. First produced in Bavaria sometime prior to 1420 and named after the German word meaning "to store," lager beer develops a tangy, effervescent taste from being properly aged. It is made only with bottom-fermenting yeast that had been unknown in the Americas. Philadelphia brewer John Wagner, a former Bavarian brewmaster, brought the first lager yeast into the United States in 1842 and revolutionized the American beer industry. Five years later, two Germans, John A. Huck and John Schneider, opened the first lager brewery in Chicago. In city after city, Germans became the first to brew lager. In 1850, there were 431 active breweries in the United States, and home brewing had died out.

By the time of the Civil War, lager beer constituted the favorite drink of white American males, but lager required hops. A perennial that grows on vines and a cousin of hemp, hops did not become a commercially important crop in the United States until the nineteenth century, when demand for beer made from hops skyrocketed largely because of German influence. Coincidentally, with the nation's demand for staples being met by farmers in the Ohio Valley, growers in other areas needed a profitable cash crop to stay in business. They seized upon hops. Massachusetts thus became a major hops-growing state, even exporting some of its crop to France and Germany. New York at midcentury became the leading hops grower in the nation, producing 11 million pounds annually and representing 88 percent of the total crop grown in the country. By 1850, hops were produced in thirty-three states. By the time of the millennium, hops had achieved the rank of seventy-second in a listing of the most important American crops, with the hops industry now centered in Idaho, Washington, and Oregon.

Lager beer standardized the brewing industry. It offered a moderately priced beer of sparkling appearance, great stability, light body, and lighter alcohol content than the old-style ales and porters. The popularity of lager allowed Germans to dominate the brewing industry to the point that the U.S. Brewmaster's Association titled its journal *Der Braumeister* (The Brewmaster), and German remained the official language of the U.S. Brewer's Association until 1873.

The German origins of American beer can be seen everywhere beer is sold in the German names of the brewing companies. All the major breweries began operation in the nineteenth century, switched to other products such as cereal during Prohibition, and restored themselves to full strength after repeal through skillful marketing.

The Pabst Brewing Company produces Pabst Blue Ribbon, Old Milwaukee, Colt 45, and Lone Star among its twenty-nine brands. The company started up in 1844, when Jacob Best left Mettenheim, Hesse-Darmstadt, and began brewing lager beer in Milwaukee. Frederick Pabst, son-in-law of Best's son Philip, took over the company and gave it his name in 1864 when the firm produced 5,000 barrels annually. Nine years later, Pabst turned out 100,000 barrels of beer per year. In 1951, it became the first brewer to participate in color television by sponsoring a program. In the twentieth century, it has taken over the brands of failed breweries, including Schlitz.

The Joseph Schlitz Brewing Company, founded by an immigrant from Mainz who took over another German-owned brewery, began operation in 1858. By 1870, the brewery was producing more than 12,000 barrels per year. By 1947, Schlitz sold over a million barrels annually as the leading beer producer in the world. Schlitz introduced the pop-top can in 1963, and this innovation considerably boosted sales of such brands as Schlitz and Schlitz Malt Liquor. A change in its beer recipe combined with failed advertising campaigns sent Schlitz into bankruptcy in 1981. Stroh Brewing Company of Detroit, founded by German brewer Bernard Stroh in 1850, purchased the assets of the company before it was in turn taken over by Pabst.

Frederick E. Miller, born in Riedlingen, Württemberg, arrived in the United States in 1855 after serving as brewmaster at Hohenzollern Castle in Sigmaringen, Hohenzollern. He bought a brewery in Milwaukee. In 1883, Miller's brewery became one of the first to establish a bottling plant, and it bottled 5,000 barrels annually within three years. Beers like Miller High Life and slogans such as "It's Miller Time" have made the brewery into the second largest in the United States.

Anheuser-Busch is the largest American brewer. The firm traces its roots to a brewery begun in St. Louis in 1864 under the direction of soap manufacturer Eberhard Anheuser and brewer's supply store owner Adolphus Busch, both originally from Germany. Anheuser-Busch produces thirty brands of beer, including Budweiser. Known to viewers of television commercials as the "King of Beers," Budweiser has been brewed since 1876. It has been the world's best-selling beer since 1957, and at the millennium it was distributed in more than 70 countries. One in almost every five beers sold in the United States is a Budweiser.

Americans consume millions of barrels of beer a year because Germans brought their favorite drink to the New World along with the skills to make it. Although the rise of microbreweries in the 1980s has cut into the sales of the major breweries, particularly among female consumers, most beer sold in the United States today is still made by companies founded by Germans. Of all the contributions made by German Americans to the United States, beer may be the most appreciated.

Caryn E. Neumann

See also Chicago; Milwaukee; New York City
References and Further Reading
Anderson, Will. *Beer, USA*. Dobbs Ferry, NY: Morgan and Morgan, 1986.
Apps, Jerry. *Breweries of Wisconsin*. Madison: University of Wisconsin Press, 1992.
Goldammer, Ted. *The Brewer's Handbook: The Complete Book to Brewing Beer*. Clifton, VA: KVP, 2000.
Salem, Frederick William. *Beer: Its History and Economic Value as a National Beverage*. New York: Arno Press, 1972.

BERGER, VICTOR L.

b. February 28, 1860; Nieder-Rehbach, Transylvania
d. August 7, 1929; Milwaukee, Wisconsin

The recognized leader of the Milwaukee Socialist movement from 1895 to 1928, Berger was the first member of his party elected to the U.S. Congress (1910). He emigrated to Milwaukee from Austro-Hungarian Transylvania after attending universities in the Habsburg Empire. Berger established himself as a leading figure in the Wisconsin city's German community as a German-language teacher, an officer in the Milwaukee Turners, and a participant in Socialist discussion groups.

Victor Louis Berger, Socialist, representative of Wisconsin. (Library of Congress)

After joining the fledgling party, Berger edited several Socialist newspapers. In 1898 he cofounded the Social Democratic Party of the United States, Branch 1, and was soon recognized as the unchallenged leader of the Socialist movement in the most German city in the United States at the turn of the twentieth century. Often accused of "bossism" at the local level, Berger was active in national party politics and served as a delegate to the Second International Socialist Congress in Amsterdam in 1909. He maintained contact with leading German Socialists and spoke to party assemblies in Berlin and Vienna. Once elected to Congress, Berger changed his political focus from running the local party apparatus to operating more vigorously at the national level. However, he lost his run for reelection in 1912. Berger returned to Milwau-

kee after his defeat, but he rose again as a national figure leading the antiwar faction of his party between 1914 and 1917 and ultimately facing prosecution under the Alien and Sedition Act because of his editorials opposing U.S. involvement in World War I, calling for draft resistance, and favoring peace. Shortly after standing trial in a Chicago federal court for treason, Berger ran for the U.S. Senate in Wisconsin's special election in the spring of 1918, and captured 111,000 votes in a losing cause against Progressive Party candidate Irvine Lenroot. That November, Berger scored a solid victory to win back his Milwaukee congressional seat. However, his colleagues in the House of Representatives refused to seat him by a 307 to 1 vote. Congress forced him to stand for special election, but Berger confounded his opposition in the House and won again at home in 1919. But he was again denied his House seat, gaining only seven more votes from his colleagues. Berger finally lost the regular 1920 election, yet he returned to Washington after winning in 1922 and served two more terms thanks to the easing of the "red scare" and more moderate views from his colleagues in the House. A major force in Milwaukee political affairs for thirty-five years and an active figure in the national party, Berger retired from politics in 1928.

Gareth A. Shellman

See also Espionage and Sedition Act; Milwaukee; Milwaukee Socialists; World War I and German Americans
References and Further Reading
Gavett, Thomas W. *The Development of the Labor Movement in Milwaukee.* Madison: University of Wisconsin Press, 1965.
Miller, Sally M. *Victor L. Berger and the Promise of Constructive Socialism.* Westport: Greenwood Press, 1973.

BERLIN WALL

On November 11, 1958, Soviet leader Nikita Khrushchev declared the 1944 London Protocol invalid. The Western powers of France, Great Britain, and the United States had forfeited their rights to stay in West Berlin, he said, and the latter should become an "independent political unit, a free city." Khrushchev issued an ultimatum: if Western powers would not comply with his proposal, then Moscow would sign a separate peace treaty with the German Democratic Republic (GDR) and pursue the eviction of any Allied presence from West Berlin. Ensuing diplomatic contacts (a foreign minister conference in Geneva in 1959, U.S.-Soviet summits in 1959 and 1960) partly defused the imminence of the "Berlin crisis," but tensions and military contingency preparations continued at a high level. Mainly due to U.S. initiative, in May 1961 the North Atlantic Treaty Organization (NATO) defined three nonnegotiable "essentials" from the Western perspective: the freedom of West Berlin's people to choose their own political system; an Allied military presence in the Western sectors; and unrestrained access to West Berlin through the GDR by air, by land, and on water.

During this period, the GDR's implementation of socialism at various levels of East German society, peaking between the years of 1958 and 1960, had led to a constant flow of refugees to West Berlin and West Germany through open borders in Berlin. Between 1955 and 1961, more than 200,000 East Germans annually had left the GDR, among them many skilled workers and professionals in high demand. It became clear that the GDR might not survive as a state with open borders to West Berlin. Starting in the fall of 1960, GDR pressure

on the Soviet Union to guarantee the ongoing existence of the East German "Socialist state" by closing the borders to West Berlin became ever more persistent. It eventually met Nikita Khrushchev's approval in early July 1961 when the Soviet leader had felt the time for such a measure was ripe. On August 7, 1961, GDR leader Walter Ulbricht informed the Politbüro of the Socialist Unity Party (SED) on the forthcoming implementation of long-prepared measures along the sectoral border around West Berlin. During the night of August 12–13, 1961, GDR police and *Kampfgruppen* units (worker militias) began to set up barbed wire on East German territory and surrounded the entire city of West Berlin along an approximate length of 155 kilometers (97 miles). Over the next few weeks, those provisional devices were to be replaced with walls made of brick and concrete. Of formerly eighty-one street border crossings between East and West Berlin, just seven heavily guarded ones remained. Public transportation between both halves of the city was cut off permanently. GDR propaganda praised the sealed border as an "antifaschistischer Schutzwall" (anti-Fascist protection wall) against Western aggressiveness, thereby willfully ignoring how the wall's fortifications were directed against the East German people to prevent them from leaving the GDR.

The three Western Allied powers issued a note of protest to the Soviets but otherwise saw to the upholding of the "three essentials." In fact, the erection of the wall seemed to have concluded a dangerously lingering crisis and diminished the possibility of a nuclear war over Berlin. John F. Kennedy was relieved that "a wall is a hell of a lot better than a war" (Beschloss 1991, 278). Nonetheless, the situation in

A woman stands at the Berlin Wall in west sector, after waiting three hours to see her East Berlin friends and relatives, 1961. (Library of Congress)

Berlin became extremely tense in late October 1961, when Soviet and U.S. tanks confronted each other across the Allied "Checkpoint Charlie." Soviet nuclear forces had been put on high alert, and the Kennedy administration pondered nuclear war scenarios as well. Eventually the GDR stopped its violations of Berlin's four-power status, and efforts to prevent Western allies from entering East Berlin ceased.

After his initial disappointment and irritation about Washington's lackluster reaction in August 1961, West Berlin mayor Willy Brandt finally fell in line with Kennedy and Vice President Lyndon B. Johnson, who had been sent to West Berlin to assure its population of continued U.S. support. Later Brandt would note how the brutal reality of the cold war, manifested in August 1961, inspired him to move ahead

with an *Ostpolitik* of reconciliation and accommodation with the East. Cold war confrontation had only deepened German division. The best way to overcome it was to accept realities first and work toward changing them later. Starting with the intra-German Pass Agreements from 1963 to 1966 and continuing with the GDR visa for Western citizens and tourists later on, the Berlin border became permeable at least from West to East.

The Berlin Wall itself and its vast and various hinterland fortifications became an almost insurmountable obstacle for attempts to flee into West Berlin. Only in the years immediately after 1961 did a significant number of escapes succeed, among them many attempts through underground tunnels and with the support of organized rings of *Fluchthelfer* (flight helpers). The

GDR border guard's shoot to kill order against refugees resulted in about 250–300 deaths between August 24, 1961, and February 2, 1989.

In October 1989, the GDR regime gave in to massive demonstrations in all major East German cities and frantically started various kinds of late reforms to consolidate its crumbling power. When SED Politbüro member Günter Schabowski announced a revised version of the GDR's Travel Law during an international press conference on November 9, 1989, thousands of East Germans streamed to Berlin border crossings and forced their opening. Within days, amid scenes of jubilation, people took hammers and chiseled away the wall piece by piece. City contractors began to remove large segments. Visa requirements to enter West and East Berlin were waived on December 22, 1989. Farcically, passport checks remained in place until June 30, 1990. Remnants of the Berlin Wall ended up as souvenirs all over the world. Larger chunks were shredded and utilized for road construction in Germany.

Bernd Schaefer

See also German Unification (1990); Halvorsen, Gail S.; West Berlin

References and Further Reading

Beschloss, Michael R. *The Crisis Years: Kennedy and Khrushchev, 1960–1963*. New York: HarperCollins, 1991.

Harrison, Hope M. *Driving the Soviets Up the Wall*. Princeton, NJ: Princeton University Press, 2003.

Hertle, Hans-Hermann, Konrad Jarausch, and Christoph Klessmann, eds. *Mauerbau und Mauerfall: Ursachen, Verlauf, Auswirkungen*. Berlin: Christoph Links, 2002.

Lapp, Peter Joachim. *Gefechtsdienst im Frieden: Das Grenzregime der DDR, 1945–1990*. Koblenz: Bernard and Graefe, 1999.

Uhl, Matthias, and Armin Wagner, eds. *Ulbricht, Chruschtschow und die Mauer*. Muenchen: Oldenbourg, 2003.

BERLINER JOURNAL

A weekly German-language newspaper published every Thursday, without interruption, from 1859 to 1918 in Berlin (Kitchener), Ontario.

Founded by German-born immigrants Friedrich Rittinger and John Motz, the latter serving as the paper's editor for forty years, the *Journal* saw a steady increase in circulation figures from its inception until 1909, when its readership reached a peak of over 5,000. The *Journal* was read far beyond the borders of Waterloo County; copies of the paper were distributed to major Canadian cities as well as to former inhabitants of Berlin, Ontario, who had settled in Pennsylvania, Ohio, and Michigan. The *Journal's* aim was to provide its readers with an overview of events in Europe, particularly in Germany, as well as to report on local and regional happenings. However, in its latter years, as the *Journal's* readers became increasingly established in Canada, local news outweighed foreign reports. The *Berliner Journal* absorbed three other newspapers between 1904 and 1909, and by 1916 it was the only German-language newspaper in Ontario. The *Journal* was suddenly forced to cease publication after the government of Canada issued an Order in Council on October 2, 1918, which prohibited the publishing of German-language newspapers.

More than a mere chronicle of events, the *Berliner Journal* was a key instrument in allowing German settlers to acclimatize to their new home. While maintaining a bond with the Old World by printing national and local news from Germany, the *Journal* also introduced its readers to the customs, laws, and opportunities of the New World; proceedings of the Parliament of Canada, the Canadian constitution, and detailed reports of the Canadian political scene were all relayed in German to the paper's readership. The reporting of local news and gossip, as well as the advertising of local German cultural events such as concerts, theater performances, and church gatherings, although seemingly provincial, served the important purpose of building community. Articles and editorials advocated not only pride in German language and culture but also local pride in the city of Berlin.

In his first editorial, Motz, himself an active member of the Reform Party, made a claim of the *Berliner Journal*'s intended neutrality in reference to religion and politics, with slight leanings toward the Reform Party in regard to the latter. In fact, the *Journal* proved to be a staunch supporter of the policies of the Liberal Party (which had absorbed Reform Party remnants) up to 1904, when it merged with the *Ontario Glocke* (Ontario Bell) and became more independent politically.

In respect to the political situation in Germany, the *Berliner Journal* had a rather critical stance toward the German Empire and its restrictive policies. The pro-German stance of the *Journal*'s competitors, notably the *Freie Presse* (Free Press) and the *Deutsche Zeitung* (German Newspaper), was not well received by the public; younger German generations did not want to be set apart on the basis of their cultural origins. On this matter, as on many others, the *Berliner Journal* proved to be a German Canadian newspaper, as opposed to merely being a German-language newspaper in Canada.

Agata Monkiewicz and James M. Skidmore

> **See also** Newspaper Press, German Language in the United States; Ontario; Rittinger, John Adam

References and Further Reading
Frisse, Ulrich. *Berlin, Ontario (1800–1916)*. New Dundee, Ontario: Trans-Atlantic Publishing, 2003, 251–254.
Kalbfleisch, Herbert Karl. *The History of the Pioneer German Language Press of Ontario, 1835–1918*. Toronto: University of Toronto Press, 1968.
Richardson, Lynn Elizabeth. "A Facile Pen: John Motz and the *Berliner Journal*, 1859–1911." MA thesis, University of Waterloo, 1991.

BERLIN/KITCHENER, ONTARIO

Kitchener, named Berlin prior to 1916, is located some 100 kilometers (62 miles) west of Toronto in the center of Ontario's main German settlement area. Founded by Pennsylvania German Mennonites at the beginning of the nineteenth century, Waterloo County with its center Berlin attracted many German immigrants. As one of the main recipients of German immigrants from Europe, Berlin developed into the cultural, economic, and administrative center of the German settlement area, proudly promoting itself as "Canada's German capital." Prior to World War I, German immigrants and their descendants never accounted for less than 70 percent of the local population. Facing strong anti-German feelings and actions, the community was renamed Kitchener during World War I, and by the end of the war its unique German identity had been destroyed. Kitchener's strong German ties were reinforced after World War II, when large numbers of ethnic German immigrants who had been expelled from their homelands in Eastern Europe as well as former residents of Germany proper arrived in the community. As a result, the German presence has remained strong in Kitchener to the present day. According to the census of 2001, 47,380 out of a total population of 188,160, or 25 percent of Kitchener residents, consider themselves belonging to the German ethnic group (Statistics Canada, Census of 2001).

The village, town, and then city of Berlin grew out of a little hamlet founded by Pennsylvania German pioneers at the beginning of the nineteenth century. Pennsylvania German leaders such as Mennonite bishop Benjamin Eby defined the parameters of community life during the early pioneer period, which came to an end shortly after the arrival of the first European Germans during the 1830s. The coming of the European Germans corresponded with the end of Mennonite immigration from Pennsylvania. German immigrants brought with them to the community their highly diversified trades, which formed the basis for a strong local economy during the second half of the century. They also brought with them their Lutheran faith, the German language, traditions and customs, and forms of organizations. They founded German churches and congregations, choirs, a *Turnverein* (gymnastics association), a musical society, and theater and drama groups.

By 1850 the European German presence was so predominant in Berlin that the community's earlier Pennsylvania German identity was entirely replaced by a dominating European German character. Only very few Pennsylvania Germans contributed to Berlin's developing urban lifestyle as entrepreneurs, administrators, merchants, or artisans; most chose to maintain their traditional religiously defined lifestyle instead. Berlin's development into the urban center of Waterloo County,

perpetuated by becoming the seat of that newly founded county in 1852 and its connection to the Grand Trunk Railway only four years later, contributed to the growing lack of understanding for the Mennonites' traditional agricultural and isolated way of life among Berlin's mostly European German population.

Berlin's new European German character manifested itself in local festivities such as a celebration of Alexander von Humboldt's one hundredth birthday in 1869 and the *Friedensfest* (Peace Festival) on May 2, 1871. According to contemporary sources, 10,000 Germans and non-Germans from Canada and the northern United States came together in Berlin to celebrate the end of the Franco-Prussian War and the founding of the German Empire. During the second half of the nineteenth century Berlin also hosted several *Saengerfests,* large-scale choir festivals with visiting choirs from as far away as Montreal and Detroit. Berlin's constructed European German identity culminated in 1897 with the erection of a monument to the late Emperor Wilhelm I in Victoria Park, the town's public park, making Berlin the only community in Canada honoring a foreign monarch with a monument in a public park. Under reference to Emperor Wilhelm I's bust in their park, proponents of the community's strong "German" identity usually referred to Berlin as *Kaiserstadt* (imperial city). The "nationalization" of the community's cultural life was also expressed in the founding of a *Schuetzenverein* (hunting club) and two veterans societies in which former soldiers from the German armies performed marches and public drills on official occasions. As late as January 1914, a group of about 100 Berliners, both immigrants and members of the

Canadian-born generations, celebrated the German emperor Wilhelm II's birthday in one of the local German clubs.

Despite the official image of Berlin as "Canada's German capital" and "Kaiserstadt Berlin," local society underwent significant changes during the second half of the nineteenth century as the forces of acculturation went to work in Berlin, just as in other German ethnic neighborhoods. While old immigrants and community leaders held on to their German heritage and perpetuated the community's official German image, members of the younger generations became more and more Canadian as the century progressed. They started to define themselves not as Germans living in Canada, as their parents and grandparents did, but as Canadians of German heritage. English-language services were introduced in most of Berlin's churches from the 1890s onward. Although they did not replace German as the main language, these services clearly reflected changing demographics and the processes of acculturation, separating the old immigrants from their Canadian-born children and grandchildren. Regardless of such concessions, ethnic hardliners among the community leaders (pastors, mayors, and industrialists in particular) continued to represent Berlin to the anglophone Canadian community as exclusively German, overemphasizing the links between Berlin, Ontario, and Berlin, Germany, thereby creating the false image that Berlin's Germans identified with imperial Germany rather than with their adopted homeland, Canada.

During the challenging years of World War I, Berlin was faced with the effects of this false constructed image as well as the consequences of growing anti-German sentiment and action in Canada. Despite the fact that most Berlin factories were relentlessly contributing to the war effort by producing boots, textiles, and other products for the Canadian and the Allied armies, Berlin, as Canada's most German community, even bearing the name of the enemy's capital, was at the center of anti-German feelings in Canada. A loyalty crisis developed that originated both within and outside the community. It was spurred by widespread anti-German hysteria, the presence of military recruits, and local industrialists' fear that products bearing the label "Made in Berlin" would not be able to sell anymore. Such fears were not entirely unfounded, as Berlin products were boycotted in communities such as Toronto, where signs advertising German beer brewed in Berlin, Ontario, were prohibited. Faced with growing propaganda not just against Germany but against German Canadians and Germanness as such, Berliners tried to express their loyalty to Canada and the cause of the war by any means possible: German-language education in schools, as well as German-language services in local churches, were terminated during the war. Berlin's previously German-speaking congregations hosted smokers and dinners for the soldiers of the 118th Battalion, which was garrisoned in the community and was responsible for violent attacks on Canadians of German origin not willing to fight against the land of their parents and grandparents. The local German Concordia club closed its doors in 1915 but was nevertheless ransacked and its inventory destroyed by soldiers of the 118th Battalion. As an act of demonstrated loyalty, Berlin and neighboring Waterloo became the two communities in Canada with the highest per capita contributions to the Canadian Patriotic Fund. After a bitter campaign the community changed its name from Berlin to Kitchener in 1916, after the late British minister of war, Lord Horatio Herbert Kitchener. Although Berlin passed this loyalty test, it failed in many other regards. As was the case in other Ontario regions, Waterloo County with its center, Berlin, was not able to meet overambitious recruitment numbers for Canada's overseas forces. Members of the community openly rejected conscription, and when Prime Minister Robert Borden visited Berlin in November 1917 to rally for conscription and his unionist government, he was shouted down by members of the local audience. By electing William D. Euler in the federal elections of December 17, 1917, Berlin and the riding of Waterloo North sent a declared anticonscriptionist to Ottawa, thereby reinforcing the public perception that the community's disloyal German spirit had survived the name change.

After the experience of World War I, Kitchener developed into a more mainstream Canadian city. In the interwar years German cultural life was revitalized by the founding of new organizations, but German culture did not become predominant again in the life of the community. Attempts by a recent immigrant from Germany to establish a local National Socialist group in 1933 did not meet with wide support in the community. The *Deutscher Bund,* a militant pro-Nazi group, was established in Kitchener in 1934, but lacking response from within the community, moved its headquarters to Montreal shortly thereafter. The local chapter nevertheless organized a "German reunion" in September 1934 in which the British Union Jack and the swastika were hoisted side by side. Such expressions of loyalty to Nazi Germany were, however, not representative of the community at large. By the outbreak of World War II, most Germans had been assimilated, and Kitchener was spared a repetition of the loyalty crisis that had split the community during World War I. When Canada opened its doors again to German immigrants after the war, thousands of ethnic Germans who had been expelled from their homelands in Eastern Europe made Kitchener their new home and reinforced the German presence in the community. They came from Yugoslavia, Romania, Hungary, Poland, the Soviet Union, the Baltics, and elsewhere. Together with post–World War II immigrants from Germany, they continue to contribute greatly to Kitchener's rich cultural and economic life. At present, Kitchener is home to an annual Christkindl market, German Pioneers day, several German-speaking clubs, and North America's largest Oktoberfest, attracting hundreds of thousands of visitors annually. Successful entrepreneurs and professionals have organized themselves in the German Canadian Business and Professional Organization. Due to a changed immigration pattern since the 1980s, German Canadians have developed into one of many, albeit highly visible, groups within the local ethnic mosaic of Kitchener, Ontario.

Ulrich Frisse

See also Humboldt, Alexander von; Ontario; Turner Societies; Waterloo, Ontario; Waterloo County, Ontario

References and Further Reading
English, John, and Kenneth McLaughlin. *Kitchener: An Illustrated History.* 2nd ed. Toronto: Robin Brass, 1996.

Frisse, Ulrich. "Through German-Canadian Eyes: A Revisionist Approach to the Historical Identity of Berlin, Ontario." *Waterloo Historical Society* 91 (2003): 54–81.

———. *Berlin, Ontario (1800-1916): Historische Identitaeten von "Kanadas Deutscher Hauptstadt." Ein Beitrag zur Deutsch-Kanadischen Migrations-, Akkulturations- und Perzeptionsgeschichte des 19. und fruehen 20. Jahrhunderts.* Kitchener, ON: Transatlantic Publishing, 2003.

Uttley, W. V. (Ben). *A History of Kitchener, Ontario.* Waterloo, ON: The Chronicle Press, 1937.

BERNOULLI, CARL GUSTAV
b. January 24, 1834; Basel, Switzerland
d. May 18, 1878; San Francisco, California

Scion of a prominent family from Basel who emigrated to Guatemala in 1858, Carl Gustav Bernoulli was a doctor, pharmacist, coffee planter, explorer, and amateur archaeologist of ancient Maya sites. He was responsible for the transfer of the world-famous carved wooden panels from temple ceilings in the ancient Mayan city of Tikal to his native city of Basel, where they are exhibited in the Museum of Cultures.

Bernoulli, the son of a pharmacist, studied medicine in Würzburg, Berlin, and Paris and received his doctorate at the University of Basel in 1857. After visiting the explorer and scholar Alexander von Humboldt, then in the eighty-ninth year of his life, he traveled to Guatemala in 1858. For ten years he practiced medicine in the capital. In addition, he opened pharmacies in the provincial towns of Mazatenango and Retalhuleu and acquired a coffee plantation in the province of Suchitepequez. In 1868 he removed to Retalhuleu. Bernoulli was a passionate botanist who classified the varieties of the cocoa plant in Central America, collected numerous plants in herbariums (which are still preserved in Göttingen and Basel), and carried on an extensive correspondence with natural scientists in Germany and the United States. He published articles on his travels through Guatemala as well as on medical, geographical, and botanical subjects in German journals and regularly sent Indian antiquities, ethnographic objects, and zoological species to Basel, where his friend Fritz Müller was director of the city's natural history collections.

In 1877 Bernoulli undertook a voyage to the ancient Mayan ruins of Tikal in the company of O. R. Cario, a young botanist and geographer who had been sent to Guatemala by the director of the botanical collections in Göttingen. Bernoulli and Cario assembled extensive herbariums, which formed the basis for Cario's Göttingen dissertation, and discovered the carved wooden panels in the temple ruins. With the permission of the Guatemalan government, they instructed Franz Sarg, a German planter and businessman in the Alta Verapaz region, to ship the panels to Basel via Hamburg. The full significance of these rare wooden panels has been appreciated only in recent years, when scholars succeeded in deciphering the ancient Mayan hieroglyphs and found that they contain important information on the Mayas' knowledge of astronomy.

Bernoulli was a member of the Swiss Reformed Church who openly criticized the role of the Catholic Church in Central America. The image of the Guatamalan Indians that Bernoulli drew in his letters and articles was highly negative and reveals the influences of social Darwinism and racism.

He claimed that the Indian population could only be governed by fear and attributed the chronic labor shortage on the coffee plantations to the natives' alleged natural laziness. In several petitions to the Guatemalan government, he demanded the systematic registration and surveillance of Indian laborers for the benefit of the agricultural export economy. Each laborer was to carry a passport in which his work performance was to be meticulously recorded. Sadly enough, the government of Justo Rufino Barrios took up this idea and initiated the forced recruitment and control of the Indian workforce in the 1870s. In the twentieth century, the infamous passport laws of the South African apartheid regime followed a similar rationale.

Bernoulli planned to return to Basel in 1878 but fell ill during the voyage and died in San Francisco. In recognition of his botanical work, two plants were named for him. The *Bernoullia helvetica* is a fossil plant that Bernoulli himself discovered in stone sediments near Basel, and the *Bernoullia flammea Oliver* is an orange-blossomed tree that was found in Tikal and first described in 1936.

Michaela Schmölz-Häberlein

See also Humboldt, Alexander von
References and Further Reading
Castellanos Cambranes, Julio. *Coffee and Peasants: The Origins of the Modern Plantation Economy in Guatemala, 1853–1897.* Stockholm: Cirma, 1985.
Mayer-Holdampf, Valerie. *Ein Basler unterwegs im Dschungel von Guatemala: Carl Gustav Bernoulli (1834–1878): Arzt, Botaniker und Entdecker der Tikal-Platten.* Basel: GS-Verlag, 1997.
Schmölz-Häberlein, Michaela. *Die Grenzen des Caudillismo. Die Modernisierung des guatemaltekischen Staates unter Jorge Ubico, 1931–1944. Eine regionalgeschichtliche Studie am Beispiel der Alta Verapaz.* Frankfurt am Main et al.: Peter Lang, 1993.

BERNSTORFF, JOHANN HEINRICH ANDREAS HERMANN ALBRECHT, COUNT VON

b. November 11, 1862; London, England
d. October 6, 1939; Geneva, Switzerland

Imperial Germany's ambassador to the United States during World War I.

After the outbreak of war in Europe in August 1914, Johann Heinrich von Bernstorff found himself at the center of a diplomatic firestorm in the ensuing months. His profound knowledge of the political landscape in the United States and its economic potential, together with his conviction that President Woodrow Wilson was genuinely trying to keep his country out of the European war, led to Bernstorff's desperate but unsuccessful campaign to avert a German American break. Although a skilled and eloquent diplomat and a popular person in Washington's most influential circles, he fought from a position of weakness. His own government in Berlin regularly ignored his advice, believing him to be too liberal and too pro-Western. His urgent warnings not to underestimate U.S. determination were considered to be exaggerations by his superiors in the Foreign Office. When the naval and military high commands in Berlin decided to resume submarine warfare at the end of 1916, there was nothing left Bernstorff could do to prevent U.S. entry into the war against Germany in 1917.

Bernstorff was born in London, where his father Albrecht was ambassador to the Court of St. James. Growing up in Britain, he became bilingual. When his father died in 1873, his mother returned to the family estate in northern Germany. When a family quarrel with the influential

Bismarcks kept him from pursuing a diplomatic career in his father's footsteps, he spent eight years in the military as a lieutenant, which introduced him to the social circles at the court and to Berlin salons. In 1887, he married Jeanne Luckemeyer, a German American. A year later, the restored esteem of Herbert von Bismarck made it possible for him to be stationed with the embassy in Constantinople. In 1890, Bernstorff was sent to the Foreign Office in Berlin in order to take the two-year course prior to the diplomatic examination, which he passed in February 1892. Soon after, he was assigned to the embassy in Belgrade, where he served as legation secretary; in the summer of 1894, he was transferred to Dresden, where he remained as legation secretary until the end of 1895. Bernstorff spent the next one-and-a-half years as second secretary at the embassy in St. Petersburg. In October 1897, he was named legation secretary at the Prussian legation in Munich, where he stayed for five years.

In the autumn of 1902, Bernstorff received his first noteworthy post when he was appointed counselor of the embassy in London. In Ambassador Paul Count von Wolff-Metternich zur Gracht, he found a kindred spirit who believed that it was in Germany's best interest to pursue a conciliatory policy toward its western neighbors. This view was not shared by circles around the Berlin court and the navy, but it lead to Bernstorff's being supported by liberal-minded politicians and economists back home. In the spring of 1906, Bernstorff was named consul general in Cairo. When Hermann Speck Baron von Sternburg, the German ambassador in Washington, died in 1908, Bernstorff was appointed his successor. His ceaseless efforts between 1914 and 1917 to avoid a break between the two countries, supported by President Wilson yet so thoroughly sabotaged by Berlin, destroyed his energetic optimism and left him humiliated and broken. He was forced to return to Germany in February 1917, when diplomatic relations between the two countries were severed due to the resumed submarine warfare and the Zimmermann telegram, which had been sent to Mexico by the German foreign secretary Arthur Zimmermann. The telegram's content revealed that Germany had offered the Mexican government the lost territories of the American southwest in return for an alliance in the event of an American declaration of war. The public reacted with indignation and outrage, and on April 6, 1917, the United States declared war on Germany.

In the last year of the war, Bernstorff accepted the post of ambassador to Constantinople. In October 1918, when it could no longer be denied that Germany was losing the war, he was asked to succeed Paul von Hintze as foreign secretary, but he refused the offer. In anticipation of negotiations with President Wilson, Bernstorff was ordered back to Berlin in order to share his intimate knowledge of the United States. He was appointed head of the preparatory Commission for the Peace Negotiations, and advocated acceptance of the unpopular Treaty of Versailles. After the war, Bernstorff became an unfaltering supporter of the Weimar Republic and helped to organize the Deutsche Demokratische Partei (German Democratic Party) in 1919. He represented his party in the Reichstag from 1921 to 1928.

On the international level, Bernstorff cofounded the Deutsche Liga für den Völkerbund (German Association for the

League of Nations), and served as its president for ten years. In addition, he was elected president of the World Federation of Associations for the League of Nations. From 1926 to 1933, he headed the German delegation to the Preparatory Conference for Disarmament in Geneva. As a diplomat, Bernstorff was convinced that only a policy based on mutual respect and international negotiations would prevent future wars. When several of his friends were assassinated by radicals despising the republic in the 1920s, Bernstorff began to fear for his life, as he was soon viewed as a traitor because of his ideals. After the National Socialist German Worker's Party's (NSDAP) electoral success in 1933, he went into exile in Geneva in order to escape persecution.

Katja Wuestenbecker

See also Sternburg, Hermann Speck von; Treaty of Versailles; World War I
References and Further Reading
Bernstorff, Johann H. von. *My Three Years in America.* New York: Charles Scribner's Sons, 1920.
Doerries, Reinhard R. *Imperial Challenge: Ambassador Count Bernstorff and German American Relations, 1908–1917.* Chapel Hill: University of North Carolina Press, 1989.
Tinnemann, Ethel Mary. "Count Johann von Bernstorff and German-American Relations, 1908–1817." PhD diss., University of California at Berkeley, 1960.

BISMARCK'S ANTI-SOCIALIST LAW (1878–1890)

Concerned with the growth of the Social Democratic Party of Germany (SPD) in the 1870s, Chancellor Otto von Bismarck sponsored passage in the German Reichstag of the Ausnahmegesetz zur Abwehr sozialdemokratischer Ausschreitungen (Exceptional Law for Vigilance against Social Democratic Activities, or the Anti-Socialist Law) on October 19, 1878. This law suppressed Socialist publications, issued arrest warrants for party leaders, outlawed trade unions, and suppressed public demonstrations. Its passage damaged the SPD, which rallied during the 1880s and grew to become the largest faction in the Reichstag by 1912.

A state-of-siege aspect of this law enabled the police to expel persons who were considered "dangerous to public security and order." These laws forced many Socialists and skilled workers to leave Germany for other places in Europe and North America. German immigrants swelled the ranks of American labor organizations. Waves of machinists and toolmakers, artisans and craftspeople were hired in factories in Milwaukee, Chicago, and Pittsburgh. These workers reached the New World with memories of a hostile central government, experience with a political party, and an awareness of the value of organizing labor. The most noteworthy refugees from Bismarckian repression to surface on the landscape of American socialism were the radical Johann Most and the Lassallean Paul Grottkau. Once established in the United States, the Socialist émigrés from Germany tended to be drawn to the radical fringe of labor politics. Anarchists and Socialists, most of the accused "Haymarket bombers" in Chicago were German immigrants who had left their homeland in the wake of the anti-Socialist law. An arch-foe of SPD leader Wilhelm Liebknecht, Johann Most wrote a manual on bomb making and spent much of his New York residency in Blackwell Island prison. He was arrested first in connection with the Haymarket Square bombing and stayed on the radical fringe of the working-class movement, writing in German only until his death in 1906.

Labor politics in the United States gravitated toward trade union sponsorship. Socialists scored electoral triumphs in a number of U.S. cities (Milwaukee in 1910 was their most striking victory), but the Germans fleeing from Bismarckian oppression never found a strong party base. American socialism evolved as a marginal political movement, but it was articulated with a strong German accent. Socialist newspapers were published in German by the end of the nineteenth century in New York, Chicago, and most major cities. German working-class immigrants contributed organization and ideology to American labor politics leading up to World War I.

Gareth A. Shellman

See also Anarchists; Chicago; Haymarket; Liebknecht, Wilhelm; Milwaukee; Most, Johann; New York City; Socialist Labor Party

References and Further Reading

Dominick, Raymond H. *Wilhelm Liebknecht and the Founding of the German Social Democratic Party.* Chapel Hill: University of North Carolina Press, 1982.

Lidtke, Vernon L. *The Outlawed Party: Social Democracy in Germany, 1978–1890.* Princeton: Princeton University Press, 1966.

Überhorst, Horst. *The German Element in the U.S. Labor Movement.* Bonn: Friedrich Ebert Stiftung, 1983.

BITBURG

President Ronald Reagan and federal chancellor Helmut Kohl made a highly controversial visit on May 5, 1985, to the Bitburg war cemetery to honor German soldiers who had died in World War II. Intended as a symbolic act of German American reconciliation, the ceremony provoked strong protests from U.S. veterans of World War II and the American Jewish community after approximately forty-eight graves of Waffen-SS were discovered and Reagan equated victims of the concentration camps with fallen German soldiers. German American relations suffered a temporary setback when Kohl insisted on the visit in the face of U.S. demands to release Reagan from his commitments to the chancellor.

Kohl, chairman of the Christlich Demokratische Union (Christian Democratic Party, or CDU), who had been excluded from the Western Allies' commemoration of the fortieth anniversary of D-Day in June 1984, desired a symbolic gesture of reconciliation and friendship between the former enemies of World War II. French president François Mitterand obliged by meeting Kohl at the battlefield of Verdun. During a visit to the White House in November 1984, the chancellor proposed a similar event to Reagan, to be scheduled during the upcoming economic summit in Bonn in early May 1985. Michael Deaver, the White House chief of staff, developed the program in cooperation with the federal chancellory.

The original plan called for honoring both U.S. and German graves. Since no U.S. soldiers are buried in Germany, the German war cemetery in Bitburg was chosen, mostly for its logistically convenient proximity to a U.S. Air Force base. The planners remained unaware of the presence of Waffen-SS graves. Kohl had also suggested an additional visit to the concentration camp Dachau. The White House mistakenly believed that the chancellor would prefer not to be embarrassed by being reminded of Nazi crimes, however, and removed the visit from the program.

The scandal broke when journalists discovered Waffen-SS graves at the cemetery only a few days after the Bitburg visit was announced on April 11, 1985. The Waffen-SS had been instrumental in the implementation of the Holocaust and had committed war crimes throughout Europe, including a massacre of U.S. prisoners of war (POWs) at Malmedy. By going to Bitburg, not only did the U.S. president honor the perpetrators, but also he ignored their victims by refusing to visit a concentration camp. Even worse, during a press conference Reagan equated murderers and victims when he maintained that German soldiers were victims of Nazism "as surely as the victims of the concentration camps" (*New York Times,* April 19, 1985).

For a month Bitburg remained on the front pages of newspapers and was the top news item in TV news and political talk shows in the United States. As the various fortieth anniversaries of World War II events had passed, the media had regularly published documentary accounts of the fighting and the atrocities. On prime-time TV, graphic historical footage of the liberation of concentration camps ran next to the latest on the Bitburg scandal. Published opinion was almost unanimous in its condemnation of the visit; editorials called for cancelling the ceremony or at least changing the itinerary to include a concentration camp. Instead of Reagan, an inept White House staff and a stubborn Kohl were blamed for the fiasco. Passionate opposition to the visit was widespread. Veterans' groups charged Reagan with dishonoring the sacrifices of U.S. soldiers. All major

churches condemned the visit as an insult to the victims. Both houses of Congress passed resolutions urging Kohl to rescind his invitation to Bitburg.

The strongest protest came from the American Jewish community. Jewish leaders lobbied Congress and the White House, organized protests, and spoke publicly against the visit. By honoring the perpetrators, they said, the U.S. government appeared to dismiss the suffering of millions, causing deep hurt to Holocaust survivors and descendents of victims. Outrage and deep disappointment found their expression in public remembrances of the Shoa that turned into manifestations against the Bitburg visit.

The most poignant event occurred during a White House ceremony in honor of Nobel Prize laureate Elie Wiesel's reception of the Congressional Gold Medal. On live TV he addressed the president directly and implored him to cancel the cemetery visit: "That place, Mr. President, is not your place. Your place is with the victims of the SS" (*New York Times,* April 20, 1985).

Opinion polls showed that the American public was not quite as adamantly opposed. Only a slight majority of Americans opposed the visit, whereas a strong minority approved of the effort of German American reconciliation. In Germany, Bitburg was only one issue in a larger debate about the meaning of May 8, 1945, as defeat versus liberation. Kohl, although sincere in his many statements on German historic responsibilities for Nazi crimes, adhered to the conservative predilection of stressing German victimhood. His government falsely claimed that the Waffen-SS graves only contained young draftees who could not have been involved in atrocities and maintained the popular myth that the Waffen-SS had merely been troops of honorable elite soldiers. The chancellory also feared that a retreat from the visit would benefit Soviet attempts at dividing the Western allies over their past enmity.

Kohl received support from about 70 percent of the German public, from expellee organizations, the conservative media, and his party's nationalist wing. Sharp criticism of the visit came mainly from the leftist opposition, public intellectuals, and the liberal media, who denounced Kohl's *Vergangenheitspolitik* (coming to terms with the past policy), alleging that he was attempting to rewrite history in a conservative mode. The White House staff, unable to dissuade Reagan or the Germans from the visit, tried to minimize the scandal's outfall by adding a stopover at the Bergen-Belsen concentration camp to the program. The visits to Bergen-Belsen and Bitburg on May 5 passed without any problems. Kohl and Reagan gave long, well-received speeches at the camp, while the Bitburg event was reduced to a very short wreath-laying ceremony with White House officials doing their best to limit TV coverage. Immediately following the ceremony, Kohl and Reagan visited with jubilant U.S. soldiers and Bitburg citizens at the Bitburg Air Force base, celebrating German American friendship. Live TV coverage in the United States and Germany was extensive and mildly critical.

Overall, Deaver's damage control was fairly successful. After the event U.S. opinion polls showed a slight majority approving the visit. Deaver left the White House as he had planned before Bitburg and loyally carried all responsibility for the scandal with him, leaving the president untar-nished. The painful and embarrassing issue quickly disappeared from media attention. American Jewish leaders realized that ironically Bitburg, notwithstanding the severe trauma it had caused, had helped more to raise American consciousness of the Holocaust than any educational program could have achieved.

In Germany the debate over the past took a decisive turn through the memorial speech of federal president Richard von Weizsäcker (CDU) in the Bundestag only three days after Bitburg. He insisted that May 8, 1945, could not be separated from January 30, 1933, the ascendancy of Hitler to power. In what later became the consensus interpretation, he acknowledged the suffering of many Germans, but insisted that overall May 8 meant the liberation of Germany and turned out to be for the good of all. "Die Rede" (The Speech), as it came to be known, is arguably one of the most important speeches in postwar German history and became required reading in German high schools. Weizsäcker's eloquence quickly overshadowed Kohl's Bitburg mess and smoothed the waves of a bitter debate.

Raimund Lammersdorf

See also World War II

References and Further Reading

Funke, Hajo. "Bitburg, Jews, and Germans: A Case Study of Anti-Jewish Sentiment in Germany during May 1985." *New German Critique*, no. 38 (1986): 57–72.

Hartman, Geoffrey H., ed. *Bitburg in Moral and Political Perspective*. Bloomington: Indiana University Press, 1986.

Levkov, Ilya, ed. *Bitburg and Beyond: Encounters in American, German, and Jewish History*. New York: Shapolsky Publishers, 1987.

Lipstadt, Deborah E. "The Bitburg Controversy." *American Jewish Yearbook* 87 (1987): 21–37.

BLOCH, FELIX

b. October 23, 1905; Zurich, Switzerland
d. September 10, 1983; Zurich,
Switzerland

A Swiss physicist who left Germany for the
United States in the early 1930s and participated in the Manhattan Project, Felix
Bloch was a pioneer of solid-state physics
and was awarded the Nobel Prize for his research on magnetic nuclear resonance.

Bloch studied engineering at the Eid-
genössische Technische Hochschule (Federal Institute of Technology, ETH) in
Zurich. Impressed by Peter Debye's lectures, he decided to switch from engineering to physics and mathematics. After he
received his diploma in 1926, Bloch became the first doctoral student of Werner
Heisenberg at the University of Leipzig. In
his dissertation (1928), Bloch investigated
the conductivity of metals by applying the
new methods of quantum theory. He constructed *Eigenfunctions* of electrons in the
periodic lattice potential that became fundamental to the theory of solid-state
physics, later known as "Bloch Waves."
After some time as an assistant to Wolfgang
Pauli in Zurich, where supraconductivity
had been his research topic, and a fellowship at the University of Utrecht, Bloch returned to Leipzig in 1930. Two years later,
he defended his second doctoral dissertation (Habilitation). During this time,
Bloch collaborated with Niels Bohr in
Copenhagen and worked on the theory of
ferromagnetica, as well as on metallic conductivity. When the National Socialist
German Worker's Party (NSDAP) came to
power in Germany, he resigned voluntarily
from his teaching position at the University of Leipzig.

Financed by a grant from the Rockefeller Foundation, Bloch continued his research in Rome and Cambridge. A recommendation from Bohr got Bloch a two-year
appointment at Stanford University. When
he turned down an offer to join the Hebrew University in Jerusalem in 1936,
Bloch was made full professor at Stanford.
He thus became the first professor of theoretical physics at that university. Yet Bloch
did not remain a classical theoretical physicist. He favored a close connection between theoretical and experimental
physics. Bloch performed experiments
using an X-ray tube to produce neutrons
and developed a theory of magnetic neutron scattering. From 1938 onward, he collaborated with Luis Alvarez from the University of California at Berkeley, where he
had access to a cyclotron. Using this apparatus, Bloch and Alvarez determined the
magnetic moment of the neutron. Bloch
managed to convince Stanford to acquire a
cyclotron. It was constructed from 1939 to
1941, mainly for the purpose of providing
neutrons for magnetic investigations. For
the Manhattan Project, Bloch determined
the energy spectrum of those neutrons that
were set free in the process of nuclear fis-
sion. For a few months in 1943, he worked
on the implosion problem in Los Alamos.
Afterward he joined the Radio Research
Laboratory at Harvard University, where
he worked on technologies that could prevent detection of any military objects like
ships or airplanes by radar.

After the end of World War II, Bloch
returned to Stanford University. Through
his research on ferromagnetism and magnetic moments, he became interested in
nuclear induction. Bloch was able to determine the nuclear moments of solid bodies,

fluids, and gases by measuring the "Larmor frequency" of an external alternating magnetic field. The method was called nuclear magnetic resonance (NMR) and became important in chemistry, biology, and medicine. Bloch, together with Edward Purcell, was awarded the Nobel Prize for this discovery in 1952. From 1954 to 1955 Bloch served as the general manager of the newly founded Conseil Européen pour la Recherche Nucléaire in Geneva.

Back at Stanford University, he devoted much of his time to the construction of a large linear accelerator. Continuing his research on nuclear induction, he focused on the microscopic interpretation of phenomenological parameters. During the 1960s, Bloch returned to the topic of supraconductivity. He found a comparatively simple explanation for the "Josephson effect" (a flow of electric current between two pieces of superconducting material separated by a thin layer of insulating material). Bloch continued his research until his death during a visit in Zurich.

Stefan L. Wolff

See also U.S.-German Intellectual Exchange
References and Further Reading
Chodorow, Marvin, ed. *Felix Bloch and Twentieth-Century Physics.* Houston: William Marsh Rice University, 1980.
Hofstadter, Robert. *Felix Bloch: Biographical Memoirs of the National Academy of Sciences* 64 (1994): 34–71.

B'NAI B'RITH (SONS OF THE COVENANT)

The Independent Order of B'nai B'rith is the oldest and largest Jewish fraternal order.

B'nai B'rith was founded on October 13, 1843, in New York City by eleven German Jews (Henry Jones, Isaac Rosenbourgh, Isaac Dittenhoefer, Joseph Seligman, William Renau, Michael Schwab, Ruben M. Rodacher, Henry Kling, Valentine Koon, Samuel Schafer, and Jonas Hecht). Most of them were immigrants and belonged to the traditional German Jewish congregation Anshe Chesed. Following the foundation of the order, the majority of this group broke away from the congregation and founded a Kultusverein (religious association). This association formed the basis for the Reform congregation Emanu-El of New York City. The latter became a symbol of the German Jewish desire to add decorum, worship, and respectability to traditional Jewish religiosity. In the United States the majority of the founders were active members of American lodges, such as the Masons and the Odd Fellows. Although several Jews were rejected by American fraternal orders, Henry Jones, the president of the congregation and a high-ranking member of the Odd Fellows, argued that not antisemitism but the lack of American religious forms and middle-class respectability of those applicants was the cause of their rejection. To remedy this problem and to improve the image of Jews and Judaism in the United States, he suggested the founding of a Jewish fraternal order, where the growing number of immigrant Jews could improve each other and practice a sense of community while developing a respectable American civic identity.

Indeed, the founding of a Jewish fraternal order served several needs of the quickly growing American Jewish community. First, it provided a modern platform for Jews of different backgrounds who missed a sense of social community in the American synagogue, which was a spiritual rather than a social center. Second, the founding of the order was closely connected with the introduction of the German Reform movement in the United States, which triggered increased factionalism in American Jewish congregational life and thus threatened the ethnic unity Israel was commanded by the Covenant to observe. Third, the order actively tried to familiarize immigrant Jews with the challenges of American modernity by bridging the division between community and society through its organizational setup and teachings; it actively promoted integration and the rejection of religious particularism in favor of a new civic American and Jewish identity.

The idea of the B'nai B'rith, its "civic Judaism" and construction of an American Jewish civil religion, was closely linked to the Reform movement in Judaism. Both placed Judaism in the middle of the human family and stressed the brotherly nature of human relationships, helping Jews in modern times seek universalism, take on an active role in society, and overcome traditional particularism. Nevertheless, B'nai B'rith strictly guarded its organizational and religious independence from the Reform movement, its congregations and ecclesiastic life to be able to serve as a platform to unite all Jews, no matter their religious affiliation.

The order's commitment to secrecy was subject to continuous criticism from inside and outside, especially since it did not seem in line with the universalist mission of the organization. In fact, however, its secrecy protected mainly the details surrounding the order's charitable support. This charitable engagement followed the tradition of Jewish *chevrot* (communal mutual aid societies). Although the fraternal ritual was also kept secret, as in other fra-

ternal orders, proceedings and reports of annual meetings were regularly published.

Soon after its founding, the order rapidly grew into a national organization, long before a national religious platform could be established. Therefore, the order had a tremendous impact on the shaping of an American Jewish identity and on the founding and support of the first Jewish charitable and communal institutions. These hospitals, orphanages, and manual training schools could not have been established by individual congregations given their size. Among the best know of these institutions are the Cleveland Orphan Asylum; the Philadelphia Jewish Hospital; the Chicago Jewish Hospital; the Touro Hospital in New Orleans; the National Jewish Hospital for Jewish Consumptives; the Leo N. Levi Hospital in Hot Springs, Arkansas; the Philadelphia Jewish Orphan Asylum; the Atlanta Jewish Orphan Asylum; the Jewish Orphan Asylum in New Orleans; the Manual Training School in Philadelphia; and the Jewish Home for the Aged in Yonkers, New York.

The organization was a strictly male order until 1895, when the men's organization started offering membership in women's auxiliaries. However, between 1874 and 1895 the B'nai B'rith officially recognized the Unabhängiger Orden Treuer Schwestern (United Order of True Sisters) as its sister organization.

In 1882, B'nai B'rith's success in the United States and the service of former B'nai B'rith president Benjamin Peixotto as U.S. consul in Romania (1870–1873) prompted the organization to create a network for international Jewish solidarity. Demonstrating its close relationship to German Jewry, its first lodge abroad was founded as Deutsche Reichsloge (German

Imperial Lodge) in Berlin in 1882. The German lodges served as a European stronghold and organizational center for the spreading network of lodges across Europe and the Orient, such as Cairo (1886), Jerusalem (1888), and Romania (1889). By the 1930s B'nai B'rith had grown to be the single most important international Jewish organization, providing with its "civic Judaism" a transnational network of Jewish solidarity in modernity.

After the Nazis took power in Germany, B'nai B'rith was forced to close its lodges in 1937. Because of the Holocaust the order was almost extinguished in Europe. After the Holocaust the order changed its focus to Zionism and became a staunch supporter of the newly founded state of Israel, where it established a strong foothold. During the 1960s, the order slowly started rebuilding lodges in Germany and is currently present in fifty-seven countries throughout the world. Today the organization has its headquarters at B'nai B'rith International in Washington, D.C.

In the twentieth century B'nai B'rith played a major role in American Jewish social and political life through the founding of several suborganizations, which reflect its core values of civic service and commitment. Among them are the Anti-Defamation League of B'nai B'rith (1913); the Hillel Organization of B'nai B'rith (Jewish campus organization, 1923); and the youth organizations Ahava, Zedakah, Achdut (Love, Justice, and Unity, 1924), and B'nai B'rith Youth Organization (1948). B'nai B'rith Women was established in 1909 but remained an auxiliary until 1947, when it finally gained equal membership status. In 1995 it had changed its name to Jewish Women International.

Cornelia Wilhelm

See also Antisemitism; German Jewish Migration to the United States; Judaism, Reform (North America); Unabhängiger Orden Treuer Schwestern

References and Further Reading

Moore, Deborah D. *B'nai B'rith and the Challenge of Ethnic Leadership.* Albany: SUNY Press, 1981.

Wilhelm, Cornelia. "Community in Modernity: Finding Jewish Solidarity within the Independent Order B'nai B'rith." *Jahrbuch des Simon-Dubnow-Institut für jüdische Geschichte und Kultur* 1 (2001): 297–319.

———. "Shaping American Jewish Identity: The Independent Order B'nai B'rith." *German-Jewish Identities in America: From the Civil War to the Present.* Ed. Christof Mauch and Joe Salmons. Madison: Max Kade Institute, 2003, 64–87.

BODMER, KARL

b. February 11, 1809; Zurich, Switzerland
d. October 30, 1893; Paris, France

Best known for the depictions he created of native peoples and lands while accompanying Prince Maximilian of Wied-Neuwied (1782–1867) on an expedition along the upper Missouri frontier in the early nineteenth century. The artist rendered Native Americans, flora, fauna, settlements, and topography with a wealth of realistic detail unprecedented prior to the invention of the camera, thus transforming images into "exquisite representations of life and landscape" (Wood, Porter, and Hunt 2002, 14). Historians and anthropologists value Bodmer's drawings, paintings, and prints as a visual documentary of a rapidly changing young country experiencing the emergence of an industrial society and the destruction of its natural resources and Indian cultures. Bodmer also portrayed towns such as Bethlehem, Pennsylvania, and Gnadenhutten,

Mouth of the Fox River *(Indiana), painting by Karl Bodmer, ca. 1834. Bodmer is best known for the depictions he created of native peoples and lands while accompanying Prince Maximilian of Wied-Neuwied (1782–1867) on an expedition along the upper Missouri frontier in the early nineteenth century. (New York Public Library)*

Ohio, which had been founded by German Moravians; Prince Maximilian visited these places to learn the fate of Germans who had fled persecution in their native country. After the expedition, Bodmer supervised the production of eighty-one aquatints (prints made from etched or engraved images on a metal plate) for an atlas published with the German, French, and English editions of *Travels in the Interior of North America, 1832–1834.* This two-volume work contained Maximilian's scientific observations and travel notes on topics such as slavery, politics, the environment, and the frontier.

At age thirteen, Bodmer began receiving instruction in watercolor, sketching, and engraving from his uncle, the painter

Johann Jakob Meier (1787–1858). He moved to Koblenz, at the confluence of the Rhine and Moselle rivers, in 1828. His drawings and watercolors of this region, which were published in scenic folios popular with tourists, caught the attention of Prince Maximilian; the German aristocrat, who had studied the natural sciences, needed an artist to illustrate his exploration of the American frontier. A Prussian officer recommending the young Swiss artist for the adventure found him to be healthy, aptly talented, enthusiastic about the journey, and undemanding; he had only to hone his hunting skills. Bodmer's contract with Maximilian provided for a modest salary, expenses, paper, and art materials; the artist would supply his own drawing instruments. In preparation for the journey, both Bodmer and his patron examined expeditionary and ethnographic art available at that time, including the works of American artist George Catlin.

Prince Maximilian and Bodmer left Rotterdam on May 17, 1832, arriving in Boston on July 4. En route to the Missouri River, they spent the winter at New Harmony, Indiana, a town founded in 1814 by the German religious leader Georg Rapp. While staying in this frontier scientific community, Bodmer and Maximilian used the extensive library of natural history and discussed Native Americans with eminent scientists. Bodmer also completed a large series on the town's environs. The documentary value of his work is evident in *Confluence of the Fox River and the Wabash.* Depicted in the watercolor are several Carolina parakeets; the only parrot native to the United States, this species is now extinct. In January 1833 Bodmer traveled alone to New Orleans, where he made his first drawings of Native Americans—Choctaws, Cherokees, and Chickasaws.

The actual expedition, which was fraught with the perils and hardships of frontier life, began in early April 1833, when Maximilian and Bodmer departed from St. Louis on a steamboat. Their journey extended to Fort McKenzie in Great Falls, Montana, and took them into territories that had hardly been explored. When Assiniboines and Crees attacked the Piegans outside Fort McKenzie on August 28, 1833, Maximilian and Bodmer grabbed their weapons and joined the battle. Bodmer's later sketch of the event and Maximilian's notes are considered among the most exceptional non-Indian eyewitness accounts of intertribal warfare. Afterward, armed guards often accompanied Bodmer

when he left the fort to paint. The five winter months spent at Fort Clark (Bismarck, North Dakota) proved to be the most significant and productive phase of the expedition for both Maximilian and Bodmer, in part due to their contact with the Mandan and Hidatsa tribes. Bodmer spent time with Mandan warrior friends, and his portraits of Four Bears, a prominent Mandan chief, and Two Ravens, a warrior from the Hidatsa tribe, are among his best-known works. Once again, his renderings proved to be timely historical documents. Less than one month after they left Fort Clark, two of three Hidatsa villages were destroyed by Lakotas, and in 1837 a smallpox epidemic killed all but about 120 Mandans, including Four Bears.

Although Maximilian often mentions in his journals a painting that his Swiss companion had made, no record exists of how the artist went about his work or selected particular subjects or scenes. Bodmer probably worked independently, choosing his subject matter from his own field studies and, in some cases, from Maximilian's sketches; in New Harmony and at Fort McKenzie and Fort Clark he was able to set up studios. The Native Americans he portrayed often spent hours dressing themselves for sittings, in order to show their family position or wealth. Depicting his subjects as strong and dignified, Bodmer focused on the details of their physiognomy, clothing, weapons, and decoration. He strove to produce the visual representation for his employer's scientific observations; absent in his portraits are the sentimental exaggerations often found in nineteenth-century paintings of Native Americans or the nationalist motives apparent in works of his contemporary, Thomas Cole. Bodmer did employ European conventions for his landscapes, however; romantic elements can be found in his paintings of the eastern woodlands or geological formations on the upper Missouri.

After returning to Europe in late August 1834, Bodmer established a studio in Paris in 1836 and spent nearly ten years supervising the production of the copperplate and steel engravings to illustrate Prince Maximilian's text. Both the text and the plates used for the atlas were sold by subscription; the date given in the German edition was 1839–1841, although the final installments did not appear until 1843. The prints were issued on at least three different weights and finishes of paper, in colored and also black-and-white editions (or combinations thereof). After completion of the atlas, Bodmer ended his business relationship with Maximilian, although they maintained their friendship and continued to correspond. Before relinquishing most of his American art to his employer, as stipulated in his contract, Bodmer exhibited his works in 1845. He married, became a French citizen, and in 1849 moved to Barbizon, where he associated with French landscape artists such as Jean Baptiste Camille Corot and Jean François Millet. He collaborated with Millet on an American commission for a series of lithographs of early frontier life; the project was discontinued, but four prints entitled *Annals of the United States Illustrated: The Pioneers* did appear. Bodmer won the third-prize medal at the Universal Exposition in Paris in 1855 and received honorable mention at the Salon of 1863.

Lorie A. Vanchena

See also Indians in German Literature; Pietism; Wied-Neuwied, Maximilian Alexander Philipp Prinz zu

References and Further Reading

Gallagher, Marsha V., and John F. Sears. *Karl Bodmer's Eastern Views: A Journey in North America.* Omaha: Joslyn Art Museum, 1996.

Hunt, David C., and Marsha V. Gallagher, eds. *Karl Bodmer's America.* Omaha: Joslyn Art Museum and University of Nebraska Press, 1984.

Wood, W. Raymond, Joseph C. Porter, and David C. Hunt. *Karl Bodmer's Studio Art: The Newberry Library Bodmer Collection.* Urbana: University of Illinois Press, 2002.

BONHOEFFER, DIETRICH
b. February 4, 1906; Breslau (Silesia), Prussia
d. April 9, 1945; Flossenbürg, Bavaria

German Lutheran pastor and theologian who was a Sloane Fellow at Union Theological Seminary in New York from 1930 to 1931. Bonhoeffer was at first not impressed with the state of theology at Union, confiding in a letter about the dismal state of theology in U.S. seminaries. This negative assessment of American theology was soon countered by his admiration for the manner in which some American Christians wrestled with troubling social ills and especially racial prejudice. During his year at Union, he took Reinhold Niebuhr's course in applied theology and regularly visited black Baptist churches in Harlem, especially Abyssinian Baptist Church, pastored by Adam Clayton Powell Sr. Bonhoeffer was deeply grieved by the plight of African Americans in the United States, and it is probable that his months visiting Harlem were formative in setting the terms by which he would oppose the Third Reich.

In 1931 he returned to Europe, first taking a pastorate and a university lectureship in Berlin (officially revoked in 1936), but also for brief periods serving congregations in and around London and, after 1935, teaching at illegal German seminaries. An increasingly outspoken critic of the Nazis, Bonhoeffer initially joined the ranks of the Confessing Church and was a signer of the Barmen Declaration (1934), which outlined the spiritual mission of the church in contrast to the views of the Nazi-supporting "German Christians." As his political safety withered in the tense years of late-1930s Germany, Bonhoeffer considered exile and his American friends encouraged it. Yet after traveling to New York in summer 1939 with teaching positions arranged, he changed his mind and returned to Germany with the intention of living through a difficult period of German history with the Christians of Germany. He would famously insist that "Only he who cries out for the Jews may sing Gregorian chants!" Upon his return, he became a civilian member of the *Abwehr,* a secret service of the German Army. Bonhoeffer conspired with a select group in the *Abwehr* to remove Adolf Hitler from power. His English and American theological connections made him a valuable asset in the resistance movement. His arrest in 1943 and execution on April 9, 1945, in Flossenbürg shortly before the war's end have earned him a prominent place in most accounts of twentieth-century Christian martyrs. During his visits to the United States and through later correspondence, Bonhoeffer grew close to Reinhold Niebuhr, Paul Lehmann, the Swiss theologian Erwin Sutz, the French Reformed pastor and pacifist Jean Lasserre, and the African American student from Alabama, Franklin Fisher. Despite his affinities with American neo-orthodox and liberal theology, Bonhoeffer's writings have appealed to a wide spectrum of American Christian readers.

R. Bryan Bademan

See also Germans Students at American Universities; Harnack, Mildred Fish
References and Further Reading
Bethge, Eberhard. *Dietrich Bonhoeffer: A Biography.* Rev. and ed. Victoria J. Barnett. Minneapolis: Fortress Press, 2000.
Holland, Scott. "First We Take Manhattan, Then We Take Berlin: Bonhoeffer's New York." *Cross Currents* (Fall 2000).
Zerner, Ruth. "Dietrich Bonhoeffer's American Experiences: People, Letters, and Papers from Union Seminary." *Union Seminary Quarterly Review* (Summer 1976).

BOSSE, GEORG VON
b. November 3, 1862; Helmstedt, Duchy of Brunswick
d. April 21, 1943; Rahns, Pennsylvania

A leader of German Americans committed to the notion that German immigrants and their progeny should steadfastly retain their ethnic heritage.

Essential to this endeavor for Lutheran pastor Georg von Bosse was maintenance of German language, culture, and religious practices. Von Bosse wrote books, essays, and poems on the experiences of Germans in the United States. He believed that it was possible for German Americans to live in a dual world: a German sphere of culture, religious piety, and joy in life and an American sphere that included civil and religious liberties. His beautifully written history of Germans in the United States, *Das deutsche Element in den Vereinigten Staaten* (The German Element in the United States, 1908), remains a standard work. Like most of his writings, this prize-winning book was addressed not only to Germans and others in the United States but also to Germans in Europe. He was pastor of several German Lutheran churches in the mid-Atlantic region before accepting a call in 1906 from St. Paul's German Lutheran Church in Philadelphia, where he remained until his retirement in 1930. Von Bosse was deeply committed to the struggle to maintain U.S. neutrality during World War I. In 1917 his like-minded son, Pastor Sigmund G. von Bosse, became president of the National German-American Alliance, devoted to keeping the United States out of war with Germany and to the struggle against Prohibition.

Von Bosse's early education was dominated by his highly cultivated, cosmopolitan aunt, Auguste von Bosse, a writer then well known under her pseudonym, H. Schönau. He rebelled against her by entering a special Lutheran seminary in Kropp/Schleswig, which from the 1880s to 1931 produced over 200 pastors to meet the shortage of Lutheran clerics in the United States. Central themes of this training included the need to ensure that Germans abroad maintained their language as well as loyalty to the Lutheran faith and the land of their birth.

Von Bosse arrived in the United States in 1889, served in Philadelphia for a year as assistant pastor of St. Paul's, married a young parishioner, and accepted a call from a Lutheran church in the German American town of Egg Harbor City, New Jersey, in 1891. Establishing a household that, he hoped, would be a model for German Americans, he obtained his wife's agreement that German would be the language of their home. When he first met his future wife during a pastoral call, she, like many children of immigrants, spoke to her parents in English. The two years that von Bosse spent as the head of a German orphanage near Buffalo at the beginning of the twentieth century gave him the opportunity to test on a large scale his theories of language retention. He ascertained that the major reason children were reluctant to speak German was that they felt ashamed to display the poor German learned from their parents. Von Bosse found the key to the retention of German in providing bilingual education aimed at complete fluency in both languages.

Despite von Bosse's sophistication, he saw the world in simplistic terms. Throughout the earth, he intoned in 1909, a great struggle was under way between two weltanschauungen: one Germanic, one English. He perceived the conflict in the United States as one in which "the English"—his term for monolingual speakers of English—were attempting to assimilate newcomers. Religion played a major role among the issues he addressed: English religion was, he complained, superficial, as were the English in general. Also on his list of grievances were English churches (largely secularized), English worship (too emotional), and English preaching (sensationalistic). For von Bosse, the English perceived of religion as a social force, whereas the Germans looked upon it as a matter of individual piety. He complained bitterly about the Puritans, whom he identified as the source of much fanaticism and hypocrisy, as in the temperance and Prohibition movements

Von Bosse was a German chauvinist, not inclined to compromise as had German Americans like Carl Schurz, who was involved far more deeply in American politics. Curiously, von Bosse wrote very favorable biographies of both Schurz and Charles J. Hexamer. One of two mottos von Bosse placed at the head of his history of German Americans is a version of a couplet by a nineteenth-century German poet often cited after Emperor Wilhelm II made it famous: "Und es mag am deutschen Wesen/Noch einmal die Welt genesen" (And the world may once again be saved by German virtue). Von Bosse proudly announced in 1909 that he had joined the Pan-German League.

Walter Struve

See also Egg Harbor City, New Jersey; Hexamer, Charles J.; National German-American Alliance; Schurz, Carl; World War I

References and Further Reading

Bosse, Georg von. "Die deutsche Kirche und Gemeindeschule in Amerika." In *Das Buch der Deutschen in Amerika*. Ed. Max Heinrici. Hrsg. unter den Auspicien des Deutsch-Amerikanischen National-Bundes. Philadelphia: Walther's Buchdruckerei, 1909.

———. *Ein Kampf um Glauben und Volkstum: Das Streben während meines 25jährigen Amtslebens als deutschlutherischer Geistlicher in Amerika.* Stuttgart: Chr. Belsersche Verlagsbuchhandlung, 1920.

Kloss, Heinz. "German-American Language Maintenance Efforts." In *Language Loyalty in the United States: The Maintenance and Perpetuation of Non-English Mother Tongues by American Ethnic and Religious Groups.* Ed. Joshua Fishman. The Hague: Mouton, 1966.

Luebke, Frederick G. *Bonds of Loyalty: German Americans and World War I.* DeKalb: Northern Illinois University Press, 1974.

BOVERI, MARGARET
b. August 14, 1900; Würzburg, Bavaria
d. July 6, 1975; West Berlin

Prominent German political journalist and expert on the United States from the 1940s through the 1960s.

Boveri wrote for the *Berliner Tageblatt* (Berlin Daily), the *Frankfurter Zeitung* (Frankfurt News), and the *Frankfurter Allgemeine Zeitung* (Frankfurt General News, or FAZ), as well as for cultural reviews (magazines) and Nazi propaganda minister Josef Goebbels's highbrow newspaper, *Das Reich* (The Empire). Boveri published several books on her extensive travels around the Mediterranean, the Middle East, and India and on political topics: the postwar trials of the German Nazi Foreign Ministry, an analysis of journalism in the Third Reich, and a four-volume study of treason in the twentieth century. Her ties to the United States were twofold, private as well as professional. Her mother was a successful, Harvard-educated American academic who took Boveri for extended stays to the United States and provided extensive personal contacts. The United States became the main topic of her journalistic work during World War II when Boveri was a foreign correspondent in Sweden and the United States (1941–1942). She was briefly interned as an enemy alien after the attack on Pearl Harbor but then returned to her fatherland. During the war, Boveri's nationalistic leanings led her to reject emphatically the idea of emigration, to comply with Nazi regulations on journalism, and to contemplate a position at the Third Reich's embassy in Madrid. After the war, Boveri continued to write on political and foreign policy topics relating to the United

States for the FAZ, where she was increasingly marginalized because of her strong opposition to Konrad Adenauer's integration of the Federal Republic of Germany into the West, which in her view intensified a cold war driven by U.S. motives and solidified German division.

Boveri wrote her *Amerikafibel* in the fall and winter of 1945. Published in 1946 and soon censored in the American Occupation Zone, its full title read: *America Primer for Grown-up Germans: An Attempt to Explain What Has Not Been Understood.* And indeed, the contemporary German reviewers of the widely read *America Primer* overwhelmingly praised her contribution to German American understanding and reconciliation. The future president of West Germany, Theodor Heuss, lauded in particular her explanation of the questionnaire that Americans used for denazification as "pacifying the German soul." One lonely contemporary American reviewer recognized the primer for what it was: an anti-American treatise. Under the guise of a value-free presentation, her German readers easily recognized the entire panorama of familiar anti-American clichés. Although the ostensible purpose of Boveri's *Primer* was to facilitate understanding between the defeated Germans and their occupiers, her true intent was to help her compatriots to resist any attempts of "Americanization" by strengthening the homegrown and long-standing tradition of superiority to and contempt for American civilization. Her book thus fit into the early postwar literature, together with Ernst von Salomon's *Fragebogen* (The Questionnaire) and Caspar von Schrenk-Notzing's *Charakterwäsche* (Character-washing), denouncing American denazification efforts,

although Boveri went about it in a seemingly nonantagonistic manner and, more importantly, as a recognized authority on the United States.

Michaela Hoenicke Moore

See also American Occupation Zone; Denazification

References and Further Reading

Boveri, Margret. *Amerikafibel für Erwachsene Deutsche: Ein Versuch Unverstandenes Zu Erklären.* Berlin: Minerva-Verlag, 1946.

———. *Verzweigungen: Eine Autobiographie.* Ed. Uwe Johnson. Frankfurt: Suhrkamp, 1996.

Görtemaker, Heike B. *Ein deutsches Leben. Die Geschichte der Margret Boveri 1900–1975.* Munich: C. H. Beck, 2005.

Streim, Gregor. "Berichterstatterin in den 'Landschaften des Verrats.' Margret Boveris Amerika-Darstellung aus der Kriegs- und Nachkriegszeit. Mit dem Briefwechsel zwischen Margret Boveri und Carl Zuckmayer." *Zuckmayer-Jahrbuch* 5 (2002): 475–510.

BRACKEBUSCH, LUDWIG

b. March 4, 1849; Northeim, Prussia
d. June 2, 1906; Hanover

German geographer and cartographer of Argentina.

Brackebusch studied geology at the University of Göttingen, where he received his doctorate in 1874. Shortly after, Hermann Burmeister, who was in charge of establishing the new natural science department at the University of Córdoba, offered him a professorship. In 1875, Brackebusch began teaching mineralogy and geology at this Argentinean university, where he remained for sixteen years. Together with Arthur Seelstrang, Brackebusch explored the Sierra de Córdoba and produced the first map of this mountain range. In addition, he drew maps of the Sierra de San Luis and the Sierra de Ambato in the province of Catamarca. Financed by the Argentinean state, Brackebusch began the systematic exploration of the Cordilleras on the Chilean border (Sierra de Valasco) in 1880. On the request of the government, he went on to explore the northern province of Jujuy, where he focused on the oil fields and gold mines. In 1883, Brackebusch traveled for the third time into the mountainous province of Salta in northwestern Argentina. When he returned to Germany for a visit, he used his time home to design a topographical map of Argentina on a scale of 1 to 1 million (*Mapa del Interior de la República Argentina*, 1885). In 1887, the Argentinean government asked him to produce a relief map of the country on a scale of 1 to 500,000 for the World Exhibition in Paris in 1889. To fulfill this request, Brackebusch went on a new expedition in the Cordilleras from Mendoza to Salta in order to measure the region trigonometrically and searched for selenium, oil, coal, and copper. His *Mapa de la República Argentina y de los Paises limitrofes* was 8 meters (8.7 yards) long, about 5 meters (5.5 yards) wide, and 70 mm (2.75 inches) high. It was awarded a gold medal at the World Exhibition in Paris. This map was printed for the first time in 1891 in two sheets and reduced to a scale of 1 to 1 million. Brackebusch was the first geographer to explore the geology and minerals of the Argentinean Cordilleras systematically, as well as the first to produce topographical and geological maps of those mountains.

Heinz Peter Brogiato

See also Argentina; Burmeister, Carl Hermann Conrad

References and Further Reading
"Dr. Ludwig Brackebusch." *Deutsche Rundschau für Geographie und Statistik.* Vol. 17 (1895): 39–41.
Hantzsch, Viktor. "Ludwig Brackebusch." *Biographisches Jahrbuch und Deutscher Nekrolog.* Vol. 11 (1908): 161–165.
Henze, Dietmar. *Enzyklopädie der Entdecker und Erforscher der Erde.* Graz: Akademische Druck- und Verlagsanstalt, 1978, 1:335–336.

BRANDT, WILLY
b. December 18, 1913; Lübeck
d. October 8, 1992; Unkel, North Rhine Westfalia

Mayor of West Berlin (1957–1966), foreign secretary of the Federal Republic of Germany (FRG, 1966–1969), chancellor of the FRG (1969–1974), chairman of the Social Democratic Party of Germany (SPD, 1964–1987), and chairman of the Socialist International (SI, 1976–1992). Willy Brandt was born Herbert Karl Frahm.

As long as he lived, Brandt consistently held transatlantic relations to be indispensable. He never questioned the cardinal importance of the United States or of the transatlantic alliance, holding fast to this belief, which he had adopted during World War II. Nonetheless, changes in Brandt's attitude toward the United States occured between the 1950s and 1970s, with his coming into power marking a turning point. Over these decades, he metamorphosed from an enthusiastic to a self-confident, pragmatic champion of transatlantic relations. Already during World War II, Brandt was convinced that reconstructing a democratic Germany and integrating it into Europe would be impossible without American support. In the 1950s, he was among a small contingent of politicians within the SPD who, in opposition to Kurt Schumacher and the party majority, supported the FRG's integration into the Western bloc, as well as a strong orientation toward the United States. In the early 1960s, the SPD came round to adopting this policy, ending the dissension between the party and Brandt, at that point the party's candidate for the chancellorship. Initially, Berlin and its overriding importance in the cold war proved to be pivotal for Brandt's relations with the United States. Having been elected mayor of West Berlin in October 1957, Brandt used this opportunity to consolidate ties with the United States, thus furthering his ambitions in domestic politics. In his capacity of mayor of Berlin, Brandt visited the United States in February 1958, February 1959, March 1961, October 1962, November 1963, May 1964, and April 1965. As a rule, the United States accorded him the courtesies reserved for prominent statesmen, and he met with the presidents of the time and other leading politicians. John F. Kennedy and Brandt shared a particularly close relationship.

When the Berlin Wall went up on August 13, 1961, Brandt, like so many others in West Berlin and West Germany, was disappointed by the muted U.S. response. Nonetheless, and unlike the Adenauer administration, he avoided any kind of open confrontation with the Americans, except for a letter to President Kennedy of August 16, 1961, in which he urged the president to take some action. In any case, Brandt was able to turn this situation to his advantage by presenting himself as the guarantor of stability and continuity in friendly German American relations. At the time, he knew well that his policy of détente with the Eastern bloc depended on American support.

By the time Brandt was elected the first Social Democratic chancellor of the FRG on October 21, 1969, the focus of U.S. foreign policy had already shifted from Germany and Europe to Asia. Nevertheless, the Nixon administration agreed with Germany's new *Ostpolitik* in principle while harboring some reservations about its possible long-term consequences, such as the loosening of the Atlantic pact, which might compromise U.S. influence in Europe. Consequently, German initiatives were initially met with some reservation, which diminished as Germany's negotiations proved increasingly successful and did not lead to any blocking of political activity in the East. Yet under Brandt's chancellorship, German American relations underwent a fundamental change, which had set in during the time of the Big Coalition (1966–1969). This process aimed at political emancipation from the United States. The FRG wanted to advance from junior partner to meeting the United States on an equal footing. Thus, while U.S. officials and political departments were regularly kept informed about the progress of West German negotiations with the Soviet Union, Poland, and so on, no details were discussed in advance. The Brandt government was in no doubt that *Ostpolitik* could not succeed without U.S. approval, which was especially true with regard to the status of Berlin. Friendly German American relations were thus not questioned, were praised, indeed reaffirmed in public

President John F. Kennedy and Mayor Willy Brandt of West Berlin at the White House, March 13, 1961. (Library of Congress)

speeches, and effectively stage-managed for the media, particularly during bilateral state visits. What counted were the effects: the support of the superpower United States strengthened the hand of the FRG in its dealings with the Eastern bloc, and domestically solid ties with the United States proved a boon for Brandt and his government.

As long as Brandt was chancellor, he never publicly criticized nor distanced himself from the United States. On the contrary, he lost no opportunity to emphasize the overriding importance of German American relations and close ties with the United States.

Daniela Münkel

See also Berlin Wall; West Berlin

References and Further Reading

Merseburger, Peter. *Willy Brandt, 1913–1992: Visionär und Realist.* Stuttgart: Deutsche Verlags-Anstalt, 2002.

Münkel, Daniel. "Als 'deutscher Kennedy' zum Sieg? Willy Brandt, Amerika, und die Medien." *Zeithistorische Forschungen* 1 (2004), Heft 2.

———. *Willy Brandt und die "Vierte Gewalt." Politik und Massenmedien in den 50er bis 70er Jahren.* Frankfurt am Main/New York: Campus Verlag, 2005.

Orlow, Dietrich. "Ambivalence and Attraction: The German Social Democrats and the United States." In *The American Impact on Postwar Germany.* Ed. Reiner Pommerin. Providence: Berghahn Books, 1997, 35–51.

BRAUN, WERNHER VON

b. March 23, 1912; Wirsitz (Posen), Prussia

d. June 16, 1977; Alexandria, Virginia

Rocket engineer who was of use to both Nazi Germany and the United States.

Wernher von Braun's influential aristocratic family had the resources to send him to such prestigious private schools as the French Gymnasium in Berlin from 1920 to 1925 and the Herman Lietz Schools in Ettersburg and Spiekero. He studied mechanical engineering and physics at the Technical University of Berlin and the Federal Institute of Technology in Zurich (1930–1932). Interest in space travel consumed his spare time; as a student he was a member of the Verein für Raumschiffahrt (Society for Space Travel), experimenting with rockets. Braun received a doctorate in physics from the University of Berlin in 1934 with a classified thesis about rocketry, "About Combustion Tests."

From 1930 to 1932, he was employed as an assistant at the Rocket Field Reinickendorf, and in 1934 he became the chief of the Rocket Experiment Station at Kummersdorf. When the Army Rocket Center in Peenemünde opened in 1937, he was appointed its technical director devoted to developing liquid-fueled missiles. Besides the technological innovations, Braun learned to sell his ideas to the leadership of the Third Reich. He was a member of the National Socialist German Worker's Party (NSDAP) since 1937 and was also admitted to its elite wing, the SS, in which he rose from the rank of second lieutenant to major during the years 1940–1943. His work was essential in developing the A1 to

A4 rockets. The A4 Rocket was renamed V2 (*Vergeltungswaffe,* or vengeance weapon) by Minister of Propaganda Joseph Göbbels. During the half year the V2 rocket was in active use, London was the prime target of the 1,027 missiles launched. The success of Braun's work can easily be quantified: 2,511 people were killed and 5,869 seriously injured.

Braun was arrested by the Gestapo on March 21, 1944, for what he later alleged were "anti-Nazi remarks." After two weeks, however, he was released from custody. As Soviet troops closed in on Peenemünde, Braun successfully evacuated the research and production facilities to locations in southern Germany. In the Mittelwerk, an underground factory used by the war industry, slave laborers assembled V2 missiles and other weapons under terrible conditions. More than a third of the 60,000 laborers, supplied by the nearby concentration camp Dora, died of starvation and disease.

As the defeat of Nazi Germany became inevitable, Braun and his team of rocket scientists turned into last-minute renegades. On May 2, 1945, after Braun's brother had negotiated the conditions, Braun surrendered to U.S. troops. After four months at the U.S. Army Interrogation Camp in Garmisch-Partenkirchen in 1945, Braun, together with the core of his Peenemünde team, was transferred to the United States in a move codenamed Operation Paperclip. Initially the project was to be limited to a few months. Efforts were made to cover up the team's past. These included sealing incriminating evidence of Nazi affiliation and altering conclusions of interrogations. The U.S. Army denied demands for Braun's return to Germany as a witness in trials against accused war criminals from the Mittelwerk-Dora complex. He did, however, visit Germany in the winter of 1947 to marry Maria von Quistorp, his first cousin. Braun was project director at the army's Research and Development Division at Fort Bliss, Texas, from 1945 to 1950. Using parts salvaged from the Mittelwerk, the team continued to assemble and launch V2 rockets under U.S. Army supervision. Braun was never accused of any war crimes but was repeatedly under surveillance by the Federal Bureau of Investigation. It was feared that his skills could be of interest to a remilitarized Germany.

The cold war triggered a space race in which Braun played a decisive role. In 1950, the research was moved to the Redstone Arsenal in Huntsville, Alabama, where Braun was named technical director at the Guided Missile Development Group. In 1955, Braun and his team of German scientists were granted U.S. citizenship. He was director of the Army Ballistic Missile Agency from 1956 to 1960.

Braun led the development of new generations of missiles, named Redstone, Jupiter, and Pershing, with both military and civilian potential. The cold war space race started when the Soviet Union successfully launched the satellite Sputnik 1 on October 4, 1957. U.S. military leaders increasingly understood the potential of Braun's team, which long had wished to show their technological advantage to the world. The Redstone carried the first American into space on May 5, 1961. Most importantly, Braun's team improved the U.S. capability of launching a massive nuclear attack on the Soviet Union.

Braun actively educated the American public about space exploration. Parallel to his work for the army, Braun established himself as a leading visionary for space exploration and popularized the subject in books and articles. One of his mentors was Walt Disney, who engaged the German scientist as a consultant and narrator for a series of films in the 1950s: *Man in Space, Man and the Moon,* and *Mars and Beyond.* His exceptional ability to explain the complex details of borderline science in accurate and engaging terms won him the attention and trust of President John F. Kennedy and leading military officials.

In 1960, he became director at the George C. Marshall Space Flight Center, a part of the National Aeronautics and Space Administration (NASA). His most important project was the development of the Saturn rockets. The Saturn V was used in the Apollo program and successfully launched astronauts to the moon. For his work he was honored with more than twenty honorary doctorates, and two American orders, military and civilian decorations. After retiring from NASA in 1971, Braun accepted the position of corporate vice president at Fairchild Corporation. In 1975, he entered German service again, as a member of the board of directors at Daimler Benz Company.

Tommy Tobiassen

See also Latin America, Nazis in
References and Further Reading
Lampton, Christopher. *Wernher von Braun.* New York: Franklin Watts, 1988.
Piszkiewicz, Dennis. *Wernher von Braun: The Man Who Sold the Moon.* Westport: Praeger Publishers, 1998.
Simpson, Christopher. *Blowback: America's Recruitment of Nazis and Its Effects on the Cold War.* New York: Weidenfeld and Nicholson, 1988.
Stuhlinger, Ernst. *Wernher von Braun, Crusader for Space: A Biographical Memoir.* Malabar: Krieger, 1994.

BRAZIL

Before Brazil gained independence, Germans played only a marginal role (as merchants, soldiers, and technicians) in the history of this Portuguese colony. The best-known German explorer of this early period is Hans Staden. Larger groups of Germans came to Brazil only during the colonization attempt undertaken by Dutchmen in the northeast (1630–1654) and in the process of an accelerated occupation of the Amazon region in the second half of the eighteenth century. German monks, such as Samuel Fritz, SJ (1654–

1725), Johann Philipp Bettendorff, SJ (1627–1698), Jodokus Perret, SJ (1663–1707), Aloys Konrad Pfeil, SJ (1638–1701), Hans Xaver Treyer, SJ (1668–1737), Anton Sepp von und zu Rechegg, SJ (1655–1733), and Richard von Pilar, OSB (1635–1700), were instrumental in spreading the Catholic faith among the native population. Johann Heinrich Böhm (1708–1783) created the first Brazilian army. After the construction of several fortresses in the Amazon basin, José Sebatião de Carvalho e Melo, Marquis de Pombal, prime minister of Portugal,

Major German Settlement Areas in Brazil

ordered that settlements should be established near Macapá and the village of Viçosa da Madre de Deus. For these colonies, Azoreans and ninety-one German soldiers and settlers, including two women, were recruited.

In October 1807 the Portuguese court fled to Brazil because of the advance of Napoleon's troops. The colony became the new center of the empire, and projects for its development were started. In December 1815 the United Kingdom of Portugal, Brazil, and Algarve was created. The entourage of John VI included several German scientists, engineers, and officials, who were entrusted with fostering the development of the new kingdom. The king also issued the first instructions to increase the country's population. Thus, in 1818 the first settlements of German immigrants were established in Southern Bahia and Nova Friburgo in the state of Rio de Janeiro. In the wake of the return of John VI to Portugal in 1821, Brazil became independent on September 7, 1822.

Spontaneous emigration to Brazil was practically impossible because it could not compete with the brevity of crossing from Europe to North America. The fact that a sizable migratory flow to Brazil did occur is due to the Brazilian government's directionist attitude. After Empress Leopoldine, the daughter of the emperor of Austria, Francis I, encouraged German immigration, the Brazilian government sent agents to Germany to recruit immigrants. One of these agents was Major Anton Aloys von Schaeffer. Schaeffer and other agents made promises, such as freedom of religion, full civil liberties, and equal rights, as well as a ten-year tax exemption, that did not have the approval of the Brazilian government and were partly in conflict with the Brazil-

ian constitution. Conservatives and plantation owners, however, opposed further European immigration and succeded in passing a law that stripped the government of all financing for the promotion of immigration in December 1830. The government reacted by deferring the issue of immigration to the provinces. Thus colonial legislation was passed in the province of Santa Catarina in 1836 and in Rio Grande do Sul in 1845, which was amended in 1854. In spite of that, gaps in the legislation (particularly regarding the legal status of Protestant immigrants) and other inconveniences led the Prussian state to promulgate, from 1853 onward, laws such as the von-der-Heydt'sches Reskript (Heydt Edict) of 1859, that protected its emigrants and also restricted emigration to Brazil. The Prussian law forced the Brazilian government to regulate the legal status of Protestant immigrants.

Lured by the propaganda of emigration agents and letters written by emigrants to their relatives and friends, many Germans were attracted to Brazil. The failure of the 1848 revolution forced many to leave Germany. After World War I, members of the middle class who had been ruined by inflation and unemployment emigrated to Brazil. When the Social Democrats came to power in 1919, members of the right-wing parties as well as Communist activists, members of the "Spartacus," emigrated. Among the immigrants were smaller groups that, although not having come from German territory, help to complete the panorama of German immigration in Brazil. In three different periods (1877–1879, 1890–1891, and immediately prior to World War I) many Germans from the region of the Volga River and from Volinia left their home.

German Settlements in Brazil

Locality	Foundation	Origin
Rio Grande do Sul		
São Leopoldo	1824	Hunsrück, Saxony, Württemberg, Saxony-Coburg
Santa Cruz	1849	Rhineland, Pomerania, Silesia
Agudo	1857	Rhineland, Saxony, Pomerania
Nova Petrópolis	1859	Pomerania, Saxony, Bohemia
Teutônia	1868	Westphalia
São Lourenço	1857	Pomerania, Rhineland
Santa Catarina		
Blumenau	1850	Pomerania, Holstein, Hanover, Braunschweig, Saxony
Brusque	1860	Baden, Oldenburg, Rhineland, Pomerania, Schleswig-Holstein, Braunschweig
Joinville	1851	Prussia, Oldenburg, Schleswig-Holstein, Hanover, Switzerland
Praná		
Several settlements around		
Ponta Grossa	1877/1879	Germans from the Volga River
Espírito Sanot		
Santa Izabel	1847	Hunsrück, Hesse
Santa Leopoldina	1857	Pomerania
Rio de Janeiro		
Nova Friburgo	1819	Switzerland; from 1824 onward: Hesse
Petrópolis	1845	Palatinate, Westphalia, Nassau, Moselle, Rhineland
Minas Gerais		
Teófilo Otoni	1847	
Juiz de for a	1852	Hesse, Tyrol, Holstein, Baden, Schleswig, Bavaria, Nassau, Braunschweig, Mecklenburg, Saxony

After World War II a group of Swabians from the Danube went to Brazil to start a new life.

The immigrants' place of origin shows that they constituted a rather heterogeneous group. Their total number must not have been higher than 300,000.

In Brazilian society German immigrants were marginalized from the very beginning. The German settlements were usually located in scarcely populated areas, and for this reason their contact with already established populations in the country was minimal. Elements of Brazilian culture were only adopted when they seemed to offer some kind of advantage. Ethnically homogeneous settlements emerged, where the German language and traditions were preserved. Over time, however, they went through such profound changes that a German culture of peculiar characteristics emerged. The fact that the white immigrants worked on their property and tilled the land with their own hands—until then a task regarded as slave work—was incompatible with the Brazilian mentality. Up to that time the prevailing opinion in Brazil was that manual labor was unworthy of a white man. Thus it is easy to infer that the older inhabitants of the country saw the immigrants as second-class people. The religion of many immigrants also seemed strange. The difference in religious beliefs did not make the incorporation of Protestant immigrants into society easier; this difference was precisely one of the factors of marginalization.

In 1889 Brazil became a republic. This political change brought two significant advantages for German immigrants: the "great naturalization," that is, the generalized granting of the Brazilian citizenship, and the separation of church and state. Immigrants hoped that these changes would allow for easier integration into Brazilian society. However, the opposite happened. In Brazil most descendants of German immigrants supported the Liberal Party and, additionally, were loyal supporters of the monarchy. When the republic was proclaimed, most supporters of the Conservative Party oddly moved to the Republican camp. In this way a doubly unpleasant and curious situation was created for Germans. As supporters of the monarchy, they might have expected the support of the Conservatives. But since the Liberal Party had provided the last ministers of the empire and since most Germans had been supporters of this party, that support earned them the enmity of the conservative forces, which also represented the large estate owners.

With the proclamation of the republic, Brazilian Germans were once again marginalized. The situation in Rio Grande do Sul was characteristic. When in 1893 the Federalist Revolution broke out, most Germans sympathized with the leader of the former Liberal Party, Gaspar Silveira Martins, who was at the same time the intellectual leader of the Federalists. The revolution ended with the victory of the Republican Party and the indirect defeat of the Brazilian Germans. Their political involvement, which had started with Koseritz and others, was ended. They completely withdrew from politics. In the end, a tacit agreement with the winners was reached: the descendants of German origin were allowed to preserve their German heritage in exchange for their votes. Furthermore, under the hegemony of the Republican Party, Rio Grande do Sul adopted a positivist constitution, which fully corresponded to the ideas of the French philosopher Auguste Comte and was guided by his *Système de politique positive,* according to which the state should not intervene in the intellectual life of a people. Science, art, and religion must develop independently from the state. By following the positivist motto, "Those who want may learn and those who can may teach," an enormous development of the German community schools was made possible. From 1889 to 1930 became a golden age of German culture in Brazil. The greatest progress in the struggle for the preservation of the German heritage was achieved precisely in these years. This philosophical and political change, however, turned out to be a trap. They created a cultural German ghetto for themselves and thus furthered their marginalization. After the end of the so-called Old Republic (1930) that resulted in the end of the domination of positivism in Brazil, this German marginalization was overcome violently.

Until the foundation of the German Empire in 1871, Germany had no great interest for the citizens of the various German states. Until the middle of the nineteenth century, Germans knew almost nothing about the "Germans" in Brazil. Although the Hanseatic cities did have some economic interest in the colonists, it was only in the middle of the nineteenth century that private Protestant associations became concerned with emigrants' living conditions. Even after 1871, Brazil did not matter in the foreign policy of Germany. With regard to Germans abroad, Otto von Bismarck remarked: "Germans who take off their fatherland like an old jacket are no longer Germans for me, and I no longer have any interest as a compatriot in them" (Brunn 1971, 127). However, some politicians and public opinion did not agree. Many people expected a separation of a German state from the Brazilian territory and believed that the proclamation of the Brazilian Republic would fulfill their dream of a surrogate for the colonies that Germany did not have. The revolutions that occurred in the beginning of the Republican era seemed to give them reasons for such hope. It was expected, for instance, that Brazilian Germans actively participated in the revolution and that after the separation of the southern provinces from the rest of Brazil, a German supremacy would be established there. But these hopes ignored the political position of Brazilian Germans.

After Bismarck's fall from power, the German Foreign Relations Ministry showed a greater interest in the fate of Brazilian Germans. The representatives of the German Empire were instructed to visit the German colonies and to participate more actively in public life. These measures were guided by economic interests. There was also an attempt to divert German emigration to Brazil. Only after this policy failed did the German Empire develop a more active policy regarding German colonists in Brazil. It was designed to preserve German culture in Brazil to guarantee a market for German industry. German politicians encouraged Brazilian Germans to withstand assimilation. They were ready to employ the German press, German schools, German-speaking congregations and churches, and the German navy to this end.

Attempts to exert influence on the German-speaking schools through teachers, printed materials, and financial support were very successful. Several civil and ecclesiastic organizations participated in this project and received financial support from the School Fund of the Foreign Relations Ministry of Germany. In 1906 the same ministry funded the publication of a German reading-book for schools in Brazil that had a print run of 10,000 copies. By 1914 this book had already reached its fifth edition. The policy for the preservation of German culture that was developed by the German navy should not be minimized. By the turn of the century, the visits of German ships to Brazil became routine. They were seen as an evident means of preserving contacts between Germany and Brazil's German enclaves. The crews visited German settlements in order to arouse the pride of the descendants of Germans for Germany.

The results of this policy were counterproductive, however, and contributed to the emerging fear in Brazil of a "German danger." When Germany declared war on France in 1914, Brazilian Germans enthusiastically celebrated the news. But this support was mainly a consequence of the political marginalization to which most of the Brazilian Germans were submitted in the first years of the Brazilian Republic rather than a sign of admiration for Germany's war goals. Reservists presented themselves at the consulates and attempted to reach Germany. The course of events in Europe led to public demonstrations in favor of the entente (the military alliance between France, Russia, and Great Britain) in Brazil, which in turn provoked plunders and led to outrages and abuses of Brazilian Germans. Only the intervention of Brazilian authorities put an end to it. The torpedoing of the Brazilian ship *Paraná* on April 4, 1917, led to the rupture of diplomatic relations between Brazil and Germany. After the torpedoing of two more ships on October 25, Brazil declared war on Germany. Two days later the Brazilian Ministry of the Interior sent a decree to the governors of the states with German populations. The instructions prohibited the circulation of German newspapers and ordered the closing of German schools. Finally, after the torpedoing of additional Brazilian ships, a state of siege was declared on November 17 in the states of Rio de Janeiro, Rio Grande do Sul, Santa Catarina, Paraná, São Paulo, and the Federal District.

After the end of the war and the defeat of the Germany in 1918, the idea of a strong German state that could interfere into Brazilian domestic policy had been shattered, and it was expected that Brazilian Germans would distance themselves from the "old fatherland." However, the prohibition of German-language newspapers and the closing of schools had unexpected consequences. Even though the ban on the German language was lifted after the end of war, Brazilian Germans retreated into their ethnic enclaves. During the 1920s and 1930s, they faced a new challenge with the advent of modernism and the new state policy of "Brazility," which mandated the integration of all ethnic groups into mainstream Brazilian society.

This new movement had its first great expression in the "Week of Modern Art" that took place in São Paulo in 1922. During the government of Getúlio Vargas, Brazil's ruler from 1930 to 1945, the integration of the various immigrant groups was declared the center of his social policy. Initially, a system of quotas was introduced, in which immigration was reduced to 2 percent of the total number of immigrants of each nationality that had arrived in the previous fifty years. Measures were adopted to create mixed settlements to prevent the emergence of ethnically homogeneous units. Vargas made the development of a national educational system a priority of his government. In addition, schools that were considered "foreign schools" were requested to conform to state requirements. First the government demanded the teaching of all disciplines in the national language, and later the teaching of any foreign language to students below the age of twelve was prohibited. These measures were particularly significant for Brazilians of German descent because of the network of schools in which German was the first language of instruction in all subjects.

After 1933, Brazilian Germans became the target of Nazi propaganda. National Socialist (NS) organizations were created in the towns, and agents infiltrated the Brazilian German associations. The state of Rio Grande do Sul, for instance, was organized as a *Kreis* (district) of the National Socialist German Worker's Party (NSDAP) with a *Kreisleiter* (district leader). Brazilian German companies that did not sympathize with the National Socialist movement were boycotted, fund-raising campaigns for the *Winterhilfswerk* (Winter Aid Organization) were organized, and conferences and public demonstrations on the major National Socialist holidays were promoted. The NS movement showed a particular interest in the Brazilian German associations. The NSDAP attempted to infiltrate and influence these societies by paying the fees of its members. As soon as a majority of members favored National Socialism, an assembly was called together. This assembly decided then to affiliate the association to the NSDAP and to the Verband Deutscher Vereine (Federation of German Associations), which in turn was affiliated to the Verband Deutscher Vereine im Ausland (Federation of Foreign German Associations).

The Brazilian Constitution of November 10, 1937, prohibited all political activities and, in the beginning of 1938, banned all foreign political parties. Since the NSDAP could no longer work officially in Brazil, it went through the German consulates. But the intervention of the police reduced all activities to a minimum. These measures were followed by the deportation of some Germans and the imprisonment of Brazilian German leaders. Although until 1939 the nationalization measures implemented by Brazilian authorities were moderate, during World War II repressive measures were taken, and some government officials went too far. The publication of German newspapers was prohibited. It was forbidden to speak German in public. German books and documents were confiscated from the homes of Brazilian Germans. German libraries were destroyed, weapons were confiscated from shooting societies, and Germans were imprisoned and put in confinement. The torpedoing of ships and Brazil's declaration of war on Germany led to outrages and abuses of the German population. Practically all Brazilian Germans became the target of anti-German excesses.

The experience of World War II, a time that was seen as a period of persecution, continued to have consequences after the war. The Brazilian Germans felt that they were second- or third-class citizens, even after the ban on the German language was lifted, and the German press resumed its publishing activities in 1946. Only the passing of time changed this perception. Animosities decreased, and the mobility of society, the emergence of a modern media complex, and other factors led the Brazilian Germans to increasingly feel like an integral part of Brazilian society.

Martin Norberto Dreher

See also Brazil, German Exile in; Brazil, Religion in; Brummer; Forty-Eighters; Fritz, Samuel; German Migration to Latin America (1918–1933); German-Speaking Migration to the Americas; Koseritz, Karl von; Latin America, Nazi Party in; Markgraf, Georg; Volga Germans in the United States; Von-Der-Heydt'sches Rescript

References and Further Reading

Brunn, Gerhard. *Deutschland und Brasilien (1889–1914)*. Cologne: Böhlau, 1971.

Dietschi, Theophil. "Vom Werden und Wachsen der Riograndenser Synode." *Estudos Teológicos* 1956: 6–20, 32–50; 1957: 13–32.

Dreher, Martin. *Igreja e Germanidade*. São Leopoldo: Ed. Sinodal, 2003.

Iotti, Luiza Horn, ed. *Imigração e Colonização: Legislação, 1747–1915*. Caxias do Sul: EDUCS, 2001.

Müller, Jürgen. *Nationalsozialiamus in Lateinamerika: Die Auslandsorganisation der NSDAP in Argentinien, Brasilien, Chile, und Mexiko, 1931–1945*. Stuttgart: Verlag Hans-Dieter Heinz, 1997.

Oberacker, Carlos Henrique. *A Contribuição Teuta à Formação da Nação Brasileira*. Rio de Janeiro: Editora Presença, 1968.

Schröder, Ferdinand. *A Imigração Alemã para o Sul do Brasil até 1859*. São Leopoldo: Ed. UNISINOS, 2003.

BRAZIL, GERMAN EXILE IN

Although Brazil is the largest country in Latin America and is built upon emigration, it took in only a small number of the Germans (about 16,000 people) who had to leave Nazi Germany between 1933 and 1945. In 1930, when Getúlio Vargas became president and after the suppression of a Communist insurgency in 1935, he established an authoritarian government. On November 10, 1937, Vargas declared the creation of the "Estado Novo," dissolved parliament, banned all political parties, and abolished basic civil rights. In his foreign policy, the new dictator initially moved closer to Nazi Germany and Fascist Italy but abandoned this strategy by 1942. Brazil even declared war against the Axis powers and sent troops to participate in Italy's liberation in 1944.

With the exception of Mexico, most Latin American countries, including Brazil, treated German refugees as normal immigrants who had to fulfill certain criteria set by the immigration authorities. Well-educated engineers, scientists, and wealthy people were preferred over those without such qualifications. Beginning in 1937, racist and antisemitic motives influenced immigration policies as much as a general suspicion that German immigrants could include spies. However, in spite of these hurdles, many German Jews were able to enter the country, in most cases with tourist visas. Furthermore, Jews used falsified documents such as faked baptism certificates to circumvent the racist restrictions of Brazilian immigration law. However, deep antisemitic feelings prevented the Brazilian government, when asked by the Pope, to issue 3,000 visas for non-Aryan Catholics. With 16,000 German and Austrian immigrants, Brazil was second to Argentina and closely followed by Chile.

The majority of German refugees settled down in Brazil's urban centers—in its capital Rio de Janeiro, in the emerging industrial center São Paulo, and in the cities of Curitiba and Porto Alegre. The agricultural settlements in Resenda, 320 kilometers south of São Paulo, and Rolândia were an exception to this pattern. Rolândia was founded well before 1933 in the middle of the jungle in the state of Paraná. It became a haven for anti-Fascist Catholics and Jews and has become over time a model community for the successful economic and social integration of refugees.

About one-third of all German refugees came from white-collar and trading professions, and a further 20 percent belonged to the academic, administrative, and service sectors. Since there was no need for these professional qualifications in Brazil, about two-thirds of all immigrants had to find employment in a new profession. Many immigrants took two or three jobs to survive. There was no financial help from the Brazilian government, and only Jewish support organizations granted material or financial help. German refugees had founded 187 small and medium-size enterprises, restaurants, bed and breakfasts, auto garages, workshops, and factories by 1940. These enterprises employed about 6,000 people, most of them refugees themselves. Physicians, lawyers, and professors had a much harder time adjusting since there were restrictions on practicing these professions, and the different legal, cultural, and intellectual climate prevented quick integration of newcomers. The language barrier was also a factor for these professionals.

In spite of a latent official antisemitism that limited the immigration and integration of Jewish refugees, the social, charitable, and cultural activities of Jewish communities and of Jewish charitable organizations prevented the isolation and social degradation of German Jewish refugees. Some of these organizations were the Congregação Israelita Paulista (Jewish Community of São Paulo, or CIP) in São Paulo, the Associação Religiosa Israelita (Association of Jewish Religion, or ARI) in Rio de Janeiro, and the Sociedade Israelita Brasileira de Cultura e Beneficência (Cultural and Social Society of Brazilian Jews, or SIBRA) in Porto Alegre. Since the government had outlawed the use of languages other than Portuguese in religious ceremonies, synagogue services had to be in Portuguese only. Although this requirement suggested a swift assimilation into Brazilian culture, the religious service still followed German and Austrian traditions very closely. German-speaking immigrants did not integrate into the existing Sephardim and Ashkenazi communities but established their own communities with their own German traditions. These Jewish communities became the center of an extensive network of organizations for women, youth, culture, and sports, as well as charitable organizations to help the poor and old. This network has survived in part to the present day.

Besides the local charitable associations, a few national relief organizations for Jewish refugees also sprang up. The most important one was the Comissão de Assistência aos Refugiados Israelitas da Alemanha (Committee for the Support of German Jewish Refugees, or CARIA), which handed out financial assistance to newly arrived immigrants. About 50–60 percent of its budget came from other Jewish relief organizations such as the American Jewish Joint Distribution Committee (JDC), and about 40–50 percent of the remaining funds were collected among Brazilian Jews.

Political activities of German refugees were very limited but were permitted throughout the 1930s. Financial difficulties posed the strongest obstacles to political organization and the distribution of information. The anti-Fascist newspapers *Tribüne* (Tribune) and *Freie Presse* (Free Press), both printed in São Paulo, did not survive beyond their debuts. Fritz Heller, a former editor of the *Leipziger Zeitung* (Leipzig Newspaper), who attempted to found *Gegenwart* (Today), also failed. The Friends of the Gegenwart dissolved quickly. The only successful paper was a newsletter edited by the Liga für Menschenrechte (League for Civil Rights). This organization, founded by Fritz Kniestedt, published the newsletter under various names until both the organization and the paper were outlawed in 1937.

Political organizations offered a home for political refugees, ethnic Germans who lived abroad and despised the Nazi dictatorship, and German Jewish refugees who still hung on to their homeland. In 1935, the Notgemeinschaft Deutscher Antifaschisten (Emergency Organization of German Anti-Fascists) was founded with groups in Rio de Janeiro, São Paulo, Curitiba, Rio Negro, and Pelotas. In 1942, it became part of the Movimento dos Alemães Antinazis (Movement of German Anti-Fascists). This movement had much in common with the committee Das Andere Deutschland (The Other Germany), which brought together German Social Democrats. Competing with this organization was the Movimento dos Alemães Livres (Movement for a Free Germany), which was related to the Communist Bewegung Freies Deutschland (Movement for a Free Germany) in Mexico. However, all these organizations together had no more than a few hundred members. After the ban on all political parties and the enforced prohibition of political activities by foreigners in 1943, these organizations ceased all their activities. Only after the end of the war and the end of the Vargas dictatorship in 1945 did these organizations engage once again in politics. The Freie Deutschland was reinstated and the Vereinigung deutscher Sozialdemokraten in Brasilien (Association of German Social Democrats in Brazil) was formed. The latter group engaged in collecting donations for the starving German population and sending care packages to their former homeland.

Besides these left-wing organizations, there were also bourgeois, Christian, conservative, and even right-wing circles active in Brazil's German refugee community. The former vice chancellor, minister of justice, and minister of the interior Erich Koch-Weser worked on a constitution for postwar Germany from exile in Brazil. The members of the former Zentrum (Center Party), Hermann Matthias Görgen, Johannes Schauff, and Johannes Hoffmann, kept political Catholicism alive. Since Brazil was one of the few Catholic countries to which German refugees could escape, it was especially attractive to Catholic priests who had to leave Germany and the occupied parts of Europe—among them Father Paulus Gordan, the Benedictine monk Desiderius Schmitz, the Jesuits Walter Mariaux and Walter Lutterbeck, and the Austrian Cistercian monk Alois Wiesinger.

Brazil also provided a new home for the followers of Otto Strasser's dissident Nazi organization, Schwarze Front (Black Front). They remained, however, very limited in their political activities and did not achieve any significant influence among German refugees. Among Austrian exiles who began to distance themselves from German refugees' organizations after 1943, Christian conservative circles and even monarchists had some influence.

Cultural activities engaged in by German refugees were limited because of political restrictions and because the use of the German language had been banned in public. Vargas hoped that outlawing German speaking in public would accelerate the integration into Brazilian society of Germans, both new refugees and older German settlers who had come to the country before World War I. Furthermore, forced integration would allow for better control of this part of the population. Since most refugees were busy simply surviving, there was little time left over for cultural activities. The social and cultural network of associations, clubs, restaurants, orchestras, theaters, cabarets, newspapers, and cultural performances, so typical of the other exile and immigration centers in Latin America, did therefore not exist in Brazil.

Nevertheless, many Germans and Austrians left their imprints on Brazilian society. Some writers and journalists successfully published their work in Portuguese. The journalists Fritz Heller, Ernst Feder, Anatol Rosenfeld, and Otto Maria Carpeaux (Karpfen) worked as columnists, literary critics, and experts on economic questions for Brazilian newspapers. Frank Arnau wrote poetry and detective novels in Portuguese. However, outside the world of newspapers and journals, German writers remained nearly unknown. Leopold

Andrian-Werburg, Paula Ludwig, Richard Katz, Fritz Oliven, Ulrich Becker, and others were not even recognized by the Brazilian public. The only exception was Stefan Zweig. After he had to leave Germany in 1934, Zweig went to Great Britain. In 1936, he embarked on a lecture tour through Latin America, participated at the PEN Congress in Buenos Aires, and visited Brazil, where he was surprisingly welcomed as a guest of the state by Vargas. After some time in the United States and a second lecture tour through Argentina and Uruguay in 1940–1941, Zweig decided to settle down in Petrópolis, near Rio de Janeiro, in September 1941. Vargas transformed Zweig's tourist visa into a permanent visa— a rare gesture for an immigrant of Jewish origin at that time. In exchange and as a sign of his appreciation, Zweig published his book *Brasilien: Ein Land der Zukunft* (Brazil: A Land of the Future, 1941), which praised and romanticized Brazil. The book is seen as an homage to Getúlio Vargas and even considered to be commissioned by him. However, Zweig could not feel at home in Brazil. The social and cultural isolation, the lack of intellectual communication, the loss of "the world of yesterday" in Europe, and other motives caused him and his wife to commit suicide on February 23, 1942. Zweig's exceptional position in Brazil was based on political protection, not on literary success. The pompous state funeral organized by the Vargas regime proved that point impressively.

German painters and actors were somewhat more successful than their fellow poets and journalists. The painter Eleonore Koch became famous in artists' circles, and the Austrian Axel von Leskoschek influenced generations of Brazilian wood carving artists. The actors Wolfgang Hoffmann-Harnisch, Werner Hammer, and Willy Keller became important directors at Brazilian theaters. A small number of psychoanalysts, biochemists, social scientists, and economists received positions at Brazilian universities and introduced new academic disciplines.

There are no statistics available about how many Germans returned to Germany from Brazil and how many remained in that country. Furthermore, many German refugees migrated from poorer and politically unstable countries, such as Bolivia and Paraguay, to the prosperous southern part of Brazil. Many Jewish families went to the United States, Australia, and South Africa and, after 1948, to the newly established state of Israel. The few Germans who returned to Germany after 1945 were mostly political refugees without a Jewish background. Among them were Johannes Hoffmann, who became prime minister of the Saar territory, and Hermann Matthias Goergen, who served in the West German parliament from 1957 to 1961. Johannes Schauff traveled back and forth between West Germany, Brazil, and South Tyrol and occupied an important role as intermediary between the governments of different countries. Wolfgang Hoffmann-Harnisch published several books about Brazil. Some refugees who remained in Brazil became correspondents for German newspapers and used their knowledge about the country and its people to report about their new home.

Patrik von zur Mühlen

See also Brazil; Huebsch, Ben W et al., and Viking Press; Intellectual Exile

References and Further Reading

Carneiro, Maria Luíza Tucci. *O anti-semitismo na era Vargas: Fantasmas de uma geração (1930–1945)*. São Paulo: Brasiliense, 1988.

Furtado Kestler, Izabela. *Die Exilliteratur und das Exil der deutschsprachigen Schriftsteller und Publizisten in Brasilien.* Frankfurt am Main: Peter Lang, 1992.

Hirschberg, Alfred. "The Exonomic Adjustment of Jewish Refugees in São Paulo." *Jewish Social Studies* 7 (1945): 31–40.

Lesser, Jeff. *Welcoming the Undesirables: Brazil and the Jewish Question.* Berkeley: University of California Press, 1995.

Levine, Robert. "Brazil's Jews during the Vargas Era and After." *Luso-Brazilian Review* 1 (1968): 45–58.

Pinkuss, Fritz. "Um ensaio acerca da imigração judaica no Brazil após o cataclisma de 1933 e da Segunda Guerra Mundial." *Revista de História* 50 (1974): 579–607.

Reutter, Lutz Egon. *Katholische Kirche als Fluchthelfer im Dritten Reich: Die Betreuung von Auswanderern durch den St. Raphaelsverein.* Recklinghausen: Paulus Verlag, 1971.

von zur Mühlen, Patrik. *Fluchtziel Lateinamerika: Die deutsche Emigration 1933–1945: Politische Aktivitäten und soziokulturelle Integration.* Bonn: Verlag Neue Gesellschaft, 1988.

BRAZIL, RELIGION IN

German immigration challenged Brazil's established Catholic religion. Until 1808 the country had been closed to foreigners, all European people with the exception of Portugues people. Portuguese were considered indigenous people. The arrival of European immigrants resulted in a discussion about the status of the Catholic religion as the state religion. Article 5 of the 1824 Constitution established that "the Roman Apostolic Catholic religion will continue to be the Empire's religion. All other religions will be allowed with their domestic or private worship service, in houses designed for this purpose, without any appearance of a temple." Congressmen, senators, and public servants had to swear an oath to defend the state religion.

The advent of the republic in 1889 resulted in the separation of church and state. This represented a profound change for the Catholic Church: its issues would no longer be settled by the state but in civil society and mainly within the religious community itself. After the proclamation of the republic and the influx of non-Catholic immigrants from Europe, the Catholic Church needed to learn how to coexist with other religions, since there was at least theoretically equality and freedom for all cults. However, there were more changes. Under slavery, the catechesis and baptism of slaves had been entrusted to slave owners. Religion was a matter of tutelage. The arrival of immigrants fostered resistance to this tutelage, particularly where the immigrants replaced slave labor: these immigrants did not accept the religion of the planters. In Rio Grande do Sul and Santa Catarina, the Catholic Church was forced to accept that small farmers could establish their own religious organization by choosing their own religious leaders and religious calendar.

Immigration and new political conditions forced the Catholic Church in Brazil to choose new forms of action. Immigration ended religious exclusiveness. Although Brazil in 1808 had opened its ports to "friendly nations," religion was not influenced by this economic move. When in 1819 King João VI invited Swiss settlers to come to Nova Friburgo, he limited his invitation to Catholics. However, some of the Catholic immigrants had been Protestants who, immediately after the arrival of the first Protestant minister in 1824, returned to the Protestant congregation. In the constituent assembly of 1823, some of its members proposed the separation of church and state and freedom of religion. It certainly was on the basis of this trend that the Brazilian government's agent promised full freedom of religion to Germans who were willing to emigrate to Brazil. After the constituent assembly was dissolved, Emperor Pedro I promulgated the constitution, which stated in article 5 that the Roman Apostolic Catholic Church would remain the state religion.

Thus, Protestants were tolerated but could not be elected to public office and were subject to imprisonment if they attempted to propagate their beliefs. As such, they faced a situation in which they were actually second-class citizens. How could they obtain an identity card if only Catholicism was an official religion and only baptisms performed by a Catholic priest were recognized? Often the simplest solution was for the government to pressure them to convert. When larger groups of Protestant settlers were concentrated in the same area, however, the imperial government provided pastors for them, although in insufficient numbers.

Nonetheless, there were problems. In 1864 Pastor Hermann Georg Borchard was arrested in São Leopoldo because he had led a funeral procession wearing his clerical robe. According to the government official in charge of the case, he was trying to propagate his Protestant religion and thus violated the constitution. The situation of Protestant marriages was even worse since there was no registry office for them. The only valid marriage was a Catholic one. Those who did not want a Catholic ceremony lived in concubinage and had illegitimate children, who were not allowed to inherit the property of their non-Catholic parents. When the marriage of Protestants was at last legally regulated, a decree dated October 21, 1865, demanded that the children of mixed marriages be baptized in the Catholic Church. Nonetheless, this decree was a step forward, since it allowed non-Catholics to legally marry in the presence of a pastor and ensured that their marriage had the same legal standing as a Catholic marriage.

Other problems remained, however. For example, all cemeteries belonged to the Catholic Church. Dissident Christians could not be buried in them. Only the first republican constitution of 1891 changed this situation by declaring the cemeteries to be public. For this reason, Rio Grande do Sul created cemeteries next to chapels, and in São Paulo field cemeteries were established.

The immigrants profoundly altered the physiognomy of religion in Brazil. Aside from the Protestant episodes that occurred in the sixteenth century (in Rio de Janeiro) and the seventeenth century (Dutchmen in the northeast), the nineteenth century brought to Brazil for the first time on a permanent basis Lutherans, Anglicans, Baptists, Presbyterians, Muslims, Buddhists, and social and political dissidents such as Carbonari, Liberals, Socialists, Anarchists. Catholics who came from Switzerland, Bavaria, the Palatinate, Veneto, Tyrol, or Poland barely acknowledged Brazilian Catholics as their equals in faith. The church they found in Brazil had been formed in the struggles with the Moors. It was a church of tournaments, in which Iberian, Azorean, and Jewish Christian traditions had been mixed with African and indigenous traditions. The mass of the Catholic population was made up of slaves, who, as such, had never had the right to legitimately constitute a family. The only sacrament they knew was baptism. Because they could not form families, they also did not see the family as the place where religion is conveyed and prayers and devotions are practiced. This Catholicism knew another kind of family, which emerged on the basis of the baptism of infants. The unwed mother who brought the child to baptism was the "co-mother" of her master, if he had fathered the child, or other slaves. The godfather and godmother replaced the nonexistent family or, rather, constituted a new family. A spiritual kinship was created. Thus, the "co-father" did not marry the "co-mother." To become the "co-father" of a former enemy was a way of sealing the reconciliation. Such an alliance and reconciliation was sealed and ratified by the church. To German Catholic and non-Catholic immigrants, these customs seem mysterious.

Throughout the first four decades of the nineteenth century, none of the German territorial churches showed any concern for German immigrants in Brazil. It was only in the wake of Prussian economic expansion—the search for markets—that such concern emerged, although it was motivated by economic interests and not by religious concern. In the 1860s German missionary societies sent pastors and missionaries not only to preach the gospel to the immigrants but also to preserve their German character. In this respect the intervention of consular authorities, particularly of Prussia and Switzerland, was important.

The Holy See and the Brazilian episcopate hoped to use German and Italian Roman Catholic immigrants to reform Brazilian Catholicism according to the restoration model by subjecting it to a romanization process. This project was challenged by the parishes that were already occupied, it failed to obtain the resources to maintain the priests involved in it, and individual foreign priests were entering the settlements, partly as immigrants. The solution was to completely entrust the parishes in colonization areas to missionaries (German Jesuits and Franciscans). Although the settlers welcomed the clergy, conflicts emerged quickly. How should the self-organization be combined with the instructions given by the parson or bishop? What should be done about the ecclesial practices that often were unorthodox in the eyes of the priest who had an absolutely clerical view of the church? What about the "lay priests"? Soon repression set in, and the original church experience was destroyed. Lutheran immigrants had similar experiences. When ordained pastors arrived from Germany, the people who had led the congregations were dismissed as "pseudo-pastors."

The immigrants, both Lutherans and Catholics, experienced simultaneously the Europeanizing of their religious beliefs and ways of worship. Among the Lutherans there was also an effort at "Germanizing" the immigrant population. Pseudo-pastors and pseudo-priests were dismissed. In the case of Catholics, the "empires of the divine," which were places of worship associated with the Feast of the Eternal Divine Father of Jewish-Christian origin, were transformed into parsonages or schools. All property was registered as belonging to the parish and later the curia. The new congregations and apostolates began to shape the new form of the church: a sacramental one. The process of romanization and reform of Catholicism and the struggle for equal rights started with the arrival of German immigrants. It resulted in a significant change in the physiognomy of Brazilian Catholicism.

Martin Noberto Dreher

See also Brazil

References and Further Reading

Davatz, Thomas. *Memórias de um Colono no Brasil 1850, tradução, prefácio e notas de Sérgio Buarque de Hollanda.* São Paulo: Livr. Martins.

Diel, Paulo Fernando. *"Ein katholisches Volk, aber ein Herde ohne Hirte": Der Anteil der deutschen Orden und Kongregationen an der Bewahrung deutscher Kultur und an der Erneuerung der katholischen Kirche in Süd-Brasilien (1824–1935/38).* Sankt Augustin: Gardez! Verlag, 2001.

Dreher, Martin N., ed. *Imigrações e História da Igreja no Brasil.* Aparecida: Ed. Santuário, 1993.

———, ed. *Populações Rio-Grandenses e Modelos de Igreja.* São Leopoldo: Sinodal, 1998.

———, ed. *500 anos de Brasil e Igreja na América Meridional.* Porto Alegre: Edições EST, 2002.

Prien, Hans-Jürgen. *Evangelische Kirchwerdung in Brasilien.* Gütersloh: Gerd Mohn, 1989.

BRECHT, BERTOLT

b. February 10, 1898; Augsburg, Bavaria
d. August 14, 1956; East Berlin

Eminent German left-leaning playwright who became famous for his creation of the epic theater and who was exiled to the United States during World War II.

Born Eugen Berthold Friedrich Brecht, he was the son of Berthold and Sophie Brecht. In 1914, his first poems appeared in the *Augsburger Neusten Nachrichten* (Augsburg Newest News) under the pseudonym Berthold Eugen. After graduation in 1917, Brecht began to study medicine in Munich, where he attended Arthur Kutschers's seminars on theater. However, Brecht was forced by World War I to interrupt his studies. For a short time, he served as a medical orderly in Augsburg (1918). In the same year, Brecht wrote his first theatrical work, *Baal.* Shortly thereafter, Brecht began writing drama reviews for the *Volkswillen* in Munich. Altogether, twenty-seven reviews and polemics would appear between 1919 and 1921. Brecht also began work on the play *Trommeln in der Nacht* (Drums in the Night), for which he won the Kleist Prize. The play, produced in 1922, explores class conflict in the form of the Spartan Revolution. On November 4, Brecht married the opera singer Marianne Zoff and moved with her to Berlin. In 1923 Brecht's play *Im Dickicht der Städte* (In the Jungle of the Cities) opened in Munich.

While in Berlin, Brecht worked with Carl Zuckmeyer as a dramaturge under Max Reinhardt in the Deutscher Theater. In December 1924, Brecht began writing the play *Mann ist Mann* (Man Equals Man). During this time, he also met and began to work together with Elisabeth Hauptmann. On September 25, 1926, *Mann ist Mann* premiered both in Darmstadt and Düsseldorf. Shortly thereafter, Brecht divorced Marianne Zoff. In 1927, *Hauspostille* (Manual of Piety), a collection of Brecht's poems from the years 1915–1926, was published.

In 1928, Brecht began working with the composer Kurt Weill on the rewriting of John Gay's play, *Beggar's Opera. Die Dreigroschenoper* (The Threepenny Opera), which opened on August 31 and was considered to be Brecht's first major success. In the play, Brecht makes use of epic theater, which does not strive to make the audience identify with the characters. Instead, the play attempts to establish critical distance through a process of alienation. Through this alienation effect (*Verfremdungseffekt*), the audience awakens to a critical consciousness of society's structures and the need for social change. On April 10, 1929, Brecht married Helene Weigel. In that same year, he began work on *Das Badener Lehrstück vom Einverständnis* (The Baden Cantata of Consent), which premiered July 28 in Baden-Baden. The first concert production of *Lindbergflug* (The Flight of Lindberg) took place in Berlin. Brecht's opera, *Aufstieg und Fall der Stadt Mahagonny* (Rise and Fall of the City Mahagonny) premiered in Leipzig in 1930. During this time, Brecht began filming *Kuhle Wampe*. After the Nazis came to power in 1933, Brecht and his family fled from Germany to Denmark.

During his exile, Brecht began writing poetry that is almost exclusively anti-Fascist in tone. He also worked on various emigrant newspapers. In 1934, he began writing the *Dreigroschenroman* (Three Penny Novel). Two years later, Brecht was stripped of his German citizenship. In June 1935 he took part in the First International Writer's Congress in Paris. At this time, he began working with Ruth Berlau. In 1937, Brecht wrote *Furcht und Elend des Dritten Reiches* (Fear and Misery of the Third Reich). On October 16, *Die Gewehre der Frau Carrar* (Seqora Carrar's Rifles) premiered in Paris. Brecht also took part in the Second International Writer's Congress. In 1938, Brecht finished *Das Leben des Galilei* (The Life of Galileo). He moved to Sweden in May 1939. A month later, a collection of Brecht's poems, the *Svendborger Gedichte* (Svendborg Poems), was published. Brecht also began work on *Mutter Courage und ihre Kinder* (Mother Courage and Her Children) and *Das Verhör des Lukullus* (The Trial of Lucullus). After the march of the Nazis into Denmark and Norway, Brecht fled to Finland in 1940, where he finished

most of the work on *Der guter Menschen von Sezuan* (The Good Person of Szechwan). From there, Brecht finally moved to the United States.

In 1941, Brecht began work on *Der aufhaltsame Aufstieg des Arturo Ui* (The Resistible Rise of Arturo Ui). While in the United States, Brecht met many other German exiles living in Los Angeles, among them Thomas Mann and Theodor Adorno. He also met many Hollywood stars, such as Charles Chaplin and Fritz Lang, and wrote screenplays, including the Fritz Lang production, *Hangmen Also Die* (1943). Brecht also wrote *Der kaukasische Kreidekreis* (1944, The Caucasian Chalk Circle) and *Schweyk im Zweiten Weltkrieg* (1943, Schweyk in the Second World War). After Hiroshima and Nagasaki were bombed on August 6, 1945, Brecht altered the play *Das Leben des Galilei*. When the play first appeared in Denmark, Brecht presented Galileo as an independent scientist. However, in the American version, *Galileo Galilei*, Galileo's scientific work appears as an instrument that serves only the government. In 1947, Brecht was called before the House Un-American Activities Committee (HUAC) in Washington. The next day, Brecht flew to Switzerland.

In 1948, Brecht settled in East Berlin, where his first postwar publication, *Kalendergeschichten* (Tales from the Calender), appeared. In 1949, Brecht and his wife established the Berliner Ensemble. Four years later, he was elected president of the German PEN Center. In the same year, his poetry cycle, *Buckower Elegien* (Buckow Elegies), appeared. Together with other intellectuals, Brecht helped found the Deutsche Akademie der Künste (German Academy of the Arts). In May 1953, Brecht was elected president of the PEN

Center East and West. Two years later, he was awarded the Stalin Prize in Moscow.

Kerri Pierce

See also Adorno, Theodor Wiesengrund; Intellectual Exile; Lang, Fritz; Mann, Thomas; Reinhardt, Max; Zuckmayer, Carl

References and Further Reading

Brecht, Bertolt. *Brecht on Theatre: The Development of an Aesthetic.* Trans. John Willet. New York: Hill and Wang, 1964.

Ewen, Frederic. *Bertolt Brecht: His Life, His Art, and His Times.* New York: Citadel Trade, 1967.

Fuegi, John. *Bertolt Brecht: Chaos, According to Plan.* Ed. Christopher Innes. New York: Cambridge University Press, 1987.

BREMERHAVEN

Founded in 1827, Bremerhaven is a port city (it gained "city" status in 1851) lying on the right bank and estuary of the Weser River in northern Germany. The port is a part of the German state of Bremen. Along with the free Hanseatic city of Bremen, Bremerhaven became the largest port for European emigration during the nineteenth and twentieth centuries. From 1830 until 1960, more than 7 million European emigrants traveled through Bremen and Bremerhaven.

At the dawn of the nineteenth century, the Bremen economy had declined from its Hanseatic glory days. The city suffered from an unfavorable balance of trade with the United States. Ships from the United States brought tobacco and cotton to Bremen, but because of Bremen's lack of exportable goods, these ships left the port carrying ballast. This arrangement changed drastically after the poor harvests of 1816–1817 triggered the first major emigration wave of the nineteenth century. As emigrants traveled to the port in increasing numbers, ship captains realized that they could increase revenue by substituting emigrants for the ballast. With this, the emigrant trade had begun.

The rapid growth of emigration posed many social problems for the various German states. It was far from certain that cities would allow (let alone *encourage*) emigration through their gates. Many state governments denounced the new phenomenon for fear that the emigration would promote the influx of noncitizen paupers who would become charges of the state. The Bremen Senate, however, recognized the economic potential of the emigration trade and acted early. By passing such legislation as the groundbreaking Emigration Act of 1832, the Senate took an active role in regulating the quality of emigrant conditions. Bremen's longtime rival upon the Elbe River, Hamburg, would eventually follow Bremen's example but would never approach Bremen's dominance.

The clearest example of Bremen's proactive enhancement of the emigrant trade was the purchase and development of what would become Bremerhaven. At the very onset of the emigration boom, Bremen had had a serious problem. The Weser River was rapidly silting up. Bremen was in jeopardy of losing its famed key to the world because large ships no longer could reach its docks. The Bremen Senate initially responded by negotiating with the Oldenburg port town of Brake to ship Bremen goods, but the Oldenburg government soon stepped in and banned the practice. Realizing that a more stable and permanent solution was necessary, the Bremen Senate, under the direction of Mayor Johann Smidt, purchased land from the Kingdom of Hanover. After the transaction was completed in 1827, construction began on the new Bremerhaven (or "Bremen port") located approximately 40 miles down the Weser from the mother city. On September 12, 1830, the first ship arrived in the new port.

The development of Bremerhaven became inextricably linked with European emigration. The city swelled with ship merchants, dockworkers, shipbuilders, sailors, emigration agents, and of course, emigrants. Many of the emigrants had used up all their money in their journey to the port and simply drifted because they could not afford a spot on board the ships. Moreover, even the emigrants who had their tickets were often forced to wait in the city, sometimes for months, before embarking on the transatlantic journey. In order to house these emigrants more efficiently, the Senate, in conjunction with the Bremerhaven merchant Johann Georg Claussen, opened the Emigrant House in 1849 (the establishment closed due to financial troubles in 1865). The docks were constantly transformed in order to cater to the needs of new ships—especially with the arrival of the steamship. During the 1850s, a new harbor was constructed in order to accommodate the new, larger ships. Within the next few decades, the steamers from the North German Lloyd shipping line established a dominance that would last well into the twentieth century. By 1855 Bremen (with Bremerhaven) surpassed the French port of Le Havre as the leading emigration port for Germans.

After the mid-1890s, the socioeconomic climate improved in Germany, and the number of German emigrants declined considerably. However, Bremerhaven continued to draw a multitude of emigrants. From the 1880s until World War I, emigrants from eastern and southeastern Europe moved through the port in increasing numbers. Emigrant accommodations within the city improved with the opening of the Emigrant Halls in 1907. The flow of emigrants slowed to a trickle during World War I but quickly regained its former volume after the restoration of peace. The interwar years witnessed not only the continued emigration from eastern and southeastern Europe but also a resurgence of German emigration. During the Nazi era, the port became the exit point for thousands of Jews, who by 1939 accounted for 90 percent of the total emigration stream.

During World War II, much of Bremen and Bremerhaven was destroyed. After the conclusion of the war, most of the emigrants who moved through Bremen and Bremerhaven were European refugees or displaced persons. This emigration was conducted primarily through the actions of international organizations with the use of foreign ships, not as a part of German trade. By the 1960s, this emigration ceased. Emigration no longer plays a significant role in the Bremerhaven economy. The city continues to serve as a major German trading port, however, and also specializes in shipbuilding and the fishing industry.

.

Kevin Ostoyich

See also German-Speaking Migration to the Americas; Hamburg; Norddeutscher Lloyd

References and Further Reading

Armgort, Arno. *Bremen—Bremerhaven—New York: Geschichte der Auswanderung über die Bremischen Häfen.* Bremen: Steintor, 1991.

Engelsing, Rolf. *Bremen als Auswandererhafen, 1683–1880.* Bremen: Carl Schünemann Verlag, 1961.

Historisches Museum Bremerhaven. http://www.historisches-museum-bremerhaven.de.

Scheper, Burchard. *Die Jüngere Geschichte der Stadt Bremerhaven.* Bremen: J. H. Schmalfeldt, 1977.

Walker, Mack. *Germany and the Emigration, 1816–1885.* Cambridge, MA: Harvard University Press, 1964.

BRUMMER

German mercenary group in Brazil during the 1850s.

After Manoel Ortiz Rosas took power in Argentina and embraced an aggressive foreign policy that included wars against its neighboring countries Uruguay, Paraguay, and Brazil, the government in Rio de Janeiro decided to seek the help of mercenary troops from Europe. At the end of the 1840s, the government sent a representative to Hamburg, where a large number of volunteers from Schleswig-Holstein, who had fought for the independence of these two duchies from the Danish king in the 1848–1849 revolution, had just been discharged. These volunteers were liberal in their political views and had hoped for the creation of a union of all Germans. The Brazilian government offered these disgruntled volunteers the opportunity to leave Germany for Brazil, where they would serve in the army in exchange for land to be given to them upon completion of four years of military service. Based on this agreement, approximately 1,800 volunteers and 50 officers left for Brazil in 1851. These Germans were subsequently called "Brummer." This name derived from the German word for the noise copper coins made when they were thrown to the ground. These copper coins were used to pay these German mercenaries.

After the military campaign against Argentina in the La Plata area, these German mercenaries were discharged and received land grants in the province of Rio Grande do Sul. Unlike the German settlers who had emigrated to Brazil before 1840 and who were mostly of peasant background, this second wave of German immigration to Brazil included people with a high level of education who were politically liberal and Protestant. Most of them became leading figures representing the Brazilian Germans. These military volunteers were the social basis for the political, economic, cultural, and religious elite within the Brazilian German subculture.

The Brummer worked as teachers, pastors, and journalists and started enterprises that would dominate economic life in Brazil. More important, they encouraged the Brazilian Germans to form their own political organizations. Some of them were elected to the state legislature during the 1880s. However, their influence was not limited to the Brazilian German subculture; they brought with them new political, religious, and philosophical ideas, which influenced and transformed the entire Brazilian society. During the time of the Brazilian Empire (1822–1889), Catholicism was the state religion, and the Catholic faith influenced and dominated intellectual life. By bringing laicism, liberalism, evolution, and freemasonry to Brazil, the Brummer provided the intellectual basis for the modern state in Brazil. Karl von Koseritz is regarded as the foremost member of this group.

René Gertz

See also Argentina; Brazil; Koseritz, Karl von
References and Further Reading
Schmid, Albert. *Die "Brummer."* Porto Alegre:
A Nação, 1949.

BRÜNING, HEINRICH
b. November 26, 1895; Münster
(Westfalen), Prussia
d. March 30, 1970; Norwich, Vermont

German chancellor from 1930 to 1932 who was exiled to the United States after Adolf Hitler became chancellor of Germany.

Historians disagree greatly on the role he played in the downfall of the first German democracy between 1930 and 1933. His tenure as chancellor in depression-ridden Germany has been interpreted in drastically different ways. Some historians consider it the last attempt to save the Weimar Republic, whereas others see it as the first step in the dissolution of the first German republic.

After he had graduated from the Paulinum Gymnasium in Münster, Brüning entered law school at the University of Munich. After one semester he transferred to the University of Strasbourg to study philosophy, history, German literature and language, and political science. During his time in Straßburg, Brüning supported the cooperation between Protestants and Catholics and, influenced by the historian Martin Spahn, adopted a strongly pro-Prussian nationalist political position. From 1911 to 1913, Brüning studied in London and Manchester, where he was introduced to the British parliamentary system and Toryism. In 1914 he finished his dissertation on the economic and legal conditions of the English private railway companies with a discussion of the question of their nationalization. One year later, he was awarded a doctorate from the University of Bonn. Although he was considered unfit for active duty because of his nearsightedness, Brüning volunteered in 1914. During his three and a half years of service on the western front, he was wounded twice and received the *Eisernes Kreuz* (Iron Cross), second and first class.

Germany's military defeat destroyed Brüning's world. Since he had trusted in the abilities of the German High Command, defeat and revolution came as a great surprise to him. Disliking the new republican system, Brüning decided not to pursue an academic career but instead became active in the Catholic Center Party. His involvement on behalf of former front-line soldiers provided a base for his successful political career. In early 1919 he received a post in the newly created Prussian Social Welfare Ministry. Brüning, together with Adam Stegerwald, organized the melding of all non-Socialist trade unions into the Christian National Trade Union. In 1921 he became the leader of this trade union organization and edited its newspaper, *Der Deutsche* (The German). During the French occupation of the Rhineland in 1923, Brüning organized the passive resistance of the German population. The experience of hyperinflation, which was accelerated by their passive resistance, traumatized him. In 1924 he was elected to the German parliament and quickly earned a reputation as expert on finance and tax issues. In December 1929, he was chosen as leader of the Center Party faction in parliament.

On March 30, 1930, Reich President Paul von Hindenburg appointed Heinrich Brüning as chancellor of a cabinet that was based on Article 48 of the Weimar Constitution. This marked a turning point in German history and a break with parliamentary custom. The new Brüning cabinet operated independently of the German parliament, relying entirely on the emergency powers of the president. Brüning used his extraordinary powers to introduce a draconian policy of deflation. Facing one of the greatest economic crises in German history, Brüning insisted on cutting spending and increasing taxation. To get rid of the reparation payments imposed on Germany in the Treaty of Versailles was his highest priority. By fulfilling the demands of the Allies to the letter, Brüning intended to show that Germany was incapable of meeting their demands. Accepting a much higher degree of unemployment and impoverishment of the German population than necessary, Brüning was not interested in policies to ameliorate crises, since economic betterment would have prevented him from convincing the United States, Great Britain, and France that Germany could no longer pay reparations. Brüning's policy led to a much deeper economic crisis and the disillusionment of large parts of the German populace with democracy. In his memoirs, published in 1970, Heinrich Brüning stated that his goal of abolishing Germany's obligation to pay reparations was only the first step in his larger political program, which included a general reform of Germany's constitution and the restoration of the Hohenzollern monarchy.

The economic collapse in summer of 1931 and Brüning's deflationary policy made him one of the most hated politicians in Germany. After he lost his support among German industrialists, and his plans for a customs union with Austria failed, Hindenburg began to search for a replacement for Brüning. After Brüning banned the paramilitary organizations of the Nazi movement, Sturmabteilung (SA, Stormtroopers) and Schutzstaffel (SS, Elite Nazi organization) on April 13, 1932, and after he clashed with Hindenburg over the issue of aid for eastern Prussian estate owners, General Kurt von Schleicher convinced Hindenburg to dismiss Brüning.

The efficacy of Heinrich Brüning's chancellorship has been hotly debated among historians. For some it was the end of the Weimar Republic; for others it was the last attempt to preserve the republic. However, Brüning's economic policy contributed to an enormous increase in support for the National Socialist German Worker's Party (NSDAP). It was during his tenure that Adolf Hitler's party became a mass party, which slowly but surely dominated German political life. Brüning's attitude toward the Nazi movement was ambivalent and contradictory. Before 1933 he supported the idea of inviting the NSDAP into a coalition government. After Hitler was made chancellor at the end of January 1933, Brüning opposed the Enabling Act but voted in its favor on March 23, 1933. On May 6, 1933, he took over the leadership of the Center Party. Two months later, he was forced to dissolve his party in order to prevent its banning.

In May 1934 Brüning left Germany because he feared for his life. He arrived in the United States in 1937 via Holland and Switzerland. There he accepted a professorship in political science at Harvard University. He had to endure the criticism of left-wing émigrés since Brüning had refused to speak out publicly against the Hitler dictatorship and since he did not participate in any exile organization. However, he unsuccessfully tried to warn European governments of the danger of German expansionism. Brüning accurately predicted the course of German aggression and warned the British government that appeasement would not satisfy Hitler. After the outbreak of World War II, Brüning, frightened by the discussion of retribution against Germany and especially the Morgenthau Plan, lobbied U.S. politicians in an attempt to convince them that reconstruction of Germany was needed. After the end of the war, Brüning traveled back to Germany twice, in 1948 and 1950. He was pleased to see the political unification of Catholics and nationalist Protestants in the newly established Christlich Demokratische Union (Christian Democratic Union) under the leadership of Konrad Adenauer in West Germany. He rejected the offer to run for a seat in the West German parliament. In 1951, he accepted a chair in political science at the University of Cologne. Between 1951 and 1955 he taught at the University of Cologne and at Harvard University. Brüning disagreed with Adenauer's policy of integrating West Germany into the North Atlantic Treaty Organization (NATO) and objected to the incipient materialism of West Germans. After his retirement in 1955, Brüning decided to return to the United States. In 1957 he bought a small house in Norwich, Vermont, where he lived until his death.

Michael Rudloff

See also Great Depression; Intellectual Exile; Morgenthau Plan; Shuster, George Nauman; Treaty of Versailles

References and Further Reading

Mannes, Astrid Luise. *Heinrich Brüning: Leben, Wirken, Schicksal*. Munich: Olzog,1999.

Morsey, Rudolf. *Brüning und Adenauer. Zwei deutsche Staatsmänner.* Düsseldorf: Droste, 1972.

———. *Zur Entstehung, Authentizität und Kritik von Brünings "Memoiren 1918–1934."* Opladen: Westdeutscher Verlag, 1975.

Patch, William L. *Heinrich Brüning and the Dissolution of the Weimar Republic.* Cambridge, UK: Cambridge University Press, 1998.

BUFFALO

At any one time during the second half of the nineteenth century, about 1 percent of the German immigrants living in the United States resided in Buffalo, New York. Though advocates of German culture in the United States such as Karl Heinzen and Theodore Sutro berated the community in Buffalo for its lack of theater and literary culture, Buffalo's community was one of the wealthiest and most politically prominent emigrant German communities in the world. Today, however, there is no sign of a German community within the city limits.

Pennsylvania Germans such as Martin Mittag and Samuel Helm settled along the eastern shore of Lake Erie as early as the 1790s. But John Kuecherer, a water carrier who arrived from Baden in 1817, was commemorated later as the city's pioneer German. After the completion of the Erie Canal in 1825, Buffalo became a commercial center and a stopover for immigrants and goods heading west. The German population grew rapidly. German immigrants established their first church, St. John's Lutheran, in 1829, and their first newspaper, *Der Weltbürger* (The Cosmopolitan), in 1837. Breweries, incorporated *Vereine* (clubs), distinctly German Catholic churches, and a Lutheran seminary were all established before the European revolutions of 1848 sent many more settlers to the city.

The Germans incorporated themselves fairly successfully into the city, winning privileges and accepting responsibilities. They purchased much of the city's east side, which according to Buffalo's *Commercial Advertiser* on June 12, 1857, was as American as the "Duchy of Hesse Cassel." The timing and extent of their immigration served to unseat nativist politicians, help compete with rival Anglo-Americans in Fourth of July festivals, and win a special reception when President-elect Abraham Lincoln visited the city in 1861. German households also sent a higher proportion of young men into the Civil War than the city's Irish and Anglo-Americans, though not as high a percentage as African Americans. One German battery led by Michael Wiedrich won special distinction in the war and acclaim at home. City officials integrated the teaching of the German language into the curriculum of the primary schools in 1866.

In 1873, a local physician declared that the Germans of Buffalo had become a great power. Respected more than before and ever more numerous, the Germans began to assume a position of leadership in the city itself. In 1871, the city's Germans celebrated the unification of Germany with a festival declared by the *Buffalo Post* on May 30 to have been the most "grand, imposing, glorious, and never-to-be-forgotten demonstration" in the city's history. Two years later, the mobilization of the city's German *Vereine* (clubs) overturned a movement to eliminate the German program in the schools. One of the *Verein* leaders, Philip Becker, subsequently was elected mayor of Buffalo in 1875, 1885,

and 1887. By World War II, Buffalo had elected nine German American mayors, more than any other major city in the United States. In 1904, an east side basketball team, appropriately called the "Germans," won what amounted to the world championship title during the St. Louis Olympic competition. By World War I, the German banks, hospitals, and churches in the city's skyline attested to the significance of a German element that during the late 1870s crested in influence, accounting for half of the city's population.

But with the decline of nativism and an increase in working-class unrest, the solidarity of the city's Germans also dissipated in the 1870s. Marxist newspapers such as the *Die Arbeiterstimme am Erie* (The Worker's Voice on Erie) in 1878 and the *Buffaloer Arbeiter Zeitung* (Buffalo Workingman's News, 1885–1918) called for a revolution that would overthrow the government and the capitalist order. German Catholicism that had begun in Buffalo as a vocal attempt in the 1840s and 1850s to wrest the city's largest church from French pioneers and Irish bishops became more conservative and inner-directed by the 1870s. By 1900, German Catholicism in Buffalo was an empire marked by numerous otherworldly gothic spires, hundreds of *Vereine,* about twenty primary schools, and a population greater than the Mormon element of Salt Lake City. The clubs of the more liberal Germans also advanced, with the culmination of their work being the building of a new music hall for the city in 1883. Many leading Germans, such as Jacob Schoellkopf, the first businessmen to win the right to harness the power of Niagara Falls, and Philip Becker acquired impressive degrees of power financially, politically, socially, and even in denominational affairs. They helped lead a city that was a pioneer in the development of electrical energy and had more per capita millionaires than any other by 1900.

By the early 1900s, amid signs of achievement, there was also a growing sense of disappointment among the city's German leaders. The immigrants were dying off. Leading *Vereine* of the nineteenth century, such as the *Turnverein,* the *Liedertafel,* and the German Young Men's Association dropped precipitously in membership. A leading soap manufacturer, William Lautz, declared that the teaching of German in the public schools had been a failure and that the "strange drama" of language loss had occurred in many German families. In the face of these realities, however, Germanophiles staged a wakeup call to German Buffalo. In 1904, a coterie of professionals tied to the German department of the public schools, the city's German hospitals, and its German banks instituted the city's first German Day and formed a federation that affiliated with the German American Bund, formed three years before in Philadelphia.

Uncertainty reigned as the community found the United States increasingly hostile to Germany and inching toward an alliance with Great Britain and France. Some said that the community had emerged from the doldrums of the late nineteenth century. Outspoken pro-German groups like the Bund and the Harugari showed increases in membership, the circulation of local German newspapers grew, and the political power of the Germans appeared to be on the rise. By the time of U.S. entry into World War I, Louis

Fuhrmann was in his seventh year as mayor, the city had four parks with distinctly German names, and the number of students taking German in the public schools had reached its highest level. But a climactic disenchantment followed. Telling incidents, not widespread enough to inflame, raised the cost of remaining German. Patriotic hoodlums broke up a meeting of the Harugari. One Friedrich Winter was stabbed for buying a German newspaper. Pretensions of Germanic greatness had attained a mythic status. But Germany began to lose the war, and with its loss went the utility and prestige of having ties to it. During World War I, newspapers such as the *Buffaloer Arbeiter Zeitung,* the *Demokrat* (The Democrat—a *Weltbürger* offshoot, 1837–1918), and the *Freie Presse* (Free Press, 1860–1914) folded. The local bund tried in vain to survive in 1918, after finally pledging support for the U.S. war effort. An Anglo-American graduate of Yale, George Buck, defeated Louis Fuhrmann, and many parks, hospitals, and banks lost their German names.

Buffalo's German American community emerged from the war with a single daily, the *Volksfreund* (People's Friend, 1868–1954), the once proud Buffalo Orpheus, a number of regional societies, and a scattering of churches where the German language was still a mainstay. The breweries and brewer's union that had maintained the German language in their transactions were decimated by Prohibition. The area once hailed as the "Great German East Side" now consisted of two neighborhoods—the Orchard and Schiller Park. Buffalo's Polish community moved north into the German quarter, as many of German descent joined Americans of English and Irish descent in moving into neighborhoods on the far north and south sides.

As the older establishment of pioneers and liberals died, a new, more conservative German American culture emerged during the 1920s. Frank X. Schwab, a two-term German Catholic mayor (1922–1929), hosted German American leaders and helped revive the German Day celebration in 1922, four years before the return of that festival to Cincinnati. Schwab's Buffalo remained wet. The mayor fired the policemen who had enforced Prohibition and rewarded agents who helped destroy the Ku Klux Klan. When the Depression came in 1929, nostalgia flourished more conclusively. Four new German literary societies arose in Buffalo during the late 1920s and early 1930s, and associations such as the Herwegh singing society and the local alliance of *Vereine* reassembled. By the mid-1930s, it was not a lack of enthusiasm that concerned German American leaders but fanaticism. A pro-Nazi group, the Friends of the New Germany, emerged in Buffalo in 1933. Though the inner cadre of this group consisted of only about thirty-six young men and four women—almost all of them immigrants—they won sympathizers from many in the community who dreamed that the local *Deutschtum* (the German community) could be revived. In the early days, both Joseph Eltges, a German Catholic owner of the *Volksfreund,* and the scion of the wealthy Schoellkopf family Jacob Schoellkopf II, proffered time and public tributes on behalf of local Nazis.

Public condemnation of Nazism and Germany itself, however, upstaged this second revival completely, and Buffalo's *Deutschtum* fell from the rank of a nationality to a dispersed ethnic group. By the time Hitler plunged Europe into war in 1939, local Nazis were so hated that local German American politicians such as Frank Schwab and Edwin Jaeckle were agitating for their suppression. From 1941 to 1945, the U.S. Justice Department prosecuted local Nazis, while the Buffalo Federation of German Societies maintained a low profile. After the war, the *Volksfreund* appeared irregularly and no longer presumed to give advice to German speakers. The last German neighborhoods lost their character, and the oldest section, the Orchard, became a slum known as the Fruit Belt. Only a few German societies and churches persisted, with many accepting non-German members. Due to a remarkable decline in the city's population in the late twentieth century and to a suburban exodus, there is today no recognizable German neighborhood in a city that 130 years before was half German.

Andrew Yox

See also Cincinnati; Friends of the New Germany; Hexamer, Charles J.; National German-American Alliance; Schwab, Frank X.

References and Further Reading

Gerber, David. *The Making of an American Pluralism: Buffalo, New York, 1825–1860.* Urbana: University of Illinois Press, 1989.

Yox, Andrew. "Decline of the German-American Community in Buffalo, 1855–1925." PhD diss., University of Chicago, 1983.

———. "The Parochial Context of Trusteeism: Buffalo's Saint Louis Church, 1828–1855." *The Catholic Historical Review* (October 1990): 712–733.

———. "Bonds of Community: Buffalo's German Element, 1853–1871." *Coming and Becoming: Pluralism in New York State History.* Ed. Wendell Tripp. Cooperstown: New York State Historical Association, 1991a, 185–208.

———. "The Fall of the German-American Community: Buffalo, 1914 to 1919." *Immigration to New York*. Eds. William Pencak et al. Philadelphia: Associated University Presses, 1991b, 126–147.

BUFFALO BILL

By the end of the nineteenth century, millions had taken part in a common experience promising to transport them to the real American West: Buffalo Bill's Wild West show, which toured Europe and the United States extensively during the late nineteenth and early twentieth centuries. Throughout its thirty-three-year existence, this vibrant show blurred the lines separating entertainment spectacle and history, creating an experience that seemed to be "the real thing." Presiding over the show was one of the best-known Americans of the day and one of the first modern international celebrities: Buffalo Bill. Numerous cultural and political luminaries saw it, such as Queen Victoria, Emperor Wilhelm II, Pope Leo XIII, and Karl May, as well as hundreds of thousands of other spectators from all walks of life. It served as inspiration for Puccini's opera *La Fanciulla del West* (The Child of the West) and numerous western dime novels. In short, it aroused enthusiasm and passion on both sides of the Atlantic for over three decades and helped mold a German understanding of the American West.

Although best known for his Wild West shows, Colonel William F. Cody (also known as Buffalo Bill or in Germany as Büffel-Wilhelm) gained a fair degree of fame in the United States before he organized his first Wild West show in 1883. He had previously ridden for the Pony Express

and Majors and Russell, fought in the Civil War as a Union soldier, driven a stagecoach, hunted buffalo to feed the Kansas-Pacific Railroad's work crews, served as a scout for the U.S. Cavalry, prospected for gold, engaged in several major battles against American Indians, and acted in several melodramatic theatrical productions. As a result of his exploits he received the Congressional Medal of Honor and was elected to serve in the Nebraska state legislature. Contemporaries commonly believed that he had truly experienced firsthand the settlement of the western frontier. Due to his exploits and the resulting accolades he achieved, he and a business partner, Nate Salsbury, thought him the perfect person to organize a show promising easterners a glimpse of the quickly vanishing frontier. The initial successes the show achieved in the United States led Cody and Salsbury to expand it to Europe for several seasons. Following successful tours in Britain, France, and Italy, the show went to Germany in 1890–1891.

The show offered a spectacle that amazed its German observers. When the company arrived in a German city, crowds gathered to see the unloading of the train's cargo and watch the parade as it went to an open space in the city. So impressed were the observers by the rapidity with which the show assembled corrals and tents that the Prussian military sent officers to document specifically how the troupe accomplished this feat so quickly. Following the arrival at the designated open space, the company set up a camp, complete with tepees, corrals, stagecoaches, and tents. The public was allowed to roam these grounds for free and meet the company's celebrities. The show itself was a series of acts, each

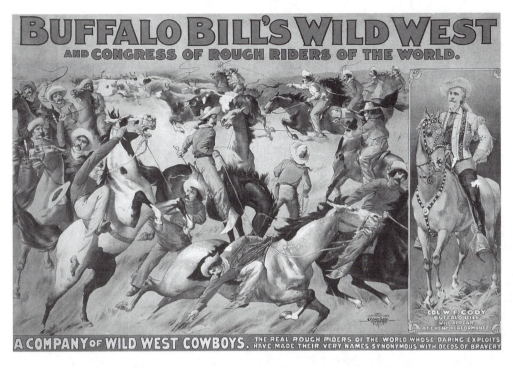

Circus poster showing cowboys rounding up cattle and portrait of Colonel W. F. "Buffalo Bill" Cody on horseback. (Library of Congress)

demonstrating a mythologized aspect of the western frontier such as the job of a Pony Express rider, life in a Native American village, gunfights, and horse taming. The Wild West show allowed German audiences the chance to see things, people, and events they associated with the American West that they had long imagined but had probably never seen. Examples included Native Americans, cowboys, Mexican vaqueros, buffalo, broncos, and displays of lassoing. Several of the show's most popular star performers during the German tour were Annie Oakley, Jim Larson, Jonnie Baker, Red Bear, Black Heart, and Eagle Horn. The show had a full itinerary in Germany. By the end of its travels it had performed in the German cities of Munich, Dresden, Leipzig, Magdeburg,

Brunswick, Hanover, Berlin, Hamburg, Bremen, Cologne, Düsseldorf, Frankfurt, Stuttgart, Karlsruhe, Strasbourg, Dortmund, Duisburg, Baden-Baden, Mannheim, Darmstadt, Koblenz, and Aachen. Moreover, it visited the Austrian cities of Innsbruck and Vienna.

Although the show obviously presented a romanticized vision of the American West—replete with such clichés as gunfights and Indian war dances—its promoters claimed that it represented an actual portrait of the western landscape. Moreover, Cody's actual participation in the drama further blurred the lines separating fact and fiction. For its own part, the company purposely attempted to confuse German audiences. A disclaimer in the Wild West's German program read, "We have only real personalities, only true, no false equipment. . . . [the performance] depicts a great, romantic and nevertheless realistic picture of the time, that though now over, still lives in memory. . . . Here is no theater production, one sees here actual life, as it was in the west . . . a genuine, unadulterated [ungeschminkt] picture of the past—the fighters and wild riders of the prairie" (Shealy 2003, 11). German newspaper reviewers of the production seem to have accepted the assertion that they were in some ways seeing an objective portrayal of life in the American West. They described it as a combination of performance, historical reenactment, circus, and educational opportunity. On seeing the performance, a reviewer effused, "One feels nature—the wild, powerful, unbounded nature of the Prairie. That is something completely different from the most beautiful, impressive circus." Another reporter wrote that "one gets a real living picture of the hunting- and Indian-life of the North American prairie," and yet another reporter told his readers, "If you would hold that Col. W. F. Cody is a loud charlatan, you are very mistaken" (Shealy 2003, 23, 45). The show powerfully influenced many Germans' conception and understanding of the American West.

Cody always asserted that the reason for his international tour was to serve as a type of cultural ambassador from the New World to the Old, in order that Europe might think more highly of the United States. In this respect, he must have been pleased with the reaction of German audiences. According to Cody and other members of the troupe, German audiences attended the productions with more enthusiasm and interest than their European counterparts. The visit of the Wild West to a city often left in its wake groups of hobby clubs devoted to exploring aspects of American Indian culture or life in the West. Moreover, numerous contemporary articles relate stories of girls pretending to be Annie Oakley and men injuring themselves as a result of trying to duplicate the show's stunts. Interestingly, the movement of performers across the Atlantic Ocean occurred in both directions. Following the show's tour through Germany, it returned to Chicago to take part in the World Exposition of 1893. Wilhelm II allowed a detachment from the Prussian military to accompany the troupe and perform their riding abilities before American audiences.

Gregory Paul Shealy

See also Indians in German Literature
References and Further Reading
Blackstone, Sarah J. *Buckskins, Bullets, and Business: A History of Buffalo Bill's Wild West.* New York: Greenwood Press, 1986.
Kasson, Joy S. *Buffalo Bill's Wild West: Celebrity, Memory, and Popular History.* New York: Hill and Wang, 2000.
Moses, Lester George. *Wild West Shows and the Images of American Indians, 1883–1933.* Albuquerque: University of New Mexico Press, 1996.
Reddin, Paul. *Wild West Shows.* Urbana: University of Illinois Press, 1999.
Shealy, Gregory. *Buffalo Bill in Germany.* MA thesis, University of Wisconsin at Madison, 2003.

BUND DEUTSCHER FRAUENVEREINE (FEDERATION OF GERMAN WOMEN'S CLUBS)

On March 29, 1894, the Bund Deutscher Frauenvereine (BDF, or Federation of German Women's Clubs) was founded in

Berlin. It was the first umbrella organization with the specific aim of connecting and centralizing the broad spectrum of women's interests and concerns. The idea for such a federation had originated in the United States. In 1893, several prominent German women's rights activists—Anna Simson, Hanna Bieber-Böhm, Auguste Förster, and Käthe Schirmacher—had attended the International Women's Congress at the Chicago World Fair and had familiarized themselves with the perspectives, strategies, and organizational forms of the American women's movements. Taking the National Council of Women as their model, they had returned to Germany with the plan to bring together, under one organizational roof, as many different women's clubs as possible and thus to extend the movements' political reach and influence. The World Fair in Chicago and the resulting formation of the BDF can thus be considered the formal beginning of German American organized women's cooperation.

In addition to the National Council of Women in the United States, the BDF was also indebted to the International Council of Women (ICW), which was founded in Washington, D.C., in 1888. The meetings of the ICW happened in the context of a lively, more informal transatlantic exchange. At the end of the nineteenth century, travel times between the United States and Europe had shrunk to five days on an ocean liner, although distance and cost often still constituted considerable obstacles, both for individual women and the organizations of which they were part. Nevertheless, many professional contacts were established, and individual friendships developed. One prominent example

was Jane Addams, the founder of the settlement movement, who traveled to Europe in 1883 as part of her "finishing tour." She visited Ireland, England, the Netherlands, Italy, Greece, Austria, France, Switzerland, and Germany. This journey, intended as the final step of her formal education, turned into the initial impulse for her later dedication to social reform. Two years later, she again visited Europe (this time especially England, Germany, Italy, and Spain) and brought back the idea for Hull-House. During this second trip, Addams collected information on women's situation and the state of the women's movements in these European countries, being especially impressed by German social reform. And Addams was not alone in her interest and engagement. Other reformers of the Progressive Era—among them Florence Kelley, Alice Hamilton, Mary Church Terrell, Mary Kingsbury Simkovitch, and Emily Greene Balch—repeatedly traveled to Europe, often including visits to Germany. Most of them had initially come on study or finishing tours but later deliberately sought contacts with German reformers. Many saw in German institutions and reforms models to take back and implement on their side of the Atlantic. Especially the German educational system and an insurance legislation that emphasized social responsibility seemed worthy of emulation.

In turn, German women familiarized themselves with the goals and perspectives of the American women's movements during their travels to the United States. Addams in particular became a role model for the prominent positions women could occupy within social reform. Hull-House in Chicago was considered one of the most

attractive destinations of politically interested European travelers; even Bertha von
Suttner, Austrian writer, pacifist, and first
recipient of the Nobel Peace Prize, stopped
there. German women also took advantage
of the opportunity to inform American
women of their activities at home because
most American activists had only a sketchy
understanding of the situation in Germany, despite the general enthusiasm that
accompanied these transatlantic connections. And several prominent German
women's rights activists managed to be acknowledged in the United States for their
ideals and goals; Alice Salomon in particular established herself in American circles
as an expert on German social policies and
published widely in American journals.

ICW and BDF shared the idea of bringing together and accommodating a wide variety of women's interests; accordingly, both
organizations' statutes were intentionally
vague and flexible. The ICW's corresponding secretary, Teresa Wilson, expressed
both apprehension and enthusiasm when
she described this strategy of noninterference in the Quinquennial Report of the
ICW for 1899 as both "our stumbling-block
and our pride—our stumbling-block because of the difficulty we experience in explaining precisely by rule and measure what
we are and what we want, and our pride because this very vagueness enables us to be
all-embracing" (Rupp 1997, 19). In a similar vein, paragraph 2 of the BDF's founding
documents determined that the federation
should explicitly refrain from interfering in
its member societies' internal affairs.

This policy of noninterference, however, was not easy to maintain, as the various groups' perspectives and goals differed
widely and often resulted in conflicting demands. In Germany, the bourgeois
women's movement alone was divided between radicals and moderates, and Socialist
and conservative women constituted independent factions outside middle-class organizing. In addition, Prussian law prohibited women, high school students,
apprentices, and "insane" persons—until
1908—from being members of political
organizations. This law had far-reaching
consequences for the formation of an organized women's movement in the German
Empire because it forced all women's organizations to project an explicitly nonpo-
litical image in order to prevent being shut
down by police. This was especially detrimental to the Socialist/Social Democratic
women's movement because their support
for the rights of female workers was, as far
as the state was concerned, undoubtedly
political. Socialist women's societies and
their members were thus constantly under
observation, running a high risk of persecution and/or prohibition.

Despite these difficult political circumstances and its highly contested beginnings, the BDF quickly developed into a
very powerful organization. Before World
War I, membership grew surprisingly fast.
With 65 member organizations in its first
year, it grew to include 137 organizations
with about 70,000 individual members in
1901. In 1913, it consisted of 2,200 organizations and approximately 500,000
individual members. In 1933, the National Socialists tried to incorporate the
BDF in its own women's organization; to
avoid this development, the BDF chose to
disband.

Kerstin R. Wolff

See also Addams, (Laura) Jane; International
Council of Women

References and Further Reading

Gerhard, Ute, and Ulla Wischermann. *Unerhört: Die Geschichte der deutschen Frauenbewegung.* Reinbek bei Hamburg: Rowohlt, 1990.

Greven-Aschoff, Barbara. *Die bürgerliche Frauenbewegung in Deutschland, 1894–1933.* Göttingen: Vandenhoeck and Ruprecht, 1981.

Herminghouse, Patricia. "'Wohl auf Schwestern!' Schnittpunkte der deutschen und amerikanischen Frauenbewegung im 19. Jahrhundert." *Deutsch-amerikanischen Begegnungen: Konflikte und Kooperation im 19. und 20. Jahrhundert.* Ed. Frank Trommler and Elliott Shore. Stuttgart: Deutsche Verlagsanstalt, 2001, 103–116.

Rupp, Leila J. *Worlds of Women: The Making of an International Women's Movement.* Princeton: Princeton University Press, 1997.

Schüler, Anja. *Frauenbewegung und soziale Reform: Jane Addams und Alice Salomon im transatlantischen Dialog, 1889–1933.* Stuttgart: Franz Steiner Verlag, 2004.

BURGESS, JOHN WILLIAM

b. August 26, 1844; Cornersville, Tennessee

d. January 13, 1931; Newport, Rhode Island

American political scientist. After studies in Germany, John William Burgess became professor at Columbia University and a major influence in the creation of political science as a graduate academic discipline in the United States.

Burgess grew up in Tennessee in a slave-holding but pro-Union family. In the Civil War he served with the Union as scout and quartermaster. After the war he studied at Amherst College, from which he graduated in 1867. He studied law with a law firm in nearby Springfield, Massachusetts, and was admitted to the bar in 1869. He did not practice but joined the faculty of Knox College. From 1871 to 1873 Burgess studied law, history, and political science at the universities of Göttingen, Leipzig and Berlin, where he had Johann Gustav Droysen, Theodore Mommsen, Heinrich von Treitschke, Rudolf von Gneist, and other leading scholars of the day as teachers. A companion in his study trip was Elihu Root, later U.S. secretary of state. Upon his return to the United States in 1873, Burgess taught history and political science at Amherst until 1876, when he joined the faculty at Columbia University. In 1880, together with Nicholas Murray Butler, Burgess established the School of Political Science at Columbia University, which replicated German educational models. The school soon commenced publishing the *Political Science Quarterly.* In 1890 Burgess published his most important academic work, *Political Science and Comparative Constitutional Law,* and became dean of the Faculty of Political Science in 1890. He remained in that position until his retirement in 1912.

Burgess's relationship with Germany and with German culture can be seen as part of his mission in life. During the Civil War, Burgess vowed to himself that he "would devote [his] life to teaching men how to live by reason and compromise instead of by bloodshed and destruction" (*Reminiscences* 1934, 29). He sought to acquire in German universities "the education which would fit [him] for the life work which [he] had chosen for himself" (*Reminiscences* 1934, 86). In 1906 Burgess became the first Roosevelt Professor of American History and Institutions at the Friedrich Wilhelm University in Berlin. When World War I broke out, Burgess wrote several newspaper articles and two books in which, as he later stated, he sought to express the idea "that as a neutral nation, we ought to understand how the parties involved viewed the war, and thus maintain our neutrality intelligently" (*New York Times,* December 17, 1918, p. 2). For his empathetic treatment of the German position, Burgess endured sharp criticism. When the United States entered the war, the secretary of war banned Burgess's two war books. After the war, Burgess was repeatedly among the first named in Senate hearings as a source of pro-German sentiment.

James R. Maxeiner

See also Göttingen, University of; World War I

References and Further Reading
Burgess, John W. *Political Science and Comparative Constitutional Law.* 2 vols. Boston: Ginn, 1890–1891.
———. *Reminiscences of an American Scholar: The Beginnings of Columbia University, with a Forward by Nicholas Murray Butler.* New York: Columbia University Press, 1934.
Farr, James. "Burgess, John William." *American National Biography.* New York: Oxford University Press, 1999, 3:940–941.

BURMEISTER, CARL HERMANN CONRAD

b. January 15, 1807; Stralsund (Pomerania), Prussia
b. May 2, 1892; Buenos Aires

German geographer and explorer of Argentina.

Hermann Burmeister studied medicine at the University of Halle, where he received his doctorate in 1829. Four years later, Burmeister finished his *Habilitation* (postdoctoral degree) at the University of Berlin. In 1837 he was appointed honorary professor for zoology at the University of Halle. At this point, he had already been recognized as a very successful scholarly author for his *Grundriß der Naturgeschichte* (Basics of Natural History), published in ten editions between 1833 and 1868; his *Handbuch der Naturgeschichte* (Handbook of Natural History) in two volumes, published in 1837; and his *Geschichte der Schöpfung* (History of Creation), published in eight editions between 1843 and 1872. In 1848, Burmeister was elected as deputy of the newly created German National Assembly in Frankfurt am Main. Disappointed by the failed 1848 revolution, Burmeister asked for a sabbatical from his university and embarked on an extensive journey through South and Central America.

After Alexander von Humboldt had arranged for funding from the Prussian government, Burmeister left Germany for South America in 1850. In order to carry out some paleontological research in Brazil, Burmeister traveled from Rio de Janeiro via Nova Friburgo to Lagoa Santa and visited the provinces of Rio de Janeiro and Minas Gerais. However, a broken leg prevented him from accomplishing all that he had planned for this trip. Back in Germany, Burmeister published several books about his encounters in Brazil, among them *Reise nach Brasilien* (Journey to Brazil, 1853); *Landschaftliche Bilder Brasiliens* (Landscape Pictures of Brazil, 1853); *Systematische Übersicht der Tiere Brasiliens* (Systematical Overview over the Animals of Brazil, 1854–1856), in three volumes; and the *Erläuterungen zur Fauna Brasiliens* (Remarks about the Fauna of Brazil, 1856).

In 1856, Burmeister returned to South America for geological and paleontological research as well as for observations of the climate, fauna, and birds. Between 1856 and 1860, he spent most of his time in northern Argentina. However, he also went on research trips from Buenos Aires to Rosario and through the Pampas to Mendoza. In Mendoza, Burmeister spent about thirteen months in 1857–1858 in order to investigate the fauna and to take meteorological measurements. His book, *Über das Klima der Argentinischen Republik* (About the Climate of the Argentinean Republic, 1861), was a direct result of this research. For about nine months, Burmeister led the life of a farmer in Paraná. In June 1859, he embarked on his second big journey into the northern parts of Brazil. From Rosario, he reached Córdoba, Tucumán, and Catamarca before he crossed the Andes into Chile. Burmeister was the first European to take this path across the Andes. In Chile, he boarded a ship bound for Europe.

Burmeister was able to correct European's topographic knowledge about South America. His eye for detail and his excellent abstract thinking skills enabled him to produce the first comprehensive description of the physical geography of the La Plata states in his book *Reise durch die La Plata-Staaten mit besonderer Rücksicht der Argentinischen Republik* (Travel through the La Plata States with an Emphasis on the Argentinean Republic) in two volumes (1861). Burmeister's extensive travels matched his extensive scope of knowledge and publications. In addition to books on paleontology and zoology, he published works on biology and climate research. Burmeister is known as the founder of the geoscientific explorations of the La Plata states and as the best specialist of the physical geography of Argentina.

Soon after his return, Burmeister finally decided to emigrate to Argentina for health reasons. In 1862, he took over management of the Museo Público in Buenos Aires, which he transformed into one of the world's most impressive paleontological collections. In 1870, he established the natural science department at the University of Córdoba and recruited German academics for the university (among them was Ludwig Brackebusch). Burmeister published an uncounted number of articles in journals as well as many books. His most important and comprehensive treatment of South American geography was the *Physikalische Beschreibung der Argentinischen Republik* (Physical Description of the Argentinean Republic, 1875), which he dedicated to his patron and friend Domingo Faustino Sarmiento, the president of Argentina. His last expedition brought him to Patagonia in 1887. Upon his death, he received a state funeral in Argentina for his service in the geographic exploration and investigation of that country. Eight years later, a memorial made from white marble and erected in Buenos Aires at the shore of the Rio de la Plata was dedicated to Burmeister.

Heinz Peter Brogiato

See also Argentina; Brackebusch, Ludwig; Humboldt, Alexander von

References and Further Reading

Henze, Dietmar. *Enzyklopädie der Entdecker und Erforscher der Erde.* Graz: Akademische Druck- und Verlagsanstalt, 1978, 1:409–412.

Hermann Burmeister: Ein bedeutender Naturwissenschaftler des 19. Jahrhunderts. Stralsund 1993 (Meer und Museum; vol. 9).

Ratzel, Friedrich. "Burmeister, Carl Hermann Conrad." *Allgemeine Deutsche Biographie.* Leipzig: Duncker and Humblot, 1903, 47:394–396.

BUSINESS, U.S.–THIRD REICH

Well before the the 1941 Trading with the Enemy Act set legal prohibitions on trade with Axis nations, General Motors and Ford Motor Company disregarded anti-Nazi public sentiment and vigorously competed for Nazi military contracts. In 1938 General Motors president Alfred Sloan publicly stated that as an international business, General Motors ought to conduct its international operations in purely business terms without consideration of the political ideologies or policies of nation-states. Referencing contemporary debate surrounding international relations with Adolf Hitler's Third Reich, Sloan's commentary reflected a general philosophy shared with Ford Motor Company executives of both political apathy and tacit support for the Nazi regime. Although General Motors and Ford executives were not the only prominent Americans supportive of Nazi Germany before the war, including such household names as Joseph Kennedy, Prescott Bush, and Charles Lindbergh, their corporate actions just prior to and during the war have been a source of recent legal and public inquiry. The story of General Motors, Ford Motor Company, and the Nazi authorities is not simply one of totalitarian coercion by a monolithic state but of complex motivations tempered by acts of consensual collaboration and corporate greed in adopting a "business as usual" attitude under the Third Reich.

Like many industrialists worldwide, executives at General Motors were generally intrigued with Hitler and supportive of his economic policies. Throughout the 1930s, it was not uncommon for top General Motors executives like Alfred Sloan, William Knudsen, or vice presidents James Mooney and Graeme Howard to make public statements in support of Hitler and Nazi Germany. After a trip to Germany in 1933, Knudsen referred to the Third Reich as one of the great miracles of the twentieth century. In 1938 James Mooney, along with Henry Ford, Charles Lindbergh, and Benito Mussolini, received the Grand Cross of the German Eagle, the highest award available to foreigners to reward invaluable service to the Third Reich. In 1940 Howard wrote a book entitled *America and a New World Order* that supported Hitler's corporate-friendly economic policies; a piece that placed Howard on an FBI surveillance list throughout the war.

General Motors played an important role in prewar military production and the sharing of advanced technologies with the Third Reich through its German subsidiary, Adam Opel AG. As consumer spending decreased before the war, General Motors sought new production markets through military contracts. In 1935 the Wehrmacht encouraged General Motors to open a new truck plant in Brandenburg, producing the "Opel Blitz" truck exclusively for the German armed forces. The Brandenburg plant had an annual production capacity of 25,000 trucks for the Nazi military. In order to protect General Motors' investments from "nationalization" by the Nazis and to keep profits up, James Mooney negotiated a deal with the Nazi authorities in Berlin to convert all Opel production to war materials in 1940. Outside of basic production before the war, General Motors technologies became vital to Nazi military strategy. In a 1977 interview with Bradford Snell, Hitler's minister for armaments Albert Speer asserted that without the synthetic fuel technology provided by General Motors to IG Farben at the request of the Nazi regime, Germany would never have even considered invading Poland.

Henry Ford, inspired by the fabricated *Protocols of the Learned Elders of Zion,* purchased a small newspaper in 1918 called the *Dearborn Independent* and set aside $10 million to finance his public exposure of a "Jewish plot against humanity." Faced with consumer boycotts and a pending lawsuit for slander, Ford discontinued the publication of his newspaper in 1922 and focused upon spreading his antisemitic tracts through the international publication of his book, *The International Jew: The World's Foremost Problem.* Ford's book, a piece still praised and published by antisemites worldwide on the Internet, also caught the attention of men like Adolf Hitler, who came to deeply respect and admire Ford as an industrialist and fellow antisemite. The Nazi Party distributed a German translation of Ford's book and Hitler himself kept a large photo of Ford in his Munich office, stating once in a 1931 interview that he considered Henry Ford to be his personal inspiration. During the Nuremberg trials Baldur von Schirach, leader of the Hitler Youth program, stated he developed his antisemitic views at the age of seventeen not from reading Hitler's *Mein Kampf* (My Battle), but from Ford's *The International Jew.*

In 1938 Ford Motor Company's German subsidiary Ford-Werke AG began producing troop transport trucks for the German military. General Motors had faced certain challenges under the Third Reich due to the foreign ownership of Adam Opel AG, whereas the Opel company had been manufacturing in Germany since 1862 and had a long-standing German identity. Since Ford-Werke AG was an American-built and -owned company, Ford felt threatened by the nationalist sentiment of the German public and Nazi authorities and felt compelled to convert its production facilities to fulfill military contracts. In order to protect its subsidiary, Ford forged closer bonds with the Nazi Party and IG Farben, each corporation owning large shares in each other's foreign subsidiaries to protect their investments from state interference or liquidation. This process of "Germanizing" the business came in the late 1930s under direction from Ford management in Dearborn, showing loyalty to the production needs of Hitler's government while maintaining a majority American ownership. Continued American involvement had a dual benefit for Ford and the Nazis, allowing the Nazis to exploit Ford technologies and resources while Ford exerted control and influence on its subsidiaries in occupied territories in the event of Nazi European expansion.

Although both General Motors and Ford Motor Company claim to have played a vital role to the Allied powers in armament production throughout the war, boasting to be "the arsenal of democracy," it is clear that neither corporation can claim a guilt-free record in their relations with the Third Reich. As Allied troops began their push through western Europe, they were astonished when they encountered an enemy that was driving trucks and jeeps built by General Motors and Ford. Once German cities like Cologne were liberated, Allied soldiers found large numbers of slave laborers residing at a Ford-Werke plant that had been virtually untouched by Allied bombing raids that had leveled the rest of the city. After Europe began its postwar path to economic recovery and restored consumer spending, General Motors and Ford Motor Company assumed a leading and profitable role in the European automotive market, while many of their prewar competitors faded into obscurity.

Joel Lewis

See also Ford, Henry Augustus; Lindbergh, Charles; World War II

References and Further Reading

Billstein, Reinhold, Karola Fings, Anita Kugler, and Nicholas Levis. *Working for the Enemy: Ford, General Motors, and Forced Labor in Germany during the Second World War.* Ed. Nicholas Levis. New York: Berghahn Books, 2000.

Higham, Charles. *Trading with the Enemy: The Nazi American Money Plot, 1933–1949.* New York: Barnes and Noble Books, 1983.

Reich, Simon. *The Fruits of Fascism: Postwar Prosperity in Historical Perspective.* London: Cornell University Press, 1990.

Turner, Henry A. *German Big Business and the Rise of Hitler.* New York: Oxford University Press, 1985.

CAHENSLY, PETER PAUL

b. October 28, 1838; Limburg an der
Lahn, Hesse
d. December 25, 1923; Koblenz, Prussia

Founder of the St. Raphaels-Verein zum
Schutz der katholischen deutschen Auswanderer (St. Raphael Association for the
Protection of German Catholic Emigrants), which he served as general secretary and later as president.

Peter Paul Cahensly was a central figure in the "nationality question" within the
American Catholic Church. He served in
the Abgeordnetenhaus (Prussian House of
Delegates) from 1885 to 1915 and in the
Reichstag (German parliament) from 1898
to 1903.

After completing his merchant apprenticeship, Cahensly traveled to the French
port city of Le Havre, where he lived from
1861 until 1868. While in Le Havre he
witnessed the hardships that emigrants
faced. Inspired by the actions of a German
missionary priest, P. Lambert Rethmann,
whom he met while working for the St.
Vincent de Paul Society, Cahensly decided
to lobby for the improvement of emigrant
conditions in Europe's port cities. During
the annual *Katholikentage* (Catholic Days),

he called upon the General Assembly of
German Catholic Societies to take an active role in providing spiritual, moral, and
material help for emigrants in the prominent ports Antwerp, Le Havre, Bremen,
and Hamburg. His efforts led to the formation of the St. Raphaelsverein at the
General Assembly in Mainz in September
1871.

Cahensly provided the new association
with financial support and served as its first
general secretary (and later as its president
from 1899 until 1919). He met with emigration authorities and government officials in the port cities and drafted annual
reports on the enforcement of emigration
regulations. In 1883 he traveled incognito
to the United States in steerage so that he
could gain firsthand experience of the miserable emigrant conditions. While in the
United States, Cahensly toured the "German Triangle" of the Midwest and the large
cities of the East Coast, drumming up support for emigrants along the way. The main
American headquarters of St. Raphaels-
verein, the Leo House (named after Pope
Leo XIII), was opened in New York City in
1889. Eventually branches of the association sprouted throughout the United
States.

During the 1880s and 1890s, Cahensly's name became synonymous with a particular view in a debate within the American Catholic community. Cahensly believed that German Catholics were losing the faith in the United States because the American church did not adequately cater to the needs of its national minorities. German Catholics, he argued, needed German priests who spoke German with their congregation. Thus he helped draft and then presented Pope Leo XIII with the Lucerne Memorial (1891), which recommended that the American church be districted upon national rather than geographical lines and that bishops should be selected in proportion to the size of the respective national immigrant communities. Pope Leo XIII eventually rejected the Lucerne Memorial, but his decision did not prevent bickering within the American Catholic Church. "Americanist" Catholics, who were predominantly liberal and Irish, denounced what they called "Cahenslyism" as an affront to the catholicity of the church and an encroachment of German Catholic politics onto American soil. Cahensly did in fact represent the German Catholic Center Party (Zentrum) in both the Prussian House of Delegates and would later become a member of the German parliament. He denied that his stance on the national question in the American church was politically motivated and maintained that he had only the spiritual interests of German Catholics in mind. The St. Raphaelsverein (after 1977, *Raphaels-Werk*) continues to aid emigrants to this day.

Kevin Ostoyich

See also St. Raphael's Association for the Protection of German Catholic Emigrants

References and Further Reading

Barry, Coleman, J., OSB. *The Catholic Church and German Americans.* Milwaukee: Bruce Publishing, 1953.

Gleason, Philip. *The Conservative Reformers: German-American Catholics and the Social Order.* Notre Dame: University of Notre Dame Press, 1968.

Roemer, Theodore, OFM Cap. *The Catholic Church in the United States.* St. Louis: B. Herder, 1950.

Schenk, Heinrich, and Victor Mohr. *Das Erbe Cahenslys: Festvortrag zum 150. Geburtstag Peter Paul Cahenslys.* Hildesheim: Bernward Verlag, 1989.

CANADA, GERMANS IN (DURING WORLD WARS I AND II)

By 1914, the over 400,000 people of German descent in Canada constituted the Dominion's third-largest ethnic group after the British and French. Most of the German speakers in Ontario—including the sizable Mennonite population—had been Loyalists, although the roots of the small German population in Nova Scotia predated the American Revolution. Almost half of Canada's Germans and most of the newcomers were pioneer farmers in the prairie provinces, including 20,000 Mennonites. Many of the non-Mennonite Germans in the west had lived in the United States, and most of the rest had come from ethnically German enclaves in eastern Europe. Less than one-fifth were German-born. Religion, not ethnicity, defined German settlements, and since German Canadians employed the German language primarily for religious purposes, the need to maintain it as a barrier against assimilation was less noticeable than among other immigrants. Nonetheless, the overwhelmingly rural—and hence isolated—nature of German settlement in the west and the ethnic homogeneity characteristic of "block" settlement helped preserve cultural identity. Only the more recent immigrants from eastern Europe had been exposed in any significant way to *völkisch* thought and felt part of a "German nation."

In the older, established German communities of British Columbia and Ontario, successful business and professional men were part of the local "establishment," politically and otherwise. German cultural clubs flourished in most urban centers. In Berlin, Ontario, the country's most "German" city, the birthdays of the Emperor Wilhelm II and Queen Victoria were both celebrated as civic holidays. The German Canadians in these long-settled communities saw no contradiction between loyalty to Canada and admiration of German culture.

In the early years of the century, "nativism" (or Anglo-conformity) was a growing force in western Canada. As John Dafoe, editor of the influential *Manitoba Free Press,* editorialized in 1910: "We must Canadianize this generation of foreign-born settlers, or this will cease to be a Canadian country in any sense of the term" (May 10, 1910). Dafoe could have easily substituted British for Canadian. Yet as "preferred" immigrants, Germans were seldom a nativist target. However, from the Boer War (1899–1902) onward, Anglo-Canadians began to see their German neighbors as being in league with Berlin and the emperor. Like their lively weekly press, most German Canadians—regardless of their European origins—sympathized with Germany, naively arguing that

it was as natural for them to feel loyalty to Germany as for British immigrants to support their "old country."

By 1914, half of the German Canadian population was Canadian-born, and only 20,000 were not naturalized (that is, not British subjects). Overall, the "German" community in Canada was markedly heterogeneous, with no cohesive ethnic identity and with rare exception, only a cultural—but not a political—affinity for "the Fatherland." The outbreak of World War I marked the end of innocence for Canada's German population as the much-favored settlers and citizens found themselves vilified overnight. Canada would wage war against not only Germany but also "Germanness." In fairness, the Canadian government faced a difficult situation. The Dominion's population included half a million people from countries at war with the British Empire, many of them only recently arrived. Incautious statements favorable to the German and Austro-Hungarian cause had been made by some newspapers and community leaders. Canada bordered the neutral United States, where millions more who were sympathetic to the British Empire's enemies resided. The realization that some German and Austrian reservists were slipping into the United States and thence back to Europe further heightened suspicions. Despite Ottawa's initial pledge that "immigrants of German nationality quietly pursuing their usual avocation . . . should continue in such avocation without interruption," public tolerance rapidly eroded (Entz 1976, 58).

Anglo-Canadian animosity focused on "enemy aliens," of whom Germans quickly became the most loathed. The experience of the 10,000-strong community in Winnipeg, Canada's third-largest city, was typical. Efforts to create a German Canadian identity, so central to the community's activities prior to 1914, had to be abandoned. Indeed, churches were the only German cultural institutions not to show a marked decline in participation, and even some of them cut back on German-language services. The outbreak of hostilities ignited a wave of vandalism against German property, and many workers of German descent were fired. Local merchants and consumers boycotted German products and businesses. Some members of the community were even assaulted on the street. Most foreigners—like the Ukrainians and Poles—were quick to display their loyalty to the British cause as a group, but Germans were reluctant, instead trying to lie low. Although no evidence of spying was ever unearthed, fears of German fifth columnists became rampant. Daily the warlike nature of the "Huns" was hammered home in the press. Ottawa supplied every newspaper with a copy of the British *Report of the Committee on Perceived German Outrages,* which breathlessly accused the German army of "murder, lust and pillage . . . on a scale unparalleled in any war between civilized nations" (Thompson 1991, 6). Meanwhile, German cultural attainments were everywhere denigrated. The idea that "Kaiserism" and militarism embodied the will of the German people was universally accepted. Winnipeg's Germans were bewildered by their portrayal in the English-language press but powerless to do anything about it. The city's Germans, who had been trying to integrate before the war, now had less contact than ever with their English-speaking neighbors.

In Ontario, German Canadians voluntarily closed many of their schools, and most refrained from using their language in public. After bitter controversy and repeated eruptions of violence against German-operated businesses and institutions as well as ordinary citizens, the people of Berlin voted to rename their city the suitably patriotic Kitchener in 1916.

For many western Canadians, loyalty and cultural and linguistic uniformity became synonymous during World War I. Public pressure finally achieved the abolition of all bilingual schools in Manitoba in 1916. Alberta and Saskatchewan followed suit two years later. Public schools were seen as the mill that would take immigrant children and "turn them out with the stamp of the King and the Maple Leaf" (Thompson 1991, 8). Such displays of nativism were not just aimed at Germans. Nonetheless, many reacted by shedding their identity—Braun became Brown, and Schmidt Smith. Several western communities with German names adopted less offensive identities—Dusseldorf, Alberta, became Freedom, and Prussia, Saskatchewan, was renamed Leader. Still, many other towns in heavily German-populated areas resisted the tide.

Throughout the war, jittery Canadians invariably linked accidental disasters like the burning down of the parliament buildings in 1916 to the "hidden hand" of the "enemy alien." Harvest time reliably brewed a spate of rumors that the crop would be torched. Newspapers repeatedly warned of a German American army massed to invade, with "enemy aliens" secretly drilling in Canada to assist them. In reality, German Canadians posed no security threat, and there was no evidence during the war of their involvement in fifth column activity.

Naturalized Germans or Austrians who tried to prove their loyalty by enlisting were usually rejected. The University of Toronto dismissed three German faculty members, and miners in Fernie, British Columbia, struck rather than have to work alongside Germans. Scattered acts of violence against German property and individuals occurred virtually everywhere and usually involved soldiers. Forcing Germans on the street to kneel and kiss the Union Jack was a favored measure. Many of the accusations leveled against German Canadians were cruelly ironic, such as the case of a Lutheran pastor in Ontario denounced for preaching in German whose son was serving in France.

Although governments rarely encouraged or approved outbreaks of vigilante justice, prosecutions were rare, and all gradually succumbed to an outraged public's demands that they "deal" with the "enemy alien." The War Measures Act (1914) had given the federal government powers of "arrest, detention, exclusion and deportation" of individuals and specifically denied the rights of bail and habeas corpus to anyone arrested "upon suspicion that he is an alien enemy." From 1915 onward, such persons—80,000 registered, a large proportion of them Germans—had to report monthly to local authorities, and their movements (and bank accounts) were strictly monitored. Altogether Ottawa interned nearly 8,000 Canadian residents for varying periods, including almost 1,200 Germans. Internment and registration applied only to the unnaturalized, and the great majority of the internees were impoverished Ukrainians.

German-language newspapers continued to publish. The War Measures Act incorporated a censorship law, but Ottawa refused to muzzle the German-language press. Instead, the government closed down "defiant" papers and had local officials and the Royal North West Mounted Police monitor the others. The chief censor quickly extracted a pledge that nothing would be published "unduly to cause exultation among German readers" (Entz 1976, 58). Editors walked a fine line. When Conrad Eymann, editor of *Der [Saskatchewan] Courier,* urged his German Canadian readers to become more involved in Canadian life "from a thoroughly loyal Canadian standpoint," his apparent advocacy of political involvement was not well received (April 24, 1915). So-called returned men (mostly wounded veterans) led a growing chorus to silence the "enemy press"—*Der Courier*'s offices were ransacked by such protestors twice in 1917 alone. When the Great War Veterans Association, ardently patriotic and strongly nativist, called in 1918 for the immediate closure of all German-language publications—with the veiled threat that they would do it themselves if Ottawa dragged its feet—Prime Minister Robert Borden acted. In September, an order-in-council prohibited publication "in any enemy language."

The reinforcement crisis of 1917 produced a Unionist government of English-speaking Conservatives and Liberals committed to conscription for overseas service. Although principally aimed at French Canadians, conscription made the predicament of "enemy aliens" much worse. The War-Times Election Act (1917) disenfranchised all Germans (and other "enemy aliens") who were naturalized but had arrived after 1898, which included the vast majority of Germans in western Canada. All Mennonites lost the vote without exception. Both groups were also exempted from the draft. The measure was one of several adopted to ensure a Unionist victory at the polls in December 1917. Returned soldiers and many others thought the government had let the "enemy aliens" off too lightly. "Left to fatten on war-time prosperity," they argued, saying it was time to conscript these people for industry at a private's pay (Thompson 1991, 9). In contrast to German Canadian business and professional people and urban workers who had suffered badly during the war, German-speaking farmers generally had done well—their sons stayed home, and agricultural prices were high. German Canadians in Ontario did not lose the franchise and scored a rare political victory when William D. Euler, the mayor of Kitchener, won election to the House of Commons in 1917 on an unapologetically pro-German Canadian and anticonscription platform. By 1917–1918, the "war increasingly came to be viewed," according to Art Grenke, "as a struggle, not between armies, but between forces of British and Allied justice and righteousness, and the Germans forces of darkness and autocracy." To its credit, the federal government did not accede to the more extreme demands of the nativists and patriots during the last two years of the war, but public opinion would not have stopped it.

The last year of the conflict brought exhaustion at home and a wave of strikes. Frightened upper- and middle-class Canadians branded labor unrest as "bolshevism," which was denounced as a German-inspired war strategy. Although German Canadian workers who participated in strikes were just following the lead of their unions, their actions were offered as clear evidence of a malign Teutonic plot. The banning of meetings in German and the suppression of the German-language press that occurred in the last months of the war were both ostensibly aimed at the Bolshevik menace. The red scare ensured that many anti-German measures remained in place through 1919.

As David Smith aptly put it, people of "enemy alien" origin became a problem for the Canadian government from 1914 to 1918 "not because they were disloyal . . . but because many native-born Canadians suspected them of being disloyal" (Smith 1969, 436). Although many of the measures taken against Germans had been part of the prewar nativist agenda, fear of and hatred toward the "enemy alien" nurtured by wartime patriotism had helped to legitimize government action. The impact of the oppression suffered during World War I was deep and lasting. The ethnic pride and traditional self-esteem of German Canadian communities plummeted to a point where even those United Empire Loyalist families who before 1914 had been proud of their German descent suddenly renounced it. At least 100,000 German Canadians claimed Dutch or Austrian ethnicity in the 1921 census. The prewar belief in "German culture" was discarded, with the result that Germans became one of the most assimilated ethnic groups in Canada during the 1920s and 1930s. Indeed, most wanted nothing more than to be left alone. The government restored the franchise in 1920, and the 1919 prohibition against German immigration was dismantled in 1923. Public opinion, however, would have kept the door firmly closed.

The militant Anglo-Canadianism spawned in World War I set the cultural tone during the interwar years and constituted a far more virulent form of nativism than anything the "foreign-born" had encountered before World War I.

The 1931 census showed 474,000 Canadians of German descent. Although only about one in ten were from Germany, most Anglo-Canadians continued to feel that all Germans were culturally homogeneous and had their political roots there. Eight years later, only 16,000 of the Germans in Canada were not naturalized, and large numbers of these were Jewish, Austrian, or Czech refugees. The reopening of German immigration had led to an influx of both Mennonites and non-Mennonites from Russia during the 1920s. Of the 90,000 post–World War I German immigrants in the Dominion in 1939, 80 percent had taken up farming in the West (McLaughlin 1985, 13).

Nazi Germany made a major—if disorganized—effort to proselytize among these newcomers after 1933. The National Socialist German Worker's Party (NSDAP) itself and the Deutsche Arbeitsfront (DAF, or German Labor Front) attempted to recruit German citizens, while the Deutscher Bund Kanada (German Association of Canada), a thinly disguised cultural and social club established in 1934, aimed at the naturalized (and by now predominantly Canadian-born) population. Membership in the DAF and Nazi Party never exceeded 500 and 140, respectively. As for the Bund, it claimed perhaps 2,500 members, including Mennonites and devout Lutherans who joined for nostalgic and cultural reasons rather than ideology. For many of the *Russlaender* (Russian) Mennonites who had fled Russia in the 1920s, the Nazis' anticommunism exercised strong appeal. Most German-language newspapers—with several Roman Catholic exceptions—were sympathetic or at least benign toward the "new Germany," a stance that would come back to haunt them after 1939.

Overall, however, Nazism was never able to gain a large following among German Canadians. Although significant numbers of ethnic Germans undoubtedly sympathized in one way or another, the raving about Jews, Communists, racial purity, and even the preservation of the language was of little relevance to German Canadians during the Great Depression. Furthermore, the communities were divided geographically and otherwise and remained profoundly affected by the anti-Germanism of World War I. By the late 1930s, the vast majority of Germans in eastern Canada and a growing number in the west had ceased to identify themselves as Germans, dooming any effort to promote a *völkisch* ideal and making Nazism itself seem "foreign."

Such success as the Nazis did achieve was assisted by the apathy of the Canadian government and non-German population. The Bund's appeal lay primarily among the young, economically marginal, and generally disaffected recent German immigrants. Bund promoters, by continuously refuting anti-Nazi arguments in public, actually heightened the awareness of the Nazi threat among both German Canadians and the larger population. More overtly Nazi initiatives like setting up swastika clubs generally fizzled in the face of nativist opposition. The shock of the 1938 *Reichskristallnacht* and the undeniable prospect of war by 1939 finally began to alert Canadians to the "threat" of domestic Nazism.

Throughout the 1930s, "refugee" was a code word for Jew in Ottawa. Amid depression and dust bowl conditions, newcomers were unwelcome in Canada, least of all Jews. Proportionately, Canada had the worst record of any country in accepting German Jewish refugees. French-speaking Catholic Quebec was openly opposed, a view that the Liberal Party government of Mackenzie King felt it dare not ignore, but antisemitism ran deep in English-speaking Canada, too. Making "refugee" policy fell to a few antisemites in the bureaucracy, with predictable—and tragic—results. Ottawa mostly offered sanctimonious expressions of sympathy and promises to study the problem. The small Canadian Jewish community lacked confidence and was divided over how to influence the system. Canada's response to the 1938 Evian Conference starkly revealed the country's position—even a proposal to admit some 5,000 German and Austrian refugees, the "better kind of Jew," over four years, with the costs paid by Canadian Jewry and none of the refugees to be settled in Quebec, was spurned by Ottawa. *Reichskristallnacht* forced public opinion to confront Nazi brutality, and the government appeared to be on the verge of finally helping on "humanitarian" grounds, only to back down again. Instead, Ottawa agreed to admit 200 families of anti-Nazi (and predominantly Roman Catholic) *Sudeten* Germans, not the least to deflect mounting international pressure to take Jews. As late as 1939, the government, with no significant public opposition, turned away the liner *St. Louis* with its pitiful cargo of 907 German Jewish refugees. Following strict regulations to the letter, Ottawa would not even provide temporary transit for German Jews bound for the United States.

The war changed nothing. About 2,600 "friendly" alien internees from Britain were accepted by Canada in 1940. Among them were many German refugees, including Klaus Fuchs, a future atomic spy. Ottawa, however, deemed them all suspect, and with tasteless irony, interned them with domestic Nazis for two years. Only the desperate need for skilled labor led to their gradual release. British requests to have thousands of German Jewish child refugees temporarily admitted were brusquely turned down, though thousands of British children were welcomed with open arms.

While Canada did not officially declare war until September 10, 1939, a week after Britain, the proclamation of the Defence of Canada Regulations (DCR) under the War Measures Act a week earlier sent shudders through Canada's German community. Under the DCR, the justice minister could detain without charge anyone who might act "in any manner prejudicial to the public safety or the safety of the state." Once again, habeas corpus was suspended. Ominously, the government also granted these sweeping powers to provincial and municipal authorities who were likely to be much less scrupulous in their application. Whether naturalized or not, all Germans who had arrived after 1922 had to register.

The Royal Canadian Mounted Police (RCMP) had made a halfhearted effort during the late 1930s to identify the "suspect" elements within the German Canadian population. The force's real interest was chasing "Reds"—a preoccupation the war would not change—and few German Canadians were involved in left-wing activities. Lacking contacts in the community or even language skills, the handful of officers assigned to the task had not gotten very far. Mere membership in the Bund could find one portrayed as a dangerous Nazi agent. However, in the absence of anything better, the list compiled haphazardly by the RCMP became the master guide in the fall of 1939. During the first months of the war, English Canadian opinion pushed politicians and bureaucrats to destroy the German conspiracy within, and Ottawa and the authorities responded hurriedly, though rarely out of any legitimate security concerns. The first 303 arrests—most of them ordinary farmers and workers—were made on September 4, six days before Canada officially declared war. In camera judicial reviews followed, and with them the first releases for lack of evidence.

Widespread reports of fifth columnists during the blitzkrieg of western Europe convinced skittish Canadians that such activities might be rife at home, derailing government plans to liberalize the DCR. The ensuing public uproar was fed by RCMP paranoia—even Eskimos, the Mounties claimed, had been recruited, and thousands of dangerous agents were likely on the loose. The force quickly assembled a new and longer list of "enemy alien" suspects, mostly via denunciations. By mid-1941, however, everyone's attention turned to the Japanese Canadian community in British Columbia. From 1942 onward Ottawa steadily released German Canadian internees and held only 89 in custody at war's end. In December 1942 all naturalized Germans in Canada were exempted from reporting because of their "exemplary good behavior." Six months later the armed forces authorized their enlistment. Forty citizens of German descent were denaturalized during the war, but the process was so poorly received by German Canadi-

ans—a vital Liberal electoral constituency—that the King government quietly discontinued the practice. Altogether, a total of 847 Germans and German Canadians were detained, modestly lower than the World War I numbers.

During World War II, policy toward German Canadians was much influenced by a small group of diplomats in the Department of External Affairs who advised the prime minister. They subscribed to the view that Nazism was a minority criminal conspiracy even in Germany, let alone Canada—hence it was only necessary to arrest the "real" Nazis. Neither King nor his ministers personally saw German Canadians as depraved or untrustworthy in the mass, and their obsession with maintaining national unity meant the government would try to avoid overreacting. In addition, the wartime emphasis on home front economic achievements helped German Canadians—who were already quite assimilated—to "fit in." The relatively light military losses incurred through mid-1943 helped keep down anti-German feeling as well. Finally, unlike World War I, when from Wilhelm II to humble peasant, all had been "Huns," during World War II the majority of the Anglo-Canadian public made a distinction between Adolf Hitler and his followers on the one hand and the majority of ordinary German people—and German Canadians—on the other.

Most German organizations, certainly the ones not suppressed as Nazi fronts, quickly professed their loyalty, and many wisely suspended operations. In most areas, Lutheran churches ceased using German in services and proclaimed their loyalty to King George VI. A steady flow of German Canadian enlistments—for example, Albert Hoffmeister served with distinction in command of an armored division—helped defuse suspicion. It helped greatly that most of the English-language press generally refrained from the anti-German vituperation so prevalent a generation earlier, instead stressing the government line that but for a few bad apples, German Canadians were loyal. Beginning in 1941, the Wartime Information Board (WIB) began targeting immigrant communities, including German ones, to support the war. As the title of WIB pamphlets and radio programs asserted, they were *Canadians All.* Nativists and overzealous patriots in the guise of chambers of commerce, service clubs, farmers' organizations, unions, and of course the Royal Canadian Legion throughout the west protested the lack of "sufficient arrests." Unlike World War I, however, vigilantism and rioting did not accompany the rhetoric.

The sense of camaraderie that the war effort fostered generally worked to undermine class and ethnic barriers. Although most German Canadians benefited from this, Mennonites and Hutterites became the object of heightened hostility. In 1939 there were 110,000 Mennonites scattered across Ontario and the Prairies. German-speaking and pacifistic, their practice of "die Stillen im Lande"—being quiet in the land—was unlikely to save them from discrimination. Though some had been arrested and imprisoned from 1917 to 1918, and there had been serious friction with non-Mennonite neighbors, the Borden government had accepted their claim of conscientious objector status and honored pledges made to earlier Mennonite settlers that they would not be conscripted. Still, no such promise was given to the *Russlaender* Mennonites who immigrated to Canada during the 1920s.

Mennonite leaders failed to reach a consensus when they met in the spring of 1939 to discuss a common stand in the event of another war. Although the *Russlaenders* were generally prepared to serve as noncombatants, the majority adhered to the traditional position on nonparticipation, shunning even alternative service if it was directly related to the war. Conscription for home defense, introduced in June 1940, posed a serious problem. Apart from those groups given carte blanche exemption, initial negotiations with government officials over alternative service did not go well. There were isolated cases of vandalism, Mennonite public school teachers lost their jobs, and German-language classes had to be terminated as anti-Mennonite feeling intensified.

Resolving the alternative service impasse was crucial, and the timely intervention of Agriculture Minister James Gardiner, a former Saskatchewan premier sympathetic to the Mennonite situation, avoided a crisis. Ottawa granted a form of civilian alternative service in late 1940 that served as an acceptable compromise. When the men were initially confined to working in national parks, public opinion dismissed the waste of labor. Although many Mennonites were prepared and indeed sought to do more, progress in making this possible was painfully slow. In 1943 the government, confronted with a desperate labor shortage, finally sent most Mennonite conscientious objectors to work on farms or in industry where their cooperative spirit and work ethic earned general admiration. Later that year, Mennonites were allowed to enlist in the army medical services. Over 7,000 Mennonite men accepted alternative service, and many others simply went to work in war industries.

The most telling statistic involved the more than 3,000 who enlisted in the armed forces, most as combatants. Bearing arms caused much conflict in (and between) Mennonite communities. Many of those who enlisted were shunned by their congregations or found it impossible to reintegrate after the war. Even alternative service broadened horizons. For many Mennonites, male and female, leaving home was a frequent—and often permanent—experience during World War II.

Whereas Mennonites' willingness to cooperate in the war effort in tangible ways won them at least grudging acceptance, the more isolationist and uncooperative Hutterite community, who adamantly refused any form of alternative service, was much resented and harshly treated. In Alberta, the home of most of Canada's Hutterites, the government attempted to restrict their land-ownership, finally succeeding in 1947.

By any measure—language use and retention, residential and occupational segregation, marriage patterns, or membership in ethnic churches and associations—among German Canadians all but the Hutterites were more assimilated into the Canadian mainstream in 1945 than in 1939. Although some of this process had been economically driven, much was attributable to wartime pressure. And although the situation was significantly better than it had been a generation earlier, it was painful enough, especially since "none of these [German] minorities ever constituted a serious threat to Canadian security," as John Thompson argued. "In all cases the war emergency provided the justification for internment, but policies were built upon long-established patterns of prejudice established in peacetime" (Thompson 1991, 17).

At least the absence of bitter anti-German tensions within Canada during World War II made the postwar adjustment of German immigrants easier. The onset of the cold war, coupled with basic Canadian decency, led to the acceptance of 50,000 displaced persons in 1947 and 1948, primarily from Western-occupied Germany and mostly German refugees from east of the Oder-Neisse Line. By 1950, Ottawa permitted citizens of West Germany to immigrate, and during the next twenty years, almost 300,000 arrived.

The "enemy alien" experience in the two world wars, of which German-speaking Canadians bore a disproportionate share, had a profound ethno-cultural impact on their community. Gerhard Bassler, a leading historian of the period, pointed out: "While English Canada participated in the world wars with an unprecedented 'national' euphoria and emerged from them with a new sense of nationhood, a large segment of Canadian society, including the population of the entire German-Canadian mosaic . . . was left the opposite experience. Its members were ostracized as 'aliens' and penalized for their non-English cultural and ethnic identity. [Their] experience [during eleven years of war] and, as a result, [their stigmatization] for many more years, made generations of German Canadians eager to renounce their visible ethnicity and heritage" (Bassler 1990, 42).

By the 1960s, while "Germans" were still the third-largest identifiable ethnic group, they were among the best integrated, least vocal, and least politically active ethnic groups in Canada. Certainly the two wars played a central role in this transformation.

Pat Brennan

See also Berlin/Kitchener, Ontario; Fuchs, Klaus; Nova Scotia; Ontario; Papen, Franz von; S.S. *St. Louis;* World War I, German Prisoners and Civilian Internees in; World War I, German Sabotage in Canada during

References and Further Reading

Bassler, Gerhard P. "Silent or Silenced Co-founders of Canada? Reflections on the History of German Canadians." *Canadian Ethnic Studies,* 22, 1 (1990): 38-46.

Entz, W. "The Suppression of the German Language Press in September 1918 (with Special Reference to the Secular German Language Papers in Western Canada)." *Canadian Ethnic Studies,* 8, 2 (1976): 56–70.

McLaughlin, Kenneth. *The Germans in Canada.* Ottawa: Canadian Historical Association, 1985.

Smith, David. "Emergency Government in Canada." *Canadian Historical Review,* 50, 4 (December 1969): 429–448.

Socknat, Thomas. *Witness against War: Pacifism in Canada, 1900–1945.* Toronto: University of Toronto Press, 1987.

Thompson, John. *Ethnic Minorities during Two World Wars.* Ottawa: Canadian Historical Association, 1991.

Wagner, Jonathan. *Brothers Beyond the Sea: National Socialism in Canada.* Waterloo, ON: Wilfrid Laurier University Press, 1981.

CANADIAN MILITARY FORCES IN WEST GERMANY

At the end of World War II, Canada left a small occupation force in Germany that was integrated into the British Army of the Rhine (BAOR). This contingent, based on the 2nd Canadian Infantry Division, was withdrawn in 1946. The acceleration of the cold war in the late 1940s, particularly the Berlin blockade and the Communist takeover of Czechoslovakia, led Canada to reassess its place in the postwar world order. A charter member of the North Atlantic Treaty Organization (NATO),

Canada initially earmarked a division-sized force to be deployed in the event of war in Europe. Overzealous Royal Canadian Air Force (RCAF) leaders then committed, without receiving approval first, twelve jet fighter squadrons and twelve light jet bomber squadrons. The Canadian government retracted the initial offer but agreed to build and commit twelve fighter squadrons. The situation in Korea, however, prevented the deployment of the Canadian division to serve with NATO. Suffering from the effects of an isolationist prime minister, William Lyon Mackenzie King, the army had been pared down after 1945 to a cadre and continental defense force. New formations had to be raised during "peacetime." Consequently, the initial Canadian land force commitment to NATO consisted of a division, with one brigade group deployed forward in West Germany and two brigade groups based in Canada to be sent as reinforcements if the cold war went "hot."

The 27th Canadian Infantry Brigade Group (CIBG) landed at Rotterdam on November 21, 1951. At the time, there was concern that Korea was a feint for a major Soviet overt and covert attack on Western Europe. At the same time, the United States deployed four divisions by sea. These actions served as a deterrent maneuver to demonstrate transatlantic solidarity and to give some steel to the lightly equipped occupation forces. Operation Panda, as the 27 CIBG deployment was called, sent the Brigade directly to serve with Northern Army Group (NORTHAG) in Hanover on the East German border. Soon after, in early 1952, the first RCAF Sabre squadrons deployed by air across the Atlantic Ocean to Europe in Operation Leap Frog. Initially, 1 Air Division RCAF consisted of ten Sabre squadrons. It had numerous bases in Europe: the West Germany–based squadrons were located at Zweibrücken and Baden-Soellingen.

Both formations were part of NATO's Integrated Force. The 27 Brigade was part of I (British) Corps as an independent formation (one out of ten brigades in the corps), whereas 1 Air Division was nearly 25 percent of 4 Allied Tactical Air Force's (4 ATAF) fighter strength. The brigade group redeployed to the Soest-Hemer-Iserlohn region outside of Cologne by 1953. Operationally, the brigade's role was to shape the battlefield and force the advancing Soviets to pile up on several obstacles, which would present a target of sufficient density to warrant using nuclear weapons. This would offset the crushing Soviet conventional capability located on the other side of the Iron Curtain. At that time, the entire brigade rotated with the Canadian-based units every three years, and RCAF squadrons rotated personnel through the European-based squadrons. Consequently, 27 Brigade was relieved by 1 Brigade, 2 Brigade, and 4 Brigade in the 1950s. By 1958, the decision was made to keep 4 Brigade in place and rotate units through it.

The Canadian brigade participated in annual exercises alongside allied NATO forces. The purpose of these exercises, in addition to preparing for war, was to present a deterrent posture to the Warsaw Pact and to stiffen up the European allies in a myriad of ways. For example, surplus Canadian equipment was transferred to the Dutch and French armies. Training exchanges and *Partnerschaft* relationships were established with *Bundeswehr* units. The emergent Luftwaffe (air force) acquired Canadian-built F-86 Sabres and trained alongside Canadian pilots in the NATO aircrew training program. Reconciliation between Canadians and Germans at the national as well as personal level was facilitated by these expanding contacts. The presence of an effective, salient Canadian military contribution numbering 12,000 people plus their dependent communities was a critical aspect of Canada's NATO commitment in West Germany. The West Germans were not alone in confronting the massive threat on the other side of the Iron Curtain, and this fact was demonstrated time and again as the Centurion tanks of the Canadian brigade and the F-86 Sabre fighters of 1 Air Division patrolled the skies. In time, four squadrons of CF-100 Canuck all-weather fighters, usually reserved for the air defense of North America, were deployed to serve with 1 Air Division. In general, the role was to engage in aerial combat to gain air superiority and to escort nuclear strike aircraft headed for interdiction targets.

Changing NATO strategy with regard to nuclear weapons had a direct impact on Canadian forces stationed in West Germany. Canada had always favored a NATO nuclear strategy, and the Europe-committed forces started training as early as 1951 to operate on a nuclear battlefield. Almost all exercises incorporated the nuclear dimension into them. The decision by the Eisenhower administration to implement nuclear sharing arrangements with NATO allies altered the Canadian force structure. Honest John free-flight rockets were made available to the brigade by 1961, and with the reduction of British forces in BAOR, Canada's contribution became even more numerically significant in that one surface-to-surface missile battery amounted to 25 percent of the Honest John batteries in I (British) Corps.

On the air side, the Canadian government accepted a nuclear strike role for 1 Air Division, which meant scrapping the F-86 and CF-100 fighters and reducing the air commitment from twelve squadrons to eight. Canada chose the Lockheed F-104 in 1959–1960. Built in Canada under license, the CF-104 Starfighter equipped six strike and two reconnaissance squadrons. All aircraft had the ability to deliver nuclear weapons: the strike squadrons could carry weapons with a yield of 1 megaton. In 1966, the government of Charles de Gaulle demanded the removal of Canadian nuclear weapons delivery units from French soil. Canadian nuclear operations were conducted from Zweibrücken, Baden-Soellingen, and eventually Lahr, which was traded for the Canadian bases in France. Indeed, the decision by Canada to acquire the F-104 airframe influenced other NATO allies to do the same so they could access the nuclear stockpile. The Luftwaffe also adopted the Starfighter as its nuclear strike aircraft, and Germany's relationship with Canada prospered.

The Berlin crisis of 1961 prompted Canada to prepare to reinforce 4 Brigade in West Germany with one of the Canada-based brigades: 3 Brigade was readied for action in the summer of 1961, and shipping was on the verge of being called up when the crisis subsided. In a year, the Cuban missile crisis almost escalated out of control. At that time, Canadian general Jean V. Allard was commanding a British division that included 4 Brigade. A tripartite but non-NATO organization called LIVE OAK had been established to forcibly open the Berlin access routes in the event of blockage. Allard's British division was earmarked to handle LIVE OAK tasks, and it moved to Helmstedt when the crisis

broke. Ultimately, the force was stood down when the Soviets turned their ships back. At this point, the CF-104 squadrons were in the process of deploying to West Germany and were not yet prepared to execute nuclear operations. However, 4 Brigade had its Honest John rockets prepared if the situation escalated: the brigade moved to its deployment areas near the Harz Mountains in case the Warsaw Pact attacked.

It would not be the last time. In 1968, the Czech crisis "Prague spring" generated a massive Soviet reinforcement of its forces in East Germany through Poland. This prompted a NATO alert, with NATO nuclear forces on quick reaction alert loading up with their weapons and ground units deploying to survival areas. Again, 4 Brigade (now 4 Canadian Mechanized Brigade Group, after it had been re-equipped with armored personnel carriers, self-propelled guns, and a Centurion tank upgrade) moved off at high speed to its defensive positions forward of the Weser River.

The 1960s were the heyday of Canada's military commitment to NATO in West Germany. In terms of numbers and quality, the air and land forces were significant contributions to NATO security. One Air Division boasted 33 percent of 4 ATAF's nuclear strike capacity and approximately 10 percent of the air-deliverable nuclear weapons in Allied Command Europe. Four Brigade retained 25 percent of I (British) Corps' nuclear capacity, and one-eighth of its conventional capacity. Canadian pilots were assigned high-risk targets (command-and-control sites, missile sites) because of their superior skills, and Canadian soldiers were tasked to cover a dangerous gap that developed in

NORTHAG due to Belgian withdrawals from their sector.

By 1970, however, two factors emerged to reduce the effectiveness of Canada's NATO forces in West Germany. NATO strategy shifted to "flexible response," which reduced dependency on nuclear weapons in favor of fighting conventionally as long as possible first and then using nuclear weapons if that failed. The election of Pierre Elliott Trudeau and the subsequent defense review unleashed antinuclear and anti-NATO thinking in the cabinet and among elements of the bureaucracy. In theory, the reduction in nuclear forces should have been accompanied by an increase in conventional forces in order to implement the new strategy. Instead, Trudeau decided to cut nuclear forces and at the same time reduce conventional forces. Outright withdrawal from West Germany was averted when a compromise was struck between anti- and dissident pro-NATO cabinet factions. The number of CF-104 squadrons was reduced from eight to three, and those three squadrons were redeployed as conventional attack squadrons. The base at Zweibrücken was closed, leaving Lahr and Baden-Soellingen as the primary Canadian air bases. Four Brigade lost its Honest John rockets and then was slashed in half, from three infantry battalions to two, with the tank regiment and artillery regiment each cut in half. To make matters worse, the salient contributions to forward defense in NORTHAG that 4 Brigade made became moot when the brigade was forced to relocate to Lahr and Baden-Soellingen bases. The remnants of 4 Brigade were assigned to a vague reserve role for Central Army Group (CENTAG), and all saliency was lost.

It took the Trudeau government five years to realize that its policy was flawed. Instead of taking action to correct it, however, cosmetic improvements were made to satisfy West Germany's leadership, which was pressuring Canada to remain effective players in the defense of the NATO Central Region. For example, a minimalist number of Leopard tanks were purchased in 1978 to equip 4 Brigade, replacing aging Centurions. In time, the Trudeau government was replaced. In 1983, the Mulroney government pledged to reinvigorate Canada's NATO commitment. Numerous improvements were made to 4 Brigade, including improved antitank capability, better mobilization plans, and the adoption of a clear mission on the intercorps boundary on the Czech border between VII (US) and II (German) Corps, a critical juncture. CF-104s, not designed for close air support operations, were crashing far too often on training missions, so the New Fighter Aircraft project was initiated in the late 1970s. In time, the CF-18 Hornet was selected. Three squadrons totaling forty-eight aircraft were deployed to Baden-Soellingen by 1985. The CF-18 was multirole: it could conduct air superiority operations as well as air-to-ground missions, though the propensity was for aerial combat.

The disappearance of the Warsaw Pact as a result of peaceful revolutions in Eastern Europe caused the Canadian government to reconsider its military engagement in West Germany. Beginning in 1990, Canadian forces withdrew from West Germany. Two CF-18 squadrons from Baden-Soellingen, plus an infantry company to guard them were deployed to Bahrain in the fall of 1990 as part of the operations Desert Shield and Desert Storm. Units of 4 Brigade (this included 4

Combat Engineer Regiment and a composite Royal Canadian Regiment/Royal 22nd Regiment battalion group) joined the United Nations Protection Force (UN-PROFOR) in the spring of 1992, which was deployed as a peacekeeping force in Croatia. By 1993, the CF-18s flew back to Canada, and the remnants of 4 Brigade closed out, unit by unit.

Sean M. Maloney

See also U.S. Bases in West Germany; World War II

References and Further Reading

Bashow, David L. *Starfighter.* Stoney Creek: Fortress Publications, 1991.

Maloney, Sean M. *War without Battles: Canada's NATO Brigade in Germany, 1951–1993.* St. Catharines: McGraw-Hill Ryerson, 1997.

———. "Berlin Contingency Planning: Prelude to Flexible Response, 1958–63." *Journal of Strategic Studies* 25, no. 1 (March 2002): 99–134.

Milberry, Larry. *The Canadair Sabre.* Toronto: CANAV Books, 1986.

Morin, Jean, and Richard H. Gimblett. *Operation Friction: The Canadian Forces in the Persian Gulf, 1990–1991.* Toronto: Dundurn Press, 1997.

CARRANZA, VENUSTIANO

b. December 29, 1859; Cuatro Ciénegas, Coahuila
d. May 20, 1920; San Antonio, Tlaxcalantongo

President of Mexico during the last years of World War I who found himself courted by Germany, which was seeking an ally geographically close to the United States.

Venustiano Carranza held various political positions in Porfirio Diaz's Mexico, but in 1909 he joined forces with Francisco Madero to overthrow the long-standing dictator. Carranza remained loyal to Madero when the latter assumed the presidency. After Madero's death in 1913, Victoriano Huerta, a general under Madero, assumed power. Carranza did not agree with Huerta's dictatorial methods and led one of the many rebellions against the new regime. Woodrow Wilson, who became president of the United States in 1913, adamantly opposed Huerta and refused to recognize his adminsitration's legitimacy. With increased pressure from opposition, including the United States, Huerta fled Mexico. The power vacuum created by Huerta's flight left Carranza and Pancho Villa as the most likely successors. Washington chose to support Carranza, and Wilson sent General John J. Pershing into Mexico to capture Villa. Although the punitive expedition failed, Villa's powers slowly diminished, allowing Carranza to establish supremacy.

After six years of fighting, the revolutionary leadership concluded that it was time to legitimize their cause. A congress met at Querétaro in November 1916 and eventually drafted the Constitution of 1917. Special elections were held in March 1917, in which Carranza won the presidency easily. Carranza's appointment did little to ease tensions between the United States and Mexico. As World War I raged in Europe, it became increasingly likely that the United States would enter the fray against Germany. Most Latin American nations prepared to ally with the United States, but Carranza believed the best course for Mexico was to remain neutral. Germany, much like the United States, wanted Mexico on its side and decided to pursue an alliance.

Venustiano Carranza (left), president of Mexico, 1917–1920, shown with with G.F. Weeks. (Library of Congress)

One of the pivotal events of Carranza's presidency occurred when the British intercepted a telegram from the German foreign secretary, Arthur Zimmermann, intended for the Mexican government. The "Zimmermann telegram" set forth a scenario for Germany and Mexico to forge a formal alliance. Germany asked that Mexico attack the United States, should it attack Germany. In return, Germany, after winning the war, would make sure that Mexico received back lands that the United States had taken in the nineteenth century. Carranza turned down the German offer, as he continued to prefer a path of neutrality, especially given the fragile nature of the Mexican state. When word got out in the United States, after newspapers published the telegram, citizens were outraged. This event, coupled with Germany's resumption of unrestricted submarine warfare, led the United States to declare war on Germany on April 6, 1917.

Melvin Duane Davis

See also Mexico; World War I

References and Further Reading

Hart, John Mason. *Revolutionary Mexico.* Berkeley: University of California Press, 1987.

Knight, Alan. *The Mexican Revolution.* New York: Cambridge University Press, 1986.

Richmond, Douglas. *Venustiano Carranza's Nationalist Struggle.* Lincoln: University of Nebraska Press, 1983.

CASABLANCA CONFERENCE/ UNCONDITIONAL SURRENDER

At the end of the British American conference in Casablanca, January 14–23, 1943, Franklin D. Roosevelt, with Winston Churchill at his side, explained that the elimination of Axis war power meant their unconditional surrender. This proclamation was the one war aim pertaining to Nazi Germany that the Allies publicly announced during the war. It was immediately criticized by the American media as a wholly negative one that would only stiffen the German resolve to fight and thus prolong the war and increase American casualties. Indeed, "unconditional surrender" proved an encumbrance to psychological warfare. In subsequent explanations British and American leaders stated that this policy did not mean the enslavement of the German people. Roosevelt clarified that "unconditional surrender" did not mean the destruction of the enemy population, but he emphasized that it did aim at the destruction of Nazism, fascism, and militarism. There was, however, little disagreement among political and military officials over the validity and purpose of the formula.

Roosevelt, who had been a member of the Wilson administration during World War I, had regarded the armistice with Germany ending that war to be a mistake that had given rise to the "stab-in-the back legend" of a German army undefeated in

Casablanca Conference at Casablanca, French Morocco, Africa. The "unconditional surrender" announcement. President Roosevelt, with Prime Minister Winston Churchill at his side, reads to the assembled war correspondents, January 1943. (Library of Congress)

the field. In U.S. wartime planning the term "unconditional surrender" had been discussed approvingly from the time the United States entered World War II. Soon thereafter, Roosevelt announced that no compromise could end the current conflict, thus also ruling out any substantive contacts and negotiations with the German resistance to Adolf Hitler. Domestically the president intended his announcement to quell a public outcry, especially among the liberal media and intellectuals, over a negotiated deal his administration had struck in November 1942 with the French Fascist admiral Jean-Francois Darlan to prevent resistance against the Allied troops after their landing in North Africa (TORCH). Similarly, the Soviet ally had to be reassured that Britain and the United States were determined not to enter into separate deals with parts of the German leadership. In addition to public apprehension over the demand for unconditional surrender, sections of the U.S. government, such as the emigrant-staffed Research and Analysis Branch of the Office of Strategic Services, pointed to the troublesome effects of the unconditional surrender policy from a psychological warfare point of view, especially when compared with the Soviets' alternative strategy of holding out a prospect of democratic self-rule, as embodied in the Free Germany Committee.

Michaela Hoenicke Moore

See also Tehran Conference; U.S. Plans for Postwar Germany; World War II

References and Further Reading

Casey, Steven. *Cautious Crusade: Franklin D. Roosevelt, American Public Opinion, and the War against Nazi Germany.* Oxford: Oxford University Press, 2001.

Klemperer, Klemens von. *German Resistance against Hitler. The Search for Allies Abroad, 1938–1945.* Oxford: Clarendon Press, 1992.

O'Connor, Raymond G. *Diplomacy for Victory: FDR and Unconditional Surrender.* New York: W. W. Norton, 1971.

CATHOLIC WOMEN'S UNION

The Catholic Women's Union (CWU), established in 1916, modeled itself closely on the Katholischer deutscher Frauenbund (KDF, or Catholic German Women's Organization) as a result of the organization's almost exclusively German American membership and its emphasis on ethnic issues. The CWU remained under the jurisdiction of the male German Catholic Central-Verein (CV), whose St. Louis–based national headquarters it shared. By the early 1920s the Catholic Women's Union, along with many other women's groups, had affiliated with the National Council of Catholic Women, based in Washington, D.C., as part of the larger trend toward centralizing lay groups. The CWU followed an ethnically based model of Catholic activism, drawing heavily from German reform influences. It emphasized a maternalist ideal to assist working women and the poor and opened its membership to working women, although both the membership and leadership of the CWU tended to be middle class. Though socially conservative on many issues, the CWU occasionally challenged both the authority and indifference of the clergy and hierarchy. By engaging in social reform programs, middle-class women, many of whom were mothers, sought to extend their maternalism to the poor or working classes and to channel their leisure time and material wealth into more acceptable ends. They could, moreover, increase the visibility of Catholic women in voluntary work without entering the more controversial arena of suffrage activism and other women's rights issues.

Although the orientation and goals of Catholic women's groups remained removed from traditional politics, they often became active on issues pertaining to modernity, social morality, and the family. In the early twentieth century, several groups took stances against a number of issues, including birth control measures, suffrage, the Child Labor Amendment, divorce, and immoral entertainment and dress. Women justified their involvement in these groups on the basis of defending their home and moral beliefs, as earlier generations of middle-class Protestant women had justified their involvement in temperance and in other issues.

German American Catholic women in the early twentieth century organized their reform efforts around the principle of home protection, and they chose St. Elizabeth of Thuringia as their patron saint. St. Elizabeth, who lived in the early thirteenth century, was the daughter of a king. After her early marriage, she devoted herself to charitable pursuits, including work with lepers and the poor, as well as relief efforts for flood and famine victims. She died a widow at age twenty-four, after having established a Franciscan Hospital in Marburg, and became widely known as the "Patroness of the Poor." By adopting her as its symbol, CWU leaders sought to emphasize the selflessness of their programs, their compassion toward the poor, the universality of charity among females, and the common ethnic bond between St. Elizabeth and the members of their organization.

The CWU emerged in 1916 to complement the existing male CV. Key lay leaders and members of the hierarchy, in-

cluding Milwaukee archbishop Sebastian Messmer and Chicago archbishop James Quigley, supported the creation of a woman's group. But the initiative also encountered resistance from some within the CV, who believed that women should not have a public role. In the coming years, CWU members found that they needed to defend their work to those male clergy, bishops, or laity who were hostile or indifferent to their organization. By 1925, the CWU had 50,000 members in branches in nineteen states and a national budget of $45,461. Although the most active groups were concentrated in Wisconsin, Illinois, Texas, and Missouri, the CWU also formed branches in Arkansas, New Jersey, Connecticut, and several other states where the German American population was proportionately small.

Although the domestic ideology of CWU members seems inspired by the middle-class Protestant separate spheres ideology of mid-nineteenth-century America, their views on Catholic social reform drew extensively from central European influences. Because the German ethnic identity was a strong focus in both the male and female *Vereines* (clubs), these women appropriated models of social action that existed in Europe, as well as responding to secular, Protestant, and Catholic trends within the United States. In fact, many bourgeois women in late nineteenth-century Germany articulated a similar view of "social motherhood" that emphasized the responsibility that middle- and upper-class women held for poorer women in their communities.

Despite their emphasis on domesticity, members of the CWU simultaneously acknowledged that many mothers had no choice but to remain in the workforce.

They advocated the expansion of day care facilities for children, such as those of the St. Elizabeth Settlement in St. Louis, and promoted the establishment of a mother's pension program. Although, like Pope Leo XIII, they condemned socialism, the CWU and *Central Verein* also proved quite critical of modern capitalism and its effects on the working class and poor. Much of the rhetoric in the CWU emphasized the unique prerogative that women, as mothers and wives, held for extending their influence throughout society, except in ways that involved traditional political activities. German Catholic women believed that as females they were uniquely able to influence society while remaining within the domestic sphere. This domestic sphere was not limited, however, to the private home.

Unlike other Catholic women's groups in the United States, German American women readily acknowledged the existence of class differences within society; although other Catholic lay groups implicitly recognized divisions between its members and those they sought to assist, they did not refer to them in class terms. Many of the initiatives undertaken by the CWU in the early twentieth century were patterned on those of Catholic women's organizations in Germany, particularly the KDF, which was established in 1903. Members of the KDF and CWU forged relationships between their two groups, shared many of the same views on social issues, and launched similar charitable efforts. The CWU viewed German organization members as part of a larger transatlantic movement, and several KDF members visited CWU leagues throughout the United States. One difference between the leaders of the German organization and the American one was the more modest economic position of those in the United States. For example, the leadership of the Wisconsin German Catholic League, a CWU affiliate, was comprised mostly of wives and daughters of businessmen.

The CWU's major work involved the development of a traveler's aid network. The programs targeted rural German Catholic women who had left their homes for work in cities such as Milwaukee and Chicago; these reformers sought to create a network of affiliated traveler's aid societies. This particular emphasis of the CWU also proved similar to that of Catholic women's organizations in Germany. There, women's groups claimed to have benefited 2 million working women and had launched a network to protect young women at railroad stations and ports, like others developed for Catholic immigrants in the United States and elsewhere.

Anti-German sentiment permeated American society during World War I, leading the New York branch of the CV to suspend its conventions in 1917 and 1918. Yet the CWU did not discuss the issue of divided loyalties in their publications. The Wisconsin branch of the CWU referred only obliquely to the issue in its statewide publication, when it announced that it had changed its name from *DRK Frauenbund von Wisconsin*/GRC Women's League to the less ethnic-sounding Catholic Women's League of Wisconsin. It also reported on the success of liberty bond drives, underscoring the CWU's loyalty to the United States.

As part of its objection to modern social influences, the CWU actively opposed birth control laws and the Child Labor Amendment and had its members write letters to their political representatives to express their views on those topics. The CWU and CV advocated the creation of mother's pension programs, health insurance, and other maternal assistance programs. The programs that they advocated would have had a far greater impact than the Sheppard-Towner Act (1921), which provided federal matching funds to states for the provision of prenatal and infant care, child care clinics, and visiting nurses. Yet CWU members in Wisconsin sent at least one petition opposing the Sheppard-Towner bill to a Wisconsin congressman, arguing that the bill would allow the federal government to take away power from local and state agencies. The fear that it would remove the social stigma against unmarried motherhood might have influenced their decision. CWU members also viewed the Child Labor Amendment as a potential infringement of parental authority and distributed pamphlets urging Catholics to oppose it.

Another major controversy arose among CWU leaders in the early 1920s, with the emergence of the National Catholic Welfare Council (NCWC) and National Council of Catholic Women (NCCW), the national lay groups sponsored by the hierarchy after World War I. The CWU members viewed those organizations suspiciously as a threat to the identity, agenda, and vitality of their own group. Although ultimately the CWU affiliated with both the NCWC and NCCW, CWU members voiced their resentment that the NCCW sought to engage in work pioneered by the CWU. Ultimately, in the wake of anti-German sentiment resulting from World War I and the creation of the NCCW in 1920, the CWU moved away from its strong ethnic identification and toward greater uniformity with other Catholic women. In 1924, the CWU replaced as its patron saint St. Elizabeth, an ethnic as well as religious symbol, with Saint Mary, Our Lady of Good Counsel, a universal Catholic saint.

Deirdre M. Moloney

See also German American Women's Organizations; German Catholic Central-Verein

References and Further Reading

Gleason, Philip. *The Conservative Reformers: German-American Catholics and the Social Order.* Notre Dame, IN: University of Notre Dame Press, 1968.

Moloney, Deirdre M. *American Catholic Lay Groups and Transatlantic Social Reform in the Progressive Era.* Chapel Hill: University of North Carolina Press, 2002.

Sachße, Christof. "Social Mothers: The Bourgeois Women's Movement and German Welfare-State Formation." *Mothers of a New World: Maternalist Politics and the Origins of Welfare States.* Eds. Seth Koven and Sonya Michel. New York: Routledge Press, 1992, 136–158.

Spael, Wilhelm. *Das katholische Deutschland im 20. Jahrhundert: Seine Pionier-und Krisenzeiten, 1890–1945.* Würzburg: Echter-Verlag, 1964.

CENTRAL PARK

Since its creation in 1858, Central Park has been one of New York City's landmarks. The first landscaped public park in the United States could not have been envisioned, let alone built, without a profound knowledge of German garden theory and German garden design. In fact, the aesthetic and social principles that governed Frederick Law Olmsted and Calvert Vaux's design for Central Park can be traced back to German landscape architecture: the understanding of the park as a national work of art, as a succession of landscape paintings often bearing national connotations, and as a symbol of democracy that offers a public space where all social classes can meet.

It was a German philosopher and professor of aesthetics, Christian Cayus Lorenz Hirschfeld (1742–1792), who was the first person worldwide to articulate and substantiate the need for a public park designed for all social classes and financed by the government. He explored this idea in his groundbreaking book, *Theorie der Gartenkunst* (Theory of Garden Art, 1779–1785), a five-volume work that Olmsted owned and heavily relied upon—both for content and style—in his own writing and his park design. The English Garden in Munich was the first realization of Hirschfeld's social principles, a landscaped park that Olmsted visited several times and on which he lavished much praise.

New York City was growing rapidly in the 1840s. Urbanization and its consequences, such as the inhumane and unhygienic conditions of tenement housing, bred fatal epidemics. The influx of American farmers and European immigrants in search of better job possibilities led to fierce competition for employment, often resulting in poverty and leading to riots and crime. Wanting to exercise control over the lower classes as well as believing in nature's therapeutic ability to civilize the riotous classes, members of the upper class expressed the urgent need for a public park. In 1853 the state legislature authorized a public park financed by the city government. A space of 843 acres filled with rocky outcrops and therefore undesirable for building purposes was designated as parkland. The oblong park site in the midst of Manhattan, stretching from 59th Street to 106th Street, was extended to 110th Street in 1863, and reaching from Fifth Avenue on the east side to Eighth Avenue, today is called Central Park West, on Manhattan's west side.

To ensure the best possible results for the design of Central Park, a contest was held in 1857. It was the first landscape design competition in the United States. Frederick Law Olmsted (1822–1903), an autodidactic landscape gardener and former journalist, and his partner Calvert Vaux (1824–1895), a British-born architect, won the competition when their design entry "Greensward," beat out thirty-two competitors. Characteristic of their design were the pastoral and picturesque landscapes, the extensive sweeping meadows (Sheep Meadow, East Meadow) juxtaposed with wooded rugged-rocky terrains (the Ramble, as well as landscape around the lakes called Loch and Pool) planted with indigenous vegetation. Four transverse roads crossing through the park were mandatory in the design. Olmsted and Vaux deliberately lowered them below park level so as to avoid disrupting, visually or acoustically, the three-dimensional landscape paintings they had created. They also relied to a great extent on the terrain's natural pictorial qualities and deliberately kept the architecture sparse.

Olmsted was not the only designer of Central Park; neither was Vaux. Both men counted on the tremendous botanical knowledge and the artistic sensibilities of German gardeners whom they assigned leading positions in the Central Park administration. Ignaz Anton Pilat (1820–1870) in particular, but also Wilhelm Fischer (1819–1899) and Eugene Achille Baumann (b. 1821), who had received a thorough education in Germany and had already been well established in New York, were instrumental to the park's realization.

Olmsted and Vaux relied on the German philosopher Christian Cayus Lorenz Hirschfeld for their social vision for the

Central Park Summer, *by John Bachmann. A New York City landmark, Central Park could not have been envisioned, let alone built, without a profound knowledge of German garden theory and German garden design. Central Park's 44 bridges (here, Bow Bridge) were focal points of Olmsted's and Vaux's effort to make the park function as a national monument. (Library of Congress)*

park, but they resorted to the celebrated German landscape gardener Hermann Heinrich Fürst von Pückler-Muskau (1785–1871) for the aesthetics. The pictorial language the German aristocrat employed designing his expansive estate in the southeastern town of Muskau (1815) bears distinct national connotations. To make Central Park "a great work of art of the Republic," the American designers and their German gardeners resorted to the national aspects of Pückler's pictorial language. In fact, Olmsted's partner Charles W. Eliot would later identify Pückler-Muskau's pictorial language as a "national style," urging American landscape architects to adopt it.

The national aspects of Pückler's pictorial language consist of the naming of things to evoke the historical past, in Pück-

ler's case, his aristocratic genealogy, but he also makes references to German mythology by naming old oak trees "Thor" and "Odin." Further, Pückler's deliberate use of indigenous rock as building material and his use of indigenous plants were meant to imbue the park visitor with national pride about the native vegetation. Olmsted and Vaux singled out nature as the nation's greatest cultural resource and the most potent expressive vocabulary. Like Pückler, Olmsted and Vaux used indigenous vegetation to display the tremendous diversity of flora in the United States and, by doing so, educated the park visitors and encouraged them to take national pride in their native plants. In employing nature as pictorial language, they alluded to the country's history as "Nature's Nation" (Miller 1967) at a time when the United States was becoming an increasingly industrial nation. Their adoption of Pückler's national principles is further exemplified by their use of local building material. The bridges and rustic seats were often made of the gneiss and Manhattan schist found in the park.

The park's forty-four bridges, too, were focal points of Olmsted's and Vaux's effort to make the park function as a national monument. The bridges' design, building material, location, and above all their quaint names (Pine Banks Arch, Huddlestone Arch, Springbanks Arch, Oak Bridge) are intended to evoke the nostalgia for American rural life. Explicit allusions to, for instance, the Natural Bridge, a natural and national monument Thomas Jefferson describes in his *Notes on the State of Virginia* (1784–1785), express the designers' intention to make Central Park a national monument as well.

Olmsted and Vaux also customized the park's landscape to preserve and document the lost landscape of the nation. Just as the painters of the Hudson River School painted the Catskill Mountains, the White Mountains, and the Adirondacks exactly when they were being destroyed by tourism and industrialization, Olmsted and Vaux evoked the very same landscapes in the park. They provided allusions to those exemplary terrains for two reasons: first, in accord with their understanding of the park as a succession of landscape paintings, they wanted to create a "picture gallery" of the most celebrated American landscapes. Second, they wanted to provide those who could neither afford to go to galleries nor to make a trip to the Catskill Mountains with at least a suggestion of the famous landscapes en miniature. Their goal has been amply realized. To this day more than 25 million people visit this outdoor picture gallery, an oasis amid a chaotic, bustling, sensorily exhausting metropolis, each year.

Franziska Kirchner

See also Landscape Architects, German American

References and Further Reading

Beveridge, Charles Eliot, and David Schuyler, eds. *The Papers of Frederick Law Olmsted.* Vol. 3: *Creating Central Park, 1857–1861.* Baltimore: Johns Hopkins University Press, 1983.

Kirchner, Franziska. *Der Central Park in New York.* Worms: Wernersche Verlagsgesellschaft, 2002.

Miller, Perry. *Nature's Nation.* Cambridge, NY: Cambridge University Press, 1967.

Miller, Sara Cedar. *Central Park: An American Masterpiece.* New York: H. N. Abrams, 2003.

Rosenzweig, Roy, and Elizabeth Blackmar. *The Park and the People: A History of Central Park.* Ithaca: Cornell University Press, 1992.

CHAMISSO, ADELBERT VON

b. January 30, 1781; Boncourt Castle, France
d. August 21, 1838; Berlin, Prussia

German romantic author: participated in the Russian exploration of Alaska, Hawaii, and California.

With the objective of discovering a subarctic navigable passage across North America, the Russian brig *Rurik,* under the command of captain Otto von Kotzebue, set sail from Kronstadt, Russia, in the summer of 1815. This voyage took Kotzebue and crew across the Atlantic Ocean, around Cape Horn, and into the Pacific Ocean. The *Rurik* sailed up to the Bering Strait, making the first of its two visits to Alaska in summer 1816. From there it sailed south to San Francisco Bay, remaining there for approximately one month.

The ship next paid its first visit to Hawaii, arriving in the then Sandwich Islands in the fall of 1816. After approximately three weeks, it sailed westward, before again turning north for the second visit to Alaska in the summer of 1817. Ill health and harsh weather forced the captain to abandon his objective of finding a passage through the Arctic, and the crew eventually headed home, passing once more through the Hawaiian Islands. The voyage ended when the *Rurik* arrived home in St. Petersburg in the summer of 1818.

A good account of this journey was provided by resident naturalist and romantic writer Adelbert von Chamisso. Chamisso, best known for *Peter Schlemihl's wundersame Geschichte* (Peter Schlemihl's Miraculous Story) and numerous poems, published in 1836 a two-volume edition of his journey, consisting of his journal and a series of essays and observations of the voyage. This story is one of many travelogues from the period, in which much of the Pacific Ocean was first being thoroughly explored by Europeans. Through Chamisso, the reader benefits from having a naturalist and a romantic poet telling the story. His volumes contain rich details, not only of the flora and fauna he encountered but also of the people he met. For example, the reader learns of Chamisso's hikes through the Hawaiian Islands, along with similar wanderings in the Aleutians. The books include an account of a botanical excursion in Hawaii, in which he walked through a fertile valley behind Honolulu (Hanaruru), picked some beautiful grasses he had not seen before, and encountered considerable grief because he had actually picked rice during the first year it had successfully grown in the islands.

Chamisso discusses indigenous customs and relations among the Russians—who were not popular in the Hawaiian Islands—Spanish, other Europeans, and Americans. The indigenous peoples of Hawaii generally enjoyed and had fun with Chamisso, causing him once to say "Arocha," a customary peaceful salutation, incessantly. The author's response displayed his good nature toward the peoples he met. In California, Chamisso witnessed negotiations between the Spanish governor and the Russians who were encroaching on Spanish territory. Although the Russians were not the only power that violated Spain's claims in that region, they had a settlement near San Francisco, which the Spanish wanted vacated. Chamisso's command of languages provided him an important role in these negotiations: although no decision was made over the settlement's future, both parties decided to issue a document that would be sent to the Spanish and Russian royal courts. This essentially solved the problem, at least during Chamisso's stay in California.

In addition to his journal of this voyage, Chamisso also wrote several essays about his experiences. One of these provides more details of his stay in California, including weather patterns and the plight of the local peoples. There are descriptions of the animals of the region, including the ferocious brown bear, along with wolves, foxes, goats, and stags. The problems faced by the local peoples were more serious, resulting from a Spanish policy that also kept the region underpopulated and sapped California of its potential for trade and shipping. The mission system was more problematic, especially because of its exploitation of the native peoples. The so-called savages faced serious troubles, and found their histories, customs, beliefs, and languages treated with contempt by the mission priests. Indeed, Chamisso notes that the local peoples were dying at alarming rates from disease and the lack of sufficient medical help. Chamisso knew he could do little to help the peoples he encountered, but he hoped that someone who followed his expedition would be able to learn more about the local cultures of the area.

Chamisso was fortunate throughout his journey. His efforts to collect fossilized ivory, human skulls, stuffed birds, and models of whales were greatly aided by his sympathetic captain, who provided extra storage. When Chamisso safely arrived home, he wrote about his journey and left history not only with a literate account of his travels but also with a sizable collection of specimens for the museumgoers of Berlin.

David E. Marshall

See also Indians in German Literature; Kino, Eusebius Franciscus; Travel Literature, Germany-U.S.

References and Further Reading
Chamisso, Adalbert von. *A Voyage around the World with the Romanzov Exploring Expedition in the Years 1815–1818 in the Brig Rurik, Captain Otto von Kotzebue.* Honolulu: University of Hawaii Press, 1986.

CHEWING GUM

Since the end of World War II, chewing gum has had an important place in the collective memory of Germans. It is a symbol of the new beginning after the war and a result of the U.S. occupation of parts of western Germany. Americanization of West German society during the 1950s brought Coca-Cola, chewing gum, and rock 'n' roll to a young generation that was starving for entertainment and willing to experiment with new and unusual cultural imports. The history of chewing gum in the Federal Republic of Germany (FRG) is the history of the product developed by the Wrigley's Company, which was founded in 1891 in Chicago. Wrigley's established its first German production facility in 1925 in Frankfurt am Main, where it produced the PK gumball. However, in 1932 Wrigley's had to close its German outlet because of increasing difficulties importing necessary raw materials and the financial problems related to Germany's obligations under the Treaty of Versailles and the Great Depression. After 1933, Wrigley's chewing gum could still be distributed and purchased inside Germany. However, it was no longer produced there and had to be imported. Wrigley's opened an import and distribution bureau at Berlin's famous Unter den Linden Boulevard for marketing purposes. In contrast to Coca-Cola, however, Wrigley's renamed its product: chewing gum became *Kaubonbon* (chewable candy).

The image of the American GI chewing Wrigley's gum became an icon in European culture during and after World War II. For some time, Wrigley's decided to send its entire production to the U.S. soldiers engaged in the European and Asiatic theatres of World War II. As well as Coca-Cola, chewing gum became symbolic of U.S. resolve to win the war. It was to give the U.S. soldier psychological support during combat. Scientific studies had proven that chewing helped to decrease stress. Furthermore, chewing gum became important in winning the trust of the defeated civilian population. U.S. soldiers who handed chewing gum to German children were no longer seen as enemies but as sympathetic

German Wrigley's gum advertisement. (Wrigley Germany)

men. For the Germans, chewing gum and American cigarettes functioned as currency on the black market.

Gum-chewing U.S. soldiers provided Wrigley's with an invaluable opportunity to advertise and market its product. The GIs became, involuntarily, pioneers for the advertisement of Wrigley's spearmint gum. In later years, Wrigley's sold twice as much chewing gum in the southern part of Germany, the former American Occupation Zone, than in the northern part where the British had been in charge of administration. However, chewing gum was a luxury product for most people in postwar West German society. No worker could afford Wrigley's chewing gum, sold at ten Pfenning a piece and fifty Pfenning a package. Because it was treated as a luxury product, it was subject to certain import limitations. In the long run Wrigley's conquered the German market, and its chewing gum became a staple among young children after the economic recovery of West Germany. It quickly rose to the top of chewing gum producers in West Germany (Unterhachingen, near Munich, became the German headquarters) and continued to dominate the market. To correctly pronounce the product name was certainly a challenge for West Germans. In the 1950s, an analysis among customers revealed that there were at least twelve different pronunciations. Subsequently, Wrigley's engaged in an advertising campaign focused on its product name. In these advertisements, consumers could read the shortened version "Rigley's" instead of "Wrigley's," and spearmint was rewritten as "Speer"-mint. Since 1959, Wrigley's has printed on its product's wrapping the German term *Kaugummi* (chewing gum).

Since chewing gum was identified with Americanization as much as Coca-Cola, blue jeans, and rock 'n' roll, it became the target of protest and resistance by conservative cultural critics. Their opposition toward the gum-chewing younger generation combined traditional cultural stereotypes about American society with the fear of a degeneration of culture caused and symbolized by chewing gum. The chewing of gum has been used by generations of youngsters to silently protest traditional norms of behavior and paternalistic limitations of freedom. Nevertheless, conservative critics did not succeed in their endeavor to rid Germany of chewing gum. Today, it is part of a multi-billion-dollar health and cosmetics industry. Chewing Wrigley's spearmint gum is said to provide fresh breath and clean teeth and even to help fight the desire to smoke.

Hilmar Sack

See also American Occupation Zone; Americanization; Coca-Cola; Consumerism; McDonald's Restaurant

References and Further Reading

Aaseng, Nathan. *Business Builders in Sweets and Treats*. Minneapolis: Oliver Press, 2004.

Davies, Henry. "Deutsche Wrigley." *All around Wrigley* (Fall 1985): 8–11; (Winter 1985): 9–11; (Spring 1986): 6–9.

Lee, Norma E. *Chewing Gum*. Englewood Cliffs, NJ: Prentice-Hall, 1976.

CHICAGO

Important urban center of German migration in the United States during the nineteenth century.

Chicago's history illustrates the full impact of the dramatic social, demographic, and economic changes American society and economy underwent in the second half of the nineteenth century. Compared with other cities in the Midwest, Chicago was a latecomer, but its growth was breathtaking. Within a few years it rose from a small settlement along the frontier to the dominant metropolis of the American continent. Chicago's booming economy attracted hundreds of thousands of immigrants from Europe and internal migrants from the American Northeast. Between 1880 and 1890 alone, Chicago's population doubled from 500,000 to over 1 million, making Chicago the second-largest city in the United States and the fifth-largest in the world. Between 1890 and 1900 almost 80 percent of Chicago's inhabitants were foreign-born or children of immigrants (Philpott 1978, 7–8). Even for the United States, this was an unusually high proportion. The rise of Chicago went hand in hand with a growing degree of social disorder. Mass immigration and rapid social change, accompanied by several economic recessions, caused social unrest. During the last third of the nineteenth century, Chicago became the site of the worst outbursts of urban violence in the United States.

Chicago's rise depended on three connected factors: location, investment, and immigration. Chicago was incorporated as a city in 1837 with just 4,000 inhabitants. From the 1850s to the 1870s, Chicago emerged as a strategically located traffic hub, halfway between the seemingly unlimited raw materials and agricultural products of the West—in particular lumber, grain, and meat, which were processed in Chicago—and the markets on the East Coast and beyond. The Civil War proved a catalyst driving the rise of Chicago against its main rivals, the river cities Cincinnati and St. Louis. Both cities were too close to the military action and suffered from trade blockades caused by the war. Chicago became the main production and supply center for Union troops west of the Alleghenies. After the war, Chicago developed into the leading railroad hub of the American continent and a strongly expanding industrial center. In 1850, the city of Chicago already counted 30,000 inhabitants, in 1870, 300,000, and in 1900, 1.7 million. Although the processing industries such as meat packing gradually began to move west before the turn of the century, Chicago remained a distribution center with an innovative service sector and, more importantly, a financial marketplace where the commodity prices were fixed.

Chicago's largest immigrant group during the decisive second half of the nineteenth century was Germans. However, today few traces recall the presence of tens of thousands of German-speaking immigrants in Chicago. A prominent Goethe Monument on the northern edge of Lincoln Park dedicated before World War I, a small Schiller statue, and streets named after Johann Wolfgang von Goethe and Friedrich Schiller on the near North Side are the most visible traces, apart from Chicago's cemeteries, where thousands of graves with German inscriptions can still be found. Further northwest, on Lincoln Square, a few remnants of post–World War II immigration remain: a popular German restaurant, a small souvenir shop, a delicatessen, and nearby, a *Konditorei* (bakery). However, the area is not a German neighborhood; most of the immigrants who lived there during the 1950s and 1960s have moved to the suburbs. Although streets and buildings in Chicago recall the names of famous immigrants of other ethnic backgrounds, once-famous German

immigrants like the doctor and Forty-Eighter Ernst Schmidt, publisher and politician Anton Casper Hesing, newspaper editor and politician Lorenz Brentano, Civil War general Edward Salomon, and many others are forgotten.

Around 1900, shortly after the decline of the strong German transatlantic migration, the Germans and their still vibrant ethnic life were much more visible in Chicago. Yet U.S. entry into World War I in 1917, which went hand in hand with a massive anti-German propaganda campaign, seemingly obliterated the ethnic life of the Germans within a few weeks. The famous Germania Club was renamed Lincoln Club, the Bismarck Hotel became the Hotel Randolph, the large German Hospital changed its name to Grant Hospital, and so on. Almost all street names referring to German persons, cities, and regions were changed by the city council. German as the official language was dropped by many associations and disappeared from most immigrant church pulpits. And like many Americans, quite a few Chicagoans anglicized their German-sounding names. Nevertheless, it would be too simplistic to trace the virtual disappearance of the Germans in Chicago to 1917.

The German presence in Chicago was never as dominant as in the three cities of the so-called German triangle surrounding Chicago (Milwaukee, Cincinnati, and St. Louis) or as in many of the smaller cities and towns throughout the Midwest. In Chicago, Germans certainly represented the largest immigrant group in numerical terms during the second half of the nineteenth century: in 1850, they numbered about 1,000, or 17 percent of Chicago's population; in 1870, about 52,000, or 17.5 percent; in 1900, about 170,000, or

10 percent. However, Chicago also attracted large numbers of Irish, English, Bohemian/Czech, and Scandinavian immigrants, and, after 1880, eastern European Jewish, Polish, Italian, and Greek immigrants. By the turn of the century, the number of German immigrants was declining significantly. Moreover, as elsewhere in North America, German immigrants were far from being a homogeneous group. They arrived throughout the nineteenth century from different regions in Germany and came for different reasons. Regional and religious differences often went hand in hand. German speakers were Protestant, Catholic, and even Jewish. German immigrants influenced by socialism, a strongly growing group in Chicago since the early 1870s, were openly atheist or agnostic; others were freethinkers. The borders of the German group in Chicago were constantly shifting, reflecting to some extent that even after 1871 Germany was rather a broad cultural concept than a national state with clearly defined borders. In the dynamic setting of Chicago, ethnic categories were not fixed. Germans overlapped with several other ethnic groups, especially from east-central Europe. Many Bohemian immigrants, for instance, spoke German, as did Austrians, some Poles and Scandinavians, and most Jews who arrived before the 1870s. In addition, immigrants who did not identify themselves as German were still categorized as Germans by others.

It is hardly surprising, therefore, that most attempts to lump together Germans and their numerous *Vereine* (associations), ranging from the Turners to many literary societies and religious congregations, were short lived. The so-called Beer Riot of 1855—a violent protest by German and Irish immigrants against a ban of the public sale and consumption of alcohol by the city—strengthened the cohesion of the German group. Conflicts over Prohibition laws were symbolic battlegrounds over the place of (German and Irish) immigrants in mid-nineteenth-century American society. In 1856, German immigrants led by Forty-Eighters organized a cultural center called the Deutsches Haus (German House), which served as a focal point for many of the German associations for several years before it lost its appeal. Many Germans in Chicago identified with the newly founded Republican Party. German opinion leaders in Chicago, especially the editors of the leading German daily, the *Illinois Staatszeitung* (Illinois State Newspaper), George Schneider, Eduard Schlaeger, and Lorenz Brentano (all Forty-Eighters) were prominent Republicans in Illinois.

During the Civil War, many German-born Chicagoans fought for a mostly German unit, the 82nd Illinois Volunteer Infantry Regiment, which was led by the famous Forty-Eighter Friedrich Hecker and later by the German Jewish Chicagoan Edward Salomon. The regiment, which fought at Gettysburg, included companies made up of Jewish and Scandinavian immigrants, respectively. The loose organization of the German group and its many facets made it inclusive for many groups, not least German-speaking Jews. Even though the small Jewish community in Chicago as such remained distinct from the German community project, individual Jews like banker Henry Greenebaum, lawyer Julius Rosenthal, and rabbi Emil Hirsch were among the leaders of the Chicago Germans. The huge 1871 German victory parade on the occasion of the end of the

Franco-Prussian War and German unification was organized in Rosenthal's office and led by Greenebaum. Like the Beer Riot of 1855 and the raising of the 82nd Illinois Regiment, the 1871 parade proved to be a rallying point for the heterogeneous German group.

German-speaking immigrants lived all over Chicago. During the 1850s and 1860s, the main German neighborhood was the Near North Side. Following the disastrous Chicago fire in 1871, many Germans moved farther to the north; during the 1880s and 1890s, ethnic German neighborhoods could be found in particular on the Northwest Side along Milwaukee Avenue. At first glance, the Chicago fire represents the worst-case scenario of social disorder in the modern American city. Large parts of Chicago burned down within a few hours, and thousands of people of all social backgrounds lost their homes. Federal troops were dispatched to Chicago to safeguard law and order. German immigrants were particularly hard-hit, as the fire destroyed in particular the German North Side and thus weakened the cohesion of the German immigrants in the city. The Chicago Relief and Aid Society discriminated against many immigrants, especially those who did not speak English. The philanthropic Deutsche Gesellschaft (German Society), in later years known as the German Aid Society, which had been established in 1854 to support immigrants from Germany, Austria, and Switzerland, could only assist a few of the worst-off victims of the fire.

Before the 1920s, most bakers, butchers, and brewery owners (and brewery workers) in Chicago were German immigrants. Several Germans "made it," becoming successful and wealthy businesspeople.

Even before the turn of the century, growing numbers of German immigrants rose into the middle class. But throughout the nineteenth century, most Germans were manual workers. Unlike other European immigrants in Chicago, a large proportion of the Germans arriving between the 1840s and 1870s were skilled in different fields, often having been trained as artisans. German women often worked as domestic servants, usually starting at a young age. German men and women arriving after the Civil War found jobs as industrial workers. During the 1870s, Socialist German immigrants led efforts to organize a radical workers' movement in the city, which was influenced to some extent by anarchist ideas. Chicago was still recovering from the fire when two serious recessions hit the nation in 1873 and in 1877, displacing hundreds of immigrant workers from their jobs. The recession of 1877 led to strikes and serious violence in Chicago, and again federal troops were brought in to quell the disturbances. The 1877 strikes were the first in a series which culminated in the 1886 Haymarket riot and the 1893 Pullman strike. In both instances Chicago saw the worst urban workers' riots in the nation's history.

Several cultural institutions in Chicago can be traced back to German founders, most famously the Chicago Symphony Orchestra, which was founded by conductor Theodor Thomas in 1891. During the nineteenth century Chicago counted numerous well-attended German-language theaters and many small German music and literary societies. Several of the largest German American newspapers, such as the *Illinois Staatszeitung* or the *Abendpost* (Evening Post), which had readers throughout the Midwest and beyond, were published in Chicago. After the turn of the century, however, the vibrant German ethnic life in Chicago gradually lost its momentum, becoming less German. The slow erosion of the still large German American community network from within was caused by the decreasing immigration of German speakers, the loss of German as a spoken language among the second generation, and declining membership in the *Vereine*.

In retrospect, the inherent structural weakness of the Chicago German community, which from the start had been more project than tangible reality, and the post-1900 erosion of German ethnic life mitigate the seemingly massive impact of the U.S. declaration of war against Germany in 1917. In Chicago, moreover, the anti-German campaign of 1917 must be seen within a specific interethnic political context. In 1914, leading Chicago Germans facing a growing disintegration of German ethnic life instrumentalized the war to rally Germans once again. They managed to bring thousands to the streets supporting the German cause. Throughout 1915, several large rallies were held in support of the German war effort. Although Jewish and Irish immigrants who opposed Russian and English oppression of their kin in Europe initially expressed sympathy, Polish and Czech immigrant leaders who were supporting efforts for national independence in Europe were deeply offended. A series of small, sometimes violent interethnic incidents paralleling to some extent the war in Europe ensued. In 1917, Poles and Czechs, now backed by official U.S. policy, took revenge for the Teutonic arrogance.

After World War I, Chicago Germans played a rather subdued role. The German *Vereinsleben* (activities of associations) did not entirely disappear but was organized much more inconspicuously than before 1900. The German-language *Abendpost,* for instance, was published into the 1950s. During the 1930s, the pro-Nazi German American Bund was active in Chicago, one of its most important centers. However, the impact of the Bund was limited, and the organization lost its appeal even before U.S. entry into World War II. As a result of persecution by the Nazis, several famous German and German Jewish emigrants moved to Chicago during the 1930s. Among them was the Bauhaus architect Ludwig Mies van der Rohe, who taught at the Illinois Institute of Technology and emerged as a leading proponent of the influential international style. Mies and his students played a major role in shaping the modern image of Chicago and, in fact, of most modern cities in the Western world with their office buildings. A number of influential intellectual and academic exiles from Germany taught and studied at the University of Chicago; for example, the historian Hans Rothfels, the physicist and Nobel Prize laureate James Franck, and Stefan Heym, who took a masters degree in the German Department during the 1930s and became a leading German writer after the war. During the 1960s, famous exile scholars like the theologian Paul Tillich and the philosopher Hannah Arendt taught at the University of Chicago.

Tobias Brinkmann

See also Addams, (Laura) Jane; Altgeld, John Peter; Anarchists; Bauhaus; Cincinnati; 82nd Illinois Volunteer Infantry Regiment; Forty-Eighters; German American Bund; Haymarket; Hecker, Friedrich; Heym, Stefan; Illinois; *Illinois Staatszeitung;* Intellectual Exile; Judaism, Reform (North America); Mies van der Rohe, Ludwig; Salomon, Edward S.; Socialist Labor Party

References and Further Reading

Avrich, Paul. *The Haymarket Tragedy.* Princeton: Princeton University Press, 1984.

Brinkmann, Tobias. "*Von der Gemeinde zur Community*": *Jüdische Einwanderer in Chicago, 1840–1900.* Osnabrück: Rasch, 2002.

Cronon, William. *Nature's Metropolis: Chicago and the Great West.* New York: W. W. Norton, 1991.

Holli, Melvin G. "German American Ethnic and Cultural Identity from 1890 Onward." In *Ethnic Chicago: A Multicultural Portrait.* Ed. Melvin G. Holli and Peter d'Alroy Jones. Grand Rapids: W. B. Eerdmans, 1995, 93–109.

Philpott, Thomas L. *The Slum and the Ghetto: Neighborhood Deterioration and Middle-Class Reform, Chicago, 1880–1930.* New York, Oxford: Oxford University Press, 1978.

Seeger, Eugen. *Chicago: Die Geschichte einer Wunderstadt.* Chicago: M. Sternand, 1892.

Seeger, Eugen, and Eduard Schlaeger. *Chicago: Entwickelung, Zerstörung, und Wiederaufbau.* Chicago: M. Stern, 1872.

Smith, Carl. *Urban Disorder and the Shape of Belief: The Great Chicago Fire, the Haymarket Bomb and the Model Town of Pullman.* Chicago: University of Chicago Press, 1995.

CHILE

During the middle of the nineteenth century, the Chilean government made a deliberate effort to recruit German immigrants to settle the sparsely populated south. Those settlers, together with individual urban dwellers (mostly businesspeople and professionals) who immigrated to Chile during the nineteenth and twentieth centuries and the descendants of both groups, constituted approximately 30,000 German-speaking residents by the mid-twentieth century. They included Chilean-born, naturalized, and permanent German residents. By the early twenty-first century, the German-language newspaper *Condor* reported a weekly readership of 15,000 to 20,000. This numerically small group has enjoyed remarkable economic success while retaining the German language, culture, and institutions, as a result of the tolerant Chilean state's absence of suppression of the language and cultural institutions of the Germans, or any other nationality, even during the two world wars.

Conquered by Spain in the sixteenth century, Chile declared its formal independence in 1818. During the colonial era, very few Germans entered. Bartholomé Flores (variously called Barthel Blümlein or Bartholomäus Blumen), a literate carpenter from Nuremberg in Spanish service, became alderman, legal counsel, and in 1549 treasurer in Santiago. Beginning in the early seventeenth century, German Jesuits and members of other religious orders entered the country. Prior to and shortly after Chile's declaration of independence, a trickle of German merchants settled in the urban areas, and by 1822 the first German trading company had been established in Valparaiso. Systematic immigration by Germans began around the mid-nineteenth century. Approximately 10,000 to 11,000 Germans entered Chile between 1850 and 1900. Half of those were married, and families with five or more children were not uncommon. Children born in Chile were, by law, considered Chilean citizens. By 1907, it was estimated that 30,000 Germans and their descendants lived in Chile. Proportionally, German immigrants were numerically unimportant. According to statistics from 1917 (Converse 1979, 302) most immigrants were Spanish, followed by Italian, German, British, and French immigrants.

Looking to Europe and North America, South Americans observed economic development based on healthy agriculture and rapid industrialization from the efforts of skilled and trained European farmers and artisans. This led the Argentine Juan Bautista Alberdi to utter his popular aphorism "to govern is to populate." The Chileans Benjamín Vicuña Mackenna and Vicente Pérez Rosales became instrumental in promoting liberal immigration policies and colonization projects beginning in the 1840s. Earlier, Bernhard Eunom Philippi (Bernardo Philippi), while in Prussian employ, collected flora and fauna, mapped Chile's south, and participated in the Chilean expedition to win the Straits of Magellan. He gained military honors, served temporarily as governor of that region, and proposed colonization of Chile's south by Germans to the Chilean government after exploring the densely forested areas of Llanquihue. Eventually appointed to Germany as official agent for immigration to Chile between 1848 and 1852, he recruited mostly from around Hesse Cassel, his home region. These settlers, on land purchased in and around Valdivia, were soon joined by groups from throughout Germany, arriving from Silesia, Württemberg, Westphalia, Brandenburg, Saxony, Hanover, and Hamburg. German Bohemians settled Nuevo Braunau.

In 1852, the Chilean Vicente Perez Rosales was sent to Germany as consul general, where he recruited additional colonists, especially among the middle class. He considered families more stable than single men and included the latter only if they were members of families. The first recruited and subsidized group consisted of 180–200 Catholic families who had agreed to pay their own way in exchange for a promise of land around Lake Llanquihue; loans and tax exemptions; and aid for German priests, teachers, and doctors to keep settlements homogeneous. However, land around Lake Llanquihue could not yet be reached, and the land around Valdivia was no longer free. Immigrants with capital had bought properties around Valdivia, built homes and shops, and engaged in trade and commerce, developing it into a thriving urban community. Additional ships arrived at the coastal Forts of Corral where the immigrants lived miserably in the fort's casemates until they finished building a road to Lake Llanquihue. Puerto Montt, on its southern edge, was established in 1853. Each family had to clear the forest to receive their parcels of land, credit, seed, oxen, a cow, and other supplies. By 1861, several communities had developed around the lake. Further north, the lands of the Frontera had originally been planned to remain in the hands of the indigenous population. Earlier, small, adjoining German settlements had failed because of the Indian rebellions of 1859. After successful military operations against the Mapuche (Araucanian) Indians, new colonization laws were passed to free Frontera land for settlement by Europeans, including Germans, who for the most part chose not to farm there.

A few smaller mixed groups, financed by the Chilean government, had been settled on the Chiloe Peninsula in 1895, but many of the Germans left by 1903 and, together with additional Germans and Europeans from throughout South America, established Huefel-Comuy at the edge of the Frontera between 1905 and 1912. In 1924 new colonization laws were passed, and the government settled Catholic Bavarians in

Peñaflor and several other small settlements. A private group of 230 from Siegburg an der Lahn bought land east of Parral in 1961. The Colonia Dignidad contributed to economic development of the area and assisted the indigenous population with modern farming. After the initial establishment of immigrant settlements in the south, the Germans and their descendants spread and by 1895 were found throughout Chile. After 1910 the purchase of land became more difficult.

In agriculture and trades, German immigrants and their descendants contributed to economic development. Ibero-Chilean preference for land in central Chile had facilitated German settlements in the south, where the landscapes resembled those of their homeland. In Chile as in most of South America, where huge but uncultivated landholdings and landless peasants were the rule, the German settlers introduced the concept of family farms. Agriculture flourished in the Lake District, and by 1932 the biggest farms belonged to families with German names in Valdivia, Puerto Montt, and Puerto Varas. The immigrants had brought limited financial assets but made up for that with human capital. Most of the farmers concentrated on beef cattle and dairy herds, followed later by hogs, and by 1924–1925 they produced 75 percent of Chilean butter, much meat, and enough hides to supply all of Valdivia's tanneries (Converse 1979, 317).

For the most part, the immigrants were literate and skilled. Prior to emigration, many had prepared themselves for their new lives in Chile by learning additional trades. The raw materials produced by farmers as well as the forests provided for the growth of industries: leather goods, shoe factories, lumber, sawmills and paper mills, grain mills, and breweries. Candles and, after the importation of bees, honey were often produced by women immigrants. Many of the goods had previously been imported at high prices. Finally, the raising of cattle and hogs resulted in the establishment of slaughterhouses and the production of meat products such as hams and sausages for exports.

German entrepreneurs flourished in many communities, especially in the hotel and restaurant business and machine and repair shops. Many of Chile's pharmacies and pharmaceutical businesses were run by German immigrants and their descendants. A long list of companies and merchant houses established in the late nineteenth and early twentieth centuries by German immigrants and their descendants were later joined by German branch firms. Immigrants not only provided but also promoted a market for German imports and sales.

During the two world wars, Allied statutory or black lists interrupted German Chilean, German, and other Axis businesses by imposing trade embargoes. In response, the German Chamber of Commerce (now Camara Chileno Alemana de Comercio e Industria) was established in 1916. After its temporary demise during World War II, it received its juridical persona or legal recognition in 1950, once again furthering German and Chilean trade.

The establishment of schools became imperative for the German settlers, who were aware that literacy contributed to the success of such small minority groups. In the absence of sufficient Chilean schools, particularly in the isolated areas of Chile's south and the Frontera region, the immigrants established fifty-two schools, which were primarily secular but included a few religious schools. Although they were financed primarily by German Chileans they were, with interruptions during the two world wars, subsidized by Germany with teachers and books.

Beginning in the early 1930s, German Chilean youth became targets of Nazi propaganda. With the active encouragement of teachers from Germany, most of the secular schools adopted Nazi curricula, and existing youth groups were modeled after the Hitler Youth. After 1938, the Chilean government insisted on compliance with state requirements (e.g., 85 percent of the teachers had to be Chilean citizens). A proposed Chilean law to establish Spanish as the only primary language, however, was defeated as being unconstitutional. In the 1970s, encouraged by resumed bonds with Germany and aid, the schools became socially responsive toward indigenous cultures and the disadvantaged. Still today, German private schools are renowned for providing an excellent multilingual education.

German was spoken almost exclusively in the isolated lake communities, but in mixed communities most Germans soon became bilingual, often mixing German and Spanish. During the twentieth century, the young began to prefer Spanish, but many Chileans of German descent are still able to converse in German. Although insisting on the additional use of Spanish in the schools, organizational protocols, and publications during World War II, the Chilean state never discouraged the use of German or any other foreign language.

In the south only a few German newspapers, except for some local and religious papers, succeeded between 1886 and 1928. Most news was spread by word of mouth. In urban central Chile, Valparaiso, and Santiago, the *Deutsche Zeitung fuer Chile* (German Newspaper for Chile) succeeded three earlier papers, including the first German paper in Valparaiso in 1870, and was published until diplomatic relations between Chile and Germany were severed in 1943. In 1938, the Deutsch-Chilenische Bund (DCB) or Liga Chilena-Alemana (German Chilean Association) began publication of *Condor*, combining its publication with several existing smaller papers, in the attempt to distance the German Chilean community from National Socialist Germany. For a while after1943, *Condor* faced difficulties, but it expanded and still publishes today as a weekly German-language paper.

Of about 20,000 to 30,000 German-speaking people living in Chile in the mid-1930s, approximately 60 percent were Protestant and 40 percent were Catholic. In part because of resistance by German bishops, Chile's demand for only Catholic immigrants soon changed. Although Chile permitted religious freedom, Protestant churches could not build towers or install bells. Catholic immigrants were served by priests and members of religious orders, including many German-speaking monks.

American aid helped build the first German Protestant church in Osorno in 1863. By the 1930s, local congregations had established about fifteen German Protestant congregations. Because of German subsidies and pastors sent by Germany, those Protestant congregations fell under the influence of the Foreign Office for Church Affairs of the Reich during the 1930s. After 1960 and the establishment of the Chilean Synod, the Protestants once again cooperated with the Protestant Church in Germany, this time in an ecumenical movement that emphasized social responsibility. Only one congregation in the south temporarily broke away in protest against such liberal changes. On the other hand, German Catholics were considered part of the Chilean Roman Catholic Church and participated in its activities from the time of their arrival in Chile. Communities established specific associations to support schools, churches, and hospitals. German freemasons helped establish the German Hospital in Valparaiso in 1877, and Hamburg merchants founded a hospital in Concepcion in 1897. In 1907 Puerto Varas established a hospital with German doctors and Mallinckrodt nuns and nurses. The large, modern German Hospital Aleman in Santiago opened in 1917, followed by additional hospitals throughout Chile, including in Colonia Dignidad. The statutes of the hospitals required that members of all confessions, nationalities, and both genders be served. Self-help organizations assisted widows, orphans, and stranded seamen and established voluntary insurance funds. Germans and other European immigrants organized voluntary fire departments, which had been almost unknown in South America.

Purely social, cultural, and recreational organizations were abundant. Almost all communities, rural and urban, had a local German club (*Deutscher Verein*), which provided *gemütliche,* or congenial ambience for social and cultural events. Some of the elegant urban clubs had libraries and dining facilities for business meetings as well as social or official meetings with Chileans. Women's clubs were involved in cultural and charitable activities, including the support of nursing homes. Singing clubs and choral and instrumental groups were common in most communities. Athletic and sports clubs, including gymnastics, soccer, rowing, hiking, bowling, and marksmanship, abounded.

German Chilean graduates of Chilean universities in Santiago, Valparaiso, and Concepcion founded fraternities to help maintain the German language. In the late 1930s, the members of the oldest and probably the most liberal pro-German but anti-Nazi fraternity, the Burschenschaft Araucania, became instrumental in preventing the worst excesses of Nazi influence and preserving traditional German Chilean institutions. After World War II, the fraternities concentrated on the young and Chile's social problems.

The Liga Chilena Alemana (German Chilean Association) had been created as an umbrella organization in 1916 in response to Allied propaganda and blacklists, to protect German Chilean institutions, especially the schools, to lobby for Chilean neutrality, and to protect the interests of German citizens. Nazi infiltration and ideology held the Liga and many of its member associations captive between the early 1930s and May 1938. Then, prudent German Chileans excluded German citizens and extricated the Liga, schools, organizations, and especially youth groups from Nazi control. After Chile's diplomatic break with Germany in 1943, the Spanish language was adopted for Liga protocols, and the bylaws were changed to conform to Chilean law. Nowadays, Liga still supports the German schools and promotes German Chilean cultural institutions and programs in an effort to preserve the positive vestiges of German culture.

Although German immigrants were not required to serve in the military, some German colonists and descendants did serve in the militia. Mostly they provided medical help in the Valparaiso German

Hospital during the 1891 Civil War. In that war, the German captain Emil Körner, hired in 1885 by the Chilean government to train the Chilean military, led troops of the winning Congressionalists, the faction German Chileans had not favored. He was promoted to general chief of staff and returned to Germany in 1910. During both world wars, some young German Chileans joined German citizens who left to serve in the German military, although it was illegal for the Chilean-born to do so.

Chile's tolerance not only promised but facilitated naturalization, while permitting dual citizenship. Naturalized German Chileans entered the civil service as municipal administrators (i.e., Puerto Montt and La Union), educators (e.g.,Valdivia), and mining engineers. Before the turn of the century, German Chileans were elected as mayors (i.e., Valparaiso and Osorno), aldermen (twelve of fifteen in Puerto Montt, four of ten in Osorno), and councilmen (Valparaiso and La Serena). By 1890, several sons of immigrants held seats in the Chilean congress. Although he was not a citizen, Bernhard Philippi was appointed governor of Magellan. After 1898, a few noncitizens were permitted to enter the civil service and hold municipal offices in special cases.

Christel Converse

See also German Migration to Latin America (1918–1933); German-Speaking Migration to the Americas; Philippi, Bernhard Eunom; Printing and Publishing

References and Further Reading

Blancpain, Jean-Pierre. *Les Allemands au Chili: 1816–1945.* Cologne: Böhlau Verlag, 1974.

Converse, Christel. "Die Deutschen in Chile." In *Die Deutschen in Lateinamerika.* Ed. Hartmut Fröschle. Tübingen: Erdmann Verlag, 1979, 301–372.

———. "Culture and Nationalism among the German-Chileans in the 1930s." *MACLAS: Latin American Essays,* no. 4 (April 1990): 117–124.

Converse, Christel Krause. "The German Immigrants and Their Descendants in Nineteenth-Century South America." MA thesis, DePaul University, 1974.

———. "The Rise and Fall of Nazi Influence among the German-Chileans." PhD diss., Georgetown University, 1990.

Tenenbaum, Barbara, ed. *Encyclopedia of Latin American History and Culture,* vol. 1, New York: Charles Scribner's Sons, 1996.

Young, George F. W. *Germans in Chile: Immigration and Colonization, 1849–1914.* New York: Center for Migration Studies, 1974.

CINCINNATI

Cincinnati is considered the the most Teutonic of American cities. Germans shaped Cincinnati's development from its earliest years. The frontier Ohio River fort Losantiville (1788) was strategic as German Baptists, or "Dunkers," who had come to Pennsylvania in 1719 and settled upriver at Columbia. David Ziegler, born in Heidelberg in 1748, moved to Pennsylvania before the American Revolution and then, having gained the rank of major in the Continental Army, commanded Fort Washington in 1790, the year the outpost was named Cincinnati. Martin Baum (1765–1831), from Alsace, arrived in 1795 via Maryland. By 1810, he had established a general store, a mill, and the first bank, sugar refinery, and iron foundry in the West, recruiting Germans from eastern cities. Baum's barge *Cincinnati* broke the round-trip speed record to New Orleans in 1811 before he invested in steamboats. He founded the Western Museum; a subscription library; schools; and the Society for the Promotion of Agriculture, Manufacturing, and Domestic Economy. Despite the 1818–1819 panic and mill fires in 1823 and 1835, Baum prospered as industry boomed by 1830 in the "Queen City of the West," incorporated as a city in 1819.

Germans made up 5 percent of the city in 1830 when immigration from Germany as well as from the East Coast escalated. The German population jumped from 23 to 27 percent from 1840 to 1850. Friedrich Hecker, German nationalist and hero of the failed 1848 revolution, arrived to cheering crowds in New York and then Cincinnati, where he settled, serving as a magnet for thousands of fellow Forty-Eighters.

Cincinnati became the nation's second-largest industrial city, its population swelled by arrivals from the Rhineland, Baden-Württemberg, and Bavaria. Working-class newcomers settled north of the center and east of the Miami–Erie Canal in 110 blocks dense with three-story brick tenements, townhouses, and shops intermingled with gardens and punctuated by church spires. Germans made up 60 percent in Uber dem Rhein (Over-the-Rhine), the German neighborhood in the city, and a fourth of the city's 115,435 inhabitants in 1850, occupying professions such as shopkeepers, bakers, tailors, and woodworkers. Tradespeople called "mechanics" made the city a printing and machine-tool center. The less skilled found jobs as the city became a pig-slaughtering and pork-packing center nicknamed "Porkopolis."

Germans who had been truck farmers around the city's periphery made Pleasant Ridge a suburb, attracting more Germans with life centered on the Evangelical Lutheran Church in the 1870s. They moved up the Millcreek Valley into Cor-

ryville, annexed to Cincinnati in 1870. From 1870 to 1890, German immigration numbers were high. The city had the nation's third-largest Germanic population, 45 percent, in 1900; only Hoboken (55.7 percent) and Milwaukee (64 percent) had a greater concentration of German residents. Twelve percent, or 38,308 of the 325,902 Cincinnatians, had been born in Germany. In 1900, the city listed over 200 German physicians and 167 lawyers, along with prominent industrialists, businesspeople, and politicians (Hurley 1982, 104). After World War I, immigration nearly stopped. During World War II and after, only a small number of German Jews who fled Nazi Germany; Danube Swabians, Pomeranians, and Silesians; and others displaced by Soviet occupation made their way to the city. The 1970 U.S. Census revealed German as the native language of 55,000 out of the city's 451,455.

Political Influence

David Ziegler won election as council president in 1802 as the village was incorporated, before it became a city. Martin Baum was elected mayor in 1807 and 1812. The city printed ordinances in German in the 1830s. Admitted to the bar in 1849, Johann Bernhard Stallo (1823–1900), who arrived from Oldenburg in 1839, became a Court of Common Pleas judge. After coming under attack from the nativist Know-Nothing Party in the 1840s, many Germans joined the new Republican Party after 1856. Know-Nothing xenophobia peaked in the 1850s, tainting local politics and erupting in violence with nativist cries of "Kill the Dutch" in 1855 as German militias barricaded Over-the-Rhine for three days of rioting. Know-Nothings failed to rid public schools of German. Liberals gained clout by electing ten of their members to City Council in 1852 and loosened Sabbatarian restrictions. Hecker and Stallo supported the largely German 9th Ohio Volunteer Infantry Regiment with 1,500 militia and Turnerites. Under Prussian officer August von Willich (1810–1878), *Die Neuner* (The Nines) was distinguished in the Civil War. Willich was honored in Washington Park by a 1873 portrait statue by Leopold Fettweis, inscribed in German, "1848. 1861. By word and deed [he fought] for the people's freedom in his old and new native lands."

Germans won many political offices. Gustav Tafel (1830–1908) was born in Munich and settled with his grandparents in Cincinnati in 1849. After working as a printer, he became the *Volksblatt* (People's Newspaper) city editor in 1855 while studying law. Admitted to the bar in 1858, he served as colonel in the 9th Ohio, before he won election to the state legislature in 1866. Elected mayor in 1897 on a "fusionist" ticket to modernize the water and sewer systems, he served one term, until 1900.

Wielert's Pavilion (1873), the leading beer garden, provided a *Stammtisch* (round table) as headquarters for George B. Cox, the Republican "boss" dominating local politics from 1884 to 1912, when Rudolph K. "Rud" Hynicka and August Herrman took over the "machine." Political groups also met in the Germans' Central Turner Hall behind Wielert's.

Charles Fleischmann (1835–1897), a German Jew who got rich from distilling liquor and yeast production, founded the Market National Bank, served as Ohio governor William McKinley's adviser, and became a prominent philanthropist. His son Julius (1872–1925) served as mayor (1900–1905), pledging businesslike management. He began free kindergartens in public schools and built the first public bathhouse in 1904. Leopold Markbreit (1842–1909) became mayor in 1908, continuing Fleischmann's progressive policies. Born in Vienna, he immigrated in 1848 and became a lawyer. After serving in the Civil War, he edited the *Volksblatt* for years after 1886 and served as waterworks commissioner (1896–1907) before Republicans chose him as mayoral candidate. When he died in office in 1909, the city staged tributes in German and English.

German Jew Frederick S. Spiegel (1858–1925) was a one-term Republican mayor (1914–1915). Born in Prussia and educated in a Westphalia gymnasium, he came via Alabama and graduated from the Cincinnati Law School while editing the *Freie Presse* (Free Press). He entered public service in positions including chairman of the Public School Committee on German language. While a judge of the Superior Court (1902–1913), Spiegel headed several *Vereine* (associations). Backed by the waning Cox machine, George Puchta (1860–1937), born in Cincinnati of German-born parents and a machine tools businessman, won the mayorality (1916–1917) with the largest plurality ever. Preoccupied with looming war, Puchta organized a municipal war council to support the federal effort before returning to his business.

Despite the Germanophobia during and after World War I, long-assimilated German American civic leaders regained prominence in politics after World War II. Edward Nicholas (Eddie) Waldvogel (1895–1954), a Catholic born in the city with a résumé of public positions and civic service, was elected mayor in 1953. Eugene

Ruehlmann, a Western Hills lawyer of German descent, was mayor from 1967 to 1971 and championed urban renewal. Gerald Norman (Jerry) Springer (1944–), the child of German Jewish parents who fled from Nazi Germany to New York, moved to Cincinnati after he had received a law degree in 1968. The liberal Democrat served on the City Council, had an interim mayoral term in 1974, and won election as mayor (1977–1978) before going on to a career as a TV talk show host. His 2003 decision not to run for Congress from his hometown won national coverage.

Diverse Religion

Local Germans were religiously divided— freethinkers, various Protestant sects, Catholics, and Jews. German and Swiss followers of Ulrich Zwingli founded Cincinnati's first German Protestant congregation, St. Johannes Kirche (Saint John's Church) in 1814 and built a Gothic church in 1868, later called St. John's Unitarian.

German liberals fought with orthodox Catholics and Protestants. Stallo led freethinkers in the legal fight to keep the Bible and hymns out of public schools in the 1830s. Celebrating Christmas in the German way was opposed by many Anglo-Saxon Protestants. A radical, anticlerical Socialist from Vienna, Frederick Hassaurek, became a leader of the *Freimännerverein* (Freemen's Society). His anti-Catholic attacks inflamed Turners to demonstrate against the papal nuncio's 1853 visit.

Wilhelm Nast (1807–1899), born in Stuttgart, immigrated in 1828 and converted to Methodism, bringing it to Cincinnati in 1835. He edited the weekly *Der Christliche Apologete (The Christian Apologist)* (1839–1894) to promote fundamentalism, Sabbatarianism, and temperance. Cincinnati became the home of German Methodism.

Northern Germans built the Deutsche Evangelische St. Paulus Kirche (St. Paul's Evangelical Church, 1850), with its steeple topped by a gilded rooster. The Deutsch Evangelisch Reformierte Salem's Kirche (Salem Evangelical Reformed Church, 1856) erected a German Gothic brick church in 1867, with its spire topped by a gilded Angel Gabriel. Concordia Lutheran (later Prince of Peace) built a brick Gothic church in 1871. Philippus Evangelical and Reformed Lutheran (1891) had a golden fist with finger pointing to heaven atop its church.

German Catholics founded Holy Trinity parish, including a school, in 1834. The Swiss-born priest Johann Martin Henni (1805–1881) founded St. Marien Kirche (St. Mary's Church) in 1842. German architect Franz Ignatz Erd built it, then the largest in the Ohio Valley, with stained glass from Bavaria and German paintings. Its 170-foot "broach spire" had the city's oldest public clock. Father Joseph Ferneding moved from St. Mary's to found St. Johannes parish in 1845 in a German Romanesque brick church and then the less affluent St. Paul's in the 1850s. *Henni's Wahrheits-Freund* (Henni's Friend of Truth, 1837) became the nation's first German Catholic newspaper to counter the anticlericalism of German freethinkers.

Although the city had only 150 Jews in 1830, an influx of 10,000 came from Germany by the 1860s. Most of the newly arrived migrants settled in the West End. Leaders championed "modernized" laws and ritual. Isaac Mayer Wise (1819–1900) left Bohemia for the United States in 1846.

He settled in Cincinnati in 1854 and made the city a center for Reform Judaism. Wise worked with the K. K. Ben Yeshurun (Children of God) synagogue, which was the home to the Minhag America prayer book and rabbinical education. Together with Rabbi Max Lilienthal, he published *The Israelite* (1854) and *Die Deborah* (1855–1903). They established rabbinical training at the Hebrew Union College (1876), which ordained the first American rabbis in 1883. Emphasizing "religious community" and ethical monotheism rather than the law "not adapted to the views and habits of modern civilization," they minimized ritual, held the Sunday rather than Saturday Sabbath, integrated women in family pews, and had mixed choirs. They eliminated keeping kosher and cultural traits that would make them "stand out" from the mainstream.

German Cultural Life

An 1838 law introduced German into public schools. Cincinnati's Germans used and preserved their language at home while speaking English in the outside world, thus making their urban culture bilingual. Although *Die Ohio Chronik* (The Ohio Chronicle) began publishing in 1826, most Germans read the *Tägliches Cincinnatier Volksblatt* (Daily Cincinnati People's Paper, 1836), the only German daily in the United States for almost a decade. There were three other German papers by 1850. Unionists preferred the *Arbeiterzeitung* (Worker's News Paper); radicals liked the *Republikaner* (Republican). A radical, anti-clerical Socialist, Frederick Hassaurek, fled to Cincinnati from Vienna in 1848 to publish *Hochwächter (The High Watchman)* "an organ for intellectual enlightenment and social reform." He later became editor of

the *Volksblatt,* which remained the major newspaper until World War I, survived only by the *Freie Presse* (Free Press, 1874).

Stallo fostered the German Reading and Culture Society (1844) after studying at St. Xavier College. German Freimännervereine (freethinkers' societies) organized Das Deutsche Institut (The German Institute, 1846), staging four plays a week until the Civil War. Stallo promulgated Hegelian philosophy through a study circle and the publication of his own books *The General Principles of the Philosophy of Nature* (1848), *State Creeds and Their Modern Apostles* (1872), and *Concepts and Theories of Modern Physics* (1881), earning renown in Germany as his era's most significant philosopher of science.

Heinrich Arminius Rattermann (1832–1923), who immigrated from Ankum in 1846, edited the monthly *Der Deutsche Pionier* (The German Pioneer, 1874–1885), which was published by the city's largest association (1869–1887), making it a top journal of German American culture and history. He also edited the *Deutsch-Amerikanisches Magazin* (German American Magazine) and contributed to literary life by writing forty-four books, hundreds of articles, and countless poems.

Friedrich Hecker organized the first American *Turnverein* (Turner Society, 1848) in Cincinnati to foster "refined humanity" through physical exercise and intellectual development, which had the motto *Mens sana in corpore sano* (a sound mind in a sound body). This concept goes back to the founder of the modern *German Turnerbewegung* (Gymnasts Movement), Friedrich Ludwig Jahn, who in 1811 amid Napoleonic invasions articulated a philosophy to prepare for democratic freedom. Hecker opened a small *Turnhalle* (Turner

Hall) in 1850 and then the large, central Turnhalle in 1859 with an athletic club, a concert room, and theater.

Germans formed the *Schützenverein* (Shooting Club) in 1831. Civil War veterans expanded the association, incorporated in 1868 with 250 members, each holding $500 in stock to buy a hill northwest of the city as a shooting park, or *Schützenbuckel*. Opened as a public beer garden, it had beer and wine cellars, a dance pavilion, swings, and bowling alleys. Germans held their annual *Schützenfest* there until 1873.

From the Haydn Society in 1822 and first *Männerchöre* (male chorus) in 1838, Germans enriched urban life with dozens of singing societies, bands, and orchestras. The first annual *Sängerfest* (singing festival) took place in 1849. Crowds enjoyed music of the German masters at the *Löwengarten* (Lion Garden, 1860–1872). Clara Baur (1835–1912), born in Württemberg, founded a Conservatory of Music in 1867 that was modeled after the Stuttgart Conservatory. Rattermann helped found the American *Sängerbund* (Association of Singing Clubs), wrote German opera librettos, and hosted a salon for intellectuals. The city's *Sängerbunds* built the *Sänger Fest-Halle* (1870) opposite Washington Park, with a seating capacity of 5,000. Germans crusaded to expand the use of their language in public schools. The Board of Education formed the German English Normal School in 1871 to train German-language teachers. By 1890, about half of all students studied German, although it was optional. The system had 175 German teachers in elementary schools and four in high schools by 1900, who reached over 18,000 pupils. Dr. Heinrich H. Fick (1849–1935), who came to Cincinnati in 1864, became assistant superintendent in 1901 and headed the German English Normal School until he retired in 1915. Fick devised a bilingual curriculum, the "Cincinnati Plan," used in many cities along with his textbooks.

German Americans created an extensive cultural and social network that was not well liked by their Anglo-Saxon neighbors. Germans faced hostility from the American Protestant Society, which disliked the recreational "Continental Sunday," called "a high carnival of drunkenness," and championed temperance to counter the German culture of beer. Germans successfully rallied against the "Puritan Sabbath" and Sunday closing laws: "Kamf gegen die Sabbathfrommelei" (Battle against the Puritan Sabbath). The 1890 Cincinnati City Directory listed 1,810 saloons, only a few non-German. For those living in cramped domestic quarters and even for the prosperous with parlors, such places provided informal, recreational "living rooms" as well as community centers.

Cincinnatians, including women and children, consumed 40 gallons of beer a year per capita in 1893, 24 over the national average. They drank during vaudeville at Hubert Heuck's *Volkstheater* (People's Theater, 1875). Georg Rapp's Highland House (1876) had panoramic views from its Mount Adams restaurant, beer garden, picnic grounds, concert hall, theater, and bowling facilities inside and outdoors for 8,000 at a time. Moritz Eichler's ornate Clifton House had extensive gardens, plus a concert hall and hotel. In that heyday, seventeen beer gardens staged concerts—Hildebrand's, Kissell's, Schickling's, and others. Wielert's Pavilion (1873), the most fashionable, boasted an immense interior and beer garden lined with busts of Ludwig van Beethoven, Johann Wolfgang

Goethe, Felix Mendelssohn-Bartholdy, Johann Wolfgang Amadeus Mozart, Friedrich Schiller, and Franz Schubert. Michael Brands's orchestra was the nucleus of the Cincinnati Symphony Orchestra (1895).

All prospered until World War I and its aftermath squelched Cincinnati's German culture for decades. Most Germans who arrived after World War II assimilated quickly, even more so than those before, although the *Verein der Donauschwaben* (Society of Swabs from the Danube) celebrated its first festival in 1956. Cincinnati hosted the Forty-first National Saengerfest in 1952. The roster of Cincinnati Symphony conductors reveals ongoing German influence—Fritz Reiner, Eugene Goossens, Max Rudolph, Thomas Schippers, and Michael Gielen. Even Jesus Lopez-Cobos, director in the 1990s, had been music director of the Berlin Opera before he came to Cincinnati.

Shaping the City

From frontier days, Germans shaped the city's infrastructure. Merchants formed the Covington and Cincinnati Bridge Company in 1846, hiring engineer John Augustus Roebling and his firm to build the first bridge over the Ohio River. Amos Shinkle, a coal merchant, expedited the project financially and politically in 1856. Construction stalled during the panic of 1857, as Irish workers quit and the Civil War intervened. The world's longest suspension bridge was completed in 1866 as 120,000 people, over half of Cincinnati's population, walked across it.

Andrew H. Ernst helped found the Cincinnati Horticultural Society (1843), which was responsible for major urban beautification, especially after the 1852 arrival of Prussian landscape gardener

A view from Covington, Kentucky, shows the Roebling suspension bridge spanning the Ohio River to Cincinnati. (Corbis)

Adolph Strauch (1822–1883), who designed estates in the new suburb of Clifton, redeveloped Spring Grove as a garden cemetery, and then created the city's first public parks in 1870 and 1872. Their friend, Andreas (Andrew) Erkenbrecher, founded the Association for the Acclimatization of Rare Birds. Supported by the local German press and advice from the Berlin zoologist Alfred Edmund Brehm, Erkenbrecher incorporated the Cincinnati Zoological Society (1873), modeled after the Frankfurt Zoo. Strauch advised German designer Theodore Findeisen on the layout. Animals were sent by Carl Hagenbeck in Hamburg. The nation's second zoological gardens opened in 1875, twice the size of that in Philadelphia, which had opened the year before. Hagenbeck's agent, Sol Stephan, helped spawn other American zoos, promoting Hagenbeck's idea of barless enclosures. Johann (John) Hauck, a brewer who came from Bergzabern in the

Palatinate in 1852, saved the bankrupt zoo after Erkenbrecher's death in 1885.

Architects Alfred Fellheimer and Stewart Wagner designed Union Terminal (1933), an art moderne masterpiece with an *infundibuliform* (funnel-shaped) interior, to handle 216 trains per day. Weinhold Reiss, born in Karlsruhe in 1886 and trained in art in Munich, designed its huge mosaic murals of Ohio settlement, transportation, and local industrial workers, executed by the Ravenna Mosaic studios of Berlin and New York. Some of them were moved to the airport in 1973.

German Beer Breweries

Immigrants imported the process of *lagering* beer developed in the 1830s by Gabriel Sedlmayr in Munich and Anton Dreher in Vienna, which used chilled processing to produce a carbonated brew lighter than English beers. By 1840, eight small Cincinnati breweries made Lagerbier. As more Germans immigrated, breweries grew to eleven in 1848, sixteen in 1856, and thirty-six in 1860, including six of the nation's twenty largest by 1870. Local production soared from 354,000 barrels (1 barrel holds 32 gallons) in 1870 to 656,000 in 1880 to 1,115,000 in 1890.

Christian Moerlein (1853) opened a barrel factory in 1862, which became the city's largest brewery by the 1880s, with buildings of German Romanesque Revival "round-arched style" in three Over-the-Rhine blocks. After Moerlein installed an ice machine in 1876, annual production leaped from 60,000 to 98,000 barrels. Moerlein opened a pioneering bottling plant in 1895 to ease shipment problems, advertising Old Jug-Lager Krug Bier as "Exhilarating, Stimulating, Re-Juvenating, Wholesome, Delicious and Pure." Its reputation

spread nationally in the 1890s, producing 350,000 barrels of "National Export" and "Old Jug Lager."

Conrad Windisch joined Gottlieb and Henry Muhlhauser to found the city's second-largest brewery in 1866, producing 175,000 barrels a year by 1890. Louis Hudepohl and Fred Kotte bought the Koehler Brewery in 1885. It had a hundred employees and annual production of 40,000 barrels in 1902 when Hudepohl died, leaving the business to his wife and five daughters, who carried on, shifting to make near beer and soft drinks during Prohibition and thus preserving one of the city's only three surviving breweries. Daughter Celia and her husband John O. Hesselbrock revived and automated it in 1932 as Hudepohl-Schoenling. Their Christian Moerlein brand became the first American beer to pass Germany's rigid purity law, the *Reinheitsgebot,* in 1983 (Hurley 1982, 190).

World War I and Its Impact

The Deutscher Staatsverband (German State Association) held its annual picnic in Chester Park on August 1, 1914, when Cincinnati's German American population learned about the outbreak of war. After a telegram was read that announced the declaration of war by Germany, all participants sang "Die Wacht am Rhein" *(The Watch on the Rhine).* Many recent emigrants supported imperial Germany's policies, but the German American establishment embraced American patriotism. The *Freie Presse* assailed Woodrow Wilson's neutrality and the German-Austrian-Hungarian Aid Society raised funds for "iron" for the Central Powers.

After the United States entered the war, Cincinnati's police banned German in public meetings; and many *Vereine* were closed. The City Council anglicized thirteen Germanic street names, from Bismarck to Montreal, Berlin to Woodward, Hamburg to Stonewall, Bremen to Republic, German to English, and so on. So did many families and societies. The German Mutual Insurance Company became Hamilton County Fire Insurance. Its statue of "Germania" was shrouded in black, draped with the American flag, then rechristened "Columbia," with "E Pluribus Unum" inscribed on her cape. The German National Bank took the name Lincoln. The Staatsverband became the American Citizens League. Vigilantes destroyed German inscriptions on buildings. The Alien Property Custodian seized suspect German businesses.

The American Protective League enforced a ban on German-composed music. The German Theater was closed. Public school students taking German dropped from 13,856 in 1916 to 7,546 in 1917. Ohio eliminated elementary German in 1918, firing most "Hun tongue" teachers and censoring those remaining. The library purged German books and periodicals from its shelves. Cincinnati's Germans spoke English in public and raised $95,000 for a 1918 Liberty Bonds Crusade. The *Volksblatt* folded in 1919 after raids by federal agents; the *Freie Presse* held on until 1924. The last German-language church, Philippus Protestant, adopted English in 1921.

Prohibition seemed the coup de grace in 1920, closing twenty-six breweries and countless saloons and beer gardens. Wielert's became the Gildenhaus Funeral Home. John Stenger's restaurant, founded in 1893, closed and was not revived by his son until 1934. The Gambrinus Stock Brewery, founded by Christian Boss in 1867, folded in 1922.

A unified German community never recovered its prewar vibrancy. German was not taught in elementary schools; but six teachers gave lessons in the Central *Turnhalle*. The Catholic Kolping Society revived the shooting sport in 1923 through the Schuetzenclub. Fifteen churches had services in German in 1935 and used the language in Sunday schools. Amusement parks revived German Days in the 1930s; Coney Island attracted 38,000 for one in 1938. The German Literary club met upstairs at the restaurant founded in 1872 by German-born baker Anton Grammer. The walls of this restaurant were decorated with *Wirtstube*-style murals of Rhineland landscapes in the 1940s. Today, the Downtown Council attracts thousands to a mid-September Oktoberfest of beer brats (bratwurst), metts (*Mettwurst*), and German music on Fountain Square. Even though the National Municipal League named Cincinnati an "All American City" in 1981, the city revived and retains its place as the most Teutonic of American cities.

Blanche M. G. Linden

See also American Civil War, German Participants in; Beer; Forty-Eighters; German Jewish Migration to the United States; Hecker, Friedrich; Judaism, Reform (North America); Landscape Architects, German American; Newspaper Press, German Language in the United States; Roebling, John Augustus and Washington Augustus; Strauch, Adolph; Turner Societies; Verein; Willich, August von; Wise, Isaac Mayer

References and Further Reading

Clubbe, John. *Cincinnati Observed: Architecture and History*. Columbus: Ohio State University Press, 1992.

Dobbert, Guido A. *The Disintegration of an Immigrant Community: The Cincinnati Germans, 1870–1920*. PhD diss., University of Chicago, 1965.

Engelhardt, George W. *Cincinnati: The Queen City, 1901.* Cincinnati: Young and Klein, 1982.

Hurley, Daniel. *Cincinnati: The Queen City.* Cincinnati: Cincinnati Historical Society, 1982.

Sarna, Jonathan D., and Nancy H. Klein. *The Jews of Cincinnati.* Cincinnati: Center for Study of the American Jewish Experience, 1989.

Tenner, Armin. *Cincinnati Sonst und Jetzt.* Cincinnati: Mecklenburg and Rosenthal, 1878.

Tolzmann, Don Heinrich. *The Cincinnati Germans after the Great War.* New York: Peter Lang, 1987.

Tolzmann, Don Heinrich, ed. *Festschrift: German-American Tricentennial Jubilee: Cincinnati 1983.* Cincinnati: Cincinnati Historical Society, 1982.

Wimberg, Robert J. *Cincinnati: Over-the-Rhine.* Cincinnati: Ohio Book Store, 1987.

CLUSS, ADOLF

b. July 14, 1825; Heilbronn am Neckar, Württemberg

d. July 24, 1905; Washington, D.C.

One of the leading architects, engineers, and city planners in nineteenth-century Washington, D.C., Adolf Cluss was also a social reformer and journalist. He fled Germany for the United States after taking part in the failed revolution of 1848. Cluss was born into a family of wealthy craftspeople and winegrowers. He attended school in Heilbronn and became a carpenter. In 1846, he was employed in Mainz as "second architect" at the Hessische Ludwigsbahn, Rhine-Hessen's first railroad. In Mainz, Cluss was involved in the Turner movement and organized the Arbeiterbildungsverein (Workers Educational Organization), which offered workers free classes and access to Socialist literature. He also contributed to *Der Democrat,* the weekly journal of the Arbeiterbildungsverein, and was one of three delegates from Mainz to the convention of the Frankfurt Parliament in 1848. Cluss had met Karl Marx and Friedrich Engels in 1847 and stayed in touch with them for many years, exchanging letters on an almost weekly basis. Until the failed revolution of 1848 forced Cluss to emigrate, he was a regular contributor (under the pseudonym of C. Lange) to the *Deutsche Brüssler Zeitung* (German Brussels Newspaper), a Communist biweekly newspaper that informed German refugees about democratic activities in Europe.

After arriving in the United States in September 1848, Cluss spent several months in New York City before his interest in politics brought him to Washington, D.C. His skills secured him employment with the U.S. Coastal Survey, and while stationed at the Washington Navy Yard, he attended sessions of the nearby U.S. Congress. Cluss lobbied for better working conditions in the Navy Yard. At the same time, he joined the left-liberal Washington *Turn-Verein* (Turner Association) and got involved with publishing its journal, the *Turn-Zeitung* (Turner Gazette); he also contributed numerous articles to political organs including the London *People's Paper* and the New York journal *Die Reform (The Reform).*

The second half of the 1850s was a turning point in Cluss's life. In 1855 he became an American citizen, and that year he joined the Treasury Department as a draftsman, which started his career as an official architect in the U.S. capital. Cluss married Rosa Schmidt, a fellow immigrant from his hometown, on February 8, 1859. His conflicts with other members of the German émigré community further contributed to his transformation from a German activist and social reformer to an architect who attempted to realize his reformist ideas through building, engineering, and urban planning.

In 1862 Cluss started his own architecture firm with Wilderich von Kammerhueber, another German immigrant. Although some of the early commissions were for the military, the office also designed the first public school building in Washington, D.C., the Wallach School.

Over the years, Cluss contributed as an innovative engineer and architect to Washington's system of free public schools, which would be unsurpassed in the nation. The excellence of his work was recognized in the United States and abroad. Cluss was awarded a Medal for Progress in education and school architecture at the World's Exposition in Vienna in 1873 for his design of Franklin School. His school designs also won prizes at international expositions in Philadelphia (1876), Paris (1878), and New Orleans (1884). Cluss's schools, which included many engineering innovations such as modern heating systems and light-filled classrooms, were seen as both functional and attractive and influenced architects into the early twentieth century.

As chief engineer of the Board of Public Works in the District of Columbia (since 1872), Cluss designed a modern sewer system and implemented comprehensive plans for a modernization of the city's gas and water infrastructure. He also pursued the "parking" of Washington's streets by narrowing roadways and planting trees and grass along wide avenues.

Among Cluss's many projects were eight churches with characteristic split-level plans (with classrooms on the ground level) and three major markets (Alexandria City Hall and Market House, Center Market, and Eastern Market). In the 1880s,

Adolf Cluss established himself as one of the most experienced and innovative museum architects in the United States. His designs included the Army Medical Museum, extensive exhibition spaces in the Agriculture and Patent Office buildings, and the reconstruction of the Smithsonian "castle." His architectural masterpiece was the National Museum (today the Arts and Industries Building) on the National Mall. It opened to the public in 1881 and was designed in a modernized Romanesque style that featured a red brick façade enlivened by colored glazed bricks that were meant to resemble woven cloth, perhaps inspired by Gottfried Semper's theory of textile as the original wall material.

There can be no doubt that Cluss's influence on Washington, D.C., architecture was decisive in the period after the Civil War, when the U.S. capital redefined itself and grew from a seat of government to a major national city. Shortly before Cluss's death, changing architectural tastes and new technological demands led to the replacement of most of his buildings. Cluss's signature Victorian red brick architecture gave way to a neoclassicism where marble and limestone were dominant. However, his impact is still visible today in the schools and row houses on Capitol Hill, as well as his designs on the National Mall.

Christof Mauch

See also Landscape Architects, German American

References and Further Reading

Beauchamp, Tanya Edward. "Adolph Cluss: An Architect in Washington during the Civil War and Reconstruction." *Records of the Columbia Historical Society* 48 (1971–1972).

Lessoff, Alan, and Christof Mauch, eds. *Adolf Cluss, Architect: From Germany to America.* New York: Berghahn Books, 2005.

COCA-COLA

After pharmacist John S. Pemberton invented a stimulating new soft drink in 1886, his carbonated and caffeinated creation quickly rose to national and worldwide prominence. It became not only an integral part of everyday life in the United States, but also the American national drink and a defining element of twentieth-century American culture. The drink, the brand's logo, and the Coca-Cola bottle, created by Alexander Samuelson in 1915, turned into symbols of consumerism and the American way of life. Admired by some, despised by others, Coca-Cola faces a large number of cultural critics who consider its enormous success to be the Coca-Colonization of the world. Both sides, however, agree that the success of Coca-Cola is evidence of the value and symbolic power of a worldwide and decades-long advertising campaign. The new concept of a brand was one of the most important product innovations in the history of the consumer society, and Coca-Cola paved the way for the new worldwide culture of brands.

In 1929, the first Coca-Cola vending machines were installed in Germany. Only one year later, the German branch of the Coca-Cola Company was founded in Essen. This company was an essential element in the economic and cultural Americanization of German society. Before World War I, Germans considered the United States to be a distant land of dreams, a place that held their hopes for freedom after emigration. This attitude changed with Germany's defeat and the arrival of American loans, companies, and products. After Germany's economy stabilized, American companies and products pushed their way into the German market.

Coca-Cola, Wrigley's Chewing Gum, and Kellogg's Corn Flakes became staples in the homes of affluent families. Their appearance fed the discourse about the place of American products in everyday life and about the advantages and disadvantages of Americanization. Even after 1933, American products were not banned but further constituted an integral part of German consumption. Initially, Coca-Cola with its advertisements promising leisure, freedom, and fun seemed to contrast the political and ideological climate of Nazi Germany. Subsequently, some Nazi dignitaries who considered the American soft drink to be un-German made their doubts public and demanded an end to the continuous presence of Coca-Cola. Nevertheless, the Coca-Cola Company developed and nurtured a close and friendly relationship with the German government. This became evident in the rare legal exception that allowed Coca-Cola to use bottles that did not comply with the standardized measurements set by the German Reichsflaschenverordnung (the imperial law about the standard measurements of bottles). Only between 1942 and 1949 was production of Coca-Cola inside Germany halted because of lack of raw materials.

Coca-Cola's big breakthrough in Germany came after World War II, when Coca-Cola plants followed U.S. soldiers who were stationed there. After the founding of the West German state and the Wirtschaftswunder (economic miracle), Coca-Cola won over a significant group of new customers with its slogan "Mach mal Pause!" (Take a Break!). This slogan captured the attention of millions of busy, hardworking West Germans who longed for joy after years of war, destruction, and reconstruction. This 1950s Coca-Cola slogan, repeated again and again in advertisements, reached an unprecedented level of fame by entering the German vocabulary as an unchangeable and oft-quoted saying. It is now used by German speakers to ask somebody to take a break from work and career or to sarcastically interrupt somebody's never-ending monologue. In the 1970s and 1980s, new English slogans, such as "Enjoy Coca-Cola" and "Coca-Cola is it," were introduced to customers who could then consider themselves "cooler" and happier because they were consuming the only "right" drink, the one everybody else was drinking.

After 1989 and the fall of the Berlin Wall, Coca-Cola expanded into the former German Democratic Republic (GDR). Even more than in post–World War II West German society, Coca-Cola was not just a drink in East Germany. It was considered a symbol of the triumph of Western capitalism, and the bottles and cans were collected as trophies. Drinking Coca-Cola in the former Eastern European Communist countries thus became a symbolic and reassuring act of integration into the Western world, and the substitute cola that had been produced for years in the GDR did not stand a chance.

Alexander Schug

See also Americanization; Chewing Gum; Consumerism; McDonald's Restaurant

References and Further Reading

Beyer, Chris H. *Coca-Cola Girls: An Advertising Art History.* Portland: Collectors Press, 2000.

Domentat, Tamara. *Coca-Cola, Jazz, und AFN: Berlin und die Amerikaner.* Berlin: Schwarzkopf und Schwarzkopf, 1995.

Rose, Rogger, and Patra McSharry Sevastiades, eds. *Coca-Cola Culture: Icons of Pop.* New York: Rosen, 1993.

Watters, Pat. *Coca-Cola: An Illustrated History.* Garden City, NY: Doubleday, 1978.

Coca-Cola's 1955 slogan "Mach mal Pause!" ("Take a Break!") captured the attention of millions of busy, hardworking West Germans who longed for joy after years of war, destruction, and reconstruction. (Deutsches Historisches Museum, Berlin)

COLOMBIAN GERMAN AIR TRANSPORT COMPANY

see Sociedad Colombo-Alemana de Transportes Aéreos

COMMITTEE ON PUBLIC INFORMATION

President Woodrow Wilson created the Committee on Public Information (CPI) by executive order on April 14, 1917, nine days after Congress declared war on Germany. The primary purpose of the CPI was to unify public opinion in favor of the war effort, explain the justification for U.S. entry into the military conflict, and to spread the message of the United States' selfless war aims across the North American continent, as well as Europe. Under the leadership of George Creel, a progressive and reform-minded newspaperman from Missouri, the CPI became a public relations agency that used every form of communication to bring the government's message to the people.

The CPI enlisted thousands of volunteers who educated Americans about the facts of the war and German militarism. Famous writers and leading historians prepared circulars and leaflets and supplied the nation's press with feature articles defining American ideals, purposes, and war aims. The Speaking Division sent famous speakers, including U.S. veterans, several Belgians, and the Blue Devils from coast to coast, describing life on the front and German atrocities. The Four-Minute Men, a group of 75,000 volunteer speakers, addressed audiences with brief four-minute speeches during reel changes in movie theaters and explained why the United States entered the war. Speeches, motion pictures, billboards, pamphlets, and cartoons presented the enemy, Germany, as a murderous aggressor and as an obstacle to the civilized world and justified U.S. entry into this global conflict as good fighting evil. This emotionally charged promotion of American values and nega-

tive portrayal of Germany not only created a willingness to sacrifice life and money for the war effort but also resulted in hatred and intolerance to everything German and un-American.

The CPI also established a Division of Work with the Foreign-Born to shape and unite the attitudes of the foreign-born. The CPI targeted immigrants from fourteen European countries, but German immigrants and their descendants received particular attention through the German Bureau. Creel enlisted famous immigrants as writers and speakers to combat ignorance about the United States and bring the truth about the war and American ideals to the foreign-born. These writers supplied the foreign-language press with articles about education, industry, religion, agriculture, and institutions to project a true picture of American democracy and its devotion to peace and unselfish aims in the war. Speakers and writers emphasized that the war was a fight with Wilhelm II and his government, not with the German people.

In October 1917 the CPI also established the Friends of German Democracy in the German Bureau for the purpose of keeping the German-born loyal to the United States. It appointed Franz Sigel, the son of the Civil War hero Franz Sigel, as its president to recognize the loyalty German Americans had demonstrated in the past. Prominent, loyal German American authors wrote pamphlets and articles, such as "Democracy, the Heritage of All," "German Militarism and Its German Accusers," "Lieber und Schurz: Two Loyal Americans of German Birth," "On Loyalty, Liberty, and Democracy," and "American War Aims and Peace Program," which reached an estimated 2 million German readers. The Friends of German Democracy also sent letters and appeals to groups in Switzerland, who were able to smuggle many of them into Germany. These articles aimed to incite opposition to the war and urged the people of Germany and Austria to overthrow their old rulers and to establish pro-democracy governments. At the same time, the German Bureau also collected valuable information on various German organizations and the German-language press in the United States to learn how German propaganda had been able to make headway and how the U.S. government might be able to stop it.

The CPI not only fought to unite American public opinion against Germany and for the war effort but also aimed to persuade world opinion in favor of the Allies. Creel and government officials believed that for years preceding the war, Germany had been secretly building a publicity machine, in the United States and elsewhere, designed to spread pictures of Germany's vast industrial, commercial, and military power and to spread lies about the United States. To counter this impact and to provide European countries with information explaining American ideals and war aims, the CPI opened offices and established wireless service throughout the world, including Mexico City, Paris, Bern, Rome, Madrid, Lisbon, Tokyo, and Beijing. President Wilson's speeches and CPI pamphlets, posters, and movies received worldwide circulation. Well-known authors such as Ida Tarbell and William Shepherd wrote short articles describing the nation's history and its social and industrial progress and emphasizing U.S. patriotism, self-sacrifice, and goodwill toward allied nations. Several articles also exposed German methods of propaganda. The Foreign Press Bureau translated and mailed them to the foreign press. The office in Bern, Switzerland, was one of the busiest. Getting news into the Swiss press appeared to be one of the best ways to get news into Germany because Germans read Swiss papers, German papers quoted from Swiss papers, and rumors circulated freely between Switzerland and Germany.

The CPI also had full control over the foreign distribution of American movies. By requiring foreign movie houses to purchase entertainment films with war pictures, the CPI was able to distribute the committee's own movies and became convinced that it ran the German propaganda film industry out of business. George Creel believed that the CPI succeeded in destroying the German misinterpretation of the United States as a materialist country and turned the most misunderstood nation in the world, the United States, into the most popular.

Petra Dewitt

See also Lieber, Francis; Schurz, Carl; Sigel, Franz; World War I; World War I and German Americans

References and Further Reading

Blakey, George T. *Historians on the Homefront: American Propagandists for the Great War.* Lexington: University Press of Kentucky, 1970.

Cornebise, Alfred E. *War as Advertised: The Four-Minute Men and America's Crusade, 1917–1918.* Philadelphia: American Philosophical Society, 1984.

Mock, James R. *Words That Won the War: The Story of the Committee on Public Information, 1917–1918.* Princeton: Princeton University Press, 1939.

Ross, Stewart Halsey. *Propaganda for War: How the United States Was Conditioned to Fight the Great War of 1914–1918.* Jefferson, NC: McFarland, 1996.

Vaughn, Stephen. *Holding Fast the Inner Lines: Democracy, Nationalism, and the Committee on Public Information.* Chapel Hill: University of North Carolina Press, 1980.

CONQUISTA

Germans played a minor but nevertheless notable role in the European expansion to the New World. In the first half of the sixteenth century, when Spain embarked on the conquest of the Central and South American mainland, merchant houses from the south German imperial cities of Augsburg and Nuremberg were among the most important bankers of the Spanish crown. In 1519, the Augsburg firms of Jacob Fugger and Bartholomäus Welser financed the election of Charles V as emperor of the Holy Roman Empire, and over the next three decades the Fuggers, Welsers, Herwart, and Sebastian Neidhart, among others, continued to advance large sums to the Spanish crown. These financial activities paved the way for direct participation in transatlantic commerce and the conquest of the South American continent.

Initially the German firms set up warehouses (factories) in Seville, the Spanish entrepôt for trade with the West Indies. In 1525 the printer Jacob Cromberger and his son-in-law Lazarus Nürnberger were the first Germans to receive permission to enter the American trade, which had until then been exclusively reserved for Spaniards. Lazarus Nürnberger sent agents to the island of Santo Domingo, where they exported sugar and precious metals and imported textiles, metal goods, and books. One of his agents on Santo Domingo, the carpenter Bartholomäus Blümel (Flores) from Nuremberg, traveled to Peru in 1536, accompanied Pedro de Valdivia on the expedition that led to the conquest of Chile (1540–1541), and acquired an extensive landed estate there. Lazarus Nürnberger also traded in pearls and slaves and represented the interests of leading south German merchant houses in Seville.

Even before Charles V opened the American trade to foreign merchants in 1526, the Welser representatives Ambrosius Talfinger and Georg Ehinger received permission to travel to the New World and establish a factory on Santo Domingo. In March 1528 Heinrich Ehinger and Hieronymus Sailer, acting for the Welsers, concluded a treaty with the emperor that gave them jurisdiction over the territory that became known as Venezuela. Ehinger and Sailer agreed to build three fortresses, found two towns, and settle each of them with 300 colonists. Moreover, they were to administer the province, distribute land among the colonists, and Christianize the Indians. In return, they received a number of special privileges. These included the right to transport 4,000 African slaves across the Atlantic, mining concessions in Venezuela and the neighboring province of Santa Marta, monopolies on Venezuela's foreign trade and on the production of salt, tariff reductions, and the right to send three commercial vessels directly from South America (Santo Domingo) to Flanders.

Since no documents concerning the Welsers' plans for Venezuela have been uncovered, their motives remain obscure. Some scholars have claimed that the firm, which was also engaged in mining activities in Saxony and Bohemia at the time, was primarily interested in exploiting precious metals, and the Welsers did send about fifty miners from Saxony to the New World. Others have argued that the firm's primary aim was the conquest of a rich Indian civilization. Most likely, the Welsers initially considered a range of economic options that also included plantation agriculture and trade in tropical goods. In any case, the Welsers' governors and military leaders in Venezuela—Ambrosius Talfinger, Nikolaus Federmann, Georg Hohermuth, and Philipp von Hutten—soon fixed their attention on the extraction of booty from the region's Indians and conducted a series of military expeditions into the interior parts of Venezuela and neighboring Colombia. The origins of the myth of El Dorado, an Indian cacique whose body was ritually covered with gold, lie in these *entradas,* which may have covered a total distance of 20,000 kilometers (about 12,500 miles).

Ambrosius Talfinger founded a settlement on Lake Maracaibo on his first expedition in 1530 and was killed on his second *entrada* to the interior parts of the province in 1532. Nikolaus Federmann, whose narrative of his first expedition through the *llanos* (lowlands) of southeastern Venezuela has survived, came closest to the goal of conquering a rich Indian people on his second *entrada,* when he succeeded in crossing the Andes to the Colombian valley of Cundinamarca. Unfortunately for him, the Spanish conquistador Goncalo Jiménez de Quesada had arrived there before. Although Quesada, Federmann, and a third conquistador, Sebastian de Benalcázar, jointly founded the city of Bogotá in 1539, Spain eventually rejected the Welsers' claims to Colombia. The last and longest of the expeditions was headed by Philipp von Hutten, a Franconian knight who had already participated in Georg Hohermuth's 1535–1538 foray, and Bartholomäus Welser the younger. Their arduous five-year journey (1541–1546) was a complete failure in economic terms, and upon their return the two leaders were murdered by rival Spanish officers. The crown suspended the Welsers' jurisdiction in 1546 and, after extensive litigation, officially took the province away from them a decade later.

Contemporaries like the clergyman Bartolomé de las Casas and later Spanish chroniclers have accused the Welser governors and captains general of treating the Indians with particular brutality and savageness. Although their accounts are often biased, the German conquistadors were certainly no less hesitant than their Spanish counterparts to recruit Indian laborers by force, torture and kill natives, and loot and burn their villages. During the 1530s and 1540s, the Indian slave trade was one of the major activities of the Venezuelan colonists. Why the Welsers abandoned other economic goals in favor of conquest remains a matter of debate, but there is evidence that the provincial governors, who were indebted to the firm and interested in quick profits, discouraged and even sabotaged a more farsighted policy of colonization and development.

Compared to the Welsers, the role of other German merchant houses in the conquest of South America was much more limited. For a while the Fuggers were interested in obtaining a South American province for themselves. In 1531 their representative Veit Hörl even negotiated a treaty with the Spanish crown that would have given the firm jurisdiction over present-day Chile, but it was never ratified. Four years later, the Nuremberg branch of the Welsers and the Augsburg merchant Sebastian Neidhart financed and outfitted two ships of the fleet that carried the Spanish conquistador Pedro de Mendoza and his army to the La Plata region. Mendoza founded the city of Buenos Aires but did not discover the rich Indian civilization he had hoped for. One

of the roughly eighty German participants, the Bavarian Ulrich Schmidel,
wrote an eyewitness account that constitutes one of the most important sources
on this phase of Spanish colonization.

Mark Häberlein

See also Mining; Schmidel, Ulrich
References and Further Reading
Bitterli, Urs. *Die Entdeckung Amerikas: Von
Kolumbus bis Alexander von Humboldt.*
Munich: C. H. Beck, 1991.
Friede, Juan. *Los Welser en la Conquista de
Venezuela.* Caracas: Ed. Edime, 1961.
Häberlein, Mark, and Johannes Burkhardt,
eds. *Die Welser: Neue Forschungen zur
Geschichte und Kultur des oberdeutschen
Handelshauses.* Berlin: Akademie Verlag,
2002.
Simmer, Götz. *Gold und Sklaven: Die Provinz
Venezuela zur Zeit der Welser-
Statthalterschaft, 1528–1556.* Berlin:
Wissenschaft und Technik-Verlag, 2000.

CONSTRUCTION
see Aufbau

CONSUMERISM

Consumer patterns in Germany and America have always been intertwined with
other aspects of culture. Objects and their
ownership don't just provide comfort, they
are also markers of identity. Thus throughout the twentieth century, the adoption of
American consumerism (or mass consumption), and its cultural repercussions, was a
subject of heated debate. It remains so
today. The close relationship between
American culture and mass consumption
has spurned argument over the nature of
Americanization in Germany, the level at
which Americanization is actually modernization, and whether counter-Americaniza-
tion measures are necessary in order to preserve cultural heritage.

The debate over mass consumption
first grew in Germany in the years following World War I, when industrialists
sought to discover how the United States
obtained its economic success. Proposals
for postwar economic reforms were rooted
in the Fordist model, but lifestyle and
mass consumption were also key to these
discussions as Germans sought to discover
at what level culture, as well as technology
and Tailorist methods of management,
was formative. It was believed that the key
to economic success also lay in American
culture and society. Thus class structure,
the emancipated American woman, and
daily life in the United States became subjects of popular debate. Critics of Americanization, however, feared the effects of
this change, as American culture became
increasingly associated with a monoto-
nous, homogenous mass consumption
that was held up against traditional German culture (*Kultur*). They were concerned over the way that popular culture
material such as American cinema and
jazz music challenged established social
and political orders. Film was one of the
most effective avenues through which
American consumer cultural values were
spread. By the 1920s, approximately 60
percent of the films shown in Germany
were American (Pells 1997, 16). Coinci-
dently, however, the transmission of
American values through cinema was ultimately both an American and a German
effort, beginning especially with the
growth of fascism in Germany. German
cinematic talent left to escape increasing

social restrictions or was imported to play roles in American films. The result is that German actors, directors, and composers played a large role in American cinematic classics of worldwide renown, such as *Gone With the Wind* (1939) and later *Casablanca* (1942).

The debate over consumerism continued between trade unionists and workers who saw mass consumption as democratizing and elites who feared such changes and rejected the effect mass consumption had on class structure. However, in the end, American influence was largely psychological only, affecting familial relationships and societal actions. It sold to Germans because it reflected many of the appealing American myths: individuality, success, progress, and optimism. Americanism was also attractive to Germans because it was not European; embracing American values was not seen as incorporating a competing culture but rather as a necessary, inevitable modernization. The American model need not be emulated outright but was something that could be modified to match German needs. Thus Weimar industry was modernized without the mass consumption stemming from expanded markets, decreased cost, and wage reform. Americanism was Germanized.

The influence of American consumerist practices changed in the years following World War II. As West German disposable incomes began to increase during the 1950s, people began to spend a larger percentage of their earnings on luxury items—many of which were made in the United States and associated with the American lifestyle. The purchase of an automobile, especially an American brand, became a symbol of the American dream.

Whereas car ownership had formerly been an outward expression of the sharply stratified nature of German society, ownership of cars by a wider group of people was indicative of the growing middle class. It was also during these postwar years that Germany became Coca-Cola's most important foreign market. American-style advertising paired Coke with cars and that which they represented. Change, however, did not result in the replacement of one culture with another. Though cultural critics such as Francis Otto Matthiessen were alarmed by his German students' preference for Coke over beer, drinks in Germany today that consist of a mixture of Coke and beer are an expression of the way American culture is reused after appropriation.

The American government influenced German consumer habits at this time, as American culture and corporations had gained a foothold in West Germany during the occupation years. The place of American culture in Germany was central to Germans' increasing acceptance of mass culture. Whereas Germans had rejected mass consumption after World War I because of its homogenizing, anticultural aspects, the United States had waged a cultural initiative in Europe following World War II that altered German conceptions of American culture. Marshall Plan funds, for instance, paid for the study of American industry and managerial methods; meanwhile, Germany was also the front line in the fight against communism in Europe and the center for many cultural initiatives by the United States. Cultural programs attempted not only to combat communism and sell democracy but also to change German habits and traditions. This is not to say that American culture has been absorbed in its original form or without protest. Germans who feared cultural change and a unifying of the masses (reminiscent of the Nazis' mass politics) suggested that the building of culture from the bottom up, as opposed to the top down, was inferior. Companies such as McDonald's and MTV have tailored their products to the German market and have been widely accepted. Nonetheless, anti-American sentiment in this regard continued throughout the twentieth century.

In the 1960s, American movies and music gained in popularity, especially through the adolescent revolt against high culture and their expression of this through consumer products. Ironically, American popular culture and consumer habits became for German youth a symbol for the opposition of America. It had come to be associated with hegemony in the world and thereby also the older German generation of the war years. German youth expressed their affinity with the rebellion of American minorities and youth through American products.

German and American consumption practices shifted again in the 1980s, when an improved German economy, coupled with the growing frustration of American consumers with the quality of products, increased sales of German products such as cars, which had long been associated with quality and craftsmanship. The influence of the German automotive industry in the United States is also apparent in late-century mergers and buyouts, such as the takeover by Germany's Mercedes of the major American car manufacturer Chrysler.

Meanwhile, in the media, the privatization of German television in the 1980s led to commercials and an increase in American programming; German media has been increasingly influential in the United States as well, however, as evidenced in purchases and partnership agreements between American and German media companies, such as the buying of American media outlets by Bertelsmann, one of Germany's largest media and publishing companies. Much like American producers of popular culture in Germany earlier in the decade, Bertelsmann tailors products to its American audience. The turn of the twenty-first century saw additional sales of iconic American media companies, such as the purchase of Jim Henson Company by Germany's EMTV and Merchandising AG, as well as growing competition between media giants such as Kirch Group in Germany and Rupert Murdoch in the United States. Thus it becomes more difficult to differentiate who is creating consumer and popular cultural products and from which side of the Atlantic Ocean the influence in mass consumption is coming.

Stacy Dorgan

See also Coca-Cola; Foreign Policy (U.S., 1949–1955), West Germany in; Hollywood; McDonald's Restaurant; Volkswagen Company and Its VW Beetle

References and Further Reading

Nolan, Mary. *Visions of Modernity: American Business and the Modernization of Germany.* New York: Oxford University Press, 1994.

Pells, Richard. *Not Like Us: How Europeans Have Loved, Hated, and Transformed American Culture since World War II.* New York: Basic Books, 1997.

Rogers, Everett M., and Francis Balle, eds. *The Media Revolution in America and in Western Europe.* Norwood, NJ: Ablex Publishing, 1985.

Willett, Ralph. *The Americanization of Germany, 1945–1949.* London: Routledge, 1989.

COOPERATIVE FOR AMERICAN REMITTANCE TO EUROPE/COUNCIL OF RELIEF AGENCIES LICENSED FOR OPERATION IN GERMANY

Both the Cooperative for American Remittance to Europe (CARE) and the Council of Relief Agencies Licensed for Operation in Germany (CRALOG) were founded after World War II. Their primary task was the collection of donations in the United States for the purpose of distributing humanitarian aid to Europe. CARE was an independent enterprise created by nongovernmental American aid societies, whereas CRALOG was an umbrella organization for a number of nongovernmental, mostly religious societies.

CRALOG and CARE used different methods to attract and collect donations. The organizations that participated in CRALOG collected food, clothing, and medication independently of CRALOG and transported the aid to the designated U.S. port, from which it was shipped to Germany. CRALOG was responsible for organizing the transport from these U.S. ports to Germany. In the case of CARE, U.S. citizens could order and pay for aid packages that CARE would send in their name to a specified receiver in Europe. Only a small number of CARE packages did not have a specified receiver and could therefore be distributed among Germans in need at the discretion of the welfare organizations.

American donations sent to Germany by CARE and CRALOG were distributed by nongovernmental social welfare organizations in Germany, most of which were affiliated with churches: Caritas with the Catholic Church and the Hilfswerk der Evangelischen Kirche in Deutschland (Aid Organization of the Evangelical Church in Germany) with the Protestant Church. The Deutsche Rote Kreuz (German Red Cross) and the Arbeiterwohlfahrt (Workers Social Welfare) did not play a major role in this distribution of American donations. Donations were delivered to social aid institutions, such as asylums or refugee camps, and to local donation centers. In the case of the donations provided by CRALOG, local authorities and representatives of the social welfare organizations and the church decided how to distribute the aid. Nevertheless, CRALOG insisted that the distribution had to follow American regulations. CARE packages were simply sent to the receiver by mail and picked up in local distribution centers. Recipients of these packages had to sign a statement acknowledging the receipt of the package. This receipt was mailed to the American donor as proof that his or her donations had been received by the individual specified.

From the beginning, CRALOG was established as an aid organization exclusively for Germany. CARE was responsible for all of Europe, although Eastern European countries did not receive or often rejected such help for political reasons. Nevertheless, far more than half of all CARE packages were destined for Germany. This geographic imbalance was due to the high number of German Americans involved in ordering CARE packages for their relatives in what was left of Germany.

In the two years from summer 1946 to summer 1948, CRALOG alone organized the shipment of more than 40,000 tons of aid to Germany. In this period, more than 3 million CARE packages were sent to Germany. When CRALOG closed down its operations in Germany in 1962, it had brought more than 300,000 tons of aid to

CARE packages for Reichsbahner. American donations sent to Germany by CARE and CRALOG were distributed by nongovernmental social welfare organizations in Germany, ca. 1945–1947. (Deutsches Historisches Museum, Berlin)

Germany. CARE, which shut down its operations in 1960, was responsible for having sent about 83,000 tons of aid to Germany. Although U.S. governmental aid in food and privately sent packages surpassed the donations given to Germans by CARE and CRALOG, both organizations played a decisive role in providing assistance for the people in need. In the beginning, large segments of the population received support from CARE and CRALOG. Later, after the foundation of the Federal Republic of Germany and the beginning of Germany's economic recovery, refugees from the former East Prussia, Pomerania, and Silesia as well as prisoners of war returning from Russian captivity received most of the aid.

Although CRALOG sent much more aid to Germany than CARE, it is the latter that is still remembered by Germans. The individualized approach to helping people in need provided the basis for personal relationships across the Atlantic. This was something that CRALOG could never achieve. Nevertheless, CRALOG and CARE contributed a great deal to the improvement of the relations between West Germany and the United States. From a German point of view, American help aided the emergence of positive feelings toward the former enemy among broad segments of West German society. Unfortunately, American aid also helped enshrine an attitude according to which Germans viewed themselves as victims of

National Socialism and avoided any discussion of guilt and responsibility. From an American point of view, the delivery of aid helped change the perception of Germany among Americans. Immediately after the war, a majority of the American population was in favor of harsh retribution. Reports about the desperate situation of the German population provided by CARE and CRALOG helped to change this attitude and were partially responsible for the reemergence of a positive perception of Germany as the new ally in a worldwide struggle against communism. The outbreak of the cold war led to increased pressure by the American government on nongovernmental aid organizations. Since the number of private donations decreased throughout the 1950s, CRALOG and CARE relied more and more on governmental financial support and thus became dependent on political decisions by the government. The American government continuously attempted—rather unsuccessfully—to use aid provided by CARE and CRALOG as a political weapon in the cold war.

Gabriele Lingelbach

See also Reconstruction of West Germany
References and Further Reading
McSweeney, Edward O. P. *Amerikanische Wohlfahrtshilfe für Deutschland, 1945–1950.* Freiburg: Caritas Verlag, 1950.
Sommer, Karl Ludwig. *Humanitäre Auslandshilfe als Brücke zu atlantischer Partnerschaft: CARE, CRALOG und die Entwicklung der deutsch-amerikanischen Beziehungen nach Ende des Zweiten Weltkriegs.* Bremen: Selbstverlag des Staatsarchivs Bremen, 1999.

COUNCIL FOR A DEMOCRATIC GERMANY

The Council for a Democratic Germany (CDG) was founded in New York City in May 1944 by German émigrés with different political affiliations in order to add an organized voice of "the other Germany" to the American public wartime debate and in the hope of influencing the official U.S. planning for postwar Germany. Its purpose was not to prefigure a kind of government-in-exile, but rather to advocate a constructive European-wide peace settlement based on continued Allied cooperation. The groups' organizing committee comprised nineteen left-liberal political and cultural representatives (among them Bertolt Brecht, Hermann Budzislawski, and Paul Hagen) under the chairmanship of the Protestant theologian Paul Tillich. The sixty cosigners of the council's original declaration included a wide range of German artists, academics, religious representatives, and political—especially labor—activists. Party affiliations ranged from the Catholic Center Party through various liberal parties to Socialists and Communists (e.g., Friedrich Baerwald, Ernst Bloch, Lion Feuchtwanger, Paul Hertz, Fritz Kortner, Peter Lorre, Heinrich Mann, Erwin Piscator, Wolfgang Stresemann, and Carl Zuckmayer). Although primarily an organization of emigrants and refugees, the council was publicly supported by a group of American intellectuals long active in public campaigns against the Third Reich and favoring a constructive peace with defeated Germany (John Dewey, Horace M. Kallen, Reinhold Niebuhr, Dorothy Thompson, Rabbi Jonah B. Wise, and others).

The council had a significant precursor in an earlier German American advocacy group with which it shared both personnel and political aims: the American Friends for German Freedom (AFGF), with its indefatigable research director Karl Frank, alias Paul Hagen (who represented the Socialist Neu-Beginnen, or "New Beginning" group), as well as Max Lerner, Dorothy Thompson, Thomas Mann, and Paul Tillich as prominent executive members and Reinhold Niebuhr as chairman. Preceding the CDG by almost a decade, the AFGF had its origins in left-liberal intellectual and Jewish European–dominated trade union circles. The AFGF made significant contributions to both public and official debates on the Third Reich through its substantive research output, based on extensive contacts in the German underground, and its regular publications. Many of its members never quite gave up hope for a popular revolt within Germany against the Nazi terror and in general insisted on that nation's own ability for democratic renewal.

Like the AFGF, the council continued to fight in the public debate of 1944–1945 on two fronts: against both the Moscow-inspired German Communists and the American hard-liners on the German question, the "Vansittartists." Responding directly to the enunciations of the Nationalkommitee Freies Deutschland (NKFD, or National Committee for a Free Germany), established in Moscow in 1943, the Socialist and liberal exiles in the United States rejected the Moscow group's direct appeal to the German army as falling far short of the necessary democratization. In its public declarations the council accepted a collective German responsibility for the Nazi crimes, including the need for restitution. It was in similar agreement with Allied war plans in its indictment of Prussian German militarism. The council insisted, however, on a distinction between the Nazis and their supporters and the German people themselves, clinging to the hope that the latter would, at least in the final phase of the war, join in the defeat of Nazism. The reconstruction of a democratic Germany should be left to Germans themselves. The council strongly argued against any plans for dismemberment and partitioning, as first discussed in Tehran, as well as the kind of deindustrialization that the Morgenthau Plan envisioned. Instead it held out the vision of a supranational European unity as a prerequisite for postwar peace, anticipating continued cooperation within the international anti-Hitler coalition and expecting that Anglo-American liberal democracy would be supplemented by farther-reaching social welfare measures. For a few intense months, committees and subcommittees of the council drafted memoranda for the political, economic, and cultural reorganization of Germany's postwar democracy. By 1945, however, the council, which had never attained sufficient public or official attention, faltered under the combined pressure of a general realization of the extent of German war crimes and the first signs of inter-Allied tension. In contrast to its Soviet counterpart, the NKFD, the council did not become an instrument of U.S. policy toward Germany; indeed, the Roosevelt administration for the most part ignored it, just as it rejected all substantive contacts with any German opposition to the Nazi regime. The late arrival and feeble voice of the council on the American scene illustrates that German exiles were hardly a politically relevant force.

Michaela Hoenicke Moore

See also *Aufbau;* Brecht, Bertolt; Fromm, Erich; Intellectual Exile; Lorre, Peter; Mann, Thomas; Morgenthau Plan; Neumann, Franz L.; Tehran Conference; Thompson, Dorothy; U.S. Plans for Postwar Germany; Vansittartism; Zuckmayer, Carl

References and Further Reading

Koebner, Thomas, Gert Sautermeister, and Sigrid Schneider, eds. *Deutschland nach Hitler: Zukunftspläne im Exil und aus der Besatzungszeit, 1939–1949.* Opladen: Westdeutscher Verlag, 1987.

Langkau-Alex, Ursula, and Thomas M. Ruprecht, eds. *Was Soll Aus Deutschland Werden? Der Council for a Democratic Germany in New York, 1944–1945.* Frankfurt: Campus Verlag, 1995.

Radkau, Joachim. *Die deutsche Emigration in den USA: Ihr Einfluss auf die amerikanische Europapolitik, 1933–1945.* Düsseldorf: Bertelsmann, 1971.

DARMSTAEDTERS (THE FORTY)

Darmstaedters, or "The Forty," were a group of thirty-four young men from the county of Baden in Germany, who emigrated to the United States in 1847 to form a utopian/Communist settlement in Texas called "Bettina." About 130 idealistic, utopian communities of all types were established in the United States between 1663 and 1860. Most of these communities were located in Ohio and the upper Mississippi River valleys, the Great Lakes region, and the mid-Atlantic. Bettina was the one-hundred-and-twenty-fourth—the first in Texas but not the last.

The United States in general and Texas especially had inspired young German idealists for years. With his romantic description of Texas and the heroic deeds of the Texans in their struggle for independence, Charles Sealsfield had pointed the way for those who were looking for a better place to live. His novel *Das Cajütenbuch oder nationale Charakteristiken* (The Cabin Book, or National Characteristics) was first published anonymously in two volumes in Zurich, Switzerland, in 1841. The novel was received with great enthusiasm.

Five men emerged as the guiding spirits of the Darmstaedters: Gustav Schleicher, Ferdinand von Herff, Hermann Spiess, Friedrich Schenck, and Julius Wagner. Outwardly the Darmstaedter (or Gesellschaft der Vierziger [Society of the Forty], as they were called sometimes, too, because of their original number), were represented by Spiess and von Herff, who had originally founded this group seven years earlier. Their first idea had been to establish a German colony in Wisconsin or Iowa, but contact with the Verein zum Schutze deutscher Einwanderer in Texas (Society for the Protection of German Immigrants in Texas, or Adelsverein) made Spiess and von Herff change their plans. They knew, however, that their Communist "touch" would probably alienate the leading men of the Adelsverein. This was true, as the secretary of the Adelsverein, Dr. Ernst Grosse, had written in 1846 that the governments were afraid of the ghost of communism. For this reason they did not use the word "Communist" to describe their projected settlement in public while they were still in Germany. Count Carl of Castell-Castell from the Adelsverein, Hermann Spiess, and Ferdinand von Herff signed a contract in Wiesbaden on February 11, 1847, which promised the group free transport to their land, free food until their first harvest, 320 acres of free land of their own choice on the grant of the Adelsverein for everyone, and free tools and materials for farming and construction for every settler. To guarantee every one of the Darmstaedter a place to live in Texas, this group was given 500 acres of land on the grant land of the Adelsverein, wherever they chose, for free. In case the settlement plans failed, another 500 acres would be given this group for free. The contract also stated that the group of the Forty under the leadership of Spiess and von Herff was independent from the Adelsverein and therefore not under the control of the society's officials in Texas. According to the contract, Spiess and von Herff were allowed to enlist other German immigrants to join them. Bringing a group of 600 settlers or more would establish the right of the Forty to settle permanently on the land of the Adelsverein legally.

With the help of the Adelsverein, young men from various backgrounds and with varying levels of education sailed from Hamburg to Galveston in May 1847, moved over land to New Braunfels, and from there traveled to the land they had been promised on the north bank of the Llano River on the Fisher-Miller Grant—not far from Fredericksburg, Texas, another German immigrant settlement. Having arrived on this spot on October 1, 1847, they started to build log cabins and called the place Bettina—in honor of the woman who had become one of their guiding spirits, the German author and social visionary Bettina von Arnim. From the beginning, the Forty had divided the work according to the various skills of each member. Some went on hunting trips to provide the group with meat. Other members cut trees, mended the houses, washed the dishes, and worked in the fields. After a short while, though, the group began to disintegrate, and more and more members left. By 1850 the Darmstaedters had been dissolved. Some had returned to Germany, others had moved to various other states of the union, and a few remained in Texas, where some gained prominence, such as Ferdinand von Herff; Gustav Schleicher, who became Texas's senator in Washington, D.C.; Friedrich Schenck; and Jacob Küchler. The reason for Bettina's failure was mainly internal discord. Having based their settlement project on Communist ideas as articulated in Étienne Cabet's philosophical novel *Voyage en Icarie: roman philosophique et social* (Voyage to Icaria, a philosophical and social novel), published in Paris in 1840, they could not agree on a fair distribution of responsibilities and products. Thus, the "forty" became one of the many idealistic Socialist communities in the United States in the nineteenth century that failed shortly after its establishment. Bettina is commemorated, along with the nearby *Adelsverein* settlements of Castell and Leiningen, by a state historical marker placed in 1964 on the north side of the Llano River across from Castell.

Andreas Reichstein

See also Adelsverein; Fredericksburg, Texas; New Braunfels, Texas; Sealsfield, Charles; Texas; Weitling, Wilhelm

References and Further Reading

Bestor, Arthur Eugene, Jr. *Backwoods Utopias: The Sectarian and Owenite Phases of Communitarian Socialism in America, 1663–1829.* Philadelphia: University of Pennsylvania Press, 1950.

Lich, Glen E. *The German Texans.* San Antonio: University of Texas Institute of Texan Cultures, 1981.

Reichstein, Andreas. *German Pioneers on the American Frontier.* Denton: University of North Texas Press, 2001.

DAVIS, ANGELA YVONNE
b. January 26, 1944; Birmingham, Alabama

American cultural theorist, scholar, activist, and advocate of civil rights for African Americans in the United States.

Angela Davis was largely influenced by the ideas of her mentor, Herbert Marcuse. In return, she influenced and inspired the student movement in the Federal Republic of Germany (FRG) and was held in high regard by the German Democratic Republic (GDR) for her fight for civil rights and work for the Communist cause.

Her parents, Frank and Sally Davis, were teachers and had many Communist friends who brought Angela in contact with Communist youth groups, which she joined. She left home at the age of fifteen after she received a scholarship from the American Friends Southern Negro Student Committee to attend Elisabeth Irwin, an integrated private high school in New York, where she began to study Socialist and Communist philosophies. She was particularly interested in mass movements designed to overthrow political domination by elites.

In 1961 Davis won a scholarship to Brandeis University, where she studied French literature. Her junior year she studied at the Sorbonne. Back in Brandeis for her senior year in 1964, she read philosophy with Marcuse, who became her graduate adviser and mentor. His notion, that only independent intellectuals could become revolutionary leaders, was readily accepted and used by the student movement in the United States and Europe. Marcuse introduced Davis to the neo-Marxist theories of the Frankfurt School and sent her to the Institute for Social Research in Frankfurt am Main after her graduation. There she studied with Marcuse's former colleagues, Theodor Adorno, Jürgen Habermas, and Oskar Negt, from 1965 to 1967. Living with Socialist student leaders in the so-called Factory she experienced the heyday of the German student movement. While studying in West Germany, she repeatedly visited the GDR, where she met representatives of the Communist Party (CP) of the United States.

Away from home, she closely followed the emergence of the civil rights movement. After her return to the United States, Davis worked on her doctoral dissertation under the supervision of Marcuse, who was then teaching at the University of California at San Diego. She became politically active with the Black Panthers, the Student Non-Violent Coordinating Committee, and Ron Karenga's US-organization in graduate school. In 1968, she joined the CP of the United States and committed herself to the work in the all-black section called the "Che Lumumba Club," In order to fulfill the requirements of her doctorate, Davis had to teach for one year and was appointed to the faculty at the University of California at Los Angeles in 1969. After learning of her membership in the CP, the governing body of the university, the Board of Regents, and the governor of California, Ronald Reagan, wanted her out of the university. After a battle in court, Davis was dismissed. In 1970 Davis was charged with conspiracy, kidnapping, and homicide because one of her friends, Jonathan Jackson, had used guns registered in her name in an unsuccessful attempt to free a prisoner during a court session in the Marin County Center in San Rafael, California, on Aug 7. After Davis had been arrested, a worldwide campaign began for her defense. Angela Davis Solidarity Committees had been founded in East and West Germany. At school, East German kids drew pictures of her, signed them with "Freedom for Angela Davis," and sent them to the president of the United States, Richard Nixon. In West Germany, the Angela Davis Solidarity Committee in Frankfurt am Main staged a petition to President Nixon to free her.

On June 4, 1972, the jury acquitted her of all charges. Angela Davis became a symbol for the struggle of the "other," leftist America in the GDR. Kindergartens were decorated with her picture; schools were named after her. When Davis was finally set free, East Germans felt that they had accomplished something. When she came to participate in the Tenth World Youth Games in 1973 in East Berlin, which were held under the motto "Anti-imperialist Solidarity, Peace, and Friendship," she was at the center of the celebration. These games, also labeled "red Woodstock," attracted 8 million visitors with 25,000 international participants. They were to demonstrate East Germany's new openness to the world.

Davis's mentor, Marcuse, had supported the solidarity campaign on behalf of Angela Davis after she was arrested. He spoke at the Frankfurt am Main solidarity conference organized for her by the Offenbach Socialist Office, the largest independent group of the New Left in West Germany. However, he disagreed with her orthodox communism, which did not allow for criticism of Stalinism in Eastern Europe. For Davis, this issue was complicated since the Eastern European Communist countries had supported her struggle for freedom.

After her release from prison, Davis taught black philosophy and women's studies at San Francisco State College, Stanford University, and Claremont College. In 1980 and 1984 she ran on the Communist Party ticket for the vice presidency. Since 1991 she has been teaching history of consciousness at the University of California. In 1994, she received the distinguished honor of an appointment to the University of California Presidential Chair in African American and Feminist Studies. She left the CP in the same year, when she realized that that body could not be reformed and freed from doctrinaire thinking. To fill the void, Davis focused her energies on the Conference Committees for Democracy and Socialism in the United States that she cofounded. In an interview with *Neues Deutschland* (New Germany) in 2003, she described the solidarity, especially from East Germans, that she had experienced during her time in prison, as a major motivation in her ongoing fight for her political and social activism. In 2004, Angela Davis was a tenured professor teaching the history of consciousness at the University of California at Santa Cruz, an interdisciplinary program that encompasses philosophy, literature, and history. In Germany, Angela Davis Solidarity Committees, like the Frankfurt am Main one, are still active and engage in the ongoing fight against political oppression, though their influence is very limited. Angela Davis's legacy as symbol of the "other" America is still important in the former GDR.

Christiane Rösch

See also Adorno, Theodor Wiesengrund; Frankfurt School; Marcuse, Herbert

References and Further Reading

Davis, Angela Yvonne. *If They Come in the Morning: Voices of Resistance*. New York: Third Press, 1971.

————. *Angela Davis: An Autobiography.* New York: International Publishers, 1984.

Marcuse, Herbert. *Die Studentenbewegung und ihre Folgen: Nachgelassene Schriften.* Vol. 4. Springe: Verlag zu Klampen, 2004.

Nadelson, Regina. *Who Is Angela Davis? The Biography of a Revolutionary.* New York: P. H. Wyden, 1972.

DAWES PLAN

A U.S.-led plan to revive the German economy so that Germany could pay the reparations it owed the Allies as a result of losing World War I, the Dawes Plan was the result of the work of a committee of economic experts appointed by the Allied Reparations Commission in November 1923. Named for its chairman, American financier Charles G. Dawes, the Dawes Committee issued a report in April 1924 that called for lower reparations payments as part of a comprehensive reform of the German economy. Never envisioned as a long-range solution for Germany's economic problems, the Dawes Plan provided stabilizing reforms that enabled the German economy to grow and prosper, allowing Germany to make regular reparations payments to the Allies, primarily Britain and France, who in turn made war debt payments to the United States. The Dawes Plan operated until 1929, when it was replaced by the Young Plan, a new U.S.-led effort to reduce Germany's reparations burden. By the time the Young Plan began, however, the effects of the Depression, which had originated in the United States, had spread to Germany, ending the economic boom of the late 1920s and creating the conditions for the electoral successes of the National Socialist German Worker's Party (NSDAP).

The Dawes Plan was borne out of the international financial situation created by World War I, which saw the United States emerge as the world's dominant economic power, enabled Britain and France to emerge victorious but financially exhausted, and left Germany in political and economic chaos. Article 231 of the Treaty of Versailles required Germany to accept responsibility for starting the war and causing all the damages suffered by the Allied and Associated (the United States) governments during the conflict. As a result of this "war guilt" clause, Germany was required to pay reparations for all the damages it inflicted upon the civilian populations of the Allied and Associated powers. On April 27, 1921, the Allied Reparations Commission announced at its London Conference that Germany must pay a total reparations bill of 132 billion gold marks ($32 billion). The Allies had already determined that Germany would pay the majority of reparations (52 percent) to France, Britain would receive 22 percent, Italy 10 percent, and Belgium 8 percent; while the lesser Allied nations received varying percentages of the remaining total. Allied experts believed the German economy could tolerate the expense of the reparations, which could be met through in-kind and cash payments, the latter being raised by a combination of new taxes and spending reductions.

The experts were correct in theory but wrong in practice. A politically and economically stable Germany could have made the scheduled payments, but the Weimar Republic in 1920 was neither: the republic defeated a left-wing rebellion in 1919, survived a right-wing coup attempt in 1920, and inherited a large budget

President and Mrs. Coolidge, standing on steps beside Mr. and Mrs. Charles Gates Dawes, June 30, 1924. (Library of Congress)

deficit and highly inflated currency from the former imperial regime, which used deficit spending to finance the war. Hated by the Left and the Right, the republic was also held in contempt by much of the general population, who blamed it for conducting Germany's surrender to the Allies and agreeing to the onerous terms of the Versailles Treaty, especially the "war guilt" clause that forced Germany to pay the massive reparations debt. Given this attitude, it was unlikely that Germany would move quickly to fulfill its reparations obligations—any German government that tried to relieve this debt by raising taxes would not survive for long. Instead, successive Weimar governments resorted to inflation as a means of raising cash to pay off debt.

This strategy seemed to work at first: the German economy expanded with the initial injection of new money, and in August 1921 the German government paid the first installment of 1 billion marks as demanded by the terms of payment of the "London Ultimatum," as the Reparation Commission's plan of April 1921 came to be called by the Germans. As inflation increased, however, Germany received less and less value for the marks it sold on the international currency market, where it had been buying foreign currency to pay reparations. At the end of 1921, the centrist government of Chancellor Joseph Wirth asked the Allies for a moratorium on reparations as the mark dropped in value to 192 to the dollar. The Reparations Commission finally agreed to a moratorium on monetary payments in November 1922 after the Wirth government, which fell that month, reported that new payments were impossible given the terrible state of the mark, which now stood at 3,500 to the dollar. France, however, insisted that Germany continue to make payments in kind. In January 1923, after the Germans failed to deliver a portion of the in-kind payments on time, the French government of Premier Raymond Poincare ordered troops, to occupy the Ruhr industrial region along with troops from Belgium.

As the occupation progressed, the German government, now led by Chancellor Wilhelm Cuno, adopted a policy of "passive resistance" that encouraged Germans living in the Ruhr to refuse to work for the occupiers, who were forced to bring in their own workers to run German factories. Although a popular reaction that encouraged national unity, passive resistance led to economic disaster in Germany: the already heavily inflated mark spiraled into hyperinflation when the Reichsbank declared it could no longer risk using Germany's dwindling gold reserves to support the worthless currency, which the Cuno government continued to print in order to support the millions of Germans now unemployed due to passive resistance. By August 1923, when the Cuno government was replaced by a cabinet led by Gustav Stresemann, the mark had fallen to 3.5 million to the dollar; it would reach 160 million to the dollar in September and drop to 4.2 trillion to the dollar before the Stresemann government began to bring inflation under control in November.

The collapse of the mark ensured that Germany would not be able to resume reparations payments, intensifying an international financial crisis that began with the German reparations defaults of 1922. Without reparations, the Allies argued they could not afford to pay on the $10.3 billion war debt they owed the United States, whose citizens demanded their government collect the debt. In 1923, that government was led by the Republican Warren G. Harding (died August 2, 1923) and Calvin Coolidge, whose secretary of state, Charles Evans Hughes, realized that Allied war debt repayment depended on solving the reparations issue. As early as December 1922, Hughes had endorsed the idea of turning over the problem of German reparations to a committee of financial experts, including Americans, who would develop a plan for German payment based on Germany's ability to pay. The inclusion of Americans on such a committee was somewhat controversial, given the fact that American politicians, beginning with Woodrow Wilson, refused to equate the payment of reparations with the issue of Allied war debts, which the American people believed should be paid whether or not the Germans could make reparations payments to the Allies. Hughes's idea received little attention from the Allies until the fall of 1923, when the crisis of the German economy was at its worst.

On November 20, 1923, the Allied Reparations Commission created two committees made up of experts from the United States, Britain, France, Italy, and Belgium, who were entrusted with the task of proposing solutions to the German economic crisis in order to establish a manageable system of reparations payments. The first and more important of the two committees was headed by Charles G. Dawes, an American banker and future vice president of the

United States, and included another American, Owen D. Young, among its members. The Dawes Committee was supposed to devise a plan to balance the German budget and stabilize the mark. Meeting for the first time on January 14, 1924, the Dawes Committee went on to hold fifty-three meetings until April 9, 1924, when the committee delivered its final report. Dubbed the "Dawes Plan" by the press, the committee's report stressed economic rather than political solutions to Germany's problems: an annual system of lower reparations payments, new taxes and financial reforms aimed at balancing Germany's budget, a reorganization of the Reichsbank, a gold-based German currency, and a series of international loans (mostly from the United States) to Germany.

The Dawes Plan emphasized that a German recovery was contingent on maintaining the economic unity of Germany. This point was clearly a criticism of the Franco-Belgian occupation of the Ruhr and the continued Allied occupation of the Rhineland. With their own country in financial crisis, the French finally agreed to withdraw their troops from the Ruhr in August 1925 (Belgium left as well), a year after the formal adoption of the Dawes Plan by the Allies and Germany. The Dawes Plan's reforms stabilized the German economy and enabled the Weimar Republic to experience a period of substantial industrial growth from 1925 to 1929. The U.S.-backed loans allowed Germany to make its required annual reparations payments to the Allies, who in turn used the reparations money to make payments on the war debt they owed to the Americans. This system began to collapse, however, with the coming of the Great Depression in 1929, which encouraged the Allies

and the United States to adopt the Young Plan that year. Named for its chairman and former member of the Dawes Committee , Owen D. Young, the Young Plan drastically reduced the total German reparations bill, but it had little effect on the Depression, which ravaged the German economy in 1930. The NSDAP benefited from the unpopularity of the Young Plan and the popular discontent brought on by the Depression to win big in the Reichstag elections of 1930, becoming the second-largest political party in Germany.

R. Boyd Murphree

See also Great Depression; Treaty of Versailles; World War I
References and Further Reading
Dawes, Rufus C. *The Dawes Plan in the Making.* Indianapolis: Bobbs-Merrill, 1925.
Ellis, L. Ethan. *Republican Foreign Policy, 1921–1933.* New Brunswick, N.J.: Rutgers University Press, 1968.
Hardach, Karl. *The Political Economy of Germany in the Twentieth Century.* Berkeley: University of California Press, 1980.
Schuker, Stephen A. *The End of French Predominance in Europe: The Financial Crisis of 1924 and the Adoption of the Dawes Plan.* Chapel Hill: University of North Carolina Press, 1976.

DECKERT, FRIEDRICH KARL EMIL

b. February 26, 1848; Taucha, Saxony
d. October 1, 1916; Dornholzhausen, Hesse

German geographer of North America.

Before entering the University of Leipzig to study geography, Emil Deckert worked as a teacher. In 1883, he finished his graduate studies with the defense of his doctoral thesis on the creation of railway networks in Germany. After having received his doctoral degree, Deckert dedicated himself to research on trade and colonial geography. In 1885 he published his book *Die Kolonialreiche und Kolonisationsprojekte der Gegenwart* (Colonial Empires and Colonial Projects of Our Days). From 1884 to 1885 he embarked on his first extensive trip through North America. Once home in Germany, he resumed teaching and then later published the popular science magazine *Globus* from 1888 to 1890. Herein Deckert published several articles about the United States on topics such as North American caves and the Great Salt Lake. In 1891 he decided to return to North America, this time accompanied by his family. Until 1899 he moved around, acquainting himself with the subcontinent. While still in North America he published several regional-cultural studies (e.g., *Die neue Welt* [The New World], 1892; *Cuba,* 1899) and several essays about the climate, geomorphology, hydrography, and cultural, infrastructural, and economic-geographical aspects of life in North America, Mexico, and the West Indies. In 1892, Deckert reprinted a selection of his earlier articles in his book *Die Neue Welt: Reiseskizzen aus dem Norden und Süden der Vereinigten Staaten sowie aus Canada und Mexiko* (The New World: Travel Sketches from the North and South of the United States, Canada, and Mexico). Deckert was recognized by his colleagues as the "best German expert on North America," and Wilhelm Sievers asked him to write the part on North America for his *Allgemeine Länderkunde* (General Regional Geography, 1904). This particular volume, first published in 1904 and reprinted several times, became the standard German work on North America. As such, it enabled

Deckert to pursue an academic career. In 1906 he was appointed professor for economic geography (*Wirtschaftsgeographie*) at the Academy of Social and Economic Sciences in Frankfurt am Main, where he taught until his death in 1916. Before his death, he published his last book, *Die Länder Nordamerikas in ihrer wirtschaftsgeographischen Ausrüstung* (The Geographic-Economic Character of North America's Countries, 1916). No other German geographer before World War I devoted himself so intensively to the exploration and investigation of North America.

Heinz Peter Brogiato

See also Sievers, Wilhelm
References and Further Reading
Maull, Otto. "Emil Deckert." *Geographische Zeitschrift* 23 (1917): 57–62.
Roemer, Hans. "Friedrich Karl Emil Deckert." *Neue Deutsche Biographie.* Berlin: Duncker andand Humblot, 1957, 3:549.

DENAZIFICATION

The policy of eliminating all traces of National Socialism (NS) from postwar Germany through public and private sector purges; the most controversial of all U.S. policies in its zone of occupation.

Pursued between 1945 and 1948 by the four occupying powers (the United States, Great Britain, the Soviet Union, and France), U.S. denazification policy was initially the most sweeping and punitive. Denazification was enormously unpopular among Germans, and by 1952, the West German government had authorized the reinstatement of thousands of Germans who had lost their positions in the purges and formally terminated denazification.

During the war, the United States, Great Britain, and the Soviet Union agreed that postwar Germany would be democratized, demilitarized, decartelized, and denazified. After the war, however, each occupying power (which by then included France) pursued denazification in different ways, their respective policies shaped by three factors: (1) the manner in which each occupier administered its zone; (2) its particular conceptions of National Socialism's relationship to German society; and (3) the emerging conflict between the wartime Allies. U.S. and Soviet policies were initially the most extensive and ideology driven, though their guiding assumptions about German society and their ultimate objectives were very different. France, and especially Great Britain, tended to take a more pragmatic and often more lenient approach.

In 1945, most U.S. policymakers expected a brief occupation. Given tremendous domestic political pressure to demobilize and the U.S. Army's unwillingness to assume long-term responsibility for civil affairs in occupied Germany, U.S. officials decided that the Germans themselves would have to bear the bulk of the responsibility for their nation's physical, political, and economic reconstruction. Yet they also assumed that a democratic future and lasting peace depended upon the elimination of all traces of NS from German society. U.S. denazification policy mandated either the automatic arrest or removal of a given individual from public or private sector employment, based on whether he or she had belonged to the NSDAP or had supported the dictatorship in more than a "nominal" manner. This policy of categorical removals reflected a conception of NS as having its foundations mainly in Germany's most influential institutions: the party, the state (which included the educational establishment), the military, and industry. In practice, however, all adult Germans were to be subject to the denazification policy.

In the very first stages of the occupation, denazification was only one of the many responsibilities assigned to local military government detachments. Soon, however, "Special Branch" units were created to handle the purges. Every adult German was required to complete a lengthy questionnaire (*Fragebogen*), detailing the subject's personal, professional, and political past. To discourage falsification, the questionnaires themselves contained the warning that the Allies had possession of NSDAP records, against which answers would be checked. Occupation and counterintelligence officials would then review the completed questionnaires and make a recommendation for retention or dismissal. By June 1946, Special Branch teams had collected 1,613,000 questionnaires and had ordered the barring or removal from employment of 373,762 persons.

The sheer magnitude of the purges, the inability of the military government to handle the workload, and much negative publicity in the American press led the military governor, U.S. Army general Lucius D. Clay, to hand over primary responsibility for denazification to the Germans. By June 1946, 316 local civilian tribunals (*Spruchkammern*) had been created, with anti- or at least non-Nazi Germans selected to preside over the cases and pass judgments. Regional German Ministries for Political Liberation provided the main oversight of the tribunals, though the verdicts were subject to approval by U.S. officials. Once again, every adult (some 13.5 million people in the American zone) had to fill out a background questionnaire (the *Meldebogen*, a much shorter version of the *Fragebogen*) and submit it to his or her local *Spruchkammer.* The tribunal would place the defendant in one of five categories: (1) major offenders; (2)activists, militarists, and profiteers ("Belastet"); (3) less incriminated; (4) followers or fellow travelers ("Mitlaeufer"); and (5) exonerated. Most defendants were categorized as "followers." Penalties ranged from short prison terms to temporary barring from employment to nominal fines.

From the beginning, the policy suffered from many problems, above all that of reconciling the desire for a brief occupation with the perceived necessity of an extensive purge. This dilemma divided U.S. officials, many of whom viewed the purges as obstructing physical and political reconstruction, whereas others believed an uncompromising purge was a necessary step toward a stable and peaceful postwar Germany. Hence policy enforcement was often uneven as occupation officials with differing conceptions of Germany's past and future struggled to maintain security, restore civic life, and carry out denazification.

The sheer magnitude of the program also presented insurmountable difficulties. Millions of files and hundreds of thousands of cases had to be processed, and there were simply too few qualified U.S. and German personnel available to do the job. The vagaries of policy enforcement in occupied Germany led to many negative press reports in the United States about the "failures" of denazification. Such reports pressured Clay to widen the scope of the purges in 1945, which in turn exacerbated the administrative burden and heightened animosity among the Germans.

The unpopularity of the purges among Germans was yet another major problem. Prominent German intellectuals

and church officials labeled the policy unjust, and it was ridiculed in the German press. Many held that denazification amounted to a charge of "collective guilt" and did not take into account the complexities of life under a dictatorship. Many also believed that numerous criminals had been allowed to go free, whereas those with allegedly little or even no real connection to NS were prosecuted. The new democratic German political leadership in the western zones—most notably Konrad Adenauer—understood that the objects of denazification proceedings were now their constituents and pressured U.S. authorities to bring the program to an end. Not surprisingly, then, within only a few years of West Germany's creation in 1949, the new government in Bonn allowed those who had lost their positions in the purges to regain their jobs and ended the denazification program altogether.

The *Spruchkammer* process also suffered from a number of fundamental weaknesses. The caseload remained overwhelmingly large, and U.S. officials noted a lack of qualified Germans committed to carrying out the letter of the law. The accused relied on affidavits (known derisively as *Persilscheine,* after a popular brand of detergent) from mutually reinforcing personal networks, thus distorting the evidentiary basis for making reasonably objective judgments. Above all, the use of affidavits turned denazification from a means of removing former Nazis from influential positions in society into a political and legal whitewash. Thousands of former Nazis who underwent a *Spruchkammer* trial could thereafter be reinstated to their former jobs and would be under no compulsion to account for or discuss their pasts in public.

Finally, the emerging cold war between the former wartime Allies compromised the Allies' original intentions with regard to the purges. The U.S., British, and Soviet governments, for instance, raced to obtain former Nazi intelligence officers and scientists for their respective military, scientific, and commercial establishments. As four-power agreement over Germany's future failed to materialize, the Americans, British, and French on the one side and the Soviets on the other sought to secure the allegiance of Germans in their respective occupation zones. This meant far less emphasis on reckoning with the past in the form of unpopular war crimes trials and denazification and a greater emphasis on reconciliation and reconstruction. This development, combined with the tribunal process many flaws, led the United States to relinquish oversight of denazification in 1948.

Steven Remy

See also Nuremberg Trials; U.S. Plans for Postwar Germany; World War II
References and Further Reading
Boehling, Rebecca. *A Question of Priorities: Democratic Reform and Economic Recovery in Postwar Germany.* Providence, RI: Berghahn Books, 1996.
Bower, Tom. *Blind Eye to Murder: Britain, America, and the Purging of Nazi Germany—A Pledge Betrayed.* London: Little, Brown, 1995.
Frei, Norbert. *Adenauer's Germany and the Nazi Past: The Politics of Amnesty and Integration.* New York: Columbia University Press, 2002.
Remy, Steven P. *The Heidelberg Myth: The Nazification and Denazification of a German University.* Cambridge: Harvard University Press, 2002.
Vollnhals, Clemens, ed. *Entnazifizierung: Politische Säuberung und Rehabilitierung in den vier Besatzungszonen 1945–1949.* Munich: Deutscher Taschenbuch Verlag, 1991.

DIESELDORFF, ERWIN PAUL
b. 1868 Birthplace: unknown
d. 1940 Place of death: unknown

Erwin Paul Dieseldorff, a native of Hamburg, was one of the wealthiest and most influential coffee planters and merchants in the Alta Verapaz region of Guatemala in the early twentieth century. Before migrating to Guatemala in 1888, he had been trained in the international trading firm of his uncle, C. W. Dieseldorff, in London. In Central America he began his career working for another uncle, H. R. Dieseldorff, who had a mercantile business in Cobán, the regional capital of the Alta Verapaz, and imported consumer goods and ironware from Birmingham and Manchester. In addition, he volunteered at several German coffee estates (*fincas*) and learned how to grow coffee. Endowed with a substantial inheritance, Dieseldorff soon became one of the largest estate owners in the Alta Verapaz. Around 1897 the Dieseldorff family, which included several brothers and nephews, already owned about 52,000 acres and 600,000 coffee trees and operated coffee-processing facilities (*beneficios*) in Cobán, San Pedro Carchá, and Panzós. The value of their land was estimated at 750,000 German Reichsmark. Dieseldorff continued to expand his estate in the following decades, and the family was among the few Germans who escaped expropriation by the Guatemalan government during World War II.

In addition to his business activities, Dieseldorff had a lively interest in science and archaeology. During his early years in Guatemala, he accompanied the geographer Karl Theodor Sapper on some of his expeditions through Central America. His travel experiences strengthened his interest in botany and archaeology. He collected and studied medical plants in the Alta Verapaz and experimented with their commercial production. In 1908 he published a guidebook for prospective coffee planters in the northern regions of Guatemala. Three volumes on the culture and religion of the ancient Maya civilizations were published in Germany between 1926 and 1933. Dieseldorff also wrote several articles on Maya archaeology.

His personal papers, scientific collections, and business correspondence are located in the Dieseldorff collection of Tulane University Library in New Orleans. They also include historic manuscripts like a sixteenth-century copy of the "Golden Legend" of the Kekchí Maya. Moreover, he collected dictionaries of Indian languages, manuscripts of Indian dance dramas, and drawings of Mayan ruins. He corresponded with German geographers, ethnologists, and archaeologists like Karl Theodor Sapper and Eduard Seler, as well as with Frederic W. Putnam (1839–1915), director of the Peabody Museum archives at Harvard University.

Michaela Schmölz-Häberlein

See also Sapper Family

References and Further Reading

Náñez Falcón, Guillermo. "Erwin Paul Dieseldorff, German Entrepreneur in the Alta Verapaz of Guatemala, 1889–1937." PhD diss., Tulane University, 1970.

Schmölz-Häberlein, Michaela. *Die Grenzen des Caudillismo: Die Modernisierung des guatemaltekischen Staates unter Jorge Ubico 1931–1944: Eine regionalgeschichtliche Studie am Beispiel der Alta Verapaz.* Frankfurt am Main: Peter Lang, 1993.

Wagner, Regina. *Los alemanes en Guatemala, 1828–1944.* Guatemala City: Editorial IDEA, 1991.

DIETERLE, WILLIAM
b. July 15, 1893; Ludwigshafen am Rhein, (Bavarian Palatinate), Bavaria
d. December 8, 1972; Ottobrunn, Bavaria

U.S. film director, born Wilhelm Dieterle

An eclectic filmmaker and producer, Wilhelm Dieterle grew up in Germany and began his artistic career as an actor for Max Reinhardt, onstage in Berlin, in 1921 (*A Midsummer Night's Dream*) and onscreen for director Leopold Jessner and Paul Leni (*Hintertreppe* [*Backstairs*], 1921), Paul Leni (*Das Wachsfigurenkabinett* [*Waxworks*], 1924), Friedrich Wilhelm Murnau (playing Valentin in *Faust,* 1926), and many others, appearing in some sixty silent films mainly between 1920 and 1930. In Germany, Wilhelm Dieterle directed fifteen films from 1923 to 1931. He was the first director who ever produced a biographical film, *Ludwig der Zweite, König von Bayern* (Ludwig II, King of Bavaria, 1929).

In 1930, Wilhelm Dieterle emigrated to the United States, where he released more than fifty feature films under the Americanized name of William Dieterle. The genres varied: dramas, musicals, adaptations from classics (*The Hunchback of Notre-Dame,* 1939), and film noir (*Portrait of Jennie,* 1948). In 1935, William Dieterle teamed with Reinhardt, and they codirected a flamboyant film version of William Shakespeare's *A Midsummer Night's Dream* (1935), with the music of Felix Mendelssohn. Although it was a commercial failure, this big-budget film was acclaimed by critics, and it remains the only film production made in the United States by Max Reinhardt. In Hollywood, William Dieterle also worked with actor Paul Muni for two major biographies of French celebrities: *The Story of Louis Pasteur* (1935) and *The Life of Emile Zola* (1937). This second production won the Oscar for best picture in 1937. He also directed Bette Davis in an early version of the Dashiell Hammett novel *The Maltese Falcon,* titled *Satan Met a Lady* (1936). During World War II, Dieterle was the cofounder of an anti-Nazi magazine, *The Hollywood Tribune,* and helped many Jewish refugees arriving in the United States from Germany. William Dieterle returned to West Germany in 1959, working for minor productions, either in film, television, and later for theater festivals (Bad Hersfeld; Munich).

Yves Laberge

See also Hollywood; Leni, Paul; Murnau, Friedrich Wilhelm; Reinhardt, Max

References and Further Reading

Gemunden, Gerd. "Dieterle, William." GERMAN 43: Exiles and Émigrés. http://www.dartmouth.edu/~germ43/resources/biographies/dieterle-w.html (accessed May 11, 2005).

The German-Hollywood Connection. www.germanhollywood.com (accessed May 11, 2005).

Passek, Jean-Loup, ed. *Dictionnaire du Cinéma.* Paris: Larousse, 1998.

DIETRICH, MARLENE MAGDALENE

b. December 27, 1901; Berlin-Schöneberg, Prussia
d. May 6, 1992, Paris, France

Marlene Dietrich became one of the first and brightest movie stars. Her career endured for decades, challenging stereotypes about gender and age, until she became an international classic. She grew up in a wealthy family near Berlin. After her dreams of becoming a violinist were quashed by a wrist injury, she joined the chorus line of a traveling musical review in 1921. She entered Max Reinhardt's innovative drama school, taking small roles in German films and onstage with his theater company. Dietrich married Rudolf "Rudy" Sieber, a Czech production assistant, in 1924 and had a daughter, later the actress Maria Riva. Although never divorced, the couple lived separately until Sieber's 1976 death.

Dietrich became a popular leading lady in German films, many co-starring Emil Jannings: *Napoleons kleiner Bruder* (*The Little Napoleon,* 1922), *Tragödie der Liebe* (*Tragedy of Love,* 1923), *Die Freudlose Gasse* (*The Joyless Street*), *Manon Lascaut* (both 1925), *Der Juxbaron* (*The Imaginary Baron,* 1926), *Eine DuBarry von heute* (*A Modern Du Barry,* 1927), *Wenn ein Weib den Weg verliert* (*Cafe Elektric,* 1927), *Ich küsse Ihre Hand Madame* (*I Kiss Your Hand, Madame,* 1929), and *Der Schiff der verlorenen Menschen* (*The Ship of Lost Souls,* 1929). Magazines compared her to Elisabeth Bergner and Greta Garbo. American director Josef von Sternberg chose her to star as seductive dance-hall vamp Lola Lola with Jannings in his *Der blaue Engel* (*The Blue Angel,* 1930), filmed in both German and English. The heroine impervious to romance, her songs epitomized sultry independence in a husky voice that became her trademark: "Ich Bin die Fesche Lola" (I'm Fancy Lola) and "Ein Richtiger Mann" (Tonight I'm Looking for a Man). "Ich Bin von Kopf bis Fuss" (Falling in Love Again . . . Can't Help It) became her theme song. The role won her international fame and a contract with Paramount Pictures.

She left her husband and daughter to come to Hollywood as von Sternberg molded Dietrich's glamorous, sensuous, mysterious persona. He called her his "puppet" and directed her to lower her voice an octave, claiming to control "the depth of her thoughts" (Mordden 1983, 106). Her films included *Morocco* (1930), as a cabaret singer opposite Gary Cooper; *Dishonored* (1931), as a street walker turned spy; *Blonde Venus* (1932), opposite Gary Grant with a "Hot Voodoo" number she performed in a gorilla suit; *Shanghai Express* (1932), a $3 million box office success; and *The Scarlet Empress* (1934), as Catherine the Great. Von Sternberg's wife Riza sued Dietrich for alienation of affection and libel, but Dietrich won the case by bringing her husband and daughter to the United States. Work with von Sternberg lasted through *The Devil Is a Woman* (1935), again as a cabaret singer.

Already she had made *Song of Songs* (1933), directed by Rouben Mamoulian. She continued with *Desire* and *The Garden of Allah* (both 1936), the latter produced by David O. Selznick. While filming *Knight without Armor* in England (1937), Nazi agent and ambassador Joachim von Ribbentrop approached her with Adolf Hitler's personal appeal to return to Germany to make films. Hitler banned her films due to her refusal, and she became a U.S. citizen that March.

Photoplay described Dietrich "of the heavy-lidded, inscrutable eyes" in a 1931 article, "Charm? No! You Must Have Glamour." So popular was she that her mannish leisure pants created an unprecedented vogue among young American women. Scenes of her provocatively veiled in her cigarette smoke made smoking seem sexy and fashionable. Women tweezed eyebrows as she did and sucked lemons to keep their mouths tight but could not afford her other beauty secret—the half-ounce of real gold dust Max Factor put in

Motion picture advertisement for Hermann Sudermann's The Song of Songs *with two illustrations of Marlene Dietrich, February 25, 1933. (Library of Congress)*

her hair for glitter during filming. She was the image of the independent woman for decades, challenging convention, hinting at secrets of multiple liasons, even bisexual. She staged a "comeback" for Universal as Frenchy, a western saloon singer, opposite James Stewart in *Destry Rides Again* (1939), making "[See What] the Boys in the Back Room [Will Have]" a hit song (Mordden 1983, 110). Costume films followed: *Seven Sinners* (1940), *The Flame of New Orleans* (1941), *Manpower* (1941), and *The Lady Is Willing* (1942). In 1942, she co-starred with John Wayne and Randolph Scott in *The Spoilers* and *Pittsburgh*. She played a seductive harem dancer in *Kismet* (1944). During the war, she starred in war bond drives and entertained troops for the U.S.O., even near combat, over

500 times. She accompanied Allied troops into the Bergen-Belsen concentration camp to liberate her sister. She made anti-Nazi propaganda broadcasts in German, later winning the U.S. War Department Medal of Freedom (1947) and the Chevaliere medal of the French Legion of Honor.

After she played a gypsy in *Golden Earrings* (1947), the media in 1948 dubbed her "the World's most glamorous grandmother" as her daughter gave birth to a son. She then made a string of films: *A Foreign Affair* (1948), as an ex-Nazi in Berlin's ruins in the dark comedy for Billy Wilder; *Stage Fright* (1950), singing "La Vie en Rose"; *No Highway in the Sky* (1951); *Rancho Notorious* (1952), playing a saloon singer; *The Monte Carlo Story* (1957); *Witness for the Prosecution* (1957), as the wife of a murder suspect; *Touch of Evil* (1958), as a gypsy fortune-teller; and *Judgment at Nuremberg* (1961), as a German aristocrat for Stanley Kramer. She had cameo roles in *Around the World in Eighty Days* (1956), *Paris When It Sizzles* (1964), and *Just a Gigolo* (1979).

Dietrich starred in two weekly radio dramas, *Cafe Istanbul* (1952) and *Time for Love* (1953). Into the 1970s, she epitomized glamorous aging, an unprecedented image. She forged a new career as a popular, sultry, world-weary cabaret performer and recording star with her trademark spoken/singing style at venues in Las Vegas, London, Paris, Moscow, Tel Aviv, and Berlin. Old friend Maximilian Schell made the film *Marlene* (1984) with her voice-over commentary because she refused to appear on camera.

Dietrich lived most of her life in Paris and retreated to seclusion there for the last thirteen years of her life, dying of kidney failure at age ninety. Reluctant bureaucrats ceded to her desire to be buried in Friedhof III cemetery in Berlin-Friedenau. She left her memorabilia to the City of Berlin. In 2002, Berlin declared her an honorary citizen, "an ambassador for a democratic, freedom-loving and humane Germany" who personified "reconciliation."

Blanche M. G. Linden

See also Films (German), American Influence on; Hollywood; Jannings, Emil; Reinhardt, Max; Sternberg, Josef von

References and Further Reading

Dickens, Homer. *The Films of Marlene Dietrich*. New York: Citadel, 1971.

Frewin, Leslie. *Dietrich: The Story of a Star*. New York: Avon, 1967.

Higham, Charles. *Marlene*. Norton, 1977.

Mordden, Ethan. *Movie Star: A Look at the Women Who Made Hollywood*. New York: St. Martin's Press, 1983.

Sternberg, Josef von. *Fun in a Chinese Laundry*. New York: Macmillan, 1965.

DIMENSION²

Independent bilingual literary magazine. Edited by Ingo R. Stoehr. Editorial offices are currently located in Nacogdoches, Texas.

The magazine aims to give an English-speaking audience immediate access to the whole spectrum of contemporary literary production in the major German-speaking countries of Austria, Germany, and Switzerland. Exclusively devoted to contemporary German-language literature, *Dimension²* prints German original texts and their translations into English on facing pages. Literary texts include prose, poetry, and drama; short texts, such as poems and short prose, are published in full, and longer texts, such as novels and theater plays, in excerpt. Although the focus is on creative literature, the magazine also publishes interviews with authors, publishers, and literary scholars; essays on literary and cultural issues; and black-and-white reproductions of artwork.

So far the magazine has published over 200 authors, ranging from young talents who saw their first publication in English translation to well-established writers, including Günter Grass, Hans Christoph Buch, Hans Magnus Enzensberger, Barbara Frischmuth, Ludwig Harig, Rolf Hochhuth, Sarah Kirsch, Günter Kunert, Botho Strauß, Uwe Timm, and Christa Wolf. In a similar way, the translations are done by a wide range of practioners: some are graduate students at the beginning of their career; others are well-respected translators and scholars, such as Reinhold Grimm, Burton Pike, A. Leslie Willson, and the late André Lefevere.

Each volume consists of three issues (January, May, and September) of approximately 140 to 160 pages each, and each issue is unified by a special focus. For the first five volumes, the January issues focused on new publications from the previous fall, including interviews with publishers, such as Siegfried Unseld, Michael Krüger, and Daniel Keel; the May issues introduced literary archives, including the German Literary Archives in Marbach and the Swiss Literary Archives in Berne; and the September issues presented literature with a thematic focus, such as the image of the New Germany (after unification), America, the classical tradition, and the Third World. Beginning with volume 6, the basic publication plan was made more flexible to allow for double issues, such as on poetry and the literature of the years 1999 to 2001 (the turn of the millennium).

Dimension² prints approximately 700 to 900 copies per run. Publication is made possible by two factors: government support and volunteer work. From the inception of *Dimension²,* the German government's agency for international cultural exchange, Goethe-Institut Inter Nationes, has supplied generous support with a standing subscription, accounting for about half the magazine's subscription base. Individual issues have also received additional support from the Swiss Cultural office, ProHelvetia; the Deutscher Literaturfonds in Darmstadt; and the Austrian Bundeskanzleramt (Federal Chancellory) in Vienna. In spite of this support, publication of *Dimension²* also depends on the magazine's various contributors forgoing pay: editor and translators volunteer their services, and authors and publishers grant copyright free of charge on a one-time and nonexclusive basis.

Dimension² has been published since 1994, but the superscript 2 in its title pays tribute to its tradition: it is the successor publication to *Dimension,* which was founded in 1968 and edited by A. Leslie Willson at the University of Texas at Austin. In 1994, the same year *Dimension* ceased publication, the first issue of *Dimension²* appeared.

Ingo R. Stoehr

See also Literature (German), the United States in; Literature (German American) in the Nineteenth Century; Literature, German Canadian

References and Further Reading

Dimension²: Contemporary German-Language Literature. http://members.aol.com/germanlit/dimension2.html.

DOBRIZHOFFER, MARTIN

b. September 7, 1717; Friedberg
(Bohemia), Austria [Frymburk], or Sept.
7, 1718; Graz
d. July 17, 1791; Vienna, Austria

Jesuit and early ethnographer who served in Paraguay.

The birthplace and the date of birth for Martin Dobrizhoffer are not entirely certain. In 1734 Dobrizhoffer joined the Jesuit order and was dispatched as a missionary to Paraguay in 1748. Here the order had organized a huge, coherent territory, in which the native population of the Guaraní could live and work in secure settlements (Reductions) and be protected from the raids of the slave traders. However, the continued existence and protection of these Jesuit settlements was endangered because the prosperous Reductions provoked envy among the European settlers, who desired cheap labor. Dobrizhoffer arrived in Paraguay at a time when the Jesuit state was already in decline and the Reductions were repeatedly and violently attacked by slave traders. He lived about eighteen years with native tribes in Paraguay. His first assignment was to serve among the Mocobi in San Xavier (north of Santa Fé). From there, he was sent to live with the Abipón in San Hieronymus and later in Concepción. Last of all, he was ordered to take over the administration of the new Reduction "Zum Heiligen Rosenkranz und St. Karolus" (Holy Rosary and St. Charles) at the Rio Paraguay.

The Abipón were a martial people who had recently moved into settlements and allowed themselves to be baptized. Nevertheless, they were continuously involved in warring among themselves and with neighboring tribes (Toba and Mocobi). Dobrizhoffer learned the language and the habits of life of the Abipón; his fundamental work *Historia de Abiponibus* appeared in 1783–1784 in three volumes in Latin and German and was translated into English in 1822. Contemporaries considered it to be the most important book at the time about Paraguay, the Jesuit state, and the activities of missionaries. Because of his strict factual treatment of the Abipón's customs and traditions, Dobrizhoffer paved the way for the ethnological investigation into the cultures and societies of the native tribes in South America. After the rescission of the Jesuit state in 1767, Dobrizhoffer had to leave Paraguay and returned to Austria, where he—after the breakup of the order—was appointed court chaplain by Maria Theresia in 1773.

Heinz Peter Brogiato

See also Argentina; Paraguay
References and Further Reading
Egghardt, Hanne. *Osterreicher entdecken die Welt. Forscher, Abenteurer, Idealisten.* Vienna: Pichler, 2000, 92–106.
Henze, Dietmar. *Enzyklopädie der Entdecker und Erforscher der Erde.* Graz: Akademische Druck- und Verlagsanstalt, 1983, 2:82–83.
Otruba, Gustav. "Dobritzhoffer, Martin." *Neue Deutsche Biographie.* Berlin: Duncker andand Humblot, 1959, 4:6–7.

DOHMS, HERMANN GOTTLIEB

b. November 3, 1887; Sapiranga, Rio
Grande do Sul
d. December 3, 1956; São Leopoldo, Rio
Grande do Sul

Lutheran church leader who studied theology at German universities and who published the *Deutsche Evangelische Blätter für Brasilien* (German Evangelical News for Brazil).

During his study of theology at the universities of Basel, Leipzig, and Halle with Konrad von Orelli, Paul Heinrich Wilhelm Albert Mezger, Paul Wernle, Albert Hauck, Martin Kähler, Ferdinand Kattenbusch, and Friedrich Armin Loofs, Dohms discovered the theology of Friedrich Daniel Ernst Schleiermacher, Martin Kähler, Albert Ritschl, and Ernst Troeltsch. From 1914 onward, he worked as a parish pastor in Cachoeira do Sul, Rio Grande do Sul, where he published the *Deutsche Evangelische Blätter für Brasilien,* the most important German-language magazine in Brazil. There he founded the Pre-Theological Institute, an institution that was later moved to São Leopoldo. In 1935 he also became the president of the Synod of Rio Grande do Sul, the church of the Lutherans in that state. In 1946 he founded the Lutheran Seminary (the present-day Lutheran School of Theology), also located in São Leopoldo, where he taught systematic theology. Acting as the leader of the presidents of the other Lutheran synods in Brazil, Dohms founded the Federation of Synods in 1949, whose name was changed to the Evangelical Church of the Lutheran Confession in Brazil in 1952. Having been deeply influenced by Johann Gottfried Herder, Troeltsch, Ritschl, and Kähler, Dohms also dealt with the issue of the relationship between church and ethnicity. His efforts to build the Evangelical Church of the Lutheran Confession in Brazil must also be understood from this perspective. His studies were devoted to the influence of German Protestant theology in Brazil, Auguste Comte's positivism, the Brazilian political parties, and the rights of ethnic minorities in South America and particularly in Brazil. In this context he was interested in issues related to the citizenship of German immigrants and their descendants in Brazil but also in their right to preserve the German cultural legacy. The impact of the nationalization policy of Getúlio Vargas on the communities of immigrants, World War II, and the discussions in the German *Kirchenkampf* (church struggle), including the transference of the confrontation between *Deutsche Christen* (German Christians) and *Bekennende Kirche* (Confessing Church) to Brazil, effected a profound reorientation in his thinking, leading him to emphasize the need of the Lutheran Church to be a church in Brazil and the opening to the ecumenical world.

Martin Norberto Dreher

See also Brazil; Brazil, Religion in; Germanism in Rio Grande do Sul

References and Further Reading

Dreher, Martin N. *Igreja e Germanidade.* 2nd ed. São Leopoldo: Editora Sinodal, 2003.
Dreher, Martin N., ed. *Hermann Gottlieb Dohms: Textos Escolhidos.* Porto Alegre: EDIPUCRS, 2001.

DUDEN, GOTTFRIED
b. 1785; Remscheid (Westfalia), Prussia
d. 1855; Remscheid (Westfalia), Prussia

Gottfried Duden was the author of *Bericht über eine Reise nach den westlichen Staaten Nordamerikas und einen mehrjährigen Aufenthalt am Missouri in den Jahren 1824, '25, '26 und '27. In Bezug auf Auswanderung und Überbevölkerung* (*Report on a Journey to the Western States of America and a Stay of Several Years along the Missouri during the Years 1824, '25, '26, and '27,* published in English in 1829), which prompted many German-speaking settlers to move to Ohio, Indiana, Illinois, and especially Missouri.

In 1824, Duden had acquired 270 acres of land in present-day Warren County, close to the Missouri River and some 20 miles west of Saint Louis. Different from most settlers, he possessed sufficient financial means to live the life of a gentleman farmer for the next four years—apparently with only limited success in agriculture—before returning to Germany to publish his experiences in the form of thirty-six letters to an unnamed German friend. The book, although comprehensive, detailed, and accurate in the descriptions of his travels and sojourn in Missouri, often digresses into lengthy philosophical and sociopolitical comparisons between life in the wide expanses of the Missouri River valley and life in Germany. Many disaffected persons in Germany and Switzerland read it and began to organize emigration societies employing Duden's advice. It obviously appealed to those living in the overpopulated area of Duden's home region of the Rhineland, as well as to more affluent and educated readers throughout Germany and Switzerland with a desire to found homesteads based on nineteenth-century ideas of bucolic life abroad.

The popularity of Duden's book during his lifetime is attested by successive publications, first in Elberfeld, Germany, in 1829, followed by a second revised edition in Bonn in 1834; two special editions, sponsored by the Swiss Emigration Society, appeared in St. Gallen in 1832 and 1835. No further editions followed because apparently reactions had come in from settlers, who upon their arrival in the United States had found Duden's descriptions too glowing and optimistic. This prompted Duden to publish "Selbst-anklage Wegen seines amerikanischen Reiseberichts zur Warnung vor fernerm leichtsinigen Auswandern (Self-Recrimination because of his American Travel Report to Caution Everyone against Frivolous Emigration, 1837).

Portions of Duden's *Report on a Journey* were first published in English from 1917 to 1919 by William Bek in successive issues of the *Missouri Historical Review*. A thoroughly annotated, but in some places tedious, English translation of the entire *Report on a Journey*, under the general editorship of James W. Goodrich, appeared in 1980. It also includes Duden's essay "Concerning the Nature of the North American United States or: Concerning the Bases of the Political Situation of the North Americans." In it, Duden lays out his theory that sparse population and a conducive natural environment are the reasons for the perfect living conditions awaiting the settlers in the Missouri River valley. In comparing them to the conditions in his homeland, he states that the miracle of a beggarless society "occurs in a country where passports are unknown, where one can travel thousands of miles without once being asked one's name, where, although all the ordinary police protection common in Germany is altogether lacking, theft, robbery, and swindling are rare. . . . In America, Europe can recognize the results of its own overpopulation" (Duden 1980, 239f.). "A Postscript for Emigrating Farmers and for Those Who Contemplate Commercial Undertakings" is also included in the edition. It briefly gleans the most salient pieces of advice from the thirty-six letters: the most advantageous travel routes, either via New York and Baltimore overland or through New Orleans and then by steamboat up the Mississippi River; the cost of the respective travels; the means of payment; the best ways of carrying money; the minimum financial resources needed for a successful enterprise; and those items best brought along from Europe versus those that can be bought more cheaply in the United States are some of the points discussed.

From a current perspective, Duden's glowing description of life along the Missouri River is naïve, filled with nineteenth-century German romantic notions of an untrammeled existence in an unspoiled wilderness that is just beginning to be opened to the uses of civilization. There are exceptions, however. His twenty-eighth letter deals with the many diseases to which a settler may be exposed and the lack of medical care, and his fifteenth letter allows a rare glimpse of the dangers and difficulties faced by the frontier settler, who is plagued by ticks, is bitten by rattlesnakes, and may lose his property to a raging forest fire. Immediately following in letter sixteen, in a manner reminiscent of Jakob and Wilhelm Grimm's "Little Red Riding Hood," Duden describes several dogs attacking a captured wolf, a "beast of prey," that is being tortured and eventually destroyed by neighbors. Duden displays ambivalence toward this act of cruelty. There seems to be no ambivalence, but rather a bit of national pride, when he asserts that the descendents of Englishmen "proclaim without hesitation that they like the German immigrants best, whereas complaints about the Irish are common, as they are prone to be intemperate, lazy, and quarrelsome" (Duden 1980, 41).

The *Report on a Journey* is not only an excellent sourcebook about frontier life in Missouri in the 1820s. For an American readership, it also reveals interesting and often still relevant perceptions of the United States as seen from abroad. In addition, it proves that some problems perceived as new today have existed for almost two centuries. One example is Duden's passing comment about the Electoral College, where he notes in 1829 that people want to elect the president directly and no longer go through representatives (Duden 1980, 152).

Klaus Dieter Hanson

See also Travel Literature, Germany-U.S.
References and Further Reading
Boone-Duden Historical Society. "Local Map of Boone Duden Historical Society." http://www.rootsweb.com/~moboonhs/map.html (accessed July 19, 2004).
Duden, Gottfried. *Report on a Journey to the Western States of America and a Stay of Several Years along the Missouri (during the Years 1824, '25, '26, and 1827)*. Ed. and trans. James Goodrich. Columbia, MO: State Historical Society of Missouri and University of Missouri Press, 1980.

DUNT, DETLEF
b. May 7, 1793; Lütjenburg, Holstein
d. 1847; Columbus, Texas

Author of one of the earliest German guidebooks to Texas, *Reise nach Texas, nebst Nachrichten von diesem Lande für Deutsche, welche nach Amerika zu gehen beabsichtigen* (Journey to Texas: With Information about This Land for Germans Planning to Go to America), in 1834. Dunt's book reflects the growing German interest in Texas as a possible destination for emigrants even before the founding of the Republic of Texas in 1836. Dunt, who was born Detlev Thomas Friedrich Jordt, publicized the presence of Germans in

Stephen Austin's colony in Texas, most notably the settlement of Friedrich Ernst in Industry. Dunt's book is an important source for the early history of European and American settlements in Texas.

The book belongs to a particular genre of literature, the emigrant guide that flourished in the nineteenth century. These works address "how-to-do-it" questions beginning with who should emigrate, where the emigrant should go, what should be taken, and what is better purchased abroad. Dunt recounts that a Scot he met in Texas confirmed what many Americans who had traveled throughout the United States had told him: Texas, which still belonged to Mexico, was far superior to any part of the states for European settlers. As Dunt explains, it was possible in Texas for a male head of household to acquire a vast land grant. Dunt cautioned that to obtain the maximum grant, the immigrant must not only be married but have his wife with him.

Dunt had not done well economically in Germany. He was still living in eastern Holstein in 1819 when he married a woman from the duchy of Oldenburg to the west. The marriage records note that his deceased father had been simply a *Kaufmann* (merchant or businessman), a term that without enhancement usually denoted a small businessman. Dunt's first three children were born in the town of his own birth. In 1827, before the birth of a fourth child, he applied to the authorities in Oldenburg for permission to settle in the duchy. The request was denied until his father- and brother-in-law, both surgeons, filed affidavits that, if necessary, they would support him and his dependents to prevent the family from becoming a burden on public funds. Dunt moved with his family to Berne/Wesermarsch, a small locality near the town where his wife's father resided.

Enticed by fellow Oldenburger Friedrich Ernst's open letter of 1832 about the attractiveness of Texas, which circulated widely in parts of northern Germany, Dunt departed for Texas via Bremen on November 20, 1832. After sojourns of a few weeks in both New York and New Orleans, he arrived in Texas early in May 1833. He returned to Oldenburg in the fall of 1834.

Almost two years elapsed before he carried out his plan, announced in his book, to emigrate to Texas, and then he failed to follow his own advice to bring his wife and take advantage of the generous land grants to which husbands accompanied by spouses were entitled. In February 1836, he and his two sons, aged thirteen and fifteen, set out for Texas, leaving his wife in Oldenburg with the couple's two daughters, aged seven and ten—perhaps to care for the older daughter, who died the following year. In 1844 Dunt's wife and their surviving daughter were still in Oldenburg, although by then they resided in Bockhorn/Wesermarsch, where the wife's father lived until his death in 1843. Dunt himself made at least one more round trip between Texas and Oldenburg. The record of his surviving daughter's confirmation in 1844 lists him as present at the ceremony in Bockhorn and as an innkeeper in nearby Berne/Wesermarsch. His stay in Germany must have been brief. In 1846 his wife emigrated to Texas with their daughter, now seventeen, as well as a young man, the son of a postal employee in Oldenburg, whom the daughter married the following year. Officiating at the wedding in September 1847 as justice of the peace was Dunt's old friend Friedrich Ernst of Industry, Texas. It is unclear from the records whether Dunt lived long enough into 1847 to see his daughter marry.

Walter Struve

See also Ernst, Friedrich; Texas; Travel Literature, Germany-U.S.
References and Further Reading
Brenner, Peter J. *Reisen in die Neue Welt: Die Erfahrung Nordamerikas in deutschen Reise- und Auswandererberichten des 19. Jahrhunderts.* Tübingen: Niemeyer, 1991.
Görisch, Stephan. "Die gedruckten 'Ratgeber' für Auswanderer: Zur Produktion und Typologie eines literarischen Genres." *Hessische Blätter für Volks- und Kulturforschung* 17, 1985, 51–70.
Struve, Walter. *Germans and Texans: Commerce, Migration, and Culture in the Days of the Lone Star Republic.* Austin: University of Texas Press, 1996.

DUTCH

It is often said that the use of the word *Dutch* by English-speaking people to refer to Germans was the result either of a confusion of identities or an attempt to pronounce the German word *Deutsch,* which, it is assumed, the Germans used to describe themselves. These explanations do not hold up under scrutiny. Of course, there were cases of confusion, but in the seventeenth century, when German settlers began to arrive in substantial numbers in Britain's North American colonies, the term *Dutch* still had meanings that have disappeared and are forgotten today.

The terms *Deutsch* and *Dutch* are closely related cognates, but prior to the nineteenth century—and even prior to the unification of Germany in 1871—many migrants from the German states were not prone to describe themselves as *Deutsch,* even to strangers. They were more likely to refer to the territorial state from which they came. In some instances their sense of religious identity transcended the designation of homeland, as was often the case with Amish, Mennonites, Dunkers, Jews, and Moravians—to mention only a few. The "Pennsylvania Dutch," the German Americans whose ancestors came mainly from the Palatinate and Lower Rhine regions and settled mostly in eastern Pennsylvania in the seventeenth and eighteenth centuries, often did not recognize the term *Deutsch* as applicable to themselves, even after the unification of Germany. With sarcastic wit they referred, in their German dialect, to the new arrivals as *Deitschlänner* (*Deutschländer* in standard German); that is, people who were constantly talking about *Deutschland,* a political entity created long after the ancestors of the Pennsylvania Germans departed for the New World.

The use of *Dutch* as a synonym for *German* antedates British settlement of North America. In the late Middle Ages and early modern period, *Dutch* included both Germans and Dutch. It referred to people speaking a group of closely related Germanic languages. This usage pertained mainly to inhabitants of the Holy Roman Empire and distinguished two kinds of "Dutch" people on the basis of geography, culture, and, critically, language: "High Dutch (*Hochdeutsch*)," or "High German" in today's English usage; and "Low Dutch (*Niederdeutsch*)," or "Low German" in today's usage. The English language did not distinguish Netherlanders from other speakers of "Low Dutch," except by specifying the province, locality, or region.

War and political change in the sixteenth and seventeenth centuries created a strong need to distinguish Netherlanders from other "Low Dutch." The successful wars for independence waged by the northern provinces of the Low Countries led to the creation of the Republic of the United Provinces. Their withdrawal from the Holy Roman Empire and their independence were confirmed by the Peace of Westphalia in 1648. The English language responded by increasingly restricting the term *Dutch* to people from the Netherlands. The corresponding shift in Dutch was different. The term *duytsch,* or *duits,* the Dutch cognate of *Dutch* and *deutsch,* was restricted to Germans and no longer included Netherlanders or their language. The Netherlanders now referred to their own language as *Nederlands.*

The refrain of an old drinking song that I learned in college on the edge of the Pennsylvania German region expresses clearly some of the distinctions once made between various uses of *Dutch.*

> O, the Highland Dutch,
> And the Lowland Dutch,
> The Rotterdam Dutch,
> And the Goddamn Dutch,
> Singing glorious, glorious!
> One keg of beer for the four of us,
> Thank God there are no more of us,
> O, glorious! O, glorious!

In this song "Highland Dutch" stands for the Austrians and South Germans. The "Lowland Dutch" are the northern Germans. And the "Rotterdam Dutch" refers to the inhabitants of the Dutch Republic or the Kingdom of the Netherlands.

English-speaking colonists and their descendants were carrying on traditional usage when they persisted in referring to Germans as *Dutch* in colonial America and beyond. An often overlooked reason why this label has stuck so well is that the confusion has often been useful to German Americans. For example, during both world wars the Pennsylvania Dutch seemed to many Americans to have nothing to do with Germany. General John J. Pershing, commander of U.S. forces in Europe, went a step farther when he, like some other Pennsylvania Germans, attempted to prove that his Palatine ancestors were actually French; they or their ancestors were presumably French Protestants who found a temporary haven in the Palatinate before emigrating to America.

There is still another reason why the term *Pennsylvania Dutch* has survived the efforts of many scholars over many decades to eradicate it. A distinctive culture developed and persisted in some parts of Pennsylvania and nearby upper southern and middle western states. Both other German Americans and other Americans have perceived of this culture, especially in its Amish and Mennonite forms, as distinctly different from any other German culture.

Walter Struve

See also German Unification (1871); Pennsylvania; Pennsylvania German (Dutch) Language

References and Further Reading

Yoder, Don. "Palatine, Hessian, Dutchman: Drei Bezeichnungen für Deutsche in Amerika." *Hessische Blätter für Volks- und Kulturforschung. Neue Folge der Hessischen Blätter für Volkskunde* 17, 1985, 191–213.

ECKENER, HUGO

b. August 10, 1868; Flensburg (Schlesvig),
Prussia
d. August 14, 1954; Friedrichshafen
Baden, Württemberg

The world's most prominent advocate of
rigid airship flight between the world wars,
whose spectacular zeppelin voyages helped to
rebuild German ties with the United States.

Eckener's early career as a journalist
brought him into contact with Graf Ferdinand von Zeppelin, whose dream of lighter-
than-air flight he adopted with enthusiasm.
During World War I, Eckener assumed control of the Zeppelin Works in Friedrichshafen. After the war, he arranged a deal to
deliver an airship to the United States as an
"in-kind" payment in war reparations,
thereby skirting Allied disarmament provisions and keeping his plant and its skilled
employees at work. After flights across the
Atlantic, around the globe, and into the
Arctic in 1924, 1929, and 1931, respectively, he was lionized as a national hero in
Germany and revered around the globe. His
political convictions and aims for the zeppelin brought him into conflict with the Nazis,
who forced him out of public life. He strove
in vain to rekindle international interest in
airships after World War II.

An indifferent student as a youth, Eckener grew more interested in intellectual
pursuits as a young adult. He studied economics, philosophy, history, and psychology
at the universities of Berlin, Munich, and
Leipzig, where he earned a doctorate with a
dissertation in what today would be known
as experimental psychology. During the
1890s and early 1900s, he worked as a journalist and editor, first in Flensburg and then
at Friedrichshafen in southern Germany,
where he resettled for health reasons at the
end of the 1890s. He worked there as a correspondent for the *Frankfurter Zeitung*
(Frankfurt Newspaper), writing commentary articles as well as music and art criticism. Friedrichshafen was also the center of
Graf Zeppelin's experiments with rigid airships, and Eckener was assigned to cover
Graf's earliest, and mostly failed, efforts.

A string of zeppelin crashes at first reinforced Eckener's skepticism about the future of the airship. He gradually developed
a fascination with the great machines, however, and, after a personal meeting with
Zeppelin in 1908, accepted the Graf's offer
of a position in charge of public relations to
help counter expert criticism from prominent physicists and engineers. Eckener then
played a key role in directing the attention
of German naval authorities toward the

long-distance reconnaissance potential of the airship. He helped establish the Deutsche Luftschiff-Aktien-Gesellschaft (DELAG, or German Airship Corporation) and in 1911 was licensed as an airship pilot. From that point on, he directed the training of pilots for the corporation and assumed an increasingly preeminent role in the zeppelin program.

Eckener directed the training of naval airship commanders during World War I, but the zeppelin was an acute military disappointment. Although the unrivalled range of the airship made it useful for marine reconnaissance and a few successful raids were carried out over England, the huge size and relatively slow speed rendered the airship quite vulnerable. Over half of Germany's naval airships fell victim during the fighting to enemy fighters, storms, and lightning.

At the war's end, Allied authorities seized the newly built passenger zeppelin LZ 120 and mandated size restrictions on future construction which would have meant the end of airships capable of carrying passengers. Desperate to save what he viewed as his life's work, Eckener offered to build a large new airship for delivery to the Americans in lieu of monetary reparations for the airships German ground personnel had destroyed to prevent them falling into Allied hands. As he had anticipated, U.S. authorities—particularly naval personnel—were eager to accept the proposal. The American Goodyear company, a rival to the German airship program, had produced in the airship ZR 1 a vessel considered by most experts to be technically inferior to the German product.

Thus empowered to legally circumvent Allied aircraft construction restrictions, Eckener in 1923 and 1924 built the colossal LZ 126, which he personally piloted across the Atlantic to Lakehurst, New Jersey, in October 1924. The ocean crossing was a spectacular success, covered by an intensive international publicity campaign engineered in part by the media-savvy Eckener himself. New York stopped in its tracks to watch the passing of the airship, and half a million people greeted the arrival of the LZ 126 (soon to be the *Los Angeles*) at Lakehurst. Eckener was given a ticker tape parade through Manhattan and received by Calvin Coolidge at the White House as the "modern Columbus."

Eckener's success made him a hero in Germany as well, and he built upon it. With help from the government and a national fund drive, he built the *Graf Zeppelin,* the world's largest airship. In August 1929, Eckener flew the new *Graf Zeppelin* around the world, profiting from the sale of newspaper rights, winning the "Special Gold Medal" of the American National Geographic Society, and evoking a huge popular response where the airship touched down in Tokyo and Los Angeles. This was followed by an Arctic flight in collaboration with the Russians in 1931, another pioneering success. Eckener was now so popular that the Social Democrats seriously discussed running him as a presidential candidate in 1932 against Adolf Hitler.

With the rise of the Nazis, however, and the still-mysterious explosion of the Hindenburg at Lakehurst in 1937, Eckener's airship program was doomed. He himself was forced into retirement from public life, and his beloved airships were scrapped by the Nazis. After the war, he tried without success to revive international interest in the airship and spent the last years of his retirement composing his memoirs.

David Murphy

See also Treaty of Versailles; Zeppelin
References and Further Reading
Botting, Douglas. *Dr. Eckener's Dream
Machine: The Great Zeppelin and the Dawn
of Air Travel.* New York: Henry Holt,
2001.
De Syon, Guillaume. *Zeppelin! Germany and
the Airship, 1900–1939.* Baltimore: Johns
Hopkins University Press, 2001.
Eckener, Hugo. *Im Zeppelin über Länder und
Meere.* Flensburg: Verlagshaus Christian
Wolff, 1949.
Itataliaander, Rolf. *Hugo Eckener: Ein
moderner Columbus.* Konstanz: Verlag
Friedrich Stadler, 1979.

*Gertrud Ederle swam the English Channel, August 6,
1926, in the record time of 14 1/2 hours. She is the
first woman ever to have accomplished this feat. Here,
William Burgess, her trainer, is shown greasing Ederle
down before her start. (Bettmann/Corbis)*

EDERLE, GERTRUD
b. October 23, 1906; New York City
d. November 30, 2003; New York City

Born to German immigrants in New York
City, Ederle was the first woman to swim
the English Channel in 1926.

Ederle was raised in the German section of New York's West Side, a second-
generation German immigrant with working-class roots. Her father Henry was a
butcher and her mother a housewife and
caregiver to their six children. Trudy, as her
family called her, was a tomboy who
learned to swim at the family cottage in
New Jersey when she was nine, though she
claimed she did not learn to swim correctly
until she mastered the crawl stroke that
carried her across the English Channel.

Tutored by the Women's Swimming
Association of New York, whose coach discovered her talent, she won her first swimming competition at fifteen. One year later
she beat the men's record for the classic 21-
mile race from Manhattan's Battery to
Sandy Hook in New Jersey. Between 1921
and 1925 she held twenty-nine amateur
and world records in women's freestyle

events, winning three medals at the 1924
Paris Olympic Games.

Ederle's first attempt to swim the channel in 1925 ended unsuccessfully. After
nine hours her trainer, who claimed Ederle
was too nauseated to continue, pulled her
protesting from the water. A year later on
August 6, 1926, Ederle returned to Cape
Griz-Nez on the coast of France for her second attempt, this time with financial backing from Captain Peterson of the *New York
Times* and *Chicago Tribune.* Wearing an
outfit customized by her sister Margaret—
red bathing cap, two-piece swimsuit, wrap-
around goggles—and slathered with lano-
lin and lard to protect against jellyfish and
cold water, she battled the 21-mile crossing
for fourteen hours, thirty-one minutes.
High winds, driving rain, and shifting tides
forced her to swim an arduous extra 14
miles. When her concerned father begged
her to retreat into the accompanying boat,

she replied "what for?" and kept on swimming until she saw welcoming bonfires off the coast of England. A roaring crowd who had gathered to celebrate her accomplishment greeted her. Overnight, the newspapers would claim, she had become the most famous woman in the world. Ederle had shown it could be done, triumphing over the prevailing view that opposed competitive athletics for women due to their presumed physical inferiority.

Eschewing the public spotlight, she traveled to Germany to visit her father's relatives. While Ederle was there, another female swimmer accomplished the channel swim, thus diminishing the magnitude of Ederle's achievement in the eyes of the media. Nonetheless, she returned home to a massive celebration, first in New York Harbor to the din of swooping airplanes and steamship sirens and then up Broadway to a ticker tape parade. At City Hall, the mayor compared her achievement to Moses crossing the Red Sea, Caesar crossing the Rubicon, and Washington crossing the Delaware.

The media was not slow to size up the "Queen of the Waters" and "America's best girl" as the ideal type of American womanhood while at the same time underscoring her sturdy German features and working-class origins. A telegram from the United German Societies of Americans of German Descent proclaimed their pride that the first woman conqueror of the channel was a German American, a butcher's daughter who grew up to be a Queen.

Ederle's ambition stopped short at the channel shore. Her potential professional career was badly mismanaged, and offers of lucrative theater and swimming engagements came to naught. A red roadster promised to her by her father was one of the few tangible incentives she received for her swimming achievement. She was traumatized by her triumph and celebrity status and suffered a nervous breakdown at the age of twenty-one. She was also dogged by misfortune, injuring her back, which severely limited her mobility, and then becoming deaf, which she blamed for her growing shyness and lack of confidence.

During World War II, Ederle became an instrument technician for American Overseas Airlines at La Guardia and later volunteered to teach deaf children to swim. Around the same time she was appointed to President Dwight D. Eisenhower's Citizen's Advisory Committee on the Fitness of America's Youth and in 1965 was inducted into the International Swimming Hall of Fame. Her last public appearance was in 1976 on the fiftieth anniversary of her historic channel swim. She lived on until she was ninety-seven, living quietly in New York with two female companions and then at the Christian Health Care Center in New Jersey, where, confined to a wheelchair, she was surrounded by her trophies.

Christiane Job and Patricia Vertinsky

References and Further Reading
Benjamin, Philip. "Then and Now: Gertrude Ederle, First Woman to Swim the English Channel Still Gets Fan Mail." *New York Times,* August 6, 1961, 58.
Gallico, Paul. "Gertrude Ederle." *The Golden People.* New Jersey: Doubleday, 1965.
Trumbull, Walter. "Queen of the Waters." *St. Nicholas* 53 (October 1926): 1114.

EGG HARBOR CITY, NEW JERSEY

Although never close to fulfilling the objectives of its founders in the 1850s that it become a German metropolis with a

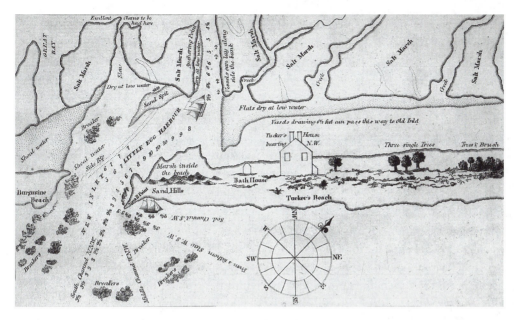

Nautical chart of Little Egg Harbor, New Jersey (1822). Egg Harbor City has the distinction of long being reputed the most German town in America. As late as 1900 virtually everyone in Egg Harbor spoke German. (New York Public Library)

world-class harbor, Egg Harbor City has the distinction of long being reputed the most German town in the United States. As late as 1900, virtually everyone in Egg Harbor spoke German.

The proposals for this haven of Germandom were formulated in the wake of Know-Nothing Party nativist agitation, which included violence against German and other immigrants in mid-nineteenth-century America. But altruistic concerns were intermingled with material objectives. A group of prominent Germans in Philadelphia, a center of nativist activity, served as architects of a grandiose plan for a large commercial and industrial center with a seaport and an agricultural hinterland in southern New Jersey. Crucial to these plans was the newly opened Camden and Atlantic Railroad between Philadelphia and the new resort of Atlantic City. Egg Harbor is about 30 miles southeast of

Philadelphia and would be a rail stop enroute to Atlantic City. Egg Harbor was designed to benefit the Camden and Atlantic by increasing its freight and passenger business. Some Philadelphia businesspeople of German descent were actively involved in both the rail line and the new "city."

Serious planning for what became Egg Harbor began in late 1854 with the founding in Philadelphia of a corporation, the Gloucester Farm and Town Association, which purchased some 38,000 acres of pine woods. The first settlers arrived within a year or so. The association issued stock, initially at $300 and later at $400 per share. Each share entitled the purchaser to a 20-acre farm, as well as a town building lot. A town lot alone cost $78. The construction of public buildings, schools, parks, streets, and much more was promised.

The association's aggressive publicity campaign included extensive advertising in newspapers in many U.S. cities. A promotional pamphlet printed in German in 1859 by the association offers insights into a mentality shared by many nineteenth-century German emigrants and prospective emigrants. The brochure enunciated the goals of the project: "A new German home in America. A refuge for all German countrymen who want to combine and enjoy American freedom with German *Gemütlichkeit.* . . . A place to develop German folk life, German arts and sciences, especially music" (Cunz 1956, 11).

The actual development diverged greatly from the association's promises. Egg Harbor succeeded as little as another product of Philadelphia Germans—Hermann, Missouri—founded two decades earlier. In 1860 the population of Egg Harbor stood at 789; by 1890 it had scarcely doubled. The planners had expected the town to spread northeastward to the Mullica River, which, it was assumed, would somehow be made navigable for large ships. But the "city" never grew to the river, and no port was constructed.

The settlers' dismay at the wilderness they encountered upon arrival led to the formation of an organization demanding that the board of directors in Philadelphia make good on the association's promises. Unlike Hermann, Missouri, where an analogous struggle ended with the severance of all links between settlers and the sponsoring organization, the Philadelphia masters of Egg Harbor yielded some power by revising the constitution of the Gloucester Farm and Town Association to provide for representation of the actual settlers on the board.

The town survived largely by cultivating grapes and making wine, for which it became widely known. Another major source of employment was tailoring. Big city shops sent garments for finishing work. As in other German settlements, a myriad of musical groups, choirs, gymnastic societies, dramatic clubs, literary societies, and fraternal orders flourished.

Like Hermann, Missouri, and Fredericksburg and New Braunfels, Texas, Egg Harbor provides an example of unfulfilled nineteenth-century German aspirations to create a new, better Germany in the United States. Although Egg Harbor never fulfilled its designers' ambitious plans, it remained overwhelmingly German speaking until the twentieth century. A small influx of Italians, many of whom were attracted by the wine industry, provided some diversity without altering the basic character of the town. But as the twentieth century advanced, the town became Americanized in speech and culture. Beginning in 1916, the proceedings of the city council were recorded only in English, no longer in both English and German. The German Lutheran Church in Egg Harbor did not shift to keeping its records in English as well as German until 1932. By then, most of the several other churches in town had gone over to record keeping in English only.

The loss in language was accompanied by modest growth in the number of residents. From 1,808 in 1900, the population stood at 4,546 in 2000. But the town has retained part of its heritage. Where else in the United States could one find street after street named for German composers, as well as many a street with an ancient Greek or Latin name?

Walter Struve

See also Fredericksburg, Texas; Hermann, Missouri; New Braunfels, Texas

References and Further Reading

Bosse, Georg von. *Ein Kampf um Glauben und Volkstum: Das Streben während meines 25 jährigen Amtslebens als deutsch-lutherischer Geistlicher in Amerika.* Stuttgart: Chr. Belsersche Verlagsbuchhandlung, 1920.

Breder, George F. *Egg Harbor City: 1855–1905, Goldenes Jubiläum, Sept. 16–19.* Egg Harbor City: Deutscher Herold, 1905.

Cunz, Dieter. "Egg Harbor City: New Germany in New Jersey." Society for the History of Germans in Maryland. *Annual Report* 29 (1956): 9–30.

EHRENREICH, PAUL MAX ALEXANDER

b. December 12, 1855; Berlin, Prussia
d. April 4, 1914; Berlin, Prussia

German ethnographer and anthropologist who traveled extensively to Brazil and Argentina and conducted comparative research on Native American mythology.

Paul Ehrenreich received his doctorate in medicine from the University of Berlin in 1880. Under the influence of Rudolf Virchow, he turned to the study of ethnology and anthropology. From 1884 to 1885 Ehrenreich toured Brazil for the first time and visited the Botokude in the two states, Espírito Santo and Minas Gerais. Based on his observations, Ehrenreich published *Ein Beitrag zur Charakterisitk der botokudischen Sprache* (A Contribution to the Characteristics of the Botokudian Language) in 1896. In addition, he was the first European to report about the delta region of the Rio Doce.

From 1887 to 1888 he participated as an anthropologist and photographer in the second Xingú Expedition led by Karl von den Steinen. This expedition brought him from Buenos Aires via Cuyabá to the native tribes of the Bakairi, Nahuquá, Mehinaku, Auití, Yaulapití, and Kamayurá. Ehrenreich collected about 1,235 artifacts from these tribes and donated this ethnographic collection to the Museum für Völkerkunde (Ethnological Museum) in Berlin. After a stay in Cuyabá during the rainy season, the expedition traveled to the Bororo, which had been forced to settle in a reserve.

After the expedition was dissolved, Ehrenreich continued his research independently in the area of the Rio Araguaya-Tocantins and the Rio Purus. Further, he explored the eastern parts of the mountainous Matto Grosso. His journey led him from Cuyabá and Goiás to Leopoldina and via the Araguaya to Belém. He wrote about his encounters on this trip in his *Südamerikanische Stromfahrten* (South American River Voyages, 1892).

Ehrenreich drastically corrected topographic knowledge about South America and presented his results in a chart on a scale of 1 to 1 million (1892). He carried out ethnological and linguistic studies with the Karayá and published the results in *Beiträge zur Völkerkunde Brasiliens* (Contributions to the Ethnology of Brazil, 1891) and *Anthropologische Studien über die Urbewohner Brasiliens, vornehmlich der Staaten Matto Grosso, Goyaz und Amazonas (Purus Gebiet)* (Anthropological Studies about the Native Population of Brazil, Especially of the People in the Provinces of Matto Grosso, Goyaz, and Amazonas [Purus region], 1897). After his return, he received a second doctorate (DPhil) from the University of Leipzig in 1895. In 1911 he received a professorship of ethnology at the University of Berlin. Further exploration voyages led him to India, East Asia (1892–1893), and North America (1898 and 1906). During the later trips, Ehrenreich compared his findings in Brazil with the new findings in North America and published his book *Die Mythen und Legenden der südamerikanischen Urvölker und ihre Beziehungen zu denen Nordamerikas und der alten Welt* (The Myths and Legends of South American Native People in Their Relation to Those of North America and the Old World, 1905). In his later years he devoted himself mainly to the study of mythology, publishing *Die allgemeine Mythologie und ihre ethnologischen Grundlagen* (The General Mythology and Its Ethnological bases, 1914) and his *Die Sonne im Mythos* (The Sun in Mythology, 1915).

Heinz Peter Brogiato

> **See also** Argentina; Brazil; Steinen, Karl von den
>
> **References and Further Reading**
> Henze, Dietmar. *Enzyklopädie der Entdecker und Erforscher der Erde.* Graz: Akademische Druck- und Verlagsanstalt, 1983, 2:158–159.
> Zerries, Otto. "Ehrenreich, Paul Max Alexander." *Neue Deutsche Biographie.* Berlin: Duncker and Humblot, 1959, 4:354.

EICHMANN, KARL ADOLF
b. March 19, 1906; Solingen, Prussia
d. May 31, 1962; Ramleh, Israel

German Schutzstaffel (SS) lieutenant-colonel in charge of the Gestapo Section IV B4 for Jewish Affairs who implemented and administered the operational apparatus behind the deportation and deaths of Jews to extermination camps in the sixteen German-occupied territories during World War II. After the war, Adolf Eichmann escaped to Argentina, where he lived peacefully and undiscovered for about ten years before he was captured by MOSSAD and tried in Israel.

Eichmann's Protestant middle-class parents relocated from Solingen to Linz, Austria, upon the death of his mother. He failed to complete his engineering degree, but his studies taught him to be particularly meticulous in his endeavors. He began his working life as a laborer and salesman. He worked for the U.S.-based Vacuum Oil Company from 1927 to 1933. He found his true vocation when he joined the Austrian army and the National Socialist German Worker's Party (NSDAP) in 1932; he served as a Schutzstaffel (SS) corporal at Dachau concentration camp in 1934. Thereafter he joined the Security Service (SD) where his performance in devising a solution to the "Jewish problem" garnered attention from his superiors, Heinrich Himmler and Richard Heydrich. To better understand his prey, Eichmann undertook an in-depth self-study course of Jewish history, faith, and culture; Zionism; and the Hebrew and Yiddish languages.

By 1938 Eichmann was ordered to Vienna, where he established the Central Office of Jewish Emigration with the aim of addressing the "Jewish problem." In exchange for an exit visa, Jews met with forced emigration, extortion, and bribery. As the Reich's expert on Jews, Eichmann became director of the Gestapo Section IV B4 of the Security Office (RHSA), making him solely responsible for the Department of Jewish Affairs and evacuation. From this position, Eichmann implemented the Final Solution (*Endlösung*), based on directions from the Wannsee Conference of January 20, 1942, that he had helped to organize.

Before Eichmann's elevation to director, Jews were shot and buried in common graves that caused seepage and proved unsanitary. To spare his SS troops this inhumane sight, he turned to using gas; first in mobile van units and later in concentration camps. He introduced Zyklon B, which was far less costly than one bullet per Jew. Victims were gassed in supposed shower rooms, and their bodies were then incinerated in camp ovens. Eichmann was a zealot in this job; he complained about unmet death camp quotas. He reported to Himmler that some 6 million Jews had met their deaths under his supervision.

After the collapse of the Third Reich, U.S. troops captured Eichmann near Ulm on May 7, 1945, wearing the uniform of a Luftwaffe airman second class and carrying the identity of Adolf Karl Barth. He fled the camp, knowing very well that he would be discovered sooner rather than later. In August 1945 the Americans captured Eichmann again and confined him to Oberdachstetten camp. The Americans still had no knowledge of whom they held in custody because he was using the alias of SS Lieutenant Otto Eckmann, 22nd Calvary Division. On January 5, 1946, Eichmann escaped with forged identification under the name Otto Neninger. He then went underground. In 1950, Eichmann reached Austria and then Italy, where he received a refugee passport as Ricardo Klement, posing as a German national from Bolzano, Italy. Eichmann obtained an Argentine visa and moved there in 1950; his family arrived later.

On May 2, 1960, Israeli secret service agents found Eichmann living on Garibaldi Street in Buenos Aires. The spectacular kidnapping of Eichmann and his secret abduction to Israel engendered considerable global interest. Eichmann was charged with crimes against humanity and stood trial from April 2 to August 14, 1961. He was found guilty on December 2, 1961, and hanged in Ramleh prison on May 31, 1962.

Annette Richardson

See also Argentina; Latin America, Nazis in
References and Further Reading
Arendt, Hannah. *Eichmann in Jerusalam: A Report on the Banality of Evil.* New York: Penguin Books, 1994.
Harel, Isser. *The House on Garibaldi Street: The Capture of Adolf Eichmann.* London: Deutsch, 1975.
Loziwick, Yaacov. *Hitler's Bureaucrats; The Nazi Security Police and the Banality of Evil.* London: Continuum, 2002.
Reynolds, Quentin J. *Minister of Death: The Adolf Eichmann Story.* London: Cassell, 1961.
Russell of Liverpool, Edward. *The Record: The Trial of Adolf Eichmann for his Crimes against the Jewish People and against Humanity.* London: Heinemann, 1962.

82ND ILLINOIS VOLUNTEER INFANTRY REGIMENT

The 82nd Illinois Volunteer Infantry Regiment fought for the Union during the American Civil War and included numerous German volunteers. The men who joined the regiment chose to become members and were not forced to join because of any federal government conscription requirements. The regiment was created at Camp Butler, Springfield, Illinois, on September 26, 1862, and was mustered into service a month later. The 82nd started that autumn with nearly 1,000 men, the usual regimental strength, and would end the war with barely 300 soldiers three years later. The regiment was divided into eleven companies, A through K, with Company C being composed entirely of German Jews. More than two-thirds of the men were German immigrants living in the Chicago area, with a significant number of recruits residing in the Belleville area of southern Illinois. Two prominent German soldiers, Friedrich Hecker and Edward S. Salomon, created and commanded the regiment throughout the war. The 82nd fought in both the eastern and western theaters of the Civil War, participating in the battles of Chancellorville, Gettysburg, Mission Ridge, and Atlanta; Sherman's March to the Sea; and the campaign of the Carolinas. By war's end in 1865, the recent German immigrants were recognized as soldiers who had fought with great pride and distinction.

The German volunteers in the 82nd Illinois differed socially and economically from one another. German immigrants from the predominantly agricultural regions of their homeland settled in southern Illinois because of the favorable farming conditions there. Farmers who did not have the ability to purchase land in a German province found that elusive opportunity in Belleville, Illinois. Skilled and semiskilled German laborers, however, were more likely to settle in Chicago, where their previous work experience could develop into economic opportunities. They became the dominant ethnic group in the manufacturing and mechanical industries. Upward social and economic mobility was easier in the Midwest than it was on the East Coast of the United States during the 1840s and 1850s. As a result, German immigrants

found it easier to integrate themselves into American culture in the Midwest.

Regardless of their economic and social standing, the Germans volunteered to join the 82nd Illinois for numerous reasons: to protect northern Republican Party ideas under attack by the South, to raise their status both politically and socially in the community, to have an adventure, and to make money. Additionally, many recruits joined the regiment out of the simple pride of being patriotic Americans, even if they were recent immigrants. Their newfound country had provided them with the opportunity to reach many of their dreams and goals, and the Civil War allowed them to repay that debt. Ethnic pride entered into the recruitment equation as well. In Chicago, the Germans disliked the Irish and wanted to make sure their enlistment numbers were higher than those of the Irish. Their neighborhoods faced stigmatization by the city if enough men did not enlist in the recruitment quotas. Moreover, a draftee was not entitled to any of the volunteer recruitment bonuses that were common at the time.

Colonel Friedrich Hecker and Lieutenant Colonel Edward S. Salomon were responsible for helping to create and organize the 82nd Illinois in 1862. Before the Civil War, Colonel Hecker lived in Belleville, Illinois, and Lieutenant Colonel Salomon resided in Chicago. The two Germans had previously served together in the 24th Illinois Regiment. Germans throughout Chicago and southern Illinois quickly filled the enlistment quotas when they learned who was in charge of the 82nd Illinois Regiment. Salomon was responsible for helping to create an entire company exclusively of German Jews, which would be nicknamed the Concordia Guards after the recruitment hall. Finally, on September 26, 1862, the 82nd Illinois was formally created at Camp Butler, Illinois, and integrated into the Union army on October 23. In December 1862, the 82nd Illinois was attached to the First Brigade, Third Division, 11 Corps of the Army of the Potomac under the command of their fellow Germans, Generals Alexander Schimmelpfennig and Carl Schurz.

The early months of 1863 witnessed the 82nd Illinois's participation in what was known as the "Mud Campaign"—a series of movements throughout Virginia that eventually brought them to Chancellorsville. The Battle of Chancellorsville in May 1863 was a terrible defeat for the Army of the Potomac. The men of the 82nd Illinois, however, performed bravely during the attack upon them by Confederate general Stonewall Jackson. They were able to keep the Confederate forces in check as the Union army retreated. The 82nd paid a high cost in defending the retreating Union troops—Colonel Hecker was wounded while attempting to rally his men, and 156 men were counted as casualties.

Two months later, the 82nd Illinois was again in the middle of an historic battle. The Battle of Gettysburg, from July 1 through July 3, 1863, allowed the Union army to regain the pride it had lost at Chancellorsville. The first day of battle quickly turned against the Union army north of the town, forcing them to retreat through the town and rally their forces on Cemetery Hill. Colonel Hecker was still recovering from his wounds at Chancellorsville, which presented Lieutenant Colonel Salomon with the opportunity to lead the 82nd. Under his command, the 82nd provided protection for the Union artillery batteries on the plains north of town, covered Union regiments retreating through Gettysburg, and positioned themselves facing Confederate troops on Cemetery Hill. The second day brought little relief for the 82nd. The regiment confronted a group of Confederate sharpshooters on the outskirts of town and participated in the twilight battle to protect neighboring Culp's Hill. The third day of the battle occurred south of the 82nd Illinois's position, allowing the men to only witness the Confederate charge against the well-entrenched Union line. The resounding defeat of the Confederates forced them to forget their plans of invading the North and made them retreat back into Virginia. The 82nd continued its pursuit of the Confederate forces until the fall, when it was transferred with the 11 Corps out west.

Throughout October and November 1863, the 82nd faced off against Confederate generals Longstreet and Bragg in Tennessee, participating in the Battle of Mission Ridge. In December, the regiment was encamped in Lookout Valley and a month later reorganized into the new 20th Corps, part of the Army of the Cumberland. Hecker, who was now a general, resigned in March 1864, transferring command of the regiment to Salomon. From May until July, the 82nd worked its way through the South toward Atlanta, Georgia, contributing in the siege of the Confederate stronghold for the rest of the summer. On September 2, Atlanta fell to the Union forces, and within days the 82nd was part of the occupation force assigned to guard Confederate prisoners, defend the city, and partake in the supply foraging expeditions. The men's stay in Atlanta lasted until the middle of November 1864, when they became the rear guard for General William Sherman's March to the Sea. Within a month, the 82nd had reached the defenses of Savannah, Georgia. The 82nd continued its sweep through the Deep South, conducting operations through the Carolinas during the early months of 1865. Finally, on April 16, the men learned that the Confederates had surrendered and that the war was over. They made their way to Washington, D.C., to join in the victory festivities and participate in the Army's Grand Review.

Marc Dluger

See also Chicago; Hecker, Friedrich; Salomon, Edward S.; Schimmelpfennig, Alexander; Schurz, Carl

References and Further Reading
Andreas, Alfred Theodore. *History of Chicago.* Vol. 2. New York: Arno Press, 1975.
Keil, Hartmut, and John B. Jentz, eds. *German Workers in Industrial Chicago, 1850– 1910: A Comparative Perspective.* DeKalb: Northern Illinois University Press, 1983.
Meites, Hyman L. *History of the Jews of Chicago.* Chicago: Chicago Jewish Historical Society, Wellington, 1990.
Pierce, Bessie Louise. *History of Chicago: From Town to City, 1848–1871.* Vol. 2. New York: Alfred A. Knopf, 1940.
Tortorelli, Susan. "82nd Illinois Infantry Regiment History: Adjutant General's Report." http://www.rootsweb.com /~ilcivilw/history/082.htm (cited October 9, 2002).

EINHORN, DAVID

b. November 10, 1809; Dispeck, Bavaria
d. November 2, 1879; New York, New York

German American Reform rabbi and editor of the *Sinai.*

David Einhorn received his rabbinical training at a traditional yeshivah in Fürth, where he earned an official rabbinical diploma. He also received a secular education and studied philosophy at the universities of Erlangen, Würzburg, and Munich. Introduced to the methods of critical enquiry and *Wissenschaft* (science) in the philosophy of religion, he moved away from Jewish orthodoxy and was rejected from the rabbinate by both religious and secular authorities in Bavaria.

In 1842 he was hired as a rabbi in Birkenfeld, in the grand duchy of Oldenbourg. Five years later he succeeded Samuel Holdheim, a radical supporter of the German Reform movement, as chief rabbi in Mecklenburg-Schwerin. For a few months he served as rabbi of a radical Reform congregation in the city of Pest, Hungary, until that congregation was closed down by the government.

For Einhorn, Judaism could never be static but was constantly adapting to the challenges of the times and demonstrated the capacity for continuous development. He stressed what he called the "essence of Judaism"—the spirit of pure humanity— which he regarded to be older than Jewish nationhood. Therefore, he concluded, Judaism had from its beginning commanded its followers to overcome its national exclusiveness and serve as an ethical example for humankind.

Left without opportunities in Europe, Einhorn left for the United States with his wife and two daughters in 1855, having been invited by Har Sinai congregation of Baltimore, Maryland, the country's first Reform congregation, to serve as their rabbi. His arrival coincided with the Cleveland Conference, a rabbinical meeting in

1855, organized by Isaac M. Wise and Isaac Leeser, who sought a religious platform for national unity in American Judaism. Having suffered from the influence of established religious authority, which prevented changes in Judaism, and having failed to secure the development of Jewish Reform thought because the all-embracing communal structures in Europe (*jüdische Einheitsgemeinde*) thwarted religious compromise on the congregational level, Einhorn instantly understood that American religious structures would provide an unique environment where a modern Judaism could flourish. Thus, here he fiercely opposed the attempt at a national religious union and the establishment of a "synod." He cherished the individualism of the American congregation and believed that only in this climate of religious liberty could Reform Judaism develop fully according to its principles. Critical to America's scholarly potential, Einhorn sought to maintain a close intellectual relationship to German Jewish thinkers, such as Abraham Geiger and Samuel Holdheim, which he considered essential to the maintenance of theological and philosophical Reform principle. In 1856 he founded the monthly periodical *Sinai* (1856–1862) to disseminate his thoughts in the United States and published his prayer book, *Olat Tamid.*

An uncompromising champion of abolition, Einhorn was forced to flee from Baltimore in 1861. He settled in Philadelphia and served as the rabbi of the congregation Kenesseth Israel. In 1866 he moved to New York City to lead the congregation Adath Israel, later Temple Beth El. At the Philadelphia Rabbinical Conference in 1869, Einhorn stressed the messianic nature of American Reform Judaism. By dominating the conference, Einhorn made a future union of American Jews on theological grounds, as envisioned by Wise, impossible.

His thinking gained greater influence after his death through his sons-in-law, Kaufmann Kohler and Emil Hirsch, who were married to Johanna Einhorn Kohler and Mathilde Einhorn Hirsch, respectively. These two men shaped the American Reform movement theologically from the "Pittsburgh Platform" (1885), a rabbinical conference that took place in Pittsburgh. Its results served as a basis for what used to be referred to as "Classical Reform." Classical Reform stressed Reform principle (Judaism's basis as spirit, not law, so that continuous religious progress could be achieved) over communal unity. In Pittsburgh, Reform Jews defined themselves as a community of belief. It gave up the idea of Jewish nationhood and instead stressed Jewish identity as *American* Jews. The Pittsburgh Platform called for a "living Judaism," which was reflected in active social service. This interpretation opened a mutual interest with American groups in the dominating social gospel movement. Finally, the conference decided to use Einhorn's prayer book *Olat Tamid* as a model for the *Union Prayer Book* of the American Reform movement and thus secured Einhorn's lasting influence on the American Reform movement in Judaism.

Cornelia Wilhelm

See also Judaism, Reform (North America); Kohler, Kaufmann; Wise, Isaac Mayer
References and Further Reading
Friedland, Eric L. "'Olath Tamid' by David Einhorn." *HUCA* 45 (1974): 307–332.
Greenberg, Gershon. "The Messianic Foundations of American Jewish Thought; David Einhorn and Samuel Hirsch." *WCJS* (1975): 215–226.

Kohler, Kaufmann, ed. *David Einhorn, Memorial Volume: Selected Sermons and Addresses.* New York: Bloch, 1911.

Meyer, Michael A. *Response to Modernity: A History of the Reform Movement in Judaism.* Detroit: Wayne State University Press, 1990.

EINSTEIN, ALBERT
b. March 14, 1879; Ulm, Württemberg
d. April 18, 1955; Princeton, New Jersey

The most eminent physicist of the twentieth century of German Jewish background, Albert Einstein emigrated to the United States in 1933. He revolutionized physicists' understanding of space and time with his special theory of relativity (1905) and general theory of relativity (1915). His light quantum hypothesis (1905) contributed largely to the establishment of quantum physics and revolutionized the wave and particle theory of classical physics.

After conflicts with the authoritarian German school system, Einstein left Germany for Italy at age fifteen and in 1895 he went on to Switzerland, where in 1896, he finished school in Aarau, Switzerland, and entered the Technical University of Switzerland (ETH) in Zurich to study physics and mathematics. Upon graduation in 1900, Einstein failed to secure an academic career. He worked instead as a substitute teacher. From 1902 to 1909, he was employed as an evaluator for the Patent Office of the Swiss government in Bern. During these years, Einstein defended his first and second doctoral (*Habilitation*) dissertations, in 1905 and 1909, respectively. In 1905 he published three ground-breaking papers on the light-quantum hypothesis, the Brownian mo-

tion, and electrodynamics. These publications paved the way for his academic career. In 1909, Einstein was appointed extraordinary professor of theoretical physics at the University of Zurich. In 1911, he accepted a full professorship at the German University of Prague. From 1912 to 1914, Einstein taught at the ETH. Invited by leading German physicists in Berlin, he moved there in 1914. In Berlin, Einstein became a full member of the Prussian Academy of Sciences and was made director of the Kaiser Wilhelm Institute of Physics in 1917, which freed him from teaching obligations. The Berlin years were the peak of Einstein's scientific and social recognition. However, he also became the target of political and antisemitic attacks by German right-wing and racist politicians. When Adolf Hitler was appointed chancellor in January 1933, Einstein, who was giving guest lectures in the United States, decided not to return to Germany. Opposing the new political system, Einstein cancelled his membership in the Prussian Academy of Sciences. Until his death, he remained in the United States and worked as a fellow at the newly founded Institute for Advanced Study in Princeton, New Jersey.

After a British solar eclipse expedition in Africa confirmed essential parts of Einstein's general theory of relativity, he quickly became world famous and also attracted the attention of scholars on both sides of the Atlantic Ocean. Yet, his first trip to the United States was connected not to his scientific achievements but to the Zionist cause. In 1921, Einstein traveled with Chaim Weizmann to the United States to collect donations for the Zionist movement and for the founding of Hebrew University in Jerusalem. During this visit, he received his first honorary doctorate

Albert Einstein receives from Judge Phillip Forman his certificate of American citizenship, October 1, 1940. (Library of Congress)

from Princeton University. He also met influential American scholars such as Robert Andrew Millikan, the most important U.S. physicist at that time. It was Millikan who invited Einstein at the beginning of the 1930s for several research stays at the California Institute of Technology in Pasadena (Cal Tech).

Although he held the scholarly climate in Berlin in high esteem, Einstein had thought about leaving Germany since the beginning of the 1920s. The political climate of the Weimar Republic, right-wing trends, and increasing antisemitism were responsible for his growing alienation from German society. In the summer of 1932, he had readily agreed to accept an appointment at the Institute for Advanced Study in

Princeton. The industrialist Abraham Flexner had founded the institute to give scientists the opportunity to pursue research projects without teaching obligations. This appointment allowed Einstein to keep his position in Berlin and spend the winter semester at Princeton Institute. When the Nazis seized power, Einstein was in Pasadena working at Cal Tech. He immediately denounced the new political system and pointed out the persecution of Jews and of political dissenters in his home country. In his resignation letter to the Prussian Academy of Sciences (April 5, 1933), Einstein wrote that he would not live in a country where citizens could not enjoy equality in the face of the law, nor freedom of opinion and teaching. Einstein was one of the very few German scholars who immediately attacked the Nazi dictatorship.

After a short stay in Europe, Einstein returned to the United States in the fall of 1933. From his exile in the United States, Einstein continuously criticized the political terror and antisemitic propaganda of the Nazi system. He used his position as a recognized scientist to help persecuted and exiled colleagues. During World War II, Einstein also served as a scientific adviser to the U.S. Navy. In 1939 he supported the initiative of Leo Szilard and Eugen Wigner, two émigrés from Berlin, to inform President Franklin D. Roosevelt of the possibility that Nazi Germany could develop an atomic bomb and to suggest that Americans should begin a similar project.

Einstein was not involved in the Manhattan Project partly because of his lack of expertise in nuclear physics and partly because the Federal Bureau of Investigation (FBI) felt that he might be politically unreliable. It concluded its investigation of Einstein in the summer of 1940 with this evaluation: "In view of his political background, this office would not recommend the employment of Dr. Einstein on matters of a secret nature, without a very careful investigation, as it seems unlikely that a man of his background could, in such a short time, become a loyal American citizen" (Jerome 2002, 39). The FBI was suspicious of his German past since "in Berlin, even in the political free and easy period of 1923 to 1929, the Einstein home was known as a Communist center clearing house. Mrs. and Miss Einstein were always prominent at all extreme radical meetings and demonstrations." These baseless accusations were not new to Einstein. The political police in Germany and the right-wing

press had come to the same ridiculous conclusion during the 1920s.

Freedom and civil liberty were central to Einstein's political convictions. He not only attacked Nazi Germany and Stalinist Russia for their annihilationary policies, he also criticized the state of civil liberties in the United States. The McCarthy era reminded Einstein of the right-wing extremism of the 1920s. His support of the civil rights movement in the United States made him a hero in liberal circles and a villain to conservative, right-wing politicians. Some of the latter even wanted to take away his U.S. citizenship and throw him out of the country since he did not hide his left-leaning, humanistic opinions. For instance, in the 1930s, he took the side of the Popular Front government of Spain and supported the "Friends of the Lincoln Brigade," who fought in the Spanish Civil War against Francisco Franco. His uncompromising anti-Nazism and support for any anti-Fascist organization, including Communist and pro-Soviet groups, did not make him many friends within the American establishment. Einstein met public resentment when he aligned with the civil rights movement and engaged together with the singer Paul Robeson and the ethnologist William du Bois in the antilynching movement. All these activities made Einstein a political outsider who became the target of Secret Service investigations at the beginning of the 1950s.

After the bombing of Hiroshima and Nagasaki, Einstein demanded a ban on nuclear weapons. He favored the creation of a world government that would find peaceful solutions to conflicts between nations and states. He became one of the most vocal critiques of the ensuing cold war and was one of the authors of the Russel-

Einstein-Manifesto that became the basis for the Pugwash movement, a movement that since 1957 brought together scientists from different countries and political backgrounds to discuss the dangers of nuclear weapons, general disarmament, and world security. However, the FBI was less concerned with Einstein's position on international problems and more with his statements concerning domestic policy. Einstein criticized the judicial system, which was based on the idea of equality but sometimes failed to meet that ideal. Racism was the "worst American disease" to him. In particular, he criticized the activities of Senator Joseph McCarthy and branded his investigations as a modern-style Inquisition. The FBI considered Einstein a danger since his prominence could compel other Americans to follow his example and to speak out against the injustices of American society. J. Edgar Hoover was personally involved in the attempt to prove Einstein's Communist leanings. He considered him to be the lynchpin of a supposedly Communist spy network that he wanted to uncover. In the end, it was his prominence and the lack of conclusive evidence that saved Einstein from becoming another victim of McCarthyism.

Dieter Hoffmann

See also U.S.-German Intellectual Exchange; Wigner, Eugen(e) Paul

References and Further Reading

Fölsing, Albrecht. *Albert Einstein: A Biography.* New York: Viking, 1997.

Jerome, Fred. *The Einstein File: J. Edgar Hoover's Secret War against the World's Most Famous Scientist.* New York: St. Martin's Press, 2002.

Pais, Abraham. *"Subtle Is the Lord": The Science and the Life of Albert Einstein.* Oxford: Oxford University Press, 1982.

Sayen, Jamie. *Einstein in America: The Scientist's Conscience in the Age of Hitler and Hiroshima.* New York: Crown, 1985.

ENCYCLOPAEDIA AMERICANA

The first modern encyclopedia designed and published in the United States according to international standards established in Europe in the first quarter of the nineteenth century was the work of the German American Francis (Franz) Lieber (1798 or 1800 to 1872), an eminent jurist, political scientist, and polymath. With its thirteen volumes, the *Encyclopaedia Americana, Popular Dictionary of Arts, Sciences, Literature, History, Politics and Biography, Brought down to the Present Time; Including a Copious Collection of Original Articles in American Biography; on the Basis of the Seventh Edition of the German Conversations-Lexicon,* was published in Philadelphia from 1829 to 1833 and became an instant success with the American reading public, notably among the professional class. During the following decades, the *Encyclopaedia Americana* was published in numerous editions in different places by different publishers and was widely used in all parts of the country until the time of the Civil War. Its significance is twofold. First of all, it represents the successful transfer and adaptation of the German type of encyclopedia, namely Brockhaus's twelve-volume *Allgemeine deutsche Real-Encyclopaedie für die gebildeten Stände* or *Conversations-Lexikon* (Universal German Encyclopedia for the Educated Classes, 1827–1829), to the needs and circumstances of the United States, and in the process it evolved into a truly American reference work. At the same time, it functioned over many decades as a widely accepted source of information, not only about things American but also about the history and culture of the principal European nations of England, France, Germany, Italy, the Netherlands, Portugal, Russia, and Spain.

Lieber had derived the rationale for his enterprise from "the wants of the age," which he saw as not confined to the new American republic but as a common trait of all modern Western nations. The speed with which political changes now took place; the accelerating pace of scientific discoveries, where "science gathers contributions from every quarter of the globe " (vol. 1:iv); and the increasing facility of communication among nations with the rapid spread of information had enormously enlarged the field of civilization and therefore required a new type of work that would furnish the general reader with all the information necessary to keep abreast of these developments. The Brockhaus *Reallexikon* (encyclopedia) had successfully filled that need in Germany and other European countries (it was translated into Danish, Dutch, Swedish, and French). Now Lieber wanted to create a "repository of knowledge" relating to the United States and to all branches of knowledge that could be of value to an English and American readership and include "all subjects of general interest on the continent of Europe" (vol. 1:v). The *Encyclopaedia Americana* was thus explicitly designed by Lieber to venture beyond the traditional historical and cultural reach of the English encyclopedias that had been in use in the United States until the early 1800s.

Lieber's plan for such a work won immediate approval and strong support among the New England intelligentsia, notably from the group of recent graduates of the University of Göttingen in Germany, who shared and expressed a view of a future American national culture independent from that of Great Britain and in whose plans the adaptation and utilization of German cultural ideas and achievements played a vital part. They included George Bancroft; Edward Everett, professor of Classics at Harvard and subsequently its president; and George Ticknor, the first professor of Romance Languages and Literatures at Harvard. In Göttingen they had been students of the new historical and philological disciplines for which the university was famous and had absorbed the Herderian notions of nationhood and national culture upon which these disciplines had been erected. Upon their return to the United States, they used these new ideas to construct their own notion of an American national culture. They found their mouthpiece when Everett assumed the editorship of the prestigious *North American Review*. An essential part of their program was the attempt to enlarge the American cultural horizon beyond the one they had inherited from their former colonial masters. The journal published important articles by Bancroft, Alexander, and Edward Everett, which introduced the American public to major German authors such as Johann Wolfgang von Goethe, Friedrich Schiller, and Johann Gottfried Herder. Lieber, who had made contact with the group upon his arrival in Boston in 1827, shortly saw himself play the double role of mediator of German culture in this country and participant in the new American nationalist movement whose cultural and political ideals he shared. Supplied with strong letters of support from the Göttingen alumni, he convinced Mathew Carey, of Carey, Lea, and Carey of Philadelphia, arguably the most prominent publishing house in the country at the time, to accept his proposal for an American encyclopedia and sign a contract with him.

Setting up shop in Boston with Carey's support, he hired an assistant editor

(E.Wigglesworth), and went about his task employing up to a dozen translators at a time. Yet to make the work truly an American encyclopedia required the removal of hundreds of articles from the original Brockhaus encyclopedia, the rewriting of hundreds more, and the creation of an equal number of new entries. He succeeded in securing American contributors who were experts in their respective fields, the most prominent among them Joseph Storey, associate justice at the Supreme Court, who contributed over 120 pages on American legal topics. Also in need of treatment were the topics of Native American languages and American history, biography, economy, geography, mineralogy, and flora and fauna. Robert Walsh, editor of the *American Quarterly,* agreed to write the biographies of prominent Americans; Moses Stuart, theology professor at Andover and an expert on German biblical hermeneutics, wrote and/or translated many of the articles on religious topics; Edward Everett was responsible for the Greek and Roman classics; and George Ticknor covered modern European letters and literatures, in particular those of Italy and Spain. John Pickering of Salem, Massachusetts, who, together with Peter S. Duponceau, president of the American Philosophical Society in Philadelphia (also a contributor), belongs among the founders of American linguistics, was commissioned to write a lengthy article on the North American Indian languages. To inform the American public about the forthcoming work, Lieber in 1828 had an eight-page prospectus inserted in the *North American Review.* In 1829 the first volume appeared, and by 1830 volume 5 had been published, but the final volume (13) was not published until 1833 because the task had

proven more demanding and complicated than the editor had first anticipated. Writing to his German correspondent Wilhelm von Humboldt, who belonged to the European network of friends and informants with whom he had stayed in contact after his arrival in this country (Wilhelm and his brother Alexander both were accorded entries in the encyclopedia), Lieber likened the *Encyclopaedia Americana* project to a jealous mistress who mercilessly claimed his time. In order to bring the work up to date on the latest political developments, as promised in the title, Lieber felt obliged to write extensive accounts of the Greek Revolutionary War, the July Revolution of 1830 in France, the establishment of the Kingdom of Belgium in 1831, and the English Reform Act of 1832.

Upon completion, the shape of the work was determined as much by the standards required for the modern encyclopedia as by the editor's decisions on what to include and exclude; his choice of contributors; and his educational background, intellectual culture, historical understanding, and philosophical and political beliefs and opinions. Although the work, in order to represent the political map of the time, contains articles on most European nations, their respective treatments differ noticeably in type and density of information offered. "Germany," with nearly 34 pages, would seem to surpass "Great Britain," with a mere 26 pages, were it not for an additional 6.5-page entry "England" (with an entry on the English language) and another 5.5 pages on "Scotland." Belgium, mentioned only briefly in volume 1 (the country did not exist yet in 1829), was given a 15-page treatment in the appendix to volume 13. Poland, although not an independent state, received an entry of over 10 pages because, Lieber argued, it possessed a clear ethnic, cultural, and linguistic identity. The entry "Prussia," in contrast, consists of only 7.5 pages and includes critical comments on the heterogeneous nature of the Prussian state. "Russia" has 33 pages, against "Spain" with 24 and "Portugal" with about 17, whereas "Italy" takes up nearly 45 pages. However, the lengthiest treatment—over 100 pages—was given to "France." Its extraordinary length (including several appendices) was not due to a predilection of Lieber for France or French civilization, but resulted from his view of the current state of affairs in Europe as the consequence of the French Revolution and its aftermath: the rise of Napoleon, his conquest of Europe and eventual defeat, the order imposed at the Congress of Vienna with its restoration of the monarchical system on the continent, the opposition it encountered in various countries, and the developments in France that led to the July Revolution of 1830. The latter was seen by Lieber as an encouraging sign that other countries, in particular Germany, might follow suit and move toward a democratic and representative form of government. The developments in France were therefore depicted within the larger European context, and much of the lengthy account devoted to them read more like a history of modern Europe than French history. Not surprisingly, Lieber used these articles in a separate publication.

Yet upon closer examination, the apparent preponderance of France over the rest of the European nations dissipates, and a persistent German presence emerges. The very structure and organization of the work in fact displays its German descent. Besides the entry "Germany," we find a veritable plethora of different articles dealing with German literature, philosophy, theology, science, scholarship, music, and painting that convey mostly state-of-the-art information and open new vistas that had not been available in the country until then. In addition, many articles pertaining to topics such as Greek and Roman civilization or the entries on general literary topics, such as the ballad, the drama, the epic, the concept "romantic," and the substantial article on literary history—areas in which the Germans had taken the lead—relied heavily on German scholarship. Often, German scholars and critics, like August Wilhelm and Friedrich Schlegel, are quoted verbatim. The same holds true for the articles on Homer and the English poet William Shakespeare. The list of German authors represents a substantial enlargement of the literary horizon of the New England Göttingen alumni, whose interest was focused on classical authors like Herder, Gotthold Ephraim Lessing, Goethe, and Schiller. Now for the first time information was made available on the mainstream of writers that make up the literary history of Germany. Thus new names were added to the canon that had been established by Madame de Staël in her influential book *De L'Allmagne* (Germany, 1813; Amer. ed., 1814). Besides entries on authors such as Clemens Brentano, Gottfried August Bürger, Heinrich Wilhelm von Gerstenberg, Salomon Gessner, Johann Wilhelm Gleim, Johann Christoph Gottsched, Friedrich von Hagedorn, Albrecht von Haller, Friedrich Maximilian Klinger, Friedrich Gottlieb Klopstock, Lessing, Martin Opitz, Jean Paul Richter, Novalis (Friedrich von Hardenberg), Ludwig Tieck, on the medieval Nibelungen poem and, of course, Goethe and Schiller, we encounter names not mentioned by de

Staël, such as Ernst Moritz Arndt, Simon Dach, Paul Fleming, Christian Fürchtegott Gellert, Paul Gerhardt, Andreas Gryphius, E. T. A. Hoffmann, Ludwig Christoph Hölty, or Johann Anton Leisewitz. Throughout, entries are organized around the biographical data for each figure; their important works are given with a few descriptive and (or) evaluating comments, mostly from a moralizing, liberal, political point of view. Thus Arndt is praised for having contributed to the liberation of Germany from Napoleonic rule "by his bold and patriotic writings" (vol. 1:386), and Novalis's *Hymns to the Night* we are informed "have the greatest merit," though we are not told why. About Klopstock we learn that as a lyric poet, he belonged among the most successful of any age, so that "he may well be called the Pindar of modern poetry" (vol. 7:377).

The treatment of Germanys philosophy and theology, though uneven in its coverage, proved to be more consequential than that of its literature. It raised issues and evoked ideas that preoccupied the minds of the New England intelligentsia at the time, providing them with strong indicators for the making of a new philosophical outlook beyond traditional empiricism or Calvinism that would be articulated by the Transcendentalists (Ralph Waldo Emerson and Theodore Parker) during the following years and decades. Among the articles on German philosophers, those on Gottfried Wilhelm Leibniz and Immanuel Kant are the longest. The entries on the idealists Joahnn Gottlieb Fichte, Georg Wilhelm Friedrich Hegel, and Friedrich Wilhelm Joseph Schelling contain no more than biographical and scant bibliographical data and generalizations, though some of Schelling's main ideas are discussed in an article on the German philosophy of nature. Fichte is praised chiefly for his patriotism and ethical stance. Schelling and Hegel were still alive at the time, as was Goethe. The entry on Leibniz, "one of the most celebrated scholars and philosophers Germany has ever produced" (vol. 7:490), by contrast, discusses the details of his life and his achievements in various fields, from mathematics, logic, and physics to metaphysics. Here the emphasis is placed on his rationalist, antiempiricist stance, notably his doctrine of innate necessary truths. In his article on Kant, Lieber uses formulations that evoked this Leibnizian doctrine when he describes key notions in that thinker's *Kritik der Reinen Vernunft* (Critique of Pure Reason). He employs expressions first introduced by de Staël to account for Kant's position at a time when no English or French translations were yet available. Formulations much like these by Lieber later entered into the core writings of the American Transcendentalists: Kant having discovered "the fundamental laws of the mind," ascertained the "exact number of these original or transcendental ideas or, imperative forms." These we do not derive from experience, but rather "we acquire experience" by them. Of the mind's three departments, the senses are "passive," whereas the understanding displays "spontaneous activity," yet reason shows "the highest degree of mental spontaneity" (vol. 7:305–306). Remarkably, Friedrich Heinrich Jacobi, "a distinguished German philosopher," receives more attention than any of the idealist thinkers or Lieber's former teacher, Jakob Friedrich Fries. On account of the "religious glow " of his metaphysical writings, Jacobi has been called "the German Plato," and Friedrich Daniel Ernst Schleiermacher is lauded for having "done much for the intellectual and religious advancement of his countrymen." Georg Christoph Lichtenberg is described as "the greatest natural philosopher, and wittiest writer Germany has produced." But these men are surpassed by Herder, to whom "Germany is deeply indebted in almost every branch of literature" (i.e., in theology, philosophy, literature, and history) and "who brought before the public the poetry of past times of Europe and Asia" (vol. 6:274f.). Yet the entries on European philosophers, taken singly or together, regardless of nationality, only insufficiently convey the importance that was attributed by the editor of the *Encyclopaedia Americana* to German philosophy. In the article "Philosophy" (Appendix, vol. 10:594– 604), the exceptionality of German thought is maintained and its reach extended beyond the traditional sphere of philosophy. The Germans had acquired through their philosophy "a spirit of scientific liberty, unknown in other nations," a spirit that pervaded "the best of their works on religion, on literature, on natural philosophy" . . . "and may well challenge comparison." Madame de Staël had already expressed similar views, as would the Transcendentalists later.

In its compilation of the scientific knowledge produced in the different European nations, the *Encyclopaedia Americana* included a significant contingent of German scientists and scholars, many of whom were connected with the University of Göttingen. Besides the mathematician Karl Friedrich Gauss and Johann Friedrich Blumenbach, founder of modern anthropology, we find representatives of the historical-philological disciplines, such as the orientalist Johann Gottfried Eichhorn, the classicist Christian Gottlob Heyne, the philosopher and literary historian Friedrich Bouterwek, and the historian Arnold Hermann Heeren, some of whose works had been translated and published in this country by his former student Bancroft. Lieber included entries on the German linguists Jakob Grimm, Heinrich Julius Klaproth, Johann and Friedrich Adelung, and Johann Severinus Vater—the latter two were involved with the beginnings of American linguistics. This new discipline (in which Lieber possessed strong personal interest) was represented by John Pickering, with his article on the American Indian languages (Appendix, vol.6:581–600, subsequently translated and published in Germany), and by Peter S. Duponceau, with entries on the German Moravian missionaries in Pennsylvania, Johann Gottlieb Ernst Heckewelder, and David Zeisberger and their pioneering work on Indian languages and customs. Lieber also included a lengthy and personal article on the historian Berthold Niebuhr, his former teacher and benefactor (231 lines). His desire to join German and the American traditions can be gathered also from his treatment of the U.S. legal system. Thus, the article on the jury system consists of two parts: one, the translated Brockhaus text by a German legal scholar who also discusses the weaknesses of the system, and the other, a contribution by the American judge Storey. This entry illustrates in an exemplary fashion how the *Encyclopaedia Americana* could be both product and vehicle of the multifarious process of German American cultural transfer it helped set in motion and sustain.

A distinct weakness of the work derives from the the disproportionate length of its articles devoted to the lives of American political and military personalities. Thus, the entry on Benedict Arnold, American general and turncoat during the American Revolution, takes up almost 10 pages, whereas Aristotle and René Descartes are compressed into 2 pages each, and the poet John Milton occupies a mere 2.5 pages. Yet on balance, the work, with its approximately 8,000 pages and 20,000 articles, proved a highly practical and effective compilation of knowledge. Its ready availability and low price contributed to its success—its contents equaled that of thirty-six to forty-eight English octavo volumes, which would have cost about $150, whereas the price for the entire thirteen-volume set was a mere $32.50. It sold throughout the entire country and abroad, with sales reaching 100,000 sets over the years. Presidents Andrew Jackson and Abraham Lincoln owned one, as did Emerson and his writer friends; Alexis de Tocqueville received one as a gift from the editor himself. The work helped enormously "to republicanize," as one reviewer put it, the knowledge that once had been the privilege of a few. It was above all the rapid expansion of the United States during the decades following its first publication that rendered the work outdated by the time of the Civil War.

Kurt Mueller-Vollmer

See also Adelung, Johann Christoph; Bancroft, George; Everett, Edward; Göttingen, University of; Humboldt, Wilhelm von; Lieber, Francis; Ticknor, George; Transcendentalism; Vater, Johann Severin

References and Further Reading
Freidel, Frank. *Francis Lieber: Nineteenth-Century Liberal.* Baton Rouge: Louisiana State University Press, 1947.
Mueller-Vollmer, Kurt. "German-American Cultural Interaction in the Jacksonian Era: Six Unpublished Letters by Francis Lieber and John Pickering to Wilhelm von Humboldt." *Die Unterrichtspraxis,* no. 1 (1998):1–11.
Neal, John. "Encyclopaedia Americana." *North American Review* 34 (1832): 262–268.
Perry, Thomas Seargeant, ed. *The Life and Letters of Francis Lieber.* Boston: James Osgoodand, 1882.
Pochmann, Henry A. *German Culture in America: Philosophical and Literary Influences, 1600–1900.* Madison: University of Wisconsin Press, 1957.
Schäfer, Peter, and Karl Schmitt, eds. *Franz Lieber und die deutsch-amerikanischen Beziehungen im 19. Jahrhundert.* Weimar: Böhlau, 1993.
Walsh, Robert. "Encyclopaedia Americana." *American Quarterly Review* 6 (1829): 331–360.

ENDE, AMALIE (AMELIA) VON
b. June 19, 1856; Warsaw, Russia
d. August 25, 1932; New York, New York

A student of the German American writer and activist Mathilde Franziska Anneke, Amalie von Ende was exposed to radical ideas and that exposure was reinforced by her marriage with German-born (Georg) Henrich von Ende (1847–1879), a journalist with Communist leanings, in 1876. Until her husband's death, she collaborated with him on a number of radical journalistic ventures. She was an important German American writer, journalist, translator, composer, musician, teacher, and lecturer.

At the age of six, Amalie von Ende arrived in Milwaukee, where she received early training in music. Following her move to Chicago, she started the German

American Young Ladies Institute, a boarding school for girls that adhered to progressive pedagogical principles. She remained principal of that school until 1893, when she moved to New York City and became the most significant and prolific cultural mediator between Germany and the United States in her time. In leading German and American papers and journals such as *Das Literarische Echo* (Literary Echo) and *The Bookman,* she informed American, German American, and German readers about the complex literary and cultural developments in the respective fin-de-siècle societies, often from a comparative angle.

In 1898, von Ende introduced a German audience to Emily Dickinson by translating four of her poems for a German American magazine and two for a German magazine. A board member of Horace Traubel's Walt Whitman International, an organization assembling friends and enthusiasts of Walt Whitman, she was an ardent advocate for Walt Whitman and worked hard and very successfully for his reception in Germany. Her intense interest in music never subsided; in New York, she was known as a pianist; she also composed several songs, which were published in Germany.

Always critical of Prussian nationalism and militarism and a feminist pacifist who demanded the replacement of patriotism by matriatism, von Ende became deeply disillusioned with Germany after the outbreak of World War I. The number of her journalistic contributions declined after 1914, and she increasingly took to the lecture circuit, which led her to most major colleges and universities on the East Coast, where her lectures and presentations were highly acclaimed. Von Ende's work was informed by a then-rare, inclusive, and antielite notion of culture, clearly anticipating the multicultural revisions of canons toward the close of the twentieth century.

Walter Grünzweig

See also Anneke, Mathilde Franziska
References and Further Reading
Grünzweig, Walter. "Cries of Distress: Emily Dickinson's Initial German Reception from an Intercultural Perspective." *The Emily Dickinson Journal* 5, no. 2 (1996): 232–239.
Müller, Manuela. *Amalie von Ende: Wegbereiterin des interkulturellen Journalismus. Porträt einer Mittlerin und Grenzgängerin zwischen den Kulturen.* Diplomarbeit, Department of Journalism, Universität Dortmund, 1998.

Ephrata

A monastic community of Sabbatarians in northern Lancaster County, Pennsylvania, Ephrata was founded in the late 1720s by (Georg) Conrad Beissel (1691–1768). During its peak period in the middle decades of the eighteenth century, the community may have numbered over 300 people. Its members wrote numerous religious hymns, developed a style of choir singing that profoundly impressed visitors, and left a rich legacy of illuminated manuscripts. They also constructed large monastic buildings whose architecture is thought to reflect religious symbolism. Ephrata attracted numerous visitors and the attention of European observers even in Beissel's time. One of the most famous German exiles in the twentieth–century United States, Thomas Mann, incorporated a passage on Beissel and the choral music of Ephrata into his novel *Doctor Faustus* (1947). Today the remaining buildings are among the

Pennsylvania German culture area's major tourist attractions.

The tenth child of a baker from Eberbach in Palatinate who was orphaned as an eight-year-old, Conrad Beissel spent his youth in abject poverty. He was reportedly apprenticed to the baker's trade and came to Heidelberg as a journeyman, where he had a conversion experience in a pietist circle in 1715. Three years later, he was apparently expelled from the Palatinate as a religious dissenter and lived with radical pietists in the Hessian principality of Isenburg-Büdingen for some time. In 1720 he emigrated to North America and apprenticed himself to a weaver in Germantown, Pennsylvania. A year later he moved to the still sparsely settled Conestoga region, where he sought to live the solitary life of a hermit. In 1724 Beissel received baptism from the Dunker Peter Becker and subsequently became the leader of the Dunkers, a radical pietist group practicing adult baptism by immersion, in the Conestoga area. Beissel gradually moved away from basic Dunker teachings, however, when he began to honor Saturday as the divinely ordained Sabbath and advocate celibacy. The renewed baptism of six members of his congregation in 1728 marked his break with the Dunkers. Four years later, Beissel moved to a solitary cabin on the banks of Cocalico Creek, but his adherents followed him and established their own dwellings. Single men and women lived in hermit cabins, while the so-called householders lived together in family units. This distinction between celibates and householders became a basic feature of life at Ephrata.

In 1735 the community built the first monastic house for female celibates, whom Beissel organized into the Order of Spiri-

W.P.A. poster promoting the Ephrata Cloister, Lancaster County, PA. It reads, "Ephrata: Visit the ancient cloisters of the early German pietists in Lancaster Co., Pennsylvania," ca. 1936–1941. (Library of Congress)

tual Virgins. A few years later, a communal house was constructed for the male celibates, who were organized as the Zionitic Brotherhood. In a veritable building boom, a number of additional buildings were erected until midcentury, and Beissel's evangelizing attracted new converts, including the Reformed pastor Peter Miller and Pennsylvania's Indian agent Conrad Weiser. Under the direction of the brothers Israel and Samuel Eckerlin, Ephrata also entered a phase of economic expansion: mills and workshops were built, and a printing press was acquired in 1745.

Beissel's emphasis on celibacy has been traced to his peculiar understanding of the androgynous nature of God and the first man. In Beissel's view God combined male and female characteristics in perfect balance, the female attributes being embodied in the conception of the divine virgin Sophia. The sexual difference between man and woman was interpreted as a consequence of original sin and humanity's fall, and Beissel promoted chastity and discipleship as the way to eventual reunion with God. A prolific author of theological and poetic works, Beissel developed a highly original mystical language to convey his sense of the presence of God. Beissel's theology of redemption and rebirth and his eschatology drew on continental European sources, particularly on the mystic Jacob Boehme and the radical pietist writers Johann Georg Gichtel and Gottfried Arnold, and the community sought to express these concepts in its religious life and material culture. Life at Ephrata was structured by rituals like baptism by immersion and communal love feasts, and the celibates practiced an ascetic lifestyle that involved a sparse, mostly vegetarian diet, the tonsuring of heads, the wearing of white, hooded garments, and extended nightly prayer sessions.

Conrad Beissel's charismatic personality attracted numerous people, but his autocratic and occasionally erratic demeanor also caused repeated conflict. As early as 1745, Beissel expelled Israel Eckerlin, the leader of Ephrata's communal economy, who may have become too influential for his taste. His final years were overshadowed by legal conflicts over property rights and challenges to his authority. After Beissel's death in 1768, Peter Miller became the leader of the celibates, but the community was already in decline, and the last celibate woman died in 1813. Of the various offshoots of the Ephrata cloister established during the eighteenth century, all were short lived except the Antietam/Snow Hill congregation in south-central Pennsylvania, which flourished throughout the nineteenth century.

Mark Häberlein

See also Germantown, Pennsylvania; Mann, Thomas; Pennsylvania; Pietism; Weiser, Conrad

References and Further Reading

Alderfer, E. Gordon. *The Ephrata Commune: An Early American Counterculture.* Pittsburgh: University of Pittsburgh Press, 1985.

Bach, Jeff. *Voices of the Turtledoves: The Sacred World of Ephrata.* University Park: Penn State University Press, 2003.

Carpenter, Delburn. *The Radical Pietists: Celibate Communal Societies Established in the United States before 1820.* New York: AMS Press, 1975.

ERNST, FRIEDRICH
b. June 18, 1796; Neustadt-Goedens, Grand Duchy of Oldenburg
d. May 16–July 10, 1848; Industry, Texas

One of the earliest German settlers of Texas when it still belonged to Mexico, prior to the Texas war for independence and the establishment of the Republic of Texas in 1836.

Friedrich Ernst was instrumental in the emigration of many other Germans to Texas in the nineteenth century. In 1831 Stephen F. Austin, proprietor of "Austin's Colony," granted Ernst a league of land (ca. 4,428 acres) in what is today Austin County. On the west bank of Mill Creek, Ernst founded the town of Industry, arguably the earliest surviving German community in Texas. Only months after his arrival, he wrote an open letter (dated February 1, 1832) to a friend in his homeland, calling for Germans to settle in Texas. This letter was published in at least one newspaper and circulated widely in manuscript form in northern Germany. Ernst described Texas as a land without winter, with soil requiring no fertilizer, and with a climate akin to southern Italy's. His appeal received still wider distribution when Detlef Dunt's guidebook for German emigrants to Texas, *Reise nach Texas: nebst Nachrichten von diesem Lande für Deutsche, welche nach Amerika zu gehen beabsichtigen* (Journey to Texas: With Information about This Land for Germans Planning to Go to America, 1834), reprinted it with much additional material encouraging emigration to Texas.

The man known to history as Friedrich Ernst was born Christian Friedrich Ernst Dirks in a small community in the grand duchy of Oldenburg in northwestern Germany. He came from modest origins; his father was a gardener in the ducal gardens. The younger Dirks also acquired a knowledge of gardening. He married well; his father-in-law was a judicial official in another small town in Oldenburg. Ernst worked as a clerk in the ducal post office. In the fall of 1829 he left Oldenburg with his wife and their children. After arriving in New York late in 1829, the family ran a boarding house there for a year, long enough to be recorded in the census of 1830 under their new surname, "Ernst."

From New York, Ernst and his family set out for Missouri in February 1831 under the influence of Gottfried Duden's popular book, *Bericht über eine Reise nach den westlichen Staaten Nordamerikas und einen mehrjährigen Aufenthalt am Missouri in den Jahren 1824, '25, '26 und '27. In Bezug auf Auswanderung und Überbevölkerung* (Report on a Journey to the Western States of America and a Stay of Several Years along the Missouri during the Years 1824, '25, '26, and '27, 1829). One of the earliest handbooks instructing Germans how to emigrate to Texas, Duden's book focused on the wonders of that territory. En route to Missouri, the Ernsts changed course and sailed to Texas via New Orleans at a time when Stephen F. Austin was seeking to gain European settlers for his colony in Texas.

Working together with another German, Charles Fordtran, whom he met in New York, Ernst developed a little German colony within Austin's. In 1838 he officially laid out the town he called "Industry" and sold town lots there. By then he had a substantial truck garden and a large orchard. Some historians have gone so far as to attribute the introduction of orchardry in Texas to Europeans, particularly Ernst. He became known also for the cigars he had made in a small "factory" on his premises. His other crops included cotton, as well as maize for both animals and humans. Early on he traded a quarter of his land for about a dozen cows, and before long he was raising hogs and chickens. Like many other early settlers, he was a man of many trades. He is reported to have run a store in Industry at some point. About 1840 his wife opened a hotel—the term at first expressed more wish than reality—in the large new house he built in Industry. By the mid-1840s, part of the large stream of German immigrants moving up from coastal regions to the interior of Texas passed through Industry, and not a few of them, especially officers and representatives of the sponsor of much of this stream, the Adelsverein (Society for the Protection of German Immigrants in Texas), were guests at the hotel. In 1842, immediately prior to the great surge in the volume of German emigration to Texas, perhaps as many as several hundred Germans were living in Industry and its immediate vicinity. By 1860, the town itself may have increased to as many as 1,400. In 2000 its population was a mere 304. Valiant efforts have been under way to preserve what is left of the historic settlement. When Ernst died in 1848, he left only a modest estate, valued in the dollar of the day, at some $3,400. The man who had abruptly departed his native duchy twenty years earlier had become the founder of a town in Texas, justice of the peace for the western section of Austin County, and member of the County Commissioner's Court of Appeals (a body whose main concerns were building roads and encouraging the operation of ferries).

Walter Struve

See also Adelsverein; Duden, Gottfried; Dunt, Detlef; Texas

References and Further Reading

Biesele, Rudolph L. *The History of the German Settlements in Texas, 1831–1861.* San Marcos: German-Texan Heritage Society, 1986.

Lindemann, Ann, James Lindemann, and William Richter, eds. *Historical Accounts of Industry, Texas, 1836–1986.* New Ulm: New Ulm Enterprise Printing/Industry– West End Historical Society, 1986.

Struve, Walter. *Germans and Texans: Commerce, Migration, and Culture in the Days of the Lone Star Republic.* Austin: University of Texas Press, 1996.

York, Miriam Corff. *Friedrich Ernst of Industry.* Giddings: Nixon Printing, 1989.

ERTL, HANS

b. February 21, 1908; Urschalling am Chimsee, Bavaria
d. October 23, 2000; La Dolorida, Chiquitania, Bolivia

Pioneering cameraman, filmmaker, and mountaineer Hans Ertl worked with directors Arnold Fanck (1889–1974), Günther O. Dyhrenfurth (1886–1975), and Luis Trenker (1892–1990) to develop the mountain film genre for German cinema (*Freiburger Schule* [Freiburg School]). Collaboration with director Leni Riefenstahl (1902–2003) on *Olympia* yielded innovations that included work with a handheld motion picture camera and the first recorded underwater film footage. Travel to South America in the 1950s led Ertl to produce documentaries on the culture of indigenous Bolivian people.

Coming of age in the Bavarian Alps, Ertl developed an affinity for mountaineering and an interest in filmmaking. Expected to follow in the family business, Ertl enrolled at the Kaufmännische Fachhochschule (Business College) in Munich to study business in 1930. After only one year of study, Ertl left college to work with Fanck, founder of the German mountaineering film genre (*Bergfilm* [Mountain Film]). Ertl traveled with Fanck's production team to Greenland to assist as cameraman and stunt actor in the mountaineering film *SOS Eisberg* (SOS Iceberg, 1933). Further work in the genre of *Bergfilm* followed with camera work for Dyhrenfurth's *Der Dämon des Himalaya* (The Demon of the Himalayas, 1935). It is Ertl's early work with Fanck and his subsequent development of the mountaineering film that established him as a member of Fanck's *Freiburger Schule* of filmmaking.

On the set of *SOS Eisberg*, Ertl developed an important relationship with the actress and aspiring director Leni Riefenstahl. Ertl's friendship and collaboration with Riefenstahl on Fanck's films led her to favor him as lead cameraman for *Tag der Freiheit—Unsere Wehrmacht* (Day of Freedom—Our Army, 1935). Their collaboration continued in Riefenstahl's epic documentaries *Olympia* (1938) and *Olympia II* (1938). It was during his period of collaboration with Riefenstahl that Ertl developed his most innovative cinematic techniques. While shooting promotional footage for the 1934 Winter Olympic Games, Ertl's pioneering work with a handheld camera presented audiences with the perspective of a ski jumper while in flight. Further, while documenting the diving competition for *Olympia,* Ertl recorded the first known underwater film sequences. After completing work on Riefenstahl's films, Ertl joined director Luis Trenker's team as cameraman for *Liebesbriefe aus dem Engadin* (Love Letters from Engadin, 1938) and collaborated with Arnold Fanck on *Ein Robinson* (1940) in Chile.

Ertl's plans to return to Chile for an independent film project in 1939 were thwarted when he was forcefully drafted into the *Wehrmacht* (Armed Forces). During World War II, Ertl worked primarily as a war correspondent for the Propaganda Ministry. From 1939 to 1945 Ertl documented General Erwin Rommel's desert campaign in northern Africa, as well as battles in the Caucusus and on the western front. He also served as cameraman for the propaganda films *Glaube und Schönheit* (Faith and Beauty, 1940), *Der Sinn des Lebens* (The Meaning of Life, 1940), and *Sieg im Westen* (Victory in the West, 1941).

After the war, Ertl returned to filmmaking, directing *Nanga Parbat* (1953), a documentary of Herman Buhl's successful ascent of Nanga Parbat in the Pakistani Himalayas. Disappointed by the failure of *Nanga Parbat* to garner the coveted German Film Prize, Ertl withdrew from public life in Germany and settled in Bolivia. In 1954 Ertl embarked with his family on an Andes-Amazon expedition to locate and photograph Inca cities in the Bolivian jungle. Following the successful completion of his expedition, Ertl released the documentary film *Vorstoß nach Paititi* (The Charge into Paititi, 1955) and wrote two books recording his experiences. *Paititi* (1955) traces Ertl's progress through the Amazon and describes his discovery of Inca ruins. A book of photography, *Arriba, Abajo: Vistas de Bolivia* (High and Low: The Vistas of Bolivia), followed in 1958. Together with daughter Monika, Ertl produced a second documentary on South American culture, *Hito Hito* (1958), in which they recorded the culture of the now extinct Sirino Indians. After failing to complete his final film, Ertl retired from filmmaking. He settled near Santa Cruz, where he became a cattle farmer. In the 1980s Ertl wrote two memoirs: *Meine wilden dreißiger Jahre* (My Wild Thirties, 1982) and *Hans Ertl als Kriegsberichter* (Hans Ertl: War Correspondent, 1985). During his lifetime, Ertl also published numerous articles on South American culture and mountaineering. Two documentary films on Hans Ertl's life have been made: *Hans Ertl—Bolivien Urwald* (Hans Ertl—Bolivian Jungle, 1981) and *Der Gratwanderer—Die Erinnerungen des Hans Ertl* (Wanderer on the Edge: Hans Ertl's Recollections, 1995).

Marta Folio

See also Hollywood

References and Further Reading

Ertl, Hans. *Meine wilden dreißiger Jahre: Bergsteiger, Filmpionier, Weltenbummler.* München: Herbig, 1982.

Fanck, Matthias. "Der letzte Gipfel. Erinnerungen an den Abenteurer Hans Ertl." *Süddeutsche Zeitung,* November 9, 2000.

Heissenberg, Claudia. "Der alte Mann im Urwald—und andere Geschichten aus Bolivien." Heinz-Keun-Stiftung, 1998. http://www.heinz-keun-stiftung.de /pdf/jahr13/jahr13_14.pdf (accessed summer 2004).

Semper, Franck. "Hans Ertl in Bolivien." 2000. http://www.sebra-verlag.de /aktuelles/hertl.htm

ESCHWEGE, WILHELM LUDWIG VON

b. November 10, 1777; Aue (near Eschwege), Hesse
d. February 1, 1855; Wolfsanger, Hesse

German mining expert who contributed to the industrialization of Brazil.

Wilhelm Eschwege studied law and economy at the University of Göttingen and geology at the University of Marburg. After he had gained practical experience in the mining industry, in 1802 Eschwege took over the directorship of the ironworks company Foz d'Alge in the Portuguese province of Estremadura. In 1810, he was appointed a member of the Academy of Science in Lisbon and entered into the service of the Portuguese government in Brazil, where until 1821 he was primarily active in Minas Gerais. Within ten years he established twenty-eight ironworks, thereby founding Brazilian metallurgy. In 1817, Eschwege was appointed general director of goldmining in Brazil and director of the imperial mineralogy cabinet. Aside from his job in the mining industry, he also laid the scientific foundation for the study of mineral deposits and became "the father of Brazilian geology." He produced the first geological profile of Brazil and the first colored geological map of Minas Gerais, and he was also the first to conduct barometric measurements. Eschwege is responsible for naming itabirite and itacolumite. In addition to his pioneering work as a geologist, he also carried out early research into Brazilian ethnology (among the Botokude and Coroado).

Eschwege was among the first to point out the destructive impact humans have on nature. He publicly demanded an end to the destruction of Brazil's tropical forests. After his return to Europe, he split his time between Portugal and Germany, where he was active as a mining expert. Eschwege used the remaining part of his life to document his scientific findings from his time in Brazil. He wrote several books, including *Journal von Brasilien oder vermischte Nachrichten aus Brasilien auf wissenschaftlichen Reisen gesammelt* (Journal of Brazil, or Mixed News from Brazil Collected on Scientific Journeys, 1818); *Geognostische Gemählde von Brasilien* (Geological Pictures from Brazil, 1822); *Brasilien, die Neue Welt* (Brazil, the New World, 1824); *Beiträge zur Gebirgskunde Brasiliens* (Contributions to the Lore of Brazil's Mountains, 1832); and *Pluto Brasiliensis. Eine Reihe von Abhandlungen über Brasiliens Gold-, Diamanten- und anderen mineralischen Reichtum* (Pluto Brazil: A Series of Essays on Brazil's Gold, Diamonds, and Other Mineral Wealth, 1833).

Heinz Peter Brogiato

See also Brazil; Mining
References and Further Reading
Beck, Hanno. "Wilhelm Ludwig von Eschwege." *Neue Deutsche Biographie.* Berlin: Duncker and Humblot, 1959, 4:652.
Henze, Dietmar. *Enzyklopädie der Entdecker und Erforscher der Erde.* Graz: Akademische Druck- und Verlagsanstalt, 1983, 2:181–183.

Toussaint, Friedrich. "Wilhelm Ludwig von Eschwege (1777–1855), a German Engineer of Mining and Metallurgy in Portugal and Brazil." *History of Technology* 22 (2000): 155–169.

ESPIONAGE AND SEDITION ACT

On June 5, 1917, just two months after the United States entered World War I, President Woodrow Wilson enacted the Espionage Act, duly passed by Congress, into law. This act was intended to catch and punish spies, in particular German spies, and to stop the subversive activities of foreign enemies. Debates over the bill demonstrated that many members of Congress feared that Germans in the country were spies and believed this bill was necessary to safeguard and protect the nation's defense secrets.

But this statute went far beyond outlawing behavior such as spying for the enemy, willfully sabotaging war production, and promoting the success of the enemy. It also gave the government the tools to silence people who expressed opposition to the administration's efforts to fight a war that aimed to make the world safe for democracy. The most negative paragraph of the Espionage Act stated that anyone who made "false statements with intent to interfere with the operation or success of the military or naval forces" or caused or attempted to cause "insubordination, disloyalty, mutiny, or refusal of duty in the military or naval forces of the United States, or shall willfully obstruct the recruiting or enlistment service" could receive a "fine of not more than $10,000 or imprisonment for not more than twenty years or both" (40 Stat. 217 [1917]). Prosecutors and the courts used this section of the Espionage Act to charge and convict individuals suspected of committing disloyal activities and making subversive statements.

Article 12 of the Espionage Act prohibited the sending through the mails of any material "advocating or urging treason, insurrection, or forcible resistance to any law of the United States." This gave Postmaster General Albert Burleson the authority to determine what were mailable and what were treasonous publications and to ban such subversive material from the mails. In effect, the Espionage Act allowed one government official to silence the foreign-language press, in particular the German-language papers, and to coerce it to change its position on the war. Most German-language newspapers had opposed U.S. entry into World War I, but not all had supported Germany. However, the threat of loosing mailing privileges convinced most papers to rapidly change their editorial policy, to become more patriotic, and to conform to the national position on the war or to suspend publication.

By the spring of 1918, in response to growing violence and intolerance directed at suspected enemies within the United States, public officials began to demand stronger laws against spies and disloyal acts. Claiming that the Espionage Act had not brought about enough convictions and had not succeeded in wiping out sabotage and treasonous behavior, representatives and senators passed the more severe Sedition Amendment to the Espionage Act on May 7, and Wilson signed it into law on May 16, 1918. It made it a crime to "willfully utter, print, write, or publish any disloyal, profane, scurrilous, or abusive language" about the U.S. government, the Constitution, the flag, or armed forces or to use "language intended to cause contempt, scorn, contumely, or disrepute." It also made it illegal to obstruct the sale of war bonds, to advocate the success of the enemy, or to "urge . . . any curtailment of production . . . essential to the prosecution of the war" (40 Stat. 553 [1918]). Any publicly voiced criticism of government policy could be interpreted as pro-German sentiment and was punishable by fines up to $20,000, or twenty years' imprisonment, or both. The Sedition Act thus broadened the power of the Espionage Act not only to stop the overt acts of German spies and saboteurs but to also eliminate the unpatriotic words of any opponent to the war.

The Espionage and Sedition Act was intended to ensure loyalty and conformity while the United States dealt with a national crisis. The zealous enforcement of these laws also made it increasingly difficult to distinguish between a German spy or traitor and a person who simply criticized U.S. war policies. As a result, more than 2,000 law-abiding citizens of German birth, workers, and individuals who expressed an opinion critical of the government's war effort were arrested and prosecuted for having made pro-German and disloyal statements. About half of them were convicted, and hundreds of aliens were deported. These acts were very effective in silencing immigrants, the foreign-language press, and opponents to the war and in restricting their civil liberties.

Petra Dewitt

See also Newspaper Press, German Language in the United States; World War I; World War I and German Americans; World War I, German Prisoners and Civilian Internees in

References and Further Reading
Jensen, Joan M. *The Price of Vigilance.* Chicago: Rand McNally, 1968.
Peterson, H. C., and Gilbert C. Fite. *Opponents of War, 1917–1918.* Madison: University of Wisconsin Press, 1957.
Zieger, Robert A. *America's Great War: World War I and the American Experience.* Lanham, MD: Rowman and Littlefield, 2000.

EUGENICS/EUTHANASIA

The eugenics movement, both in the United States and in Europe, had its roots in Charles Darwin's theory of evolution and the application of this theory to human beings. But Darwin's ideas were not the only impetus behind the development of eugenics. This movement was also influenced by early criminology, scientific racism, and sociological studies of the poor. Each of these strands blended together gave rise to the eugenics movement, whose goal was to improve the genetic pool through selective breeding, thereby eliminating the weaker elements in society and reinforcing Darwin's ideas regarding the survival of the fittest. These weaker elements were to be found often in one or more of the following categories: the working class, the mentally or physically handicapped, those with a criminal record, and non-Caucasians and/or Jewish people. Scientists, working together with politicians and social workers, developed public policy regarding sterilization and, in the case of Nazi Germany, murder, all under the guise of furthering and strengthening certain genetic qualities of the human race. However, although many intellectuals and scientists in the United States dismissed these early theories by the interwar period, in Germany they found fertile ground with the rise to power of Adolf Hitler.

In the mid-1800s, several European intellectuals wrote about the possibilities of eugenics and reinforced their ideas with contemporary assumptions about the inequality among classes and races, neither of which could be proven scientifically. The French thinker Joseph-Arthur de Gobineau proposed a hierarchy of races in 1853 in his work *The Inequality of Human Races.* He believed that the pattern of human history evidenced the struggle between the races and demonstrated that certain races (white Europeans) were destined to greatness, whereas other races (nonwhites) were destined to be ruled or controlled by the superior races. He emphasized what he perceived as the dangers in race mixing, which he labeled as degeneration, conjecturing that it would weaken the purer, stronger white race. This theory of degeneration, according to de Gobineau and Benedict Augustin Morel, stated that weak hereditary characteristics would worsen with each successive generation; if a man suffered from a nervous disorder, then his child would be neurotic and his grandchild would be insane. Given the extensive European global empire structure, de Gobineau believed that the mingling of Europeans with non-Europeans presented a serious danger to the superior place of Europeans. His work began a pattern of science buttressing prevailing stereotypes and beliefs that persisted into the middle of the twentieth century and that led in multiple directions, including sterilization and murder.

De Gobineau's racial hierarchy was perpetuated by other European intellectuals such as the German composer Richard Wagner; his son-in-law, Houston Stewart Chamberlain; and Paul de Lagarde. This trio of thinkers believed that the Jewish "race" was the most degraded of all and warned of their enormous potential for corrupting the "purer" races. These beliefs led to the coining of a new word, anti-semitism, in 1879 by Wilhelm Marr. Prior to this time, when referring to hatred of Jews, the term *Judenhass* was used. However, tying into the desire to link racism with science, these intellectuals saw the need for a more modern term that emphasized the supposed race of Jews, rather than their religion. For this strain of eugenicists and racists, Jews represented the most degenerate of all the races, given to parasitical behavior. The process of Jewish assimilation into European culture, sparked by the Enlightenment and the Napoleonic Code, hastened their fears that Jews were infiltrating Western Christian society and contaminating its racial purity through intermarriage.

Criminologists such as the Italian professor of legal medicine, Cesare Lombroso, were also key figures in the early development of eugenics. He theorized that criminals were people whose physical and mental capacities had not fully developed. He identified certain physical characteristics, such as a sloping forehead, long arms, large incisors, and lack of symmetry in facial features, and patterns of behavior, such as emotionality and inconstancy, as indicators of stunted development and one's tendency toward immoral and/or criminal acts. He also labeled certain groups within society as hereditarily predisposed to criminality, including both the handicapped and gypsies. He presented his ideas in his 1863 work, *Genius and Madness,* which argued that criminality was habitual because it was hereditary. Criminals with his identified physical and behavioral characteristics were a constant threat to society and could never be reformed; therefore, he recommended that they be put to death by the state. Lombroso's ideas found favor in the United States with many American scholars, particularly those who managed prisons and asylums.

Another key figure in the intellectual development of eugenics theory was the Englishman Francis Galton. In his work, *Hereditary Genius* (1869), Galton posited that the racial health of a people was dictated by their natural, inherited characteristics and formulated thirteen criteria on which people should be judged. The way to ensure national strength was to encourage those with all or most of his identified characteristics to have many children, while dissuading the hereditarily weak from giving birth. Within the so-called positive characteristics were many stereotypically middle-class attributes such as character, work ethic, height, and intelligence. His work was read widely across Europe and the United States.

Within the United States, the early proponents of the eugenics movement were clustered around those who cared for the mentally and/or physically handicapped or criminals and those who studied the roots of poverty and immorality. Its underpinning was threefold: the Progressive Era, which sought to eradicate ills, corruption, and weaknesses in society and politics; the growing belief that heredity dictated strengths and weaknesses in human development; and increasing anti-immigrant sentiments, particularly directed against immigrants from southern and eastern Europe. This manifested itself in the form of mandatory sterilization laws and laws preventing marriage between people labeled as "degenerate" in the early 1900s. Prisons, asylums, and homes for delinquent youth became "laboratories" for testing basic assumptions about degeneracy and heredity.

In the United States, the most common "cure" was to remove these lesser beings from the gene pool by forced sterilization and/or castration. This extreme measure was first instituted by F. Hoyt Pilcher, the superintendent of the Kansas State Home for the Feebleminded. In the mid-1890s, Pilcher castrated forty-four boys and sterilized fourteen girls to stop them from procreating. Medical science soon thereafter offered the less extreme options of tubal ligation and vasectomy. This part of the movement culminated with the Indiana legislature passing the first law mandating the sterilization of habitual criminals, the mentally handicapped, and rapists who were housed in a state institution, once their case had been reviewed by a panel of experts. By 1917, a total of sixteen states (including Indiana) had passed such legislation (California, Connecticut, Iowa, Kansas, Michigan, Nebraska, Nevada, New Hampshire, New Jersey, New York, North Dakota, Oregon, South Dakota, Washington, and Wisconsin). In the interwar period, fourteen additional states enacted forcible sterilization laws (Alabama, Arizona, Delaware, Idaho, Maine, Minnesota, Mississippi, Montana, North Carolina, Oklahoma, Utah, Vermont, Virginia, West Virginia). By 1931, more than 12,000 people in the United States had been sterilized (Haller 1984, 133–134, 137, 141).

Another strand was the prohibition of the marriage of certain types of people. In 1896, Connecticut passed legislation forbidding the marriage of a mentally handicapped person, the first such legislation in the United States. By 1905, five other states (Kansas, New Jersey, Ohio, Michigan, and Indiana) had enacted similar laws, some with even further-reaching restrictions, such as forbidding alcoholics to get married. By the mid-1930s, laws prohibiting the marriage of mentally handicapped persons existed in forty-one states, of epileptics in seventeen states, and of alcoholics in four states. With these actions, the United States became the first government to endorse compulsory sterilization laws.

In the early 1900s, Charles Benedict Davenport founded a series of institutions, including the Eugenics Records Office and the Eugenics Research Association, at Cold Spring Harbor, Long Island. Davenport was trained as a biologist, anthropologist, and eugenicist and worked closely with well-established racist theorists such as Madison Grant. Under his leadership and that of his institutions' manager, Harry Hamilton Laughlin, they influenced the development of public policy on sterilization, marriage prohibition, and decreasing immigration, the last most notably through the Immigration Restriction Act of 1924. In the 1930s, Laughlin and Davenport praised the sterilization laws passed by the Third Reich in their newsletter, *Eugenic News.* In addition, Davenport published his research in German scientific journals and served on two journals' editorial boards throughout the 1930s, severing his ties much later than most other American eugenicists.

In addition to the exchange of scientific information via publications, eugenicists held a series of meeting in the early 1900s that allowed them to meet and share ideas directly, through the International Society for Racial Hygiene (ISRH), an organization heavily influenced by German eugenicists, which first met in Dresden in 1907 and later in London in 1912. Although these contacts were temporarily lessened due to World War I, they emerged once more in the 1920s, as scientists in Germany were strengthening their support for legislation dealing with those "unworthy of life." German scientists remained isolated from the international eugenics movement until 1925, when Germany was reintegrated into the international community. An important result of renewed contact was extensive financial assistance given by the Rockefeller Foundation in the 1920s and 1930s to support German research in eugenics and to provide funds for the Kaiser Wilhelm Institute for Psychiatry and the Kaiser Wilhelm Institute for Anthropology, Eugenics, and Human Heredity. These two German institutes pushed for government support and legal processes to ensure the genetic health of Germany and played a central role in the formation of public policy. In 1932, the Prussian Parliament held discussions on a proposed sterilization law, based on those of multiple American states and Switzerland. The drive to institute eugenics at the national level began shortly after President Paul von Hindenburg appointed Adolf Hitler as chancellor of Germany on January 30, 1933.

For scientists (centered in the German Society for Race Hygiene and these two aforementioned institutes) and the National Socialist German Worker's Party (NSDAP), racial purity and good birth were of utmost importance. They feared that the strongest and purest people within society were having too few children, while the weakest people were having too many. Therefore, they instituted policies and programs to reverse this imbalance. One element of their policy was the development of the *Lebensborn* (Well of Life) program, under the leadership of the Schutzstaffel (SS). This program began as a series of boarding homes for unwed mothers of pure Aryan race and developed over the 1930s into a selective breeding program. After women gave birth, the state encouraged them to leave the children in its care. At least 12,000 children were born into the *Lebensborn* program between 1938 and 1945. A second part of this program coordinated the selection of racially pure children from eastern European countries occupied by the Third Reich, who were taken from their homes and adopted by German families. Estimates of the number of kidnapped children range from 100,000 to 250,000 (Carlson 2001, 328).

The sterilization program of the Third Reich began in July 1933, when the German Reichstag passed the Law for the Prevention of Progeny with Hereditary Diseases. It stated that anyone with a hereditary illness could be sterilized against his or her will if a medical expert determined that he or she was likely to produce children with a serious hereditary defect and was based on several state laws passed in the United States. According to this law, hereditary illness was characterized by one of the following conditions: congenital feeblemindedness, schizophrenia, manic depression, hereditary epilepsy, Huntington's chorea, hereditary blindness or deafness, serious physical deformities, or chronic alcoholism. The majority of people sterilized against their will were deemed congenitally feebleminded, yet no clear, scientific definition and/or test existed to detect this condition. Decisions were, therefore, often arbitrary. A person could recommend himself or herself for sterilization, but the vast majority of the recommendations came from physicians, nurses, or the administrative heads of homes, hospitals, and prisons.

The decision to sterilize someone in Germany was made by a newly created Hereditary Health Court, which was composed of one judge and two physicians. If the court decided in favor of sterilization, there was no path of appeal, and the court did not consider whether the person was in favor of the sterilization or not. Some 300,000 German citizens had been sterilized under this program by 1939; during the course of the war, an additional 50,000 to 75,000 people underwent forcible sterilization. Therefore, approximately 0.5 percent of the German population was directly affected by this program (Friedlander 1995, 30).

In the United States, some American scientists began to question the path that Nazi eugenicists had chosen, marking a widening gap in practice and support between the two scientific communities. By the late 1930s, American scientists such as Franz Boas, a prominent anthropologist and professor at Columbia University, directly and publicly attacked the policies and beliefs of the Third Reich. Within mainstream organizations such as the American Eugenics Society, social eugenicists took positions of power away from racial eugenicists. Scientific support for sterilization laws and practice was not waning; rather, there was a shift in focus from sterilization based upon race or anti-semitism to sterilization based upon social factors such as government support for larger families of "superior" genetic background. Indeed, forced sterilization continued in the United States until the 1970s, totaling more than 62,000, of which more than 20,000 (32 percent) were sterilized by the state of California (Haller 1984, 141).

The Third Reich's eugenics program led directly to mass murder through the euthanasia program known as T-4, which killed mentally and physically handicapped children and adults, and the Holocaust, which built upon this mindset of eliminating those seen as "lesser," or genetically inferior. The German and American scientific communities were reconnected after World War II during the Nuremburg Doctors' Trials, held in 1946. These trials focused on medical professionals who were involved in the T-4 program and/or medical experiments conducted in concentration camps and killing centers. However, U.S. prosecutors did not charge those involved with the forced sterilization of more than 3,500,000 German citizens, making a distinction between "genuine" eugenics and the mass killings. In the long term, these German eugenicists, even many who were involved with mass murder, were quickly reintegrated into the international scientific community, often with the assistance of U.S. scientists.

Laura J. Hilton

See also Antisemitism; U.S.-German
Intellectual Exchange

References and Further Reading

Barkan, Elazar. *The Retreat of Scientific Racism: Changing Concepts of Race in Britain and the United States between the World Wars.* Cambridge: Cambridge University Press, 1992.

Carlson, Elof Axel. *The Unfit: A History of a Bad Idea.* Cold Spring Harbor: Cold Spring Harbor Laboratory Press, 2001.

Friedlander, Henry. *The Origins of Nazi Genocide: From Euthanasia to the Final Solution.* Chapel Hill: University of North Carolina Press, 1995.

Haller, Mark. *Eugenics: Hereditarian Attitudes in American Thought.* New Brunswick: Rutgers University Press, 1984.

Kühl, Stefan. *The Nazi Connection: Eugenics, American Racism, and German National Socialism.* New York: Oxford University Press, 1994.

Mosse, George. *Toward the Final Solution: A History of European Racism.* Madison: University of Wisconsin Press, 1985.

EVERETT, EDWARD
b. April 11, 1794; Dorchester, Massachusetts
d. January 15, 1865; Boston, Massachusetts

Everett is primarily remembered today as the "other" orator at Gettysburg, when Abraham Lincoln delivered his historic address, and secondarily as the holder of numerous public offices, as well as the presidency of Harvard College, but he is not widely known as a cultural intermediary between Germany and the United States. In fact, Everett was among the early contributors to the wave of enthusiasm for the German language and literature that swept the New England intellectual elite in the early nineteenth century. After his graduation from Harvard in 1811 and a brief ministerial career, Everett accepted a newly endowed chair of Greek literature at his alma mater, an appointment that allowed him to travel and study in Europe prior to assuming his teaching responsibilities. Accompanied by his friend, George Ticknor, he left for Europe in 1815 and returned four years later. After a brief tour of Europe, the two nascent scholars enrolled at the University of Göttingen, which, thanks largely to their influence, was to become a de facto graduate school for Harvard graduates who were later to gain prominence, such as George Bancroft, Joseph Green Cogswell, and John Lothrop Motley. Everett immersed himself in his studies with prodigious enthusiasm and energy, concentrating on Greek, while studying subjects as diverse as modern history, civil law, Hebrew, and German language and literature. While in Germany he found time to write book reviews for the *North American Review,* the most important of which was a forty-five-page review of

Edward Everett, ca. 1863. (Library of Congress)

Johann Wolfgang von Goethe's *Dichtung und Wahrheit* (*Poetry and Truth*), considered to be the first important article on Goethe written in an American journal. After completing his PhD in 1817, probably the first American to receive that degree at Göttingen, Everett returned to Harvard in 1819. During his brief teaching career, he introduced German philological methodology to his students of Greek.

As a student and young professor, Everett clearly made a substantial contribution to American understanding and appreciation of German culture. This was especially true in the case of Goethe, who had been known primarily through indifferent translations of *The Sorrows of the Young Werther* (1774) and selected passages from *Faust*. During their stay at Göttingen, he and Ticknor had undertaken a

pilgrimage to Weimar, where they had an interview with Goethe. Even though Everett viewed Goethe as somewhat stiff and cold, he persisted in his admiration of him. In his review of *Dichtung und Wahrheit* (1817), Everett made a plea for a greater understading of the poet, while comparing some of the passages in *Faust* with the writing of William Shakespeare. While in Germany, Everett also laid the groundwork for the subsequent German collection at the Harvard library. With a grant of $500 from the Harvard College, he purchased German grammars and dictionaries, Greek lexicons, and other works. He also began negotiations with Goethe to acquire his writings, which culminated in the eventual purchase through Joseph Cogswell of a twenty-volume edition of Goethe's works for the library. During his teaching career at Harvard, Everett was also editor of the *North American Review,* in which he published reviews of several German authors. During the same period, he translated a prominent Greek grammar and a reader, which reflected current German scholarship, for the benefit of his students.

In spite of such promise as a teacher and scholar, Everett decided by 1824 to turn his abundant energies to public life, virtually terminating his intensive involvement in German culture. His change of career was partly attributable to his dissatisfaction with teaching immature youths and partly because of his admiration for Daniel Webster, who became Everett's mentor. As Webster's protégé, Everett became a member of the House of Representatives, governor of Massachusetts, and ambassador to Great Britain. After his return from England, he became president of Harvard College from 1846 to 1849. When Webster died in 1852, Everett succeeded his mentor as secretary of state until 1853 and then served briefly as senator from Massachusetts (1853–1854). One of his last acts of public service reflected his student days at Göttingen, where he and Ticknor had been favorably impressed with the extensive university library. Inspired by these impressions, he joined Ticknor in founding the Boston Public Library and served as president of its board from 1852 to 1864. In this way, too, Germany played a role in the legacy that Everett left to his city and nation.

John T. Walker

See also American Students at German Universities; Bancroft, George; *Encyclopaedia Americana;* Göttingen, University of; Motley, John Lothrop; Ticknor, George

References and Further Reading

Bartlett, Irving H. "Edward Everett Reconsidered." *New England Quarterly* 69, no. 3 (September 1996): 426–460.

Frothingham, Paul Revere. *Edward Everett: Orator and Statesman.* Boston: Houghton Mifflin, 1925.

Long, Orie. *Literary Pioneers: Early American Explorers of European Culture.* Cambridge: Harvard University Press, 1935.

Pochmann, Henry A. *German Culture in America: Philosophical and Literary Influences, 1600–1900.* Madison: University of Wisconsin Press, 1957.

F

FAR EAST, U.S.-GERMAN ENTENTE IN THE

During the presidency of Theodore Roosevelt, the intensity of diplomatic relations between the United States and the German Empire reached a climax. A series of diplomatic clashes taught the Germans not to underestimate U.S. imperialism. Simultaneously, as the situation in Europe darkened, German desire to call upon U.S. goodwill grew constantly and was expressed, for example, during the First Moroccan Crisis. German attempts to reach some kind of alliance or at least close cooperation with Washington in order to guarantee the integrity of China in 1907 and 1908 followed this vein. The episode clearly reveals the basic fruitlessness of German-U.S. cooperation during Roosevelt's presidency.

After the conference of Algeciras in 1906, which had amply demonstrated the utopian character of German American cooperation, Berlin's disillusionment did not last long. Already in May of the same year, Chancellor Bernhard von Bülow had outlined his conception of the future, emphasizing the need to rely on Germany's own power. Yet, he also named the Allies and potential friends that the empire had left. In this list the United States was promi-

nently included. The perceived urgency of a rapprochement with the United States grew because of Germany's increasing isolation or—speaking in the contemporary terminology—"encirclement."

In 1907, the Far East was the region where Berlin's diplomatic failures seemed to lead to dangerous developments. A whole series of agreements among major powers, like France and Japan, Russia and Japan, and finally even Great Britain and Russia with regard to China, in combination with the existing alliances, made Germany's containment seem complete. Due to the imminent end of the Manchu dynasty, the partition of China seemed more likely than ever before. In Berlin, the Foreign Office and Wilhelm II feared exclusion from the Chinese market and sought the help of the only power besides Germany that had not yet concluded an agreement, the United States.

Because of the diplomatic situation, German hopes were not completely unfounded. Economic rivalries in the aftermath of the Russo-Japanese War had revealed deep tensions between the United States and Japan. Late in 1906, discrimination against Japanese schoolchildren in San Francisco led to open protests by Tokyo. While Roosevelt was able to allay these tensions by an exchange of diplomatic notes—the so-called gentleman's agreement—the press continued to play on "yellow peril" notions.

From the German point of view, it was natural that Berlin should cooperate with Washington. Keeping the door open to allow trade with all countries had been the declared policy of the United States in China for several years. Now, in 1907, with its European competitors united against her, Germany sought to replace the United States in the Chinese question and announced that it worked for the same objective.

One of the measures to win U.S. support was to try to arouse suspicion and fear against the other great powers. Thus, Wilhelm II in September 1905 wanted to palm off his favorite "yellow peril" picture, accompanied by a frank letter about the topic, on Roosevelt. Yet, the German government resolved to wait for an U.S. initiative for closer contacts.

By the end of 1906, when reports about the heightened possibility of a conflict between the United States and Japan reached the Foreign Ministry in Berlin, such a U.S. initiative seemed likely. By the end of October, the embassy in Washington reported that Roosevelt had brought up the topic of a probable war himself and had asked for some information on the Japanese navy. Roosevelt's wish for data was fulfilled in early November, and Ambassador Hermann Speck von Sternburg was instructed to encourage the president's mistrust in a careful manner. In February 1907, Sternburg reported growing anti-Japanese feelings in the United States. He also stressed the fact that U.S. leaders supported the conciliatory policy of the presi-

dent because of the inferiority of the U.S. Navy in the Pacific Ocean.

New racial conflicts in San Francisco in May and the conclusion of the Franco-Japanese agreement in early June made an alliance with the United States even more likely. Indeed, public opinion in the United States as well as in Europe became more and more convinced that a war against Japan was inevitable. In addition, the German envoy in Beijing began to warn against the threat of Japanese expansion and suggested examining the possibility of cooperation with the United States, Russia, and China to prevent this eventuality.

In July, Germany informed Roosevelt about the substantial increase in Japanese immigration to Mexico. The reports speculated that Japan was moving troops into Mexico in order to be able to wage an effective land war against the United States. President Roosevelt, however, thought the idea of a Japanese invasion via Mexico absurd. Nevertheless, Berlin succeeded in keeping Roosevelt's distrust alive, and the president concluded that there was indeed a tendency toward war in Japan, but that it was no immediate threat.

Partly because of Sternburg's personal approach to diplomacy with his friend Theodore Roosevelt and his distorting reports home, the impression of U.S. nervousness about Japanese policy in China remained alive in Berlin. Indeed, the ambassador's reports encouraged the German government to find out if the United States showed an interest in countering the Anglo-French-Japanese alliance in China. In autumn of 1907, a Chinese offer for cooperation with Germany arrived, and the Germans wanted to extend it to the United States. Indeed, the Germans had reason to believe in the success of their diplomatic maneuvers. At the end of 1907, preparations for the cruise of a U.S. battleship fleet around the world were in full swing. The cruise seemed to heighten the risk of war since the Japanese reaction was not easily predictable. But again the president expressed his polite but firm reserve toward the German offers, and again Sternburg's reports created a very different impression in Berlin.

Thus, although realizing that a formal alliance was impossible, German diplomacy hoped for at least a joint declaration about the integrity of China. Even this symbolic cooperation became unlikely when tensions between Japan and the United States gradually subsided. By the summer of 1908, chances of reaching the desired agreement had almost vanished. A decisive factor for Roosevelt's rejection of the German scheme was his desire to keep peace with Japan and reach an understanding with that country. In late November the Root-Takahira agreement between the United States and Japan was concluded. An exchange of notes guaranteed the maintenance of the status quo in the Pacific Ocean and support for the open door as well as the integrity of China. Hence, the United States had basically concluded the same type of agreement with Japan as Russia and France had done earlier. Instead of cooperating with Germany against the rest of the world, Roosevelt had joined the camp of the opponents.

Stefan Rinke

See also Sternburg, Hermann Speck von; Venezuelan Crisis

References and Further Reading

Esthus, Raymond A. *Theodore Roosevelt and the International Rivalries.* Waltham: Regina Books, 1970.

Menning, Ralph R. *The Collapse of "Global Diplomacy": Germany's Descent into Isolation, 1906–09.* PhD diss., Brown University, 1986.

Pommerin, Reiner. *Der Kaiser und Amerika: Die USA in der Politik der Reichsleitung, 1890–1917.* Cologne: Böhlau, 1986.

Rinke, Stefan. "A Misperception of Reality: The Futile German Attempts to an Entente with the United States, 1907–08." In *Theodore Roosevelt: Many-Sided American.* Ed. Natalie A. Naylor. Interlaken: Heart of the Lakes Press, 1992, 369–382.

FAUPEL, WILHELM
b. October 29, 1873; Lindenbusch (Lower Silesia), Prussia
d. May 1945; Berlin (?), Prussia

German officer who was a crucial figure in military relations to Latin America in the period prior to and after World War I. As a right-wing political figure and president of the Ibero-Amerikanisches Institut in Berlin, Faupel also gained publicity as the coordinator of Nazi cultural policy toward Latin America in the 1930s and 1940s.

At age eighteen Faupel joined the German army and went through a typical military career, which lasted until the end of the nineteenth century. In 1900, however, because of his knowledge of Russian, he was commanded to translate for the German forces engaged in the Boxer rebellion in China. Four years later he volunteered to participate in the German colonial war of extermination against the Herero and Nama tribes in South-West Africa (1904–1906). After his return to Germany in 1907, Faupel was made general staff officer. In 1911 he joined a group of German military instructors for the Argentinean army. He stayed in Buenos Aires as instructor at the war academy until 1913.

During World War I, Faupel served as a general staff officer. In May 1918, he was one of the organizers of the successful offensive of the "Chemin des Dames," which killed thousands due to the massive use of toxic gas. For this achievement, Faupel was awarded the highest military decoration, Pour-le-Mérite, in August 1918. Immediately after the war, Faupel acted as a mediator between revolutionary soldiers and the army command. In addition, he became an important leader of the counterrevolutionary movement in Germany, founding the Freikorps Görlitz (or Freikorps Faupel) in January 1919, which actively participated in fighting against the Socialists in Munich and in the Ruhr region. Faupel also supported the abortive right-wing military coup against the Weimar Republic in March 1920.

In 1921 Faupel had to leave the German army due to the restrictions of the Treaty of Versailles and returned to Argentina. At the Río de la Plata, Faupel was informally hired as adviser by General José Félix Uriburu who, in 1923, was promoted to inspector general. Faupel managed to contract a group of old comrades willing to serve in Argentina despite the provisions of the peace treaty that prohibited German officers from serving in a foreign army. Until 1926, when he finally gained the rank of general in the German army, Faupel commanded these so-called *informantes civiles*. He was a crucial figure in the secret arms trade at the Río de la Plata. After the fall of Uriburu, Faupel had to leave Argentina but became inspector general of the Peruvian army a year later. Again, with the help of his traditional aides, he set out to reform the army structure, but again his measures provoked the resistance of Latin American officers, who rejected the foreigners' influence. In 1929, the German contingent under Faupel had to resign.

Back in Germany during the Great Depression, Faupel held various positions in right-wing associations. After the Nazis' rise to power, Faupel was appointed president of the Ibero-Amerikanisches Institut in Berlin in 1934. From that position, Faupel became the chief coordinator of German cultural relations to Latin America. In 1936 Adolf Hitler sent him as ambassador to Franco's Spain, but Faupel had to be recalled because of diplomatic difficulties a year later. Until the end of the war, Faupel continued to lead the Ibero-Amerikanisches Institut. His institution gradually lost importance due to the declining role of Latin America in Nazi strategic planning. In May 1945, together with his wife, Faupel probably committed suicide in Berlin.

Stefan Rinke

See also Argentina; Latin America, German Military Advisers in; Latin America, Nazi Party in; Treaty of Versailles

References and Further Reading

Gliech, Oliver. "Wilhelm Faupel: Generalstabsoffizier, Militärberater, Präsident des Ibero-amerikanischen Instituts." In *Ein Institut und sein General: Wilhelm Faupel und das Ibero-Amerikanische Institut in der Zeit des Nationalsozialismus*. Eds. Reinhard Liehr, Günther Maihold, and Günter Vollmer. Frankfurt am Main: Vervuert, 2003, 131–279.

Rinke, Stefan. *"Der letzte freie Kontinent": Deutsche Lateinamerikapolitik im Zeichen transnationaler Beziehungen, 1918–1933.* Stuttgart: Heinz, 1996.

FEDERATION OF GERMAN WOMEN'S CLUBS

see Bund Deutscher Frauenvereine

FEININGER, ANDREAS
b. December 27, 1906; Paris, France
d. February 18, 1999; New York, New
York

Pioneer of photojournalism who became famous for his black-and-white photos of American metropolises such as New York City and Chicago.

Feininger was the oldest of the three sons of the American painter Lyonel Feininger and his wife Julia Lilienfeldt. Two years after his birth, the family moved to Berlin-Zehlendorf. In 1919 a position was offered to Feininger's father at the newly founded Bauhaus School in Weimar, which became the new home of the family for almost a decade. Weimar had a seminal influence on the younger Feininger. There he developed his love for nature and freedom and a dislike for compulsion and authority. As a sixteen-year-old he left grammar school and registered as a student at the Bauhaus, where he received his certificate as a cabinetmaker in 1925. Afterward he took up his studies in architecture at the Bauhaus, which had by then moved to Dessau. Here his interest in photography was awakened and his talent discovered. In 1929 Feininger graduated summa cum laude from his studies in architecture. Being an American and a Jew, it was not easy for him to find a job in Germany during the Great Depression. For a short time he worked in Dessau and later in Hamburg. In 1931 he ran out of work and traveled in his Opel sports car through Europe, taking pictures. With the help of a friend of his father, he finally found work in Paris. After it became impossible for him to continue his work in France, he settled in Stockholm, Sweden, for some years, where he held a position as architectural photographer. There he married the Swede Wysse

Hägg on August 30, 1933. In September 1935 their son was born. Once again, the political situation forced him to leave the country. Finally, in 1939, at the age of thirty-three, Feininger and his young family emigrated to New York, where his parents had already settled two years before.

In the United States Feininger was lucky: regardless of his inability to speak English, and despite his old-fashioned photo equipment, he was hired by the Black Star Picture Agency as an all-round photographer for a guaranteed $20 a week. His pictures were sold to newspapers and magazines. This job enabled him to take pictures of anything he was interested in and to get to know New York City. After one year Feininger left the agency and accepted an offer to work as a freelance photographer for *Life* magazine. In January 1943 he became editorial photographer of the magazine, a position he held for almost two decades, until 1962. In that position, he had the opportunity to use the latest equipment and take advantage of the magazine's laboratory, with its specially trained experts. Andreas Feininger produced almost 400 stories for *Life* magazine.

After Feininger left *Life* magazine, he worked on his own, publishing several books and teaching at New York University in 1972. By the year of his death Feininger had published more than fifty books, many of which had been translated into other languages. He had received a great number of prizes and awards for his photography. His pictures have been and are still presented in uncountable solo and group exhibitions in many famous museums and public collections in the United States and Europe and are familiar to a large audience from motifs on posters, postcards, and calendars.

Annette Hofmann

See also Bauhaus; Photography
References and Further Reading
Buchsteiner, Thomas, and Otto Letze, eds.
Andreas Feininger: That's Photography.
Ostfildern-Ruit: Cantz, Hatje Verlag,
2004.

FESTIVITIES, GERMAN BRAZILIAN

During the second half of the nineteenth century, German immigrants in Rio Grande do Sul created a system of celebrations rooted in German tradition. In 1863, the first *Sängerfest* (choir competition) was hosted by the Sociedade Orpheu in São Leopoldo. During the 1870s, the *Kaiserfeier,* which was dedicated to Emperor Wilhelm I, was added to the German calendar of festivities. Beginning in the 1890s, several associations, such as the Verband deutscher Vereine (Association of German Societies, created in 1886), the Turnerschaft von Rio Grande do Sul (Turner Societies of Rio Grande do Sul, originated in 1895) and the Deutscher Sängerbund Rio Grande do Sul (German Singing Association, founded in 1896) organized festivities on a regular, mostly annual, basis. Cities such as Porto Alegre hosted these events, which followed carefully detailed programs. Their formal, hierarchical character became obvious in the production of *Festschriften* (commemorative books on the occasion of an anniversary of an organization), which prescribed, regulated, and settled the organization of the festivities. From 1890 to 1941, the main celebrations were dedicated to Emperor Wilhelm II, Otto von Bismarck, and Friedrich Ludwig Jahn, who founded the *Turnerbewegung* (Gymnasts Movement). They included choir performances, shooting practice, and gymnastics and celebrated historical events concerning both Germany and the German immigration to Brazil, among them January 18 and July 25.

On March 22, 1872, the birthday of Wilhelm I, the first *Kaiserfeier* was organized in Porto Alegre. This celebration was dedicated to the German emperor and the unification of Germany in 1871. It was intended to create an emotional bond between German Brazilians and the newly formed German nation. This *Kaiserfeier* was held, with few interruptions, every March 22 from 1872 to 1887. It included popular parties (*Volksfeste*) on the Wilhelmshöhe, a small countryside property that belonged to the Hilfsverein (Aid Association), and dinner parties in hotels and other establishments owned by Germans. The climax of the *Kaiserfeier* came in 1887 with the celebration of the emperor's ninetieth birthday. This event began with the sending of a congratulatory telegram to the monarch on behalf of Porto Alegre's Germans, followed by a Protestant church service and a mass in the Catholic Church. Afterward, a festive procession brought the participants to the Wilhelmshöhe, where a concert was given, speeches in honor of the emperor were made, and patriotic songs, such as "Heil Dir im Siegeskranz" (Salute Dear Victory), "Wacht am Rhein" (Guard on the Rhine River), and "Was ist des Deutschen Vaterland?" (What Is the German's Fatherland?), were sung. The celebration ended with the return of the procession and dinner parties in various societies, such as Gesellschaft Germania (Society Germania), Leopoldina, and Gemeinnütziger Verein (Mutual Help Society).

After Wilhelm II was crowned emperor in 1888, the *Kaiserfeier* in Porto Alegre continued from 1889 to 1917. The celebration, dedicated to Wilhelm II, occurred annually on January 27, Wilhelm II's birthday. It consisted of concerts, dinner, and/or breakfast parties at the Salon Preussler. Many German societies, including the Germania, Gemeinnütziger Verein (Association for Mutual Benefit) and Deutscher Krieger-Verein (German Veterans Association), held parties to honor the emperor. As of 1900, the Verband Deutscher Vereine was in charge of organizing the *Kaiserfeier* according to the *Fest-Commers* (a guidebook that contains the rituals for these festivities) manner. These celebrations offered only men a chance to socialize. Women were invited to participate for the first time in 1916.

The *Fest-Commers* followed a set agenda throughout the annual celebrations. It always started with a musical opening, a moment of saluting the guests, toasts (*Trinksprüche*) to the emperor, festive speeches to the person being honored and to Brazil, declamation of German patriotic poems, instrumental music and choir presentations, the singing of the Brazilian National Anthem, and the sending of a congratulatory telegram to Wilhelm II. The *Kaiserfeier* focused on the celebration and exultation of Emperor Wilhelm II, who was deemed the personification of German national unity. The speakers glorified Wilhelm II's achievements in politics, economy, and foreign policy. The commemoration served to strengthen the ties of German Brazilians with Germany proper. To this end, Wilhelm II made donations for German schools in Brazil and stated that he considered Germans living abroad the pioneers of German commerce and culture. Between 1889 and 1917, *Kaiserfeiern* were held in Porto Alegre, São Leopoldo, Pelotas, and Rio Grande. From

1920 to 1922, the *Kaiserfeier* was organized as a festive commemoration by the Deutscher Krieger-Verein in Porto Alegre and again restricted to men. Its objective was to show loyalty to the abdicated emperor and to protest the Treaty of Versailles.

The second most important event, held in Porto Alegre and São Leopoldo, was the *Turnfest*. Dedicated to gymnastics, this celebration was organized by the Turnerschaft of Rio Grande do Sul in the years 1896, 1899, 1901, 1903, 1907, 1921, 1929, and 1935. The 1935 *Turnfest* was integrated into the Turnerschaft's fortieth anniversary celebration and into the festivities related to the Farroupilha Revolution centennial. The celebrations dedicated to gymnastics had as a central objective to revere a cultural practice that was considered an instrument for the formation of the German character and the maintenance of Germanity (*Deutschtum*). Gymnastics was believed to have a moral content: it was seen as reflecting seriousness and a sense of duty, two of the virtues that were part of the German identity. The organizers intended to promote solidarity among Germans and to tighten the ties with Germany through gymnastics. The creation and organization of the *Turnfest* was related to the role gymnastics societies and *Turnvater* (the father of gymnastics) Jahn played in the process of German unification. During the Napoleonic occupation of all of Germany, Jahn had revitalized gymnastics with the objective of strengthening the national conscience, thus preparing the youth to fight for Germany's unification.

The *Turnfest* usually started on a Friday and ended on a Monday. The protocol included the reception for the participating teams; the *Fest-Commers;* the sportive competition in different disciplines, among them floor and apparatus exercises, high jump and triple jump, rhythmic gymnastics, and fencing; and a dancing ball on Sunday, which included an awards ceremony and was followed by a *Katerfrühstück* (hangover breakfast). The *Fest-Commers*, which was usually scheduled for the Saturday, followed an official program determined by the organizing committee of the *Turnfest* and included a musical opening, a salute to the participants, festive speeches on behalf of Brazil and Germany, gymnastics and fencing performances, male choir presentations, and the performance German songs and poems. Even though women participated in the sportive competitions, the *Fest-Commers* was a strictly male event.

Another kind of periodic celebration was the *Sängerfest,* organized by the Deutscher Sängerbund Rio Grande do Sul. This event took place in Porto Alegre in 1898; in São João do Montenegro in 1901; in Hamburgerberg (present-day Hamburgo Velho) in 1905 and 1909; in São João do Montenegro in 1912; in Hamburgerberg in 1916; in Porto Alegre in 1924, on the occasion of the festivities to celebrate the German immigration centennial; and in Novo Hamburgo in 1935. The *Sängerfeste* were established to celebrate and cultivate the tradition of choir singing and German folksongs. The *Sängerfest* lasted for two days, usually Saturday and Sunday, and its program centered on the competition among choirs. In general, the event began with the reception of the contestants, followed by a festive evening. Sunday was dedicated to the morning practice of the choirs, the fraternization lunch, the party opening, the festive speech, and the presentation and competition of the choirs. In

the evening there was the announcement of the winners and the award ceremony.

In the 1920s the celebration of the *Deutscher Tag* (German Day) in Porto Alegre on January 18 became a permanent event of the festivities calendar. Its celebration occurred continuously from 1923 to 1937. The Verband deutscher Vereine was in charge of organizing this event, which was always held during the evening in the Turnerbund premises in Porto Alegre. The *Deutscher Tag* commemorated German unification and the foundation of the German Empire on January 18, 1871. It showed solidarity with Weimar Germany, which had been humiliated by the terms of the Treaty of Versailles.

The *Deutscher Tag* was celebrated according to the *Fest-Commers*. It began with a musical opening, normally a piece performed by an orchestra or sung by a choir; salutation to the guests; declamation of patriotic poems; the singing of the Brazilian and the German national anthems and, from 1934 on, the "Horst-Wessel-Lied" (Horst-Wessel Song); performance of the choirs from the singing societies; living pictures portraying German history (Germania, Otto von Bismarck, Friedrich II, Barbarossa, Hermann der Cherusker, and the river Rhine); festive speeches dedicated to Brazil and Germany; and gymnastics exercises on the bars and rhythmic dances. The past was explored in search of events and experiences that could be locally represented and used as identity traces and reference points of a common memory. The purpose of the *Deutscher Tag* was highlighted in the festive speeches, which focused on the desire to form a great German Empire based on German *Volk* (folk) and German blood. The belief in Germany's rebirth and in the emergence of a führer (leader) who could lead the German people to their destiny was defended. During the 1930s, Adolf Hitler was glorified as a guide for both the people and German youth.

Der 25. Juli: Unser Tag (The Twenty-fifth of July: Our Day) was one of the annual festivities with the greatest geographical and public reach. Celebrated for the first time in 1924, it commemorated the arrival of the first German immigrants in São Leopoldo in 1824. It glorified German culture and German contributions to Brazilian economic development. In 1934, General Flores da Cunha decreed July 25 a state holiday in Rio Grande do Sul. From 1934 to 1941 the commemoration occurred in practically all places where German immigrants and their descendants had settled, among them Feliz, Novo Hamburgo, Panambi, Passo Fundo, Pelotas, Porto Alegre, São Leopoldo, Sapiranga, and Taquara. Die Kommission pro 25. Juli (The Committee for July 25), formed by the main German leagues and societies, such as Verband Deutscher Vereine, Riograndenser Synode (Organization of German Associations, Synod of Rio Grande do Sul), and Volksverein für die deutschen Katholiken in Rio Grande do Sul (Association for German Catholics), centralized the planning and organization of the celebration. According to the organizing committee, July 25 was to begin with a morning awakening with drums, songs, or bells; a festive church service; a fraternization lunch; a procession from the main street to the place of the event, which should be a wide open place; a march including the schools, the societies, and the gymnasts in order to hoist the flags; a salutation; gymnastics presentations, choir performances,

and several games; and an evening party at the ballroom with musical performances, choirs, declamation of poetry, festive speeches, plays, and/or movies. The pieces to be presented were to reflect the immigrants' way of life and to awaken the participants' curiosity about their origin. The program included plays, such as *Deutsche Wandern nach Brasilien* (Germans Emigrating to Brazil) by Clara Sauer, which tells the story of a German immigrant family from a rural area and their life in Brazil.

All these events and commemorations contributed to the identification process of German immigrants and their descendants in Rio Grande do Sul. The celebrations were based on a unifying structure that congregated the participants around an assembly of symbolic forms and rites. For the celebrating community, the festival's primary function was to remind them of their ethnic origin and heritage, thus ensuring and strengthening their feeling of ethnic belonging. Organizing events, singing, practicing gymnastics, and recollecting dates and personalities were not only a way to activate the memory and the culture but also a kind of representation and differentiation of the celebrating group from Brazilian society.

Imgart Grützmann

See also Brazil; German Unification (1871); Treaty of Versailles

References and Further Reading

Grützmann, Imgart. *A mágica flor azul: A canção em língua alemã e o germanismo no Rio Grande do Sul.* Doutorado em Letras, Faculdade de Letras, PUCRS, 1999.

———. "Do que tu herdaste dos teus antepassados, deves apropriar-te, a fim de possuí-lo": O germanismo e suas especificidades." *Relatório de pesquisa recém-doutor apresentado à FAPERGS.* Porto Alegre, Maio de 2001.

Rambo, Arthur B. *Reconstructing the Fatherland: German Turnen in Southern Brazil.* London: Frank Cass Publishers, 2001.

Ramos, Eloísa Capovilla da Luz. *O teatro da sociabilidade: Um estudo dos clubes sociais como espaços de representação das elites urbanas alemãs e teuto-brasileiras: São Leopoldo, 1850/1930.* Doutorado em História, Instituto de Filosofia e Ciências Humanas, UFRGS, 2000.

Silva, Haike Kleber da Silva. *SOGIPA: Uma trajetória de 130 anos.* Porto Alegre: Palotti, 1997.

Tesche, Leomar. *A prática do Turnen entre os imigrantes alemães e seus descendentes no Rio Grande do Sul: 1867–1942.* Ijuí: Unijuí, 1996.

Weber, Roswitha. *As comemorações da imigração alemã no Rio Grande do Sul: O 25 de Julho em São Leopoldo 1924/1949.* Mestrado em História, Instituto de Filosofia e Ciências Humanas, UFRGS, 2000.

Wieser, Lothar. *Deutsches Turnen in Brasilien: Deutsche Auswanderung und die Entwicklung des Deutsch-Brasilianischen Turnwesens bis zum Jahre 1917.* London: Arena, 1990.

FILM AND TELEVISION (AMERICAN) AFTER WORLD WAR II, GERMANY IN

Since 1945 American films, and later television, have mainly portrayed German people as Nazis, mad scientists, Communists, or some combinations of them. Given that Hollywood films and television programs have traditionally been much more influential in shaping American perceptions of historical events than any other media, Hollywood's propagation of German culture in negative terms has cultivated a German legacy that remains largely negative to this day in the United States. This negative summation of Germany and Germans overlooks the crucial role Germans have played in the growth of science, literature, music, and education throughout history while also ignoring the close cultural relationship between Germans and Americans dating back to the late 1600s.

But Hollywood's main goal has always been to entertain and not to educate, and since World War II the most entertaining portrayal of Germany has been that of Nazism. American portrayals of Nazism in film began before the United States even entered the war, when the Three Stooges lampooned Adolf Hitler in seven short films from 1937 to 1944. Charlie Chaplin produced the only full length anti-Nazi movie (*The Great Dictator,* 1940) before the United States declared war on Germany. Until the present, a steady stream of anti-Nazi movies have been produced, perpetuating the notion that all Germans are Nazis at heart regardless of the passage of time.

The most numerous form of anti-Nazi films have been the many World War II battle films, which began in the mid-1940s. Since then there have been over sixty full-length feature films focusing on the American and Allied struggle against Nazism. The 1950s, 1960s, and 1970s produced a roughly constant flow of anti-Nazi battle films, including *The Desert Fox* (1951), *The Guns of Navarone* (1961), *The Dirty Dozen* (1967), and *A Bridge Too Far* (1977). Given the extent of German war crimes, the violent blitzkrieg, and the memory of the Nazi death camps, the American image of Germany after the war was justifiably negative. But the sheer volume of anti-Nazi films produced over the years has, in the American mind, reduced the rich legacy of German culture spanning hundreds of years down to the atrocities committed by the Nazi regime, which spanned a mere twelve years.

Beginning in the 1960s, Hollywood began producing several films that combined the popular image of the Nazi with that of a new threat—German communism. The Berlin airlift (1948), the partitioning of Germany (1949), and the building of the Berlin Wall (1961) all helped foster the notion of a "good" capitalist West Germany and a "bad" Communist East Germany in American popular culture and, of course, in movies by the mid-1960s. Although Nazism was still the dominant perception of Germans in that decade, it began to take on a secondary and often comical role as newer threats of German Communist spies and atomic annihilation predominated. In *Dr. Strangelove* (1964), for example, the title character is a former Nazi scientist advising the United States on nuclear arms matters while constantly having to curb his habit of saluting in Nazi fashion. *The Spy Who Came in from the Cold* (1965) combines the threat of Nazism and German communism. This theme resurfaced as late as 1991 in *Star Trek VI: The Undiscovered Country,* when a militaristic Klingon general argues, "We need breathing room!" to which the heroic Captain Kirk retorts "Hitler—1939." In the same conversation the Klingon later remarks, "We are all cold warriors in space."

By the 1970s, serious films focusing on the threat of Nazism began to decrease, but many movies continued to be produced containing Nazi overtones. The most successful American movie series of all time, *Star Wars,* began in 1977 and contained strong Nazi themes. By the end of 2005 the *Star Wars* series will have included six major blockbuster films that follow the rise and defeat of an evil intergalactic empire led by an opportunistic chancellor who is only elected after he invents a military threat to an otherwise peaceful republic. The chancellor then declares emergency powers, names himself emperor, and creates an army of invading "Stormtroopers" to destroy any resistance to the empire. The 1970s also saw a spate of films about former Nazis in hiding after World War II, including *The Odessa File* (1974) and *Marathon Man* (1976).

Nazi overtones are apparent in many popular 1980s and 1990s movies as well. In two of the three Indiana Jones movies, *Raiders of the Lost Ark* (1981) and *Indiana Jones and the Last Crusade* (1989), the title character battles evil Nazis for possession of magical religious artifacts during World War II. The Oscar-winning *Sophie's Choice* (1982) relates the story of a Jewish man's and a female Polish Auschwitz survivor's relationship in the postwar United States. Several 1990s movies were produced with direct anti-Nazi storylines, including *Schindler's List* (1993), *Saving Private Ryan* (1998), and *The Thin Red Line* (1998). More recent movies such as *Enemy at the Gates* (2001) have kept anti-Nazism alive in twenty–first century United States culture.

The second most popular American stereotype about Germany after Nazism is the idea that Germany is the home of the world's worst mad scientists. This is the oldest stereotype about Germany in films, beginning with the first Frankenstein movie in 1909. Since then, scores of Frankenstein movies have emerged from Hollywood, including the classic *Frankenstein* (1931), *The House of Frankenstein* (1944), the comedic *Young Frankenstein* (1974), and the more recent *Frankenstein* (1994) starring Robert De Niro. Several other films set in the postwar period have combined the German mad scientist concept with the familiar Nazism threat. In *They Saved Hitler's Brain*

(1963) and *The Boys from Brazil* (1978), for example, postwar Nazi scientists in hiding attempt to revive the Third Reich by reviving Hitler's maniacal life essence. Similarly, in *Splash* (1984), a former Nazi scientist now living in the United States attempts to capture a beautiful mermaid for evil biological experiments.

American television portrayals of Germany are similar to that in films in most regards, except that television programs about Germany have been more numerous and somewhat more lighthearted. As with films, the most popular German stereotype on television has been that of Nazism, but beginning in the late 1950s, several programs cast the Nazi threat in a comical light. From 1959 to 1973 the popular children's cartoon *The Adventures of Rocky and Bullwinkle* had as its main villain a character named "Fearless Leader" who sported latent Nazi insignia. The 1953 movie *Stalag 17,* a comedy about Allied prisoners of war (POWs) in World War II Germany, spawned a popular television series from 1965 to 1971 called *Hogan's Heroes,* which lampooned Nazism by having the American POWs constantly outsmart the ignorant but loveable Colonel Klink and Sergeant Schultz.

The most common type of programs dealing with Germany after 1945, however, has been the numerous television documentaries about World War II and Nazism. Portrayals of Nazism reached somewhat of a peak in the 1970s with the airing of *Hitler: The Last Ten Days* (1973) and *Holocaust* (1978). Fictional programs about Nazism have been less popular and include *The Winds of War* (1983) and *Hitler's Daughter* (1990), both based on popular books. Although serious fictional and documentary programs about Nazism were more numerous than the few comedy series of the 1960s, the comedies were, in the long run, more influential in American culture, especially since they were immortalized in syndication and continue to air today.

Jeff Stone

See also Hollywood
References and Further Reading
Abramson, Abraham, project coordinator. *New York Times Film Reviews.* New York: New York Times, 1970–1975, vols. 3–7.
Barclay, David E., and Elisabeth Glaser-Schmidt. *Transatlantic Images and Perceptions: Germany and America since 1776.* Washington, DC: German Historical Institute, 1997.
Gorman, Lyn, and David McLean. *Media and Society in the Twentieth Century: A Historical Introduction.* Malden, MA: Blackwell Publishers, 2003.
Hanson, Patricia King, and Stephen L. Hanson. *Film Review Index.* Phoenix, AZ: Oryx Press, 1986, vols. 1–2.

FILM (GERMAN), AMERICAN INFLUENCE ON

German film, its images, and its institutes cannot be understood without reference to the international framework, in which the United States has held a principal role. Already before World War I, German filmmakers and distributors had imitated American technology and cinematic conventions and had struggled to distinguish their products from those made in the United States. The twofold endeavor of the German cinema—to recognize and adopt the "good" aspects of American film and to create a distinctive "German" film—continued into the Weimar Republic and the Nazi era. The privileged position of the American film industry in post–World War II West Germany increased the local filmmakers' challenge. By the 1990s, they needed to find a way into the hearts of German spectators, who had gradually become accustomed to American film conventions and eventually found it easier to identify with the consumer society's cultural values promoted in American blockbusters.

The significant work of local inventors and filmmakers such as the Skladanowski brothers, Oskar Messter, and Herman Foesterling notwithstanding, the German film and its cinematic imagery were always notably influenced by international practices and conventions. In its first decade (roughly, 1895–1906), German cinema was established, like its American equivalent, as an exhibition-led industry. Import, rather than production of films, was a common practice due to its comparatively low costs. American films and distinctive "American" genres—such as the Western—are reported to have been popular in Germany at the beginning of the 1900s (for example, Edwin S. Porter's *The Great Train Robbery*, 1903). From this early stage on, American companies had shown great interest in the German film market and were concerned with satisfying it. Edison Manufacturing Company, for instance, had a representative in Berlin as of 1906.

Concurrently with the international film industry, German film's second decade witnessed two major institutional changes: the development of an efficient distribution system and the emergence of a feature-length narrative film. Both changes contributed to the establishment of a local production industry, which needed to struggle for its share against foreign imports. Already in this early stage, the American film industry was marked both as the most ferocious rival and as an ideal the Germans should follow.

In the years before World War I, 25–30 percent of the films shown in Germany were American, whereas only 10 percent were German productions. (Saunders 1994, 20–21). In order to improve their products' popularity, local filmmakers started to imitate American cinematic conventions (for example, the technique of cross-cutting parallel lines of action). Formulas from popular genres, as well as a "star" system, started to appear in the German film market. "Sauerkraut" Westerns, for instance, were being produced in Germany in accordance with Hollywood editing and plot-line conventions before World War I (unfortunately, very few traces of these films have survived; we know of films such as Viggo Larsen's *Der Pferdedieb* [*The Horse Thief*, 1911] only from descriptions in the trade press). At the same time, filmmakers also sought to develop a distinctive "German" style, in order to distinguish their product from its foreign competitors. This strategy was compatible with the approach favored by contemporary intellectuals (mostly, though not exclusively, common among conservatives), who identified film as expression of non-German characteristics (e.g., American capitalism). Prewar German intellectuals often called for a construction of a new film, one that would help to build a (better) German nation.

World War I had a decisive role in the way the German film industry developed; it also made a significant contribution to the nature of American influence. After declaring its neutrality, the United States continued to export films to Germany; until 1916 American moviemakers still referred to Germany as a "fruitful market." Once its country was engaged in the war, the American film industry shifted its distribution efforts to the non-European world (a move that promised its hegemony in the postwar international market). The administration of Woodrow Wilson attributed an important role in the war efforts to film and the images it distributed. "Film," according to Wilson's statement from 1916, "lends itself importantly to the presentation of America's plans and purposes" (Thompson 1985, 94). Following his command, a Division of Film was launched, not only to make films that would present German soldiers as "a mass of Kaisers, primitive animals," but also to fight the German film industry. When the division was closed in 1918, its administrator announced that it had achieved its goal—the "elimination of the German film."

The reality, however, was more complicated. Despite the severe crisis following World War I in the early 1920s, the German film industry was the strongest in Europe and the only one that sought to challenge Hollywood's hegemony. One of the main reasons was the founding of Universal-Film-A.G. (UFA) in 1917. This production and distribution company was founded in collaboration with the military high command in order to help the war effort—to supply the Germans with means to counter American propaganda endeavors. When the German fight came to an end with a dreadful defeat, UFA was already a conglomerate of numerous film companies and filmmakers, including many of the greatest talents in Europe. These gifted men and women had another advantage: due to a ban on American movies declared by the German government, they could experiment with artistic styles and cinematic expressions—with a much lower risk of loss in the local market.

The ban on Hollywood's films, however, did not halt their influence on Ger-

man cinema. American films were always a point of reference to filmmakers and moviegoers: the reputation of the American film, the constant writing about it in German magazines, and the small number of films that were screened in Berlin in spite of the ban were enough to maintain Hollywood as a real and unavoidable challenge. Interestingly, German films enjoyed sensational success in interwar America, before American films met a similar reception in Germany. American audiences' enthusiastic response to Ernst Lubitsch's *Madame Du Barry* (*Passion,* 1919) and *Anna Boylen* (*Deception,* 1920) and later on to Robert Wiene's *Das Cabinet des Dr. Caligari* (*The Cabinet of Dr. Caligari,* 1920) and Fritz Lang's *Der Müde Tod* (*Destiny,* 1921), for instance, had a tremendous impact on the evolution of German film in the first half of the 1920s.

During the postwar years, the high rate of inflation in Germany made the export of German films immensely more profitable than leaning on the profits of the local film market. Censorship and local tax policies made the need to sell German movies abroad exceedingly urgent. The necessity to find a profitable "niche" in the international market caused German filmmakers to look for a way to distinguish their products from Hollywood's goods. The formula was found in films such as *Caligari* and *Destiny* (the slogan "this is the Germany we love" accompanied the latter's screening in newspaper reviews all over the world). A "German" way of filmmaking was now identified with characteristics such as expressionist stylization; powerful, irrational protagonists; and often a departure from "classical" cinematic conventions. Thus, freedom to experiment and the urgent need to export were responsible, to a large extent, for the peculiarities of German films of the early 1920s. It is important to note that the success of German films in the United States also had a destructive impact on the industry: many of the most talented German filmmakers left to find glory in Hollywood (Ernst Lubitsch, Friedrich Wilhelm Murnau, and Paul Leni are a small sample for this "first wave" of German filmmakers in the United States).

In 1922, with the end of the ban, a flood of American films reached Germany—mostly cheap slapstick comedies and melodramas. The need to compete—again—with American products led local producers and artists to enhance their filmmaking and marketing strategies. Once again, classical conventions were adopted and imitated: by 1925, for instance, continuity editing, a Hollywood norm, was practiced constantly in German films. Also the drive to make "films [that] America would never do"—as Lang described the motivation for his celebrated *Metropolis* (1927)—was growing stronger. The alleged contrast between "American technology" and "German artistic skills," which was observed by German filmmakers and intellectuals alike, served as a marketing strategy, as well as a persuasive argument in the discourse about the characteristics of German identity.

Economically, however, this strategy failed; the appeal of the German film could never surmount Hollywood's international attractiveness. In 1924, when the stabilization of the German currency started to diminish inflation, German exports were no longer lucrative; American exports to Europe became much more gainful. Under these circumstances—intensive struggle over market share with Hollywood, inside and outside Germany, and lower profit on

exports—the German film industry found itself on the edge of bankruptcy. In Austria, for instance, the German market share decreased from 90 percent to one German film for every eight American ones (Thompson 1985, 104).

Between 1923 and 1927, the American presence in the German film industry was immense. It reached its peak with the foundation of "Parufamet," an agreement between UFA and the American studios Paramount and MGM. This collaborative contract relieved UFA from its enormous debts in exchange for American influence over the German distribution market. These occurrences contributed to the "Americanization" of the German moviegoers' taste: Charlie Chaplin, Douglas Fairbanks, and Mary Pickford were adored equally by the masses and intellectual elites; American movie stars and filmmakers published their contemplations regularly in German magazines; and local movie "stars" were rated according to American standards (Harry Piel, perhaps the most popular German movie star in the 1920s, was known as "the German Fairbanks"). When Alfred Hugenberg, a conservative businessman, gained control over UFA in 1927, the collaboration with American studios gradually ceased. Hollywood continued to cherish the potential of the German market in the early 1930s, as seen in the intensive endeavor to solve technological and legal difficulties in order to facilitate screening of American sound films to German audiences.

Hollywood's efforts notwithstanding, state regulation and audience taste protected the German film industry from collapse. It is noteworthy that by the end of the 1920s, the German film industry was regaining significant popularity and had registered remarkable artistic achieve-ments. The American market share in Ger-many was comparatively low, about 30 per-cent, and some notable filmmakers and actors—for instance Paul Martin, Josef von Sternberg, and Emil Jannings—even came back from Hollywood to work in Berlin (the illustrious *Blue Angel*, released in 1930, was directed by Sternberg and starred Jannings).

The rise of National Socialism caused a second wave of emigration from Germany. This group contained many filmmakers and actors, such as Fritz Lang, Billy Wilder, Marlene Dietrich, and Peter Lorre, who ar-rived in Los Angeles and eventually re-turned to Germany to make films after World War II. The Nazi rise to power was not, for many of them, the only reason for emigration to Hollywood, but they gained a reputation as "fugitives," which helped them to develop their career in the United States, especially when Adolf Hitler was perceived as a global threat.

Hitler and Joseph Goebbels, who adored American movies and were reported to watch them repeatedly, acknowledged the important influence film might have on public opinion. Goebbels gave film a crucial role in the new regime and declared his ambition to create "pure" German cin-ema. Nevertheless, the first years of the Nazi reign did not mark a clear rupture in American influence over the German film industry. Despite famous assertions by Goebbels, who declared that German films should not look like those of any other na-tion, Nazi cinema had consciously adopted Hollywood's conventions. Film magazines continuously reported about American films, often in an enthusiastic tone. Con-trary to official statements, the Nazi film industry continued Weimar's tendency to emulate the stylistic and cultural conven-tions of the United States, as can be shown in films such as *Glückskinder* (Children of Fortune), made by UFA in 1936. As a re-sult of the film industry crisis that year, calls to "learn from Hollywood" became ever louder. A close look at Nazi films re-veals that imitation was common but lim-ited to specific aspects of American films (such as escapist qualities and efficient marketing methods). Film scholars often indicate differences in emphasis between "classical" Hollywood films and popular genres in those of the Nazi era, which were expressed in esthetical choices (mise-en-scène, camera movement, etc.) rather than in dialogues and plots.

Until 1940—late into the National Socialist regime—American films could be seen in Berlin. During World War II, Ger-man films repeated the World War I pro-duction tendency on both sides of the At-lantic: films served as a way to distribute war propaganda and supply escapist enter-tainment. Two weeks after the war was over, regular screenings of movies started in the parts of Germany under American occupation. Both among the Western Al-lies and Germans themselves, the image of the Germans as "easily manipulated" by mass media was popular. This perception caused the United States to pay close at-tention to the German film industry and the imagery it distributed to the "weak-minded" Germans.

Once again, by the second half of the 1940s, a flood of Hollywood products found an enthusiastic audience. Interest-ingly, it was the United States that stopped Hollywood from completely taking over the German film market. The restrictions placed by American officials were meant to allow Germany a chance to develop a (considerably) independent film industry. This "new" industry was to a large extent a continuation—in the personnel and the stylization—of the recent past. Certainly, essential changes were made in subject matters, and, in addition, American conventions and imagery were readopted. The spectators, now presented with American and German movies, crowded the cinema halls: by the mid-1950s theater owners sold 817 million movie tickets to Germans each year (Fehrenbach 1995, 118).

In the middle of the 1950s a new movement of "angry young men" raised its voice against the residues of the Nazi era in German cinema. This movement, coming out of the "Cine-Club" of the big cities, combined the struggle against old Nazis with one against American influence. It called for the "purification" of German film from formulas created by "Hollywood or UFA." The German film should (re)construct itself, according to this movement, by returning to its "essentials"—those of the "art film," as opposed to the "popular" American film.

The debate about the formation of a mass consumer society, symbolized by the United States, stood at the core of West German discourse on identity during the immediate postwar era. Within this context, the call for "genuine" German films came not only from the Left but also from conservatives. The German church, which had a significant role in the reconstruction of West German culture and politics, decried the American influence over German popular film.

Despite the feelings they stimulated among conservatives and anti-capitalists, popular genres of West German cinema in the 1950s were not mere duplications of American conventions. *Heimatfilme*, for instance, a genre that traditionally presented the German countryside as the authentic opposition to the non-German modern city, continued to be remarkably fashionable. Moreover, American cinematic conventions were not adopted wholeheartedly even in distinctive "American" genres. The 1950s German melodramas, such as Erich Engel's *Liebe Ohne Illusion* (Love without Illusions, 1955), for example, had some elemental differences—in visual stylization and the cultural values they promoted—from their American equivalents. Despite the unprecedented control of American studios over the West German film market, before the 1970s the popularity of local films, based on local cinematic traditions and cultural background, was higher than that of American ones.

In the German Democratic Republic (GDR), the American influence was obviously weaker. Filmmakers were acquainted with American productions, at least until the 1960s, but the East German market was not controlled by Hollywood, and the Socialist administration encouraged manifestations of "Socialist" principles in stylistic and plot-line developments. The American way of moviemaking was a point of reference from which filmmakers were inspired and from which they also sought to differentiate themselves. Along with their enhancements of "Socialist genres," these filmmakers also borrowed and modified American ones. Like its American counterpart, the extremely popular GDR Western, the *Indianerfilm*, portrayed the struggle between the American white man and the native "savage" on the frontier. Instead of telling the white man's conquest story, however, the *Indianerfilme* depicted Native Americans as a harmonious, precapitalist society that had to fight against (the white man's) capitalism.

In West Germany, where the American presence was a lot more evident, local filmmakers felt they should make a drastic break in order to distinguish themselves. In February 1962, during the West German festival of short films in Oberhausen, twenty-six young filmmakers declared the death of "the old film" and announced their belief in a new one. The New German Cinema, they proclaimed in the famous "Oberhausen Manifest," would be free from "the usual conventions . . . from commercial influences . . . from the dominance of interest groups." Though it was not their sole concern, the enemy that was indicated here was, mainly, American involvement in the West German film market. Once again, the inability to compete—economically—with Hollywood was combined in the New German Cinema with the conviction that American films were based on cultural conventions that were foreign to the essence of German identity.

By the 1970s, the defeat of West German cinema by Hollywood was evident. Throughout the post–World War II era, Hollywood had taken advantage of American leverage in Germany to make it a most profitable export market, but until 1971 the German share of box office was higher than the American. Yet by the early 1970s, the German share had decreased dramatically. This shift is mainly due to the reorganization of Hollywood's European distribution network in the late 1960s, the rise of television (which meant younger movie spectators), and the new dominance of "American" cultural values over traditionally "German" ones.

The New German Cinema grew out of these unfortunate circumstances. It did,

however, "free" itself from the constraints of the market to a certain extent. Governmental funding and television screenings freed German filmmakers from box office evaluation. The New German Cinema developed "art films" that sought to explore and undermine popular (Hollywood) cinematic conventions and to establish an essentially "German" film (which meant un-American). Art films were not the only reaction of German filmmakers to the rising appeal of American films. International cooperation, production of films that targeted teenagers, and sex-centered films participated in the endeavor to gain market share in the face of the latest changes in audiences' nature and taste.

Some West German films of the 1980s also adopted contemporary "American" conventions: *Die Unendliche Geschichte* (The Never Ending Story, 1984), for instance, presented a male protagonist with supernatural powers who pursues personal goals. These characteristics display the shift in cultural values from "German" self-sacrifice and the sense of duty and social responsibility to "American" self-fulfillment. At that time, an American-style "star" system developed in German mainstream cinema. After the international success of German popular and art cinema in the early 1980s, many German talents again left to work in Hollywood in the 1990s—e.g., Wolfgang Petersen (director, *Air Force One*, 1997), Roland Emmerich (executive producer, *Independence Day*, 1996).

In the 1990s even Hollywood could not rely solely on its home market for profits. In addition to the efforts to sell in the international market, German producers realized they desperately needed to find an audience among television spectators and video store consumers. In order to compete in these markets, German filmmakers often sought inspiration in new popular genres, such as the sitcom, which was influenced by American television conventions and proved to be popular among television spectators. Other films were shot especially for international distribution companies by integrating American themes, fitting (American) genre expectations, and occasionally using English titles and references to popular American films.

The tradition of the "author film," which was one of the major ideals of the New German Cinema, has reached beyond the 1970s. It is noteworthy, however, that American companies controlled the distribution of the films made by Werner Herzog, Volker Schlöndorf, and Wim Wenders and thus made profit from these allegedly independent film productions. The unification of Germany brought a larger local market for German productions. Typical "German" genres have gained a substantial share in the market since 1996. Nevertheless, American domination of the German film market was secure; during the 1990s, an American blockbuster could easily attract 4–5 million German spectators, whereas the most successful *Autorenfilme*—which supposedly maintained distinctive "German" characteristics—could expect less than one-tenth of this number.

Ofer Ashkenazi

See also Americanization; Consumerism; Dietrich, Marlene Magdalene; Herzog, Werner; Hollywood; Indian Films of the Deutsche Film Aktiengesellschaft; Jannings, Emil; Lang, Fritz; Leni, Paul; Lorre, Peter; Lubitsch, Ernst; Murnau, Friedrich Wilhelm; Sternberg, Josef von; Wilder, Billy; World War I

References and Further Reading

Elsaesser, Thomas, and Michael Wedel, eds. *A Second Life: German Cinema's First Decades.* Amsterdam: Amsterdam University Press, 1996.

Fehrenbach, Heide. *Cinema in Democratizing Germany: Reconstructing National Identity after Hitler.* Chapel Hill: University of North Carolina Press, 1995.

Garncarz, Joseph. "Hollywood in Germany: The Role of American Films in Germany." In *Hollywood in Europe: Experience of a Cultural Hegemony.* Eds. David W. Ellwood, Rob Kroes, and Gian Piero Brunetta. Amsterdam: VU University Press, 1994.

Krämer, Peter. "Hollywood in Germany/Germany in Hollywood." In *The German Cinema Book.* Eds. Tim Bergfelder, Erica Carter, and Deniz Göktürk. London: British Film Institute, 2002.

Saunders, Thomas J. *Hollywood in Berlin: American Cinema and Weimar Germany.* Berkeley: University of California Press, 1994.

Thompson, Kristin. *Exporting Entertainment: America in the World Film Market 1907–1934.* London: BFI Pub. 1985

FILM (GERMAN), THE IMAGE OF THE UNITED STATES IN

"American" landscapes and people have appeared repeatedly in German film from its emergence until today. The German cinematic depiction of the United States was grounded, from the very first stage, in the discourse of German cultural identity. Distinctive American scenery (skyscrapers, "Indian" raids) and characters (the gangster, the capitalist entrepreneur) were presented as a means to identify and create Germany's image of itself. Cinematic imagery of the United States fluctuated throughout the twentieth century, as the U.S. role in international politics evolved and German identity was reconstructed after World Wars I and II.

Several conventions are commonly found in German film portrayals of the United States throughout this time. They can be best described as a set of dualities within which the United States and Americans are described. First, the United States was envisaged both as the absolute "Other"—against which "Germanness" could be measured—and as a reflection of Germany's essential characteristics. Second, in most cases, the United States and Americans were portrayed as an idea or a fantasy rather than as an actual reality. Usually this idea was illustrated as a utopian or a dystopian concept; in many cases, as we see below, the United States was envisaged as both utopian and dystopian at the same time. Third, the depiction of the United States was based on the duality of a hypermodern society (e.g., rush hours in the modern city, cars, airplanes) and a premodern society (the "tribal" way of life, the moral system of life on the frontier). Once again, many times the United States was represented as an ongoing tension between these two poles: primitivity was often detected within the ultramodern civilization.

German filmmakers recognized the appeal of American images and made use of them since their earliest film productions (starting in late 1895). Frequently, they did so while imitating American conventions of representation and genre formulas. The German cinematic images of the United States, however, bore some essential differences from the American films they emulated. German Westerns, for instance, were arguably unique in emphasizing the male protagonist as a rebel against and liberated from respectable bourgeois values. These films, therefore, placed their protagonist within a premodern setting of the Wild West frontier, while providing him with ambitions that were a fundamental part of the ethos of modernity.

The cinematic depiction of the United States became more momentous during and especially after World War I. When the United States became an influential world power and an international economy leader, the manner in which the United States was represented in the films of the defeated and economically dependent Germany became critical. Hereafter the dualities mentioned above are more visible.

Fritz Lang's *Die Spinnen* (The Spiders, 1919/1920) is a good example that uses all three conventions. The tensions between hypermodernity and premodernity, utopia and dystopia, and otherness and self-reflection can be seen in its depiction of his American protagonist, Kay Hoog, and his rivals, the criminal organization the "Spiders." The tension between the modern and the primitive aspects of the United States is represented symbolically in the bandits' headquarters, which is placed in tunnels underneath San Francisco: they are a dark force, invisible inside the modern city, threatening to undermine its stability. Furthermore, the "Spiders" employ Asian warriors who use premodern weapons and martial arts. Yet, being in the United States, the "Spiders" also use hypermodern technology, such as small, hidden cameras, within the primitive setting of the underground city.

The utopian-dystopian axis is manifested, in one instance, in an American nightclub scene in the first part of the film. The Americans here—in sharp contrast with post–World War I Germans—seem almost pampered and concerned mainly with the results of a forthcoming sailing race. Into this modern capitalist heaven enters a most beautiful and dangerous woman—Lio Sha—one of the leaders of the Spiders, who intends to undercut this carefree civilization. Sha's role in this scene is identical with the above-mentioned underground city: an undetectable but almost omnipotent evil that transforms the heavenly appearance into a mere façade, a hell in disguise.

German spectators, most likely, found it hard to identify with the oblivious Americans on the screen. Lang illustrates this lighthearted society, which was seen as the outcome of modern technology and a modern economic system, as devoid of morals, self-centered, and unable and unwilling to comprehend its surroundings. Despite their advanced technology and prosperity, the Americans seem to lack certain cultural qualities, which match the old German concept of *Kultur*, traditionally used to identify "German" characteristics. Kay Hoog, the male protagonist, seems to be an ideal mixture, however: he seeks a more "authentic" way of life while using the latest technological advances and his abundant wealth. This character might be read as an indication of the potential of the German individual in the modern, post–World War I era.

The three concepts through which "America" was represented can be found in many films in the years following World War I. The sixth part of Joe May's *Herrin der Welt* (Mistress of the World, 1920), for instance, is filled with images emphasizing the modernity of New York City: unprecedented architecture and especially rapid movement of cars, people, and information. In this film, while it is visually fascinating, the modernity of the United States is chaotic and irrational and therefore contains some characteristics that are typically "primitive." A similar conception can be seen in *Metropolis* (1927). This film contains no indication of the place or the time of the events onscreen. Nevertheless, director Fritz Lang and producer Erich Pommer

describe their initial encounter with New York City's skyline as they first approached by boat as the inspiration for this celebrated film. The utopian and dystopian aspects of the big city are envisaged in the coexistence of an upper-city (once more, a modern capitalist's heaven), and an underground city (of the machine operators). A "heart" is needed in this city—according to Thea von Harbou's script—in order to unite the ones who profit with the ones who suffer from the technological achievements. Without the "heart," which is insinuated to be foreign to (American) civilization, the way to primitivity is short—as demonstrated in the violent uprising that almost destroys both the upper and the underground cities.

American characters often appear on the German screen in the 1930s as tremendously rich people who have come to Germany seeking adventures and business opportunities. The wealth and beauty of the Americans are often combined with naïveté and incapability—as is the case with the young American girl in Harry Piel's *Jonny Stiehlt Europa* (Jonny Steals Europa, 1932). When the Americans try to retrieve Europa, their stolen horse, they realize they cannot do it without the wit and strength of Jonny, the German protagonist. In the end, Jonny falls in love with the American girl, thus indicating how successful German and American cooperation is not only functional but also based on similarities in their nature. This film clearly demonstrates the symbolic value of the characters—the rich American capitalist and his daughter, the horse Europa, and the German male, Jonny: in the race to gain control over "Europa," Germans and Americans should unite their cultural potential and acknowledge their similarities.

The search for similarities and the representation of the tension between similarities with and differences from the United States, goes beyond the Weimar Republic era (1918–1933). In early Nazi films, such as *Der Tunnel* (The Tunnel, 1933) and *Der Verlorene Sohn* (The Prodigal Son, 1934), the encounters between Germans and Americans take place on American soil. In the former, German dynamite experts share an American engineer's vision of advancing humanity (by digging a tunnel under the Atlantic Ocean). In the latter, the German protagonist finds himself sleeping on a street bench in New York City during the Great Depression, right next to an American World War I veteran. Quickly we learn that they share not only a comparable past but also a passive attitude toward war experiences and their duty to serve, and furthermore, their hopeless future seems to be the same.

The portrayal of the United States in Luis Trenker's *Der Verlorene Sohn* moves between utopia and dystopia. In the beginning of the film, the United States offers a promise of wealth and adventure: the German protagonist learns from his geography teacher and from visiting Americans about their enchanting homeland. When he is in New York, he is introduced to the images of skyscrapers and rapid movements, which the German moviegoer by now identifies with American hypermodernity. Soon, however, the German protagonist finds that this modern heaven hides misery and despair, hunger, and the loss of morality (he himself has to steal in order to eat). The hypermodernity is revealed to be a thin veil above the actual backward morals of everyday life and the primitive behavior needed to survive. Even when the protag-

onist's luck changes and he becomes rich and famous, he still recognizes his inability to cope with the American way of life and returns to his loved ones. It is important to note that he does not return to Germany as a whole, but to the village and to its premodern festival. In this film "America" seems to symbolize the alleged industrial modernity of any big city, even a German one, as opposed to the "genuine" German spirit, which manifests itself in the rural, lofty *Heimat* (a concept that relates both to the German national identity—the nation's "homeland"—and to a manifestation of a nostalgic longing to and identification with the local community and its traditional way of life, which allegedly flourished in the "German" landscapes in the past).

Der Verlorene Sohn and *Der Tunnel*, like other films of the Nazi era, continued one tradition of the Weimar era (of films such as Paul Martin's *Ein Blonder Traum* [A Blond Dream], 1932): portraying the United States as a German object of desire. The protagonists in these films seek to find wealth and fame in the United States, and, particularly, a partner. Whether a lover or a business companion, the partnership is usually bound to fail; the German protagonist, who is willing to convert his lifestyle and values to American ones, discovers in the end the worthlessness of the American way of life. Only when the German protagonists stick to their *Kultur* do they find a compatible American companion. The cooperation of the German expert and the American engineer in *Der Tunnel*, against the workers' demands for better working conditions, is a good example of such a partnership. The American partner, just like the German, can elevate himself above the values of the modern mass culture (including Socialist protests and market rules of global capitalism)—together they create a covenant between two *Übermenschen* (Supermen).

The United States and Americans continue to be symbols of a deceptive redemption in German film after World War II. In Wolfgang Staudte's *Die Mörder Sind Unter Uns* (*The Murderers Are among Us*, 1946), the first German post–World War II feature film, a message of hope is delivered by an American. This message, however, arrives too late—after his recipient dies. Americans in the immediate postwar era are depicted both as a promise for an unknown, better world and as incompetent to fulfill this promise.

Compared to the substantial presence of American soldiers on West German soil in the postwar years, their almost complete absence from German films is remarkable. Billy Wilder, a German filmmaker who emigrated to Hollywood before the war, put this GI presence at the core of his movie *A Foreign Affair* (1948). Though it was an American production dealing with conflicts in American society and designed for an American audience, this film also manifests some of the traditional characteristics of German cinema's portrayal of "America." The Americans here seem to be the main (maybe the only) hope for a better future; nonetheless, they are hypocrites and opportunists, easily manipulated and bureaucratic. Strangely enough, these are the same characteristics that Americans attribute to Germans. In order to improve the image of the United States in West Germany, several "educational" films were made in the late 1940s and early 1950s in which the fear from and the resentment toward Americans are discussed, and the essential

similarities between the Germans and the Americans are emphasized.

Comments on the destructive and the constructive qualities of the United States, together with fundamental differences and similarities, continue to preoccupy the . filmmakers of the West German New Cinema. In *Im Lauf der Zeit* (*Kings of the Road*, 1976), Wim Wenders famously coined the line "the Yanks have colonized our subconscious." "America" here represents pop culture, as the protagonist cannot get the lyric of a pop song out of his head. We can read this line as a continuation of the traditional criticism in Germany of American society and its shallow cultural values and achievements. Nevertheless, this scene should be read also as an example of a more complicated image of the United States in the films of the generation of filmmakers who matured during the Adenauer era: after all, it was Wenders himself who called the same American popular music his "lifesaver" as an adolescent. According to Wenders, for his generation, American culture was both a refuge and liberator from the Nazi past and from the historical "amnesia" of older Germans.

When the challenge of the recent past became more and more crucial to the reconstruction of German identity, the New German Cinema began to increasingly use the United States as an image that relates to memory and forgetfulness, guilt and forgiveness. In Rainer Werner Fassbinder's *Die Ehe der Maria Braun* (*The Marriage of Maria Braun*, 1979), for instance, the killing of an American soldier serves as a means to win the protagonist's husband's forgiveness for her allegedly disloyal behavior during his captivity in Russia. The presence of Americans (on the screen and in the cultural consciousness) make it impossible to overlook the recent past. Other films stress the connection between Americans and the ability to forget. When Bruno Ganz awakes in a hospital with no recollection of how he got there in Reinhardt Hauff's *Messer im Kopf* (*Knife in the Head,* 1978), he says, "An American in my situation would probably take a gun and shoot blindly out of the window." For him the "American" is an action hero of the movies—the lack of memory would not prevent him from functioning in his conventional manner.

These two films envision the United States as a threat to the reconstruction of German identity. In *Messer im Kopf* the collective amnesia of the Germans regarding the circumstances that led to their present situation would render them eventually identical to the United States, which arguably acts without the burden of the past. Fassbinder's film, on the contrary, criticizes the U.S. role in mastering Germany's past. According to Fassbinder and others, such as Edgar Reitz, the educational and cultural efforts that were invested by the United States in postwar Germany have prevented the Germans from producing their own collective memories and narratives of their past and hence have limited their ability to construct their own identity. Like Wenders in his film *Im Lauf der Zeit,* Fassbinder argues in *Die Ehe der Maria Braun* that the American presence is truly redemptive because it is the sole replacement for the Germans forgetfulness; at the same time, this substitute is, eventually, illusive and foreign to the genuine German identity and needs. In presenting this dual message, Fassbinder's film may resemble the films of the early 1930s.

In early German films the United States was often a location for one episode

in an adventure travel tour, a remote place—like India, South America, and other stops along the protagonist's way—that emphasizes the protagonist's uniqueness through encounters with foreign cultures. German characters continued to travel to the United States in the films of the New German Cinema. The encounter here is based on a closer acquaintance with Americans and, obviously, loaded with tension between antagonism toward and admiration of the American way of life. The travelers who come to the United States in Werner Herzog's *Stroszek* (1977) look for salvation in what is supposed to be the ultimate "other" reality, compared to the one in Berlin. In the end they find in Wisconsin the same patterns as in Germany. Like other films of that period, *Stroszek*'s protagonists are not redeemed but enlightened: by noting the similarities between the United States and Germany, they gain a clearer view of themselves; the German identity, once again, can construct itself while gazing on its "American" reflection.

The tendency to displace the discourse of German identity in the American arena was not unique to filmmakers of the "New German Cinema." The highly popular *Indianer Filme* (German Westerns)—in West and East Germany alike—provided German film audiences with new imagery of the American Wild West and its inhabitants. This imagined American frontier gave way to reflections about the ideal qualities of individuals and their community, to which the Germans should aspire. Thus, for instance, East German Westerns emphasized the precapitalist's qualities of the Native American community, which found itself in a fierce struggle against greedy, white capitalists. This emphasis also highlighted the indifference of filmmakers to the actual reality in the Wild West, the actual way of life in the tribes and the differences between them.

We should not overlook, however, the reflective quality of the images of the United States and Americans for the German filmmakers themselves, who were part of a national film industry that sought to differentiate itself from and associate itself with Hollywood's success. We can understand those images as a displacement of their antagonism and competition with the American film industry on the one hand, and their need to rely on Hollywood's cinematic conventions and distribution methods in a search for legitimization on the other. Films such as Wenders's *Der Amerikanische Freund* (*The American Friend,* 1977) can be read easily in this vein: an American swindler convinces a German framemaker to betray his moral values (that is, to commit murder) by convincing him he is mortally ill and by promising him a great sum of money that would support his family in a way he would never be able to do otherwise. In order to stress the link between himself and the American "dreams industry," the American friend dresses and talks like the hero of a Hollywood Western, and in his diary he cites a well-known American slogan—by now a cliché—"there is nothing to fear but fear itself." Wenders uses it as if it was a superficial cliché, but, of course, it holds several layers of historical and cultural meaning, which cannot be discussed here. Only at the end of the film, after he murders for the American, does the German protagonist try for the first time to revolt and prove his own free will. His rebellion, nonetheless, is meaningless and lasts for only a few minutes, until his own

death. Evidently, Wenders has contempt for not only the intervention of Hollywood in the local film market but also for the superficial image of the United States that was established in German and international popular culture.

Even if the motivation for the depiction of the United States and Americans was the struggle of the New German Cinema filmmakers for legitimization of their films, their products finally coincided with the discourse of German identity and its reconstruction in the second half of the twentieth century. The United States continued to be a unique "other," one that could be a mirror for German identity. During the years before World War II, the United States was used often as a place that—fascinating as it was—gave a better assessment of the homeland's superiority. In the second half of the twentieth century the United States continued to attract the confused protagonists, but the insights they gained through an encounter with "America" became more complex, in concert with the new complexities of German identity after the Nazi regime.

Ofer Ashkenazi

See also Indian Films of the Deutsche Film Aktiengesellschaft; Lang, Fritz; Wenders, Wim; Wilder, Billy

References and Further Reading

Elsaesser, Thomas. *New German Cinema: A History.* New Brunswick: Rutgers University Press, 1989.

Göktürk, Deniz. "How Modern Is It? Moving Images of America in Early German Cinema." In *Hollywood in Europe: Experience of a Cultural Hegemony.* Eds. David W. Ellwood, Rob Kroes, and Gian Piero Brunetta. Amsterdam: VU University Press, 1994.

Rentschler, Eric. "How American Is It: The US as Image and Imaginary in German Film." *Persistence of Vision,* no. 2 (Fall 1985): 5–18.

FIRST MOROCCAN CRISIS (1905–1906)

German *Weltpolitik* (world politics) and U.S. expansionism brought a significant change to the relationship between Berlin and Washington at the turn of the twentieth century. The tradition of mutual sympathy gradually developed into a state of hostility. During the Venezuelan crisis of 1902–1903, friction between Germany and the United States reached a climax. After 1903, changes in the international power constellation, such as the shaping of the entente cordiale between Great Britain and France, made Washington's goodwill more valuable for the German government. During the First Moroccan Crisis in 1905–1906, which developed from Franco-German rivalries in North Africa, German foreign policy was to a large degree based upon the belief in U.S. support.

Until 1900, Germany's economic interest in Morocco had been negligible, and Chancellor Otto von Bismarck repeatedly confirmed that Germany did not have any special claim on that country. Hence, French influence was allowed to grow steadily. The Moroccan sultans became dependent on loans from Paris, which led to talks about the acceptance of French predominance in Morocco by France, Great Britain, and Spain in 1902–1903, culminating in the conclusion of the entente in 1904.

At this point, the German government gave up its traditional policy of noninvolvement in the matter and began to challenge French claims in Morocco. Berlin reacted to the demands of the pan-German Right and to the growing German economic interests in North Africa. In addition, Chancellor Bernhard von Bülow hoped to thwart the threatening Anglo-French alliance.

What Germany needed was a powerful backer, preferably one that could influence Great Britain. According to Bülow and his advisers, the cessation of English support would mean the breakdown of French policy. The United States seemed to be the ideal partner since it had shown interest in Morocco. Moreover, with Ambassador Hermann Speck von Sternburg, Germany seemed to have a direct channel to the U.S. president. In the negotiations that followed, fueled by the diplomatic dispatches of Sternburg, wishful thinking rather than rational estimations about U.S. willingness to risk involvement in Morocco determined German foreign policy. The belief in the president's support became the "keystone" of German plans.

By the middle of 1905, the specter of a Franco-German war over Morocco was looming large after Wilhelm II had personally visited Tangier and thus emphasized German claims on Morocco. Although the North African country was not really important for Germany, what mattered was to show the French that Germany was a decisive power in global politics and one that could not simply be bypassed—not even with British support.

Under heavy diplomatic pressure, U.S. president Theodore Roosevelt finally agreed to mediate a conference with all powers involved in order to prevent a European war. Yet in spite of Berlin's hopes, the president was determined to act as a neutral intermediary between the rivals. Roosevelt made it clear that he expected the Germans not to quibble over minor details. With the conference scheme secured, Ambassador Sternburg made the far-reaching commitment—presented in the form of a personal message from the emperor to the president—that Germany would be willing to back up Roosevelt's decision in case of Franco-German differences.

The conference was scheduled to open in January 1906 in Algeciras. By that point, the German diplomatic situation had deteriorated to such a degree that the only aim of the German government now was to save face and avoid complete diplomatic isolation. Yet negotiations during the conference soon led to a deadlock because of the uncompromising French and German plans about how to reorganize the Moroccan police and financial systems. In February, when the whole conference threatened to fail and war seemed imminent, President Roosevelt reacted by using the former commitment of the German ambassador to force Germany into accepting the French proposal.

Essentially, the results of the conference showed the failure of German diplomacy. Although Moroccan sovereignty and equal rights for all trading interests were confirmed, the country soon came into the formal sphere of French influence. More important, however, was the strengthening of the entente cordiale and the initiation of an Anglo-Russian rapprochement. Algeciras had openly demonstrated German isolation for the first time, and the term *encirclement* gained more currency with the German public. International conferences—this seemed to be the lesson for Germany—were obviously not a good idea. German indignation with the United States was at most short lived. If only because of Germany's growing isolation in Europe, the illusion of a cordial German American relationship and possibly even an alliance continued.

Stefan Rinke

See also Far East, U.S.-German Entente in the; Sternburg, Hermann Speck von; Venezuelan Crisis

References and Further Reading

Esthus, Raymond A. *Theodore Roosevelt and the International Rivalries*. Waltham: Regina Books, 1970.

Larsen, Peter. "Theodore Roosevelt and the Moroccan Crisis, 1904–1906." PhD diss., Princeton University, 1984.

Rinke, Stefan. "A Diplomat's Dilemma: Ambassador Speck von Sternburg and the Moroccan Crisis, 1905/06." *Mid-America* 75, no. 2 (April–July 1993): 165–196.

Vagts, Alfred. *Deutschland und die Vereinigten Staaten in der Weltpolitik*. New York: Macmillan, 1935.

FLÜGEL, JOHANN GOTTFRIED

b. November 22, 1788; Barby, Saxony
d. June 24, 1855; Leipzig, Saxony

German American merchant, philologist, and lexicographer.

After a mercantile apprenticeship in Magdeburg, Johann Gottfried Flügel worked for several German trading companies and sailed to the United States in 1810, continuing his business activities on the banks of the Mississippi River. He obtained U.S. citizenship in New Orleans in 1819. Returning to Germany in the same year, Flügel settled in Leipzig, where he became lecturer (*Lector publicus*) in English at the University of Leipzig (1824–1837) and received his doctor's degree (DPhil) in 1830. He was a laborious student of English, publishing a *Grammar of the English Language* (2 vols., 1824–1826), pamphlets, and critical essays that remain a noteworthy record of the earlier period of English philology in Germany. His *Complete Dictionary of the English and German Languages* (1830, 3rd ed., 1847), enlarged, updated, and newly edited by his son Felix, also contained a great number of Americanisms and became a standard work (15th ed., 1891).

In January 1839, U.S. president Martin Van Buren appointed Flügel U.S. consul in Leipzig, thus succeeding the famous economist and Tübinger professor Friedrich List in that office. The U.S. consulate at Leipzig, founded in 1826, was of great importance for the commercial and intellectual interests of the United States in nineteenth-century Europe, since this city represented a commercial place of the first magnitude and harbored a first-rate university with a good number of American students. Its international fairs, regularly visited by American traders from New York, Philadelphia, Baltimore, and New Orleans, had become a real bridgehead of east-west trade. Flügel was unremitting in his efforts to render service to American travelers, and by his untiring industry and zeal, he intensified Saxon-American business activities as well as transatlantic scholarly contacts.

In 1846, only one year after its foundation, the Smithsonian Institution in Washington, D.C., made Flügel agent of its international exchange service for central Europe. The regents of this famous institution of learning held their German agent in high esteem for his contribution to establishing its renown throughout northern and central Europe. After his death, his son, Vice-Consul Dr. Felix Flügel (1820–1904), was put in charge of exchange matters between Germany and the United States. Subsequently, exchanges between the United States and Austria-Hungary and also Switzerland were conducted through the Leipzig agency.

Eberhard Brüning

See also American Students at German Universities; List, Friedrich; New Orleans

References and Further Reading
Brüning, Eberhard. *Das Konsulat der Vereinigten Staaten von Amerika zu Leipzig. Unter besonderer Berücksichtigung des Konsuls Dr. J. G. Flügel (1839–1855). Sitzungsberichte der Sächsischen Akademie der Wissenschaften zu Leipzig. Phil.-hist. Klasse.* Vol. 134, no. 1. Berlin: Akademie Verlag, 1994.

FOLLEN, CHARLES (KARL)
b. September 4, 1796; Romrod, Hesse
d. January 13, 1840; near Long Island Sound, New York

The first German instructor and professor of German language and literature at Harvard University ("the first American Germanist"), Charles Follen played a significant role in introducing the German language, literature, and culture to the educated elite in the United States, especially in the Boston area. Arriving in the United States in 1824 after fleeing his native Germany in the wake of his involvement in the student movement (*Burschenschaft*), Follen taught at Harvard College for a decade. As he commenced his teaching career, he began writing his own German grammar, initially published in 1828. It was the first to be used widely in American schools and eventually appeared in over twenty editions in the next three decades. In order to facilitate his teaching of literature, he published *Deutsches Lesebuch für Anfänger* (A German Reading Book for Beginners, 1828), which included selections from the writings of numerous authors, including Gotthold Ephraim Lessing, Christoph Martin Wieland, Novalis (Friedrich von Hardenberg), and Friedrich Schiller. This work, too, was used for several decades in American colleges. Follen was particularly successful in fostering a fuller appreciation of Schiller in the United States, where he had been known almost exclusively for his early work, *Die Räuber* (The Robbers, 1781). Follen's numerous criticisms of Johann Wolfgang von Goethe were at least partially responsible for diminishing the reputation of the poet in the United States. In addition to his public lectures on German literature and philosophy, Follen promoted German culture in his social contacts with the Boston elite, including the Transcendentalists. At the same time he briefly taught ethics at the Harvard Divinity School and introduced Harvard to the German gymnastics movement. Dismissed from his academic post in 1835, partly because of his support of student protests against the college president and partly because of his involvement with the antislavery movement, Follen became a Unitarian minister. In this role he became intensively involved in the antislavery movement.

Upon his appointment to the Harvard faculty, occasioned by the recommendation of the Marquis de Lafayette to George Ticknor, Follen soon acquired a wide audience as a cultural intermediary between Germany and his adopted country. As an instructor and then professor of German language and literature after 1830, he experienced increasing enrollments and received positive testimonials from students and faculty. In public addresses and his inaugural address as professor, he promoted German literature from the *Minnesänger* (Minnesingers) to contemporary authors, including Goethe, in spite of his criticism of the poet's perceived aloofness and perceptible lack of political commitment. At the same time he defended German poets and thinkers against accusations that they were skeptical, materialistic, and atheistic.

Follen also founded the Harvard German Society in 1828, which included such prominent figures as George Ticknor. In addition to his numerous public lectures on Schiller, Follen wrote an introduction to a newly published American edition of Thomas Carlyle's *Life of Schiller*. He also assisted in the introduction of German philosophers and theologians to American audiences, especially Immanuel Kant, Friedrich Ernst Schleiermacher, and Wilhem De Wette. At the same time, he also promoted German scholarship in history and psychology. On a personal level Follen had an influence on prominent Boston literary and cultural figures such as Theodore Parker, William Ellery Channing, Ralph Waldo Emerson, George Ripley, and Margaret Fuller.

Follen's life on both sides of the Atlantic was marked by his strident, uncompromising promotion of freedom and nationalism. As a student at the University of Giessen and an instructor at the University of Jena, his views had become increasingly radical to the point of advocating political assassination and terrorism. With some reason, German authorities had suspected him of encouraging the student Carl Sand in his assassination of August von Kotzebue. Shortly after his arrival in the United States, Follen joyfully embraced American nationalism and liberties, becoming a citizen and changing his name to Charles. After he had noted that American freedom was marred by slavery, he became a militant abolitionist and ally of William Lloyd Garrison, actively participating in national, state, and local antislavery organizations. Follen stopped short of advocating slave rebellions, in spite of his earlier espousal of violence. However, until his untimely death in 1840, his dogmatic and uncompromising commitment to freedom brought him into conflict with those of more moderate views. His life was cut short when his passenger ship caught fire and sank on his return trip to Boston.

John T. Walker

See also Fuller, Margaret; Muench, Friedrich; Ticknor, George; Transcendentalism; Turner Societies; U.S.-German Intellectual Exchange

References and Further Reading

Pochmann, Henry A. *German Culture in America: Philosophical and Literary Influences, 1600–1900*. Madison: University of Wisconsin Press, 1957.

Spevack, Edmund. *Charles Follen's Search for Nationality and Freedom, 1796–1840*. Cambridge, MA: Harvard University Press, 1997.

Spindler, George W. *The Life of Karl Follen: A Study in German-American Cultural Relations*. Chicago: University of Chicago Press, 1917.

Vogel, Stanley W. *German Literary Influences on the American Transcendentalists*. New Haven: Yale University Press, 1955.

FORD, HENRY

b. July 30, 1863; Dearborn, Michigan
d. April 7, 1947; Dearborn, Michigan

Most frequently associated with revolutionary Fordist production methods, Henry Ford also exerted considerable influence on German culture as a person. His immensely successful autobiography *Mein Leben und Werk* (*My Life and Work*), published in German in November 1923, left a strong impression on German culture. With more than 200,000 copies sold already during the first two years after publication, it was one of the great bestsellers in Weimar Germany and, beyond that, a canonical statement for the Weimar stabilization period, promising the transforma-

tion of "the wasteland of industry into a blooming garden."

Henry Ford was born on a prosperous farm near Dearborn in southeastern Michigan. His grandfather, John Ford, a Protestant English tenant farmer, came to the United States from Ireland in 1847. In 1879, he left his father's home and began working as an apprentice machinist in Detroit. After he married Clara Bryant in 1888, Ford became an engineer with the Edison Illuminating Company in 1891. Two years later, Ford was promoted to chief engineer. This new position gave him sufficient time to invent his self-propelled vehicle—the Quadricycle. This invention paved the way for the creation of the automotive industry. In 1903, Ford established the Ford Motor Company, which in 1908 began producing the Model T. About ten years later, Ford produced half of all American cars. To meet the growing demand, the Ford Company expanded and opened a new production facility in Highland Park, Michigan (1910). Three years later, Ford introduced the continuous moving assembly line in this outlet.

His autobiography helped to create a mythical, iconical, rather than factual Henry Ford, representing an ideal that others aimed to emulate. German businesspeople and engineers traveled to Detroit to understand how one person had created this economic empire. Their travelogues were published in Germany along with numerous other popular books on Henry Ford. German readers were primarily interested in the person and his success instead of the abstract principles of Fordism. In these books they found not only portrayals of Ford as an engineer and businessman but also as a philosopher, a visionary, and even a messiah of the modern era. His ethics of

Celebrating his 75th birthday, Henry Ford receives the Grand Cross of the German Eagle (highest Nazi award to a foreigner) for industrial accomplishments, July 31, 1938. (Bettmann/Corbis)

social service became a shining model of humane and moral behavior. Ford assured his readers that his social system would end the attractiveness of revolution and communism for workers. This corrupted image of Ford—some people in Germany regarded it as a "Ford psychosis"—basically survived even the Great Depression.

Long before the Nazis came to power in Germany, many of its members and sympathizers were highly interested in Henry Ford. Already in the early 1920s, Adolf Hitler was an admirer of this engineer and businessman. He repeatedly mentioned Ford in his speeches and later also in *Mein Kampf* (*My Battle*). This interest was in part due to Ford's business success and

philosophy but also to another publication of his, *Der Internationale Jude* (*The International Jew*), published in Germany in 1921, even before his autobiography. In 1922 this collection of blatantly antisemitic articles was already in its twenty-first printing. An abridged edition of *Der Internationale Jude* later became a standard work of Nazi propaganda. In 1938 Hitler awarded Ford the Verdienstkreuz Deutscher Adler (Grand Service Cross of the Supreme Order of the German Eagle) in recognition for his contribution to the motorization of the masses. Ford was the first recipient of this highest award of the Nazis for foreigners.

Bernd Essmann

See also Business, U.S.–Third Reich; Fordism; Great Depression

References and Further Reading

Baldwin, Neil. *Henry Ford and the Jews: The Mass Production of Hate.* New York: Public Affairs, 2001.

Klautke, Egbert. *Unbegrenzte Möglichkeiten: "Amerikanisierung" in Deutschland und Frankreich (1900–1933).* Wiesbaden: Franz Steiner Verlag, 2003.

Sward, Keith. *The Legend of Henry Ford.* New York: Atheneum, 1975.

FORDISM

Fordism is a set of principles that includes technological measures, especially mass production on the assembly line, as well as economic strategies such as supporting mass consumption by lowering prices and increasing wages. Even though this set of principles was the result of a group effort at the Ford Motor Company, it is usually associated with Henry Ford. In Germany Fordism is often considered synonymous with the modernization and the "Americanization" of German industry in particular and German culture in general. There is, however, a significant gap between the cultural and economic acceptance of Fordism. Its economic impact was mostly embraced with much enthusiasm, whereas cultural consequences were often met with strong resistance.

The economic influence of Fordism was already considerable in the Weimar Republic. In the second half of the 1920s, studies and travelogues by German observers carried the message that the American economic miracle was built on a new form of industrial organization. Especially businesspeople and engineers, but also trade unionists visited Highland Park and River Rouge, the main production sites of the Ford Motor Company. Almost all of them returned convinced that Fordism was a revolutionary concept that should be adopted in Germany.

This "second discovery of America" propagated the image of the United States as a modern society with peace between labor and capital, steadily rising wages, rapidly increasing consumption, and a hitherto undreamed-of prosperity, virtually creating a classless society. Fordism seemed to be the answer to the class conflicts and overall instability in post–World War I Germany. The success of Henry Ford and the Ford Motor Company appeared to present irrefutable evidence for the validity of this "white socialism." It was convincing not only for those afraid of Soviet-inspired "red" socialism, but also for most of the trade union leaders, who were especially impressed by the Fordist wage policy.

Weimar Germany's economic reality in the 1920s, however, was different. The country was not sufficiently developed to apply Fordist principles in the same way that had been done in the United States. After 1933, the Nazis applied some Fordist ideas in designing their car for the masses, the Volkswagen. But even here, it was not until after World War II that Fordism played a key role in the German *Wirtschaftswunder* (economic miracle), with the Volkswagen Beetle, the German Model T, as its iconic example.

Just as West Germany can be interpreted as a Fordist success story, the absence of a Fordist automobile industry had a negative effect on East Germany. As in the Weimar Republic, the lack of an appropriate economic basis for the development and production of special machines inhibited the evolution of a modern industrial structure. Even though Fordist production methods were also important in the German Democratic Republic, for example, in shipbuilding and the serial-style (prefabricated buildings, mostly high-rise) construction of apartment blocks, Fordism never became a dominant feature in the East German economy.

Even though the economic consequences of Fordism were generally embraced and considered necessary, the resulting cultural changes met with strong resistance in Germany. In the Weimar Republic, the hope for a technological revolution was accompanied by strong fears about the loss of the German cultural tradition. The modernization that attended the introduction of Fordist principles was interpreted as *Amerikanisierung* (Americanization) and invoked the fear of soulless rationalization, mass society, and mass culture, which was perceived as a threat to German *Kultur* (high culture). One typical response to that fear was that the Old World could and should adopt American technology, yet the American technological muscle needed to be purged of its soulless, materialist capitalism. Instead it should be infused with aesthetic, philosophical, and spiritual values to establish a German culture that would be superior to the modern civilization of the United States.

In contradistinction, there were also intellectuals and artists who believed that the United States was leading the world into a uniquely modern era. They considered Fordism as a cultural opportunity for Weimar Germany. One of the leading personalities was Walter Gropius, founder and director of the widely and lastingly influential Bauhaus. Representing an important

branch of modern architecture, later known as the international style, Gropius was one of those European pioneers who used machine and industrial metaphors to express their aesthetic commitment. One of his main projects was to mass-produce machine-made houses in order to fulfill the dream of inexpensive, attractive, and healthy homes for the masses. What Ford did for the automobile, Gropius attempted with his assembly-line housing, which Sigfried Giedion called a *Wohnford* (Home Ford).

It was particularly the chaotic post–World War I situation in Germany, with its fear of unrest and social catastrophe, that influenced Gropius's architectural style. However, Gropius was not simply applying Fordism. His aim was not only to create a mass product but also to infuse American technical forms with European culture, thereby aesthetically "filtering" the directness of American technology. When Gropius left Nazi Germany for the United States, aspects of an American technological style that had been transformed into a European architectural style thus were reimported into the country where Fordism originated.

Bernd Essmann

See also Americanization; Bauhaus; Ford, Henry; Gropius, Walter Adolph; Volkswagen Company and Its VW Beetle
References and Further Reading
Berghahn, Volker R. "Fordismus und westdeutsche Industriekultur, 1945–1989." In *Deutsch-amerikanische Begegnungen: Konflikt und Kooperation im 19. und 20. Jahrhundert.* Eds. Frank Trommler and Elliott Shore. Stuttgart, München: Deutsche Verlags-Anstalt, 2001, 188–204.
Hughes, Thomas P. *American Genesis: A Century of Invention and Technological Enthusiasm, 1870–1970.* New York: Viking, 1989.

Klautke, Egbert. *Unbegrenzte Möglichkeiten: "Amerikanisierung" in Deutschland und Frankreich (1900–1933)*. Wiesbaden: Franz Steiner Verlag, 2003.

Trommler, Frank. "The Rise and Fall of Americanism in Germany." In *America and the Germans: An Assessment of a Three-Hundred-Year History.* Eds. Frank Trommler and Joseph McVeigh. Philadelphia: University of Pennsylvania Press, 1985, 332–342.

FOREIGN POLICY (U.S., 1949–1955), WEST GERMANY IN

The Strategy of Integration

Between 1949 and 1955 German-U.S. relations were characterized by the step-by-step transition from military occupation to partial sovereignty. Within a short time span, the Federal Republic of Germany (FRG), founded in 1949, achieved legal sovereignty, joined the Western Alliance on almost equal terms, and completed the transition from occupied territory to ally, which marked a huge advance in Germany's return to the international community of nations.

This remarkable change in Germany's position within the international postwar system was to a large degree the result of Washington's strategic approach toward Europe in the context of the East-West confrontation. The upgrading of the FRG from occupied to allied status was the logical outcome of America's strategy of containing its Soviet adversary by uniting the non-Communist world in a system of alliances under U.S. hegemonic leadership.

In Western Europe, Washington was confronted with the simultaneous challenges of preventing the extension of Soviet power into Central and Western Europe and ensuring that Germany would never again become a threat to world peace. The U.S. response to this dual challenge was to advance the integration of the Western European states. By increasing the economic and military strength of Western Europe, integrating it politically, and revitalizing it psychologically and ideologically, the United States hoped to prevent both the expansion of the Soviet Union and the uncontrolled resurgence of Germany. This approach met the desire of many European governments to form part of a European economic and security system under U.S. leadership, a process that Norwegian historian Geir Lundestad has described as "empire by invitation" (Lundestad 1986, 263–277).

At the point of intersection between the two plans—the strategy of integration and the policy of containment—lay the German question. The U.S. policy toward Germany had two main objectives: protection against Germany and protection against the Soviet Union. These aims were conceptually interwoven and formed the basis of an approach that is now called dual containment. In order to prevent any resurgence of German militarism, West Germany was gradually but tightly integrated into the political, economic, and military structures of an emerging North Atlantic community under American leadership. At the same time, however, the integration of the young FRG also served to contain the Soviet Union. The economic and military potential of West Germany was to give the ailing western half of Europe a shot in the arm to bolster its defenses. Political scientist Wolfram Hanrieder appropriately described this dual strategic approach as "the containment of the Soviet Union at arm's length and of West Germany with an embrace" (Hanrieder 1992, 195).

The transformation of the FRG from occupied territory to ally was thus built into the conceptual framework of the U.S. containment strategy. The fact that the change took place in a relatively short period was attributable to the U.S. interests embodied in that strategy and to the increasing polarization of the international system from 1950 on.

The Politics and Economics of Integration

The founding of the West German state in May 1949 and the conversion of the Allied military governments to civilian high commissions ended the occupation period and prepared the way for the step-by-step transformation of German-U.S. relations. Although Americans and Germany's European neighbors harbored suspicions about the extent of democratization and reform achieved in West Germany during those first years, the strategy of integration required that the FRG be granted increased room for maneuver, coupled with the insistence on the strict political, security, economic, and cultural/ideational integration of the new German state into the Western community of nations.

The Occupation Statute underwent a first revision in the Petersberg Agreement of November 22, 1949. The dismantling of German industrial plants was restricted, and the FRG received the right to establish consular relations with foreign nations and to join international organizations. At the same time, it was to conclude a bilateral economic agreement with the United States on Marshall Plan aid and join the Council of Europe as an associate member. By October 1949 the FRG became a member of the Organization for European Economic Cooperation (OEEC), and the Marshall Plan agreement between West Germany and the United States was signed on December 15. By July 1, 1950, West Germany joined the Council of Europe. A comprehensive revision of the Occupation Statute, effective from March 6, 1951, not only brought virtually complete internal self-government but also permitted the establishment of a foreign ministry. In addition, the FRG was one of the six founding states of the European Coal and Steel Community (ECSC), established in Paris on April 18, 1951.

Political integration was accompanied by the reintegration of West Germany into the world economy. The European Recovery Program (ERP), commonly referred to as the Marshall Plan after the project's initiator U.S. secretary of state George C. Marshall, was implemented between 1949 and 1952. The United States and sixteen European nations participated in a program whose financial volume of $14 billion would equate $70 to $90 billion in 2005 prices. Although West Germany received only 10 percent of the program's foreign aid, the ERP helped to stabilize the country's balance of payments and enabled the import of urgently needed foodstuffs and raw materials for the reemerging industry. The Marshall Plan thus made a significant contribution to West Germany's foreign trade balance and also helped to foster a long-term recovery into the growth periods of the 1950s and 1960s. Unemployment figures gradually decreased and the economy achieved regular export surpluses. The ERP thus helped to lay the foundations for sustained economic growth, full employment, foreign trade equilibrium, and price stability. Most importantly, in West Germany the Marshall Plan had a political symbolic value that far exceeded its economic importance, as it was interpreted and is still remembered by West Germans as a sign that the United States and the Western powers were committed to the political and economic reconstruction and integration of West Germany.

With the intensification of the cold war, and in particular during the war in Korea (1950–1953), economic stabilization became an important tool of U.S. security strategy. The Marshall Plan was consequently integrated into the Mutual Security Program as West German rearmament took on priority over reconstruction. The war in Asia accelerated the transitional relationship between West Germany and the United States as it demonstrated to the Allies the urgent need for a West German contribution to European defense.

After the fall of 1949, the Soviet Union possessed a nuclear capability and its superiority in conventional weapons in Europe was now seen as an even greater threat. The founding of NATO in the same year had brought no immediate improvement in the situation as far as the West was concerned, and the military now concluded that the imbalance could be redressed only with the aid of German divisions. Another factor in favor of rearmament was that it would ease the financial burden on the West European allies. The most compelling political argument, however, was that the complete integration of the FRG into the Western Alliance would prevent, once and for all, any return to a German policy of walking the tightrope between East and West.

From the summer of 1950, the question was no longer whether West Germany would be rearmed, but what form rearmament would take. The analogy between the Korean and German situations—a distorted analogy, yet suggestive—helped to reduce gradually the reluctance of the Western powers, and of public opinion within them, to accept a German defense contribution. The West German government, especially Konrad Adenauer, saw a unique opportunity under these circumstances to gain, through a defense contribution, sovereignty and the standing of an equal partner within the Western community of nations considerably earlier than had been expected.

The French prime minister, René Pleven, put forward a plan in October 1950 in which a supranational organization, the European Defense Community (EDC), would cushion the threat West German rearmament posed to the West. The aim of the Pleven Plan was to enable West German troops to be raised without creating a West German national army. The resulting negotiations were tough and protracted and the French, in particular, took a hostile position toward the idea of West German troops that was overcome only by considerable pressure from Washington. Not until May 9, 1952, was a draft treaty finalized. While this treaty was being negotiated, the occupying powers and the FRG, whose policy naturally linked a defense contribution to the issue of sovereignty, drew up what later came to be known as the Paris Treaties, which provided for the end of the occupation and promised the West German state its sovereignty, apart from some residual Allied rights.

However, the failure of the EDC also delayed the coming of West German sovereignty. The treaty establishing the European Defense Community was signed by the foreign ministers of the participating states in Paris on May 27, 1952, but on August 30, 1954, the French National Assembly refused to ratify it. Two years of hard work, by Europeans and Americans alike, to create a European military force had come to nothing. But just three months later, in October 1954, the NATO foreign ministers agreed to accept the FRG as a member of NATO. On May 5, 1955, the Paris Treaties, which included slight modifications to the 1952 agreements, came into force. West Germany was now a sovereign state and a member of NATO.

Personalities played an important role in bringing about this quick turn of events and the rapid integration of a former enemy into the Western community of nations. In particular West Germany's chancellor Konrad Adenauer provided the U.S. side with a steadfast partner and guarantor against what they (and he) regarded as the dangerous German policy of swinging between East and West. The chancellor made complete integration with the West a cornerstone of policy and rejected all Soviet blandishments about reunification. In addition, the "Old Man" personified the spirit of European integration, pursuing reconciliation with France and lending his support to the plans for a European Defense Community. Adenauer's close ties with the United States gave him a steadily growing influence on American policy during the 1950s as relations between the two governments were particularly close in the years 1953 through 1955.

The Cultural and Ideational Foundations of Integration

From the outset, the functional integration of the FRG into the political, economic, and military structures of the Western world went hand in hand with a program designed at ideational and cultural integration. The main instrument of this intellectual reorientation was a comprehensive program of democratization beginning in 1946 and 1947. Yesterday's enemy was now to be transformed into an allied democracy on the Western model. Thus, the objective of social reform was another integral part of the strategy of dual containment. From the U.S. point of view, it was important for the sake of a stable international system—and hence for the sake of America's own national security—that West Germany should be welcomed back into the fold of the Western democracies.

The foundations of this German-U.S. success story had been laid earlier with the end of the war and the events of the early postwar years. The United States was seen to be magnanimous in victory, an image far removed from that portrayed in National Socialist propaganda. The Germans, hungry and defeated, soon came to trust the GIs, whose behavior was far different from the excesses of the Red Army. These early impressions, encouraging for the most part, were then further strengthened by the massive economic aid provided under the Marshall Plan.

The United States therefore addressed the West German people directly, through the largest cultural relations programs worldwide designed to encourage Germans to commit themselves to the West without reservation. The programs were designed to bring about profound changes in West Germany through a wide range of cultural diplomacy and propaganda, including educational exchange, information centers, media programs, exhibits, and concerts.

Between 1947/1948 and 1955 almost 12,000 Germans visited the United States (Schumacher 2000, 160). High school and university students, scholars, and professionals toured America to study the workings of a democratic society in action and return with a largely positive attitude vis-à-vis the United States and a desire to transfer insights derived from the stay overseas. The various programs were complemented by more than 1,600 U.S. experts who toured Germany during the same time period and contributed to fields ranging from municipal administration to prison reform to educational reform.

For those who could not participate in the overseas exchange programs, information centers, the so-called Amerika-Häuser (America Houses), developed into a highly popular window into the New World. By 1951 and 1952 there were 48 of these centers and more than 110 reading rooms in West Germany. The libraries played an important role, as they provided Germans with the literature that had been banned during the years of Nazi dictatorship. But the centers also offered exhibits, films, concerts, lectures, seminars, English-language instruction, and special interest programs for women, teachers, and other groups. They became cherished institutions that not only spread knowledge about the United States but also provided a framework within which Germans and Americans could reconstruct the ideational dimension of mutual friendship.

Despite the enormous success of those cultural programs, Americans were often unsure about the West German people's basic attitude to foreign policy. The major West German controversies of the 1950s—rearmament, neutrality, integration with the West, and reunification—confronted the United States with the dilemma that the newborn spirit of democracy might seriously jeopardize the strategy of dual containment. The gradual relaxing of the Western Allies' control over the FRG between 1949 and 1955 and the subversive and propagandistic activities of the Soviet Union in West Germany deepened the concerns of U.S. leaders. They reacted to this challenge with a massive propaganda offensive designed to boost the political, economic, and military integration of West Germany. This public-relations effort by the United States thus helped bring about the controlled transformation of West Germany from occupied territory to ally.

In its promotion of European integration, U.S. propaganda focused on establishing a causal relationship between German unity and European unification. Intensive individual campaigns stressing the economic, security, and cultural aspects of integration were intended to defuse the reunification dilemma as a potential disruptive force in German-U.S. relations. Enthusiasm for Europe, it was hoped, would provide the public with a psychological substitute for the deep-seated desire for national unity. As was logical, then, the Americans also supported Adenauer, who like them rejected any notions of neutrality and was committed to the wholehearted allegiance of Germany to the Western powers. The Eisenhower administration intervened in various ways in the 1953 Bundestag election campaign to improve the chancellor's prospects. At the same time, an extensive advertising campaign to promote the peaceful use of nuclear energy was designed to establish the United States in the public mind as a force for peace, relieve the widespread fears of war, and neutralize criticism of Washington's security policy. A similar purpose was served by the deliberate contrasting of the U.S. and Soviet models of society, which stressed the fundamental community of interests of the "free world" and left no doubt as to the superiority of its moral values and concept of civilization over those of communism.

In one way or the other, most West German citizens experienced American propaganda during the 1950s—through exhibitions, books, radio broadcasts, posters, or leaflets. Regular surveys designed to monitor the effect on public opinion kept the U.S. government informed of the progress of its program for Germany. The Truman and Eisenhower administrations both believed that U.S. political propaganda in West Germany played a substantial part in bringing the West German public onto the side of the West and keeping it there. The active public-relations campaign pursued by the Americans, the broad concurrence of interests between Bonn and Washington, the polarization of the international system, the activities of outstanding figures on both sides, and the United States' strategic interest in raising the status of the FRG transformed the country, within a very few years, from occupied territory to ally and so laid the foundation for more than half a century of German-U.S. cooperation.

Frank Schumacher

See also Fulbright Program; Reconstruction of West Germany (1945–1949); Stalin Note

References and Further Reading

Berghahn, Volker R. *America and the Intellectual Cold Wars in Europe.* Princeton, NJ: Princeton University, 2001.

Buchheim, Werner. *Die Wiedereingliederung Westdeutschlands in die Weltwirtschaft, 1945–1958.* Munich: Oldenbourg, 1990.

Diefendorf, Jeffrey M., et al., eds. *American Policy and the Reconstruction of West Germany, 1945–1955.* New York: Cambridge University, 1993.

Ermarth, Michael, ed. *America and the Shaping of German Society, 1945–1955.* Providence, RI: Berg, 1993.

Hanrieder, Wolfram F. "The FRG and NATO: Between Security Dependence and Security Partnership." In Emil Kirchner and James Sperling (eds.), *The Federal Republic of Germany and NATO.* New York: St. Martin's Press, 1992. 194–220.

Junker, Detlef, ed. *The United States and Germany in the Era of the Cold War. A Handbook, Vol. 1, 1945–1968.* Cambridge, UK: Cambridge University, 2004.

Large, David Clay. *Germans to the Front: West German Rearmament in the Adenauer Era.* Chapel Hill: University of North Carolina Press, 1996.

Lundestad, Geir. "Empire by Invitation? The United States and Western Europe, 1945–1952." *Journal of Peace Research* 23 (1986): 263–277.

Rupieper, Hermann-Josef. *Der besetzte Verbündete. Die amerikanische Deutschlandpolitik, 1949–1955.* Opladen: Westdeutscher Verlag, 1992.

———. *Die Wurzeln der westdeutschen Nachkriegsdemokratie: der amerikanische Beitrag, 1945–1952.* Opladen: Westdeutscher Verlag, 1993.

Schumacher, Frank. *Kalter Krieg und Propaganda. Die USA, der Kampf um die Weltmeinung und die ideelle Westbindung der Bundesrepublik Deutschland, 1945–1955.* Trier: WVT-Verlag, 2000.

Schwartz, Thomas. *America's Germany: John J. McCloy and the Federal Republic of Germany.* Cambridge, MA: Harvard University, 1991.

FÖRSTER, BERNHARD
b. January 31, 1843; Delitzsch, Saxony
d. June 3, 1889; San Bernardino, Paraguay

German teacher, antisemitic agitator, and founder of a failed colony in Paraguay.

Bernhard Förster studied history at the universities of Göttingen and Berlin. As a student he participated in the Austro-Prussian War of 1866 and the Franco-Prussian War of 1870 to 1871. After 1871 he worked as a teacher in Berlin. During the 1870s, he became fascinated with the German composer Richard Wagner, intensely studying his life and works. In the late 1870s Förster blended his nationalistic imaginations of Wagner with radical antisemitism, cultural despair, anticapitalism, and vegetarianism into a diffuse Weltanschauung. He was a cofounder of the antisemitic Deutscher Volksverein (German People's Association) in 1881 and a leading initiator of the 1880–1881 *Antisemitenpetition* (Antisemites' Petition), which called for revoking the emancipation of Jews in Germany and was enacted in 1871. The petition attracted more than 250,000 signatures. After insulting Jewish passengers in a Berlin streetcar, Förster was dismissed from his job as a teacher in 1882. A short time later, he called for founding an "ideal Germany" (without Jews) in South America. He embarked on a two-year trip to Uruguay, Argentina, and Paraguay in 1883 to find a suitable location for the "new Germania." After returning to Germany in 1885, he married Elisabeth Nietzsche (1846–1935), whom he had first met in the early 1880s. Her brother, the philosopher Friedrich Nietzsche, detested Förster's radical antisemitic leanings. Shortly after the wedding, Förster published *Denkschrift*

über die Anlage deutscher Kolonien in dem oberen Laplata-Gebiete (Manifest on the Establishment of German Colonies in the upper La Plata Region), in order to attract potential settlers. In 1886 Förster and his wife left for South America. The Paraguayan government provided Förster with land about 150 miles north of the capital Asunción, in a wilderness area, but asked for securities and the promise that he would attract at least 140 settler families. Förster carried the full financial responsibility for the project. By the end of 1887, a number of German settlers had arrived in Neu Germania (Nueva Germania), among them several families from Saxony. A year later, in the summer of 1888, Förster was still optimistic, although the number of settlers was below the target he had promised to the Paraguayan government. By then, it had become apparent that the project was badly organized. Förster's antisemitic utopia lacked investors and thus a realistic long-term perspective. Among the settlers were several pensioners who were ill-prepared for the primitive conditions and the climate. Only a few settlers were trained farmers. In 1889 the colony ran into serious difficulties, and Förster had to ask for a large loan. At the same time, he faced an increasingly impatient government. Several disillusioned settlers threatened to sue him. In June 1889, Förster committed suicide in San Bernardino near Asunción. His widow Elisabeth unsuccessfully asked the German government for help. In 1891 the colony went bankrupt. In 1892, Elisabeth Förster-Nietzsche moved back to Germany. She cared for her brother Friedrich, who had suffered a mental breakdown in 1889. During the 1890s, Förster-Nietzsche emerged as a central figure of the avant-garde art scene in Weimar. She closely guarded access to Nietzsche's papers and was thus responsible for a distorted view of Nietzsche's philosophy. Förster-Nietzsche received radical nationalists, among them Adolf Hitler, in her Weimar home. She died in 1935, at almost ninety years old.

Tobias Brinkmann

See also Antisemitism; Paraguay
References and Further Reading
Diethe, Carol. *Nietzsche's Sister and the Will to Power: A Biography of Elisabeth Förster-Nietzsche.* Urbana: University of Illinois Press, 2003.

FORTY-EIGHTERS

The Forty-Eighters were political refugees from the failed democratic revolutions of 1848–1849 in Germany. Realizing that true popular reform would never take root after the crushing of those revolutions and aware of the danger posed to their persons and careers by remaining in German-speaking Europe, Carl Schurz, Franz Sigel, Friedrich Hecker, and most of the other civilian and military leaders of the democratic forces emigrated to other countries. Many originally chose Switzerland or England, but by the mid-1850s nearly all the prominent Forty-Eighters had settled in the United States, attracted by its republican government, endless supply of jobs and natural resources, and already sizable German immigrant population. Numbering no more than perhaps a few thousand, these erstwhile revolutionaries strove to ensure in their adopted homeland what had failed in their old one: the triumph of personal freedom, democratic government,

and true equality among citizens. Throughout the second half of the nineteenth century the Forty-Eighters exerted considerable political and social influence over their fellow German Americans, particularly in the Midwest, but also significantly influenced the course of American political fortunes in general. Their importance in the creation and evolution of the Republican Party was especially noteworthy and remained their most enduring legacy.

Upon arriving in the United States, most Forty-Eighters took whatever jobs were available to them in either the port city they entered or their immediate destination. Nearly all of these men were educated in German universities and infused with the spirit of liberalism, but the exigencies of simply making a living in their new home forced many of them to temporarily set aside their intellectual and political aspirations. Franz Sigel, for instance, taught school in St. Louis for several years, and Friedrich Hecker tried his hand as a farmer in Illinois. But men such as these found themselves easily frustrated by the day-to-day routine and quickly sought out the company of other like-minded immigrants in more invigorating venues. In the larger cities, Forty-Eighters quickly assumed control of the more prominent German societies, such as the *Turnverein* (Turner Societies), *Liederkranz* (Singing Society), and *Deutsche Gesellschaft* (German Society), and began to take over the leadership of the German American press. They were not always welcome in these efforts; in the 1850s the Forty-Eighters, derisively called the "Greens" by the 1830s-era immigrants, whom they in turn labeled the "Grays," contended with German speakers from earlier immigration periods for leadership of the German American communities. The Forty-Eighters' zealous belief structure, including agnosticism, abolitionism, and various societal reforms, often conflicted with the more conservative—and Americanized—values of earlier German immigrants, such as the Grays. Especially in the eastern cities of New York City, Philadelphia, Baltimore, and Pittsburgh, the more liberal Forty-Eighters were forced either to compromise their heretofore radical beliefs with those of the conservative Germans or move elsewhere where their beliefs were more welcome. The midwestern cities of St. Louis and Chicago quickly became havens for the more outspoken among them, and by the time of the Civil War, it was apparent that the Forty-Eighter-dominated midwestern German enclaves were more radical politically than the "Little Germanies" in the East, sustaining even those who advocated socialism and communism.

Forty-Eighters such as Schurz quickly gravitated to the Whig Party, which in the early 1850s represented the spirit of reform in the United States. But as the Whig Party disintegrated over the slavery controversy in the mid- to late 1850s, the Forty-Eighters coalesced almost to a person behind the nascent Republican Party. In the Republicans the German Forty-Eighters saw the political embodiment of most of the ideals they had fought for back in Europe: economic freedom, empowerment of the average citizen, resistance to aristocratic pretensions (in Republican parlance, the "slaveocracy" of the South), and a hatred of African slavery and the society it had spawned. For the German Forty-Eighter, slavery was especially odious; it represented a threat to immigrant labor should it expand westward into the territories, pro-

vided for the existence of an aristocratic planter class, and simply repudiated the ideal of human freedom. No wonder that nearly all Forty-Eighter newspaper editors converted their papers into organs of the Republican Party and campaigned assiduously for it in the national elections of 1856 and 1860.

Whether or not the Forty-Eighters were successful in converting their fellow German Americans into Republicans is a weighty question, but most historians now believe that the elemental differences between the former revolutionaries and immigrants who arrived earlier in the United States were enough to keep a high percentage of average German immigrants from voting Republican. Additionally, older immigrants tended to be Democrats and preferred the security of the party that had traditionally welcomed and protected immigrants to the new and boisterous Republican Party, which had taints of nativism and temperance, two issues that consistently frightened immigrants in the nineteenth century. It now appears that the famous "Myth of 1860"—that the German Americans, led by their Forty-Eighter leaders, voted en masse for Abraham Lincoln and secured his election—was indeed nothing more than a myth. But there is little doubt that the Forty-Eighters were instrumental in the creation and growth of the Republican Party in several key states, especially Wisconsin (where Schurz actively campaigned), Illinois, Michigan, and Missouri. During the Civil War and afterward, Forty-Eighter Republicans succeeded in toning down the stigmas of temperance and nativism in their party and thus drew thousands of German American voters away from the Democrats and behind the banner of Lincoln.

Forty-Eighters, by virtue of their leadership status in German American social, cultural, and political life, quickly became involved in the Civil War on the Union side. For them, the secession of the southern states was nothing more than an illegal, traitorous act by slaveholding aristocrats who wished not only to continue the enslavement of the black race but also sought the virtual enslavement of free laborers, including immigrants. Friedrich Hecker, Franz Sigel, Ludwig Blenker, Alexander Schimmelpfennig, Augustus Willich, and a host of others who had seen military service in Europe enthusiastically formed ethnically German regiments in 1861–1862 and offered them, with themselves and like-minded friends as officers, to the federal service. Because these regiments were composed not only of Forty-Eighters and Republicans but also contained Democratic Germans and those opposed to Forty-Eighter dominance, however, intraethnic squabbling often handicapped their leadership. Moreover, the Anglo-American Republican leadership in Washington felt obliged to the Forty-Eighters for their help in the recent election and frequently commissioned pure politicians, such as Schurz, as colonels and generals in the Union army. The record of Forty-Eighter military leadership in the Civil War was therefore a mixed one. Sigel, for all his experience as a commander of the rebellious Democratic forces in 1848–1849, clearly underperformed at the battles of Wilsons Creek in 1861 and New Market in 1864 and managed to resign his command of the strongly German American 11 Corps, due to a piqued ego, on the eve of the Battle of Chancellorsville. Ludwig Blenker, one-time commander of an entire division of ethnically German regiments in the East, embroiled himself in political controversies with colonels under his command as well as his commander in chief, George B. McClellan, and was even accused by other Germans of indulging in extravagant luxuries while in camp. Schurz, for having no previous military experience, fared reasonably well, despite being blamed for the Union defeat at Chancellorsville in 1863, and compiled an honorable record by the end of the war. Alexander Schimmelpfennig, Augustus Willich, and Peter Osterhaus were all promoted to high command by the end of the war, the latter two playing critical roles in the final campaigns of the western theater of operations, including Sherman's March to the Sea.

After the war, Forty-Eighters resumed many of their positions of civilian leadership among the German American communities and in the Republican Party. They continued to exert a noticeable influence in national politics, especially in the later 1870s when the liberal Republicans temporarily bolted from the Republican Party out of dissatisfaction with Reconstruction in the South, among other issues. Schurz vehemently decried the abandonment of radical Reconstruction policies, particularly those that left blacks at the mercy of their former masters. In the fields of education, business, and the arts, Forty-Eighters made viable contributions to their new homeland by introducing and popularizing the kindergarten; founding private academies and supporting both German- and English-language schools; establishing the most successful (and most long-lived) breweries, piano factories, and German-language newspapers; and publishing hundreds of volumes of books on subjects as diverse as history, medicine, physics, and German literature.

A few, such as Friedrich Kapp, returned to Germany after spending several years in the United States, but even he and other reverse-émigrés agreed that German Americans would ultimately have to acculturate and amalgamate with the greater Anglo-American population. One of the last major contributions of the Forty-Eighters was their almost unilateral insistence, expressed in countless books, newspapers, and speeches, on the necessity of German immigrants becoming Americanized and blending their unique talents and gifts with those of other American citizens. Even in this philosophical crusade the Forty-Eighters were opposed by members of their own ethnic group, but in the end their prophecy triumphed.

Christian B. Keller

See also American Civil War, German Participants in; Griesinger, Karl Theodor; Hecker, Friedrich; Kapp, Friedrich; Kindergartners; Newspaper Press, German Language in the United States; Osterhaus, Peter J.; Schimmelpfennig, Alexander; Schurz, Carl; Sigel, Franz; Verein; Willich, August (von)

References and Further Reading

Brancaforte, Charlotte, ed. *The German Forty-Eighters in the United States.* New York: Peter Lang, 1989.

Hochbruck, Wolfgang, Ulrich Bachteler, and Henning Zimmermann, eds. *Achtundvierziger/Forty-Eighters: Die Deutsche Revolution von 1848/49, die Vereinigten Staaten und der Amerikanische Buergerkrieg.* Muenster: Westfaelisches Dampfboot, 2000.

Miller, Randall M., ed. *Germans in America: Retrospect and Prospect.* Philadelphia: German Society of Pennsylvania, 1984.

Wittke, Carl. *Refugees of Revolution: The German Forty-Eighters in America.* Philadelphia: University of Pennsylvania Press, 1952.

Zucker, A. E., ed. *The Forty-Eighters: Political Refugees of the German Revolution of 1848.* New York: Columbia University Press, 1950.

FRANCKE, KUNO
b. September 27, 1855; Kiel
d. June 25, 1930; Cambridge, Massachusetts

German American professor at Harvard University who promoted the teaching of German culture in the United States.

Kuno Francke was on the faculty of Harvard University's German Department (changed to the Department of Germanic Languages and Literatures in 1897) from 1884 to 1930. Along with Hugo Münsterberg, Francke was recognized widely as the foremost cultural ambassador of higher education between Germany and the United States. Unlike Münsterberg, however, Francke became an American citizen and closely identified himself with German Americans.

Francke's most significant accomplishment was the formation of the Germanic Museum at Harvard (since 1950, the Busch-Reisinger Museum). He conceived of the museum as a visual experience by which Americans could learn of German cultural achievements. In 1899 and 1900, he related his ideas to the German ambassador (and friend of Hugo Münsterberg) Theodor von Holleben and University of Berlin professor Hermann Grimm. The timing of Francke's proposal could not have been better. Chancellor Bernhard von Bülow and Emperor Wilhelm II received the proposal enthusiastically because they wished to improve relations with the United States in the wake of the Manila Bay incident (1898) during the Spanish-American War. Wilhelm II took a personal interest in the project and donated plaster casts of German statues and cultural objects. During the winter of 1902, Wilhelm's eldest brother, Prince Henry, made a two-week visit to the United States. During the royal tour, Harvard president Charles W. Eliot awarded Prince Henry with an honorary doctorate among much fanfare. Across the Atlantic Ocean and concurrent with these ceremonies, Francke met with Wilhelm II, himself no stranger to pomp and circumstance.

The museum, dedicated in November 1903, took many years and much fundraising on Francke's part to materialize. The Germanic collection was housed for many years in a former gymnasium. On June 8, 1912, the cornerstone was laid for a new building, but World War I delayed the opening of Adolphus Busch Hall (named after its main benefactor, the famous St. Louis German beer magnate) until April 1921. Designed by German Bestelmeyer, the hall combined Renaissance, Gothic, and Romanesque styles to highlight the history of German architectural achievements. Francke wished to broaden the focus of the museum to Germanic peoples (a desire that had been reflected in the transformation of the Harvard German Department itself); however, such a desire proved too ambitious given financial and spatial constraints. He did, however, continue to travel to Germany in order to procure more plaster casts for the collection. He remained the honorary curator of the museum until his death.

Kevin Ostoyich

See also Münsterberg, Hugo; U.S.-German Intellectual Exchange

References and Further Reading
Goldman, Guido. *A History of the Germanic Museum at Harvard University.* Cambridge: Minda de Gunzburg Center for European Studies, Harvard University, 1989.
Keller, Phyllis. *States of Belonging: German-American Intellectuals and the First World War.* Cambridge, MA: Harvard University Press, 1979.
Lenger, John. "Busch-Reisinger Marks a Century: The Art Museum Named for a St. Louis Brewing Family Has Weathered the Storms of Two World Wars." *Harvard Gazette,* November 6, 2003.
Ungern-Sternberg, Franziska v. *Kulturpolitik zwischen den Kontinenten: Deutschland und Amerika; das Germanische Musuem in Cambridge/Mass.* Cologne: Böhlau, 1994.

FRANKFURT AM MAIN CITIZENS IN THE UNITED STATES

The historical ties that bound Frankfurt and the Americas were numerous and diverse. In 1494 the letters of Christopher Columbus were printed for the first time in an illustrated volume in Basel. They were distributed at the Frankfurt fairs, which were attended by visitors from all over Europe. Frankfurt publisher Theodor de Bry's account of conquistador Hernando de Soto's exploration in 1539 of the region leading up to the Mississippi River also appeared at these fairs. De Bry created an impressive volume that included numerous illustrations and presented it at Frankfurt to a wide European audience. After the American declaration of independence from Great Britain in 1776, Frankfurt also attracted many American traders, who wanted to keep abreast of the latest products as well as purchasing goods that were in demand in America.

Texan Independence

But Frankfurt was not only a marketplace for information and a magnet for trade with the New World; there were also Frankfurt citizens who emigrated to the United States. Some of these citizens ended up playing an important role in American society. For example, in the 1830s a group of Frankfurters took part in the Texan war for independence from Mexico. One of them was Gustav Bunsen. Born in Frankfurt in 1804, he was the son of an established family. His father served as director of the Frankfurt mint, and his brother Georg was regarded as a famous educator and man of liberal convictions. His second brother Karl set up a medical practice, and Gustav followed in his footsteps when he started studying medicine at the University of Würzburg. During his studies, he became enthusiastic about the ideas of the July Revolution in France as well as the idea of Germany's unification in 1830. Instead of completing his studies in Heidelberg, he traveled to Warsaw and was engaged in the Polish upheaval of that year. He did not come back to Frankfurt until 1832. Back at home, he immediately joined the democratic Preß- und Vaterlandsverein (Association for Press and Nationality) and, together with Gustav Körner and Franz Gärth, took one of the leading positions within it. Facing a ban on their organization, Körner, Gärth, and Bunsen initiated a revolution. On the evening of April 3, 1833, during a period of heightened political tensions, a group of Frankfurt students and academic figures attacked Frankfurt's main police station. Lacking popular support, the attack failed and resulted in repressive measures by the authorities.

Gustav Bunsen and Adolph Berchelmann escaped punishment by emigrating to the United States. Several weeks after their revolt, both friends arrived in St. Clair County in Illinois. There Bunsen met some old acquaintances from Frankfurt, who had succeeded in purchasing fertile land in the Shiloh valley. Life was not easy for these German settlers. Not only did

they experience culture shock as well as the difficulties of learning the English language, but also they had to get by with a limited amount of resources and a much lower degree of comfort. In this regard it is easy to see why the simple agrarian life was hard for well-educated academics. For this reason, after a short while, Bunsen left the little German village, although his brother and the sister of his friend Berchelmann arrived in 1834. Berchelmann's sister was married to Bunsen and both went to Cincinnati, Ohio, which at that time was considered to be the center of German culture in the midwestern states. However, Bunsen's life as an established physician did not satisfy his political ambitions. He became increasingly interested in the conflict between the English-speaking settlers in Texas, which was then a part of Mexico. In 1835 this conflict escalated. The Texas farmers elected a provisional government led by Sam Houston. As leader of the movement for independence, he asked for the help of the Union and proclaimed that anyone who was willing to fight for their cause would be not only justly but also richly rewarded.

Bunsen joined the rebel army and traveled into the crisis area in November 1835. He took part in the siege of the capital of the province that had been occupied by the Mexican army. After the settlers had successfully conquered San Antonio, Bunsen joined the rather hopeless campaign against Mexico. In spite of the harsh criticism, by members of the rebel army, sixty-four rebels, including Bunsen, voted for this military action, which ended in a fiasco. For the man who several years before managed to attack the German Union with only fifty amateurish revolutionaries, sixty-four well-armed riders seemed sufficient enough to attack the Mexican Republic. Not surprisingly, their expedition failed, and Bunsen lost his life right at the beginning of this battle.

The Forty-Eighters

The immigration of the so-called Latin farmers of the 1830s was only the advance guard of a much larger wave of emigration that followed after the failed revolution of 1848–1849. Numerous radical democrats decided to leave for the United States. One was Gustav Adolph Roesler, the man who had arranged a short ceasefire during the bloody street fights in Frankfurt in September 1848. After his dramatic escape, he reached New York in 1850 and settled together with his family in Milwaukee. There Roesler published a political magazine that supported the Whig Party and agitated against slavery. He later moved to Quincy, Illinois, and established another local newspaper before he fell victim to cholera in 1855.

To help people from the Frankfurt region in their transatlantic migration, influential Frankfurt citizens founded the Frankfurter Verein zum Schutz der Auswanderer (Frankfurt Association for the Protection of Emigrants) as a branch of the Nationalverein für deutsche Auswanderung und Ansiedlung (National Association for German Emigration and Settlement) on December 12, 1848. Its purpose was to organize individual as well as group emigration in a safe and modest way, preferably via a German harbor. Furthermore, the association aimed to help the emigrants in every step of the process toward their final settlement. Some of the more well-known members of the Frankfurt association were the liberal lawyer Wilhelm Stricker, the geographer and publisher Georg Varrentrapp, and the freemason Heinrich Franz Rosalino. In the very first stages of the association they supported the project of Consul Fleischmann for colonization and the creation of a depot for emigrants in "Mitschigan" (Michigan). Fleischmann not only demanded farming settlements but also industrial ones because he believed that in the long run they would require less support in terms of materials and goods. He therefore initiated the emigration of craftspeople under the assumption that their labor would prove beneficial to economic progress in the United States. In his opinion, their contribution would be greatest if organized into small factories or larger associations of handicrafts. Between 1850 and 1870 the association supported the emigration of more than 500 people each year. The majority of them were journeymen.

Economic considerations spurred an interest in the United States among Frankfurt bankers, who established business connections and branches in American cities. There were three distinct phases in the process of establishing financial connections between Frankfurt and the United States. The first phase was in the 1820s and 1830s, when the Rothschilds successfully installed representatives of their banking house in New York City. From 1833 onward, August Belmont took over this role. Belmont had learned the banking business under his original name of August Schönberg in the banking house of the Frankfurt Rothschilds. When he went to New York, he changed his name to French to distinguish himself from the crowd of German Jews already living in Manhattan. Belmont established the firm of August Belmont and Company. Backed by the Rothschild family, August Belmont rose to power and influence in the business and social life of New York. He gave opulent dinners and extravagant feasts, displayed his wealth, drove an elegant coach, invested in racehorses, and was among the founders of the racecourse at Jerome Park. As befitted one of his station, Belmont bought a luxury palace on Fifth Avenue, was accepted as a member of the Union Club, and gained a leading position in the Democratic Party. Moreover, Belmont became an Austrian consul general. But above all, he successfully managed the Rothschild's investments in cotton, tobacco, Union and state bonds, railways, and a broad spectrum of industrial loans.

The second phase came in the 1860s, when Frankfurt banking houses financially supported the Union in the Civil War. This was a major turning point for the Frankfurt bankers. While London banking houses sympathized with the South and took over the majority of the Confederate issues, Frankfurt became the second-largest outlet for U.S. government bonds in Europe. Frankfurt banking houses with strong business ties to New York held nearly 40 percent of the debts incurred by states of the Union, which rose from $90 million to $2.74 billion between 1860 and 1865. Among these banking houses were Seligmann & Stettheimer, Lazard Speyer-Ellissen, Philipp Nicolaus Schmidt, Karl Pollitz, and M. A. Gruenebaum & Ballin. By the time the Union won the upper hand, its bonds were quoted at an astonishing 73 percent and upon redemption brought "hundreds of millions" in profits to their shareholders, providing the basis for many of the city's latter-day great fortunes. Among these companies, it was J. and W. Seligman that benefited the most from their American business investments.

Based on the model of the Rothschild family, the Seligmans founded branches of their bank in London, Paris, and New York and led eventually to them being referred to as the "American Rothschilds."

The third phase of established financial ties between Frankfurt and the United States came after the business in governmental loans. Investors who had immigrated to the United States from Frankfurt changed their strategy and invested heavily in American railroad construction. The huge rail network of 300,000 kilometers stretched across the American capital market, and it soon became clear that the input of European capital was a necessity. Once again Frankfurt's banking houses and their branches in the United States led by emigrants played an important role in this part of finance business. One such success story is that of Charles Hallgarten, who began his career in financing railroads and then returned to Frankfurt as a wealthy banker. There he initiated numerous philanthropic projects. He founded, for example, the Aktiengesellschaft zum Bau kleiner Wohnungen (Joint Shareholder Association for the Construction of Small Tenement Housing). Another Frankfurt American was Wilhelm Bonn. At the age of twenty he was sent to New York to familiarize himself with the American finance market and to sell U.S. war bonds on the German market. He speedily built up his career in New York, ending up as director of the banking house of Speyer and Company, which was a subsidary branch of Lazard Speyer-Ellissen. Later on he founded his own banking firm, Ruette and Bonn, which successfully financed the transcontinental railway lines. Like Hallgarten he returned to Frankfurt at the age of forty-two and settled in a luxury villa in the Frankfurter Westend, located in the same neighborhood as Hallgarten.

The most important Frankfurt banker in New York was Jacob Schiff, who gained a leading position in the investment banking house Kuhn, Loeb, and Company. Coming from an old Jewish Frankfurt family, he went to school at the Jewish Reform school "Philanthropin" and afterward to the Orthodox *Realschule* (secondary modern school) of the Israelitischen Religionsgesellschaft (Jewish Religious Association). He completed his courses in business and trade and then emigrated to the United States in 1865. There he became an employee of the New York banking firm Frank and Gans. But Schiff was ambitious, obstinate, and a tough opponent in his business dealings. Two years later, together with Henry Budge, he founded the banking firm Budge, Schiff, and Company. But his real career began when he entered the banking house of Salomon Loeb. In the beginning he served as speaker of the company and recognized the tremendous importance of transportation for the industrial development of the United States. He gained entry into the railroad business in his own unique way. He becme an expert not only in railroad financing but also in the daily business and technical matters of railroads. When he had reached the point where he could fully grasp all the details of running a railroad company, he felt the time had come to begin competing with John Pierpont Morgan, who was the top banker in the U.S. banking hierarchy at that time. Schiff succeeded in gathering together the necessary capital for the speedy industrialization of the United States by making use of his strong ties to

Europe and Germany. After a while he controlled the Great Northern, Union Pacific, Pennsylvania, Illinois Central, Chicago, and Milwaukee railroad companies. Under the leadership of Schiff, Kuhn and Loeb developed into the second-largest investment banking house in the United States behind the Morgan trust.

Schiff's life was characterized by a deep religiosity, modesty, impatience, punctuality, and respect for hierarchy. In the realm of politics he voted for the Republican Party. More important than his political leanings in the United States were his ties to his German Jewish heritage. Like many of the migrants from Frankfurt, including Seligmann, Speyer, and Hallgarten, Schiff regarded himself as a German Jew, a "Yahudim." They sent their children to German universities and employed German tutors and German doctors. They married German, and they went, with the help of the Hamburg-Amerikanische-Paketfahrt-Aktien-Gesellschaft (HAPAG) (Hamburg-American Parcel Shipping Joint Stock Company), to Germany every year and met each other in the German spas of Baden-Baden, Karlsbad, and Marienbad.

Although Jacob Henry Schiff remained a Frankfurt citizen at heart, he stayed in the United States for the rest of his life and committed himself to working for American Jews as well as for American culture. Schiff spent no less than $100 million on philanthropic and political reform, making large donations to the Metropolitan Museum of Art, the Natural History Museum in New York, and the Bronx Zoo. He financed professorships at Harvard, Cornell, and Columbia universities, enabled the Public Library of New York to establish a Judaica collection, and initiated both the creation of the Jüdische Gesellschaft für Geschichte (Jewish Society for History) and the Jüdische Publikations Gesellschaft (Jewish Publication Society) in 1892. In addition, he also founded the Hebrew Union College and Talmud-Thora schools on New York's east side and in downtown New York. At the end of his life, he donated a professorship for German culture at Cornell University. Jacob H. Schiff's career was a symbol of the growing importance of American Jewry in American society.

Ralf Roth

See also American Civil War, Financial Support of Frankfurt Bankers for; German Jewish Migration to the United States; Koerner, Gustave Philipp; Milwaukee; New York City; Schiff, Jacob Henry

References and Further Reading

Arnsberg, Paul. *Jacob H. Schiff: Von der Judengasse zur Wallstreet.* Frankfurt am Main: Verlag Waldemar Kramer, 1969.

Hale, Douglas. "Ein Frankfurter Revolutionär im texanischen Unabhängigkeitskrieg." *Archiv für Frankfurts Geschichte und Kunst* 57 (1980): 151–166.

Heyn, Udo. *Private Banking and Industrialization: The Case of Frankfurt am Main, 1825–1875.* New York: Arno Press, 1981.

Katz, Irving. *August Belmont: A Political Biography.* New York: Columbia University Press, 1968.

Kirchholtes, Hans-Dieter. *Jüdische Privatbanken in Frankfurt am Main.* Frankfurt am Main: Verlag Waldemar Kramer, 1969.

Lustiger, Arno. *Charles Hallgarten: Leben und Wirken des Frankfurter Sozialreformers und Philantropen.* Frankfurt am Main: Societäts Verlagsanstalt, 2003.

Roth, Ralf. *Stadt und Bürgertum in Frankfurt am Main: Ein besonderer Weg von der ständischen zur modernen Bürgergesellschaft 1760 bis 1914.* Munich: Oldenbourg, 1996.

FRANKFURT SCHOOL

Friedrich Pollock and Max Horkheimer founded the Institute of Social Research in Frankfurt am Main in 1923. Through an inheritance from his father, Felix Weil contributed 120,000 deutsche marks to the new institute, which was affiliated with the Johann-Wolfgang Goethe University. Its first director was Kurt Albert Gerlach, who was succeeded by Carl Grünberg in the first year of the institute's existence. Grünberg was a professor of political and legal studies at the University of Vienna. While there, he edited the *Archive for the History of Socialism and the Workers' Movement* for a while. He supported the institute's desire for an interdisciplinary approach to the problems found in bourgeois society. In his opening address, he emphasized that the institute would pursue research over instruction, unlike most German universities, and would use a Marxist methodology in its studies.

As time passed, the group began to incorporate new members: Karl August Wittfogel, Franz Borkenau, and Julian Gumperz, all of whom were Communists. Around the end of the twenties, Leo Lowenthal and Theodor Adorno joined Horkheimer and Pollock as members of the institute. Later, Erich Fromm, through his friendship with Lowenthal, also joined the group.

In 1927 Grünberg stepped down as director due to physical ailments. Horkheimer became the new director in 1930 and was given a chair in social philosophy at the university. He created a journal for the institute, the *Zeitschrift für Sozialforschung* (*Journal for Social Research*). In the first issue, Horkheimer reiterated the interdisciplinary nature of the institute. He looked at the fissure of knowledge and blamed it on the current social situation. Horkheimer claimed the monopolistic nature of capitalism was at fault and believed it could be overcome only by a sociological understanding of current historical conditions. He believed a social science was needed to create a method to help overcome the current social forces.

Increasingly aware of the possibility of exile due to the political situation, Horkheimer, with the financial support of Albert Thomas, opened an office in Geneva, which Lowenthal was in charge of establishing. In 1932, Herbert Marcuse joined the group and helped with the creation of the Geneva office. By February 1933, the Geneva office had twenty-one members, and the name of the group was changed to the International Society for Social Research. Its main members included Horkheimer, Lowenthal, Pollock, Franz Neumann, Fromm, Adorno, and Marcuse.

In April 1933, Horkheimer was released from his duties at Frankfurt University. Afraid the Nazis would soon take over Geneva, he journeyed to New York in May 1934 to meet with several of his friends at Columbia University. Soon thereafter, they allowed the institute to be affiliated with the university and even donated a building for its work. At the same time, Felix Aldan, the publisher of the *Zeitschrift für Sozialforschung,* discontinued its publication due to his fear of the Nazis. He moved his operations to Paris in September 1933 and continued publishing the journal even when the Nazis took over Paris in 1940.

The institute was able to maintain its identity because of the money Felix Weil contributed when he arrived in New York in 1935. There, he donated another

$100,000 so that the institute could remain secure and free from any obligations throughout the 1930s. Gradually, all the important members of the group began to move to New York, including Marcuse, Lowenthal, Pollock, Fromm, Neumann, and Adorno. In the United States the institute began work on a new methodology for studying cultural, social, and economic structures. This methodology became known as critical theory, a materialist theory based on the premise of social praxis, where theory is put into action.

Horkheimer, who had been studying Georg Friedrich Wilhelm Hegel, Immanuel Kant, Arthur Schopenhauer, and Friedrich Nietzsche, realized the dangers of systematic philosophy. In his study of Kant, he came to see how the individual must never be lost in his or her relation to the totality. He began to question the existence of the absolute and even the notion of identity itself. In Hegel, he found that thought exists only in the socioeconomic conditions of human beings. His encounters with Kant, Schopenhauer, and Nietzsche helped Horkheimer to develop critical theory. Unable to see individuals as free, he saw them instead as entities controlled by various forces. Because of these beliefs, he claimed critical theory saw social realities as a process that can never be finished, nor could there ever be a definitive social being. For Horkheimer, critical theory became a critique of bourgeois society that would examine social realities rather than the current façade they fashioned.

Horkheimer and Adorno saw the regulated and automated aspects of modernity as a step toward the abolition of all that is human. Lowenthal believed the entertainment industry and consumer culture were destroying the identity of the masses. Marcuse, influenced by both Sigmund Freud and Marx, felt that the major institutions of modern capitalist society were destroying the autonomy of the individual and believed only art and aesthetics could save the world from false consciousness. For even though art may not create revolution, it is, nevertheless, a work of unending rebellion against the status quo.

For the majority of the Frankfurt group, Auschwitz revealed the progressive stages of science and reason. It showed them how the world is moving toward barbarity rather than the authentically human. They felt contempt for the bourgeois life because of its indifference to the madness of the times. For them, the end of Enlightenment thought was technological progress and the mastery of nature, which led to the illusion that there was no other possibility for living. After achieving control over nature, human beings' attention would naturally turn to the conquest of humanity. With reason tied to technology, social technology would soon follow. Seeing the problems associated with capitalism, along with the disintegration of liberal thought and the beginning of the authoritarian threat to society, they continued to develop a social philosophy throughout the 1930s.

In the 1940s, Horkheimer began to look first at Hegel's influence on Marx, especially the belief that Hegel's dialectic was materialist in nature. Through his studies of Schopenhauer and Nietzsche, Horkheimer came to doubt Hegel's notion of absolute truth. He opposed Hegel's systematic philosophy, with its belief that identity is found in the dialectic of subject and object. Instead, he believed the totality could eliminate subjectivity altogether. Most of all, he stressed the importance of reason and action. However, reason was not to be used to find a transcendental truth. It was not absolute and could only be found in social realities. Moreover, praxis, or social action, must come first, for truth was relative and could not be identified or classified as a static concept.

Like Horkheimer, Adorno was also influenced by existential philosophy. Adorno's first publication was on Søren Kierkegaard's aesthetic. Referring to Kierkegaard's definition of aesthetics as the relationship between subject and object and not merely the study of art, Adorno could no longer fathom absolute truths, nor could he conceive of a systematic philosophy. For Adorno, truth could only be found in the dynamics of subject and object. Like Horkheimer, Adorno believed truth could only be found in contingent social relations. He felt that it was only there that the subject could be saved from complete annihilation.

Studying Martin Heidegger yet firmly committed to Marx, Marcuse found that Heidegger looked carefully at contingency and historicity in its relation to social realities and found that these realities create within the self a desire to realize authenticity through action. However, Marcuse found that Heidegger overlooked how social conditions could hinder the self's ability to realize its own authenticity. Turning to Marx, he realized that the upper classes were the only ones who could act decisively in the way Heidegger described this form of action, and as a result, only revolution would make possible a world in which everyone could act authentically. Capitalism made this new society impossible. As Marx explained, revolution was not only about economic conditions but also about the awareness of true essences. And perhaps more importantly, it was through labor that these essences could be discovered.

Although the influence of the members of the Frankfurt School on American critical theory has not been fully examined, there is evidence of their influence. For instance, Adorno had essays printed in *The Kenyon Review* and *The New Left Review*. Horkheimer has had important parts of his writings translated into English, and at the same time, he wrote numerous essays in the *Studies of Philosophy and Science*. There have also been numerous essays written about both the school and its members in *Commentary, Dissent, Sewanee Review, Daedalus,* and *Salmagundi*. Many of their ideas now have been introduced to contemporary American thought through the writings of Frederick Jameson, Terry Eagleton, and others.

While living in the United States, the members of the Frankfurt School continued to publish their writings in German, especially in the *Zeitschrift für Sozialforschung,* and as a result their influence seemed negligible. If for no other reason, however, the Frankfurt School gained considerable influence through the writings of Marcuse, Fromm, and Neumann, each of whom had his own set of followers. Their influence can also be felt in their attempt to help refugees coming into the country during the 1930s and 1940s. Many of these refugees were intellectuals, and many of them became professors at American universities. Finally, their work and ideas have had a considerable influence on German philosophical and sociological thought. Through this influence, they were able to teach a whole new generation of German students. Some, like Jürgen Habermas, would become members of the institute and build on its former members'

work to create their own important and influential theories.

After the war, the Frankfurt School's writings became of considerable importance to German students and intellectuals. Horkheimer himself was asked to return to Frankfurt University in 1947, and on July 13, 1949, he accepted a position as chair of philosophy and sociology, the same chair he lost in 1933 when Adolf Hitler came to power. All the original and remaining members of the institute gradually returned to Frankfurt, except for Leo Lowenthal, who remained in the United States with his new wife and his new position with the Voice of America.

Jim Varn

See also Adorno, Theodor Wiesengrund; Frankfurt am Main Citizens in the United States; Horkheimer, Max; Intellectual Exile; Marcuse, Herbert; New York City

References and Further Reading

Friedman, George. *The Political Philosophy of the Frankfurt School.* Ithaca: Cornell University Press, 1981.

Held, David. *Introduction to Critical Theory: From Horkheimer to Habermas.* Berkeley: University of California Press, 1990.

Martin, Jay. *The Dialectical Imagination: A History of the Frankfurt School and the Institute of Social Research, 1923–1950.* Boston: Little, Brown, 1973.

Schirmacher, Wolfgang, ed. *German Twentieth-Century Philosophy: The Frankfurt School.* New York: Continuum, 2000.

Wolin, Richard. *The Terms of Cultural Criticism: The Frankfurt School, Existentialism, Post-structuralism.* New York: Columbia University Press, 1992.

FREDERICKSBURG, TEXAS

Established in August 1845 as a way station for German immigrants en route to the colonial lands granted by the Republic of Texas to the Society for the Protection of

German Immigrants in Texas (Adelsverein for short).

Located approximately 70 miles west of Austin, Fredericksburg is situated on the southern edge of the Texas hill country. The commissioner-general of the Adelsverein, John O. Meusebach, felt that the organization's principal community of New Braunfels was too far away from the actual colonial lands to serve as an adequate starting point for would-be settlers. Thus he sought to establish another village in closer proximity to the lands intended for colonization. Meusebach dubbed this new settlement Fredericksburg, in honor of Prince Friedrich of Prussia, a leading member of the Adelsverein.

Meusebach chose as the site of Fredericksburg lands at the confluence of two creeks on the southern edge of the Adelsverein's cession. These two creeks drained into the Pedernales River, some 5 miles distant, and were later named Baron's Creek, after Meusebach, and Town Creek. The land, which Meusebach purchased on credit, offered ample natural resources upon which to found a community. The town was surveyed by Hermann Wilke in the fashion of those found in the Rhineland.

The Adelsverein's colonial experiment was never a practical affair. The society greatly underfunded the enterprise, and the bourgeoisie noblemen that led the organization poorly equipped the settlers for life on the Texas frontier. Despite harsh conditions and rampant disease among the settlers, by August 1846 Fredericksburg had a population of 1,000 immigrants. Under the leadership of Meusebach, these first settlers quickly went to work building a community. In the fall of 1846 an interdenominational church was erected. Officially named the Vereins-Kirche, the structure was built in the shape of an octagon, each side of the church measuring 18 feet long with walls 18 feet high and topped off by a cupola with an octagonal roof. Due to the odd shape of the building, the Vereins-Kirche was often referred to as the Kaffeemuehle (Coffee Mill). Regular services began immediately. The church was shared by Protestants and Catholics alike, serving this purpose as well as that of school, fortress, and meeting hall for some fifty years. Today a replica of the Vereins-Kirche stands on the site of the original.

Although the new community was located deep within the territorial lands of the Comanche, the settlers remained relatively unmolested during their first two years of activity. However, Meusebach was keenly aware that if progress were to be made in moving settlers onto their land grant within the actual bounds of the colony, some form of treaty would have to be made with these nomadic Indians. The Comanche had thus far proved to be the most tenacious impediment to Spanish, Mexican, and Anglo colonization in Texas. After negotiations on March 1 and 2, 1847, held deep within Comanche territory, principal chiefs came to Fredericksburg on May 9, 1847, to sign an official treaty with Meusebach, ensuring that German settlement could take place in the Texas hill country with relative safety.

Meusebach had wisely chosen his location for Fredericksburg. By the time he stepped down as commissioner-general of the Adelsverein on July 20, 1847, the town had a population of 2,000, a wagon road had opened to Austin, and more than fifteen stores were in operation. The following year saw the establishment of the federal garrison at nearby Fort Martin Scott.

Old St. Mary's Catholic Church, San Antonio Street, Fredericksburg, Gillespie County, Texas, 1934. (Library of Congress)

The presence of U.S. troops only 2 miles east of Fredericksburg provided both security to the populace and a ready market for their dry goods and surplus agricultural products. Despite a recent outbreak of cholera, in 1849, the year after the Treaty of Guadalupe Hidalgo was signed, Fredericksburg's prosperity was further bolstered when the U.S. government established one of only four roads to the Rio Grande River valley through the burgeoning community.

In December 1847, 150 residents of Fredericksburg drew up a petition requesting that the Texas legislature create a new county out of massive Bexar County, with Fredericksburg as its seat. Originally planners thought to name the county Germania, but finally requested that the legislature call it Pierdenalis, after the Pedernales River. Legislators, instead, created Gillespie

County on February 23, 1848, named for Robert A. Gillespie, who died in the Mexican-American War at the Battle of Monterrey. All the officers of this new county were initially German immigrants with one exception: the county clerk, who was from Kentucky.

Life in Fredericksburg throughout the nineteenth century was typified by the population's commitment to religion and education. As Fredericksburg became a regional community center, prosperous farmers from throughout the area began building so-called Sunday houses so that they might have lodgings when coming into town for church services. In 1848 the Catholic congregation of the Vereins-Kirche formed their own church, which was supplanted by the Marienkirche (St. Mary's Church) in 1860, one of the most prominent landmarks in Fredericksburg. The Methodist congregation formed their own church at about the same time. In 1852 the Lutheran congregation formed Zion's Evangelical Lutheran Church, the first Lutheran church in the Texas hill country.

Johann Leyendecker, a professional teacher from Nassau, established the first school in the Vereins-Kirche in the fall of 1847. Classes were taught in German, at a tuition rate of $1 per quarter. The Vereins-Kirche was a drafty classroom ill-suited to learning, and the rapid succession of teachers were forced to hold other jobs in order to earn a livelihood. In 1856 a formal, city-sponsored public school was formed with a regular teacher's salary and classes taught in English. By this time Catholic and Lutheran parochial schools had also been established.

In 1876 the German Methodist Church founded Fredericksburg College. Intended as an institution of higher learning, it served the community for only a brief period, with its campus incorporated into the Fredericksburg Independent School District in 1884. In 1909 St. Anthony's College was established under the auspices of the Catholic congregation for the continuing education of young boys. It was dissolved in 1923 when the establishment of St. Mary's High School rendered it obsolete.

Despite its relative prosperity, Fredericksburg remained an isolated community throughout the nineteenth century. The peace sustained through this isolation was broken by the onset of the Civil War. Like many American communities, the hill country Germans were divided by secession and war. Although most Germans were opposed to slavery and remained loyal to the Union, several notables, including Charles Nimitz, grandfather of Admiral Chester Nimitz, sided with the Confederacy. Nimitz came to prominence in 1852 with the founding of the Nimitz Hotel on the main street in Fredericksburg, which today serves as the National Museum of the Pacific War.

In contrast to Nimitz, who served with honor and distinction, a group of Confederate irregulars known as Die Haengebande (Hangman's Band) emerged around ringleader J. P. Waldrip. Waldrip and his gang terrorized the community in the name of the Confederacy, stringing up those who resisted. They even targeted Nimitz when he attempted to draft Haengebande members into the regular service. James M. Duff also troubled hill country Germans. As the head of a group of Confederate irregulars, he conducted raids into the hill country and was responsible for the massacre of German Union loyalists at the Battle of the Nueces near present-day Comfort, Texas, on August 10, 1862.

Fredericksburg regained much of its isolation after the close of the Civil War. German remained the principal language spoken throughout Gillespie County. The county's first newspaper, *Wochenblatt* (Weekly Sheet), established in 1877, was in German only. However, population growth, the advent of the railroad, and finally the onset of World War I served to open up the community once and for all. World War I, more than any other historical event, forced the hill country Germans to break their ties with the Old World, largely for good. They quickly moved toward English-only schools and newspapers and sought to aid the war effort in any way possible as a demonstration of their patriotism, even making the ultimate sacrifice. The first American killed in France in World War I, Lieutenant Louis Jordan, was a native of Gillespie County.

Today Fredericksburg is best known for its cadre of annual festivals, sponsored by the numerous clubs common in German communities, such as the Easter Fires Pageant, Founders Day, A Night in Old Fredericksburg, Oktoberfest, and Weihnachten. Since the 1970s descendants of the original German immigrants in Fredericksburg have created a revival of German culture in the community. The Fredericksburg Heritage Foundation and Gillespie County Historical Society have been founded to further this mission. Visitors are treated to a *Maibaum* (maypole) on the town square illustrating prominent events in Fredericksburg's history. A plethora of "Sunday houses" and other original structures complete with Old World *Fachwerk* (framework) architecture are scattered throughout the town, which has become a tourist Mecca to those visiting the Texas hill country. In 2000 the population of Fredericksburg was 8,911.

Jerry C. Drake

See also Adelsverein; Meusebach, John O.; New Braunfels, Texas; Nueces, Battle of the; Texas
References and Further Reading
Biesele, Rudolph Leopold. *The History of the German Settlements in Texas, 1831–1861.* Austin: Von Boeckman Jones, 1930.
Biggers, Don H. *German Pioneers in Texas: A Brief History of their Hardships, Struggles, and Achievements.* Fredericksburg: Fredericksburg Publishing, 1925.
Department of History, Southwest Texas State University. *Fredericksburg: Guidebook to the Historic German Hill Country.* San Marcos: Southwest Texas State University Press, 2003.
King, Irene Marschall. *John O. Meusebach: German Colonizer in Texas.* Austin: University of Texas Press, 1967.
Newcomb, W. W., Jr. *The Indians of Texas: From Prehistoric to Modern Times.* Austin: University of Texas Press, 1961.
Roemer, Ferdinand. *Texas with Particular Reference to German Immigration and the Physical Appearance of the Country.* Trans. Oswald Mueller. San Antonio: Steward Printing Company, 1935.
Zelade, Richard. *Hill Country: Discovering the Secrets of the Texas Hill Country.* Austin: Texas Monthly Press, 1983.

FREIHEIT (FREEDOM)

Freiheit was one of the longest-running anarchist periodicals. For over thirty-one years, from 1878 to 1910, Freiheit was the foremost exponent of German-language transatlantic radicalism, first in London and then in New York. Its pages chronicled the ideological shifts occurring within the German American radical movement. *Freiheit* was largely the work of one man, Johann Most (1846–1906), an outspoken anarchist speaker and headstrong editor who rarely minced words in his call for revolutionary insurrection.

Freiheit came into being in the wake of Germany's Anti-Socialist Law of October 19, 1878, which resulted in a sweeping suppression of all Socialist activities—including publications. Hundreds of rank-and-file Socialists were expelled from Germany or emigrated voluntarily. Most ended up in London, where they organized political clubs. It was this community that pursued the need for a German propaganda paper to be smuggled back home. Exiled radicals increasingly criticized the Socialist Party leadership, which was effectively muzzled by the German government, for being unwilling to resist the state. The exiles eventually lost faith in the ability of parliamentary action to hasten social change and so turned to underground action and journalism.

In December 1878, Johann Most was expelled from Germany and sought refuge in London. A fierce critic of the Socialist elders and an experienced editor, he was persuaded by the exiles to stand at the helm of the newly founded paper *Freiheit*. The first issue appeared on January 4, 1879. Although the paper was initially a straightforward Social Democratic organ, Socialist deputies in Berlin nevertheless objected to it on the basis that it was founded without party approval.

From 1880 to 1882, *Freiheit* shifted from a Social Democratic paper to a social revolutionary paper, one that advocated decentralized activism and that no longer shied away from the rhetoric of insurrectionary violence. This shift reflected the development of the exile community itself, especially the editorial circle around Most. Russian revolutionaries, Blanquists, and Bakuninists strongly influenced this new course for *Freiheit*. On September 2, 1880, for example, readers were treated to the full text of Sergei Nechaev's *Revolutionary Catechism.*

As a well-edited mouthpiece for the Socialist exile community, *Freiheit* grew in popularity, with its circulation climbing to 1,800. It reached German and Austrian subscribers through a precarious smuggling system. Sheets were shipped in tin cans, mailed as letters to border agents, or were simply hidden in luggage. Editors further confounded customs officials by renaming each issue. Still, participation in the radical exile community was extremely dangerous.

London clubs had been infiltrated by German detectives, and some smugglers were shadowed.

In March 1881, *Freiheit* came under fire when it published an article entitled "Endlich!" ("At Last!") celebrating the recent assassination of Czar Alexander II. British prosecution of the paper landed Most in jail. Released in October 1882, he decided to move the paper (and himself) to New York, where the first American issue appeared on December 9. He assumed complete control over the magazine, aided by a core group of assistants, including Moritz Schultze, who served as interim editor whenever Most was in prison. Most traveled across the United States to recruit subscribers, hire agents, and stage fundraising events. Circulation expanded from 5,000 in 1885 to 8,000 in 1887. The bulk of those issues were still bound for Europe. A fair number also went to German American workers. In addition, the paper counted readers among Czech and Jewish anarchists in the United States. In the early 1880s, the tone had become decidedly anarchist and revolutionary, featuring articles on class warfare and the evils of American capitalism. In July 1885, the paper increased to eight pages, including advertisements for saloons, brewers, and artisans. In addition, a separate four-page European edition was published. By this time, however, many radicals felt the paper had lost its rebel spirit. Certainly, the rhetoric of violence subsided, and by 1892 Most firmly denounced individual acts of terror, although he continued his fiery idiomatic style of writing laced with tongue-in-cheek humor and High German slang.

Other than news and announcements, *Freiheit* addressed Communist anarchism, the labor movement, and syndicalism, transforming itself from a militant, combative paper into a more intellectual magazine. Among the featured authors were Jean Grave, Rudolf Grossmann, Elisée Reclus, and Helene Most, some in first-time translation. There was also room for poetry from such German Americans as Georg Biedenkapp and Martin Drescher.

During the 1890s, *Freiheit* was mired in financial difficulties mainly caused by a drop in subscriptions and rising production costs. From 1897 to 1898, Most was forced to move to Buffalo and team up with a local labor paper to save his paper. Still, Most was somehow able to keep *Freiheit* afloat. In September 1901, just moments after the murder of President William McKinley, Most unwittingly printed an old essay, "Mord contra Mord" ("Murder vs. Murder"), which supported political assassination. As a result of this unhappy coincidence, the aging Most was thrown in jail.

After Most's death on March 11, 1906, a conference was called to decide the future of *Freiheit*, now in its twenty-seventh year. A Freiheit Publishing Association was set up, which included Henry Bauer and Max Baginski. In November 1907, the association agreed to continue the paper fortnightly with Baginski as editor. Despite these last attempts, *Freiheit* finally folded for good on August 17, 1910. It was seen by many as the end of an era, the final breath of German-language radicalism in the United States, although a few other periodicals appeared until 1914.

Tom Goyens

See also Anarchists; Bismarck's Anti-Socialist Law; Buffalo; Most, Johann; New York City; Newspaper Press, German Language in the United States

References and Further Reading

Arndt, Karl and May Olson, comps. *Deutsch-amerikanische Zeitungen und Zeitschriften, 1732–1955: Geschichte und Bibliographie.* Heidelberg: Quelle und Meyer, 1955.

Eberlein, Alfred. *Die Presse der Arbeiterklasse und der sozialen Bewegungen: Von den dreißiger Jahren des 19. Jahrhunderts bis zum Jahre 1967.* Berlin (East): Akademie-Verlag, 1968.

Porter, Bernard. "The Freiheit Prosecutions, 1881–1882." *The Historical Journal.* 23 (1980): 833–856.

Rocker, Rudolf. *Johann Most: Das Leben eines Rebellen.* Berlin: Der Syndikalist, 1924. Glashütten im Taunus: Detlov Auvermann, 1973.

FREUND, ERNST
b. January 30, 1864; New York, New York
d. October 20, 1932; Chicago, Illinois

German American jurist.

Ernst Freund was born in New York City when his parents, Ludwig A. Freund and Nannie Bayer, were visiting the United States. He grew up in Germany, but upon completion of university studies in 1884, returned to the country of his birth. Freund was one of the pioneers in the field of administrative law in the United States and a founder of the University of Chicago Law School. Freund brought a perspective that was influenced by German law and legal education.

From 1875 to 1881 Freund attended gymnasium (high school) in Dresden and Frankfurt am Main. He then studied law, principally at the Ruprecht Karl University of Heidelberg, which awarded him a doctorate of civil and canon law (JUD) in 1884. He also spent two semesters at the Friedrich Wilhelm University of Berlin, where he attended lectures of comparative public law scholar Rudolf von Gneist. After his law studies in Germany, Freund went to New York City. There he attended Columbia University from 1884 to 1885 and studied public law in the department of Frank Goodnow and John W. Burgess. From 1886 to 1894 he practiced law in New York City. In 1892 and 1893 he also taught public law at Columbia University while doing graduate work that led to a PhD in public law in 1897. In 1894 he went to Chicago to join the faculty of political science at the University of Chicago. He remained at that university until his death.

Freund is remembered principally as one of the two pioneers—along with Goodnow—of the field of administrative law and also for his role in legal education. When Freund returned to New York in 1884, administrative law as a field of study was unknown in the United States and was in its most nascent of stages in Germany. Freund and Goodnow made administrative law a field of law separate from constitutional law. Freund's vision of administrative law was based on a system of statute laws. It thus had to overcome not only the common law's suspicion of administrative law but also the common law's focus on process and case law development.

In 1902 when the University of Chicago created its law school, Freund was the university president's principal adviser in the project. Harvard Law School was helping establish the school, but its dean, John Barr Ames, and the professor it was to loan to be the new dean at the University of Chicago, Joseph H. Beale, insisted on doing so exclusively in the Harvard way. That meant the teaching of law pure and simple and strictly by the study of cases. Freund

and the University of Chicago president wanted something different: legal studies as an instrument of liberal education that included subjects Harvard regarded as political science and that allowed for systematic and comparative jurisprudence. Ames felt that Freund's belief in the general methods of the German universities predisposed him against Harvard's methods. Although the University of Chicago Law School went ahead largely on Harvard's terms, German legal education through Freund had a "significant impact on the definition of American legal education" (Ellsworth 1977, 92). Today Freund's ideas about legal education find considerably more resonance than they did a century ago.

In his ideas about both administrative law and legal education, Freund juxtaposed in one person the conflicting methods of the American common law and German legal science. He wrote as an American, but with a German's perspective (Lepsius 1997, 8). From his earliest days in professional life, he extolled to Americans the virtues of systematic legislation such as was found in Germany (see, e.g., "The Proposed German Civil Code." *American Law Review* 24 (1890): 237–254.

James R. Maxeiner

See also Burgess, John William
References and Further Reading
Ellsworth, Frank L. *Law on the Midway: The Founding of the University of Chicago Law School.* Chicago: Law School of the University of Chicago, 1977.
"Ernst Freund—Pioneer of Administrative Law." *University of Chicago Law Review* 29, 755 (1962).
Kraines, Oscar. *The World and Ideas of Ernst Freund: The Search for General Principles of Legislation and Administrative Law.* University: University of Alabama Press, 1974.

Lepsius, Oliver. *Verwaltungsrecht unter dem Common Law: Amerikansiche Entwicklungen bis zum New Deal.* Tübingen: Mohr-Siebeck, 1997.

Reitz, John C. "The Influence of Ernst Freund on American Law." In *Der Einfluß deutscher Emigranten auf die Rechtsentwicklung in den USA und Deutschland.* Eds. Marcus Lutter, Ernst C. Stiefel, and Michael H. Hoeflich. Tübingen: J. C. B. Mohr (Paul Siebeck), 1993, 423–435.

FRIEDMAN, PERRY

b. September 25, 1935; Winnipeg, Manitoba
d. March 16, 1995; Berlin, Germany

Canadian folksinger and immigrant to the German Democratic Republic (GDR), where he deeply influenced East German musical culture.

After a shattered childhood, Perry Friedman was dismissed from school without a degree in 1952. Soon after his seventeenth birthday, he decided to move around North America seeking work. He left home carrying his birthday gift, a newly made banjo, with him. On his trips, deeply influenced by the famous American folk singer Pete Seeger, he started his career as a folk musician. In 1959 he gave a concert on the occasion of an international meeting of Communist parties in London. After the show, he was invited to live in East Germany by the GDR government. Friedman agreed and migrated to the GDR at the age of twenty-four.

As a guest of the government, Friedman introduced typical elements of the North American musical culture to the public culture of East Germany. He became the icon from which the youth learned techniques to play the guitar and the banjo. Furthermore, he demonstrated the impartial exposure to traditional music. Because of his high profile and his popularity, he was the ideal adviser for the Central Committee of the Freie Deutsche Jugend (FDJ, or Free German Youth). Inspired by Friedman's person and music, a new youth movement, the *Singebewegung,* emerged at the beginning of the 1960s. This new popular music inspired the youth of East Germany with lyrics relating to problems of East German society.

Seven years after his emigration, on February 15, 1966, Friedman founded the Hootenanny-Klub Berlin, which was later renamed the Oktoberklub. This club was a concertlike event consisting of a group of singers and musicians improvising live on stage. Since the day of his immigration, Friedman preached this mode of collective musicmaking in the GDR. The Hootenanny-Klub quickly became very popular and at the same time it was integrated into official ceremonies of the Sozialistische Einheitspartei Deutschlands (SED, or Socialist Unity Party of Germany) and GDR. Because of this popularity, the FDJ channeled these activities and youth movements into a new component of the cultural policy of the SED.

In 1971 Friedman returned to Canada to work for a broadcasting station, but he stayed for only five years, when East Germany's leaders invited him to the "Festival of the Political Song" in 1976. However, it was not easy for Friedman to tie into his old success. Because of changed attitudes in the East German government, he no longer received invitations to festivals. He toured West Germany, gave concerts at labor union meetings, participated in the

Ostermärsche (Easter March) movement, and played at concerts organized by the Socialist Youth, the youth organization of the Sozialdemokratische Partei Deutschlands (SPD, or Social Democratic Party). In cooperation with the FDJ he toured the GDR in the early 1980s. This successful annual event took place every October until 1987.

In spite of never losing his North American accent and because he lived for over three decades in East Germany, the GDR became his second home. His last concert took place in the Berlin Club Möwe on November 2, 1994, where he once started his career with his first concert in the GDR in 1959.

Alexander Emmerich

See also Reed, Dean
References and Further Reading
Friedman, Perry. *Wenn die Neugier nicht wär: Ein Kanadier in der DDR.* Berlin: Karl Dietz Verlag, 2004.

FRIEDRICH, CARL JOACHIM
b. June 5, 1901; Leipzig, Saxony
d. September 19, 1984; Lexington, Massachusetts

German-born scholar, most of whose long career was at Harvard University, but who spent much time in Germany before and after the Third Reich.

Through Carl Friedrich, German scholarship in the humanities and social sciences was introduced to the United States for several decades, and after World War II, he brought American approaches to politics and government to Germany— but with strong, generally unacknowledged, German roots. Best known for his work in the field of comparative politics and government, Friedrich's many books include (with Taylor Cole) *Responsible Bureaucracy: A Study of the Swiss Civil Service* (1932), *Constitutional Government and Democracy* (1941), and (with Zbigniew K. Brzezinski) *Totalitarian Dictatorship and Autocracy* (1956).

Friedrich's father was professor of surgery at the University of Leipzig. His mother, a von Bülow, came from an aristocratic family. He was the oldest of four children. World War I dealt a severe blow to the Friedrichs. The father died in a military hospital, apparently overworked by his surgical duties. Friedrich began his university studies in medicine but switched after a few semesters to social sciences and economics. He was active in the bourgeois German youth movement, a powerful force in Germany from the 1890s into the 1930s. In 1922 he undertook a trip to the United States in order to establish contacts with American academic youth. His experiences in the United States led to the founding of a major precursor of the German Academic Exchange Service. Returning to the United States the next year, he was soon to spend more time there than in Germany. In 1924 he married an American, Lenore Pelham. In 1925 he submitted his doctoral dissertation at Heidelberg University. His mentor was Alfred Weber, sociologist, economist, political scientist, and prominent brother of the great Max Weber. Friedrich hoped for a position at Heidelberg, but his ambitions were blocked by a series of problems, of which one was that he was not actually granted the doctorate until 1930. In the meantime, his contacts in the United States secured him an untenured post in Harvard University's Department of Government.

His academic rise there was rapid; he became a full professor while still in his mid-thirties.

Often Friedrich is incorrectly assumed to have been a refugee from Nazi Germany. Since he was neither Jew nor leftist—and many émigrés from Nazi Germany were both—he was not automatically considered an opponent by the Nazis. But like numerous other German-born scholars in the United States during World War II, many of whom were émigrés, he was involved in the war effort in a way that drew upon his special skills. Beginning in 1943, he taught in a school to train U.S. personnel for military government in Germany and Japan, and later he was involved in postwar military government. He has been credited with participating in the drafting of the Marshall Plan (1947). He returned frequently to Europe, especially Heidelberg, to lecture and teach. Germans have often seen him as one of the founders—or refounders—of empirically based political science in Germany.

He is best known for his exposition of the conservative theory of totalitarianism: that the similarities between Nazi Germany and Stalinist Russia far outweigh the differences. This thesis has led to much heated debate, some of it very fruitful. The fame of his book on totalitarianism and the important role played by this concept in the cold war have unfortunately diverted attention from some of Friedrich's most interesting and challenging work: his early scholarship on the political theorist Johannes Althusius (1557–1638) and his mid- to late career work on the concept of the "baroque." Althusius is important in the early modern development of the notion of the sovereignty of the people, a concept used retrospectively to justify the revolt of the Netherlands against the Habsburgs in the sixteenth century. Friedrich's scholarship on Althusius includes editions of his works. When Friedrich began working on Althusius, "baroque" was a label applied mainly to the history of architecture and the visual arts, but eventually the term was to be applied, as the great nineteenth-century historian Jacob Burckhardt did with his concept of the "Renaissance," to almost every aspect of European activity, culture, thought, music, art, and politics. We are indebted to Friedrich for a masterly exploration and synthesis of attempts to describe every major aspect of an epoch as "baroque." This achievement is embodied in his *Age of the Baroque, 1610–1660* (1952), published in the famous series "The Rise of Modern Europe," edited by the prominent Harvard historian William L. Langer.

Walter Struve

See also American Occupation Zone; Foreign Policy (U.S., 1949–1955), West Germany in

References and Further Reading

Daalder, Hans, ed. *Comparative European Politics: The Story of a Profession.* London: Pinter, 1997.
Lietzmann, Hans J. *Politikwissenschaft im "Zeitalter der Diktaturen": Die Entwicklung der Totalitarismustheorie Carl Joachim Friedrichs.* Opladen: Leske + Budrich, 1999.

FRIENDS OF THE NEW GERMANY

Nazi organization in the United States from 1933 to 1935.

The Friends of the New Germany (FONG) originated in July of 1933 with a Nazi salute. Rudolf Hess, the deputy führer of Germany, approved the ambition of

Heinz Spanknöbel, a Nazi leader from Detroit, to lead a new Nazi organization in the United States. From the beginning, the association embodied the grandiose foreign policy of Nazi Germany in the United States, and the willingness of immigrant leaders to comply with the aims of this policy. The history of FONG subsequently was tied to the interests of Adolf Hitler's new government. Germany's Nazi government funded the organization, played the role of kingmaker, and eventually succeeded in discrediting the group in the fall of 1935, after it had become a liability.

The first front man of Nazi Germany in the United States was a brash and elusive figure. An unnaturalized immigrant, Spanknöbel posed as a Seventh-Day Adventist itinerant. He was also the former leader of the Detroit office of the Gau-USA, a branch of Hitler's National Socialist German Worker's Party (NSDAP). Spanknöbel won an audience in Berlin with Hess shortly after Hitler's rise to power in 1933. The Gau officer convinced the deputy führer that he could lead an organization that would be both subservient to Hitler and winsome to Americans. He returned with a document that no other aspiring Nazi leader in the United States could gainsay: official authorization that he was now the American führer.

Spanknöbel achieved many of his goals. His "process of coordination," which delegated the right of threatening violence to the toughest of Nazis, forced the remnants of other Nazi groups such as Gau-USA, the Teutonia Association, and the Swastika League to dissolve into FONG. Spanknöbel's larger association was then structured strictly along the lines of the NSDAP in Germany. Like the NSDAP, FONG practiced the leadership principle

and maintained an *Ordnungs-Dienst* (OD, or Uniformed Service), an elite section of uniformed guards. As with Germany's NSDAP in the 1920s, FONG began to intimidate opponents, particularly in the New York City area. After threatening German American leaders with reprisals if they did not submit to him, Spanknöbel personally visited the offices of Victor and Bernard Ridder of the *New Yorker Staats-Zeitung* (New York Public News). The leader of the FONG intimated that even the Ridders would not escape the rage of local Nazis if they did not prove more sympathetic to Hitler. Victor Ridder, however, demanded that Spanknöbel leave his office, and called the police. The notoriety of the "Spanknöbel affair" had a contradictory effect. Though the rough approach to well-known German Americans created many enemies, FONG also grew in the midst of their notoriety. By October 1933, the organization was publishing newspapers in five major cities (New York, Philadelphia, Chicago, Detroit, and Cincinnati). It had about 5,000 members and would attract more in the coming years.

Though FONG, like its successor, the German American Bund, aspired for national renown, its main strength was in the New York City area. There, a large, unchurched, immigrant German population had daily contacts with the still-larger Jewish community of greater New York. The Friends of the New Germany hoped that rising hatred for the Jews would abet their infiltration of German societies, and foment a tolerance for Nazi leadership. Spanknöbel and his allies became activists in the United German Societies (UGS) of New York and nearly gained control of that organization, causing four Jewish groups to leave the federation. When it appeared, however, that a Nazi takeover of the UGS would turn German Day events (October 29, 1933) into a celebration of Nazism, Mayor John O'Brien of New York refused to grant a permit to allow German Day in 1933.

FONG succeeded all too well in inspiring hatred. During a FONG rally in Newark, the OD initiated a brawl with a crowd of hecklers. Crudely painted swastikas soon defaced a number of Jewish synagogues in the New York City area. Jews of New York began a boycott of German-made goods, and FONG served local German merchants in organizing a more conspicuous counterboycott of Jewish stores. When it became evident that the strong-armed tactics of FONG served only to alienate Americans, the foreign-affairs section of Germany's NSDAP revoked Spanknöbel's credentials, and he fled back to Germany in October 1933. In March of 1934, Congress passed a resolution sponsored by Representative Samuel Dickstein of New York City, funding a committee to investigate un-American activities, particularly those of FONG.

FONG survived its first year, as Nazis on both sides of the Atlantic still saw its existence as necessary. The foreign section of Germany's NSDAP chose a replacement for Spanknöbel, Fritz Gissibl, and nearly shelved him in turn when the group failed to shed its image as a fifth column. Gissibl, a founder of an earlier Nazi group, the Teutonia, proved less compliant than Spanknöbel. Gissibl proved willing to curtail his own power if the German Nazis insisted, but rather than leaving the country like Spanknöbel, Gissibl got a naturalized American, Hubert Schnuch, to pose as the group's new leader. Throughout 1934

FONG saw self-proclaimed führers rise against Gissibl for real control of the organization, but the latter, who could claim some support from the Fatherland, remained in control. One challenger named Ignatz Griebl, for instance, was eased out of contention by German officials who hired him as a member of the *Abwehr*, the intelligence section of the German armed services.

The irony about FONG from beginning to end was that though vetted by German Nazis, the society did little but tarnish Germany's image in the United States. Under Gissibl, FONG supported Bruno Hauptmann's unpopular effort to get a fair trial after he was accused of killing the baby of Charles and Anne Lindbergh. They opened camps, drilled young boys, chased invasive journalists from the grounds, and blared propaganda from movies and loudspeakers. By 1934, the group's presence created a stir wherever sizable numbers of recent German immigrants were found. In Buffalo, for instance, a journalistic exposé of FONG in 1934 showed that the key figure in the local effort was Gerhard Kiessow, a German consular agent. The reports spoke of power struggles; the efforts of local Nazis to take over the *Volksfreund* (People's Friend), the last German daily in the city; and a recent local rally held by the traveling Fritz Gissibl. When interviewed, Frank X. Schwab, a recognized leader of the local German community, castigated the Nazi front. He saw FONG as a German variation of the Ku Klux Klan and warned that if they tried straight-armed tactics in Buffalo, that he would die, if necessary, in the fight against them.

The decline of FONG was more related to German decisions overseas than to any cowardice or fear of unpopularity among recent German immigrants. In 1934, as Gissibl warred against competing factions, German consular agents withdrew financial support. In 1935, when Gissibl sent his brother Peter and front man Hubert Schnuch to Germany for help, Nazi officials claimed that they would do nothing to interfere in American affairs. Actually, they would interfere, but not in the way Gissibl had hoped. By this time, German ambassador Hans Luther and other observers of the American scene, such as Theodore Hoffmann, head of the Steuben Society, had convinced leading Nazis—even, it seems, Hitler—that FONG was not even kindling the enthusiasm of the rooted German American element for the new Germany. If the Nazis wanted American neutrality for a future European war, FONG was not going to be very helpful. Aware that the Dickstein committee at this time was helping to smear Germany's reputation in the eyes of Americans, Nazi officials decided that a complete renunciation of their American organization was in their best interests.

In October 1935, the Gissibl brothers and OD elite were startled to learn that the German Foreign Ministry had proscribed membership in FONG for all German nationals. This meant that a large fraction of the organization's membership would either have to quit the group or face the future confiscation of their passports and the revocation of their German citizenship. When Peter Gissibl stormed into the German consulate in Chicago and warned that his brother would personally confront Rudolf Hess about the edict, he was told that if his brother tried to go to Germany, he would be thrown into a concentration camp. Fritz Gissibl, nevertheless, booked a berth to Germany at this time and did meet with German officials. However, his trip served only to help extend the deadline for the new edict to December 31, 1935. Gissibl, ultimately true to the party who had chosen him, resigned his post and returned to Germany. He did not consign the American movement to oblivion, however, for he handpicked a successor who would become the most infamous and effective Nazi leader in American history, Fritz Kuhn. In March 1936 Kuhn reorganized FONG into the German American Bund.

Andrew Yox

See also Antisemitism; Buffalo; German American Bund; Kuhn, Fritz Julius; Lindbergh, Charles Augustus; *New Yorker Staats-Zeitung;* Schwab, Frank X.; Steuben Society of America

References and Further Reading

Berninger, Dieter. "Milwaukee's German American Community and the Nazi Challenge of the 1930s." *Wisconsin Magazine of History* 71 (Winter 1987–1988): 118–142.

Canedy, Susan. *America's Nazis: A Democratic Dilemma.* Menlo Park, CA: Markgraf, 1990.

Diamond, Sander. *The Nazi Movement in the United States, 1924–1941.* Ithaca: Cornell University Press, 1974.

Jenkins, Philip. *Hoods and Shirts: The Extreme Right in Pennsylvania, 1925–1950.* Chapel Hill: University of North Carolina Press, 1997.

FRITZ, SAMUEL
b. April 9, 1654; Trautenau (Eastern Bohemia), Austria
d. April 20, 1725; Jéveros, Peru

Jesuit who worked as a missionary in the Amazon and produced the first accurate map of the Amazon River.

In 1673, Samuel Fritz joined the Societas Jesu (Jesuits). In 1685, after an arduous two-year journey, he arrived in the Spanish colonies on the upper Amazon (Marañón) to work as a missionary among the Omaguas and Yurimagua tribes. Until 1689 he did missionary work in a vast territory between the Rio Napo and Rio Negro and founded about forty *reducciones* (secure villages where Jesuits attempted to resettle forest-dwelling natives in order to convert and train them while protecting them from attacks). While traveling into Portuguese territory in order to complain about the raids on his settlements, he was held in custody in Pará for eighteen months. Upon his return, he endeavored for over twenty years to protect his mission from Portuguese raids, but he received no support from the Spanish administration. Finally, in 1714, he was transferred to Jéveros, where he worked for another eleven years as a parish priest. The settlements and mission stations established by him were largely destroyed by the Portuguese. His scientific significance stems from the results of his trip in the Portuguese-controlled section of the Amazon. The manuscript map he drew on his return trip in 1691 accurately depicts, for the first time, the course of the stream from the headwater region to the mouth. The map was first published in 1707 in Quito in an altered form. In 1743, the French mathematician Charles Marie de la Condamine (1701–1774) brought the original to the National Library in Paris, and it was reproduced in 1893 by Gabriel Marcel.

Heinz-Peter Brogiato

See also Brazil

References and Further Reading

Egghardt, Hanne. *Österreicher entdecken die Welt. Forscher, Abenteurer, Idealisten.* Vienna: Pichler, 2000: 72–84.

Gicklhorn, Renée. "Fritz Samuel." *Neue Deutsche Biographie.* Berlin: Duncker and Humblot, 1961, 5:632–633.

Henze, Dietmar. *Enzyklopädie der Entdecker und Erforscher der Erde.* Graz: Akademische Druck- und Verlagsanstalt, 1983, 2:296–298.

FROMM, ERICH
b. March 23, 1900; Frankfurt am Main
d. March 18, 1980; Muralto, Switzerland

Eminent German psychologist, psychotherapist, philosopher, and academic teacher in the United States.

Fromm studied Jewish law and religion and graduated from Heidelberg University with a doctorate on the Jewish diaspora. He trained in psychology at the University of Munich and at the Institute of Psychoanalysis in Berlin. His Jewish family background did not play a particular role in his later professional life but necessitated emigration to New York in 1934 after employment with the Frankfurt Institute of Social Research. In the United States, Fromm once more joined that reopened institute, set himself up as a psychoanalyst, and lectured at Columbia University.

Fromm was granted U.S. citizenship in 1940 and was invited to teach at Bennington College in Vermont as well as at Yale University. He had already been inspired by the writings of Karl Marx, Johann Jakob Bachofen, and Sigmund Freud but took issue with the latter's preoccupation with unconscious drives and the supposed neglect of the importance of social factors in human psychology. In 1951, Fromm moved to Mexico City and obtained a professorship of psychoanalysis at the National Autonomous University. He subsequently became engaged in the U.S. peace movement directed against forced nuclear armament and the Vietnam War. On retiring in 1965, he edited, together with Ernst Bloch, Herbert Marcuse, and others, *Humanist Socialism,* a programmatic collection of essays establishing a connection between humanist values established in fifteenth-century Europe, like tolerance, the right to an education, and the right to free development of the mind, and Socialist thought of the time. The conclusion was, with Marx, that genuine humanism would follow from socialism.

Over the years, Fromm had developed a strong anticapitalist stance. He criticized the notion of progress as measured and evaluated by economic growth alone. In the face of technology and mechanization, informed humanist reasoning as well as unselfish love served as a counterbalance leading toward a more humane society, which, ideally, would be free of psychological oppression (*The Art of Loving,* 1956 and *The Revolution of Hope,* 1968). Work, if it dominates over humanity, is seen as an oppressing and alienating factor responsible for psychological troubles like neuroses and sadism.

Fromm had studied such negative drives in history as well as in clinical practice and published his conclusions in *The Anatomy of Human Destructiveness* in 1973. In *To Have or to Be* (1976), he analyzed the surplus society according to the American model, which, according to Fromm, favored "having" over "being." The consumption mode in combination with the emergence of mass culture and the dominance of business over private life had led, so went his line of argument, to modern human beings losing touch with life. As a result, people "have" everything but "are" nothing. The individual remained passive and turned to consumerism and toxic substances as means of compensating for existential fears of alienation and spiritual void. Fromm interpreted the manifold distractions offered by the entertainment industry and the growing sense of numbness as indicators of the longing to be reunified with one's self as well as with nature.

Markus Oliver Spitz

See also Frankfurt School; Intellectual Exile; Marcuse, Herbert; Mexico

References and Further Reading

Burston, Daniel. *The Legacy of Erich Fromm.* Cambridge: Harvard University Press, 1991.

Funk, Rainer. *Erich Fromm: His Life and Ideas.* New York: Continuum International, 2003.

Funk, Rainer, ed. *The Erich Fromm Reader.* With a foreword by Joel Kovel. New Jersey: Humanities Press, 1994.

FUCHS, KLAUS

b. December 29, 1911; Rüsselsheim, Hesse

d. January 28, 1988; Berlin (East)

German nuclear physicist who participated in the British and American projects to produce an atomic bomb and who spied for the Soviet Union.

Klaus Fuchs came from a Protestant and Social Democratic–oriented family. His father was the well-known theologian Emil Fuchs. In 1928, Fuchs finished school and began to study physics and mathematics at the University of Kiel. In 1930, he became a member of the Social Democratic Party (SPD) and in 1932 of the Communist Party (CP). After the Reichstag fire in late February 1933, he actively participated in the resistance against the Nazi dictatorship before he left Germany in the summer for Paris. By fall, he had emigrated to England, where he continued his education at the University of Bristol. There he worked with Nevill Mott, the cofounder of modern solid-state physics and later Nobel Prize winner. In 1936, Fuchs defended his doctoral dissertation on the electron theory of metals. Following his supervisor's recommendation, Fuchs went to the University of Edinburgh to work with Max Born, also a German émigré. In 1939, Fuchs defended his second doctoral dissertation in mathematics. After the outbreak of World War II, he was interned as an enemy alien in Canada. It was in the internment camp that he came again into contact with the CP—a connection he would not give up again.

Thanks to the support of influential colleagues, Fuchs was released from the internment camp early. He became an assistant to Rudolf Peierls at the University of Birmingham. There, Fuchs was introduced to modern nuclear physics. Peierls's research was the center of the British project to produce an atomic bomb ("Tube Alloy"). After Fuchs went through several background checks and had become a British citizen, he was invited to participate in this project in 1941. Two years later he was sent to the United States, where he worked first in New York and later in Los Alamos for the Manhattan Project. He was a member of the theoretical group headed by Hans Bethe. Fuchs made essential contributions to the development of the atomic bomb and was given a general overview of the entire project. Furthermore, he participated in the first discussions about a superbomb (the hydrogen bomb). Together with John von Neumann, he invented an important principle for its detonating device. In the summer of 1945, Fuchs witnessed the first successful test of an atomic bomb as well as the dropping of the atomic bomb over Hiroshima and Nagasaki. In the fall of 1945, Fuchs left Los Alamos and returned to England, where he took over the theory department in the newly established nuclear research center Harwell. There, his work focused on the development of mathematical methods for nuclear research.

Before he went to the United States in 1941, Fuchs had sought contact with the Soviet secret service. He was convinced that the Soviet Union needed his support in its struggle against Nazi Germany since the Western Allies seemed temporarily unwilling to back the Soviets. Fuchs offered to disclose information about the construction of an atomic bomb acquired during his involvement in the Manhattan Project. It is still not clear how important his knowledge was for the Russian project and how much of his knowledge he transmitted to the Russian side. Nevertheless, the knowledge from the British and American projects helped the Soviet Union to acquire atomic weapons more quickly. In December 1949, the British secret service realized that Fuchs was a spy, and he was sentenced to fourteen years in prison. A year later, he lost his British citizenship. Once released from prison in June 1959, Fuchs left England for the German Democratic Republic (GDR).

In East Germany, Fuchs was warmly welcomed and was able to continue his career as a physicist. He was appointed deputy director of the GDR's nuclear research center in Rossendorf, near Dresden and in 1972 became a member of the Academy of Science. In 1967, he became a member of the Central Committee of the Socialist Unity Party (SED)—an honor bestowed on only a very small number of scientists. During his years in East Germany,

Fuchs's research focused on nuclear physics. He was one of the most vocal proponents of the fast-breeder reactor technology, which in the end could not be realized because of economic shortages and political pressure from Moscow.

Dieter Hoffmann

See also Braun, Wernher von; Stalin Note
References and Further Reading
Goodman, Michael S. "The Grandfather of the Hydrogen Bomb? Anglo-American Intelligence and Klaus Fuchs." *Historical Studies in the Physical and Biological Sciences* 34, no. 1 (2003): 1–22.
Moss, Norman. *Klaus Fuchs: The Man Who Stole the Atom Bomb.* London: St. Martin's Press, 1987.
Tschikow, Wladimir, and Gary Kern. *Perseus: Spionage in Los Alamos.* Berlin: Verlag Volk und Welt, 1996.
Williams, Robert Chadwell. *Klaus Fuchs, Atom Spy.* Cambridge: Harvard University Press, 1987.

FULBRIGHT PROGRAM

Established in 1952, six years after the foundation of the international Fulbright program, the German American Fulbright program has so far facilitated the bilateral exchange of more than 30,000 German and American students, instructors, professors, researchers, and professionals. The Fulbright program is the only successful international exchange venture that has a clear philosophical foundation, resulting from a deep-seated dissatisfaction with the global vision of the international political leadership. In the late 1920s, J. William Fulbright, a long-term U.S. senator from Arkansas, had a series of formative experiences in both Great Britain and east-central Europe that led him to believe that it

would be necessary "to see the world as others see it." Fulbright discounted cultural and ideological differences as incidental and acquired by accident of birth and advocated programs and a mix of cognitive and personal experiences to come to understand the relativity of cultural patterns of thinking. This belief in international education as a vehicle toward peaceful global development has kept the Fulbright program largely unscathed by political developments and ensured its status as a liberal and independent force in German American relations.

Fulbright's correspondence with his friend Mike Fodor, reporting to him from Berlin, shows the senator's special interest in divided, post–World War II Germany and thus also in the German Fulbright program. Although the initial impetus of the program was certainly connected with reeducation and/or reorientation, the preamble of the 1952 agreement stressed the "mutual understanding between the peoples of the United States of America and the Federal Republic of Germany by a wider exchange of knowledge and professional talents through educational contact" (Tent 2003).

This binational balance is reflected both in the funding procedures (each side funds 50 percent of the program) and in the composition of the Fulbright board, on which both countries are equally represented. The high level of representation of Germans on the board led to a strong commitment toward the Fulbright program by many relevant German decision-makers. The presence of such organizations as the German Academic Exchange Service (DAAD), various ministries, and the German University Rectors Conference also turned the Fulbright board into a forum for dialogue and exchange in the area of the development and reform of higher education in Germany.

The impressive example of the program's founder, J. William Fulbright, has resulted in the emergence of a number of strong personalities internationally who, embodying the program, have been able to help it along in their various national contexts. The German Fulbright program has been favored by the long tenure of several well-informed officials, such as the Germans Ulrich Littmann and Rainer Rohr and the American Carl G. Anthon. Beyond its outstanding leadership, the Fulbright program has generated a large number of personalities in both countries who have brought the intercultural academic knowledge gained in the course of their stay in the partner country to bear on a specific area of expertise, whether economics, politics, or the natural sciences. However, the most important effect of the Fulbright program has been on the bilateral cooperation in the area of higher education.

Most notably, the Fulbright program has contributed decisively to the establishment of American studies as an independent field at German universities and thus helped to break the virtual monopoly English philology had on the training of secondary school teachers of English. The interdisciplinary interests of many Fulbright appointees at German universities have also extended to other areas and helped to inspire such areas as women's studies and multicultural studies. In the United States, the German American Fulbright program contributed toward the study of Germany; the German Studies "movement," although largely American in origin, was greatly assisted by special Fulbright appointments. On all levels, the Fulbright program has intensified the educational exchanges between the United States and Germany. Many key partnerships between U.S. and German universities were established as a result of Fulbright contacts, and many of the reform initiatives in the German university system came about for the same reason.

Many of the most gifted junior scholars from Germany ("excellence" being a central selection criterion) decide to stay in the United States following the completion of their "Fulbright experience." They have become some of the most productive faculty members at American research universities, and at the same time, they remain academic ambassadors for Germany in their adopted country. Indeed, junior scholars have been the most consistent focus of the German Fulbright exchange, and participation in the program was often the promising beginning of a later university career both in the United States and Germany. The Fulbright program has thus been stimulating innovative research in both countries and in many different areas.

Given Germany's previous location at the ideological dividing line between "East" and "West," it is not surprising that the German Fulbright program has always had a strategic position in European American academic relations. The "Berlin Week," established in the mid-1950s for participants throughout Germany, has gradually developed into an all-European forum for American Fulbrighters in Europe and a correspondingly interesting venue for creative dialogue and exchange.

A separate Fulbright program with the German Democratic Republic (GDR) had been established just prior to the disassembly of the Berlin Wall in 1989. It reflected the GDR's interest in improving its relationship with the United States on all levels, especially in view of the fact that support by Mikhail Gorbachev's USSR had become uncertain. However, the program was set up as an intergovernmental agreement and did not use the model of the binational commission that characterized the program in West Germany and other Western countries. The Fulbright program, with a pragmatic all-German appeal, proved to be one of the few areas in the German establishment of higher education where there was more of a spirit of cooperation than aggressive takeover and carpetbagging. It is therefore not surprising that in recent years, the German Fulbright program, now headquartered in Berlin, has also focused on the challenges connected with the accession of new members to the European Union and the dialogue with other, non-EU countries in Eastern Europe. The example the program has set in logistics, selection procedures, and philosophy has served as a trailblazer for the development of intra-European exchanges such as ERASMUS or SOCRATES and now needs to redirect its own work from a binational to the new European framework.

Beyond its traditional clientele of students and professors (the former making up the heart of the German program to the United States, the latter of the American program to Germany), the German American Fulbright program also serves assistant language teachers in secondary schools and at the college level, administrators in international education, education experts, and journalists. Added to these professional exchanges is a focus on German universities of applied sciences, the *Fachhochschulen*, which represent an important and growing segment of German higher education. Together with its active alumni association, the German Fulbright program thus continues to be the key institution in the relationship between Germany and the United States in the area of higher and professional education *and* an important player in the relationship between the two countries at large.

Walter Grünzweig

See also German Students at American Universities; U.S.-German Intellectual Exchange

References and Further Reading

Fulbright at the Start of a New Millennium. Bonn: Fulbright Kommission, 1998.

Littmann, Ulrich. *Gute Partner—Schwierige Partner: Anmerkungen zur akademischen Mobilität zwischen Deutschland und den Vereinigten Staaten von Amerika (1923–1993).* Bonn: Deutscher Akademischer Austauschdienst, 1996.

Tent, James F. "The Beginning of the German-American Fulbright Program 1952." *The First Class of Fulbrighters.* Berlin: Fulbright Kommission, 2003.

FULLER, MARGARET
b. May 23, 1810; Cambridgeport, Massachusetts
d. July 19, 1850; near Fire Island, New York

One of the best-known female writers of her century, Margaret Fuller played a significant role in introducing German literature to her friends and associates in the Transcendentalist circle, above all to her close friend Ralph Waldo Emerson (1803–1882), as well as to the educated elite in New England and beyond. Influenced by the English writer Thomas Carlyle (1795–1881) and Charles Follen

(1796–1840), she began an intensive and systematic study of German literature, while virtually teaching herself the language. From 1834 to 1838 Fuller shared what had become a passionate interest in German culture with her students at Bronson Alcott's (1799–1888) Temple School. During that time, she became increasingly immersed in her studies of Johann Wolfgang von Goethe, whom she came to regard as the greatest German writer, overcoming her initial preference for Friedrich Schiller. In 1839 her translation of Johann Peter Eckermann's (1792–1854) *Conversations with Goethe in the Last Years of His Life* (*Gespräche mit Goethe in den letzten Jahren seines Lebens, 1823–1832,* 1836–1848) was instrumental in creating a more favorable image of the poet in the United States, who was now presented as a serene and mature thinker rather than the fiery, youthful author of *The Sorrows of the Young Werther* (*Die Leiden des jungen Werthers,* 1774), a long-standing American perception. Fuller furthered this reevaluation in her preface, in which she wrote a spirited defense of Goethe and a thoughtful discussion of his strengths as an artist and literary critic. Fuller's ultimate goal was to write a biography of Goethe, a task to which she devoted her prodigious energies for a number of years but never came close to completing. However, she made further contributions to a positive reception of Goethe in articles and translations she wrote for the *Dial,* a journal associated with the Transcendentalists that she cofounded and edited for two years. In addition, she published translations and wrote articles on other German poets and writers. On the local level she regularly spoke about Goethe and other German writers in the lectures (her "Conversations") she gave to

One of the best-known female writers of her century, Margaret Fuller played a significant role in introducing German literature to her friends and associates in the Transcendentalist circle. (Library of Congress)

the women of the Boston elite from 1839 to 1844. After 1844 her public role as an advocate of German literature came to an end, as she began her career as one of the first female journalists in the United States with her employment by Horace Greeley's (1811– 1872) *New York Tribune.*

To Fuller, Goethe towered above all the German writers and poets. She defended him from the usual charge of immorality, which emerged especially from his *Die Wahlverwandschaften* (*Elective Affinities,* 1809), by maintaining that the work was indeed moral but that Goethe had framed it in accord with his personal moral code rather than that of religious authorities. She argued that he presented the world as it was, rather than as it should be, and those who were inclined to an ideal world should turn to Schiller, whom she continued to admire. Fuller presented Goethe as the best stylist in the German language, an acute observer of human beings, and an ardent believer in continuous human development. She viewed *Faust* as the summation of the great ideas of his life, and asserted that the *Wilhelm Meister* novels (*Wilhelm Meister's Apprentice Years*, 1795–1796, and *Wilhelm Meister's Travels*, 1821) were among one of the most significant educational works ever produced. Fuller also extolled Goethe's portrayal of various feminine figures in his works in her book *Woman in the Nineteenth Century* (1855). In spite of her decade of study of Goethe's works, and the voluminous notes she produced, she was unable to realize her dream of writing his biography. She eventually concluded that she could not undertake the task until she could travel to Germany and interview those who had known him. However, personal circumstances prevented her from ever visiting the land of Goethe and those poets and writers she so ardently admired.

Fuller promoted these other German poets and authors, as well as additional aspects of German culture, in her articles, reviews, and translations. She developed considerable enthusiasm for the German romantic poets and authors, especially Novalis (Friedrich von Hardenberg, 1772–1801), whose mysticism and spiritualism appealed to a prominent aspect of her complex personality. Fuller especially praised his *Heinrich von Ofterdingen* (1802) and his *Die Lehrlinge zu Sais* (*The Apprentices of Sais*, 1798). She was also fascinated by the extravagant language and exotic themes of Jean Paul Richter (1763–1825), whose *Titan* (1800–1803) she particularly admired. Fuller also translated poems by Schiller, Karl Theodor Körner (1791–1813), and Johann Ludwig Uhland (1787–1862). Her long article on the ballads of the Rhineland increased American interest in German folk poetry, the *Volkslied*. She communicated her intense involvement in German music, especially that of Ludwig van Beethoven, through a series of sketches of German composers published in the *Dial*. Realizing that her interests were more literary and artistic than metaphysical, she focused her prodigious energy on literary criticism and her translations, thereby encouraging others to follow in her footsteps. Fuller died July 19, 1850, at sea near Fire Island, New York.

John T. Walker

See also Follen, Charles; Transcendentalism
References and Further Reading
Capper, Charles. *Margaret Fuller: An American Romantic Life: The Private Years.* New York: Oxford University Press, 1992.
Pochmann, Henry A. *German Culture in America: Philosophical and Literary Influences, 1600–1900.* Westport, CT: Greenwood Press, 1978.
Vogel, Stanley. *German Literary Influences on the American Transcendentalists.* New Haven: Yale University Press, 1955.